ABC-CLIO LITERARY COMPANION

Encyclopedia of
Utopian
Literature

ABC-CLIO LITERARY COMPANION

Encyclopedia of
Utopian
Literature

Mary Ellen Snodgrass

ABC-CLIO

Santa Barbara, California
Denver, Colorado
Oxford, England

Library of Congress Cataloging-in-Publication Data

Snodgrass, Mary Ellen.
    Encyclopedia of utopian literature/Mary Ellen Snodgrass
       p.   cm. — ABC-CLIO (literary companion)
    Includes bibliographical references and index.
    1. Utopias in literature—Encyclopedias. I. Title. II. Series
  PN56.U8S66   1995   809′ .93372—dc20   95-16894

ISBN 0-87436-757-3 (alk. paper)

01 00 99 98 97 96 95 94   10 9 8 7 6 5 4 3 2 1

ABC-CLIO, Inc.
130 Cremona Drive, P.O. Box 1911
Santa Barbara, California 93116-1911

This book is printed on acid-free paper ∞ .
Manufactured in the United States of America

How hard to realize that every camp of men or beast has this glorious starry firmament for a roof! In such places standing alone on the mountaintop it is easy to realize that whatever special nests we make—leaves and moss like the marmots and birds, or tents or piled stone—we all dwell in a house of one room—the world with the firmament for its roof—and are sailing the celestial spaces without leaving any track.

John Muir
John of the Mountain, 1938

CONTENTS

PREFACE

From the first hand-scrawled cave art, the first scribble of pictographs on stone tablets, and the tentative quavering hymns to deities who turned the heavens and maintained the sun by day and the moon by night, human minds have forged into words their dreams of the perfect world. Whatever its parameter—a garden in God's new universe, Kublai Khan's oriental palace cooled by tumbling waters, Dante's *Paradiso,* a polygamous desert retreat, or an underground kingdom powered by a mythic energy that can kill or heal—the literary utopist visualizes a place where there is no cold or hunger, where all enjoy health and welcome, and where the worst of human foibles withers when pitted against the best of human virtues. Utopias appear in myriad forms and styles of literature—in scripture, bedtime stories, poems, folk and literary epics, history, novels, pastoral idylls, humans, economic diatribes, myth, short fiction, religious allegory, romance, vision, and brief verse.

Encyclopedia of Utopian Literature is intended to guide the reader through the hallmarks of utopian and dystopian writing by stressing titles, authors, characters, setting, themes, literary styles, and belief systems. Not surprisingly, textual descriptions and parameters return with regularity to the names that Western readers immediately associate with utopia. First, Plato, the initiator of the concept of "philosopher-king"; second, Thomas More, the creator of the term *utopia;* and third, the father of the modern dystopia, George Orwell, the author of a disturbing nightmare and an equally distressing beast fable—*1984* and *Animal Farm.* These pivotal works have spawned a stream of science fiction writers, fantasists, and futurists who followed the post–World War II euphoria with warnings of dreams gone lethally sour and societies teetering on moral collapse. Added to the canon are Aldous Huxley's *Brave New World,* Ayn Rand's *Anthem,* Ray Bradbury's *Fahrenheit 451,* and Yevgeny Zamyatin's *We,* a quartet of works that twist and turn the post–Industrial Revolution's technological wizardry in the light of reason to determine what humanity loses when machines replace hand labor, when hearts and souls allow conveyor-belt ethics to quell the Promethian spark.

As an aid to readers, the *Encyclopedia of Utopian Literature* provides significant study of basic terms: the Promised Land, commune, kismet, Taoism,

PREFACE

Shangri-La, Eden, Saturnalia, Camelot. Entries on style, work, and author offer thoughtful analysis of an array of great and lasting literature:

- James Hilton's Himalayan respite from an Indian uprising

- Jonathan Swift's mastery of satire and misanthropy

- Mandeville's handling of a utopic fable about bees

- B. F. Skinner's psychological study of behavior modification

- Plato's dialectics and fragmented glimpse of the failed Atlantis

- Henry Wadsworth Longfellow's contemplative paean to the mythic Hiawatha

- Karl Marx and Friedrich Engels's economic manifesto to the proletariat

- Voltaire's cursory viewing of Eldorado, the fabled City of Gold

- the forceful words and prophecies of Mohammed recorded in the Koran

- Mark Twain's depiction of medieval stodginess in Arthur's England

- the evolving role of Black Elk as holy man and support to a dying culture

- Alfred Tennyson's resetting of Arthurian lore in Christian philosophy

- Cervantes's idealistic satire of a rambling old man searching for his beatific Dulcinea

- Rabelais's outlandish medieval retreat where people do what they wish

- Alex Haley's recording of Malcolm X's autobiography, which ends in gunfire on the floor of a Harlem ballroom

- Christ's gentle Beatitudes in the Sermon on the Mount

- John Bunyan's episodic journey of Christian and Christiana to the Celestial City

- the mythic creation stories of Adam and Eve recorded in two versions in Genesis

- Plutarch's biographical study of Lycurgus, the Spartan city planner

- Doris Lessing's incisive speculative fiction depicting urban collapse

- Anthony Burgess's cynical depiction of aimless teens bent on random mayhem

- Confucius's succinct aphorisms

- Richard Adams's journey motif across an English landscape

- Lao Tzu's belief in minimalistic philosophy

- Arthur C. Clarke's regressive evolution of humans to shapeless fetuses

- the flow of a river symbolizing Hermann Hesse's merger of sorrow and joy

- the lofty ambitions of the epics composed by Homer and Virgil

To claims that the stage is an unlikely spot to develop an Edenic or hellish scheme, this volume rebuts with commentary on George Bernard Shaw's *Back to Methuselah*, Carel Kapek's *R.U.R.*, and William Shakespeare's *As You Like It*, *A Midsummer Night's Dream*, and *The Tempest*, all laced with the trappings of dream and nightmare, depending on the point of view.

Rounding out the pithier works of the masters are the less-known works of W. H. Hudson, al-Ghazali, Fra Tomaso Campanella, P. D. James, Charles Fourier, Ernest Callenbach, Oliver Goldsmith, Edward Bulwer-Lytton, Marge Piercy, Edward Bellamy, Étienne Cabet, William Morris, Torquato Tasso, and William Dean Howells alongside young adult classics—J. M. Barrie's *Peter Pan*, L. Frank Baum's *The Wonderful Wizard of Oz*, and Lois Lowry's *The Giver*.

As a fitting addition to this pageant of idylls, rambles, pilgrimages, and phantasms stand an ominous pair of twentieth-century fiction classics at the two ends of the Industrial Revolution. From the distant end, Jack London creates *The Iron Heel*, a horrific anticapitalistic anarchy fomented by the redoubtable Ernest Everhard and his doughty wife, Avis Cunningham Everhard, who close the final chapter resolved to defeat an advancing phalanx of oligarchs. At the nearer end of the era, Margaret Atwood, one of the Western world's most perceptive, unflinching feminists, plays "what if" with oddments of current cultural arrhythmias—fundamentalist fanatics grappling with failing sexual potency by killing off older women in toxic colonies and by herding together the nameless, faceless surviving breeders still capable of creating life. In boot camp lockstep, *The Handmaid's Tale* delineates the hopes and terrors of potential mothers undergoing brainwashing and assignment to a duplicitous cadre of elite studs who mouth the appropriate Bible verses on chastity and procreation while fantasizing an old-style night of love-for-sale at Jezebel's. This newest member of the male-dominated utopian/dystopian genre is a piece of fiction so chilling, so attuned to the madness bruited in the daily media that its blatant antiwomanism clicks insightfully into place among today's atrocities, paranoia, educational and spiritual malaise, soullessness, gratuitous brutality, and progressive decline in humanism.

Arranged in alphabetic order, *The Encyclopedia of Utopian Literature* offers numerous cross-references to significant studies, particularly conditioning, women in utopia, synergy, totalitarianism, sexual reproduction, economics, syncretism, prophecy, disillusion, and technology. Bibliographic notation refers the user to primary and secondary sources for more detailed perusal to amplify summaries. An extensive index allows the reader to broaden the study of a topic with insightful comparison and contrast as well as parallel reading in related entries, for example, bestiality, Brobdingnags, dystopia, *Gulliver's Travels*, Houyhnhnms, Laputa, Lilliput, satire, Jonathan Swift, and Yahoos. Overall, the book attempts to supply definition and clarity to an understanding and appreciation of a significant literary arena, the spiritual and secular paradigms that blueprint the perfect world.

 # INTRODUCTION

Harbored in the soul lies a yen for utopia, the "good place." This longing that haunts the unconscious, this desire for a respite, a stopping place, a sheltering haven free of demands and devoid of pain and death, animates the hopes of people in all places, times, stations, and professions. In most people, the yearning may remain buried in night dreams, daydreams, ritual, prayer, or brief verbal allusions. Writers, a different breed altogether, refuse to relegate the "good place" to a minuscule corner. From primeval oral traditions to current publications, writers have depicted utopia as a dream world that belongs in the forefront of creativity, where vivid word pictures alternately enlighten and chasten, dismay and delight, depending on utopia's glory, the wide separation between heaven and the here-and-now, and the behavior and worthiness of the seeker.

In the earliest forms of literary escapism, utopias center on God or gods, after-death rewards for goodness and charity, and top-of-the-mountain pavilions of the blessed. The extremes of place, surroundings, and physical and psychological topography suit the dreamer rather than the reader and give intimate testimony to the dreamer's desires:

- In mystic oriental lore, utopia has no discernible place, no measurable dimensions. As conceived by Hindus, Buddhists, and Taoists, the end of a long road of seeking re-forms the seeker into uncreated matter, much as a potter reshapes a badly molded pot back into a lump of clay. No longer endowed with a body, the spirit flees its mortal frame and departs like sun rays into a transcendent oneness with the divine.

- In Christian cosmology, wherever the soul finds and unites with God is heaven, a resplendent throne that adorns Dante's *Divine Comedy* (1320) and John Milton's *Paradise Lost* (1677).

- A more mundane version described by John Bunyan in *Pilgrim's Progress* (1678) gives an allegorical account of the quest for salvation. Bunyan's hero and heroine, Christian and Christiana, pass through fearsome obstacles and temptations on their way to Beulah Land and Celestial City, the seat of the Almighty.

Similarly, lengthy scriptural texts and commentaries, ranging from *The Book of the Dead* (fifteenth century B.C.) to Hesiod's *Works and Days* (eighth century B.C.), the *Upanishads* and Isaiah (seventh century B.C.), Genesis (950 B.C.), and Revelation (A.D. 90–95) to the more contemporary *Black Elk Speaks* (1932) and Joseph Smith's *Book of Mormon* (1830), perpetuate the soul's longing for affirmation and a promise that destruction and death do not end life. Delivered in the pithy style common to Lao Tzu, al-Ghazali, and Confucius is one of the world's most famous prescriptions for finding utopia—Christ's Sermon on the Mount, which carries a heavy warning: "For where your treasure is, there will your heart be also." His meaning is plain: Each seeker of heaven must shake off the attachment to worldly delights and concentrate on righteousness.

After humanity became citified, urbanely introspective, and tentatively atheistic, utopists turned from god on high to man on high. During the Middle Ages, the melding of valiance, honor, and fealty found its expression in Camelot, home of King Arthur, the male-centered chivalric ideal. Crisscrossed with romantic motifs of love, temptation, treachery, and revenge, the stories of the Round Table supplanted the godly utopias of early times with a pervasive, all-encompassing study of earth. Depending on the literary impetus of the writer, sanctuaries of this period departed from the religious self-denial pictured in scripture and aimed for a distinctive earthly escape. In place of the word *godly*, utopists tended toward a whole new diction—e.g., *contented, idyllic, pastoral,* and *happy*. The European Renaissance and a rebirth of humanism carried the utopian dream closer to home by stressing the worth of life. By abandoning the former eras' demands for punishment, recognition of original sin, or asceticism in place of sensual pleasure, utopists Sir Thomas More (inventor of the term "utopia"), François Rabelais, Michel de Montaigne, Johann Andreae, and William Shakespeare again altered the diction of utopia with frequent mentions of nature, delight, harmony, and joy.

Beginning in the seventeenth century, perfect worlds plunged in myriad directions, each characterizing the utopist's focus: Fra Tomaso Campanella bases his City of the Sun on an island where life is as simple as figures on a tapestry; Francis Bacon grounds his Bensalem on science; James Harrington's Oceana depicts a miniature cosmos as neatly interwoven and interdependent as clockworks. The full range of alternates appears in world pictures by British journalist Daniel Defoe and Irish prelate Jonathan Swift, whose dream worlds follow the island utopia motif:

- Defoe chooses a desert island and his hero, Robinson Crusoe, as tools of the moralist intent on a didactic lesson. Defoe's detailed plot reaches a simple conclusion: Do the best that you can and give thanks to God for work, challenge, and simple rewards.

- Swift, a troubled churchman who straddled the warring worlds of Ireland and England, grew moody and dark-visioned. Unlike Defoe's realism, his cosmos produced only ridiculous situations; his satire handicapped the fictional Lemuel Gulliver with a perverted sense of self and place, the outcome of years of travel among tiny pygmies, coarse giants, warlike residents of a floating island, and self-righteous horse-beings who denigrate humankind.

Whereas the robust Robinson Crusoe saves an endangered life and returns home with hope and gratitude in his heart, Lemuel Gulliver sinks into neurotic withdrawal, stuffs his offended nostrils with herbs, and condemns all comers, even his own family.

These spirited, imaginative other worlds precede a lengthy, disparate list of utopias and dystopias. Voltaire sets his hero Candide on a gauntlet of near misses before placing him in a garden in Turkey; in contrast, Samuel Johnson, creator of Rasselas, denies his protagonist contentment in Happy Valley and impels him back to the real world of poverty and pain. Wherever individual styles and premises prevail, writers alter the idea of heaven or its opposite to suit themselves:

- Samuel Taylor Coleridge, in an abortive attempt at a rich 300-line poem, recreates a fragment of the Edenic garden retreat of Kublai Khan, a historic Mongol warlord.

- Étienne Cabet carries the *Voyage en Icarie* (1840), his Mediterranean success story, to the heights of rational city planning, which became an obsession with other utopists of his time.

- In *Past and Present* (1843), Thomas Carlyle longs to shuck off the miseries of the Industrial Revolution and revive the unmechanized Middle Ages by following Brother Sampson's ideal—monastic absorption in hard work.

The tone and atmosphere of these dream worlds vary from Coleridge's drug-induced reverie to the workaday demands of street sweeping and garden toil to escape in Polynesian bliss. The controlling factor—the writer's mental landscape—offers an unlimited palate on which to paint the "good place."

A sharp veer from Eden to politics began in 1848 with the worker's paradise prophesied by the grim, revolutionary polemics of Karl Marx and Friedrich Engels. Outposts looked askance at the changes in their mechanized milieu and chose various avenues of accommodating themselves to busy, noisy cities and the meretricious rule of finance:

- Edward Bulwer-Lytton warns of a subterranean nation powered by *vril*, a mysterious ore.

- Samuel Butler gives the impression of creating Erewhon, a dream utopia, the reverse of which roughly spells out *nowhere*, the end of utopianism.

- Alfred Tennyson, 75 years before World War I, warns of a dystopic force—the use of flying machines to spread war.

- W. H. Hudson lapses into a melancholy blend of utopia/dystopia by introducing his hero to *A Crystal Age* (1887), a matriarchy that at first lulls him, then deludes him into unintentional suicide.

- Mark Twain brings his hero, Hank Morgan, to a similar pass in a journey backward to King Arthur's Camelot. After all-out war, Hank survives in a mystical coma before dying in his own time.

- Theodor Hertzka botches an effort to duplicate earlier utopias by describing Freiland, an unconvincing planned colony that falls short of the demands of his time.

- William Morris awakens his hero in a future era that revives England's agrarian past by abandoning factories and mechanization in favor of cottage crafts.

The wavering belief in goodness and progress prefigures the strong denunciation of human evil in the twentieth century, a time when utopia survives in the fantasy world of children's literature written by L. Frank Baum and J. M. Barrie, but collapses in the forbidding, doom-and-destruction dystopias of Jack London, Yevgeny Zamyatin, Ayn Rand, George Orwell, Aldous Huxley, William Golding, James Hilton, and Ray Bradbury.

From the blissful other worlds of centuries past, the wretched conditions preceding and following two world wars severely pruned writers' urges to look for the "good place." In numerous titles, bizarre, unexpected evils percolate through creative brains:

- Hermann Hesse places his mythic Indian hero on a riverbank to watch a rise and fall of human fortunes as arbitrary as the flow of the river.

- Alex Haley concludes the autobiography of Malcolm X, an evangelist for black pride, with his assassination in the early stages of his dreams of an Islamic unity among all races.

- Female utopists Doris Lessing, P. D. James, Marge Piercy, and Margaret Atwood write guardedly hopeful stories of terror and anarchy and of protagonists who cling to the disintegrating rim of security.

The surmise that bubbles to the surface leads the reader to question whether humankind has outlived an age-old hope for the "good place," which ebbs at a rapid pace equivalent to the sufferings, wars, pollution, and inhuman behaviors common to Homo sapiens.

If dream worlds continue their downward skid into hopelessness and self-destruction, what is the reader to conclude? A simple answer encompasses an overall explanation of literature: People write to express their responses to the times in which they live and prevailing obstacles to happiness. Some writers leap over the barriers and move into optimism for the distant future; others halt at the stop sign and contemplate how humankind arrives at such impasses. The question that inspires utopian writers today is the same question for governors, scientists, ministers, teachers, and ordinary citizens: What methods will enable societies to accommodate or alleviate the world situation? Whatever the approach, the utopist—like Teiresias, Jeremiah, and Cassandra of ancient times—serves a purpose in sounding the alarm: The "good place" may lie just around the millennium or permanently out of reach.

Encyclopedia of
Utopian
Literature

THE ABBEY OF THÉLÈME

This fanciful, ornate, fictitious setting appears in Book I of François Rabelais's raucous satire *Gargantua and Pantagruel* (1562), an episodic novel populated by picaresque caricatures and generously laced with puns and belly laughs. The antithesis of medieval rigor, control, asceticism, and piety, the Abbey of Thélème runs to excess in color, style, and variety, suggesting the delights of European salons with their perpetual gatherings of notables, gossips, clotheshorses, and literati. The imposing Abbey of Thélème is a heavily endowed retreat built by the giant Gargantua in appreciation of the kindness of monk Jean des Entpommeures. A sixteenth-century Renaissance playground, the abbey possesses neither clock nor sundial, rejects regulation by time or activity schedule, and opens its gates so that its aristocratic inmates can wander abroad as a means of widening their experience, educating their minds, and contenting their spirits.

One crucial aspect of selective utopias like that of Rabelais (as well as the exclusive utopian settings of his predecessors, particularly Plato and Castiglione) is the intense scrutiny of the application process, a measure of the author's disdain for democracy and his lack of respect for individuals. Sexism, classism, and ageism provide the major criteria: The only women admitted to the convent are "fair, well featured, and of a sweet disposition." Likewise, only men "comely, personable, and well-conditioned" settle at the abbey. Overturning the usual Catholic vows of "chastity, poverty, and obedience," Rabelais's utopian abbey demands that inmates "be honorably married, that they might be rich, and live at liberty." To woo the most promising sybarites, Gargantua promises them perfumed halls and chambers spiced with "spirit of roses, orange-flower water, and angelica."

Unlike Thomas Carlyle's *Past and Present* (1843), which views monasticism from the viewpoint of healthy, vigorous workers, Rabelais exempts his abbey-dwellers from day-to-day chores. In tune with his expansive fantasy, the building provides tapestries, damasks, cut flowers in crystal vases, canopied beds, gilt mirrors, and other extravagances not usually associated with monasticism. Outside, elegantly groomed and coiffed residents enjoy paddocks and equestrian exercise yards, an archery range, and a typical Renaissance hedge shaped into a maze, a standard convention in romantic literature that often provides lovers with a verdant spot for late-night trysts. The fountains feature classic rather than religious designs; majestic staircases grace the lavish interior. Gargantua pays 27,801 gold ingots in the shape of rams for the creation of his hexagonal, six-storied monastery. Located just south of the Loire River, the building is marked by six towers 312 paces apart. Its 9,332 rooms contain closets and private entrances. The library boasts classics in Greek, Latin, Hebrew, French, Italian, and Spanish. Outside the walls, inmates enjoy tennis courts, gardens, theaters, swimming pools, and hunting. Adorned with fretwork, wainscoting, slate, antique figures, gilt guttering, galleries, vaults, and gold and azure paint, the abbey rivals in sumptuousness the real French castles of Chambourg, Chenonceaux, and Chantilly. Yet, nobody seems to be doing the work of keeping the place clean and supplied with food.

Created as an outgrowth of Rabelais's disgruntlement with religious hypocrisy, rebellion against sour religiosity permeates the inscription of Thélème's gate with a curmudgeon's humor: The abbey claims to ward off boobs, sots, imposters, bigots, varlets, cafards, fomenters and debaters, liars, fakes, and deceivers. Also unwelcome are lawyers, clerks, scribes, pharisees, judges, and the rest of the legal community. Rabelais forbids money-grubbers, grumps, and rogues. His lengthy verse welcomes "pure, honest, faithful, true, expounders of the scriptures, old and new," a sly turn of phrase that implies his disinterest in tedious canonical scholarship. His preference for sparkly eyed, sprightly, and fashionable men and women presages a lively community exuding charm and vivacity, intent on following nature, and dedicated to a single rule: "Do as you will." (Bishop 1965; Carlyle 1977; Lewis 1969; Manguel and Guadalupi 1987; Pollard 1970; Putnam 1993; Rabelais 1955; Rabkin et al., 1983; Screech, 1980)

See also city planning; escapism; fantasy; *Gargantua and Pantagruel*; materialism; *Past and Present*; Rabelais, François; satire; women in utopia.

ADAM

The prime human figure in ancient Hebrew creation lore recorded in the book of Genesis, the Gnostic Gospels, the Kabbalah, the Koran, and Milton's epic *Paradise Lost*, Adam prefigures Christ. He is the first human being and the first male, whom Yahweh or God creates in his own image and names *'adham*, short for *'adhamah*, the Hebrew word for "earth." God shapes Adam out of earth as a potter molds clay; the significant moment in Adam's creation is the receipt of the breath of life, which God blows into his mouth.

A reflection of the fantasy of a nomadic people, the biblical story of Adam centers on stability, natural beauty, and abundance. God appoints Adam as an earthly superintendent over Eden, the prototypical utopian garden named for the Hebrew word *delight*, which is stocked with a variety of fruit trees, herbs, animals, birds, and fish. Adam's role in this idyllic setting reflects God's trust— God assigns the first man to name and care for the animals, till the garden, and

The Christian god creates Adam, the first man, in this painting by Michelangelo in the Vatican's Sistine Chapel.

tend the plants, which grow under eternally balmy conditions. Implicit in Adam's relationship with the Creator is the acceptance of a single unequivocal ban: Eat no fruit from the Tree of the Knowledge of Good and Evil.

In time, Adam ceases to revel in his pastoral haven because he grows lonely for a human companion to share it. In one version, God takes one of Adam's ribs and shapes it into Eve (or Awa in Arabic), the first female, who joins Adam in forming the first human couple and becoming the first parents. Eve proves vulnerable to the temptation of the wily serpent, an earthly persona of the fallen angel Lucifer, or Satan, who seeks to subvert God's plan for a paradise on Earth. After Adam gives in to Eve's suggestion and violates the commandment not to eat of the Tree of the Knowledge of Good and Evil, God seeks him out, demanding, "What is this that thou hast done?" According to Genesis 3:12, Adam voluntarily confesses his sin, blaming "the woman whom thou gavest to be with me, she gave me of the tree, and I did eat." Adam's flimsy rationalization comes perilously close to implicating God along with Eve as co-culprits.

In punishment for their blatant disobedience, God ends the golden age he had so generously entrusted to his earthlings by cursing the ground. He pledges to Adam and all humanity who spring from his line a life of sorrow and toil in ground that will grow thorns and thistles. Forced to sweat for his bread, Adam becomes a farmer of the dusty soil from which he was initially shaped. He is further cursed to die and be buried in the earth from which he sprang, thus symbolizing a oneness with the universe that predates the Christian concepts of forgiveness, salvation, and an afterlife in heaven. Driven from the blissful paradise on Earth and burdened with original sin and its irrevocable consequences, Adam departs from Eden in shame; he is further humiliated by siring the first murderer, Cain (whose name means spear), slayer of his brother Abel. (Alexander and Alexander 1973; Anderson 1966; Dickey 1993; Holy Bible 1958; Mays 1988; The Oxford Annotated Bible 1962; Pelikan 1992c; Turner 1993)

See also *Back to Methuselah;* creation, mythic; Eden; Eve; golden age; *Paradise Lost; Paradise Regained;* pastoral; *R. U. R.; Timaeus;* women in utopia.

 # ADAMS, RICHARD

Author of *Watership Down* (1972), a suspense-filled dystopian beast fable about tyranny and escape, Adams is a native of Berkshire, England; he used his knowledge of the wilds and indigenous creatures to flesh out the milieu of his hero, Hazel the rabbit. Born in Newbury on May 9, 1920, to Lilian Rosa Button and George Beadon Adams, a surgeon, Adams served in the military during World War II. In his mid-twenties he entered Worcester College, Oxford, and received an M.A. in history in 1948. His quarter-century career with the Ministry of Housing and Local Government stands remote from a worldly wise epic rabbit tale and the extensive canon of fantasy novels that followed: *Shardik* (1974), *Tyger Voyage* (1976), *The Plague Dogs* (1977), *The Iron Wolf* (1980), *The Girl in a Swing* (1980), and *Maia* (1984).

A resident of Whitchurch, Hampshire, Adams maintains membership in the Royal Society of Literature and has presided over the Royal Society for the Prevention of Cruelty to Animals. He is married to Elizabeth Adams, an expert in ceramic history. His success in the fiction market has brought him honorary residencies at Hollins College and the University of Florida, and a spot on the best-seller list in 1972. He has received the Guardian Award for children's literature, the California Young Readers' Association Medal, and a Carnegie Medal. Six years after the publication of his animal dystopia, Nepenthe Films released an animated color version—a realistic plunge into terror, tests of group loyalty, martyrdom, and daring. Voices for the animals were supplied by John Hurt, Ralph Richardson, Zero Mostel, and Denholm Elliott, among others. (Adams 1972; *Contemporary Authors* 1981; Gilman 1974; Prescott 1974; Smith 1974)

See also dystopia; escapism; fantasy; Hazel; humanitarianism; naturalism; prophecy; synergy; totalitarianism; *Watership Down.*

 # AENEAS

Aeneas is the handsome, devout epic hero of Rome in Virgil's lofty creation, which segues directly into Homer's Trojan lore from the *Iliad* and *Odyssey.* The story centers on a pious, thoughtful though sometimes downhearted voyager whom Hera batters with continual storms, obstructions, and disappointments. Because of his birth to Aphrodite (Greek goddess of love), Aeneas is unusually attractive. In Virgil's description,

> Aeneas stood discovered in sheen of brilliant light, like a god in face and shoulders; for his mother's self had shed on her son the grace of clustered locks, the radiant light of youth, and the luster of joyous eyes . . . (Book I)

Virgil compares this divine physical appearance to burnished ivory or precious stones inlaid in gold.

Adventure dominates the biography of Aeneas. As captain of a newly constructed fleet, Aeneas collects friends, family, and survivors of the cataclysmic fire that destroys Troy (currently known as Hissarlik, on the Asian side of Turkey) and guides them about the Mediterranean in search of New Troy, which lies at an undisclosed location to the west. Although storm-driven as far south as Libya, Aeneas is content to heed the commands of the gods who appear in dreams, visions, and disguises to provide information, inspiration, or direction. Deprived of the total picture of the elusive promised land of Hesperia, he stumbles and at times nears total despair before arriving safely in Latium, opposite the Tyrrhenian Sea on Italy's west coast.

In the early portion of Virgil's *Aeneid,* the hero relies on the experience and wisdom of his father, Anchises, a human who mated with Aphrodite, Aeneas's perpetual protector. After his father's death in Sicily, Aeneas boldly faces the terrors of the Underworld in order to hear the last of his father's advice. The most significant portion of Aeneas's journey to Hades is his visit to Elysium, the Edenic home of blessed heroes who wash themselves clean of past lives in the river Lethe, then take on new identities for subsequent ventures on Earth. As Anchises introduces them, they anticipate becoming Rome's illustrious heroes, leaders, and sages. Culminating in the Divine Augustus himself (Rome's first emperor), the entourage promises a nation supreme, more illustrious than anything the world has known.

On his return to the surface of Earth, Aeneas willingly accepts protracted war as the price of so great a nation—the Eternal City of Rome, which will house Troy's gods and perpetuate the ideals of Trojan civilization. A one-dimensional hero, he obeys the gods and his destiny, even to the point of leaving Queen Dido's hospitality as her funeral pyre smudges Libya's morning skies. Content in his role as founder of a new Troy, Aeneas refuses to allow earthly ties to a voluptuous and alluring queen to imperil his covenant with divinity. (Hardie 1986; Snodgrass 1988b; Snodgrass 1994; Virgil 1950; Williams and Pattie 1982)

See also Aeneid; disillusion; prophecy; Virgil.

 # *AENEID*

The literary epic of the Roman Empire, the *Aeneid* was composed by Publius Virgilius Naso and published posthumously in 19 B.C. The majestic sweep of

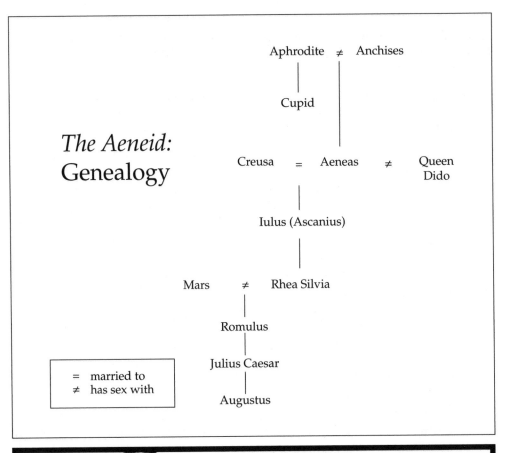

The Aeneid: Genealogy

Aphrodite ≠ Anchises

Cupid

Creusa = Aeneas ≠ Queen Dido

Iulus (Ascanius)

Mars ≠ Rhea Silvia

Romulus

Julius Caesar

Augustus

= married to
≠ has sex with

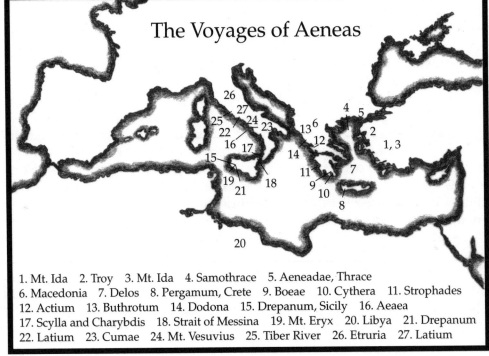

The Voyages of Aeneas

1. Mt. Ida   2. Troy   3. Mt. Ida   4. Samothrace   5. Aeneadae, Thrace
6. Macedonia   7. Delos   8. Pergamum, Crete   9. Boeae   10. Cythera   11. Strophades
12. Actium   13. Buthrotum   14. Dodona   15. Drepanum, Sicily   16. Aeaea
17. Scylla and Charybdis   18. Strait of Messina   19. Mt. Eryx   20. Libya   21. Drepanum
22. Latium   23. Cumae   24. Mt. Vesuvius   25. Tiber River   26. Etruria   27. Latium

Virgil's propagandist epic accomplishes what the poet intended: It honors Augustus, his old schoolmate and Rome's first emperor. Because Rome lacked a noble history, Virgil created one by linking the fallen Troy with the robust Roman civilization, which ruled over much of the Mediterranean world. Imitating Homer's 12-book epics, the *Iliad* and the *Odyssey*, Virgil begins Book I with a sonorous overview of the task to be accomplished by Aeneas, Rome's cultural hero, son of Anchises and the goddess Aphrodite:

> I sing of arms and the man who came of old, a fated wanderer, from the coasts of Troy to Italy and the shore of Lavinium; hard driven on land and on the deep by the violence of heaven, by reason of cruel Hera's unforgetful anger, and hard bestead in war also ere he might found a city and carry his gods into Latium; from whom is the Latin race, the lords of Alba, and high-embattled Rome.

Requesting aid of the muse, Virgil clarifies events that lead to the founding of Rome by survivors of the Trojan War. Because Hera (Zeus's consort) plots against a plan destined to destroy Carthage, she concocts a string of petty charges against the hero and his band, who carom about the Mediterranean in search of a new Troy.

Beginning *in medias res* (and at the high point of the conflict), in Book I Virgil introduces Aeneas and his faithful companion Achates. The crew is cast up in Libya on Africa's north shore after Hera forces Aeolus (the god of the winds) to wreck their ships. To lighten the survivors' distress and frustration, Aeneas, who shares their mood, promises better times:

> Comrades of hard times, we are not unaccustomed to trials. Know that these hardships are the will of the gods and that they will one day reach their appointed end. Summon strong hearts. Let no sorrow burden or dismay you. These trying days we will one day celebrate with laughing reminiscence. . . . Keep your eye to the future, when good fortune will ease the care-worn spirit.

The goddess Aphrodite (Aeneas's mother) appears and informs the men that they are approaching the kingdom of Dido, a husbandless queen whose followers toil to raise the city of Carthage. Smitten by Aeneas's radiant good looks, Dido welcomes the visitors with a state banquet. Through trickery, Venus causes Eros to wound the queen with a dart so that she will fall in love. Dizzy with passion, Dido invites Aeneas to recount the past seven years' wanderings.

In Book II, shortly after Troy's loss of Hector, their military champion, Aeneas tells of the most distressing turn of events—the departure of Greek forces from the Troad and the arrival of the Trojan horse, supposedly a divine offering. By night, Hector's spirit appears to Aeneas in a vision and warns that the wooden image is hollow and that armed Greeks will soon pour out from the trapdoor and gut the city. The ghost's instructions are clear:

> Make haste, goddess-born . . . to avoid the flames that devour the city. The Greeks even now possess the ramparts; Troy will soon tumble. . . . The dying city entrusts to you its sacred objects, its gods and future; accept this sacred trust. Sail from this carnage and search out permanent shelter. Your days will

be filled with wandering and frustration, but you alone can settle the holy remnants on safe ground.

Aeneas seizes his armor and rushes out into chaos. At the sound of thunder and the sight of a comet, he accedes to divine guidance, and against impossible odds leads his family east to safety on Mount Ida. On the way, his wife Creusa dies in the street fighting; her spirit returns to urge him to find Hesperia, the kingdom ordained by the gods. Joining the throng of survivors who cluster about him, Aeneas accepts a monumental responsibility.

In Book III, Aeneas departs from the Phrygian Mountains in a newly constructed fleet the next summer and sails north to Thrace, then south to Delos and Crete, where a divine messenger reiterates his destination:

> Hold fast to your covenant to build a shining city for a bold race. The gods intend neither Delos nor Crete for your sacred purpose. The new Troy lies to the west— Hesperia, an ancient land famed for strength. . . . Troy deserves no less.

Led only by faith, they sail blind up Greece's western coast to the Strophades Islands near Sparta, then to Chaonia, near Actium. At a chance meeting with Helenus, Troy's prophet prince, Aeneas learns that a fat white sow nursing 30 piglets under a holly tree will serve as the omen marking the crucial spot. Past Scylla and Charybdis and the Cyclopes, the Trojans reach Sicily, where Anchises, Aeneas's father and chief adviser, dies.

Book IV concludes Aeneas's poignant oral itinerary. Returned from painful memories to Dido's land at a generous banquet, he unknowingly captivates a love-starved queen. Dido ponders her infatuation for the handsome Trojan captain, who takes a seat after narrating his woeful story. For days she entertains him and beguiles him into a lyric sylvan wedding in an effort to dissuade him from leaving. By distracting him from duty, she prompts Zeus to dispatch Hermes with a heavenly reminder that the gods' will supersedes vows made to an earthly queen. Aeneas leaves his enraged lover behind and sails north. In despair, she kills herself with his sword.

As Book V opens, Aeneas and his crew assume the worst when they catch sight of Dido's flaming funeral barrow. Returning to Sicily, the fleet runs into difficulties. Men who despair of permanence set fire to the ships in hopes of ending their sea travels. Distressed by multiple problems and grieving over his father's death, Aeneas considers abandoning his mission. But his father's spirit goads him to follow his original plan of winnowing out the weak among his band and pressing on with the best of the lot. Aeneas once more sets sail, crosses the Tyrrhenian Sea, and beaches his ships at Latium.

In Book VI, the band nears Cumae, where Aeneas consults the sybil at her cave. She dispatches him to the forest to locate a golden bough by which he will enter the Underworld. When he returns with the wand, she guides him to the banks of the river Styx, where Charon the boatman ferries him to the opposite shore. Aeneas traverses the most terrifying parts of Hades to Elysium, the Edenic Fields of the Blessed, where sun and stars light the activities of wraiths who frolic to music. Aeneas reunites with Anchises; the old man weeps with joy at the sight of his son.

The poet describes in detail the wondrous future of Rome, which springs from souls who plunge into the river Lethe, escape past lives, and are fitted with new personae. Anchises names the leaders who will one day bring honor and greatness to the new Troy: Silvius, Romulus, Numa, Tarquinius, Brutus, Cato, the Gracchi, Scipio, Julius Caesar, and his nephew, Augustus Caesar, "a god's son, who shall reestablish a golden age in Latium." Freshly invigorated by the vision of so glorious a city, Aeneas returns to his fleet with purpose and vision. The remaining six books of the epic detail the brutal war that precedes the victory prophesied for Rome, the New Troy.

Similar in motif to Odysseus's Underworld search, Dante's epic journey through hell, purgatory, and heaven, and Christ's harrowing of hell, Aeneas's journey to the Underworld epitomizes Virgil's didactic purpose in writing the *Aeneid*. This confrontation with the unknown represents the ultimate test of human daring in service to an ideal. The trek across the Styx to Hades, physically and spiritually daunting, demonstrates the major character strength of the heroic Aeneas and finds him suited to his role in history. Simultaneously, Virgil presents to the reader the Roman concept of an exclusive utopian afterlife, which rewards male military heroes and rulers. (Hardie 1986; Snodgrass 1988b; Snodgrass 1994; Virgil 1950; Williams and Pattie 1982)

See also Aeneas; *Bucolics;* city planning; Dante Alighieri; didacticism; *Divina Commedia;* Elysian Fields; prophecy; Virgil.

ALEX

The victimizing and victimized central intelligence of Anthony Burgess's *A Clockwork Orange* (1962), a sadistic dystopian novel predicting a grim future for England, Alex is a smart-mouthed, amoral teenage predator without ethics or conscience. With his three pals, he roams the streets of town by night and entertains himself with pointless violent acts. His victims, the weak and undefended, fall prey to his malignant sense of fun. But Alex becomes a victim of his own gang after he upbraids Dim, the strongest and least intelligent of the foursome. The gang betrays Alex to the police and he draws a jail term.

After Alex is imprisoned in a brutal lockup, he gladly embraces a glimmer of hope—Ludovico's Technique, a rehabilitation method of applying visual avoidance training to hardened felons. After Alex is bound in a chair and injected with a powerful mind-altering drug, he proves to be a quick study of the method and fights to avoid further treatments. A luckless guinea pig, Alex cannot cope with the dystopian England he views on his release from jail, although the charity and compassion of F. Alexander, an author and humanitarian whom Alex happens to meet, briefly offsets the rejection of Alex's parents and their boarder, Joe.

Eventually the social and emotional trauma forces him back into the intransigent world of violence. In the final paragraphs, delineated in the Underworld patois of Burgess's prose, Alex signs himself into a hellish milieu and exults:

Then I was left alone with the glorious Ninth of Ludwig van. Oh, it was gorgeosity and yumyumyum. When it came to the Scherzo I could viddy myself very clear running and running on like very light and mysterious nogas, caring the whole litso of the creeching world with my cutthroat britva.

As symbolized by classical music, the dark underside of sadism once more possesses his dehumanized soul. He divests himself of conscience and self-control and sinks into escapism, content at last with "the lovely last singing movement still to come." In Alex's estimation, he accepts the cure as the narrowest yet most gratifying of perfect worlds, the cadence and melody that relieves him of self-induced torment and guilt. (Aggler 1986; Bloom 1987a; Burgess 1962; Coale 1981; Dix 1971; Mathews 1978; Morris 1971; Stinson 1991)

See also classism; *A Clockwork Orange*; conditioning; escapism; Ludovico's Technique; technology.

 # ALLEGORY

An allegory is a rhetorical device through which an author injects into a plot more than one meaning. Unlike symbolism, which is a less pervasive example of meaning intensification, allegory is a systemized arrangement of meanings forming layers of significance applicable to an entire work. For example, in *The Fable of the Bees* (1705), a satiric poem by Bernard de Mandeville, bees display human foibles and vices. The use of allegory is a form of audience control, permitting the writer to imbue characters, actions, and settings with an overlay of abstract meanings that may derive from politics, religion, or morality. The reader has the option of perusing the narrative on a denotative level or appreciating the text and the underlying allegory as well.

Interpreted from surface details, Richard Adams's *Watership Down* (1972) exemplifies an obvious surface plot—a thrilling adventure story about rabbits struggling to survive the bulldozing of their ancestral home. When human values are applied to the action, the story reveals the author's bias against totalitarianism, brutality, and violence to nature. The animals demonstrate human emotions—a need for heroic lore and divinity, delight in nature and freedom, dismay at a menace too terrifying to confront, and the fortitude to rescue other rabbits from certain death. Thus, the reader can discern in the actions of Hazel, leader of a new warren, the qualities that set him apart from the ordinary, such as sensitivity to his visionary brother Fiver, courage to combat General Woundwort (a totalitarian warlord who threatens his group's survival), logic and strategy to counter the savagery of attackers, and reverence toward the gods, who free his spirit from his body and waft it away to a peaceful, rejuvenating new life.

The most successful English allegory—John Bunyan's didactic heavenly quest *Pilgrim's Progress* (1678), a blend of pragmatism and faith—carefully arranges a series of stumbling blocks to hinder the progress of Christian on his way to salvation. The typical everyman, Christian experiences an unending battle between good and evil. He abandons his wife Mercy and defeats doubts, fears, threats, and enticements as he navigates the Slough of Despond, Vanity Fair, Doubting Castle, the Delectable Mountains, the Valley of the Shadow of Death, the Interpreter's House, the Valley of Humiliation, and a host of distractions, disillusionments, and threats. At the end of his test of faith, Christian enters Beulah Land, the chamber that precedes entrance into the Celestial City, or heaven.

Bunyan draws heavily on the richly detailed King James translation of scripture (published in 1611) to keep Christian's faith alive and his feet moving toward a righteous destination. To relieve the story of tedium, Bunyan creates menacing pitfalls, for example, the fiendish dragon Apollyon, "clothed with scales like a fish . . . wings like a dragon, and feet like a bear." He balances Apollyon with a suitable sprinkling of didactic characters whose names denote rescue, reaffirmation, good cheer, logic, strategy, belief, and anticipation (i.e., Mr. Worldly Wiseman, Giant Despair, Faithful, and Hopeful). Although the pilgrim reaches numerous cliff-hangers and teeters perilously close to acquiescence to worldliness and sin, the tone of his quest reassures the reader that Christian has what it takes to complete his mission and find acceptance in heaven.

Not all allegory is so conspicuously captioned or easily interpreted as that of John Bunyan. In 1900 L. Frank Baum, an American tableware salesman-turned-raconteur, published a best-selling children's novel, *The Wonderful Wizard of Oz*, which spooled out into a long-lived series of illustrated adventures in Oz. The Cowardly Lion, the Tin Man, and the Scarecrow, the three major characters who follow heroine Dorothy to the Wizard's palace, long to compensate for a lack of courage, heart, and intelligence. They turn to the Wizard, who proves to be a short, cowardly fake hiding behind a scary façade, a deceptive surface enabling the con artist to cow and subdue a kingdom. The seekers find themselves cured of their inadequacies through their own efforts, and Dorothy learns to value the intrinsic worth of the Kansas farm she calls home.

A less sanguine adult allegory appeared in Czechoslovakia in 1920—Karel Capek's *R. U. R.*, a diabolical creation drama set in a fantasy factory built by old Dr. Rossum, who dies before the story opens. By exploiting Rossum's synthesized protoplasm, his unprincipled son builds a factory capable of supplying the world with unemotional androids programmed to perform drudgery or form into phalanxes of mercenaries. The story acquires a touch of myth near the end when the robots, who have developed sensitivity and pride, rebel and wipe out all human exploiters except one—Mr. Alquist, whom they keep as a technician in the factory laboratory. In the play's epilogue, Alquist frenziedly works toward the creation of a new Adam and Eve, named Primus and Helena, the world's only hope of repopulation. In a final moment with the pair as they depart a perverted Eden, the godlike Alquist blesses them with a promise: "Go, Adam, go, Eve. The world is yours."

Even more disquieting than Capek's antitechnology allegory is William Golding's fearful wartime dystopia *Lord of the Flies* (1954), which opens with the crash of an evacuation plane on an unidentified Pacific isle. The castaways, including an English boys' choir, survive the bombs and terror of World War II but arrive in an Eden that they quickly turn into hell. At first the children acclimate themselves to sun, beach, swimming, fresh fruit, indolence, and inland adventures. They acquire enough stability to think through their dilemma and accept the island as a godsend. As miniature Adams, they fan out over paradise like children turned out of school for recess, eating their fill and reveling in the absence of discipline.

The rapid breakdown of the children's goodwill and their disaffection for Ralph, their titular leader, lead them to disorderly conduct, more serious infractions of courtesy and decency, and finally outright satanic acts of cruelty and murder. Newly initiated into savagery by Jack Merridew, their corrupt, power-hungry leader, the dehumanized islanders behave like monomaniacal Neanderthals; they sharpen sticks, apply clay designs to their faces, and stalk wild boar. In Chapter 8, Golding describes the confrontation between hunters and the more contemplative Ralph:

> The forest near them burst into uproar. Demoniac figures with faces of white and red and green rushed out howling, so that the little 'uns fled screaming. . . . Two figures rushed at the fire and he prepared to defend himself but they grabbed half-burnt branches and raced away along the beach. The three others stood still, watching Ralph; and he saw that the tallest of them, stark naked save for paint and a belt, was Jack.

With no wise adult counsel to dissuade them, Jack Merridew's hunters escalate their degeneracy and their love of power and destruction by slaughtering two endearing innocents—Simon, the babbling visionary, and Piggy, the overweight, asthmatic keeper of laws. A potentially catastrophic fire sweeps the island just as military rescuers arrive, simultaneously halting a third murder.

Taken as allegory, William Golding's plot cautions the reader to distrust human goodness and order, anticipate guile and inhumanity, and value discipline as a necessary control of innate bestiality. Critics have debated the source of evil in *Lord of the Flies*, caroming from Adam and Eve's original sin to the atomic war hovering in the background like storm clouds over a garden party. The dead parachutist, whose decaying remains dangle overhead and terrify the children, emblemizes a duality of soul that hovers in humankind, an outgrowth of corrupt society and faulty education. Attempting to live out the innocent vision of Jean-Jacques Rousseau's "noble savage," the children regress to barbarity because they cannot rid themselves of the nightmarish beast, the Freudian id that impels them to commit evil. As allegory, Golding's dystopia denies hope for a return to Eden, and remands the boys to a world where bad dreams predominate and sleep is never the safe refuge it was in early childhood. By example, the world states a clear message: The maker of rules is the same corrupt power that drops bombs. (Adams 1972; Bunyan 1896; Capek and Capek 1961; Cuddon 1979; Golding 1954; Holman 1981; Lovett and Hughes 1932; Mandeville 1989)

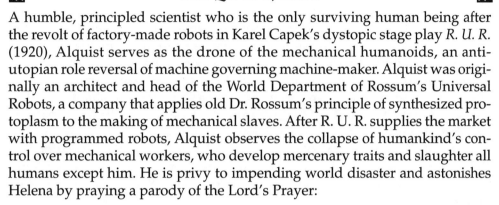

ALQUIST, MR.

A humble, principled scientist who is the only surviving human being after the revolt of factory-made robots in Karel Capek's dystopic stage play *R. U. R.* (1920), Alquist serves as the drone of the mechanical humanoids, an anti-utopian role reversal of machine governing machine-maker. Alquist was originally an architect and head of the World Department of Rossum's Universal Robots, a company that applies old Dr. Rossum's principle of synthesized protoplasm to the making of mechanical slaves. After R. U. R. supplies the market with programmed robots, Alquist observes the collapse of humankind's control over mechanical workers, who develop mercenary traits and slaughter all humans except him. He is privy to impending world disaster and astonishes Helena by praying a parody of the Lord's Prayer:

> Oh, Lord, I thank thee for having given me toil. Enlighten Domin and all those who are astray; destroy their work, and aid mankind to return to their labors; let them not suffer harm in soul or body; deliver us from the Robots . . .

Thus fueled by piety and a sense of mission, Alquist perseveres. The robots stand ready to kill him, but Radius (leader of the anarchists and spokesman for the Government of the Robots of the World) insists that Alquist, a man who "works with his hands like the robots," be spared to serve as replicator of Rossum's formula.

As his name implies, Alquist—like Daedalus, the great inventor of Greek mythology—is a courageous engineer capable of "all quests." In his laboratory, he grows frenetic, calling out the names of his predecessors as he searches for a method of synthesizing human birth. Terrified that he cannot go on without sleep, he wails, "If only there were more time—more time." His own reflection in the mirror leads him to an unsettling coming to knowledge: "Blearing eyes—trembling chin—so *that* is the last man! Ah, I am too old—too old—" Capek indicates that Alquist lacks the capability that Radius expects of him.

Radius's offer of possession of the entire earth holds no allure for Alquist. Against the odds of overwork and fatigue, Alquist prepares to dissect Radius, but, repulsed by the act of dismembering a volunteer, sinks into communion with God. He prays a simple phrase: "O Lord, let not mankind perish from the earth." His dependence on God precedes a brief sleep. At the sound of the laughter of Primus and Helena and the evidence of their tears, willingness to sacrifice, and mutual love, Alquist recognizes the prototypical couple who become the Adam and Eve of all that is left of the human world. The sight awakens hope. Like a humble parson, Alquist blesses the couple as though performing a wedding; like Yahweh of the Old Testament, he sends them forth to populate the earth. (Capek and Capek 1961; Harkins 1962; Magill 1958; Manguel and Guadalupi 1987; Massaryk 1938)

ALTRURIA

Altruria is a newly found pacifist island continent in an undisclosed part of the Southern Hemisphere in William Dean Howells's *Traveler from Altruria* (1894) and its sequel, *Through the Eye of the Needle* (1907). The surprising element of this balmy, idyllic commonwealth is its advanced notion of Christian doctrine. According to citizen Aristides Homos's narrative in Chapter 11 of *Traveler from Altruria*, an isolated form of Christian philosophy has been in practice centuries longer than the European variety because a Christian was shipwrecked on the island in the first century A.D. According to Homos, an Altrurian visitor to the United States, the castaway Christian set up a commune to bring contentment to all. The venture failed because of "misrule." At one time, monopolies like America's oil and railroad conglomerates overran his nation's economy, lacerating commoners with periods of depression, inflation, unemployment, and famine.

The doctrine of accumulation caused a rebellion, and anarchists were supplanted by a benign, evenhanded socialism. Under the new laws there was no need of paper money, which Altrurians considered a major cause of crime. All citizens worked and received what they needed, commune-style. Parliament took over mining, foundries, manufacturing, and transportation. Gradually, the Period of Accumulation died from lack of funds, and in its place rose a common cry: "Brothers all!"

At the time of Homos's visit, Altruria had reached a havenlike existence, a period of stasis suiting the needs of all. He points out that, within the four districts, high-speed electric rail service tied remote sections to each of four capitals. Foul-smelling dray animals were forbidden on roadways. Everyone was educated, and artists were revered like divinities. Business fluctuations occurred, but on a smaller scale. Crime and prostitution had ceased. People occupied unpretentious cottages and ate simply and abstemiously at refectories; these dining halls and public buildings blended utility and beauty and provided daily communion with neighbors.

Once-rampant technology gave place to a Luddite influence, which evolved into a simplicity of design, a balanced lifestyle, and a return to villages, cottage crafts, and joy in industry in the style of William Morris's altruistic utopian novel *News from Nowhere* (1890). Competition no longer stampeded the worker; three hours' work per day supplied the population's needs with useful manufactured goods, eliminating the pitfalls of overproduction. Howells notes in Chapter 12 that

> ugly towns that [former capitalists] had forced into being, as Frankenstein was fashioned, from the materials of the charnel, and that had no life in or from the good of the community, soon tumbled into decay. The administration used parts of them in the construction of [villages] . . . ; but generally these

towns were built of materials so fraudulent, in form so vile, that it was judged best to burn them. In this way their sites were at once purified and obliterated.

The slower-paced citizens coexisted in harmony, the love of God, and the assurance of salvation. Enjoying heaven on Earth and worshiping regularly at their temples, Altrurians had no fear of death and no doubts or misgivings about an afterlife. Hearing all this, Homos's friends look forward to making the far sea voyage to Altruria. Joyously, Homos replies, "Ah, you mustn't go to Altruria! You must let Altruria come to *you.*" (Bennett 1973; Cowie 1951; Escholtz 1975; Howells 1907; Howells 1957; Parrington 1964)

See also classism; Howells, William Dean; *News from Nowhere;* synergy; technology; *Through the Eye of the Needle; A Traveler from Altruria.*

THE ANALECTS OF CONFUCIUS

A collection of profound ethical and social maxims known as the *Lun Yu,* or Selected Sayings, the *Analects* were gathered by the disciples of Confucius, a Chinese sage and humanistic teacher who lived from 551–479 B.C. Extant fragments of Confucius's wisdom, a conservative text outlining the behaviors of people seeking a harmonious society, were compiled by many interpreters, each having some impact on the philosophy known as Confucianism. The syncretized *Analects,* or "Conversations," which reached its final form around the second century A.D., urges followers to comply with authority, support orderly and lawful behavior, pay taxes, honor the family, and observe charity, tradition, loyalty, subordination to those in authority, and respect for elders. In Confucius's perfect world, order evolves naturally from right-thinking, unbiased practitioners of ethics and from refinement of the follower's attitudes and behavior. The Master urges the follower "to be cautious in giving promises and punctual in keeping them, to have kindly feelings towards everyone but seek the intimacy of the Good. If, when all that is done, he has any energy to spare, then let him study the polite arts."

Similar to Plato's identification and description of morals epitomized by the deportment of the beneficent philosopher-king, Confucius deduced that rulers receive their earthly power through the intervention of divine will and should therefore serve as models of probity and lenience to ordinary citizens. To maintain the social order, Confucianism teaches followers to observe *li,* or ritual, as a stabilizing force, thus conferring on the head of the patriarchal household the rights and responsibilities of leadership. In this hierarchy, the ruler becomes the polestar, with subordinate stars paying him homage.

Confucius disdained rigid religious dogma, superstition, and the occult. Rather, he placed at the heart of his beliefs a reverence for humanity, civilization's most precious commodity. In Book 12, verse 22 of the *Analects,* he urges followers to embrace *jen,* the quality of life that sets people apart from other animals. To assure a tranquil, cooperative society, he states in verse 2: "Do not do to others what one does not wish to be done unto," a parallel to the

Christian Golden Rule. Confucius established such altruistic ideals as the foundations of a graceful, civil, cooperative society.

As these brief, pithy aphorisms were confronted by competition from other philosophies, particularly Taoism, Confucius's simple doctrines grew even stronger in popularity. By 206 B.C., the Han dynasty embraced Confucius's reasoning along with the metaphysics of *I Ching* (The Book of Changes). By A.D. 220, the decline of the Hans caused a corresponding eclipse of Confucianism. Six centuries later, during the T'ang dynasty, people again turned to *The Analects of Confucius* for spiritual guidance. This golden era of neo-Confucianism lasted into the twentieth century, when communism ruled out religious thought in China and replaced it with the edicts of Mao Tse-tung. Confucius's work remains in wide circulation throughout other parts of the Orient and in the Western Hemisphere. (Pelikan 1992a; Schwartz 1985; Thompson et al. 1991; Waley 1993)

See also Confucius; Lao Tzu; philosopher-king; syncretism; Tao; *Tao Te Ching*.

ANDREAE, JOHANN VALENTIN

German humanist, scholar and teacher, religious reformer, traveler, and utopist, Andreae wrote in Latin *Fama* (1614), a manual on the perfect college, and his epistolary, *Christianopolis* (1619), a deliberate, meticulous utopian plan for the ideal Christian city. A spindly child born on August 17, 1586, to Maria Moser and the Reverend Johann Andreae in Herrenberg, near Tübingen, Germany, Andreae came from three generations of Württemberg theologians. His father was more interested in science than his pastorage, and preferred alchemy to sermons. When Andreae was 16, his father died; Andreae's widowed mother supported the family by working as a court pharmacist.

At Tübingen University, Andreae studied music, art, mathematics, astronomy, and classical and medieval literature. He completed an M.A. in 1605 and initiated theological studies for two years, but was expelled for taking part in an obscure student insurrection. To earn his way, he traveled Europe as a private tutor until 1612. Two years later, he married Agnes Elisabeth Grüninger, settled in Vaihingen, and fathered nine children. As a Lutheran minister and court chaplain, he wrote an apologia and a variety of small pamphlets, some of which were not published until after he left the pulpit.

Visiting throughout Central Europe, Andreae assessed the strengths of medieval cities such as Herrenberg, Koenigsbrunn, Tübingen, Strassburg, Heidelberg, Frankfurt, Geneva, Vaihingen, and Calw. His gradual composition of utopian principles based on his experiences influenced him to attempt social engineering, notably the organization of dyers and weavers into trade unions and the application of progressive educational practices in his classroom. Another of his projects was the founding of the Christiani Rosencreutz, or Rosicrucians, a secret theosophical society blending mysticism, astrology, alchemy, and the occult.

Although not a Calvinist, Andreae admired John Calvin's theocracy in Geneva. He supported conservatism in public and private behavior along with the more fascist practices of censorship, spying on citizens, and a rigid system of punishment for infractions of civic law. The purpose of Andreae's well-lighted utopia was the circumvention of the darkness of original sin—the "domestic, rustic, or even paternal and inborn evil and wickedness . . . so poisonous a contagion that it spares not even those who ought to be consecrated to God. . . . " In the fictional Christianopolis, Andreae created the street lighting and a night watch to discourage crime, assure public safety, and thwart the rambunctious behaviors, assignations, and intrigues that he considered the "plots of Satan." Andreae's writings never gained the recognition of Fra Tomaso Campanella's *La Città del Sole* (1602) or Thomas More's *Utopia* (1516), but his emphasis on educational reform and intellectual inquiry influenced London's Royal Society. (Andreae 1955; Berneri 1951; Gillispie 1970; Mumford 1959)

See also Christian; Christiana; *Christianopolis*; city planning; idealism; religion; theocracy.

 # *ANIMAL FARM*

George Orwell's classic dystopian beast fable and satire, *Animal Farm* (1945) expresses the author's distaste for propagandists, tyrants, and authoritarian governments growing out of the cataclysm of World War II with its deceptively innocent allegory of Hitler, Mussolini, and Stalin and their roles in creating Nazism, fascism, and hard-line communism. The theme of this disarming idyll, set at Manor Farm, is an egalitarian struggle against human exploitation. Overlaid with irony and satire, the beasts who unseat Farmer Jones (a decadent, undependable human despot) find themselves entrenched in a dismal animal tyranny, which gains strength from a supervisory praetorian guard of pigs.

The slim novel opens with the prophetic dream of a prize Middle White boar named Old Major, who calls a meeting of all barnyard denizens—sheep, horses, cows, pigs, dogs, ducklings, plus a goat, crow, and donkey. With altruistic fervor, Old Major exhorts the animals to follow nature and rebel against Mr. Jones, their profligate master, by creating an animal society and working for themselves. The farmer disrupts their singing of "Beasts of England" with a blast from his shotgun. Three days later, the old boar dies of old age and is interred in the orchard.

Old Major's protégés—three opportunistic pigs named Snowball, Napoleon, and Squealer—set up the principles under which Animal Farm will function. They call their manifesto the Seven Commandments of Animalism:

1. Whatever goes upon two legs is an enemy.
2. Whatever goes upon four legs, or has wings, is a friend.
3. No animal shall wear clothes.

A Polish edition dust jacket of George Orwell's *Animal Farm*

4. No animal shall sleep in a bed.
5. No animal shall drink alcohol.
6. No animal shall kill any other animal.
7. All animals are equal.

On Midsummer's Eve, Mr. Jones angers the animals by drinking to excess and forgetting to tend the stock. In retaliation, they run him, his family, and workers off the place. Eager to create the perfect farm, the pigs burn whips and other evidence of human oppression. Having taught themselves to read and write, they supervise labor: They challenge the animals to surpass their former productivity under human management and retain for themselves the fruits of the harvest. Eventually, Snowball reduces the seven animal commandments to a single precept: "Four legs good, two legs bad."

In mid-October, the experimental farm suffers an unforeseen setback. Mr. Jones coalesces a party of human neighbors at the taproom of the Red Lion pub in Willingdon and the mob fuels a countermove to rout the animal rebels. Orwell heightens the satire of the melodramatic coup d'état mentality by reporting neighborhood rumors of animal torture, cannibalism, and free love. At the glorious Battle of the Cowshed, Napoleon and Snowball, a student of Julius Caesar's battlefield strategies, lead Manor Farm's pigs to victory. At the high point of the engagement, Boxer the cart horse inadvertently kills a stable boy with a blow to the skull and regrets that fighting leads to death. For his bravery, Boxer receives a medal.

Peace at Animal Farm is short-lived; Snowball and Napoleon, contenders for supreme command, fight over the building of a labor-saving windmill. When the matter comes up for a vote, Napoleon unseats Snowball by a surprise tactic—he sets nine savage dogs on Snowball, who scampers away. No longer compromised by his rival, Napoleon oppresses the animals by overworking them and reducing their rations. After the animals slave 60 hours per week plus Sundays to complete the windmill, it is mysteriously destroyed. Napoleon accuses the absent Snowball of lurking nearby, sabotaging the mill, and causing subsequent flaws in farm plans. The pigs, more firmly in power, hire Mr. Whymper as intermediary. They negotiate with humans in Willingdon and move into the farmhouse, rephrasing the Seven Commandments to accommodate luxuries for the ruling party.

Following a dismal winter, a second foray led by Farmer Frederick the next fall results in a setback when part of Animal Farm falls to human adversaries. His forces blow up the windmill, but the animals defeat them. All residents of Animal Farm rededicate themselves to rebuilding the windmill, the symbol of their utopian goals. The overachieving Boxer wears himself out with physical labor and longs to retire, but the pigs deceive him and have him removed to the slaughterhouse. Squealer, propagandist for the pigs, applies a rewriting of history (one of Orwell's chief themes in *1984*) by reporting that Boxer died in the hospital and that his last words confirmed Napoleon as leader.

Years pass; the rebel animals die off, leaving a younger generation who have no memory of Manor Farm, Old Major, or idealism. Because of their sketchy knowledge of history, Napoleon manages to deceive the animals with a new credo: "All animals are equal but some animals are more equal than others." With the assistance of his human cohort, Mr. Pilkington, Napoleon strengthens his control over the land, which he renames Manor Farm. In imitation of Jones, the pigs walk on their hind legs. The other animals, still in Napoleon's power, perceive that the tyrannical pigs resemble human beings.

A witty yet poignant literary tour de force, Orwell's engaging animal fable combines powerful elements: the revelation of intolerable farm conditions, Old Major's dream of an animal utopia, rebellion and subsequent counterrebellion, undermining of the master plan to make Manor Farm into an animal-run haven, the regressive internal strife of animals against animals, and the coercion of the lesser animals by a tyrannical superstructure whose behavior replicates that of Mr. Jones, the farm's human tyrant. A brilliant and cohesive satire composed for the enlightenment and edification of the postwar generation, *Animal Farm* symbolizes the ease with which conniving and traitorous manipulators can employ jingoism. By shifting blame, the pig cabal deceives a gullible, poorly educated nation into accepting dystopia as a subverted substitute for utopia. Just as the generations following the initial overthrow of Mr. Jones have no direct knowledge of former animals' struggles, Orwell implies that the children born after World War II will lack a clear and honest picture of the dangers of totalitarianism and fascism, the destructive forces that propelled world leaders into global war against Hitler, Mussolini, and Tojo. (Alok 1989; Calder 1987; Connelly 1986; Oldsey and Browne 1986; Orwell 1946; Snodgrass 1990)

See also bestiality; Orwell, George; satire; totalitarianism.

ANTHEM

This futuristic dystopian novella or fable was written by Russian-born American writer Ayn Rand. Although *Anthem* (1937) is firmly rooted in Rand's subtle, deterministic, often bitter philosophy, it evidences considerable influence by St. Petersburg native Yevgeny Zamyatin, author of *We* (1921). Like her Russian predecessor, Rand creates a dismal, regimented world devoid of passion, choice, and volition—a stunted microcosm in which bureaucracies stamp out initiative, creativity, and progress in their rush to control human diversity and enforce a stifling status quo. Similar to Aldous Huxley's *Brave New World* (1932), George Orwell's *1984* (1949), Margaret Atwood's *The Handmaid's Tale* (1985), and Lois Lowry's Newbery Award–winning children's dystopia, *The Giver* (1993) in its bleak emotional landscape, chilling detachment from feeling or pity, and faceless, soul-numbing despotism, the book dehumanizes characters with numbers and labels suggesting vehicle license plates, prison numbers, or death-camp tattoos, a crucial symbol exemplifying Rand's obsession with individualism and free will.

Rand moves her personae through a two-dimensional tableau of gestures and poses that justify her distaste for all forms of manacles, all obstructions to objectivism and reason. In Chapter 2, one poignant detail—the childlike nighttime cry of "Help us! Help us! Help us!" from Solidarity 9-6347—gives utterance to the insidious nature of tyranny. Doctors cannot cure the boy of the insecurity and unspoken fears the concentration camp atmosphere instills in its denizens. Solidarity 9-6347's nightmares parallel the sudden sobs of Fraternity 2-5503, who "without reason, in the midst of day or night" shakes with unexplained weeping. Housed in the same ward, the protagonist, 21-year-old Equality 7-2521, looks to the night sky and mentally escapes the barracks by willing himself into the Uncharted Forest. Rand's ironic use of a dark, ominous distant setting suggests the conventions of fable, such as the terrors of the forest and the witch's house that imperil Hansel and Gretel.

Reflecting over the past four years, Equality 7-2521 cannot shake unlawful yearnings that run counter to the state, a regressive totalitarian bureaucracy that obliterates the self so thoroughly that the pronoun *I* ceases to exist. An iron-fisted committee called the Council of Vocations lodges people in barracks, enforces mating and eugenics, and controls education and technology. Labor moves at a diminished pace because workers employ primitive tools and learn no skills to alleviate drudgery. Equality 7-2521 is so far removed from progress that he marvels at smooth, hard iron rails, an innovation belonging to an earlier time when people traveled by subway.

In this hopeless dystopian milieu controlled by sinister, do-nothing councils, numbered nonentity Equality 7-2521 struggles to attain self-fulfillment. He hides in an underground chamber, which survives from a past era known as the Unmentionable Times, and, in poor light among the remains of a subway system, keeps a diary. His words, phrased in the first-person plural, denote a longing for freedom as he crawls into the foul dampness:

> But our hand which followed the track, as we crawled, clung to the iron as if it
> would not leave it, as if the skin of our hand were thirsty and begging of the
> metal some secret fluid beating in its coldness.

After liberating himself from his oppressors, he begins to think of the self as a normal persona. His entries reveal an independent streak that avoids the collective "we" in favor of a singular individuality, a risky attitude punishable by torture and death. Memories of the Home of the Infants recall a boot-camp dormitory similar to the child warehouses in Aldous Huxley's *Brave New World*. Under constant guard, 100 children occupied a single room and lived by strictly enforced rules. Equality 7-2521 received a decade of superficial training before becoming a street sweeper, a vocation the council chose for him. In his diary, he confesses his guilt in wanting to evade regimentation and think for himself.

Rand stresses Equality 7-2521's flair for invention, an innate intellectual gift that society represses. His revolt symbolizes the psyche's war against institutionalization, which threatens to plunge the unnamed society into a new Dark Age. With scrapped laboratory equipment and oddments gathered from the yard of the Home of Scholars (an engineering collective that reinvents the candle and plate glass), Equality 7-2521 sets up his own workstation in a dank, deserted subterranean station beneath an iron grill in the City Cesspool. Nightly by candlelight, while required indoctrination sessions drone on at the City

Theatre, Equality 7-2521 bends over his primitive electrical experiments in hopes of learning more about technology, which he deems important to society's betterment. Like Daedalus, the builder of the underground labyrinth on Crete, Equality 7-2521 risks all in pursuit of ideas.

Rand's chief failure in her fable lies not in style or scope, but in the devaluation of Liberty 5-300, the sower of seeds who beguiles Equality 7-2521 with her untamed cascade of golden hair. While at work on the great road near the Homes of the Peasants, Equality 7-2521 encounters the fetching 17-year-old and is struck by the first twinges of a bittersweet, potentially doomed love. To avoid detection, he slowly makes his attraction known through tentative touches. Because the repressive Council of Eugenics allows sexual contact only during Time of Mating, Equality 7-2521 is thwarted from openly courting his Golden One. He recalls the punishment for violating state laws: Eleven years earlier, he witnessed the torture and immolation of the "saint of the pyre" for voicing the Unspeakable Word. The saint made no outcry because his tormentors had ripped out his tongue. Equality 7-2521 is unable to explain why, in the face of imminent execution, the mute, defiant saint looked directly at him with joy and pride as though singling him out to confer discipleship.

To update her version of the Daedalus and Prometheus myths, Rand calls on early scientific studies that link lightning and lodestones with electricity. In a piercing moment of chiaroscuro, Equality 7-2521 reaches a breakthrough by building a primitive electrovoltaic cell, or generator. He decides to set a precedent and demonstrate to the Council of Scholars his labor-saving device, which has the potential of lighting cities as well as illuminating the dark recesses of his superiors' fear-laden minds. One night he becomes so immersed in the interplay of light against dark that he fails to return to his dormitory on time. He refuses to reveal his venture, and is whipped and incarcerated in a brick cell. He forces his way out so that he can address the 20 council members.

Rand, who abhors collectivism, presses her protagonist to end domination through a one-man display of courage. The next day, Equality 7-2521 activates his bold plan. In Chapter 7, Collective 0-0009, serving as council spokesperson, circumvents Equality 7-2521's presentation with a single illogical dictum: "What is not thought by all men cannot be true." In a spontaneous act of desperation, Equality 7-2521 rescues himself from lashing or execution by the World Council and redeems his generator from destruction by crashing through a glass window and fleeing to the Uncharted Forest. Again, chiaroscuro presages an eminent enlightenment: Symbolically, his plunge destroys the flimsy half-light that penetrates the room. He embraces the shadows, thereby risking all for a chance to satisfy his curiosity and his yen to experiment and invent.

From the outset, Rand emphasizes the exhilarating emotional high that accompanies spiritual, intellectual, and physical freedom. Liberated from committees, overseers, and mindless dray labor, Equality 7-2521 discovers the joy in being young, strong, intelligent, and free. In a stream he glimpses the reflection of his features and muscular physique. The next day, he detects a pursuer—his Golden One. A tentative Adam, he welcomes his Eve to their Eden in Chapter 9 with hopeful words:

Our dearest one. Fear nothing of the forest. There is no danger in solitude. We have no need of our brothers. Let us forget their good and our evil, let us forget all things save that we are together and that there is joy as a bond between us.

She rushes to join him and names him the Unconquered. Blending autonomy with the will to survive, Equality 7-2521 uses a makeshift bow and arrows to kill wild birds, which he serves as their meal.

As an outspoken disdainer of the Western conventions of religion and romantic love, Rand omits sentimentality or gratitude to a deity and moves directly to sexual expression of mutual delight. Over a period of days, the pair of escapees become lovers. Beyond a mountain chain, they locate a relic of the Unmentionable Times—a two-story concrete house, which they inhabit. The Golden One, the stereotypical witless blonde, is fascinated by racks of colorful clothing from the past; Equality 7-2521 prefers the library. He learns from old texts a new word—the forbidden singular pronoun "I," which replaces the collective "we." From Greek mythology, he and Liberty 5-300 adopt the names of Titans: Prometheus, the god who steals fire from heaven to share with humanity, and Gaea, the earth mother. Before the birth of their child, Equality 7-2521 realizes the importance of self and adopts the sacred word "ego" as his goal.

Although Ayn Rand's critics lambaste her novel for its trivialization and domestication of Liberty 5-300, the story holds a place in the canon of classic utopian fare for its celebration of the indomitable human spirit. As a restrained psychological probe of the protagonist's motives and risks, *Anthem* champions the right to individuality. In Rand's microcosm, there can be no compromise with totalitarianism. The profound circumvention of human needs and desires echoes the dystopian unrest of both *We* and *Brave New World* and anticipates the flight from a controlled society in *The Giver*. A festering discontent impels the hero and heroine to accept known risk, unnamed dangers, and isolation as the price of freedom. An up-to-date Prometheus, Equality 7-2521 challenges authority and defies the oppression of the unnamed forced-labor camp that masquerades as a modern society. His mate, Liberty 5-300, serves as literary foil—the contemplative earth mother who revels in the role of helpmeet and mother and willingly accepts a less aggressive stance in the couple's rebellion against tyranny. (Binswanger 1988; Den Uyl and Rasmussen 1984; Gladstein 1984; Rand 1946; Snodgrass 1990)

See also Brave New World; conditioning; Equality 7-2521; futurism; *The Giver;* *The Handmaid's Tale;* Liberty 5-3000; Lowry, Lois; naturalism; technology; totalitarianism; *We;* women in utopia.

 # ARCADIA, OR ARCADY

A pastoral setting of the English Renaissance, Arcadia dates to an actual agricultural haven in the mountains of the central Peloponnesian plains in Greece alongside the Gulf of Argolis, reputedly Greece's oldest inhabited deme. Known for its rocky slopes, vineyards, pasturage, and grain fields, the area produces sheep and goats, dairy products, and prime fleece. In mythology, Arcadia is a center of shrines to the gods, the birthplace of Hermes, the gods' messenger, and the site of the much-ballyhooed Calydonian boar hunt, a symbolic effort that required a host of distinguished hunters to rid the pleasant groves of a ravaging beast.

In the pastoral literature cultivated for the pleasure of Alexandrian readers, utopian Arcadias flourish in the fiction and verse of Theocritus (316–260 B.C.), Bion (fl. 100 B.C.), Moschus (fl. 150 B.C.), Longus (ca. third century A.D.), as well as three major Roman poets, Ovid (43 B.C.–A.D. 18), Catullus (87–54 B.C.), and Virgil (70–19 B.C.), author of the winsome, outdoorsy *Bucolics* (42–37 B.C.). Virgil connects the promise of nature with an idyllic lifestyle by romanticizing agricultural pursuits. In Book 1 of the *Bucolics* he rhapsodizes on the Greek concept of a golden age:

> From of old Nature laid such laws upon certain regions, an everlasting covenant, what time Deucalion of old cast on the unpeopled globe those stones whence the hard race of man was born. Come therefore, from the first months of the year straight way let the strong bulls upturn the rich floor of earth, and the full strength of summer suns bake the flat clods to dust.

According to Virgil, Ceres (the Roman goddess of grain) graces each season with its characteristic pleasures and tasks. He concludes with a fond memory of the time when he sought quiet in flowery meadows and played shepherd's ditties while sitting under a shady beech.

As outgrowths of the harmony, hospitality, purity, and picturesque bucolic bliss of the golden age, classical Arcadia possesses the stereotypical shepherds' delights—simple foods, vigilance over sturdy flocks, jocular banter, flirtation with and wooing of winsome shepherdesses, and the relief of tedium and toil through singing, dancing, piping, poetic improvisation, May Day rituals, and contests of skill and strength. Characters common to the genre are Daphnis, Phyllis, and the frolicsome god Pan. The cosmology of Arcadia centers on the cycle of the seasons and the gifts of nature, both indigenous to the conventions of contentment and the traditional country scene. For this reason, Arcadia developed from a specific place to a generic term referring to any pastoral setting rich with verdant repose.

The uncomplicated plot of Iacopo Sannazzaro's 12-part *L'Arcadia* (1501), based on the idealism of a pastoral retreat, displays the setting in verse form. This motif of an Elizabethan haven colors Edmund Spenser's *Shepheardes Calender* (1579) and his masterwork *The Faerie Queene* (1596), which glorifies the person and reign of Elizabeth I. A more sophisticated version, Sir Philip Sidney's *The Countess of Pembroke's Arcadia* (usually known as *Arcadia*) (1590), replicates the pastoral idylls of Sannazzaro; so does Torquato Tasso's dramatic pastoral *Aminta* (1581).

Later writers of pastoral themes and picturesque settings follow Virgil's lead and extend the Arcadian idylls throughout Europe and America to the canon of numerous verse and prose masters. Three classic achievements in this genre are John Milton's stately masque *Comus* (1634); his *Lycidas* (1637), an elegiac pastoral masterpiece; and Alfred Tennyson's *Idylls of the King* (1888), a tribute to the peaceful landscape of King Arthur's Camelot. In more recent times, the bucolic works of Henry David Thoreau, William Wordsworth, John Keats, and William Butler Yeats return to classical Arcadian themes and locales, often as a respite from the clangor and rush of cities. In Chapter 5 of Thoreau's *Walden*, he revels in the solitude of a pastoral scene:

> Yet I experienced sometimes that the most sweet and tender, the most innocent and encouraging society may be found in any natural object, even for the poor misanthrope and most melancholy man. There can be no very black melancholy to him who lives in the midst of nature and has his senses still. There was never yet such a storm but it was Aeolian music to a healthy and innocent ear.

Like an escapee from creeping urbanism, Thoreau rejoices in the gentle peace that encroaches from all sides, freeing his spirit from difficult times and strongly contrasting political opinions that, by the end of his life, led to Civil War and the abolition of slavery. (Bell 1989; Cuddon 1979; Hammond and Scullard 1970; Holman 1981; Howatson 1991; Johnson 1968; Smith 1984)

See also Arden; Arthur; *Bucolics;* Camelot; escapism; golden age; *Idylls of the King;* Milton, John.

 # ARDEN

The bucolic setting of William Shakespeare's comedy *As You Like It* (ca. 1599), Arden is an alternative spelling of Ardennes, a forest on the borders of Belgium, Luxembourg, and France. The rural backdrop of Shakespeare's pastoral romance is a literary escape from the sophisticated, duplicitous world at court. As Duke Senior, Rosalind's father, notes in the opening lines of Act II, Scene 1, lines 4–6, 15–18:

> Are not these woods
> More free from peril than the envious court?
> Here feel we but the penalty of Adam,
> The season's difference . . .
> And this our life, exempt from public haunt,
> Finds tongues in trees, books in the running brooks,
> Sermons in stones, and good in everything:
> I would not change it.

Like Arcadia, the idyllic pasturage of Greek mythology, Arden epitomizes an established English utopia, a blissful forest populated by "many merry men [who] live like the old Robin Hood of England . . . and fleet the time carelessly as they did in the golden world." (Act I, Scene 1, lines 114–119) (Boyce 1990; Johnson 1968; Shakespeare 1959)

See also Arcadia; *As You Like It;* escapism; golden age; pastoral; Shakespeare, William.

William Shakespeare set *As You Like It* in the forest of Arden. The "old forrest of Arden" appears on a map of Warwickshire published in the early 1600s. The river Avon is also shown on the map, and Shakespeare was born in the town of Stratford-upon-Avon in Warwickshire.

ARISTOPHANES

Greek comic dramatist of the late fifth century B.C., and the most renowned funny man of ancient times, Aristophanes excelled at fantasy, burlesque, buffoonery, caricature, farce, and puns. Born to a conservative lineage around 450 B.C. in the deme of Cydathenaeon in Athens, he was the son of Philippus and Zenodora and grew up south of the mainland on the nearby island of Aegina. He began composing the first of his 55 comic dramas around 432 B.C., and in his late teens competed against the masters at the spring drama festival, where he earned five medals. As a knowledgeable satirist and parodist, he opposed the decadence that followed the Peloponnesian War by lampooning moralists (particularly Socrates and Plato), self-important aristocrats, and such notorious politicians as Cleon, the pompous tippler. In general, Aristophanes maintained a firm stance against corruption, loose morals, snobbery, violence, and war.

As a landowner and city magistrate, Aristophanes maintained a dual role as local poet and civil servant. He sired three sons—Philippos, Araros, and Nikostratos—who became comic playwrights; in 387 B.C., two years before his death, he saw them win a competition. At his passing, Aristophanes left a wealth of rollicking slapstick, allegory, and pointed invective in his *Peace, Frogs, Wasps,*

The Assemblywomen, Plutus, Babylonians, Acharnians, Banqueters, Knights, Clouds, and his most notorious—*Lysistrata,* a chronicle of women who defeat their husbands by withholding sex. Of his canon, only 11 of his works remain. His favorite play, *The Birds,* written in 414 B.C., contains one of the ancient world's strongest escapist or utopian themes: He encouraged Athenians of the postwar era to abandon compromise, democracy, and the sophists' new morality and return to simple ways. (Aristophanes 1962; Dickey 1993; Lord 1963; Magill 1958; Snodgrass 1988a; Spatz 1978; Ussher 1979)

See also The Birds; escapism; idealism; satire; women in utopia.

 # ARTHUR

This sixth-century semihistorical English king survives in legend-shrouded glory in a handsome roll call of the finest in early European literature, from Ireland to Italy and west to Germany:

- the Welsh poem *Y Gododdin* (sixth century)
- Nennius's *Historia Britonum* (late eighth century)
- the anonymous *Annales Cambriae* (late tenth century)
- the Welsh *Mabinogion* (ca. 1100)
- William of Malmesbury's *Gesta Regum Anglorum* (1125)
- Geoffrey of Monmouth's *Historia Regum Britanniae* (1140)
- Wace's version (1155)
- Chrétien de Troyes's poetic lays (ca. 1185)
- Hartmann von Aue's *Erec* and *Iwein* (late twelfth century)
- Wolfram von Eschenback's *Parzifal* (1210)
- Layamon's thirteenth-century chronicle
- *Sir Gawain and the Green Knight* (1370)
- Sir Thomas Malory's *Morte d'Arthur* (1485)

According to a tentative chronology drawn from pseudohistory, Arthur's uncle, Aurelius Ambrosius (the son of the Roman emperor Constantine), arrived in England in A.D. 470 to protect the Celts from Saxon invaders. Arthur Pendragon, illegitimate son of Ambrosius's brother Uther and Queen Ygraine of Cornwall, was born around 473, 12 years before Ambrosius's death. After Uther's crowning, Arthur remained an obscure pretender to the throne and lived at St. Albans until his father's death.

A military defeat of Saxon warlords concluded in 512 with Arthur's accession to the throne. The next year he married Guinevere and created Camelot, a walled haven in a land previously sapped by perennial wars and deluged with petty rulers, squabbling nobility, scofflaws, and assorted brigands. Against constant threats of war, Arthur's evolving military might staved off the Saxons, a power struggle that climaxed in 517 with his victory at Mount Badon. For 18 years, Camelot stood as the center of peace. Some versions depict Arthur as invincible until Mordred tricked him in an unfair fight. In 535, at the Battle of Camlann, Mordred, or Modred (Arthur's illegitimate son by his half sister

la ueille de la pentecou
ste qut tour li compaig
non de la table ronde fu

Arthur, a semihistorical sixth-century English king, feasts with Queen Guinevere and his court in an illustrated fourteenth-century manuscript from northern France.

Arthur: Genealogy

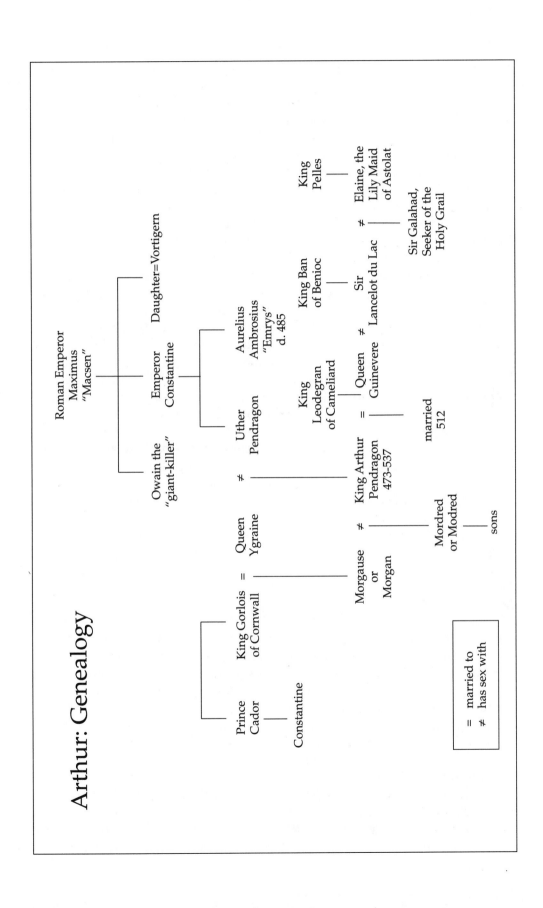

Morgan), challenged the king to open combat. Two years later, Mordred killed Arthur with a lethal thrust of Excalibur, the king's own sword.

Alfred, Lord Tennyson's lyrical 12-canto poem *Idylls of the King* (1891) features Arthur at the head of an idealized court that strives to rid Camelot of sinister elements. More Victorian than Arthurian in outlook and ethics, the work reflects Tennyson's role as England's poet laureate. In the segment that details the coming of age of Gareth (son of Lot and Bellicent), Arthur sits on his throne and, Solomonlike, holds court for complainants. After judging the case of Lynette, he dispatches Gareth, the would-be knight, to right wrongs done to the Lady Lyonors, a romanticized maiden in distress. By accepting the boon, Gareth trusts that Arthur's system of rewarding knights errant for police work will earn him a place at the Round Table.

In Mark Twain's depiction, *A Connecticut Yankee in King Arthur's Court* (1886), Arthur takes an interest in the entrepreneurial schemes of Hank Morgan, the idealistic New England forge worker who is transported across the Atlantic and back in time 13 centuries. To demonstrate to Arthur that feudalism depletes Camelot and the outlying lands by degrading workers and overtaxing farmers while fattening the coffers of church and castle, Hank disguises the king in humble attire, lops his hair, and escorts him incognito through his own realm, introducing Arthur to humble folk, artisans, peasants, beggars, and slaves. The revelation of sufferings at the cottage level redirects Arthur's social engineering and temporarily strengthens Hank's case for a democratic educational system, opportunities for laborers, a competitive marketplace, and other social improvements reflective of Twain's own time—particularly baseball teams, which reduce competition from swords and lances to bats and catchers' mitts. (Ashe 1987; Dickey 1993; Dixon 1974; Lacy 1986; Stewart 1970; Stewart 1973; Stewart 1984; Tennyson 1989; Twain 1963)

See also Avalon; Camelot; *A Connecticut Yankee in King Arthur's Court*; Gareth; humanitarianism; idealism; *Idylls of the King*; slavery.

AS YOU LIKE IT

Shakespeare's Elizabethan romantic comedy, written about 1599, is set in Arden, a pastoral Eden. During a complicated but predictable mix-up involving inheritances and banishment, two friends—Celia and her devoted cousin Rosalind, whom her father has exiled—set out from Rosalind's former palace home into the forest of Arden. Rosalind travels disguised as a man. Orlando, the maligned hero, departs with his servant Adam to the same forest. While Celia and Rosalind reside in a cottage and live the pastoral life of sheepherders, Orlando decks the trees with sheets of love rhymes dedicated to his beloved Rosalind. When the villain Oliver arrives, he falls in love with Celia.

Shakespeare tightens the plot of *As You Like It* by returning to Duke Frederick, the local authority, who is concerned that so many of his courtiers desert his halls for unknown attractions in the forest of Arden. Before the duke can investigate, he falls under the spell of a religious recluse who converts him from worldliness to spirituality. After Rosalind gives up her masculine garb, she rapidly resolves the confused alliances. Rosalind marries Orlando; Celia marries Oliver. Thus, in the style of Shakespeare's day, the play concludes with reconciliation, forgiveness, and wedded bliss.

Shakespeare's utopian theme—common to pastoral art, tapestry, literature, and music throughout Europe—idealizes the bucolic contentment of country folk. As escapist literature, *As You Like It* reflects literary conventions, notably an idealistic view of young love, the charm of living in the wild and hunting for food, and the romantic notion that certain people belong together in felicitous wedlock. Far from the cynical, exploitative political profiteering at court, the dramatis personae exist in a Renaissance pseudo–golden age, an earthly parallel to the classic mythological Arcadia and to the Eden of Genesis.

Shakespeare avoids too simplistic a contrast between civilization and nature by injecting some difficulties in Arden Forest as a token of his belief that no utopia is free of human frailties such as cruelty or manipulation, or of the dangers inherent in the food chain. In Act II, Scene 1, lines 38–42, a lord notes that, even in a blissful forest, the animals suffer from the hunter's arrow:

> The wretched animal heaved forth such groans
> That their discharge did stretch his leathern coat
> Almost to bursting, and the big round tears
> Coursed one another down his innocent nose
> In piteous chase . . .

Rosalind, the central character of Shakespeare's pastoral utopian comedy *As You Like It* was played by Katherine Hepburn in a 1950 production.

In Act IV, Scene 3, lines 111–114, Oliver applauds Orlando's bravery as he faces a snake, symbolic of Satan's disguise in Eden:

About his neck
A green and gilded snake had wreathed itself,
Who with her head, nimble in threats, approached
The opening of his mouth . . .

The scenes serve as antitheses: the deer succumbing to human hunger, the snake remaining an unseen threat by uncoiling and "with indented glides" slipping into the brush, perpetuating the natural food search by which the animal survives.

Shakespeare's utopia, although hyperbolic in its paean to Hymen (god of marriage) and mildly evocative of an idyllic, leaf-shrouded microcosm, remains earthbound with its poverty, inconvenience, and even a lurking lioness. By juxtaposing characters such as the romantic Silvius with the outspoken Corin, who recognizes the difficulties of agrarian life, the playwright departs from a strictly utopian setting, thus avoiding a saccharine stage world and allowing his play to demonstrate the beauties of a temporary pastoral escapade without overrating them. (Boyce 1990; Shakespeare 1959)

See also Arden; Eden; escapism; pastoral; Satan; Shakespeare, William; women in utopia.

 # ASCETICISM

A withdrawal from earthly pleasures including money, luxuries, possessions, sexual pleasures, comfort, society, and, at times, food and water, asceticism serves as an adjunct to Apollonian or contemplative forms of utopia. For example, bare essentials were the basis of the philosophy of John the Baptist, the wandering evangelist (and Jesus' cousin) who spread the word throughout Jewry that a messiah was at hand. Steeped in Old Testament prophecy, John insisted on immersing Jesus in the river Jordan as preparation for a holy life of teaching, healing, and martyrdom. As recorded in the books of Matthew, Mark, Luke, and John in the New Testament, John's asceticism was a necessary prelude to holy acts, which required that the body be pure of sin and unburdened of earthly longings and expectations. Jesus' baptism, symbolizing ascetic purity, prefaced an earthly ministry dedicated to serving the sick, encouraging the disheartened, and preaching the promise of an unending afterlife to those who believed.

Sprinkled throughout ancient, classic, medieval, Renaissance, and modern literature are other utopian ideals that require rigid self-control and/or self-denial as countermeasures to self-indulgence, sensuality, sybaritic luxuries, and sexual depravity.

- The Greek moralist Hesiod, author of *Works and Days* (eighth century B.C.), stresses the importance of piety and labor as easeful focuses in distressing times. Himself a contented farmer but the victim of Perses, his larcenous brother, Hesiod intends his work as a personal message to Perses about the value of virtue and devotion to the gods.

- St. Augustine, once a sinful debaucher and atheist, accepts Christianity and distances himself from the profligate life he had formerly pursued. As a man of learning and devotion to Christ, he composes a lengthy didactic text, *De Civitate Dei* (426), a compelling description of the Christian life. In Book 10, Chapter 6, Augustine says:

  > There is, then, a true sacrifice in every work which unites us in a holy communion with God, that is, in every work that is aimed at the final Good in which alone we can be truly blessed.

- Augustine urges the type of temperance described by Paul's letter to the Romans 21:1. The reward of Augustine's asceticism follows faithful Christians beyond death and brings them face to face with angels and God, the "all in all."

- Confucius's sparse, pithy *Analects* (second century A.D.) call for denial of the body as the spirit achieves oneness and harmony with nature and society. For example, he advocates a firm self-discipline in Chapter 15, Section 20, which states: "The superior man makes demands on himself; the inferior man makes demands on others." More to the point of asceticism, Chapter 7, Section 36 states: "The superior man understands what is right; the inferior man understands what is profitable."

- Al-Ghazali, a Muslim mystic, philosopher, writer, and teacher of the twelfth century from Tus in present-day Iran, withdrew from the sensual world of pleasure and wrote uplifting spiritual guides—for example, *The Alchemy of Happiness*—to assist worshipers of Allah in interpreting Islamic law and ethics.

- In *Past and Present* (1843), Thomas Carlyle's nostalgic re-creation of the medieval monastic commune of Brakelondia, Abbot Samson works out the botheration that vexes the soul by following a strict schedule of chores. Whether hoeing or praying, Samson cultivates spirituality in ordinary tasks performed in a pretechnocratic era.

- Sparse diet, simple lifestyle, and Edenic setting strengthen the subterranean city of Vril-Ya in Edward Bulwer-Lytton's *The Coming Race* (1871). The visitor who descends the shaft to their land expects darkness, yet revels in the power of *vril*, which lights the city, fuels technological advancements, heals the sick, and grows the abundant fruit that fills his plate.

- In William Dean Howells's *Through the Eye of the Needle* (1907), the sequel of *Traveler from Altruria* (1872), Aristides Homos is an emissary who studies America from the point of view of his altruistic island country. He teaches Eveleth, his American wife, to respect ascetic ways by abandoning hedonism and classism and accepting vegetarianism, frugality, and abstinence from alcoholic beverages.

- James Hilton's Father Perrault, religious leader of Shangri-La in *Lost Horizon* (1933), abstains from human contact for two reasons—his physical fragility and his preference for solitude, meditation, yoga, deep breathing, and clairvoyant trances, which are enhanced by a narcotic tea made from the *tangatse* berry. Withdrawing into an overheated upper-story room, Perrault dulls his sensual appetites as a preface to studies in self-levitation, Buddhist mysticism, and telepathy. In Chapter 7, Perrault refers to his self-denial as "the tranquil tastes of a scholar." Three chapters later, Hugh Conway, Perrault's chosen successor, rephrases the doctrine of the lamasery, less from experience than from shrewd surmise: "Perhaps the exhaustion of the passions is the beginning of wisdom." As Conway views both setting and self-denial, Perrault's retreat into mental gymnastics and contemplation must result in a quid pro quo—an exchange of worldly titillations or debauchery for the soothing, nonviolent otherworldliness that keeps him alive decades beyond the normal human span of years.

- A similar but more detailed example of religious asceticism is embodied in Siddhartha, the protagonist in Hermann Hesse's philosophical novel *Siddhartha* (1951), which follows the enigmatic Buddha character through his rebellion, search for godliness, submersion in sinful indulgence, and repeated flight to a riverside, where he adopts a simple, contemplative life as a ferryman. Hesse summarizes Siddhartha's coming awareness of serenity in terms of ascetic "preparation of the soul . . . a capacity, a secret art of thinking, feeling and breathing thoughts of unity at every moment of life." In the single word "harmony," Hesse concludes that Siddhartha has located the "eternal perfection of the world."

- Likewise, Malcolm X in Alex Haley's *The Autobiography of Malcolm X* (1965) abjures street crime, drug dealing, hustling, and other self-destructive habits after he enters prison and allies with Islam. Inspired by Mohammed's teachings in the Koran, Malcolm X simultaneously abandons lawlessness and sheds his slave name. As described in Chapter 12, in preparation for the ascetic life, he studies with spiritual leader Elijah Muhammad and bans drinking, cursing, fighting, dancing, carousing, and using dope—the very things that Mr. Muhammad taught were helping the black man to stay under the heel of white America.

  In compliance with Islam, Malcolm marries Betty Shabazz, sires a family, dedicates himself to revitalizing black faith, and devotes his talents to speaking, writing, and traveling, including a *hajj*, or obligatory pilgrimage to Mecca. On the first journey, Malcolm evolves a broadened awareness of brotherhood, which is reason enough to abandon antiwhite racism.

- In Marge Piercy's *Woman on the Edge of Time* (1976), protagonist Connie confronts a futuristic society through the telepathy of Luciente, a biologist. In her visits to his people, who face life-threatening economic and ecological decline, Connie adapts easily to their ascetic lifestyle and to the exigencies of a race that must ration goods and foodstuffs in order to survive. In the absence of work-saving technology, she observes a bucolic setting and learns from Luciente the nature of self-denial for survival: "We use up a confounded lot of resources. Scarce materials. Energy. We have to account. There's only one pool of air to breathe." Luciente concludes that death, like life, is natural—a "part of the web of nature."

- One of the strongest calls for asceticism is the artificial piety of Margaret Atwood's Gilead, the setting of *The Handmaid's Tale* (1985), where handmaidens form a class of society that follows an enforced nunlike existence. Confined to a bedroom devoid of overhead lights or reading material and supplied with bland, unappealing meals, the unnamed protagonist speaks only to servants, guards, and other handmaidens on their way to shop. With revulsion she awaits her scheduled matings with Commander Fred, the authority figure who anticipates children from successive couplings with a series of thoroughly catechized handmaidens, each brutally whipped into shape by the sadistic Aunt Lydia wielding ascetic homilies.

(Atwood 1972; Augustine 1958; Carlyle 1977; Confucius 1992; Ghazali 1964; Haley 1965; Hesiod 1973; Hilton 1933; Howells 1907; Howells 1957; King James Bible 1958; Piercy 1976; *The Qu'ran* 1992.)

See also *The Analects of Confucius;* Augustine, St.; *The Autobiography of Malcolm X;* baptism; Buddhism; *De Civitate Dei;* Confucius; Conway, Hugh; Ghazali; *The Handmaid's Tale;* heaven; Hesiod; Koran; *Lost Horizon;* Lydia, Aunt; Malcolm X; nirvana; *Past and Present;* Perrault, Father; Sermon on the Mount; Shangri-La; Siddhartha; *Siddhartha;* Sufism; *Through the Eye of the Needle; A Traveler from Altruria;* Vril-Ya; women in utopia.

ASEM, AN EASTERN TALE

A utopian romance drawn from Oliver Goldsmith's *The Bee* (1759), *Asem* is an oriental tale that focuses on Asem the Segastan misanthrope. Having been reared to love and serve his fellow humans, Asem grows disillusioned because he receives no return on his benevolence. He begins to view the human vices "ingratitude, dissimulation, and treachery" and to loathe them. Withdrawing from Segastan to a cave, Asem gathers food from the mountainside and water from a cascade. Lost in meditation of a mountain tarn, he concludes that nature is beautiful and useful, but humanity is vile and ungrateful to the Creator. Just as Asem prepares to drown himself, a ministering spirit walks across the water's surface and leads him toward wisdom. At the center of the lake, the pair sink several hundred fathoms to a sunny locale, serene and verdant. The spirit explains that, at Allah's request and under Mohammed's supervision, this netherworld took shape. The major difference between the upper and lower worlds is the behavior of the inhabitants: In the lower world they are free of vice. Asem is so thrilled that he speaks a prayer of thanks to Allah.

As Asem and his guide tour the underlake utopia, Asem questions why animals must prey on one another. The guide replies that without a control on population, animals would overproduce. Thus, nature's predations keep a check on starvation. Two disturbing events interrupt the peace of the perfect world: Squirrels chase one man; two dogs chase another. Asem is amazed that a human being could be intimidated by lesser animals. The guide replies that animals have grown too powerful and threaten human inhabitants. Asem insists that these ravagers be destroyed. The guide smiles in reply. "Where is, then, that tenderness you so lately expressed?" Asem concludes that tyranny and injustice are necessary if humanity hopes to subjugate "brute creation."

While the visitors stroll among human residences, Asem notices how humbly the houses are designed. He thanks his guide for sharing wisdom. The guide retorts, "We have no wisdom here, for we have no occasion for it." Asem comments that there is a kind of wisdom in this underlake utopia in that families dwell apart, "without society, or without intercourse." The guide explains that residents have no need of society or friendships. Asem comments that he would like at least one companion with whom to share his thoughts, but the guide declares that camaraderie is inconsistent with the philosophy of this utopia.

Asem probes further the nature of this viceless land. Encountering a man dying of consumption, he wonders why no one relieves the man's misery. His guide replies that each resident owns enough for self, but not enough for charity. Asem realizes that temperance is the single virtue of this strange land, for the people lack "fortitude, liberality, friendship, wisdom, conversation, and love." Chastened by his experience in a viceless society, Asem asks to be returned to the "very world which I have despised." Returned to normal society, he promises to avoid vice and to pity it in others. He dedicates himself to commerce, cultivates friends, and reaches his old age in "elegance, affluence, and ease." (Benét 1991; Bloom 1987e; Hopkins 1993; Johnson 1968)

See also didacticism; materialism.

ATLANTIS

This perfect island society was described by Solon in a tale heard in the courts of Sais in Egypt, by Dionysius of Miletus in "Travels to Atlantis," and in Plato's *Timaeus* (fifth century B.C.) as thriving west of the Pillars of Hercules somewhere in the Atlantic Ocean beyond the Rock of Gibraltar. In size, it was 533 kilometers by 355 kilometers and consisted of a high plain surrounded by craggy mountains. Its valleys were home to thriving villagers who mined the precious mineral oricalcum. To defend their natural resources, Atlanteans boasted a fighting force over a million in number. At one time, this elliptical island nation was deemed so powerful that it threatened the sovereignty of Asia, Africa, and much of Europe north of Tuscany. Its colonies reached as far as Greece.

At the heart of Atlantis stood its circular capital, also called Atlantis, which was surrounded by warehouses and guarded by lookouts on each side of the entrance. Ringed by three concentric canals, the city boasted an internal port and citadel at the center of dormitories and athletic fields. Subterranean tunneling and caves enabled the city to conceal its navy, which consisted of sturdy triremes, the fighting frigates powered by three tiers of slave rowers. With all its military preparedness and civic confidence, Atlantis was engulfed by seawater in 9560 B.C. As Virgil describes Atlantis's destruction in a brief passage near the end of Book 3 of the *Aeneid:* "These lands, it is said, once with violence and vast desolation convulsed, burst asunder, which once were one." Critics interpret this line as proof that plate tectonics caused a massive shift, setting off volcanoes and earthquakes and endangering life across the entire Mediterranean world.

The concept of a lost undersea city supposedly exterminated by the Great Flood, or Deluge, caused by an earthquake occurs in Pierre Benoit's *L'Atlantide* (1919). A recounting of the 1897 expedition to the Ahaggar massif of the Sahara Desert led by Morhange and Saint-Avit, the novel describes how adventurers locate writings in a cave at the base of Geni Mountain. The party discovers a lush oasis, which Dr. Le Mesge identifies as a portion of the sunken continent of Atlantis. In Sir Arthur Conan Doyle's *The Maracot Deep* (1929), nearly three decades after the French expedition's discovery, Professor Maracot locates a sealed city with a roof access surrounded by silt. Navigating the site, Maracot discovers that city streets and ruined temples survived the catastrophe that sank Atlantis. Governed by a dark-skinned race, the city depends on a lighter-skinned slave force to mine coal. A priest presides over an oven where human sacrifices are immolated in honor of the flesh-eating god Baal, or Moloch.

In these literary cosmologies, undersea Atlantis's unique feature—its advanced technology—sets it apart from lesser states. By manipulating chemicals, Atlanteans enjoy artificial coffee, tea, wine, and flour. Their knowledge of mental telepathy enables them to project memories of the past on screens. In this fashion, they teach younger generations about the time when Atlantis ruled much of the sea and subjugated coastal cities. The undersea site of Atlantis possesses a fearful ecology. Rays, sea serpents, crayfish, flatfish, a type of jellyfish, and scorpions thrive. Huge crabs and venomous eels inhabit interstices in the rocks. These oversized fauna intimidate outsiders who venture too near. (Hare 1982; Jordan 1981; Lodge 1956; Manguel and Guadalupi 1987; Nettleship 1968; Plato 1937a; Plato 1937c; Rouse 1956; Snodgrass 1988a; Warner 1958)

See also Plato; technology; *Timaeus;* Virgil.

 # ATWOOD, MARGARET

A multifaceted Canadian novelist, poet, critic, essayist, and short story writer, Atwood's best-selling novel *The Handmaid's Tale* (1986) established her as an eminent dystopian and feminist. Margaret Atwood was born on November 18, 1939, in Ottawa, Ontario, the second of three children of entomologist Carl

Edmund Atwood and Margaret Killam Atwood. In early childhood, she enjoyed romps in the north Quebec outback; at the age of seven, her family settled in northern Ontario.

Well educated with a B.A. from the University of Toronto, an M.A. from Radcliffe, and graduate studies at Harvard from 1962–1963 and 1965–1967, she came under the beneficent influence of two powerhouses: critic Northrop Frye and Jay MacPherson, a strong female role model and mentor who helped shape Atwood's philosophies of literature and feminism. From early times she composed her thoughts into pithy, tightly constructed verse. During her undergraduate years, Atwood contributed poems and articles to *Acta Victoriana* and *The Strand*, publications of Victoria College. After graduation, she served as lecturer and writer-in-residence at various Canadian, American, and Australian universities while writing prolifically. Her most famous novels—*The Edible Woman* (1969), *Surfacing* (1972), *Lady Oracle* (1976), *Life before Man* (1979), *Bodily Harm* (1981), *Encounters with the Element Man* (1982), *Unearthing Suite* (1983), and *Cat's Eye* (1989)—focus on themes of exploitation and victimization.

Chief among Atwood's studies of people—mainly women—refusing to be pawns is her dystopian feminist fantasy *The Handmaid's Tale* (1985), a futuristic

Margaret Atwood

satire that won her the *Los Angeles Times* Book Award and the title Woman of the Year from *Ms.* magazine. Subsequent honors include the Arthur C. Clarke Award, Commonwealth Literature Prize, and *Chatelaine* magazine's Woman of the Year. In 1990 *The Handmaid's Tale* was filmed by Cinecom Entertainment Group. Scripted by Harold Pinter, the movie starred Natasha Richardson as Offred; Robert Duvall and Faye Dunaway were her made-to-order family.

In recent years, Atwood continues to lecture and give public readings. In 1992 she published *Good Bones,* a collection of verse, essays, and short fiction; in 1993 her novel *The Robber Bride* was a best-seller. Currently residing outside Alliston, Ontario, she remains active in women's issues and literary circles, particularly the Canadian Authors Association. (Atwood 1972; Bergmann 1989; *Contemporary Authors* 1989; *Contemporary Literary Criticism* 1987; Davidson 1986; Dreifus 1992; Hammer 1990; Ingersoll 1991; McCombs 1988; *Major Twentieth-Century Writers* 1990; "Margaret Atwood: Interview" 1983; Van Spanckeren and Castro 1988)

See also asceticism; The Commander; disillusion; dystopia; Gilead, *The Handmaid's Tale,* Lydia, Aunt; Offred; Serena Joy; technology; women in utopia.

AUGUSTINE, ST.

A monumental figure, St. Augustine is second only to St. Paul in the formation of Christian dogma and the establishment of the Christian faith. Augustine wrote *De Ordine* (A.D. 386), *De Beata Vita* (386), *Soliloquia* (387), *De Musica* (387–389), *De Magistro* (387–389), *Narrationes in Psalmos* (392–430), *De Doctrina Christiana* (397), *Confessiones* (387–401), *De Trinitate* (397–401), *De Genesi ad Literam* (401–415), and *Retractiones* (426). But his most famous work was *De Civitate Dei* (The City of God), an influential utopian treatise that he wrote over a 13-year period from 413–426. An outgrowth of the fall of the Roman Empire and an inspirational element in the philosophical transition that enabled a dying nation to kindle new faith and vigor, this 22-book theological and social study guides future nation planners in avoiding the follies and pitfalls that destroyed Rome.

A native of the Roman province of Tagaste, Numidia (northern Africa), St. Augustine (also called Augustine of Hippo) was born in 354 to Patricius and Monica. From early childhood he came under pressure from his Christian mother to abandon his father's pagan beliefs and convert to her faith, which at first he declined. Through his parents' financial sacrifice, the boy received adequate training in Greek and Latin in Tagaste, Madaura, and later at Carthage, and focused on Plato's theories of the ideal. In adulthood, Augustine noted that Patricius wanted him to learn rhetoric but cared nothing about the spiritual impact of scholarly studies.

At age 17, Augustine and his Carthaginian mistress produced a son, Adeodatus. At the age of 23, Augustine journeyed to Rome to teach. In 384 he settled in Milan, taught rhetoric and the classics, and studied neo-Platonism under Ambrosius, a respected bishop and provincial governor. A year later,

Augustine acquiesced to his mother's command that he marry a woman more suited to his social level. At this point in his spiritual development he turned from Manichaeanism, a Persian faith blended from other religions, mythologies, and scriptures. Under the influence of Simplicianus, he embraced Christianity and was baptized along with his son (who died the next year, shortly before Monica's death at Ostia, a resort town west of Rome).

According to Augustine's autobiography, *Confessiones*, the emotional chaos of these years forced him to examine his profligate behavior. A chance reading of St. Paul's letter to the Romans, Chapter 13, affirmed his evolving asceticism and his belief that God's grace was humanity's only salvation from original sin. Augustine returned to his homeland; in 391 he entered the priesthood. Four years later he attained the post of bishop, which he held for 35 years. As a Christian apologist, he composed uplifting and substantive religious commentaries, a biography, and over 250 epistles on sin, redemption, prayer, church polity, scriptural interpretation, and dogma.

Augustine's most influential work, *De Civitate Dei*, appeared in sequential volumes. A towering symbol of the emergence of Christian faith to fill the vacuum left by Rome's political and spiritual demise, the work predicted that a New Jerusalem, as the prophets Daniel and John the Divine had foreseen, would supplant the wickedness and greed of Roman rulers. In 430, about the time of Rome's collapse and the siege of the Vandals, Augustine died in Hippo (now known as Bône, Algeria). His writings attained even greater stature after their translation by King Alfred and throughout the Reformation, especially with Martin Luther and John Calvin. (Augustine 1981; Bogan 1984; Boorstin 1983; Boorstin 1992; Burke 1984; Clifton 1992; Gilson 1983; Johnson 1968; Lawless 1987; O'Daly 1987)

See also asceticism; *De Civitate Dei*; didacticism; prophecy; religion; theocracy.

✳ *THE AUTOBIOGRAPHY OF MALCOLM X* ✳

A personal narrative of the leader of the Nation of Islam, *The Autobiography of Malcolm X* (1965) details the conversion of an American phenomenon—an orator, minister, and martyr to the cause of the Black Muslims. As the focus of a work begun by Malcolm X in interviews with Alex Haley, his collaborator, *The Autobiography of Malcolm X* details a cataclysmic era in the civil rights movement when Martin Luther King and Roy Wilkins, head of the NAACP, vied for the post of political voice for disenfranchised black citizens of the United States. Malcolm X (May 19, 1925–February 21, 1965), who ran a distant third in appeal, was born Malcolm Little, son of Grenadan Louise Little and Reverend Earl Little, a Baptist minister from Lansing, Michigan. Little's apparent murder by Ku Klux Klan members, who left his body on trolley tracks, resulted from racial animosity against the idyllic back-to-Africa initiative led by Marcus Garvey, an influential firebrand who intended to shepherd American blacks to their racial motherland.

Traumatized and uprooted after his father's death and his mother's mental collapse, Malcolm and his 11 siblings were parceled out to foster homes. He maintained the memory of his father's martyrdom on behalf of a failed political effort that resembled wishful thinking more than an actual grand-scale resettlement of blacks in the "promised land" of Africa. Malcolm's dissolute youth, spent selling marijuana, bootleg whiskey, and drugs as well as hustling numbers and prostitutes, culminated in sleazy notoriety in Boston and New York. He served part of an eight- to ten-year sentence for involvement in a biracial theft ring. Remanded at age 20 to Charlestown State Prison in Massachusetts, he pursued his education through reading, studies with his cellmate Bimbi, and correspondence with Detroit evangelist Elijah Muhammad, the backbone of the Lost-Found Nation of Islam movement.

Malcolm plunged wholeheartedly into this political and racial effort to free himself and other black Americans from coercion, manipulation, and vilification by white racists. More than a utopian scheme, the Nation of Islam was a campaign to ameliorate the damage caused by slavery and years of second-class citizenship and further complicated by self-destructive drugs, alcohol, sexual promiscuity, and crime. Ultimately, the movement intended to free the disenfranchised, who suffered humiliation and poverty through no personal shortcoming, and teach them the ways of Allah.

In Chapter 10 of his autobiography, Malcolm relates the story of Mr. Yacub, a mythic troublemaker who sprang up in the midst of the contented black nation of Shabazz:

> Mr. Elijah Muhammad teaches his followers that within six months time, through telling lies that set the black men fighting among each other, this devil race [of whites] had turned what had been a peaceful heaven on earth into a hell torn by quarreling and fighting.

To end the dissension and revitalize a former world power, Malcolm accepted Elijah Muhammad's challenge to embrace Islam and the teachings of the Koran and to work for the Nation of Islam, an ascetic religious sect that encourages self-control; fealty to Allah; abstinence from drugs, alcohol, and tobacco; and rigid marital codes requiring faithfulness to one wife, cleanliness of person and mind, and decency and honor in human relationships.

Malcolm Little demonstrated his conversion to Islam by dropping his "slave" name and adopting X as a surname to indicate the absence of the sept of his family tree that extended into Africa's dim past. Following parole in 1952, which Malcolm attained by demonstrating his piety and rehabilitation from a criminal lifestyle, he presented himself in Detroit as a potential disciple to Elijah Muhammad. After working his way up the Black Muslim hierarchy, Malcolm attained high rank as minister and propaganda specialist.

By 1963 Malcolm faced doubt in his idealistic mission because of jealousy among other sect officials. He acquiesced to an official silencing and attempted to rationalize minor difficulties, such as criticism of Elijah Muhammad's adulteries with two young secretaries, who bore him four illegitimate children. Having founded new temples and strengthened the movement with fiery speeches, Malcolm felt the need to refresh his faith by visiting the Holy Land. He followed the Islamic custom of *hajj*, a spiritual retreat to Mecca to pray among a kneeling throng of believers at the Ka'ba, or Sacred House. In holy surroundings alongside Muslim pilgrims of all races and backgrounds, Malcolm made a decided turn from the separatism and antiwhite rhetoric of his early ministry and began formulating two new ideals: pan-Africanism and world brotherhood.

Threats against Malcolm's life and the firebombing of his residence in 1964 led him to accept the martyrdom prophesied by Elijah Muhammad at the time of Malcolm's conversion. Malcolm continued to address gatherings and champion the ascetic life commanded by Islam, but he deserted Elijah Muhammad to direct his own movement, which he called Muslim Mosque, Inc., a loosely structured beginning of a sect powered by deserters of the Nation of Islam. However, his vision of pan-Africanism and world brotherhood crumpled with his own inert form. On February 21, 1965, while speaking to a gathering at the Audubon Ballroom in Harlem, Malcolm fell dead from 16 bullets pumped into his chest by three men sitting in the front row of the auditorium. Two of the men were members of the Nation of Islam. All three were found guilty of murder.

Realizing that his shift in philosophy from the separatism of the Nation of Islam was too great an ethical and theological leap for followers and the press to grasp, at the time of his death Malcolm had already begun assuring the safety of his wife Betty X Shabazz and their four daughters. Overwhelmed by pressures from various political quarters, he had pursued a formal complaint against the U.S. government of denial of black civil rights, an agenda that he intended to present to the United Nations.

The 1991 movie of *The Autobiography of Malcolm X*, filmed by Spike Lee and starring Denzel Washington as Malcolm X, renewed interest in Malcolm's visions of unity. In honor of Malcolm's martyrdom, students began studying the history of the 1960s and the selfless men and women who dreamed of a world devoid of racism. (Breitman 1965; Breitman 1967; Carson 1991; Chapman 1968; Crenshaw 1991; Gallen 1992; Goldman 1979; Haley 1965; Kly 1986; Leader 1992; Wolfenstein 1990)

See also asceticism; Black Muslims; Koran; Malcolm X; utopia; women in utopia.

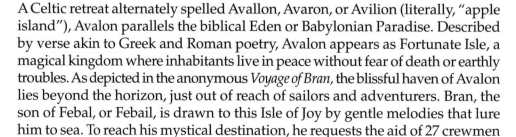

AVALON

A Celtic retreat alternately spelled Avallon, Avaron, or Avilion (literally, "apple island"), Avalon parallels the biblical Eden or Babylonian Paradise. Described by verse akin to Greek and Roman poetry, Avalon appears as Fortunate Isle, a magical kingdom where inhabitants live in peace without fear of death or earthly troubles. As depicted in the anonymous *Voyage of Bran*, the blissful haven of Avalon lies beyond the horizon, just out of reach of sailors and adventurers. Bran, the son of Febal, or Febail, is drawn to this Isle of Joy by gentle melodies that lure him to sea. To reach his mystical destination, he requests the aid of 27 crewmen and his three foster brothers. Like Odysseus and Aeneas in classical mythology, upon arrival Bran loses a sailor, who refuses to return to Ireland.

A second leg of the voyage takes Bran to the Land of Women, where he lives far beyond the normal span of years. Against the advice of the island sages, he returns home to mortality. One of the crew disobeys Bran's orders and disembarks. His aged body crumbles to dust. Bran realizes that, to maintain the effects of the island paradise, he must not risk the same demise. And so the story ends with Bran wandering among otherworldly isles, far from contact with mortals.

In Geoffrey of Monmouth's *Historia Regum Britanniae* (ca. 1135), Avalon maintains its Celtic powers as the vague westerly location of a forge capable of turning out Excalibur, the mighty sword of King Arthur. Another reference to Avalon occurs in the *Vita Merlini* (1150), in which the island of apples provides a home for nine benevolent witches led by Morgan le Fay, King Arthur's half sister. Her importance to British lore lies in a typical female role—caregiver to the king after his disastrous loss against the villain Mordred at the Battle of Camlann near the Camel River and Cadbury (the most likely site of Camelot, Arthur's mythic capital).

Tended by healing hands, Arthur is said to have withdrawn from the known world to the paradise that awaits heroes, where grapes and grain spring naturally from the soil, the climate remains eternally springlike, and human life extends to hundred-year spans and beyond. In the Irish version of Avalon, the god Manannan reigns supreme over departed souls, who find rest on the island's benevolent shores. Among these wraiths, Arthur is believed to remain mortal, growing stronger until the day that England needs him most to restore justice and peace to his people. In Guillem Torroella's version, *La Faula* (1370), the magical powers of Avalon reside in the river Tigris, in which Arthur bathes his wounds, and in annual restorative drinks from the Holy Grail, the mythic cup that held the blood of Christ.

Archaeological proof substantiates at least one Avalon of myth. In 1191 scholars located a grave at Glastonbury where a tall, regal corpse bore a sword engraved with the word "Avalonia." Thomas Malory (1416–March 14, 1471) adds to the mystery of Arthur's death by implying that Avalon was actually Glastonbury, a shelter for chaste women who treated mortal ills. As Malory reports Arthur's fate, he becomes "rex quondam rexque futurus" or, in T. H. White's translation, the "once and future king." However, Alfred Tennyson, England's poet laureate at the beginning of the Victorian era, rejects Malory's conjecture and returns to Geoffrey's lore by surmising that paradise lay across the sea to the west. As the royal vessel floats away from Bedevere, Arthur looks forward to quiet repose,

> Where falls not hail, or rain, or any snow,
> Nor ever wind blows loudly, but it lies
> Deep-meadowed, happy, fair with orchard lawns
> And bowery hollows crowned with summer sea . . .

Tended by gentle-handed maidens in this easeful bower of Avilion, Arthur intends to recuperate from "grievous wounds." A distant utopia, Avilion lies farther than Bedevere can see. He gazes as long as eyes can hold the black dot on the horizon and ears can catch the wails of Arthur's fearful attendants.

G. K. Chesterton's *Short History of England* (1917) deliberately links Celtic mythology with Christian lore. Following Christ's crucifixion at Golgotha, Joseph of Arimathea, a wealthy but secretive believer in Jesus' divinity, set sail on a mission to spread the new religion. Far west of the Mediterranean Sea, he landed at a wild western beachhead near Glastonbury called Avalon, where he planted his staff in fertile soil. From that time, the staff has put forth leaves, possibly watered by the curative waters of Chalice Well, a healing spring said to cure human ills. On Christmas Day, the rooted staff is decked in blossoms. At a nearby shrine, the cup of Christ bearing the last of his blood remained safe, guarded by Arthur's fellowship of knights, commonly called the Round Table. The cup is believed to work miracles, although the touch of divinity it holds is accessible only to the pure of heart—notably Sir Galahad, who had a vision of Christ's miraculous chalice. (Abrams 1968; Ashe 1987; Ashton 1974; Ellis 1991; Lacy 1986; Steinbeck 1976; Tennyson 1989)

See also Arthur; Camelot; syncretism; Tennyson, Alfred; women in utopia.

 BACK TO METHUSELAH

George Bernard Shaw's bitterly dystopian five-part play is a laborious and prophetic closet drama. Subtitled "A Metabiological Pentateuch," the play leaps over a chasm of time from creation to 30,000 years in the future. Named for Methuselah, an Old Testament patriarch who lived 969 years, the text projects a new religion based on myth blended with biological concepts of adaptation to environment. Shaw's use of the term "pentateuch" connects the play with the first five books of Moses, i.e., Genesis, Exodus, Leviticus, Numbers, and Deuteronomy, which contain the earliest Hebrew myths, laws, and cultural foundations.

Performed and published in 1921, the play returns to Eden, where a dead fawn signals a change in paradise. Adam and Eve contemplate the ugliness of death; the serpent, an enticingly lovely creature who interrupts their private conversation, surmises that death is offset by birth, a concept that confuses Eve. To Eve's questions, the serpent replies enigmatically, "You see things; and you say 'Why?' But I dream things that never were; and I say 'Why not?'" As the couple listen to the serpent's wily sophistry, he inspires Adam with a new feeling and gives it a name: jealousy. Brooding that the future is uncertain, Adam threatens the serpent with death if he refuses to restore faith in the future. The snake moves aside to whisper to Eve the secret of procreation.

Act II, the next domestic segment, contains Shaw's characterization at its best. The first couple face their vengeful son Cain, the prototypical fighting man who takes pride in being the murderer of his weaker brother, Abel. Cain's boastful, argumentative, blasphemous behavior causes Eve to chastise him and to disdain his theory of hero and superman. Although Cain has already murdered the gentle Abel, Eve retains hope for her remaining sons, Enoch and Tubal. At Cain's snide departing words, Adam damns him. Unfamiliar with damnation, Eve asks for a definition. Adam replies, "The state of them that love death more than life."

The rapid change of scene that opens Part II resets the play on Hampstead Heath outside London. In Shaw's incisive satire, a gathering of gentlemen discusses World War I. Franklyn Barnabas, an ex-cleric, comments to Lubin on the enigma of perpetual life in Paradise:

> Adam and Eve were hung up between two frightful possibilities. One was the extinction of mankind by their accidental death. The other was the prospect of living forever. They could bear neither.

Other conversants ponder the good and bad sides of longevity. The Barnabas brothers conclude that pure creativity is limited because human beings die too soon to develop their talents. The third part of the play, its weakest segment, moves ahead to A.D. 2170 and pursues the theme of lengthened life. By Part IV, Shaw has moved 830 years ahead to A.D. 3000, a time when England is famous for its long-lived populace.

In Part V of this convoluted study of an appropriate length for human life, Shaw introduces an indistinct summer idyll in the year A.D. 31,920. Similar to H. G. Wells's *The Time Machine* (1895) in its classic setting, the scene opens on a temple set in a grove. To the sound of flute melodies, young men and women dance in Grecian attire. This stage of human evolution finds human life springing from eggs, with the emerging embryo already matured to the late teens. People pass rapidly into full adulthood, advancing at age three or four from trivial interests to a contemplation of abstract mathematics and philosophy. For 700–800 years, these ancients survive in their idyllic state until some accident kills them.

Pygmalion interrupts the dancing couples and announces that he has created a human male and female who function in the old way, by digesting food and reproducing sexually. The man and woman appear as automata—he resembling Ozymandias, King of Kings, and she in the guise of Semiramis-Cleopatra. The pair exhibit what Shaw considers the worst of human vices—vanity, egotism, selfishness, violence, passion, cowardice, and fear of death. So depraved is the woman that she bites Pygmalion and kills him. In contemplation of such lack of civilization, the ancients conclude that human unhappiness stems from enslavement to the body.

Against the backdrop of a renewed dance, Lilith (the earth mother in Hebrew lore who has more in common with Guinevere or Aphrodite than with the ingenuous Eve) appears to muse on creation. She laments that human beings have lost the use of breast and bowels, and is dismayed at their audacity. Her complaint dominates Shaw's conclusion to this mammoth work:

> I had patience with them for many ages: they tried me very sorely. They did terrible things: they embraced death, and said that eternal life was a fable. I stood amazed at the malice and destructiveness of the things I had made: Mars blushed as he looked down on the shame of his sister planet: cruelty and hypocrisy became so hideous that the face of the earth was pitted with the graves of little children among which living skeletons crawled in search of horrible food.

Still willing to see what human life will spawn, Lilith ponders woman's greatest gift—curiosity, a parallel to Pandora and to the goddess's own interest in future developments.

The goddess concludes that stagnation is the greatest sin. She notes in her parting soliloquy: "And now I shall see the slave set free and the enemy reconciled, the whirlpool become all life and no matter." She promises to have patience with humankind, even though they waste their longevity. The moment that humanity ceases to thrive on its own possibilities and begins to kill hope and faith, she intends to end their lengthy stay on Earth by annihilating them. For the moment, she looks ahead into the endless cosmos and focuses on "its million starry mansions," many of which are empty or unbuilt. Before she vanishes from the stage, she longs for the day when her offspring shall master all creation and concludes, "It is enough that there is a beyond." (Hill 1978; Hornstein et al. 1973; Johnson 1968; Magill 1958; Negley and Patrick 1952; Shaw 1988)

See also Adam; Eden; Eve; fantasy; Genesis; prophecy; satire; Shaw, George Bernard; *The Time Machine*; women in utopia.

BACON, FRANCIS

The multifaceted politician, Platonist, natural scientist, essayist, jurist, and fablist who composed *The New Atlantis* (1627) describes a utopian society founded on scientific principle, which citizens acquire through the observation of natural phenomena at the fictional hall of science called Solomon's House. Born in 1561 to Anne Bacon, a Calvinist and classical scholar, and Sir Nicholas Bacon, keeper of the queen's seal and heir to a prestigious house, Bacon was related to important members of the advisory to Elizabeth I. As a regular visitor to court in childhood, he played with the queen's favorites and learned to survive among fawning favor-seekers, vicious gossips, and social climbers. As he grew to manhood, he earned a sullied reputation for materialism and currying favor with royalty.

Entering Trinity College, Cambridge, at the age of 12, Bacon brashly criticized his professors, particularly for their reliance on Aristotelian logic, which he deemed old-fashioned. He graduated at age 14 and began study at Gray's Inn, where he received a quality education in law. For two years he served on the ambassadorial staff of Sir Amias Paulet, traveled Europe, and studied the new ideas that were replacing scholasticism.

With the death of his father came a loss of privilege. At the age of 18, Bacon returned to England to serve as executor of his father's estate. As the youngest, he inherited none of his family's wealth and had to arrange a grant to pay the remainder of his tuition. At age 23 he achieved a seat in Parliament and, through the patronage of the second earl of Essex, made his way at court, where he bungled his rise to power by failing to ingratiate himself with Queen Elizabeth. In 1601 the fiasco of Essex's revolt against the Tudor regime forced Bacon to complete another unpleasant, demeaning task—the prosecution and supervision of the execution of his patron for treason.

After the queen's death, Bacon improved his relationship at court with her successor, James I, and was knighted. Bacon married the prominent Alice Barnham in 1607 and rose to the position of solicitor general; he also attained the prestigious post that his father had enjoyed—keeper of the royal seal. By the end of Bacon's career, although he had attained the office of Lord Chancellor and was named Viscount St. Albans, he suffered the worst of unpredictable

Francis Bacon

losses common to those who lived on the whim of the court—he was indicted for graft, fined £40,000, and imprisoned in the Tower of London. This setback cost him banishment and a loss of favor.

A prodigious observer and writer, Bacon published popular volumes of essays in 1597 and 1625. From his avocation—scientific experimentation and observation—Bacon derived the unofficial title of father of inductive philosophy, a title some critics question. His scientific works include *The Advancement of Learning* (1605), *De Augmentis Scientiarum* (1623), and his analytic exposition of induction, *Novum Organum* (1620), one of the high points of Renaissance philosophy.

An admirer of Machiavelli, a probable reader of utopists Fra Tomaso Campanella and Johann Andreae, and coiner of the phrase "knowledge is power," Bacon sought the opportunity to carry out scientific and philosophical reform in England. Composing in English, he later translated his work into Latin, the only acceptable scientific language of his day. He completed his utopian masterpiece *The New Atlantis* in 1624, but left it unpublished.

Bacon's writings emphasize a rejection of both medieval scholasticism and rote classical studies. Like his Renaissance contemporaries, he preferred to live in the real world and study its phenomena as a means of applying natural science to human betterment. He proposed a scientific consortium known as Solomon's House, or the College of the Six Days' Works, a title based on the description of creation in Genesis in which God creates the world in six days.

His insistence on empiricism cost Bacon his life. In 1626, while testing snow as a freezing agent for poultry, he caught a chill and died on April 9 at Highgate. (Bacon 1905; Berneri 1951; Hornstein et al. 1973; Johnson 1968; Magill 1958; Mumford 1959; Negley and Patrick 1952; White 1955)

See also Andreae, Johann Valentin; Atlantis; Campanella, Fra Tomaso; *The New Atlantis.*

BAPTISM

Baptism is a symbolic ritual removing the stain of an unrighteous state and conferring the promise of a blessed union with the kingdom of God. In some religions an adult or infant baptism is a requirement for acceptance into heaven. The style and ritual of applying the waters varies from faith to faith; some groups incorporate baptism, or "sprinkling," into a naming ceremony for infants and toddlers. The occasion is a joyous family event in that it demands parental accountability for the child's religious education and guarantees the reunion of the family in heaven.

Fundamentalists tend to differ on the concept of infant baptism. Some require immersion of converts, who become candidates only upon reaching the age of accountability and after a change of heart from sinfulness to acceptance of Christ as lord and savior. As the Apostle Peter warns in Acts 2:38: "Repent, and be baptized every one of you in the name of Jesus Christ for the forgiveness of your sins; and you shall receive the gift of the Holy Spirit." This style of baptism replicates John the Baptist's immersion of his cousin Jesus as described in the four Gospels of the New Testament. According to Matthew 3:1–6, John performs the ritual ablution in the river Jordan as a symbol of cleansing. Jesus rises from the water a new man because his sins are removed. He is thus proclaimed the Messiah and can actualize the ancient prophecy of Isaiah—to take on the sins of the world and unite believers with God in a blessed afterlife. Other accounts of this miraculous baptism occur in Mark 1:1–12, in which the Holy Spirit "descends upon [Jesus] like a dove," and Luke 3:2–22, in which a "voice came from heaven, which said, 'Thou art my beloved Son; in thee I am well pleased.'" In each instance, the observer describes the act as blessed.

Immersion in water echoes through literature as an earthly rebirth of fallible humans into a state of grace, e.g., as proof of the acceptance of utopian principles in Sir Thomas More's *Utopia* (1516). In William Shakespeare's *The*

Tempest (1611), connivers against Prospero have their baptism in a near-death run-in with a prodigious storm in the Atlantic Ocean off the island of Bermuda. The necessary change of heart results in Prospero's reunion with the court that despised him, forgiveness of past enmities, and the betrothal of his innocent daughter Miranda, who had previously encountered no man but her father. The play balances baptism with communion after Prospero spreads a miraculous banquet for all to partake of in pledge of brotherhood.

Modern literature often uses varying types of immersion in water as a symbolic baptism. In Ray Bradbury's *Fahrenheit 451* (1953), the hero Montag, his leg anesthetized by a hellish mechanical dog, eludes police search parties and escapes to the woods beyond Los Angeles. He plunges into the cleansing river waters, which free him from the old life that required adherence to a totalitarian government, a job as fire fighter with the duty of burning readers and their homes. The new, revitalized Montag rids himself of Beatty, a fire captain who appears to know more about Montag's inner qualms than he himself perceives.

After baptism, Montag passes from a destructive environment to a regenerative counterculture. While he floats on his back, absolved of the fear of detection and punishment, he ponders the paradox of light and fire. Illuminated and uplifted by his experience, he reaches the shallows and joins the pilgrimage of reformers by contributing his own recollection from literature—a verse from Ecclesiastes 5 in the Old Testament: "To everything there is a season."

A similar spiritual baptism launches the rejuvenation of William Weston in Ernest Callenbach's *Ecotopia* (1975). The utopian setting in the Pacific Northwest virtually rends the soul of this journalist outsider who enters forbidden territory to learn the secret of a segment of states that secede from the Union. Under benevolent house arrest engineered by President Vera Allwen, Weston wrestles with the draw of New York, his children, and his eastern mate, Pat. Pitted against these loyalties are the beauties and equities of Ecotopia and the love of a new breed of woman, Marissa Brightcloud, an assertive commune worker who teaches Weston that love should free rather than enslave. The soothing, cleansing hot-water springs plunge Weston into a blend of soul refurbishment and body reclamation. Like the human amnion and chorion, the waters shelter him safely and warmly until he chooses to be reborn as a citizen of Ecotopia. In his journal entry of June 25 he comments:

> I couldn't bear to get out, and sat neck-deep, staring at the water splashing from the pipe, listening to the complicated sounds it made. My body floated weightlessly in the warm, comforting water, feeling only the slightest of sensations.

Unaware of horizon, place, and time, he allows his escapist womb to shelter him until his choice coalesces. Like the figure of Christ rising from the Jordan River, Weston makes his "breakthrough," his physical and spiritual birth into the commune. Later, on a blanket of pine needles, he makes love with Marissa, who comments enigmatically, "Good place to conceive a child." (Alexander and Alexander 1973; Anderson 1966; Bradbury 1953; Callenbach 1975; Cavendish 1970; Cavendish 1980; Cross 1957; Eliade 1986; Hastings 1951; Holy Bible 1958; Jurji 1946; McDannell 1994; More 1963a; Wright 1971)

See also asceticism; Beatty, Captain; Beulah Land; Camelot; *Ecotopia; Fahrenheit 451*; heaven; *Pilgrim's Progress; The Tempest; Utopia.*

BARRIE, SIR JAMES MATTHEW

Barrie wrote *Peter Pan* (1904), an imaginative utopian children's classic about a fantasy island where residents never grow old. Barrie was born in the lowland village of Kirriemuir, Angus, Scotland, on May 9, 1860. The son of Margaret Ogilvy and David Barrie, a hand-loom weaver, he was the ninth of ten children. After the death of his eldest brother David in 1866, Barrie became his mother's favorite; the strong mother-son bond that colored his 77 years often led to accusations of infantilism. Critics mention this family crisis as the impetus of Barrie's biography of his mother, *Margaret Ogilvy* (1896), and of the creation of two classic characters: Wendy, the little mother, and Peter Pan, a winsome boy embodying the best of childhood traits who remains untouched by age, maturity, or death, which he characterizes as a future "great adventure."

A lover of romance and adventure, Barrie grew up in a strict Scotch Presbyterian environment, enjoyed Robert Louis Stevenson's high-sea adventure novels and James Fenimore Cooper's *Leatherstocking Tales,* and acted in local theater productions. Barrie received a worthy education from his mother's tutelage and from his brother, educator A. O. Barrie, but gave no sign of future greatness in his mediocre performance at the Dumfries Academy, which he entered at age 13.

Barrie enrolled at the University of Edinburgh, rejecting what he called "hum-dreadful-drum" professions in favor of writing. After receiving an M.A., he worked as a journalist and editor for the *Nottinghamshire Journal* and later in London under the pseudonyms Hippomenes and Gavin Ogilvy for the *St. James's Gazette* and *British Weekly.* He began freelance writing with the publication of *Auld Licht Idylls* (1888). A friend and protégé of Stevenson, Thomas Hardy, George Meredith, and Conan Doyle, he achieved fame as a fiction writer in 1891 with his novel *The Little Minister,* as well as the drama *Richard Savage.* His numerous other plays include *The Professor's Love Story* (1892), *The Wedding Guest* (1900), *The Admirable Crichton* (1902), *Quality Street* (1902), *What Every Woman Knows* (1903), and *Peter Pan: The Boy Who Would Not Grow Up* (1904), a charming work that emulates Lewis Carroll's *Alice in Wonderland,* Rudyard Kipling's *Jungle Book,* L. Frank Baum's *Wonderful Wizard of Oz,* and Robert Louis Stevenson's *Treasure Island* in that it began as unstructured storytelling for family, then went through several published versions.

Like Charles Dickens's *A Christmas Carol,* Barrie's *Peter Pan* was favored as escapist fantasy and became a traditional holiday favorite on London stages, surfacing in the United States in pirated form. The story reappeared in novel form in 1911 as *Peter and Wendy* and as an upgraded play in 1928, which became the most frequently reproduced in the canon of children's drama. As a paean to childhood, the plot amplifies Barrie's unrealistic wish: "Oh, that we were boys and girls all our lives!"

James Matthew Barrie, about 1894

At the age of 34 Barrie married actress Mary Ansell and settled into the Bayswater section of London and a country house in Farnham, Surrey. The ill-matched couple found no happiness in their childless home, in part because Mary failed to live up to Barrie's model—his mother, who died the year of her son's marriage. Although the couple remained married for 16 years, Barrie fell in love with Sylvia, the wife of Arthur Llewelyn Davies. It was for her five sons that he created the character of Peter Pan. Barrie was 50 when he divorced his wife; four months later, the widowed Sylvia Davies died before he could marry her. His last stage successes were *Dear Brutus* (1917), *The Old Lady Shows Her Medals* (1917), *Mary Rose* (1920), and *The Boy David* (1936), a tender look at the biblical character who bested the giant Goliath.

A contemporary and rival of George Bernard Shaw, Barrie earned a baronetcy and Order of Merit for his war plays, received four honorary degrees, was named lord rector of St. Andrews University in 1919, and in 1930 served University of Edinburgh as chancellor. Leaving a sizable fortune in royalties to the orphaned Davies children, whom he had adopted, Barrie died June 19, 1937, and was buried in the Barrie plot in his hometown. At his direction, his manuscripts were housed in Dumfries's Burgh Museum, and the proceeds of *Peter Pan* were left to London's Great Ormond Street Hospital. Near the Westbourne Gate in Kensington Gardens, a statue of Peter—erected in 1912 at Barrie's expense on the spot where he had walked his Newfoundland dog Luath, prototype for the dog-nurse Nana—remains a popular tourist attraction. (Barrie 1981; Carpenter and Prichard 1984; Commire 1978; Darlington 1974; Dunbar 1970; Kunitz 1942)

See also escapism; fantasy; Neverland; Peter Pan; Shaw, George Bernard; *The Wonderful Wizard of Oz.*

 # BAUM, L. FRANK

Salesman, actor, journalist, columnist, editor, and author of children's literature, Lyman Frank Baum was an early appreciator of Aesop, Hans Christian Andersen, Jacob and Wilhelm Grimm, and Lewis Carroll. He once noted that pleasing children was a worthwhile endeavor for which he received worldwide fame. Born on May 15, 1856, Baum was the seventh of nine children of Cynthia Stanton and oil tycoon Benjamin Ward Baum. He enjoyed a comfortable life in Chittenango, New York, but his childhood energies were sapped by a weak heart. Like Robert Louis Stevenson, Baum recuperated by spending dreamy hours in seclusion, studying under tutors, and reading the masterpieces of his day. He enrolled briefly at Peekskill Military Academy, but the experience brought on a heart attack. In 1871 Baum acquired a small printing press and joined with his brother Harry in publishing a newspaper that later evolved into *Baum's Complete Stamp Dealers Directory.* His aunt, actress Katherine Grayson, introduced him to the theater, which would have become his vocation had his father not insisted that he be a salesman for the family oil business. Later, after he proved to himself

L. Frank Baum

and his family that selling oil was not a good choice of career, he was drawn into theater management and wrote for a Pennsylvania newspaper.

In 1882 Baum married Maud Gage and they had four sons. He built a home in Syracuse, then moved to Aberdeen, South Dakota, to open a dry-goods store. Although this venture failed, Baum developed other interests, particularly storytelling, photography, and a love of children. He organized a baseball team for children and wrote a humorous column for the *Dakota Pioneer*. Baum moved to Chicago to write for the *Evening Post* and sell china and glassware, but the traveling-salesman work brought on a recurrence of heart problems. To stabilize his transient life, Baum devoted himself more keenly to young-adult literature and completed *Adventure in Phunniland* and *Tales from Mother Goose*. Success in the publication of a trade magazine in 1900 led him to continue writing for young readers with *Father Goose, The Songs of Father Goose, The Army Alphabet,* and *The Navy Alphabet*. From a single episode entitled "The Emerald City," Baum evolved *The Wonderful Wizard of Oz* (1900), a utopian children's fantasy for which he is best known. He followed with *The Life and Adventures of Santa Claus, Dot and Tot of Merryland, The Master Key,* and *The Woggle-Bug Book,* but none equaled the success of his earlier novel.

Baum's career turned from children's stories to film. He built a home in Hollywood, traveled in Europe and Africa, and lectured on moviemaking. Reduced to bankruptcy by 1911, he retired to a small house and garden, resumed writing children's literature, and took pleasure in his family. In 1919, still corresponding with young readers, he died of a heart and gall-bladder attack. (Baum and MacFall 1961; Baum 1983; Bewley 1970; Manguel and Guadalupi 1987; Mannix 1964; Snodgrass 1992; Snow 1954; Wagenknecht 1968)

See also Dorothy; Emerald City; fantasy; Oz; Wizard of Oz; *The Wonderful Wizard of Oz*.

 # BEATTY, CAPTAIN

Beatty is the malignant, red-cheeked, pipe-smoking fire captain in Ray Bradbury's *Fahrenheit 451*. A Machiavellian character with a passive-aggressive personality, he typifies the totalitarian control that impels fire companies to burn books and incinerate people who hoard them. In his cynical evaluation of preauthoritarian times when people could read what they wanted and savor the past, he rationalizes the suppression and ruthlessly enforced censorship of sensitive, thoughtful people through specious argument and sadistic badinage. In Part One, he summarizes the rise of a futuristic California dystopia from a disjointed comic-book bombardment of sensations and responses—"Click, Pic, Look, Eye, Now, Flick, Here, There, Swift, Pace, Up, Down, In, Out, Why, How, Who, What, Where, Eh? Uh! Bang! Smack! Wallop, Bing, Bong, Boom!" His formula for stasis is to de-energize the spirit and quell individuality: "Each man the image of every other; then all are happy."

In Part Two, Captain Beatty, a perceptive manager of firemen, indicates that he knows that protagonist Guy Montag is flirting with treason. Beatty teases Montag with a melange of lines from the Bible, William Shakespeare's *Measure for Measure*, Alexander Pope's "Essay on Criticism," and Sir Philip Sidney's *Defense of Poesy*:

> ... the crisis is past and all is well, the sheep returns to the fold. We're all sheep who have strayed at times. Truth is truth, to the end of reckoning, we've cried. They are never alone that are accompanied with noble thoughts, we've shouted to ourselves. "Sweet food of sweetly uttered knowledge. ... " But on the other hand: "Words are like leaves and where they most abound, much fruit of sense beneath is rarely found."

Himself a disillusioned idealist, Beatty copes by wearing the scornful mask, sneering at underlings, and carelessly citing stores of quotations, which proves a suspicious familiarity with a broad range of literary treasures no longer available to the public.

A failed scholar, Beatty resigns his former idealism and embraces the antiliterate dystopian state. Through savagery and the delusion that he rescues society from its failings, he maintains his distance from thinkers and dreamers who threaten his position as enforcer. The taunting, jeering smirk and habitual flicking of his lighter reveal the delight he takes in victim baiting, which forms a pun on his last name. In the novel's falling action, Montag (his literary foil) realizes the terrible truth—Beatty wants to be killed. The pressure on Montag results in poetic justice—Beatty's hideous conflagration, which shrivels him, "a torch, not moving, fluttering out on the grass," alongside his indefatigable and equally insensitive mechanical fire hound. (Bradbury 1953; Bradbury 1975; Breit 1956; Clareson 1976; Indick 1989; Johnson 1968; Johnson 1978; Knight 1967; Mogen 1986; Slusser 1977a)

See also baptism; Bradbury, Ray; *Fahrenheit 451*; idealism; Montag, Guy; technology.

BELLAMY, EDWARD

Editorialist, altruist, and novelist, Bellamy achieved success with his bestselling *Looking Backward, 2000–1887* (1887), a utopian examination of Boston in the year 2000 through the eyes of a visitor from the past. Bellamy was a substantial writer and philosopher of his day, and his futuristic novel inspired a cadre of imitators, claims of plagiarism, and rebuttals. Only two years after his classic appeared, the utopian market burgeoned with these:

- Robert Michaelis's *A Sequel to "Looking Backward" or Looking Further Forward*

- Thomas Reynolds's *Prefaces and Notes: Illustrative, Explanatory, Demonstrative, Argumentative, and Expostulatory to Mr. Edward Bellamy's Famous Book*

- Marie Adelaide Shipley's *The True Author of Looking Backward*

- Arthur Dudley Vinton's *Looking Further Backward*

The next three years brought more by Ludwig Geisaler, Conrad Wilbrandt, and J. W. Roberts. For whatever reason, Bellamy appears to have tapped a pervasive interest in world betterment, perhaps on the rise of millennial concerns for and curiosity about the twentieth century.

The son of a Baptist minister, Bellamy was born in Chicopee Falls, Massachusetts, on March 26, 1850. As a prelaw student, he read widely and attended Union College to study an appropriate mix for a utopist—economics, politics, history, and literature. Ending his college education after a year, he traveled Germany and contemplated the contrast between baronial estates and cathedrals and the misery of slums, a prelude to his interest in social reform. He began writing columns, editorials, and reviews for the *Springfield Union,* joined brother Charles in founding the *Daily News,* and reviewed for the New York *Evening Post.* His first novel, *Six to One: A Nantucket Idyll* (1878), encouraged him to delve harder into human motivation, as demonstrated by *Dr. Heidenhoff's Process* (1880). His romance titled *The Duke of Stockbridge* (1879) fell short of critical acclaim, but *Looking Backward, 2000–1887* (1887), one of America's most popular utopian novels, increased his readership, especially among the middle class.

After achieving name recognition, Bellamy formed the nucleus of a socialist movement called "Bellamy clubs" and edited the *Nationalist* and *New Nation,* journals espousing his beliefs in economic equality, brotherhood, and socialized industry. His supporters launched the People's Party, a populist movement, during the 1892 national election. During this nine-year period, Bellamy penned *Equality* (1897) as a sequel to *Looking Backward* so that he could develop some of his socialist proposals and refute misreadings of the first novel. The success of his grand schemes and plans for a National Reform Party died with the man on May 22, 1898.

Bellamy's ideas remained alive in the abstract, continued to sway European thinkers, and influenced economist Thorstein Veblen and educator John Dewey. As Erich Fromm describes Bellamy's utopism, the good society is an outgrowth of yearning for a good life, a reflection of Plato's *Republic* and the ideal of a peaceable kingdom ruled by a philosopher-king. In Bellamy's scheme, people participate willingly and rationally, selecting for themselves the behaviors that bring them joy in living. Bereft of greed and competitiveness, the characters of *Looking Backward* revel in centralized community, solidarity, and reciprocity, as demonstrated by the fair exchange of goods and services. Freed of the envy and hostile competitiveness of the marketplace, they avoid deception and manipulation in favor of the greatest good for society.

In his day, Bellamy's critics decried the bureaucratic superstructure governing his docile characters, who are mere shadows sketched in to flesh out the text from treatise to novel. Bellamy's faith in a managerial elite, like that of William Morris in *News from Nowhere* (1890), anticipates some transcendent state that exists in stasis, forever in balance despite new challenges, new discoveries, or outside interference. He assumes that the ruling class is able to satisfy all citizens by assuring material comfort and avoiding overproduction. Such shallow spirits lack a normal human drive for a creed by which to live.

This anti–Judeo-Christian faith in materialism embodies a truth that Bellamy never denied—he de-emphasized religion because he had no faith in its ability to revitalize or reward earthly activities. To Bellamy, the anticipation of heaven as reward for righteousness was not enough; the creation of a model heaven was attainable through technology and unity of purpose. In his brief postscript to *Looking Backward*, he remarks, "the Golden Age lies before us and not behind us, and is not far away. Our children will surely see it, and we, too, who are already men and women, if we deserve it by our faith and by our works." (Bellamy 1960; Bowman 1979; Bowman 1986; Magill 1958; Morgan 1945; Mumford 1959; Parrington 1964; Patai 1988)

See also golden age; *Looking Backward, 2000–1887*; Montag, Guy; Morris, William; *News from Nowhere*; philosopher-king; Plato; *The Republic*; technology.

BESTIALITY

A characteristic theme in utopias, bestiality undergirds a caste system that requires stringent, inhumane slavery. Not to be confused with beast fables, such as Aristophanes's *The Birds* (414 B.C.), George Orwell's *Animal Farm* (1945), or Richard Adams's *Watership Down* (1972), bestiality in utopian literature results from the dehumanization of a lower strata that is exploited for the pleasure and service of an elite. The classism of Aldous Huxley's *Brave New World* (1932) illustrates the utopist's need for a dray class. In his technological dystopia, controlled eugenics is easily maintained through Bokanovsky's Process, which supplies a balance of conveyor-belt fetuses, bottled and treated to equip each developing human being with an appropriate mentality. To serve the superior Alphas and Betas, the laboratory turns out Deltas and Epsilons; they are conditioned in neo-Pavlovian nurseries not only to serve in a menial capacity but to prefer it to the privileges of their betters.

Huxley follows a tradition of dehumanized serfdom that began in the eighteenth century with the prototype of the bestial utopian subgenre—Jonathan Swift's *Gulliver's Travels* (1727). A shallow observer and weak logician, Gulliver lauds the wise Houyhnhnms, an anthropomorphic race of horses, and despises the vile Yahoos, a human species who live like simians. The protagonist, whose name is a portmanteau word formed from "gullible" and "traveler," succumbs to a sorry state by trying to conceal from his horse friends his Yahoo form and nature. Gulliver's return to England so disillusions him that he lives apart from family and neighbors, whose Yahoo smell and behavior repulse him. A profoundly misanthropic Yahoo himself, he stuffs his nose to bar the offensive smell of others and attempts to change their ways to those of the wise Houyhnhnms, whom he reveres above his own kind. The dark satire of his revulsion concludes his four-part adventures with the protagonist no wiser and certainly no better off than when he began his voyages.

A similar distaste for bestial humans occurs in H. G. Wells's *The Time Machine* (1895) and in George Orwell's *1984* (1949). Wells's Eloi, a privileged class of enervated humans, have been refined through a closed breeding process to the point of human caricatures. The Eloi repress their bestial, carnivorous alter egos, the Morlocks, by forcing them to live in darkness in foul-smelling subterranean lairs and to subsist on uncooked haunches of animals. To the Time Traveller, a Morlock, set apart by luminous eyes and nocturnal habits, is a "queer little ape-like figure, its head held down in a peculiar manner." To the touch, they embody the characteristics of earthworms—cold and blind with lidless pink eyes and clammy skin.

The Time Traveller surmises that Morlocks evolved as Londoners promoted a widening gulf between workers and the elite upper class. As biologist Charles Darwin predicted, natural selection favors the subclass and threatens the existence of the overlords, or "beautiful people," a gentle, nonviolent class who must cower together at night to stave off attacks by Morlocks. In Chapter 7, the Time Traveller warns:

> The Nemesis of the delicate ones was creeping on apace. Ages ago, thousands of generations ago, man had thrust his brother man out of the ease and the sunshine. And now that brother was coming back—changed!

Orwell uses Darwinian philosophy to warn that progress has its limits and that the complete separation of the two ends of humanity simultaneously disenfranchises the Morlock and thrusts the effeminate Eloi into a life of terror. To the Morlock, the well-stocked banquet tables of the Eloi assure the under-race of tasty Eloi flesh when one of the elite race ventures out in the dark and falls prey to Morlock claws.

Similarly but with less vehemence, George Orwell's educated Londoners refer to the vigorous proletarian class as Proles, yet live contiguously with them while repressing Prole participation in society. As with Wells's Eloi, the bestial Proles become shadow beings who enjoy a freedom in their alienation that allows them certain advantages. In Book I, Chapter 7 of *1984*, Winston Smith, the protagonist, looks to the Proles for rebellion and the defeat of totalitarianism, even though there is little evidence that leadership exists for such an about-face. The poorly socialized generations who mine England's coal and whose women and children operate factories immerse themselves in gutter culture, scrape for what they want, and drown their malaise in beer.

Orwell evidences an advantage in Proledom. In a reflective moment, from the window of his rented room Winston observes the buxom grace and spirited drive of a Prole female, who sings while hanging wash on the line. Like Wells's Morlocks, who grow strong and dangerous in their underground world of machines, the Proles, who are bound to endless physical labor, remain exempt from the spying and strictures on working-class Oceanians and are less intimidated by Big Brother, the titular head of state who intimidates more in spirit than by actual physical menace. In their animal state, the Proles endure less tension than their betters and, free of totalitarian directives, can expend more energy in self-directed tasks. (Bedford 1985; Holmes 1970; Huxley 1932; Huxley 1989; Nance 1988; Negley and Patrick 1952; Orwell 1949; Swift 1958; Wells 1964)

BEULAH LAND

An easeful afterlife, the name is derived from an extended biblical metaphor described in Isaiah 62:1–4, focusing on Beulah, the Hebrew term for "married." The idyllic land offers a tantalizing respite paralleling the letting go of troubles and concerns that believers experience shortly before death. To receive Beulah Land, the righteous must undergo a celestial yielding to and marriage with Yahweh, or God. The prophet's shimmering, beguiling promise of "a crown of glory in the hand of the Lord, and a royal diadem in the hand of thy God" precedes a prediction of "thy land Beulah: for the Lord delighteth in thee."

In John Bunyan's allegorical pilgrimage to heaven in *Pilgrim's Progress* (1678), the speaker anticipates a joyous arrival in Beulah Land, a heavenly bliss outside the Celestial City. The term indicates that, prior to Christ's resurrection, faithful followers must cross the River of Death, taste bitterness, then free themselves forever from the taste. Thus baptized, the travelers remain in Beulah Land, a restful waiting area. The term evolved into a common female given name and also dots the texts of Negro spirituals. (Alexander and Alexander 1973; Benét 1991; Brewer 1899; Bunyan 1896; Evans 1817; Holy Bible 1958; McDannell 1994; Mays 1988)

See also baptism; Bunyan, John; Celestial City; heaven; *Pilgrim's Progress*.

 # BIG BROTHER

Big Brother is the remote, nebulous nether deity of George Orwell's *1984* (1949). The automata who people Orwell's realm assume that Big Brother is real, although he fails to make a corporeal appearance. Depicted on a poster in Book 1, Chapter 1 as "the face of a man of about forty-five, with a heavy black mustache and ruggedly handsome features," Big Brother gives an identity to the tyranny that restricts daily life in Oceania. He looks out above a caption reading "BIG BROTHER IS WATCHING YOU." As supreme paranoia-maker, Big Brother is the unseen presence whom propagandists tout as "an invincible, fearless protector, standing like a rock against the hordes of Asia." By Chapter 7, however, his hypnotic eyes and ubiquitous gaze oppress with a look "that penetrated inside your skull, battering against your brain, frightening you out of your beliefs, persuading you, almost, to deny the evidence of your senses." This reevaluation foretells the effect on the protagonist, Winston Smith, who seeks a respite from Oceania and the watchful, disembodied presence.

By Book 2, Chapter 9, Big Brother—still "infallible and all-powerful"—dominates telescreens. As Winston reads "The Theory and Practice of Oligarchical Collectivism," Emanuel Goldstein's commentary on the party structure that dominates Oceania, he learns that Big Brother, the apex of a triad of power, is deliberately conceived as

> . . . the guise in which the Party chooses to exhibit itself to the world. His function is to act as a focusing point for love, fear, and reverence, emotions which are more easily felt toward an individual than toward an organization.

As the book reaches its denouement, Big Brother evolves into the inverse of protection; he becomes the hellish icon that the tormented Winston Smith is forced to embrace. Both antigod and the cynical inverse of the utopist, Big Brother embodies the sinister control of the dystopian world of Oceania. His satanic role enables him to subvert human instincts into mechanical impulses through carefully programmed conditioning or torture.

As represented by his minions, O'Brien and the Thought Police, Big Brother symbolizes the anti-utopianism that emerged in the twentieth century. Perhaps so large and menacing a character in Orwell's imagination is, by style and intent, forced to float over his dystopian masterpiece like an enveloping cloud of poison gas, choking out individuality and idealism. Orwell's post-Victorian skepticism presages an era of dystopian visions, a tradition that continues in the feminist dystopias of Marge Piercy, Margaret Atwood, Ursula LeGuin, and P. D. James. Shedding faith in technology and the perfectibility of humankind, Orwell's *1984*—like Karel Capek's *R. U. R.* (1920), Eugene Zamyatin's *We* (1921), Aldous Huxley's *Brave New World* (1932), and Ayn Rand's *Anthem* (1937)—examines the technological wizardry of the twentieth century and denounces its lack of humanity and compassion and its potential for manipulation and tyranny. In a nod to Zamyatin, Orwell composed an essay in 1924 that indicated fear of the Big Brothers of the future, who would rule by exerting an immense power over individuality and truth.

Orwell's hellish dystopia has long been lionized for its predictive accuracy. Wars in Orwell's day had grown huge, unwieldy, and precise in their destruction. Such events presaged no heaven on Earth, a fact evidenced by Adolf Hitler's push for an Aryan super race and the extermination of Jews, homosexuals, gypsies, retardates, and other likely targets during World War II, as well as later forms of genocide in Afghanistan, Southeast Asia, South Africa, Bosnia, and Rwanda. Spy satellites, fiber optic cameras, wiretapping, and other insidious forms of government-initiated observation frequently earn the umbrella term of "Big Brother," a disturbingly accurate addition to the English language. (Alok 1989; Bloom 1987c; Brown 1976; Buitehuis and Nadel 1988; Calder 1987; Connelly 1986; Hynes 1974; Jenson 1984; Oldsey and Browne 1986; Orwell 1949; Stansky 1984)

See also *Anthem; Brave New World;* conditioning; dystopia; James, P. D.; *1984;* Oceana; Orwell, George; Piercy, Marge; *R. U. R.;* Smith, Winston; technology; *We.*

 # THE BIRDS

A satiric utopian farce written after the Peloponnesian War, Aristophanes's *Ornithes* (The Birds) (414 B.C.) lampoons the power plays and rampant ambition that imperiled Athens, the author's hometown. The satire centers on two levels of meaning: civic arrogance and human foibles. Because Athens had voted to expend its limited treasury on an expedition to colonize the southern and eastern shores of Sicily, Aristophanes deliberately labels the project Cloudcuckooland—a boondoggle capable of bankrupting the city-state, thus leaving it more vulnerable to Sparta, its long-term rival. On the personal level, he chooses local parasites, boobs, hangers-on, and ne'er-do-wells as minor characters to illustrate how quickly these bloodsuckers cluster around what appears to be a pleasant utopia.

Opening on the tedious political scene of the playwright's day, two old men named Euelpides ("Hopefulson" in Greek) and Pisthetairos (Greek for "Friend-Persuader") escape urban restlessness by buying a jackdaw and a crow from Philocrates, a merchant who promises that the birds will carry the men away to the land of Epops, or Hoopoe, a serene haven. The men arrive at a rocky, gorse-covered desert and doubt that they have received good advice about escaping Athens. Outside the only building, they knock at the door; a fierce, hook-nosed doorman answers. They request an audience with the Hoopoe bird.

In the receiving hall, Euelpides and Pisthetairos meet Epops, a gullible sovereign who once lived on Earth as Tereus, a mythic character whom the gods punished for seducing Philomela, his sister-in-law, and for running up debts. Transformed into a scruffy bird, Epops dispenses wisdom gained by observing the frailties and bad habits of humans below on Earth. The disgruntled Athenians press Epops to help them resettle where friendships are warm and open, and sexual liaisons are free and unencumbered by legal ties.

Epops, who claims that his kingdom is a haven for sports, feasting, and idleness, at first selects a city near the Red Sea where citizens have no need for money. Euelpides and Pisthetairos reject a place by the shore as not to their liking. They inquire about bird communities and come up with a dream utopia, *Nephelococcygia,* or Cloudcuckooland, a town in the clouds far above mortal imbroglios. Pisthetairos exults in the possibility of holding sway over the lands below. The plan appeals to Epops and his wife Procne, a mythic nightingale, but he must gain a bird consensus before enacting the plan.

Aristophanes's comic utopia does not lack its share of danger. At a meeting of the bird delegation, Koryphaios, the head fowl, scolds Epops for encouraging human habitation in their pleasant, humanfree home. So angry are they with interlopers that they threaten "death by dissection," by shredding the flesh from Euelpides and Pisthetairos's bones. Epops calls for a temporary truce and a covering of bird talons so that the Athenians can have their say before the council.

Timorously, Euelpides and Pisthetairos approach the hostile birds and placate them with compliments. Pisthetairos declares that birds lived before human creation and therefore must outrank the gods in royalty. As emblems of majesty, might, and wisdom, birds deserve to rule over humankind, he concludes. He proposes a building project—a rampart separating god and humanity. If humans object, sparrows would devour all the grain and blind the livestock; if humans allow the wall around the air, the birds would make a conciliatory gesture and obliterate the insect population. As Pisthetairos winds down his persuasive oratory, he exhorts the birds to rise above their servile state.

As the idea takes shape, Pisthetairos proposes a wall of bricks as strong as ancient Babylon. Then the birds should reestablish their ancient power by demanding Zeus's scepter. If he rejects their return to the throne, the birds should launch a holy crusade against Mount Olympus and halt all dalliances between anthropomorphic divinities and human lovers, a common theme in ancient literature. After the gods capitulate to their new masters, the birds have only to demand that human sacrificers leave offerings to the new feathered deities, with scraps going to the deposed gods.

Aristophanes lampoons the inefficiency of committees by picturing the birds quibbling over a few details. How will they settle the questions of money, which men appear to worship? Pisthetairos suggests that the birds guide human treasure-seekers to buried caches. To cement relations with earthlings, birds could report on storms and thus help the shipping industry avoid loss. As the birds warm to the plan, Pisthetairos closes with a winning gesture—praise for the birds' unaffected lifestyle, which contrasts with the gods' demands for grand edifices, sacrifices, and ritual. The birds applaud enthusiastically and, exuding nationalistic fervor, pledge to unseat the gods.

With Epops in the lead, the two Athenians move quickly to implement the plan. Epops provides them with a magic herb that grows wings on their bodies. Meanwhile, the birds exult in their ancient history, which supersedes that of humans and gods, and in their aeronautical design, which wafts them far above human reliance on the earth. At the end of their production number, the Athenians return in full-feathered glory, complete with beaks and wings.

As Cloudcuckooland begins to take shape, Aristophanes sharpens the satire. Pisthetairos superintends wall construction and priestly prayers. A poet who wants to compose a paean to Cloudcuckooland gets shoved out of the way. A seer merits a similarly unceremonious rebuff. A third meddler—Meton, the surveyor—is also unwelcome. Pisthetairos announces a new ordinance—fakery will earn the con artist a public lashing. At that, Meton beats a quick exit.

More self-important nuisances intrude on Pisthetairos's work. He circumvents an officious Athenian building inspector with a rap on the jaw and roughs up a venal politician eager to sell legal countenance for the project. These last two refuse to be quelled and require a thorough trouncing before Pisthetairos can return to walling in heaven. The chorus trills a joyful hymn to birddom and implores the judges to award Aristophanes a blue ribbon.

At this point, Aristophanes laces his comedy with potential violence and tragedy. When the wall reaches 600 feet, the birds exult at their tour de force. A herald warns that a god has sneaked past security; Pisthetairos sets the birds after him. Iris, the rainbow goddess, appears in full-color regalia, and Pisthetairos calls for her apprehension. Iris bridles at any birdling who would dare arrest a deity, and flaunts the power of her father, Zeus Almighty. Pisthetairos blasphemes the heavenly host with his contention that birds have replaced Olympian divinities. Iris warns that Zeus will fight back, but the Athenian threatens death to Zeus and rape for Iris if she should return.

Better news arrives with the next runner, who returns from Earth with an outpouring of adoration and a glittering tiara. Pisthetairos has set such a worthy example that humanity now champions anything with feathers. Birds are the rage—at worship centers, in popular ditties, as names, and as tourist attractions. With thousands of earthlings headed for heaven, Pisthetairos plunges into a frenzy of preparation, including spare wings to make the visitors feel at home in Cloudcuckooland.

A parade of immigrants passes through. The birds first welcome Parricide, a youth burdened with an unsettling misconception: He believes that he can escape earthly laws and murder his father. Crestfallen to learn that he must honor his father, Parricide blames Pisthetairos for forcing him to return to his father's house to support him through dotage. Pisthetairos soothes Parricide with a set of black wings and armaments and dispatches him to a war in Thrace.

The parade of incompetent boobs continues. After Parricide come Kinesias, the inept poet, and a spy. Pisthetairos takes pity on the poetaster by outfitting him with wings and setting him over a bird chorus to improve his tedious verses. The spy, a legalistic busybody, requests wings as a means of streamlining his profession. Pisthetairos intercedes with his cat-o'-nine-tails, drives out the seedy informer, and hauls his store of wings back to the closet.

Aristophanes grows bold in the falling action by satirizing Zeus. Prometheus, the renowned defier of Zeus, arrives to alert Pisthetairos to rumblings in the divine camp. Timidly peering out from a sheltering umbrella, Prometheus lauds the extinction of Zeus's tyranny and announces that the former lord of heaven plans to extend an olive branch. In a chummy aside, Prometheus advises Pisthetairos to hold out for a total surrender and to demand the hand of Basileia, Zeus's chargé d'affaires. With that, Prometheus slithers back to Mount Olympus.

Next appears the peace commission, composed of Herakles, Poseidon, and Triballus, a barbarian god. Poseidon acts as peacekeeper and tethers Herakles, who wants to settle the matter of power with his fists. Pisthetairos counters the trio by ignoring them and, in a bored tone, interrupts his meal with a call for horseradish. After deigning to notice the salivating embassy, he demands sovereignty over heaven, oiling the three negotiators with sweet talk but no invitation to dinner.

At length, Poseidon acknowledges that the birds deserve the royal scepter. Pisthetairos follows up the concession with a demand for Basileia, an eye-catching trophy wife who symbolizes sovereignty. At first Poseidon hedges; then, with Herakles's concurrence, he agrees. The play closes with the procession of King Pisthetairos and his lovely consort, Basileia. Birds throng to the scene and cavort about the newlyweds. The closing chorus flaunts the birds' triumph over Olympian Zeus and celebrates a happy union.

This jolly comedy, Aristophanes's best and most timely parody, retains its freshness, wit, and creativity even though it dates to 414 B.C. A second-place winner in a local contest, *The Birds* lauds the creation of a cloud haven where

Pisthetairos, through connivance and sagacity, rises to godlike power. As a dia-tribe, the play depicts the playwright's distaste for authoritarian meddling in citizens' lives, governmental malfeasance, and the free-floating malaise that permeates Athenian society. In contrast, Cloudcuckooland is devoid of greed, special interests, and violence, offering a humorous ideal, a retreat from earthly vices. (Aristophanes 1993; Dearden 1976; Ehrenberg 1943; Henderson 1975; Lord 1963; Snodgrass 1988a; Spatz 1978; Ussher 1979)

See also Aristophanes; city planning; Cloudcuckooland; Pisthetairos; religion; satire; women in utopia.

BLACK ELK

Black Elk, a medicine man and prophet, is the author of an oral Native American biography, *Black Elk Speaks* (1932), often labeled as a North American Indian bible. Because Black Elk spoke no English, the orally transmitted work was translated by his son Ben and transcribed by John Neihardt's daughter Enid from multiple interviews; John Neihardt also supplied photographs depicting a significant moment in Plains Indian history.

Born in December 1863, Black Elk, an Oglala Sioux, was a cousin of Crazy Horse, the martyred war chief who was also a prophet and priest. Originally named Hehaka Sapa, he was the fourth male of his family to carry the name Black Elk. His father was injured in the Fetterman Massacre at Fort Phil Kearney on December 21, 1866, when the Arapaho and Cheyenne joined with the Sioux to restore their homeland to its rightful owners.

In his childhood, Black Elk played war with his friends and seemed destined for an ordinary life. Then, from dreams and voices, he perceived religious stirrings in his spirit, an omen the Sioux reverenced. As *wichasha wakon*, or holy man, under Chief Red Cloud, Black Elk dedicated himself to improving life for the Sioux, an altruistic burden that ultimately brought him a bitter-sweet blend of hope and despair. Black Elk prayed to the Great Spirit that life's good road and the difficult road would continue to cross at a holy spot where ordinary life intersected perpetually with the divine.

In 1868, the year of a successful negotiation to restore tribal lands to the Sioux, five-year-old Black Elk saw a vision predicting that he would become an influential shaman and would be instrumental in reviving tribal traditions, symbolized by a hoop. Out of fear, he kept to himself his frequent communion with the supernatural voices of six elders called "grandfathers" and with sky-riders bearing flaming spears. He also concealed a disquieting sequence of out-of-body flights into the clouds.

When he was nine, he fell ill with weakness in his legs and remained in a coma or deep sleep for 12 days. During his trance, while he appeared near death, the otherworldly speakers—reminiscent of St. John in the book of Revelation or the angel Moroni's visit to Joseph Smith—promised Black Elk, or "younger brother," that he could summon a giant's power (called "the cleansing wind"), cure illness, and renew his nation's heart.

Plains Indians participate in a Ghost Dance in about 1893. Black Elk, an Oglala Sioux born in 1863, became a follower of Wovoka, a Paiute, who predicted that whites would disappear.

When Black Elk awoke, Whirlwind Chaser honored the holy aura around the boy, who ate little and withdrew from his parents to ponder the godly presence within him. The augury proved correct; by his late teens, Black Elk, who later survived the Battle of Little Big Horn, had developed his healing skills, yet was often troubled by powerful emotions and fears. Although he anticipated serving his people as a messenger of hope, by age 23 he saw much of Native American tradition destroyed by European settlers. The whites slaughtered buffalo in great numbers to strip their hides, stole Indian lands, pillaged nature, fenced in huge sections of the plains, and stampeded toward goldfields rich with promise. That year he accepted an invitation to travel to Europe with Buffalo Bill's Wild West Show in a troupe of Native American dancers who performed for "Grandmother England," the Sioux name for Queen Victoria.

In 1889, homesick and forlorn, Black Elk returned to Pine Ridge; he found his people starving because of a severe drought, his brother and sister dead, and his father dying. He was grateful that his mother, White Cow Sees, was still strong. Tentatively, Black Elk applied his healing power and found it still intact. News filtered through his tribe that the Paiute mystic Wovoka, also called Jack Wilson, had talked to the Great Spirit and learned that the whites would disappear in an apocalyptic whirlwind. Wovoka foretold that the earth would again be fruitful and serene as in the old days.

Caught up in the messianic ecstasy of the Ghost Dance that swept the Plains tribes, Black Elk experienced again the out-of-body sensation he had felt in childhood. Fellow dancers donned holy shirts said to be impervious to bullets, painted their faces red, smoked the medicine pipe, and encircled the dying tree of life. The dance purportedly put participants in direct communication with dead ancestors. The ceremony was harmless, but the white backlash to a Sioux renaissance ended disastrously. Cavalry led a massacre at Big Foot's encampment at Wounded Knee, South Dakota, on December 29, 1890. Black Elk joined in the fight between the Lakota Sioux and black cavalrymen and was wounded in the abdomen. Undaunted, he proclaimed it a good day to die.

The end of the one-sided battle at Wounded Knee forms a wretched conclusion to Black Elk's autobiography. In his final paragraphs, he recalls women and children slaughtered in the mud. The corpses, left to freeze in grotesque shapes in a winter blizzard, were examined by Dr. Charles Eastman, a Sioux physician, then interred in common graves. Black Elk, a failed prophet, felt helpless to follow his dreams of a Sioux utopia.

As demonstrated in his reflections in the postscript of *Black Elk Speaks*, the gradual erosion of religion and culture grieved Black Elk, who longed for the time when "the two-leggeds and the four-leggeds lived together like relatives and there was plenty for them and plenty for us." He concluded that the one-sided conflict at Wounded Knee was too traumatic, too debilitating a defeat to allow the Sioux a resurgence. During his interviews with John Neihardt, Black Elk's pessimism caused him to look beyond log settlements along the Powder River toward the Great Spirit and spiritual rewards for the faithful. Disillusioned, aged, and disappointed, he prayed: "In sorrow I am sending a feeble voice, O Six Powers of the World. Hear me in my sorrow, for I may never call again. O make my people live!" Black Elk died in 1950. (Brooke 1989; Brown 1970; Collier 1947; Deur 1972; Neihardt 1961; Patterson and Snodgrass 1994)

See also La Città del Sole; clairvoyance; disillusion; heaven; naturalism; religion.

BLACK MUSLIMS

A fanatically antiwhite separatist movement, also called the Lost-Found Nation of Islam, Black Muslims minister to oppressed blacks in prisons and blighted urban areas of the United States by spreading the doctrine of black superiority. A brainchild of the Depression Era, the groundwork of Black

Muslims was initiated in the early 1930s by Wallace D. Fard Muhammad, founder of an Islamic temple in Detroit. A millennialist who anticipated Armageddon (the final and cataclysmic battle between good and evil), Fard believed that the black race was destined to assume a position of power. To explain the weaknesses of twentieth-century blacks, he blamed the English language, distortions inherent in pro-white views of American history, and Christian teachings for reducing black interest in African history. To prove his vision of ascendency, he pointed out the black race's success in creating powerful and innovative civilizations in ancient times. Because blacks had internalized the Caucasian image of Christ, Fard believed that they had to redeem their cultural heritage by rejecting the white man's religion, turning back to Africa, reading the Koran, and following the dictates of Islam.

Until his mysterious disappearance in 1934, Fard influenced his successor, Elijah Muhammad. Elijah Muhammad claimed to be the messenger of Allah, god of Muslims; in his official capacity, he initiated *Muhammad Speaks,* which remains North America's most widely read black newspaper. Muhammad's most convincing disciple was Malcolm X, who deserves credit for nurturing Islamic ideals and for practicing them as an example of strong family ties and pure living. A 35-year overview of the emergence of the Black Muslims is the focus of Alex Haley's *The Autobiography of Malcolm X* (1965), a popular work successfully filmed in 1991 by Spike Lee and starring Denzel Washington in the title role.

As demonstrated by autobiography and movie, in Malcolm X's time Black Muslims earned a reputation for translating Islamic ideals to everyday life and for maintaining their ancient ascetic code of conduct, particularly for women, who cover their hair, dress demurely, and play the traditional role of wife/helpmeet/mother. The faithful abstain from lawlessness, promiscuous sex, alcohol, drugs, cosmetics, and pork; avoid involvement in the U.S. military; and discipline themselves to obedience to Allah, the god revealed in the Koran, a major source of instruction in thrift, cleanliness, and respectful treatment of black women. Black Muslims seek ways of boosting self-esteem, overcoming the "underclass" mentality, and quelling poverty, dependence on government programs, black-on-black violence, and infighting among black leaders.

Unlike the assimilationists who touted Dr. Martin Luther King, Jr., Ralph Abernathy, and the accommodating hierarchy of the National Association for the Advancement of Colored People (NAACP), Black Muslims remain outside and apart from the influence of integration and spurn any merger with white society. By establishing black-owned business and home schooling, the Black Muslims aim for self-sufficiency in a predominantly white power structure. In the 1960s, the movement had spawned 80 temples and mosques, mostly in northeastern cities, where southern blacks migrated in search of economic and educational opportunity and racial isolation in a supportive haven for non-white peoples.

After the 1965 assassination of Malcolm X, the spirited orator and disciple of Elijah Muhammad, Black Muslims battled the media stereotype of racial fanaticism and redirected their outreach toward the "black bourgeois." This shift influenced agriculture, manufacturing, and the founding of over 50 parochial schools and colleges. By the 1990s the Nation of Islam had spread into the Caribbean and Central America. Of a total population of 3 million Black Muslims, the majority reside in the Baltimore–Washington, D.C., area. (Haley 1965; Low and Clift 1981; Ploski and Williams 1989; Wolfenstein 1990)

See also asceticism; *The Autobiography of Malcolm X*; Koran; sufism; utopia; women in utopia.

BOKANOVSKY'S PROCESS

An artificial assembly-line process in Aldous Huxley's *Brave New World* (1932), this engineered system of eugenics utilizes x rays to cause fertilized eggs to bud or divide into mirror images. Similar to cloning, Bokanovsky's Process is described in Chapter 1 as creating "standard men and women; in uniform batches. The whole of a small factory staffed with the products of a single bokanovskified egg." To achieve stability and a unique form of classism, the laboratory director exults:

> One egg, one embryo, one adult—normality. But a bokanovskified egg will bud, will proliferate, will divide. From eight to ninety-six buds, and every bud will grow into a perfectly formed embryo, and every embryo into a full-sized adult. Making ninety-six human beings grow where only one grew before. Progress.

The resulting phalanx of identical twins live similar lives, think convergently, and perform identical tasks, which the laboratory director lauds as "the principle of mass production at last applied to biology."

The purpose of laboratory duplication is the stabilization of society, which will produce no individuals to question, tamper with, or sabotage the goal of the "Brave New World"—a controlled, predictable society. People who are conceived through sexual reproduction and born from a human womb, such as Linda and John the Savage, threaten societal predictability by inconsistent behavior arising from divergent thinking. These individuals are prone to refuse to submerge self in group identity and rebel against normative rules and standards. In contrast, the most desirable citizens of Utopia adhere to the world-state motto: "Community, Identity, Stability."

In Chapter 16, John, the savage from the southwestern reservation who was born vivaparously, debates the Controller, Mustapha Mond. Mond gleefully replies:

> People are happy; they get what they want, and they never want what they can't get. They're well off; they're safe; they're never ill; they're not afraid of death; they're blissfully ignorant of passion and old age; they're plagued with no mothers or fathers; they've got no wives, or children, or lovers to feel strongly about; they're so conditioned that they practically can't help behaving as they ought to behave.

So stable a system, he concludes, relies on a second line of defense—the fail-safe drug *soma*, which can quell any rebellious spirit that might erupt. The savage, whose insight into mortal weakness destroys his ability to adapt to a brave new society, recoils from the whole factory nightmare. He concludes the dialectic with a pointed riposte: "What you need...is something *with* tears for a change. Nothing costs enough here." (Bedford 1985; Holmes 1970; Huxley 1989; Magill 1958; Nance 1988; Watts 1969)

See also *Brave New World;* collectivism; conditioning; Huxley, Aldous; hypnopaedia; John; Linda; materialism; prophecy; technology.

THE BOOK OF MORMON

The Book of Mormon is one of four scriptural sources revered by Mormons, a distinctly American sect also called the Church of Jesus Christ of Latter-day Saints, headquartered in Salt Lake City, Utah. Joseph Smith, famed American sectarian and religious visionary, published the 590-page *Book of Mormon* in 1830 in Palmyra, New York. He claims that Mormonism is the "true church," as revealed by the text of *The Book of Mormon,* taken from front and back inscriptions on thin metal plates dating from 600 B.C. to A.D. 421, which Moroni completed and buried.

Moroni returned to Earth as an angel and gave the sacred works to Smith on September 22, 1827. Smith received the Urim and Thummim to interpret the unknown Egyptian language. Like the Rosetta Stone, they assisted him and his scribe, Martin Harris, in translating the scripture into its English form, consisting of 15 books originally composed by 23 writers. According to Smith, the historic plates disappeared. Some church historians believe that Smith composed the text without divine assistance.

Completed in June 1829 and verified by 11 witnesses as a divine revelation, *The Book of Mormon* relates religious history according to Mormon and his son Moroni. The text affirms that a Hebrew contingent formed the core of the first Mormons. After a godly man named Lehi left Jerusalem, he joined the family of Ishmael (Abraham's son and the patriarch of Islam) in a journey to South America. The Mormons split into two settlements: The Nephites, led by Nephi, represented God's chosen race; the Lamanites, led by Laman, chose a nomadic existence and became the aboriginal tribes of South America. (Cavendish 1970; Cavendish 1980; Cross 1957; Eliade 1986; Hastings 1951; Jurji 1946; McDannell 1994; Mullen 1966; Quinn 1987; Roberts 1985; Smith 1971; Smith 1982)

See also clairvoyance; Genesis; heaven; religion; Smith, Joseph, Jr.

THE BOOK OF THE DEAD

An anthology of the world's oldest religious writings, it is composed of ritual incantations, magic spells, prayers, and secret words. *The Book of the Dead* (fifteenth century B.C.) was placed in mummy cases or coffins and used by ancient Egyptians as a means of continuing life in the afterworld and return visits to Earth. These holy scriptures were collected from pyramid walls, coffins, and papyrus scrolls and published by priests in Heliopolis, a cult headquarters for Atum-Re, the sun god. Recorded in linear script in red and black ink, the book preserves funeral liturgy to assist the departed souls of royalty and select nobles in locating and settling in heaven. The recorded information was systematized by 30 B.C. At least 200 copies remain.

In revealing the Egyptian concept of a hereafter, *The Book of the Dead* describes the role of the sun god, a beneficent boatman similar to the Greek Charon who greets souls in the dark netherworld, comforts them in their recent departure from life, and assuages their fears of the unknown. On an island in a great subterranean river, Osiris (a god of the dead who was once an earthly king) holds court much as Hades and his judges review past lives in Homer's *Odyssey* and Virgil's *Aeneid*. Assisting Osiris are lesser gods and a monstrous hippopotamus with the jaws of a crocodile, which clamp shut on the unworthy. Thoth keeps the court record; Maat assures that the testimony is true. Horus and Anubis supervise the placement of the heart on a balance beam that weighs goodness against evil. The supplicant souls who prove their righteousness in the Hall of the Two Truths cross into an agricultural haven. (Budge 1960; Cavendish 1970; Ceram 1968; Clark 1959; Eliade 1986; Hastings 1951; Lurker 1980)

See also *Aeneid*; Elysian Fields; heaven; Virgil.

BRADBURY, RAY

A popular American science fiction writer, fantasist, visionary, and moralist, Bradbury has published short stories, screen and stage plays, poems, novels, criticism, social commentary, children's literature, and television adaptations, which can be found in over 700 anthologies. His stories have appeared on "The Twilight Zone," "Alcoa Premiere," "Alfred Hitchcock Presents," and "The Ray Bradbury Theater." Born Raymond Douglas Bradbury on August 22, 1920, in Waukegan, Illinois, Bradbury is the son of civil servant Leonard Spaulding and Esther Moberg Bradbury, a Swedish immigrant. He attended school in California and was influenced by horror films, science fiction magazines, Buck Rogers and Flash Gordon comics, fantasy, mystery, magic tricks, and illusion.

Bradbury began writing in longhand on butcher paper at age 12. He joined the Los Angeles Science-Fantasy Society, wrote under various pen names, and published a magazine, *Futura Fantasia,* which foundered after four issues. After receiving his high school diploma, he sold newspapers on the street and worked at other menial jobs to provide him with money to write. In the 1940s he composed radio appeals for Red Cross blood donors. He attended night school classes taught by Robert Heinlein, famed science fiction guru.

Under the pseudonyms Leonard Spaulding, Douglas Spaulding, and Ray Bradbury, the author has provided a wealth of short fiction and verse for popular journals and anthologies. He has achieved the widest readership for his science fiction novels and stories, notably "There Will Come Soft Rains" (1950), *The Martian Chronicles* (1950), *The Illustrated Man* (1951), *Dandelion Wine* (1957), *Something Wicked This Way Comes* (1962), *R Is for Rocket (1962), and I Sing the*

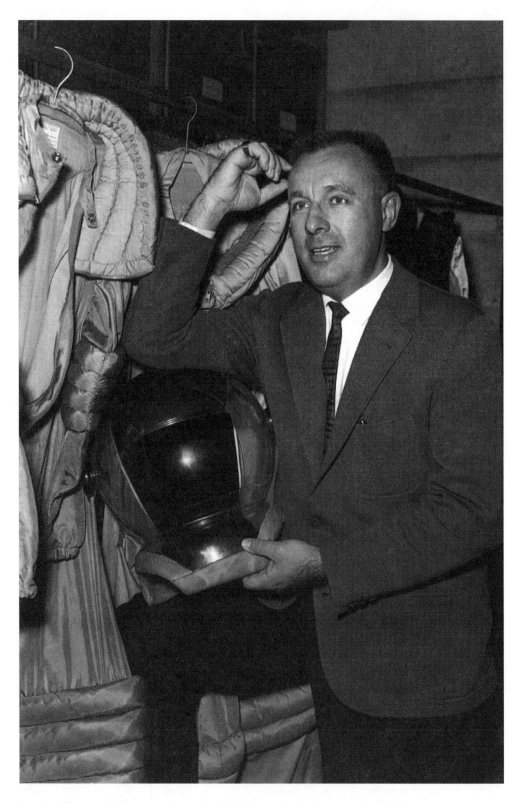

Ray Bradbury, with space costumes in a Hollywood television studio, 1959

Body Electric! (1969). The most famous, his dystopian classic *Fahrenheit 451* (1953), first appeared as short fiction in 1951. The book, which centers on the dangers of censorship, has been targeted by some parents and educators for unsuitable language, yet remains on the list of frequently assigned young-adult classics.

To counter an increasingly mechanized, dehumanized world, Bradbury encourages children to read widely and learn to value the printed word. For his skill with social satire he has received awards from the National Institute of Arts and Letters and the Boys Clubs of America; he is also the recipient of the Ben Franklin and Balrog awards and the California Gold Medal. His works—available in print, tape, film, and video—focus on two topics: whimsy and the sacrifice of humanity for progress. Following a demanding writing schedule well into his seventies, Bradbury enjoys an occasional diversion in public lectures or interviews. In addition to wife Marguerite McClure Bradbury, four daughters, and grandchildren, he devotes his energies to oil painting and watercolors, collects primitive Central American masks, and supports Los Angeles community theatricals. (Bradbury 1975; Bradbury 1990a; Breit 1956; Clareson 1976; Indick 1989; Johnson 1968; Johnson 1978; Knight 1967; Mogen 1986; Slusser 1977a)

See also baptism; Beatty, Captain; *Fahrenheit 451;* Montag, Guy; technology; "There Will Come Soft Rains."

BRAVE NEW WORLD

Aldous Huxley's acutely didactic dystopian masterpiece was published in 1932. The novel is based on the conflict between humanity's desire for stability and the individual's desire for passion and fulfillment. In the Brave New World, poverty, disease, aging, worry, and social unrest are eradicated along with despair, passion, history, literature, religion, democracy, family, and love. By examining a soulless world-state that demands the control of its citizens—body and spirit—the author emphasizes the dangers of technology-run-amok and warns of the abuse of scientific experimentation, particularly eugenics. The novel proved so provocative that in 1958 Huxley returned to the theme in *Brave New World Revisited.*

In *Brave New World,* which is set in the distant future where Utopia has triumphed for 632 years, a party of students follows the Director of Hatcheries and Conditioning and his assistant, Henry Foster, through the stifling, robotic Central London Hatchery and Conditioning Centre. An assembly-line process called "budding" systematizes human conception by replicating or cloning a single egg. Known as Bokanovsky's Process, budding produces 96 twins from a single cell. Embryos, predestined for one of five social castes, are bottled and biochemically imprinted to serve the state, which reveres a universal slogan: "Community, Identity, Stability." The global order, which bases stability on the precepts of assembly-line creator Henry Ford, limits individual capacities to the class slot each person is designed to fill by innoculating decanted embryos with chemicals to assure their success at a prescribed social level.

Only upper-level thinkers are spared the mechanized manufactory so that a small segment of Utopia will retain divergence of thought.

Upstairs in the nursery, control and indoctrination assure that growing children remain rooted in the niche for which they are created. To undergird the state economy, new members conditioned by hypnopaedia, or sleep-teaching, hear bromides and mantras repeated endlessly at pillow level, encouraging them to consume more goods, refrain from prudery and monogamy, and remain true to their caste, whether alpha, beta, gamma, delta, or epsilon. The tour concludes with the arrival of Mustapha Mond, Resident Controller for Western Europe, who emphasizes how much of human misery has disappeared since social engineering replaced the random, individualized style of procreation common to the twentieth century.

In the women's locker room at shift change, Lenina Crowne, an attractive upper-caste worker, chats with Fanny Crowne about Bernard Marx, a slightly suspect expert on hypnopaedic sleep techniques with a tendency to think for himself. Lenina divulges her plans to join Bernard on a visit to the Savage Reservation in New Mexico. Fanny disapproves of Lenina's date because of his reputation for unconventionality. Nonetheless Lenina wants to experience the exotic wilds of North America. As Bernard exits the factory, Lenina accepts the date. The two part. Lenina flies away in a helicopter to play Obstacle Golf with Henry Foster.

An introspective, tormented misfit, Bernard warms to the promise of a date with Lenina. A malcontent who disdains Utopia's promiscuity and rapturous mental void, he abstains from *soma*, a mood-lightening drug, and the time-wasting games that divert Utopians from serious thought, preferring to walk alone. This anomaly of voluntary solitude, which approaches the level of heresy, cuts him off from social contact except for friendship with Helmholtz Watson, a savvy professor at the College of Emotional Engineering and his sole confidante. Bernard accompanies Helmholtz to his house, where they bemoan the despotic regime that represses human feeling. Later, at a solidary meeting, Bernard is incapable of experiencing the transcendental unity of soul that overwhelms others as they extol "orgy-porgy." On a prevacation date, Bernard and Lenina disappoint each other: Bernard is unamused by Utopia's array of entertainments. Lenina misunderstands his opinions and questions, which threaten her mindless acceptance of utopian beliefs. Although the couple make love, Lenina wonders if Bernard's dislike of utopian values is normal. Bernard wishes that they had not rushed into bed.

Huxley creates a fearful punishment for nonconformists like Bernard. Before his vacation, Bernard secures permission from the director and receives a reprimand for nonconformity and the threat of exile in Iceland. Lenina considers canceling, but in the end makes the transoceanic rocket trip to the Indian village of Malpais, near Santa Fe, New Mexico. Bernard makes an emergency call to Helmholtz and learns that the director has indeed set in motion Bernard's ouster. The prospect of so dismal an exile sends Bernard into a panic.

By detailing the reservation's distressing effects on Lenina, Huxley reveals the profound alteration in female lifestyles in his dystopia. Despite Bernard's warnings, Lenina is unprepared for the disease, old age, filth, and insects that link pueblo culture with the pre-utopian way of life. Most unsettling is the sight of women suckling infants. On the mesa, Bernard and Lenina observe a primitive snake ritual that involves flagellation of a penitent blond Zuñi brave. The young man, also referred to as John the Savage, surprises Lenina and Bernard by greeting them in English and introducing them to his fat, scruffy mother, an outsider named Linda who was lost in the wilds before John's birth.

Bernard is entranced by Linda's story, which contrasts her utopian upbringing with the primitivism of the Southwest. Unable to cope with a predominantly monogamous society, Linda isolated herself from Indian women by seducing their husbands and staying drunk on mescal and peyote, hallucinogens derived from cactus. Twelve-year-old John, whose wretched home life made him a pariah from early childhood, absorbed himself in a collection of Shakespeare's plays, which Linda's lover Popé brought as a gift, and learned of honor, heroism, revenge, and love. Bernard, himself a loner, sympathizes with John's despair and proposes escorting John and his mother to civilization. John looks forward to visiting his mother's world, especially since the journey will keep him near Lenina.

Huxley uses this vacation as a means of joining the old world with the new. Bernard telephones ahead to Mustapha Mond that the trip has turned up two interesting specimens. Upon transport of the foursome from the London airport to the hatchery, Bernard staves off public humiliation by introducing the director to Linda and John (who is actually the director's son). Linda hugs Tomakin, the name by which she knew the director; John greets him as "Father," a repulsive term to the hatchery staff. Ridiculed and labeled a pervert, the hypocritical director resigns in ignominy.

By separating John from his mother, Huxley prepares for the alienation and despair that dominates the novel's falling action. Bernard, London's cause célèbre, escorts John about the city while Linda withdraws to television and frequent *soma* holidays, endangering her health and sanity. Bernard is reprieved from exile and wreathed in glory; he introduces John to London, which disgusts him for its absence of honesty and compassion for the working classes. To rid himself of Utopia's vapid soullessness, John returns to Shakespeare's plays, his childhood solace.

At Bernard's direction, Lenina takes John to a theater to experience "Three Weeks in a Helicopter," an insipid "feelie," which transfers character sensations to the viewer's body. After the virtual reality film, she attempts to seduce him at her apartment. Her overt sexuality enrages and disgusts him. Fearing his violent outburst, Lenina cowers in the bathroom. John's retreat from public exhibitions of a "reservation savage" deplete Bernard's popularity. Further complication results from John's friendship with Helmholtz and Lenina's attraction to John. Lenina's immodest display of nakedness and lust dismays John so completely that he condemns her forwardness by citing lines from Shakespeare.

An emergency call interrupts the debacle. John hurries away to the 60-story Park Lane Hospital for the Dying, where he tries to dissuade a stuporous Linda from overdosing on *soma* so that she can die with dignity. Her lethargy, intensified by recorded sounds, smells, colors, and light, impedes communication. John leaves in despair. On the way out of the hospital, he incites workers to abandon *soma* and tosses their drug supply out the window. Police put down the ensuing riot with *soma* vapor, mind-controlling "happy" tapes, and anesthetic squirt guns. They arrest John, Bernard, and Helmholtz.

Like John Milton's Satan and Ray Bradbury's Captain Beatty, Huxley's Mond, the star villain, serves as a worthy debater and champion for the opposition. The three miscreants receive swift judgment from Mustapha Mond. Bernard and Helmholtz are exiled with other dissenters to the Falkland Islands. John debates with the godless Mond the purpose of Bokanovsky's Process, religion, literature, and human emotion. At the high point of Chapter 17, Mond claims that belief in God is self-defeating:

> Call it the fault of civilization. God isn't compatible with machinery and scientific medicine and universal happiness. You must make your choice. Our civilization has chosen machinery and medicine and happiness.

John decries a system preferring materialism over God. He speaks the author's mind in his retort: "I want God, I want poetry, I want real danger, I want freedom, I want goodness, I want sin." Denying Mond's wisdom in removing these human essentials from the Brave New World, John dramatically accepts the side effects of nonutopian existence, then vows that he will withdraw from civilization.

Huxley orchestrates a bizarre, yet moving conclusion. Equipped with seeds, rope, pots and pans, blankets, string, nails, glue, tools, matches, and flour, John takes up residence at an abandoned lighthouse in the Wye Valley. Through doses of mustard water, repeated flagellations, and deliberate falls into juniper brambles, he purges his stomach of Utopia's pollutants and attempts to rid himself of desire for Lenina. His extreme self-torment attracts motorists, reporters, and cameraman Primo Mellon, who turns the event into a popular "feelie." A mob of depraved thrill-seekers pushes John into a mass sex-and-drug orgy. Coming to his senses, but disillusioned and beyond salvation, John hangs himself.

Like George Orwell's *1984* (1949), Huxley's powerful novel—one of the Western world's most devastating dystopian tocsins—has maintained its place in literature as it proves increasingly true. When eugenic engineering, technological control of life forces, and other insidious underminings of freedom surface in news or historical commentary, they are often lumped together under the term "brave new world," a term taken from Shakespeare's *Tempest* (1611) that has since achieved idiomatic meaning rich with negative overtones. As such, tamperings with nature—test tube babies, gender selection, amniocentesis, DNA realignment, vegetables specially engineered for the marketplace, or euthanasia—take on the ghastly perversion of creation that Huxley predicted decades earlier. (Baker 1990; Bedford 1985; Holmes 1970; Huxley 1932; Nance 1988; Negley and Patrick 1952; Watts 1969)

See also Bokanovsky's Process; *Brave New World Revisited;* conditioning; escapism; eugenics; Huxley, Aldous; John; Malthus, Thomas; Marx, Bernard; materialism; Mond, Mustapha; *soma;* technology; women in utopia.

BRAVE NEW WORLD REVISITED

Aldous Huxley's allegorical sequel to *Brave New World,* the second work was written in 1958, 26 years after the dystopian novel. The story opens with a Malthusian warning that the world has little time to control population growth and the attendant depletion of material resources. The vicious cycle of too many people and not enough food leads to social instability, provoking despotism and militarism, which draws on the glut of bodies to instigate world power struggles, fill uniforms with cannon fodder, and carry on serial aggressions. Huxley weighs several alternatives to repetitive world wars—colonization of distant planets, which he dismisses as unlikely; drugs, a short-term, no-win solution to universal misery; and eugenics for the cultivation of a sturdier, more intelligent species.

To preserve freedom, Huxley indicates that humanity must stave off an irrevocable dark age by avoiding pitfalls to enlightenment—bureaucracy, propaganda, materialism, advertising, brainwashing, alcohol, drugs, tobacco, subliminal persuaders, and hypnopaedia. From these tentacles, people must take responsibility for educating themselves. Through the combined effords of tolerance, cooperation, and learning, survivors will avoid false and outdated values as they search for truth. (Bedford 1985; Holmes 1970; Huxley 1932; Huxley 1989; Nance 1988; Negley and Patrick 1952; Watts 1969)

See also Brave New World; hypnopaedia; John; Linda; materialism; prophecy.

BROBDINGNAGS

The Brobdingnags are a race of coarse, undereducated, narrow-minded giants living on a peninsula extending westward from the coast of Alaska in Book II of Jonathan Swift's *Gulliver's Travels* (1727). As alter egos of the Lilliputians, whom Gulliver meets in Book I, the Brobdingnags balance the former race's pettiness with their coarseness and cruelty. One rare exception among the Brobdingnags is Glumdalclitch, a farmer's gentle daughter who serves as Gulliver's loving attendant. Her patient and mindful attitude toward the undersized sailor contrasts with the nation's self-indulgent queen. While the girl attends to Gulliver's needs and allows him as much dignity as possible under the absurd conditions of their variant bodies, the queen treats him as a toy, bauble, or showpiece. Using Glumdalclitch and the queen as examples of extremes in social consciousness and courtesy, Swift demonstrates a class difference in Brobdingnags, some of whom respect the minuscule man and some, like the queen's dwarf, who delight in flaunting their strength and superior height by tormenting and humiliating him.

As literary foils of the petty, squabbling Lilliputians in Book I, the Brobdingnags view Gulliver much as he viewed the Lilliputians. Upon listening to Gulliver's discourse on English history, the king of the Brobdingnags concludes that such behavior is

> . . . a heap of conspiracies, rebellions, murders, massacres, revolutions, banishments, the very worst effects that avarice, faction, hypocrisy, perfidiousness, cruelty, rage, madness, hatred, envy, lust, malice, or ambition could produce.

Concluding in disgust, the king labels Gulliver's people "the most pernicious race of odious little vermin that nature ever suffered to crawl upon the surface of the earth." This pontifical attack on a people the king has never seen demonstrates the Brobdingnags' faults of generalization, shallow thinking, complacency, and ethnocentrism. On a more timely note, Swift's words were not wasted on his contemporaries, who recognized the sting of satire directed at England and the English. (Drabble 1985; Harrison 1967; Manguel and Guadalupi 1987; Pollard 1970; Swift 1958; Woods et al. 1947)

See also bestiality; Gulliver, Lemuel; *Gulliver's Travels;* Houyhnhnms; Laputa; Lilliput; satire; Swift, Jonathan.

 # BUCOLICS

A ten-book overview of country life composed by Virgil between 42 and 37 B.C., also known as *Eclogues,* the *Bucolics* opens on a discussion of Meliboeus and Tityrus, shepherds whose serene, rural lifestyle has been altered by political unrest. Meliboeus complains that his farm has been seized by the state and awarded to a military veteran; Tityrus exults that he retains full ownership of his land. Books II and III treat the importance of work as a solace from disappointment and the use of song as a form of friendly competition.

The most famous segment of Virgil's *Bucolics* comes in Book IV, which prophesies a new golden age. Under a return reign of Saturn, lord of the Titans, a revitalized generation will descend from heaven. With the birth of a boy "in whom the iron race shall begin to cease, and the golden to arise over all the world," an era of peace and exoneration from guilt "shall free earth forever from alarm." As Virgil describes the boy, he will be nurtured in a unified blend of gods and humanity and, like a second Dionysus, will rule over a peaceful kingdom replete with twining ivy and foxglove. Goats will thrive unharmed by lions; no snake or poisonous plant shall threaten. In the glow of virtue and the heroic past, Earth will sprout corn and grapes, and oaks drip a honeyed dew.

After a brief return to militarism, the new age will produce no sea voyagers. Each country will be self-sustaining and encourage no traders from beyond its shores. This Edenic environment "shall not suffer the mattock, nor the vine the pruning-hook; now likewise the strong plowman shall loose his bulls from the yoke." On a whimsical note, Virgil adds that sheep will produce colored fleece. The poet concludes with a paean to the arising era, which inspires him to compose music that rivals Orpheus and Linus, the divine musicians of Greek mythology. In blessing, the poet urges, "Begin, O little boy."

The remaining six books return to pastoral themes of recitation, singing, and praise of green pasturage, myrtle, hazel, ash, bay, poplar, and fir, of moss, grass, and arbutus. The poet incorporates wedding songs, ritual superstitions, and Arcadian poesy. In conclusion Virgil exults, "Omnia vincit Amor," or "Love conquers all." In later ages, when Christian utopists foresaw heaven as an otherworldly paradise reserved for believers, some visionaries reinterpreted Virgil's prediction of a new golden age as a foretelling of Christ's Second Coming. Thus, Dante had reason to call upon Virgil in the *Divina Commedia* (1320) as an enlightened pagan, knowledgeable prophet, and friend to Christians. (Bernard and Alessi 1986; Dickinson 1964; Garrison 1984; Letters 1981; McDermott 1950; Snodgrass 1988b; Snodgrass 1994; Virgil 1950)

See also *Aeneid*; Arcadia; Dante; *Divina Commedia*; Eden; golden age; heaven; naturalism; pastoral; prophecy; Virgil.

 # BUDDHISM

Buddhism is an Eastern religion that encourages meditation, acquiescence, and a merger of self with the universe. Its origins date to 1500 B.C., when Aryan nomads arrived in India from Afghanistan. Bringing a culture rich in spirituality, animism, and Vedic lore consisting of ritual verses in Sanskrit, these new arrivals introduced the foundations of Hinduism. When the new religion fell into the hands of the elitist Brahmans, the resulting *Upanishads*, a companion work to the *Vedas*, formalized the dogma concerning a universal oversoul and its relation to time, fate, and suffering.

Based on the experiences of Siddhartha Gautama (563–483 B.C.), called the Buddha, or "enlightened one," modern Buddhism reformed the early rites, pilgrimages, sacrifice, and ablutions in the river Ganges. Siddhartha, a wise, introspective son of a rich man, was the chief reformer; he meditated beneath a bo tree and conceived nirvana—a simple, elusive obliteration of self that contrasts the scriptural study and good deeds of Christianity and Islam. Following extensive seeking and introspection, Buddha founded a religious faith after observing the intense suffering of the people around him. Abandoning the luxury of his wealthy, prestigious family, he practiced asceticism and contemplated all aspects of life until he achieved understanding. His cosmic view indicated that good people were reborn to a better state or incarnation free from sensual desires and ignorance. By 483 B.C., Siddhartha's sermons appeared in Pali, his native dialect, in a systematized dogma of four truths and eight right paths. The truths are interwoven statements of the human condition:

- To live is to suffer.

- Desire brings about suffering.

- An end of desire brings an end to suffering.

- Peace and harmony are accomplished through commitment to the eight-fold path.

The eightfold path—right belief, right intent, right speech, right behavior, right occupation, right effort, right meditation, and right ecstasy—results in a blissful salvation that frees the sufferer from earthly ties and the impermanence and insecurity wrought by change.

According to Hermann Hesse's philosophical novel *Siddhartha* (1951), at first the protagonist seems like a separate character from Gotama, a holy evangelist who impresses his hearers with his self-discipline and peace-loving nature, yet appears to merge as the seeker emulates the divine. Having fled home in order to put meaning in his life, Siddhartha pursues the carnality of Kamala, a knowing prostitute. After an excess of sensuality, he wearies of her allure and abandons his sybaritic life. In place of gambling, acquisitiveness, lust, perfume, greed, and other forms of sensuality and self-indulgence, he seeks peace. Depressed to the point of suicide, he flees his family and anchors himself to a riverbank beneath a tree to look inward at the turmoil of his feelings and beliefs. Under its shade, he hears the reassuring syllable *Om* resounding through his mind.

Siddhartha attunes himself to the nearby river, a symbol of the flow of human history. Its waters are ever-changing, sweeping by like human emotions, the insubstantial life force that has caused Siddhartha pain in his earlier years. He takes comfort in the river and concludes "that the water continually flowed and flowed and yet it was always there; it was always the same and yet every moment it was new." As the stream is never used up, so does the human spirit continue to produce feelings, even after death. Siddhartha listens to the river's song, a unified sound that echoes a blend of the glad and anguished voices of thousands of people. He concludes that happiness and grief are all one in the continuous flow. (Armstrong 1994; Cavendish 1970; Cavendish 1980; Clarke 1953; Dutt 1910; Eliade 1986; Hastings 1951; Hesse 1951; Jurji 1946; McDannell 1994; Pelikan 1992b)

See also asceticism; *Childhood's End*; heaven; Hesse, Hermann; nirvana; Siddhartha; *Siddhartha*; women in utopia.

 # BULWER-LYTTON, EDWARD

Bulwer is the author of *The Coming Race or the New Utopia* (1871), a satiric fantasy that features a winged, subterranean race empowerd by *vril*. Edward George Earle Bulwer, a Londoner born May 25, 1803, was the scion of a distinguished, wealthy lineage; his father died in 1807. Bulwer refused to attend Eton and studied privately before entering Trinity College, Cambridge. After completing his graduate degree in 1826, he established a light-spirited writing career in derivative verse, which he modeled after the Romantics Byron and Shelley.

In 1827 Bulwer married Rosina Wheeler, who was of such undistinguished background that he alienated himself from his family and accepted penury as his punishment. To support his family, he wrote two popular plays and novels, *Falkland* (1827) and *Pelham* (1828), a gossipy roman à clef populated by characters drawn from London society. Success raised his standard of living so dramatically that he was elected to Parliament in 1831. One of his most respected titles was *The Last Days of Pompeii* (1834), a segment of a series of realistic historical novels. The tide of his affairs turned in 1836 with a bitter separation and custody of his children after Rosina's mental collapse.

Bulwer was named a baronet at age 35. In 1843 he came into a sizable inheritance, the major portion of which was Knebworth Estate, his family's ancestral home. As a gesture of respect, he appended Lytton, his mother's family name, to his own. In 1852 he served a second term in Parliament, retired in 1866, and died at Torquay on January 18, 1873. Two years before his death, he published his last work, *The Coming Race*, a slender utopian pipe dream. (Bulwer-Lytton 1979; Flower 1973; Manguel and Guadalupi 1987; Mumford 1959)

See also *The Coming Race*; fantasy; futurism; technology; Vril-Ya.

 # BUNYAN, JOHN

Bunyan is the author of *Pilgrim's Progress* (1678), a Puritan replication of the utopian ideal known under a variety of names—Mount Zion, the land across the Jordan River, the Promised Land, Beulah Land, New Canaan, or New Jerusalem. Bunyan was born on November 30, 1628, at Elstow, Bedfordshire, and, like his father, apprenticed to the brazier, or tinsman's, trade. Poorly educated but driven by ambition, he left home after his mother's death in 1643, in part because of the negative repercussions of his father's remarriage. He served two and a half years in the military under Oliver Cromwell and his Puritan forces, who established an 11-year English Commonwealth after beheading the king, Charles I.

At age 21, Bunyan married a religious woman whose sole items of dowry were two Christian tracts. Under her influence he acquired a simple thatched cottage and abandoned cursing, lying, tippling, gambling, dancing, and carousing. A fluent teller of tales, he developed his narrative gift by reading pious tracts along with the *Book of Common Prayer* (a liturgical compendium) and the Bible. In 1653 he entered a Baptist sect hostile to the Church of England at Bedford, became a lay minister, and developed a spirited following of working-class believers. Much of his professional service was conducted in secret to prevent clashes with laws forbidding nonconformity with the state church.

After the death of his wife in the late 1650s, Bunyan married a woman named Elizabeth to provide a suitable mother for his four children. In 1660 he was arrested during an evening service and jailed for preaching without a license and against the Church of England. Given the choice between conforming to Anglicanism or going to jail, he chose the latter. He used those 12 years of solitude and inactivity as an opportunity to minister to fellow prisoners and clarify his beliefs, which appeared as *The Holy City or the New Jerusalem* (1665), *Grace Abounding to the Chief of Sinners* (1666), and *Confession of My Faith and a*

Reason of My Practice (1672). Release from prison brought a brief return to the tinker's trade and a similar accusation of preaching without a license. During a second jail term in 1676, he worked on his autobiographical masterpiece, *Pilgrim's Progress* (first published in 1678, amended in 1679, and completed in 1684). In his preface, he set forth a godly purpose: to make travelers of his readers and to direct them past melancholy, folly, and ethical riddles to the Holy Land.

In 1687 Bunyan was elevated to the post of chaplain to London's lord mayor. The next year, on August 31, Bunyan died during an evangelical tour of London. He never knew the outreach of his delightful, edifying allegory, which became the second most widely read work (after the Bible) and was translated into 100 languages. As recorded in pioneer diaries and letters, many English immigrants fleeing persecution to find tolerance in the New World crossed the prairie with only two books to give them spiritual solace—the Bible and *Pilgrim's Progress*. (Baugh 1948; Bunyan 1896; Johnson 1968; Lindsay 1969; Manguel and Guadalupi 1987; Reason 1961)

See also allegory; Beulah Land; Celestial City; heaven; *Pilgrim's Progress*; religion; theocracy.

BURGESS, ANTHONY

Scriptwriter, linguist, translator, composer, essayist, biographer, critic, children's writer, and prolific novelist, Burgess created a futuristic, authoritarian dystopia in *A Clockwork Orange* (1962). His grim fantasy was the subject of Stanley Kubrick's 1971 movie, which became a cult favorite. The film earned Oscar nominations for best picture and for Kubrick's screen adaptation and directing. Two years after the release of the film, Burgess recorded readings from the novel for Caedmon and Spoken Arts. Alarmed at media claims that his work inspired violence, Burgess distanced himself from Kubrick's exploitation of violence, and in 1974 he wrote *The Clockwork Testament*, a fictionalized overview of the book's effect.

Burgess, whose real name was John Anthony Burgess Wilson, was born February 25, 1917, in Manchester, England, of working-class Scotch-Irish Catholic ancestry. He later disavowed his ties to Catholicism. His mother, Elizabeth Burgess Wilson, was a cabaret entertainer; she died of influenza when Burgess was two. His father, tobacconist Joseph Wilson, sent him to the Bishop Bilsborrow School and Xaverian College.

Burgess wanted more than a career in shopkeeping like his father. He worked odd jobs to support himself through the University of Manchester, where he earned honors pursuing advanced degrees in literature and linguistics. During World War II he was a medical corpsman, attaining the rank of sergeant major; he also entertained at troop hospitals and rehabilitation centers by playing original piano compositions. During the war, he married his first wife, Llewela Isherwood Jones. From 1946–1950, he taught school at Birmingham University while he represented the Ministry of Education, spent four years as master of Banbury Grammar School, and trained English teachers in Malaysia from 1954–1959. In 1956 a Colonial Service doctor misdiagnosed Burgess as having symptoms of inoperable brain cancer and predicted that he had only a year to live.

Burgess returned to England for treatment and relief from the Malaysian tropical climate, and began writing the first of 50 novels in hopes of producing a cushion of royalties to support his wife, an alcoholic. Influenced by British novelists Laurence Sterne, Evelyn Waugh, and James Joyce, he produced five novels in 12 months, beginning with *A Long Day Wanes: Time for a Tiger* (1956), and a large portion of a fifth work. When the fatal illness failed to materialize, he began to suspect political collusion in his misdiagnosis, but continued writing fiction.

Chief among Burgess's works are a comic trilogy based on the adventures of F. X. Enderby, an incorrigibly infantile poet, as well as the musical version of *Cyrano de Bergerac,* a translation of Sophocles's *Oedipus Rex,* and the screenplays for *Moses* (1976) and Franco Zeffirelli's *Jesus of Nazareth* (1977). The creation of destructive gangs in *A Clockwork Orange,* his masterwork, epitomizes the rise in juvenile crime in England and parts of the Commonwealth in the early 1960s.

After the death of his first wife, Burgess married translator Liliana Macellari, lived in Italy, Monte Carlo, and Switzerland, and fathered a son, Andreas. Burgess taught at the University of North Carolina, City College of New York, Princeton, and Columbia University, and completed an autobiography, *Little Wilson and Big God* (1987). In the months preceding his death, Burgess published historical fiction based on the life of Christopher Marlowe, a tragedian and contemporary of William Shakespeare. Following a lengthy illness, Burgess died in a London hospital on November 25, 1993. (Aggler 1986; Bloom 1987a; Burgess 1962; Coale 1981; Dix 1971; Mathews 1978; Morris 1971; Stinson 1991)

See also A Clockwork Orange; conditioning; disillusion; futurism; technology.

 # BUTLER, SAMUEL

An essayist and critic, Butler is the author of *Erewhon* (1872), the dystopian forerunner of discordant, antitechnocratic works by Aldous Huxley, Ayn Rand, Karel Capek, George Orwell, H. G. Wells, and Anthony Burgess. Born in Langar, Nottinghamshire, on December 4, 1835, the son of Reverend Thomas Butler and grandson of Bishop Samuel Butler, the author was earmarked for the ministry from early childhood. In 1858 he graduated from St. John's College, Cambridge, and took up social work in London's slums. Against the wishes of his conservative father, he shunned the ministry and reentered college to study music and art. The tension at home caused him to abandon English hypocrisy, complacency, and prissiness, and to search for peace on a sheep farm in New Zealand.

The profound scientific truths in Charles Darwin's *Origin of Species* (1859) influenced Butler to renounce his Christian upbringing, although he continued to ponder the worth and meaning of religious experiences. He grew so alienated from his former life that he nicknamed himself Ishmael for the desert wanderer, the son of Old Testament patriarch Abraham and Haggar, a handmaid. At the age of 29, financed by success as a sheep rancher, Butler sold his farm and resettled in London to work on *Evidence for the Resurrection of Jesus Christ* (1865). He married Eliza Mary Ann Savage, who became his muse and in-house critic, and continued to paint and compose piano pieces while writing critical articles on Shakespeare's plays and Homer's *Odyssey*.

In 1872 Butler completed *Erewhon*, his satiric utopian classic, which proved surprisingly remunerative. Based on his travels in New Zealand, the book reflects his bias against technology. He followed with *The Fair Heaven* (1873), a defense of Christian beliefs. In 1901 he penned a more caustic satire entitled *Erewhon Revisited*, which George Bernard Shaw helped him publish. Appearing the year after his death was his masterwork, *The Way of All Flesh* (1903), a reflective, semiautobiographical examination of his rejection of Victorian prudery and of his family's harsh fanaticism, sanctimony, and rigor, which bordered on child abuse. (Butler 1968; Cannan 1925; De Lange 1925; Holt, L. 1989; Jeffers 1981; Rattray 1974)

See also Erewhon; satire; Shaw, George Bernard; technology.

CABET, ÉTIENNE

Socialist, teacher, and attorney, Cabet is the author of the French utopian novel *Voyage en Icarie* (The Journey to Icaria) (1840), which influenced visionary Edward Bellamy's *Looking Backward, 2000–1887* (1887). A product of the Napoleonic era, Cabet was born in Dijon, France, on January 1, 1788. He completed a law degree, and in 1820 joined a successful political cabal to oust the Bourbon regime. For his role in restoring Louis Philippe to power in the revolution of 1830, Cabet was appointed Corsica's Procureur Général. His antimonarchical journal, *Le Populaire* (1833), attacked royal power. Within months, threats of retaliation drove Cabet to voluntary exile in London, where he remained five years to study the utopian industrial theories of Robert Owen and Sir Thomas More's *Utopia* (1516).

Returning to France in 1839, he wrote *Voyage en Icarie* (1840), a utopian romance that attained wide readership. Named for the Greek Icarus, who died while attempting flight with manmade wings, his idyllic community requires work from all citizens, who share land and profits. Cabet was an altruistic visionary who avoided the Marxist push to establish utopia through force. His idealism gave way to an aggravated discontent with the rigid middle class because they rejected any notion of common distribution of goods and property as a means of equalizing wealth.

As a proponent of voluntary socialism and the leader of the Icarian movement, Cabet moved to Red River, Texas, in 1848 to supervise a utopian commune, but an epidemic of yellow fever thinned it out pathetically. He then helped 280 settlers to establish Icaria, an authoritarian commune in Nauvoo, Illinois, a property vacated by Joseph Smith's Mormons. After seeking U.S. citizenship, Cabet began to lose hope of broadening his appeal among Americans. His visionary philosophies failed in practice, limiting the commune's growth to 1,800 people. In 1856 he broke with dissenters—who voted him out of office—and settled with 180 followers in St. Louis, where he died on November 8. His movement continued to grow; new colonies were established at Cheltenham, Missouri; Corning, Iowa; and Cloverdale, California. The communes suffered financial ruin during the Civil War, then collapsed at the turn of the century from a lack of leadership. (Cabet 1973; Johnson 1974; Mumford 1959; Negley and Patrick 1952; Piotrowski 1935)

See also city planning; Icara; Icaria; *Looking Backward, 2000–1887;* totalitarianism; *Utopia; Voyage en Icarie.*

CALLENBACH, ERNEST

Author of *Ecotopia* (1975), a cult classic of the evolving ecological movement, Callenbach is a native of Williamsport, Pennsylvania. Born April 3, 1929, he earned a Ph.B. from the University of Chicago at age 20. After completing a master's degree in 1953, he worked as press liaison, publicity agent, and editor at the University of California at Berkeley. In the late 1950s, he edited *Film Quarter* and, after 25 rejections of his first novel, founded Banyan Tree Books to publish *Ecotopia,* which succeeded in the United States and in global markets. Callenbach's other books include *Our Modern Art: The Movies* (1955), *Living Poor with Style* (1972), and three spin-offs from *Ecotopia–The Ecotopian Encyclopedia for the 80s* (1981), *Ecotopia Emerging* (1981), and *Ecotopia: The Notebooks and Reports of William Weston* (1990). Writing in conjunction with his wife, Christine Leefeldt, he published *The Art of Friendship* (1980) and a children's book, *Humphrey the Wayward Whale* (1985). With Michael Phillips, he wrote *A Citizen Legislature* (1985), followed in 1989 by *Publisher's Lunch.* Callenbach's most recent work is *Living Cheaply with Style: Smart Ways To Live Better and Spend Less* (1992). (Callenbach 1975; *Contemporary Authors* 1988)
  See also Ecotopia.

CAMELOT

Camelot is a mythic capital in southern England that legend proclaims as the heart and inspiration of King Arthur's idealized sovereignty. During the Middle Ages, Camelot was transformed from a rather mundane castle to a structured setting, surrounded by a patchwork of wolds and oak trees, a refreshing stream, and expanses of fertile grain fields and pasturage. Featuring a Christian church as a connecting link between pagan lore and the monks who described Camelot for Christian readers, Arthur's town evolved from a sparse military enclave to the baptismal site for knights. The castle itself advanced with the times to reflect the progress of medieval architecture and gadgetry in the complexity of moats, drawbridges, portcullises, keeps, and crenellated watchtowers.
  To generations of writers, Arthur was what Plato called a philosopher-king. Grandson of the Roman emperor Constantine but burdened by the taint of illegitimacy, he ascended to the throne formerly occupied by his father, Uther Pendragon. King Arthur vowed to apply justice and morality to lift the chivalric age from its morass of crime, exploitation, rapacity, and deceit. For a symbolic residence and council hall, on the Camelot River he built the fabled stronghold of Camelot, which some archaeologists place in the wooded plains of Cadbury in southwestern England. Numerous writers have described the walled city, including Geoffrey of Monmouth in his twelfth-

century *Historia Regum Britanniae* and Chrétien de Troyes's twelfth-century *Le Chevalier de la charrete*. In Sir Thomas Malory's influential version, *Le Morte d'Arthur* (1485), Camelot represents the essence of chivalry—knighthood based on service to the populace as a police force to halt oppressors and round up brigands. According to Malory, Camelot was not at Cadbury but in southern England at Winchester, a Roman center of commerce. Displayed at this site is the inlaid top of a legless, round wooden table of dubious origin, which exemplifies Arthur's famed answer to squabbles of rank—seat all in a circle, and no one can claim the head position.

Arthurian lore returned to fashion in the Victorian literature of the 1860s and 1870s as well as in the art of the pre-Raphaelites, notably Dante Gabriel Rossetti and Edward Burne-Jones. In the most distinguished romantic version—Alfred Tennyson's *Idylls of the King* (1888)—the second canto describes the fabled city, which dazzles and delights Gareth, a boyish, would-be knight. As he rides with two farm workers toward Arthur's court, Gareth spies Camelot's spires and turrets piercing the mist. Unafraid of a city that appears like an enchanted mirage, Gareth presses on to the filigreed portal. A wise graybeard questions Gareth at the entrance to Camelot and provides the magical background of Arthur's stronghold:

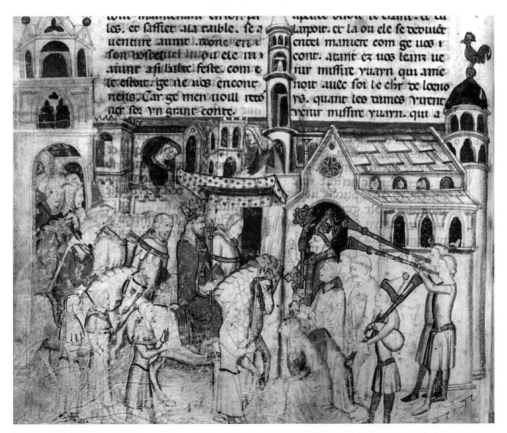

Citizens, including a bishop and musicians, greet King Arthur and his knights upon their return to Camelot; represented by a fourteenth-century Italian artist.

Fairy Queens have built the city, son;
They came from out a sacred mountain-cleft
Toward the sunrise, each with harp in hand,
And built it to the music of their harps.

Perhaps sensing that Gareth has duplicity in mind, the sage warns the youth and his attendants that Arthur demands truth of all petitioners. Inside, Gareth marvels at a rich symbolism chiseled in stone and a noble castle aiming its spire toward heaven. When knights pass in and out on official missions, "out of bower and casement shyly glanced eyes of pure women, wholesome stars of love." The people reside in an idealized atmosphere governed by their gracious, blameless king.

A second idealized Camelot opens Tennyson's "The Lady of Shalott" (1842), a chivalric poem that begins Canto 1 in "long fields of barley and of rye," woodlands, and Edenic lilies, symbols of purity that grow around the island of Shalott, which lies in sight of "many-tower'd Camelot." The size and color of the structure—a sturdy gray-walled edifice equipped with galleries, wharves, balconies, walled garden, and four watchtowers—contrasts with the quivering aspens, willowy hills, and wavy waters below. About the castle dwell barley reapers, bargemen, the Lady of Shalott at her weaving, and Sir Lancelot mounted on a war-horse, all residents of the idyllic pastoral land where warriors assure that peace reigns.

Not all Arthurian literature stresses the city itself. T. H. White's *Once and Future King* (1965) focuses on the man rather than his civic planning. Thus, Camelot takes second place to Arthur's pacified social structure, which is appropriately based on chivalry rather than might. This rendering dignifies Arthur's egalitarianism, a decided step up from his elitist predecessor's England, which was given to bloody wars and underhanded plots. Arthur asserts that militarism should not outweigh justice and that his evolving order of knights must vanquish the old-fashioned method of governance, which passed territories haphazardly from one strong ruler to the next contender.

After 20 years of strife and reshaping, Arthur succeeds in creating a state that is uniquely just and civilized for its time. As described in Book III, Chapter 25, after centuries of carnage and strife, women and children walk about Camelot without fear of harm, prelates restore the sanctity of the church, judges conduct court trials rather than the less civilized trial by ordeal, and universities flourish, rivaling those in Paris. The quality of life in Camelot improves with table manners, crockery dishes, tablecloths and napkins, imported wines, refined conversation, and musicians to play for the dinner hour. In White's words,

> In the smoky vaults, where once the grubby barons had gnawed their bones with bloody fingers, now there were people eating with clean fingers, which they had washed with herb-scented toilet soap out of wooden bowls.

The citizens, who have adapted themselves to Arthur's gentling, refer to themselves as Angle-ish or English. So appreciative is the rest of Europe that young idealists flock to Camelot from other courts. The view beyond Camelot reveals a pastoral blend of hedges, vineyards, orchards, fields, parks, outlying communities, moors, bogs, and woods. The capital's influence spreads through Sherwood, from Nottingham to York, supplying business for beekeepers, plowmen, and knights in armor, who ride forth to do the police work of Arthur's Round Table, a counsel composed of peacekeepers.

Mary Stewart restates Arthurian lore for a new generation of readers in a lyrical modern trilogy: *The Crystal Cave* (1970), *The Hollow Hills* (1973), and *The Last Enchantment* (1984). Her version casts Merlin, the enchanter, adviser, teacher, high priest, engineer, physician, and builder, in a key role. From his perspective she examines the lives of Aurelius Ambrosius, Merlin's Roman father; Uther, who is Ambrosius's brother and alter ego; and Arthur, the baseborn child of Uther and Ygraine, a handsome, savvy Cornish queen. In Book V, Chapter 3 of *The Crystal Cave*, Merlin falls deeply into one of his unpredictable trances and foresees the birth of Arthur. Like a miniature village in a snow globe, this rarefied version of a utopian state possesses a pleasantly agrarian and typically British notion of order:

> . . . the town with its bridge and moving river and the tiny, scudding ship. Round it the fields curved up and over, distorting the curved crystal till fields, sky, river, clouds held the town with its scurrying people.

To honor Ambrosius, Merlin rebuilds the Giants' Dance, a romanticized version of Stonehenge, which provides a magnificently engineered monument and equinoctial light show to honor his father, the king who invaded England and moved it closer to its destiny, and Arthur, the later king who gentles a nation too long fragmented by internal slaughters and external ravagers.

In the epigraphic verse that introduces *The Hollow Hills*, Stewart foresees Arthur as the prime mover of peace:

> He shall come
> With the spring
> In the green month
> And the golden month
> And bright
> Shall be the burning
> Of his star.

To explain Arthur's unusual appearance after 12 years of hiding until he came of age, Stewart allows some of her characters to believe the unfounded tales of the Summer Isle, a glass island known as Hy-Brasil. In Book II, Chapter 5 of *The Hollow Hills*, she refers obliquely to "the Summer Isle, which [they say] floats and sinks at the will of heaven." A transparent wonder, the island does not obscure the view of the sky, yet it supplies its mythic heroes "trees and grass and springs of sweet water."

After Arthur retrieves Excalibur from stone, he ceases to float above land and asserts the realistic mandate of his peaceable kingdom. Inherent in his idyllic vision are the seeds of Camelot's destruction. Supposedly, the castle topples under the wicked hand of Mordred, or Modred, Arthur's nephew conceived in a single incestuous coupling with Arthur's half sister Morgan. In

Book IV, Chapter 5 of *The Hollow Hills*, Merlin, who nurtures both the dream and the bitter knowledge that the dream cannot last, soothes Arthur's wrecked idealism with a suitably uplifting prophetic aphorism: "Every life has a death, and every light a shadow. Be content to stand in the light, and let the shadow fall where it will." Thus, from the beginning, Camelot is doomed to a human time span equaling the reign of its king.

American writers Mark Twain and John Steinbeck have also found Camelot a worthy utopian focus. Twain, the master satirist, describes in *A Connecticut Yankee in King Arthur's Court* (1886) a huge, picturesque castle with the stereotypical trappings of Arthurian lore. In Chapter 1, the sound of military music and the sight of plumed and helmeted knights, gorgeous banners, woven vests for the courtiers, and coordinated embellishments for their horses presage the showpiece itself—Camelot, "where men-at-arms, in hauberk and morion marched back and forth with halberd at shoulder under flapping banners with the rude figure of a dragon displayed upon them." To reach Arthur's hall, Hank Morgan (the Yankee of the title) crosses the drawbridge and enters a paved court marked at each corner by a tower. The scene bustles with people on business, servants, greeters and their acquaintances, and the movement typical of the outer courts of a busy king.

With less imagination than Twain's effort, Steinbeck's *The Acts of King Arthur and His Noble Knights* (1976) draws on Sir Thomas Malory's simplified vision of a great hall, where Arthur's council feasts, enjoys the songs of minstrels, and holds court sessions that promote justice and fairness among the populace, whatever their social class. Having quelled rivalries and violence, Arthur finds it difficult in the latter days of Camelot to govern idle, quarrelsome warriors who seek some excuse to return to service. He creates tournaments, jousts, and hunting as imitations of war, but cannot stifle the younger generation's eagerness for battle. Ultimately, the serenity of Camelot falls prey to internal rivalries growing out of the queen's adultery with Sir Lancelot of the Lake, Arthur's chief knight. (Ashe 1987; Bryant 1966; Dixon 1974; Lacy 1986; Steinbeck 1976; Stephens et al. 1949; Stewart 1970; Stewart 1973; Stewart 1984; Tennyson 1989; Troyes 1975; White 1965)

See also Arthur; city planning; *A Connecticut Yankee in King Arthur's Court; Idylls of the King;* pastoral; prophecy; satire; women in utopia.

CAMPANELLA, FRA TOMASO

An imaginative and antiauthoritarian Italian friar, Renaissance scholar, lyrical poet, neo-Platonist philosopher, pragmatic humanist, and astrologer, he wrote (in Italian) *La Città del Sole* (City of the sun; called *Civitas Solis* in Latin) (1602), which was revised and translated in 1611, 1614, and 1631. A contemporary of Galileo and Francis Bacon, Campanella was born Giovanni Domenico to a poor, illiterate family in Stilo, Calabria, on September 5, 1568. To assure his son an education, the father handed him over to Dominican monks, who introduced him to the Latin classics and trained him for the priesthood. Under their tutelage, he adopted the name Father Tomaso and began a lifetime of devotion to the church. At age 14 he was docile and obedient, but approaching manhood revealed a rebellious spirit that detested scholasticism and dogma.

His intellectual stirrings plagued his adult life. By 1586 Campanella had completed studies in science and philosophy in Morgentia, and he sought an audience at Cosenza with Bernardino Telesio (1509–1588), humanist philosopher, anti-Aristotelian, and opponent of scholasticism. Arriving after the thinker's death, Campanella took up residence at Altomonte and came under the tutelage of a rabbi who revealed to him the mysteries of the Kabbala. This compendium of mystic Zoroastrian lore, blended with Campanella's background in the traditional theology of church fathers, classical logicians, and scientific theory, resulted in disturbing writings that emphasized a basis of human experience: *De monarchia Christianorum* (1593), *Diologo politico contra Luterani, Calvinisti ed altri eretici* (1595), and particularly his *Philosophia sensibus demonstrata* (1591).

Also the author of an underground polemic titled *De Monarchio Hispanico* (Concerning the Spanish Monarchy) (1602), in youthful defiance of Spanish rule Campanella declared himself an adversary of tyranny, hypocrisy, and sophistry, and vowed "Numquam tacebo" (I shall never be silent). Church councils, suppression, and purloined manuscripts warned him that his dabblings in the supernatural challenged the authority—and patience—of the Vatican and its repressive terrorist agency, the Spanish Inquisition. At the age of 26, he was blasted for heresy and put under house arrest. Upon his release he visited Galileo in Padua; their philosophical convergence precipitated his *Apologia pro Galilaeo* (1616) and *De sensu rerum* (1620), a call for empiricism. During this sojourn, Campanella defended himself from trumped-up charges of sodomy and debating Christian dogma with a Jew. At his trial in Rome in 1596, he cleared himself of additional allegations of heresy, which were the church's major concern.

Two years later, Campanella departed from Rome, clashed briefly with ecclesiastical courts in Naples, and returned to the ghettos of Stilo. In his home monastery, he dreamed of a violent social upheaval capable of reforming a social order that relegated the bottom end to want and the upper echelons to the best of everything. His vision of a perfect world called for a contented people ruled on Earth by Spain but answerable to the church. In 1599, by launching a universal reformation based in Calabria, Campanella called on a handful of émigrés and some dissolute Dominican brothers to power the movement.

By November 8, 1599, the Vatican had mobilized against Fra Tomaso; they executed some of his minions and tossed him into a Neopolitan prison. In February 1600, after being tortured, he confessed heresy and sedition; in May he came before the Inquisition, afroth with his demented vision of anarchy. After a year of testimony, more torture, and scandal, he was condemned to life in prison for heresy, a merciful judgment that took into account his derangement and spared him public execution. Still manacled, he penned *La Città del Sole* (1602), an Italian composition reflecting the Eldorado myth. The work, calling for an enlightened commune loyal to the public good, was smuggled through his prison bars to numerous supporters. His identification with his protagonist caused him to fantasize the role of sovereign and to picture himself "walking with the crown of corn ears upon my head, wearing a Franciscan cloak, and carrying a corn sheaf as a sceptre." The fanciful manuscript remained incomplete for three decades, passing from street Italian into a more refined Latin and demonstrating his mounting conservatism against sexual depravity and human rights.

For 27 years Campanella scribbled verses, madrigals, canzonettas, and "Te Deums," which were collected in *Scelta* (Selections) (1622); he composed essays on Catholic dogma, published in 30 volumes his *Theologia* (1614), and metaphysical aphorisms in *Metafisica* (1638). At age 60, he gained his freedom through the assistance of a Spanish delegation from Madrid. He remained free for only four weeks; Pope Urban VIII had him reincarcerated in the Vatican until 1629. Free for four years this time, he met new persecution for purportedly joining a cabal against Spain. At age 70, with the help of Cardinal Richelieu, he escaped to Paris, found favor with Louis XIII and his liberal court, and spent his final three years teaching at the Sorbonne and writing and publishing sonnets and essays. Still reviled by the Vatican, he died in Paris on May 21, 1639. (Berneri 1951; Blanchet 1920; Campanella 1955; Johnson 1968; Mumford 1959; Negley and Patrick 1952)

See also Bacon, Francis; *La Città del Sole;* city planning; Eldorado; syncretism; theocracy; utopia.

CANDIDE

The wandering protagonist of Voltaire's caustic diatribe, *Candide* (1759), the title character observes the wickedness and depravity of France, Germany, Holland, England, Portugal, Italy, Paraguay, and Turkey through youthful, innocent eyes. His name suggests an ingenuous character too green and untried to anticipate corruption as he undergoes suffering, loneliness, torment, danger, and despair to reunite with his dream girl, Cunégonde, the 17-year-old daughter of a Westphalian baron. Candide (who may be the illegitimate son of his benefactor's sister) is schooled in the Leibnitzian theory that events turn out to the good, whatever their perceived evil. He looks up to his philosophy teacher, Doctor Pangloss, and sits in rapt absorption of his unrealistic teachings. Pangloss rejoins his pupil after two violent separations, including a near execution at the hands of the Inquisition. The sum of misadventures fails to deter Candide's obsession with Cunégonde.

One of Candide's most pleasant sojourns lies in the South American mountains, where he is accepted into the village of Eldorado. In serene contemplation of a peaceable realm, he listens to the 172-year-old son of the king's equerry describe a spontaneous religious system. In Eldorado all people are priests who, without prodding, "worship God from morning till night." The grateful citizens recognize that their lives are touched by God's providence and exert themselves in perpetual thank offerings.

Motivated by youthful infatuation, Candide recovers from brief periods of depression, abandons the utopian world of Eldorado to rejoin his lost love, and loses along the way the wealth his benefactors have given him. On his route east, he euphorically inscribes trees with Cunégonde's name. Like the epic hero of Miguel de Cervantes's *Don Quixote* (1615) who adores the fair Dulcinea, or John the Savage of Aldous Huxley's *Brave New World* (1932) worshiping Lenina, Candide grows more savvy to human foibles, yet remains true to his beloved, even after she loses her classic good looks from dishwashing for a Turkish slavemaster.

Trusting to the profound truth of love, Candide weathers disillusion and marries his Westphalian aristocrat. His aim achieved, he undergoes a coming to knowledge from an unlikely source: A neighboring Muslim suggests that contentment lies in his meager household, where Cunégonde cooks excellent pastry, a faithful old servant washes his linens, and Pacquette, a reformed prostitute, embroiders. At the neighbor's suggestion, Candide assuages disillusion with the world by abandoning an untenable optimism and contenting himself with the blessings of his microcosm.

Voltaire's satiric dismissal of the transcendent utopia echoes the perspective of earlier works. As in Daniel Defoe's *Robinson Crusoe* (1719), the source of Candide's rapid maturation is an appreciation of work, hope, and dedication. Also, paralleling Samuel Johnson's "Rasselas" (1759), Voltaire lauds the corner of his hero's soul that takes no stock in the greed and bloody intrigue of the worldly or in the complacency of Eldorado. For Candide, a small retreat dedicated to gardening and the circle of loved ones who share his philosophy suffice as bulwarks against whatever crises he may yet endure. Long past the age of roseate dreams, Candide the gardener propagates an appreciation of reality. (Andrews 1981; Ayer 1986; Gay 1988; Lovett and Hughes 1932; Mason 1981; Richter and Ricardo 1980; Voltaire 1961)

See also *Candide;* didacticism; disillusion; Don Quixote; Eldorado; Johnson, Dr. Samuel; materialism; Pangloss; "Rasselas, Prince of Abissinia"; *Robinson Crusoe;* satire; Voltaire, François; women in utopia.

CANDIDE

Voltaire's incisive didactic fantasy, subtitled "Optimism," was published in 1759 and earned praise that continues to the current age. The caustic story of the peripatetic Candide manages to parody adventure romances like Miguel de Cervantes's *Don Quixote* (1615) while skewering monarchy, corrupt churchmen, lechery, graft, sacrilege, and a host of other vices endemic in human society. The theme of irrepressible optimism results in guarded humor at the expense of the antihero, a bumbling boob whom Voltaire lampoons for his exuberant search for "the best of all possible worlds" against a dreary procession of natural disasters, cruelty, slavery, oppression, torture, prejudice, venality, violence, and treachery.

In the Westphalian castle of the baron of Thunder-ten-tronckh, Candide, a likable but unsophisticated youth whom the author hints is the baron's illegitimate nephew, studies under Doctor Pangloss, optimistic instructor in metaphysico-theologo-cosmolo-nigology. In daily recitation, Pangloss insists that all events work to a necessary and fitting end. Candide's residency with the baron ends after he commits a boyish indiscretion—going behind a screen to kiss the hand of Cunégonde, his host's daughter. Thus, Candide departs to make his way in the world.

Taking refuge in a nearby town, Candide meets a pair of uniformed officers who enlist him in the royal army. He learns to march, then is inexplicably beaten and imprisoned. The king of the Bulgarians extricates him so that he can war against the Abarians. Despite his height and robust youth, Candide proves unfit for battle because he detests war; he escapes from Germany to Holland, a land at peace.

Depicted as naively altruistic, Candide expects the Christian Dutch to extend welcome, but only James, an Anabaptist, treats him humanely. By coincidence, Candide reunites with Pangloss, now fallen into extreme poverty and suffering the anguish of venereal disease, which he contracted from his paramour, Pacquette. Candide learns that Bulgarian invaders have killed Cunégonde and the rest of the baron's family. With James's assistance, Candide and Pangloss sail to Lisbon, only to have their ship disintegrate offshore. Adding to their misfortunes are James's drowning and a devastating earthquake. Candide and Pangloss attend to survivors, but Portuguese scholars capture, flog, and condemn both men by auto-da-fé to burn at the stake for violating church morality. Shortly after the authorities hang Pangloss, a second earthquake ends the executions.

Voltaire pursues his plot from the foregoing cliff-hanger to an episodic series of events worthy of picaresque fiction. During the confusion, an old woman rescues Candide, salves his wounds, feeds him, and leads him to Cunégonde. She has survived the Bulgarian attack on the castle after all, and witnessed the auto-da-fé. Candide learns that for six months she has shared a residence with the Grand Inquisitor and a Jew, Don Issachar. Candide slays both men, eluding capture by galloping away with Cunégonde and the old woman. He listens to the extensive misadventures of the old woman, who claims to be the daughter of Pope Urban X, as the trio rides inland to the Sierra Morenas, then seaward to Cadiz. Candide joins a party sailing southwest across the Atlantic to Paraguay to suppress a Jesuit cabal.

Voltaire easily transfers his meandering tale from Europe to the New World. In Buenos Aires, Candide loses his fiancée to the lustful Don Fernando d'Ibarra, governor of the province. A Portuguese posse pursues him for killing the Inquisitor. Cacambo, Candide's faithful Spanish-Argentine valet, urges his master to flee to the Jesuit compound, where they meet the colonel, the chief oppressor of natives. To Candide's surprise, the man turns out to be the baron's son, a second survivor of the Bulgarian assault on Westphalia.

The ups and downs of Voltaire's comic fiction continue; Candide enjoys a brotherly reunion until he mentions that he, a commoner, intends to marry Cunégonde, a baron's daughter. Instantly, a fight breaks out. Locked in mortal combat, Candide plunges his sword into the colonel's abdomen. Disguising himself in a Jesuit robe and headpiece, he and Cacambo mount up and escape the compound. Along the way, they encounter the Oreillons, man-eaters who detest all Jesuits. Cacambo's quick action saves the duo from the cannibals, who assume them to be enemies from their priestly habits. The pair continue their trek through South America until their horses die. They board an abandoned canoe and paddle toward Cayenne, a French settlement.

Here, Voltaire allows himself some liberty with a utopian convention based on European hopes of instant wealth, a delusion dating to Christopher Columbus. High in the mountains, Candide and his servant arrive at Eldorado, a fabled utopia so far removed from civilization that its people live in contented innocence of their wealth. Candide marvels at the blissfully serene society built by Incas. But after a month of peaceful recuperation among the gold-rich Eldoradans, Candide grows restless for his lady. He ignores the king's warnings and, with Cacambo, returns toward Paraguay, carrying sheep laden with gold and jewels. Lifted by crane over the crags, the duo return to the eastward trail.

Voltaire, a dissenter from doctrinaire theological texts, centers on atrocities committed in the name of religion. Near Surinam, Candide meets a black sugar-mill slave whose foot and hand have been lopped off by a Dutch Christian. Candide concludes that life in Surinam parallels the evils of other places he has witnessed on his journey. In the harbor, Candide pays a Spanish captain for passage back to Europe—away from religious fanaticism, bigotry, and persecution. Cacambo returns to Buenos Aires to fetch the Lady Cunégonde, and Candide sails east for Italy. But before embarking, a pirate chief steals Candide's sheep, and an unscrupulous judge refuses to help Candide recover them.

Simulating the plot of Geoffrey Chaucer's *Canterbury Tales* (1385), Voltaire inserts a story line based on individual tales. Sailing first to Bordeaux aboard a French ship, Candide enlists fellow escapees from Surinam and promises to pay passage for the victim who narrates the most pathetic story. He selects Martin, an impoverished intellectual who debates philosophy with him. As is common in the novel, coincidence reunites Candide with his Eldoradan sheep. After departing from Paraguay, he observes the sinking of a Dutch vessel, which bears the pirate captain who stole his treasure. From the disaster, Candide reclaims one sheep, which he later donates to science.

Warming to the affable Candide, Martin informs him about Parisian venality, but the warning goes unheeded after a scheming abbé from Périgord mesmerizes Candide. Through connivance with a greedy actress and the marchioness of Doublestakesworthy, Candide loses at the gaming tables and is seduced and tricked out of two diamonds. The con artists post a fake Cunégonde behind a curtain as a means of defrauding Candide of more wealth. He and Martin are arrested; they gain their release and depart north immediately. As Voltaire indicates, Candide searches in vain for safe harbor. In Portsmouth, England, the winsome antihero witnesses the killing of Admiral Bynd, an English war hero who failed to kill enough of the enemy to satisfy the public demand for blood. From there Candide travels south to Venice, where he converses with a carnival of dethroned kings.

Still hopeful of reuniting with Cunégonde (who, like Dante's Beatrice and Don Quixote's idealized Dulcinea, represents all that is good), Candide looks for Cacambo, who planned to join him in Europe after rescuing the girl. Instead, Candide encounters Pacquette, the prostitute who was once Pangloss's mistress, and Father Giroflée, a malcontented monk. Candide offers money to the seedy pair. Next, Candide and Martin visit Count Pococurante, a literate Italian epicure who claims to savor joy and to avoid pain. Candide anticipates meeting a model of happiness, but finds the count to be a world-weary cynic incapable of pleasure.

When at length Cacambo appears, he urges Candide to journey to Constantinople to find the baron's daughter, who is enslaved with the old woman and washing dishes on the Sea of Marmora (modern-day Turkey). Cacambo warns that, through severe hardship and neglect, the idealized beauty has lost her youthful dewiness. At the Bosporus, Candide coincidentally locates Pangloss and Cunégonde's brother, who labor as galley slaves. Both men share fantastic tales: Pangloss escaped hanging because of a severe storm and was removed alive to a doctor's lab to be dissected, and the baron's son recovered from the sword thrust to his belly.

At Propontis, Voltaire begins to rein in his fantastic plot as Candide matures. Candide ransoms Cunégonde and her faithful companion, and despite his beloved's wrinkled, decrepit condition, he sticks to his plans for marriage. With his money gone and his dreams unrealized, he dispatches Cunégonde's brother to Rome and settles with his bride, valet, Martin, Doctor Pangloss, and the old woman on a small vegetable farm in Turkey. Pacquette and Father Giroflée return, causing Candide to reflect on the nature of vice and ill luck. From a neighboring Muslim, Candide learns how to cope with adversity— stop traveling willy-nilly, stay home, and tend his garden, a microcosm that he is more capable of managing.

Resulting from public dismay over the brutal Seven Years War, Voltaire's *Candide* is a vitriolic attack on war; it denigrates violence and excoriates false government, ecclesiastical vice, and authoritarianism. To the totalitarianism that overran France, he raised his famous outcry: "Écrasez l'infâme" (Crush the infamous). An altruist by nature, his novel demonstrates how close he came to capitulating to disillusionment in his bitter diatribe against brutality, folly, wickedness, and greed. (Andrews 1981; Ayer 1986; Gay 1988; Mason 1981; Richter and Ricardo 1980; Voltaire 1961)

See also Candide; Dante Alighieri; didacticism; disillusion; Don Quixote; Dulcinea del Toboso; Eldorado; Pangloss; satire; technology; totalitarianism; Voltaire, François; women in utopia.

 # CAPEK, KAREL

A peace-loving philosopher, journalist, novelist, and playwright, Capek wrote the prophetic dystopian play *R. U. R.* (1920), which stands for Rossum's Universal Robots, a factory specializing in servant automata. A native of Malé

Karel Capek, left, with his brother Josef, January 1938

Svatonovice, Bohemia, Karel Capek is claimed by Czechoslovakia. He was born on January 9, 1890, the son of a doctor; his younger brother, artist Josef Capek, became his collaborator. The victim of a spinal abnormality, Capek dedicated his life to learning; he studied philosophy at Charles University in Prague as well as in Paris and Berlin, and completed a doctorate in 1915.

Capek traveled widely in Europe, serving as Czechoslovakia's director of the National Art Theater. He used his post as a vehicle for experimental dramas, including *The Insect Comedy* (1921), *The Makropoulos Secret* (1922), *Factory for the Absolute* (1922), and *Power and Glory* (1937). He died on December 25, 1938, as Hitler's Reich was menacing Central Europe. His brother Josef lived to see the totalitarian rule that Capek feared. Imprisoned by the Nazis at Bergen-Belsen, Germany, Josef Capek died in April 1945, just weeks before the Allies liberated Hitler's death camps.

As author of *R. U. R.*, Capek's most famous "black utopia," he speaks out against materialism, soullessness, and modern technology, which spawned dictatorships and robbed humanity of the dignity, fulfillment, and appreciation of human labor. The play, which influenced Ray Bradbury's *I, Robot* and Arthur C. Clarke's *Childhood's End*, depicts the creation of a humanoid servant, for which Capek coined the term "robot." Through greed and titanic arrogance, the engineer Alquist narrowly escapes extinction by the superhuman species his predecessor, Dr. Rossum, created. The play concludes with a pseudo Adam and Eve, whom the author implies will repopulate the globe. (Capek and Capek 1961; Dickinson 1943; Harkins 1962; Magill 1958; Massary 1938)

See also Adam; allegory; Alquist, Mr.; Bradbury, Ray; *Childhood's End*; Clarke, Arthur C.; Eve; materialism; *R. U. R.*; technology; women in utopia.

CARLYLE, THOMAS

The Victorian era's most revered social critic, moralist, historian, biographer, polemicist, and philosopher, Carlyle is the author of *Past and Present* (1843), an earnest call for a return to the values and lifestyle of the idyllic medieval period. In his revulsion at profiteering, industrialization, pollution, and unrelenting competition, Carlyle looked to the past for a time when society functioned at its best. His selection of the Middle Ages was a literary crusade aimed at a moral and spiritual rebirth through revitalizing medieval concepts of devotion to duty and craftsmanship.

Born December 4, 1795, in Ecclefechan, Scotland, he was the eldest son of stonemason James Carlyle and his second wife Janet Aitken Carlyle. Carlyle was brought up on self-denial, Calvinistic determinism, and submission to authority. He studied at Annan Academy before enrolling at the University of Edinburgh. Rejecting his parents' hopes that he become a Presbyterian minister, Carlyle ended his formal education at age 19 and returned to his village to teach mathematics for two years. He also contributed articles to journals, including the highly revered *Edinburgh Review*. Carlyle advanced to a principalship at Kirkcaldy in 1816 before settling in Edinburgh to study law.

At age 27 Carlyle was a sickly, depressed man, wracked by self-doubt and his loss of faith in organized religion. He began composing one of his most celebrated works, *Sartor Resartus* (1835), and studied the German philosophers Emanuel Kant and Johann Fichte and the poet Johann Goethe, with whom he corresponded. Carlyle married Jane Welsh and resettled at Craigenputtock, a rural Dumfriesshire retreat, where he subsisted on meager earnings as a writer for the *Edinburgh Encyclopedia*. During his six years' work on a personal philosophy rich in respect for the individual and replete with loathing for the progressive, mechanized Industrial Revolution, Carlyle cultivated friendships with John Stuart Mill, Ralph Waldo Emerson, Jane Austen, Leigh Hunt, Walter Savage Landor, Giuseppe Mazzini, John Ruskin, and other literary figures.

The Carlyles moved to Chelsea in 1834, where he formed a literary coterie and began researching material for *The French Revolution* (1837), his first critical success. He followed with *On Heroes and Hero-Worship* (1841), a series of lectures. In 1843 he published his medieval idyll, *Past and Present*, a compelling work that exalts the Middle Ages as a time when the rigid class system of feudalism resulted in a harmonious work setting in which each citizen valued an individualized role. After serving the University of Edinburgh as Lord Rector and receiving the Prussian Order of Merit, he retired to compose his autobiography. He died in London on February 4, 1881, leaving the manuscript for

Thomas Carlyle

Reminiscences, which was published that same year. (Buckler 1958; Carlyle 1977; Greene 1971; Hodgkins 1904; Hornstein et al. 1973; Magill 1958)
    See also asceticism; classism; *Past and Present.*

 # CASTIGLIONE, BALDESSAR

Famed Milanese courtier and ambassador, Castiglione is the author of *Il Libro del cortegiano* (The Book of the Courtier) (1528), a four-book prose dialogue that offers an idealized view of the Renaissance gentleman, reflecting much of the education, manners, and effortless deportment of Castiglione himself. The book greatly influenced manners, education, and the spread of Italian humanism throughout Europe. Born to a noble Lombard house on December 6, 1478 in Casatico, Italy, Castiglione was a student of classical and Italian verse, painting, and music, growing up among the privileged Sforzas and training in Mantua under the tutelage of Francesco Gonzaga. Because of his skill with horses and his spirit, exquisite posture, and beauty, he posed equestrian-style for the painter Raphael.

Castiglione's career, begun in 1504 at a promising point in the Italian Renaissance, placed him under the mentorship of Guidobaldo da Montefeltro, duke of Urbino, and his successor, Francesco Maria della Rovere. In a privileged, palatial milieu, he enjoyed the comforts of the wealthy and the intellectual ferment of scholars, thinkers, ambassadors, travelers, and artists. In 1509 and 1511 Castiglione fought in Italian wars; for his distinguished battlefield performance, he was elevated to the rank of *conte* (count). He traveled widely and consulted with the Vatican and the Spanish court of the Holy Roman Emperor, Charles V.

Much of Castiglione's earlier writing consisted of derivative verse imitating classic form. His masterpiece, *The Book of the Courtier,* echoed the spare, emphatic style of Cicero's *De oratore* (first century B.C.) and remained in a constant state of revision from 1508 to 1528. The upper-class gentleman's handbook to the good life, Castiglione's work elaborates on an elite ideal for conversation, courtship, war, sports, appearance, manners, writing style, learning, morality, logic, self-control, dining, music, dance, and other forms of culture. At his death in Toledo, Spain, on February 2, 1529, Castiglione was commemorated as the epitome of gentility. His work, the antithesis of asceticism, circulated widely in Europe, was translated into English by Sir Thomas Hoby in 1561, and influenced the writings and style of Miguel de Cervantes, Pierre Corneille, Sir Edmund Spenser, and Sir Philip Sidney. (Castiglione 1976; Hanning and Rosand 1983; Hornstein et al. 1973; Mack 1962; Rollins and Baker 1954)

See also The Abbey of Thélème; asceticism; classism; *The Courtier*; materialism.

 "THE CAVE MYTH"

See The Republic.

 CELESTIAL CITY

The goal of the righteous who journey from the allegorical Land of Destruction toward heaven, as recorded in John Bunyan's *Pilgrim's Progress* (1678), Celestial City epitomizes the author's attention to concrete details that appeal to Christians seeking affirmation of faith. The final course to the city requires rigorous effort and strong faith. The traveler must pass over the Delectable

Mountains and wade across the bridgeless River of Death, a treacherous and unpredictable waterway of indeterminate depth that circles Celestial City. On the far shore, Pilgrim arrives in Christian's Country. From there through Beulah Land, the foyer of heaven, the elect of God wait until Christ's resurrection before they can enter the gates.

Celestial City resembles Virgil's Elysium and the biblical Eden with its verdant lawns, flowers, and orchards. The focal points of the city are streets paved with gold and the Tree of Life, which is formed of jewels and pearls. On that momentous day when Christians achieve their long-awaited paradise, a trumpet call will summon them beneath an inscription similar in style and tone to the passage of Christ's Sermon on the Mount known as the Beatitudes, which is found in Matthew 5:1–7: "Blessed are they that do His commandments, that they may have right to the Tree of Life; and may enter in through the Gates into the City." Heavenly hosts observe the procession into the eternal home, where attendants deck travelers in majestic robes and place gold diadems on their heads. (Alexander and Alexander 1973; Benét 1991; Brewer 1899; Bunyan 1896; Evans 1817; Holy Bible 1958; McDannell 1994; Mays 1988)

See also Beulah Land; Bunyan, John; Elysian Fields; heaven; *Pilgrim's Progress*; Sermon on the Mount; Virgil.

CERVANTES SAAVEDRA, MIGUEL DE

Spain's most revered writer, Cervantes is the author of the epic romance *El Ingenioso Hidalgo Don Quixote de la Mancha* (1615), sometimes called the first modern novel. Don Quixote, the Knight of the Sad Countenance, is the universal idealist, unique in world literature as the good-natured but misguided dreamer whose perfect world exists only in his visions. So benevolent is his love for humanity that this bumbling dotard and his rustic companion, Sancho Panza, have resurfaced in paintings, statuary, film, cartoon, song, legend, and musical comedy.

The fourth of seven children of ne'er-do-well hidalgo Rodrigo Cervantes, a surgeon and pharmacist at the University of Alcalá, and his wife, Leonor de Cortinas, Cervantes was born in Alcalá de Henares outside Madrid on September 29, 1547. He grew up in poverty on the ragged edge of nobility. Although his father served time in debtor's prison, Cervantes received a proper education. He read widely, particularly *Amadis de Gaula* (1509), a chivalric romance, studied with Jesuit tutors at the School of General Studies, and entered the University of Salamanca. Under Juan López de Hoyes, he received humanistic training in all forms of literature, which he began imitating.

At the age of 22, as Cardinal Giulio Acquaviva's chamberlain, Cervantes served as a Vatican aide before entering military service under Diego de Urbina. His war record reaped commendations for heroism at Tunis, Sardinia, Sicily, Naples, and Genoa; he was aboard the galley *La Marquesa* in the Gulf of Corinth at the battle of Lepanto, a Christian defeat of the Ottoman Turks in October 1571. Cervantes was so severely wounded by pistol fire that he suffered lung

Miguel de Cervantes Saavedra

impairment and lost the use of his mangled left hand. On a voyage aboard the galley *Sol,* Cervantes was captured and chained by Turkish pirates and taken to Algiers. For five years he distinguished himself by engineering a mass jailbreak to free 60 prisoners from an Arab slave pen. At his hearing in an Algerian tribunal, Cervantes claimed all the plotting as his own doing. The pasha was so impressed that he spared Cervantes's life.

After Trinitarian friar Juan Gil paid a ransom of 500 gold pieces in 1580, Cervantes returned to his Portuguese mistress in Madrid to eke out a living writing popular stage dramas. He published a pastoral idyll, *La Galatea* (1585), but did not earn enough to support his mistress and only daughter, Isabel Rojas de Saavedra. To end the constant need for money, in 1584 he married the wealthy

Catalina Salaza y Vozmediano, who was 20 years his junior. Her dowry brought him farmland, silver, and furnishings, but the marriage failed. After his father's death, Cervantes returned to his mistress and shouldered the upkeep of his daughter, sisters, and niece.

Settling in Seville and scribbling 30 plays and numerous poems for other people's novels, Cervantes accepted the lucrative post of accountant for the ill-fated Spanish armada, which fell to Queen Elizabeth I's navy in 1588. After being convicted of graft in deals involving oil and grain, he was excommunicated by the church, swindled by his banker, and imprisoned in the king's lockup in Seville. It was during this confinement that he created his master idealist, Don Quixote. Like Dante and Chaucer, Cervantes chose the language of the day—the vigorous Castilian vernacular—which he preferred to scholarly Latin or polished court Spanish. The episodic adventures of his hero, translated into French and English, attained international fame and were reprinted six times during Cervantes's life, but earned him only a small cash settlement. A parody appeared in 1614; the event inspired Cervantes to complete his work and market the whole thing as one manuscript. In 1603 Cervantes was released from prison and moved to Valladolid to live under the sponsorship of the Count of Lemos. Following a street brawl, he was humiliated and returned to jail. From 1606 until his death from diabetes on April 23, 1616, Cervantes lived in straitened circumstances in Madrid. He wrote a second segment of *Don Quixote*, as well as *Novelas Exemplares* (1613), *Viaje del Parnaso* (1613), and *Ocho Comedias y Ocho Entremeses* (1615). Depressed and sick, he died without finishing *Los Trabajos de Persiles y Sigismunda* (1617), left no will, and was interred in an unmarked grave. (Bloom 1986a; Boorstin 1992; Byron 1988; Cervantes 1957; Duran 1974; Gilman 1989; Nabokov 1984; Predmore 1990; Riley 1986; Russell 1985)

See also Dante Alighieri; disillusion; Don Quixote; fantasy; idealism; religion.

CHILDHOOD'S END

Arthur C. Clarke's problematic three-part science fiction classic was published in 1953 near the beginning of his extensive and influential career. The story blends speculative fiction with religious vision and themes of family, racism, technology, creativity, law, and interspace communication and travel. Over all reigns the question of a power struggle that not only steals Earth from its people but also transforms the next generation into a nonreactive vegetative state. Much debated in philosophical and sci-fi communities, the paradoxical novel received favorable reviews from *Atlantic, Kirkus Review,* the *New York Herald,* ALA Booklist, the *Christian Science Monitor,* and the *New York Times.*

Dramatically set on the night preceding a Russian/U.S. race into space, the plot opens on the appearance of huge, technically superior starships from a distant solar system. The ships hover 50 kilometers above "New York, London, Paris, Moscow, Rome, Cape Town, Tokyo, Canberra. . . ." The "heart-freezing" shadows remain five years; by that time, earthlings acknowledge that the navigators' intent is not military. Alien crews and benevolent Overlords take charge of the world, primitive in comparison with the advancements the aliens have left behind. People maintain limited communication with the space hierarchy through a single man—Rikki Stormgren, a lonely widower and secretary-general of the United Nations—who speaks directly to Earth's supervisor, Karellen, an undemonstrative but ostensibly supportive Overlord.

A screen separates the two during their weekly meetings. Wags in the radical underground, the Freedom League, imply that the aliens hide from human view because they are monstrously misshapen. The same witty, irreverent group lampoons Stormgren as "Karellen's office boy" and makes a weak show of kidnapping him. Stormgren challenges their plot by identifying his captors by name; Karellen secures his release. Stormgren thinks of his savior as a benevolent friend; however, on the day that Karellen makes his first physical appearance "in ebon majesty," he displays "leathery wings, the little horns, the barbed tail"—a disconcerting likeness to Satan.

Employing no violence, coercion, or interference in human activities, the Overlords use computer transmissions to promote a World Federation guided by a single formalized constitution. Within 50 years, all the starships fade into mist except the one real vehicle, which hovers over New York. In Part 2, Chapter 6, utopian aims come true—no longer do hunger, fear, disease, or war plague nations; oppression, ignorance, prejudice, and religion cease. Clarke cites the significance of global harmony:

> It was One World. The old names of the old countries were still used, but they were no more than convenient postal divisions. There was no one on earth who could not speak English, who could not read, who was not within range of a television set, who could not visit the other side of the planet within twenty-four hours.

Clarke lauds but does not elaborate on two innovations above all others—a fail-proof contraceptive and a system of blood analysis that identifies biological fathers. Other improvements streamline life on Earth: Cities are rebuilt and ground traffic thins out after travelers take to the skies in aircars. Scientific research is an outmoded endeavor. Machines and robots do most of the menial tasks. Human beings, who work 20 hours per week, strive only for extras. During this period, humanity abandons aberrant Puritanism and suspicions about Overlords; people embrace a purified Buddhism and come to expect peace and prosperity as the natural rhythm of life.

Despite these attainments, Earth's golden age does not satisfy freethinkers like Jan Rodricks, a young physics student, and Alexander Wainwright and the Freedom League, the ragtag radicals who fear the loss of earthly autonomy. The single driving force of discontent appears to be curiosity: Earth's people want to know more about the mysterious Overlords, the direction of civilization, and the makeup of outer space. At the beginning of Chapter 8, Arthur Clarke draws a meaningful conclusion about the mortal capacity for happiness:

> No Utopia can ever give satisfaction to everyone, all the time. As their material conditions improve, men raise their sights and become discontented with

power and possessions . . . there still remain the searchings of the mind and the longings of the heart.

In proof of the statement, the author introduces a disgruntled group of artists led by George Greggson and his wife Jean, son Jeffrey, and daughter Jennifer. In the group's assessment of world change, science and leisure outweigh the importance of creativity because life has lost its zest, the sparkle that underlies artistic expression. To reestablish interest in art, they move to a pair of isolated Pacific islands joined by a causeway and form two multinational colonies—Sparta and New Athens, led by Ben Salomon, a Moses figure. According to the close of Chapter 15, New Athens "hoped to become what the old Athens might have been had it possessed machines instead of slaves, science instead of superstition."

A serious contention in Clarke's novel is his belief that a transcendent power—called the Overmind—lies beyond the grasp of human thinking. Because the human brain cannot comprehend the vastness of space or the insignificance of Earth to the universe, Karellen makes a momentous demonstration for the BBC of the immensity of the heavens (Part II, Chapter 14). With emphasis on the number of stars and solar systems, he states unequivocally: "The planets you may one day possess. But the stars are not for Man." The bitter truth is tempered by a sobering ambiguity—that the golden age can last only a short time before evolution again jolts humankind toward a higher but undefined level. Karellen realizes that world harmony is nearing its end; the newest generation, exemplified by the Greggson children, demonstrates the paranormal powers that will alter irrevocably the human race.

Part III, named "The Last Generation," predicts an alteration in Homo sapiens. Through a radio broadcast, Karellen explains that his race came at just the right moment to stop earthlings from destroying themselves by misapplying nuclear energy. In a lengthy speech in Chapter 20, he explains his purpose:

> My task and my duty is to protect those I have been sent here to guard. Despite their wakening powers, they could be destroyed by the multitudes around them—yes, even by their parents, when they realized the truth. I must take them away and isolate them, for their protection, and for yours.

With some nostalgia for the race that he has come to admire, Karellen adds that the dying race "will go to its rest in peace, knowing that it has not lived in vain."

Humankind begins its transformation to a new state, one that brings people closer to a perception of the Overmind, which the Overlords serve like midwives assisting at a birth. As Karellen words his mission, he came to Earth "to till the field until the crop is ripe. The Overmind then collects the harvest." Significant to this part of the action in Chapter 22 is the return of Jan Rodricks, who has learned the number of the aliens' sun from a chance manipulation of a Ouija board. He stows away on a spaceship headed for the constellation of Carina, 40 light-years from Earth, and returns 80 years later, unaged by his adventure. As the sun dwindles, he finds only faceless, inert cocoons instead of individuals. On first view, he discerns that they are

. . . emptier than the faces of the dead, for even a corpse has some record carved by time's chisel upon its features, to speak when the lips themselves are dumb. There was no more emotion or feeling here than in the face of a snake or an insect.

The suprahuman children, naked and filthy, perform an intricate dance. In their next incarnation, they recede into a fetal state. Rodricks, the last example of Homo sapiens left alive, shudders at the altered state—the alleged "apotheosis" of the human species. To restore inner calm, he sits at a piano and plays works by Bach.

Clarke halts the plot at an undisclosed segment of evolution presaging a new life form for earthlings, which Karellen proclaims "not tragedy, but fulfillment." The new species plays with Earth's spin. The planet implodes; its light winks out. Karellen wistfully salutes the people who have been his friends. Clarke leaves to the reader a stiff set of conundrums:

- Is complete freedom from biology better than servitude to annihilation through evolution?

- Does humanity prosper by metamorphosing into an inner-directed entity that will eventually merge with the Overmind?

Rather like the paradoxical concepts of Confucius and Taoists, the submergence of individuals into the Overmind is more than anyone living can comprehend, much less evaluate. Taken on trust, the next stage of evolution may be for the best; otherwise, it must be seen as humankind's extinction. At this point in Clarke's speculative novel, the Overmind equals God or a supreme power.

Critics continue to list Clarke's work among the best of the speculative genre. Dissenters debate the open-ended plot resolution that, by definition, has no firm conclusion and, like Clarke's *2001: A Space Odyssey*, closes on an eerie, menacing nothingness. Similar in magnitude and implication to apocalyptic literature, *Childhood's End* leaves all creation on the edge of oneness with God after eons of war, disease, labor, uncertainty, and death. Clarke implies, however, that lulling humanity into a golden age is an efficient, nonviolent way of subsuming human powers and ridding Earth of the potential hazards of humankind. (Bernstein 1969; Clarke 1953; Clarke 1990; Rabkin 1979; Slusser 1977a; Sullivan 1992)

See also Buddhism; Clarke, Arthur C.; futurism; golden age; humanitarianism; Karellen; religion; *R. U. R.*; Satan; science fiction; slavery; speculative fiction; syncretism; utopia.

THE CHILDREN OF MEN

A starkly draconian dystopia by P. D. James, *The Children of Men* (1993) summons the dystopian despair of the last quarter of the twentieth century. Similar in scope and tone to Margaret Atwood's *The Handmaid's Tale*, the two-part story is told by a 50-year-old reflective diarist, Dr. Theodore "Theo" Faron, a fellow of Merton College, Oxford, whose name comes from the Greek word for god. Shortly after the violent death of 25-year-old Joseph Ricardo, the youngest man on the planet, the plot opens in Great Britain on Friday, January 1, 2021, at a nadir in human reproduction. In anticipation of a depletion of the human species, historians and antiquarians prepare their manuscripts and memorabilia for storage.

In James's bleak projection, the world started its decline when males stopped producing sperm in 1995, dubbed "Year Omega" for the last letter of the Greek alphabet. By 2008 scientists realize that the younger generation is sterile. Omega men remain tough and energetic; Omega women become laconic and withdrawn. As the median age rises, the population turns to golf and away from the fearful news of a predatory Generation Omega, the last of Homo sapiens. Frustrated scientists are unable to determine the cause of humanity's loss of fertility.

James follows utopian convention by introducing a tyrant to sort out the chaos in England. Under the guidance of Warden Xan Lypiatt, an ostensibly benign dictator protected by an ornate ceremonial ring and a praetorian phalanx known as the Grenadiers, the ruling Council goes into session on January 5, 2021, with Theo as observer. Its members include a minister of industry and production; ministry of health, science, and recreation; ministry of home affairs; and ministry for justice and state security. Resurrecting a childhood friendship with Xan, Theo (who is Xan's only living relative) flashes back to his deceased parents and his daughter Natalie, whom he accidentally ran over and killed in 1994. Theo's relationship with his wife Helena ends in 2020, after she leaves him for a younger man.

In a conference between representatives of orthodoxy and the underground, Theo agrees to meet with Julian, wife of Rolf and a member of an anti-Council that works to defeat Xan's inhumane policies. She describes the limbo inhabited by the Sojourners, a press-gang of Omegas who are urged to immigrate to England to perform the dirty work, then, at age 60, are transported back to their original countries. Luke, a second revolutionary, detests the compulsory gynecological exams and obligatory suicide for the elderly. The entire revolutionary cell protests the Man Penal Colony and looks for some spot of hope—"a resurgence of protection, comfort, and pleasure; compassion, justice, and love."

Using first-person testimony, James piles up negative evidence against Xan's regime. Miriam offers the most damning proof of misuse of power. She describes the return from prison of her brother Henry and his description of excessive punishment for a minor offense. He reports that inmates are tormented and starved. They feed on grass to keep themselves alive. Xan's bodyguard captures Henry and returns him to confinement. A week later, Miriam receives his ashes.

James develops Theo, a stereotypical, contemplative humanist, into a cautious man of action. He accepts the challenge of dissidents and inquires about these suspicious happenings. He observes a Quietus, or assisted suicide, and tries to rescue an aged woman he recognizes. A guard raps him on the head with his gun butt. Theo attempts repeatedly to save the woman, but each time the guard assaults him for his interference in the ritual. At the subsequent Council session at Southwold, Xan's associate Felicia replies to Theo's questions about the Quietus by explaining that the ritual he witnessed was botched. Before, old people were allowed to jump off cliffs. The work involved in removing bodies is streamlined into a ritual drowning in the sea, which carries away the corpses.

The Council allows Theo a second question; he wants more information about the penal colony. Felicia reports a resettlement effort, which results in no complaints. Xan adds that society can no longer afford the indulgence of crime. The others concur in a unanimity that disturbs Theo. He comments on the complaints of Sojourners. Carl, the Minister of Justice, completes the picture of a nation in the grip of fascism by stressing the positive results of civil rule. Theo replies that people need more dignity and respect than they are receiving. Xan, who refuses to justify his jackbooted approach to control, abruptly ends the session.

On a chauffeured trip to the Mall, Xan insists that Theo reveal the names of dissidents. The two men discuss how they would end their lives. Xan closes their meeting with a veiled threat against Theo's friends that they leave government to him. At the next meeting with Julian, Theo relates the abortive conversation with Xan and warns the dissidents of Xan's menace. Refusing to be cowed, Julian proposes having insurgents deliberately seek imprisonment on the Isle of Man to agitate for justice from the inside. Theo notes that Julian and her friends are unequipped to fight a tyrant like Xan. She replies that her acts are done in the name of God, a symbolic translation of Theo's name.

Faith in idealism and civil obstruction buoys James's counterculture to a showdown. Two weeks later, a folded, single-sheet flier arrives in the mail from the Five Fishes urging Britons to call an election, offer civil rights to Sojourners, abolish ritual suicide, restructure the penal colony, and stop requiring testing of citizens' fertility. Security Police call on Theo, but make no search of the premises. He continues to write in his journal and keeps it in a locked desk drawer. In March, Theo happens upon Julian in High Street near the market. He insists that they talk, but she fears that open conversation is too risky. As she walks away from him, he turns his back. Later, he confesses to his journal that he loves her. He decides to use his passport and travel about the landmarks of Europe. He intends to tear up this page before he leaves.

In Book 2, which opens in October 2021, Theo notes in his diary that he returned from Europe in September and telephoned his ex-wife. She reports the plot of the Five Fishes to free inmates from the penal colony and to depose Xan as a totalitarian monster. Theo calls the news absurd, then suffers recurring nightmares. Miriam visits his residence to report that authorities have captured Gascoigne, one of the Five Fishes who was trying to blow up the Shoreham landing stage.

In the style of dystopists George Orwell, Margaret Atwood, Lois Lowry, and Marge Piercy, James ends the novel on an ambiguous note. As Miriam leads Theo to Julian, she reports that Julian is pregnant; Theo doubts the news. Theo and Julian reunite at Oswald's Chapel, and she invites him to feel her swollen abdomen. He realizes how significant this fetus could be to the Council. She insists on giving birth in secret to keep the child safe from Xan and his storm troopers. Rolf indicates that Theo knows too many of the group's secrets and therefore must be considered a fellow dissident.

As is common to dystopias in which conflicting authority figures compete for control, *The Children of Men* ends with violence and an unclear transfer of power. The predatory Omegas capture and murder Luke in a vicious ritual. Julian acknowledges that he was the father of her child and that he died to save her. Miriam surmises that Julian loved neither Rolf nor Luke because she displays affection for Theo alone. The remaining members of the group bury Luke, and the next morning, Rolf defects. In a somber mood, Theo departs in a car taken from a local citizen and drives toward Wales. From car radio reports of their actions and of the death of the car owner's wife, the remaining Fish realize that Rolf has reached Xan and divulged incriminating information about the group. Theo blames himself for the woman's death and questions how many more must die so that this baby can be born.

At a rude shed, Miriam, the midwife (whose name calls to mind the watchful sister who set the basket containing the infant Moses in the Nile River where royalty could find him), is brutally garroted, yet the birthing provides a moment of peace and hope as Julian welcomes her son. When the child is only minutes old, Xan arrives. Julian shoves bullets into a pistol. Xan admits that he killed every group member except Julian and Theo, and that he plans to marry Julian and use the infant to sire a new race. Forced into the role of armed activist, Theo shoots Xan, then strips off the royal ring and places it on his own finger. Under the influence of supreme authority, he plans to ward off the Security Police and offer Julian and her child safe conduct. Cognizant of the ring's symbolism, the Council views Xan's body, then rejoices at the baby boy, blessed by Julian's symbolic cross blended from blood and tears.

Critics' reviews of James's dystopia are mixed. Idiosyncratic of her murder mysteries, *The Children of Men* bears the earmarks of sturdy plotting and the right dollop of suspense, but the premise is too obvious and the symbols too cumbersome. The creation of a new power in England appears to perpetuate dystopia, which passes from Xan to Theo, who now bears godlike power embodied in the royal ring. Implicit in the transfer is the greater question: How do human despots cope with a dying race? James's plaintive conclusion offers little hope that Theo and the infant can supply the answers needed by Earth's withering human population. (*Contemporary Literary Criticism* 1981b; Finn 1993; Hughes 1992; James 1958; Reading 1992; Siebenheller 1981; Symons 1992; Wangerin 1993; Wynn 1977)

See also Atwood, Margaret; dystopia; *The Handmaid's Tale;* James, P. D.; totalitarianism; women in utopia.

  # A CHILD'S GARDEN OF VERSES

See escapism.

CHRISTIAN

Laden with a rucksack of original sin on his back but guided by his ever-present Bible, this naive but stouthearted sojourner makes an episodic pilgrimage to the Celestial City. Christian's experience forms the focus of John Bunyan's *Pilgrim's Progress* (1678), a tour de force literary work combining elements from the utopian vision, suspense novel, epic, vision, folktale, and medieval allegory. Central to Christian's experiences are the emotional and philosophic ups and downs of religious faith, a faith that supports him through the final test—the fearful River of Death. By grace rather than good works, he passes the final test, wades ashore to Beulah Land, and receives the welcome that awaits the faithful—admission to Celestial City, or Paradise.

Enduring perils by means of chance encounters with such companions as Hopeful, Mr. Wiseman, and Faithful, Christian exemplifies a painful dichotomy—the man of god who is at odds with the solid family man. Throughout his journey, he berates himself for failing to dissuade his wife Christiana and their sons, Matthew, Joseph, James, and Samuel, from remaining behind in the City of Destruction, which is slated for a fiery end. Still mourning the absence of wife and children, Christian displays humanistic compassion for fellow travelers who lack the zeal necessary for so harrowing and soul-wrenching a trip. Similar to Jonathan Swift's Lemuel Gulliver, Dante's autobiographical self, Milton's Christ, and Voltaire's Candide, Christian arrives at Heaven by traversing the circuitous route of human experience. Along the way, he makes plain the pitfalls that await the backslider and the weak-willed believer. To avoid the fires of hell, he seeks a heavenly utopia—the Celestial City, the reward of the truth-seeker. (Baugh 1948; Bunyan 1896; Johnson 1968; Lindsay 1969; Manguel and Guadalupi 1987; Reason 1961)

See also allegory; Candide; Christiana; Dante Alighieri; Gulliver, Lemuel; heaven; Milton, John; *Pilgrim's Progress;* religion; Swift, Jonathan; theocracy; Voltaire, François.

CHRISTIANA

The doughty, long-suffering wife of Christian, she leads her four sons—Matthew, Joseph, James, and Samuel—from the City of Destruction to the Celestial City. After Christian pleads in vain for her to follow him to the Celestial City to avoid a heavenly conflagration, he leaves without her. Their separation proves unbearable to a woman who values monogamy and genuinely misses her mate. As a widow in mourning for her beloved Pilgrim, she changes her mind and, leading her sons, travels with Mercy the wearisome and fearful path to Paradise.

Christiana demonstrates strength of moral and religious commitment by her songs and pious words and a willingness to improve her character through prayer and good works. Significant to her triumph as a parent are her sons' wise choices of wives, who reflect the good nature of Christiana. The character grows out of John Bunyan's syncretic blend of chivalric ideals and the Christian concept of the goodwife in that she achieves much of her success through the intervention of male rescuers, notably Mr. Greatheart, slayer of giants and guide through treacherous territory. Less valiant than Christian, Christiana represents determination more than physical strength, and monogamy and motherhood over righteousness. Through her identification with the man of the house, she achieves utopia, thus embodying the seventeenth-century disenfranchisement of women and the secondary role of female Christians in matters of faith. (Baugh 1948; Bunyan 1896; Johnson 1968; Lindsay 1969; Manguel and Guadalupi 1987; Reason 1961)

See also Bunyan, John; Christian; *Pilgrim's Progress;* syncretism; theocracy; women in utopia.

CHRISTIANOPOLIS

This utopian fable about a Christian theocracy, influenced by Fra Tomaso Campanella's *Città del Sole* (1602), was written by German scholar Johann Valentin Andreae in 1619, originally named *Reipublicae Christianapolitanae descriptio,* and published in Amsterdam. A blend of naturalism and religious reform, the work evolved from serious contemplation of human needs as well as the human penchant for wickedness. Like Jonathan Swift's Lemuel Gulliver, the vagabonds in Herman Melville's *Typee,* and the shipwrecked party in Shakespeare's *Tempest,* the speaker, a seeker of goodness, contrasts this moral utopian republic with the ungodly, depraved land he deliberately left behind.

In Andreae's allegorical perfect world, Christianopolis reigns supreme as capital of a remote, rigidly moral haven where people live in communal bliss. The first-person speaker, a seventeenth-century Robinson Crusoe, boards "the good *Phantasy"* and sails on the Academic Sea in search of wisdom. Storms over the Ethiopian Sea caused by envy and calumny sink the *Phantasy,* scattering her passengers and crew to nearby islands. Of the few who survive, this "stranger on the earth" arrives at a minute islet of Caphar Salama. The island nation, a pastoral haven Andreae terms "a whole world in miniature," is richly blessed with pastures, grain fields, waterways, woods, vineyards, and animals.

After proving to border guards that he is "not a quack, or a beggar, or a stage player," the traveler attests that he values nature, the arts, history, language, and world harmony. On the strength of his promise as a worthy person, he enters the tiny walled city of Christianopolis. Built symmetrically on a fortified square 700 feet on a side, the plan calls for a moat, lookout towers, a single street and market, two rows of fireproof government buildings, mills, bakery, abattoir, and storehouses, three-storied stone residences, and a circular temple 100 feet wide. Carefully designed into the plan are an adequate supply of spring water, laboratories, armory, botanic gardens, and pharmacies, which dispense naturopathic palliatives. The most spectacular landmark is the library, 70 feet high, which contains all the lost or misplaced volumes lamented by the world.

Zoning controls town planning, which resembles a medieval fiefdom. Trade guilds use stone, metal, wood, or woven goods. The most skilled artisans live close to the center of town, with lesser workers inhabiting the far rim. Beyond this concentric arrangement of skilled and semiskilled labor lie the fields, the third realm of industry. At the heart of town a virtuous triumvirate, symbolizing the Trinity, calls on 8 men and their 64 underlings to govern the people. The constitution consists of a pair of gold-lettered tablets attesting to the godly aims of Christianopolis.

The state is founded on a true communism and a dedication to work, cleanliness, morality, and learning. By sharing limited periods of manual labor, each Christianopolite participates for a time in road building, carpentry, guard duty, and reaping, yet spends the majority of work time in a more fulfilling trade. The nation as a whole values industry and invention as a means of relieving drudgery and admires exhibitions of machinery and instructive murals. Christianopolis needs no currency. To keep the citizenry equal in property as well as social dignity and piety, the council apportions possessions by parceling out a weekly allotment of clothing, food, and tools from storehouses located in the corner watchtowers. Housing is likewise evenly distributed to the small family units, who occupy standard, well-kept apartments composed of a private kitchen and sleeping and bathing compartments. Unlike in other utopias, Andreae does not call for a public refectory, but he does require attendance at public prayers three times daily.

The populace of 400, whose clearly defined division of labor delegates them to support some area of study, exercise, or food supply, enjoys "religious faith and peace of the highest order." Citizens own little and reflect their contentment in the simplicity that the castaway praises in Daniel Defoe's *Robinson Crusoe* (1719) and Henry David Thoreau craves in *Walden* (1854). They have no need of elaborate furniture, luxury items, or servants, except for nannies and nurses for the sick. Their meager wardrobe consists of two white or gray linen outfits for summer and the same in wool for winter. The family arrangement resembles that of Fra Tomaso Campanella's *Città del Sole* in that females marry at age 18 and men at 24. Women receive the same education as men, but have no voting rights or voice in church matters. Instead of civic and religious duties, the wives remain immured in stereotypical domesticity: They clean house, serve their husbands, and concentrate on cottage industries, e.g., sewing, spinning, embroidery, weaving, and tapestry.

Conjugal relationships center on procreation rather than pleasure. Children remain at home until they enter school, where they study Greek, Latin, and Hebrew under the most virtuous elderly men and concentrate on worship, morality, and mental training. At the end of the sixth grade, like the Spartan youths of ancient Greece, the children become wards of Christianopolis and live in immaculately kept dormitories. Classes occupy half the day and alternate with domestic arts, which are taught by male and female instructors. Older students learn mystic numbers, oratory, logic, metaphysics, and theosophy. The next level of learning spotlights liturgical music played on various instruments and sung by choruses, with performances weekly and on holidays. After music come lectures in astronomy, astrology, philosophy, church history, ethics, and theology. Also emphasized are medicine, law, painting, and sculpture.

Overall, Andreae's Christianopolis teeters on the cusp of a benign totalitarian theocracy: a humane although seriously restrained artisan's autocracy for male citizens but a sexist repression of most women into the traditional role of hausfrau. The chief priest rules in matters of misbehavior, which is punished by correction rather than torture, imprisonment, or death. Andreae notes that "Anyone can destroy a man, but only the best can reform him." Thus, happiness under this intensely moral Christian autocracy is assured for men. True to his time, Andreae spares no ink on the female opinion.

The best of city life results from a careful blend of religion, learning, and justice. The juncture of these three pillars of Christianopolis results in a blessed environment. As Andreae concludes, the binding element is Christianity itself, "which conciliates God with men and unites men together, so that they have pious thoughts, do good deeds, know the truth, and finally die happily to live eternally." Andreae's idealistic utopia relies on a citywide awareness of values, the situations in which to apply these principles, and the machinery by which normal citizens can effectively demonstrate their adherence to Christianity. (Andreae 1955; Berneri 1951; Manguel and Guadalupi 1987; Mumford 1959)

See also allegory; Andreae, Johann Valentin; *La Città del Sole*; city planning; escapism; Gulliver, Lemuel; Swift, Jonathan; *The Tempest*; *Typee*; *Walden*; women in utopia.

LA CITTÀ DEL SOLE

This classic utopian treatise was written by Giovanni Campanella (1568–1639), a much maligned Dominican friar from Stilo, Italy, who taught and wrote under the name Fra (Father) Tomaso. Campanella purposely composed the original (1602) in Italian, the common tongue used by the untutored populace, rather than the more scholarly Latin. Two more versions appeared in 1623 and 1637: the first, called in Latin *Civitas Solis,* and the posthumous edition in Italian, which translates as "City of the Sun." Of the three titles, the Italian version retains the greatest following, although the Latin had greater influence on German scholars, who were impressed by Campanella's vision. Fra Tomaso was the epitome of the seventeenth-century scholarship that placed Italy at the hub of Renaissance Europe. By substituting human knowledge for church control, he created a heretical innovation: a world plan calling for the mind's awareness of its place in the universal scheme. His belief that a beneficent God draws all life toward goodness stresses divine grace as the prime mover.

La Città del Sole takes the form of a dialogue between Sir Hospitaller, grand master of a coterie of knights, and an unnamed Genoese sailor who reports his voyage to a distant utopia south of the equator. Although the inhabitants usually spurn outsiders, they allow a few visitors for a three-day sojourn, which for the seaman was enough to gain an overview of utopianism. A hilled metropolis lying near Taprobane (possibly Sumatra) in the Indian Ocean, the City of the Sun radiates a mile outward from a mesa to verdant lowlands and extends over a seven-mile circumference. Seven concentric rings, similar to the symmetry of Johann Andreae's *Christianopolis* (1619), form the residential area and are named for the planets. Along with redoubts, lookouts, and gun emplacements, the rings serve as protective moats for the inner city, a medieval citadel as practical in design as King Arthur's Camelot. Yet, the City of the Sun is not isolated—interlocking boulevards and gates fan out to the four winds.

One of Campanella's innovations in utopian city planning is the careful delineation of the human power structure and the building that fortifies the city. On entry through the ironwork of the North Gate, which can be cranked up and down by winch, a visitor looks over a 50-foot walk separating circle one from circle two. At the summit is a palace, kept safe by a double wall, one concave and one convex. It falls under the sway of Prince Hoh, or Sun, an authoritarian philosopher flanked by three allegorical acolytes: Prince Pon, Prince Sin, and Prince Mor, representing power, knowledge, and love. These staff members oversee military power and diplomatic negotiations, liberal and mechanical arts, and breeding. Prince Pon, Hoh's second in command, governs national security. Sin, the court sage, superintends an astrologer, cosmographer, geometer, physicist, rhetorician, grammarian, doctor, political scientist, and moralist.

Much of the City of the Sun and its contents are covered with recognizable symbols. Prince Sin's staff resorts to a single compendium comprised of Pythagorean wisdom. The lore of the City of the Sun—symbolized by stars, Euclidean and Archimedean figures, a world map, tablets containing foreign law codes, and alphabets—inspires wall and temple decorators and arras-makers, whose drawings serve as daily instruction. In like fashion, painted on the wall of the second circle are minerals, metals, stones, bodies of water, wines, oils, and healing nostrums. The third circle honors herbs, trees, and water animals. The fourth circle pictures birds, particularly the phoenix, alongside "reptiles, serpents, dragons, worms and insects like flies, ox-flies, and so on." The last two circles revere Earth's animals and inventions. In the final circle, the seaman records "Moses, Osiris, Jupiter, Mercury, Mahomet," as well as Jesus, his Apostles, Caesar, Alexander, and Pyrrhus. From a study of foreign language, local scholars expand their knowledge of the world and dispatch ambassadors to other countries to observe and benefit from distant customs.

Campanella assigns the role of perpetuating Sun City to the third staff member, Prince Mor, who concentrates on eugenics as well as education, healing, planting, nutrition, clothing, and courtship. The resulting human climate is a model commune, where no one owns property and all are encouraged to work the standard four-hour day and love the commonwealth as the supreme good. In simple terms,

> . . . they are rich because they want nothing; poor because they possess nothing; and consequently they are not slaves to circumstances, but circumstances serve them.

The narrator attests, "they love their fatherland with a truly amazing force." Magistrates bearing the allegorical titles of "Liberality, Magnanimity, Chastity, Firmness, Criminal and Civil Justice, Diligence, Truth, Kindness, Gratitude and Charity" oversee behavior to ward off crimes against persons. Punishments for transgressions deprive felons of food, worship, and sex "until the judge thinks that they have amended themselves."

Educators in the City of the Sun defeat elitism by reverencing pure science equally with mechanical skills. In order to select a career, four-year-olds observe local artisans in their workshops. By age seven, children study natural science; in the fields they learn husbandry and plowing and honor the plowman, who pilots wagons outfitted with windblown sails and a unique but ill-defined system of "wheels within wheels." The visiting seaman comments that "They laugh at us, who consider our workmen ignoble and hold to be noble those who have learned no trade and live in idleness and also keep in idleness and lasciviousness so many servants that it is the ruin of the republic."

The role of Hoh, or Metaphysic (an office that resembles the all-knowing role of Merlin, Arthur's wizard; the Sioux's visionary, Black Elk; Plato's philosopher-king; or the Vatican Pope), requires full understanding of world cultures, religions, and law. By comprehending the source of all knowledge and skill, the next Hoh—who, like Father Perrault of James Hilton's *Lost Horizon*, mellows during the 35 years preceding his accession—gains sufficient wisdom and patience to rule for the remainder of his life. The seaman comments that, unlike other nations' rulers, who are chosen on the basis of noble lineage, "Hoh knows too much ever to be cruel or wicked or tyrannical."

Central to the perpetuation of Campanella's utopia is control of sexuality and the strengthening of the family. As the sailor reports, citizens mock other nations that control animal mating but neglect human procreation. In the City of the Sun, casual mating is forbidden. Formal coupling is postponed until women reach age 19 and men two years beyond, a time celebrated with coming-of-age songs. However, officials allow men intercourse with sterile or pregnant women to provide sexual release. They make no similar gesture to women, who, in Campanella's time, were not accorded sexual equality. Such tolerance of physical release does not extend to sodomy, which is punished by the wearing of a shoe about the neck (symbolic of perversion) for the first offense and death for the second. Matrons coordinate procreation by mating tall with short and thin with fat to even out inherited traits. Marital relations occur every third day after proper digestion, rest, prayer, and contemplation of beauty. At the appropriate hour, which is determined by the astrologer, the matron summons the man and woman for mutual bedding.

The role of mothers, who breast-feed their offspring for two years, diminishes with weaning. In the style of the Spartan system reported by Plutarch, parents pass girl toddlers to female instructors and boys to male mentors. In accordance with Juvenal's dictum "Mens sana in corpore sano" (A sound mind in a sound body), Sun City children are expected to develop totally. After training in running, wrestling, alphabet, drawing, and languages, young people are assigned jobs appropriate to their talents. Metaphysicus, their master, names them Roman style—according to peculiarities, e.g., Pulcher (handsome), Naso (big-nosed), Cranipes (fat legs), Torvus (bent), Macer (skinny), Aureus (golden), Excellens (excellent), Strenuus (strong), Fortis (bold), or Africanus, Asiaticus, Etruscus, or other nationalities of conquered enemies.

The good life for women depends on fertility. Barren women change mates until they produce. Sterile women live freely in society but lack the honor accorded matrons, who sit at Council and attend temple rituals. This system of honor to women—a more benign arrangement than the female bondage of potential breeders in Margaret Atwood's *The Handmaid's Tale* (1985) or a similar disparagement of motherhood in Lois Lowry's *The Giver* (1993)—allows much individual freedom and the opportunity to train for the military, in which women engage alongside men. Stringent punishment awaits the female dissident: A death sentence falls on any vain woman who makes up her face or wears high heels. Rather, women are expected to remain naturally lovely by exercising to produce a clear complexion and smooth limbs. There is no parallel of punishment for men.

At the heart of Campanella's heliopolis is the sun, the life sustainer in primitive animistic culture. Residents pray to the sun four times each day—east upon arising, west at noon, south in afternoon, and north at nightfall. To emphasize their devotion to light, they reject black clothing and avoid the Japanese, who frequently dress in black. In the City of the Sun, prayers reflect the simplicity of their faith: They ask only for health and contentment for all people. Their diet, consisting of meat, butter, honey, cheese, herbs, vegetables, fruit, and moderate wine consumption, varies according to age and state of health.

Campanella works hard to spare his city from suffering. Citizens live well and encounter little disease, including gout, which was a major cause of immobility in the seventeenth century. To ease advancing age, Sun City residents live abstemiously, control diet and exercise, maintain an interest in activity, and avoid gluttony and tippling. They heal temporary discomforts with naturopathic remedies, e.g., soothing baths, trips to the country, olive-oil massage, aromatherapy, light foods, tepid drinks, herbs, meditation, and prayer. At death, each citizen's remains are incinerated so that fire will return the spirit to the only deity, the sun. There is no ritual funeral or mourning. Hoh, the chief priest, leads prayer, which always petitions the Almighty for health and happiness.

Perhaps as a result of asceticism and attention to well-being, the City of the Sun maintains an optimistic outlook. Citizens abjure lengthy trials, prisons, and torture; allow appeals of court sentences; and punish by banishing from the common table or shunning, a practice still found among Mennonites, Mormons, and the Amish of Pennsylvania. Courts whip or exile criminals, heretics, and rebels, and immure rebels in a tower. If capital punishment is required, the entire city participates. Like the biblical scenes of community executions and the rabid Particicutions of Margaret Atwood's *The Handmaid's Tale,* everyone gathers either to stone or burn the miscreant. Citizens are expected to cleanse themselves with prayer, sacrifice, and repentance.

The City of the Sun requires few codified laws; the necessary laws are inscribed alongside a list of virtues on a tablet fastened to the temple doors. Citizens are peace-loving and fight only when they must ward off an aggressor. Unwilling to proselytize less enlightened nations, they await a golden age when the whole earth will emulate their customs. To avoid smugness, Sun City citizens remain receptive to other lifestyles in the event that another nation presents a better model of the good life.

In fervid anticipation of a better world, the grand master concludes *La Città del Sole* with a fanatic's optimism:

> Oh, if you knew what our astrologers say of the coming age, and of our age, that has in it more history within a hundred years than all the world had in 4000 years before! of the wonderful inventions of printing and guns, and the use of the magnet, and how it all comes of Mercury, Mars, the Moon, and the Scorpion!

The sea captain, not so sanguine in his outlook, sourly retorts, "Ah, well, God gives all in His good time. They astrologize too much."

Severe criticism of Campanella's philosophy implies the near tyranny of Hoh's rule. At question is the creation of a lockstep municipality from rings, gates, moats, ramparts, and walls decorated with alphabets, laws, and pictures of natural phenomena. The format smacks of a picture puzzle created from oddments culled from utopian literature by Plato and Thomas More. At the heart of matters, Campanella, a bachelor like Plato and St. Augustine, cast his futuristic male in the role of monk or soldier, thus leaving unresolved a thorough explanation of his society's intimate concerns—food and reproduction—which are regulated by an intrusive state. (Campanella 1950; Johnson 1968; Manguel and Guadalupi 1987; Mumford 1959; Negley and Patrick 1952; Parrington 1964; White 1955)

See also asceticism; Augustine, St.; Camelot; Campanella, Fra Tomaso; eugenics; *The Giver*; *The Handmaid's Tale*; Hoh; *Lost Horizon*; Perrault, Father; phoenix; Plato; technology; women in utopia.

THE CITY OF GOD

See De Civitate Dei.

CITY OF THE SUN

See La Città del Sole.

CITY PLANNING

This theme is central to the more mechanistic, less spiritual or cerebral utopias and dystopias. Overall, Western literature contrasts the transcendent otherworldliness of Eastern lore in its concern for earthly civic planning, encompassing a supply of power, work, goods and foodstuffs, transportation, housing, worship, education, and defense. Ranging from tedious architectural details to a comic piling of rocks and bricks into a heavenly birdland, planned metropolises represent a variety of styles and purposes:

- Aristophanes's Cloudcuckooland in his satiric comedy *The Birds* (414 B.C.)

- the layout of Dido's new Carthage and Iulus's Alba Longa, forerunner of Rome, in Virgil's *Aeneid* (19 B.C.)

- Sir Thomas More's moated, fortressed Amaurote, the "shadow town" described by the fictional Hythloday in *Utopia* (1516)

- Francis Bacon's science-oriented town of Bensalem in *The New Atlantis* (1627)

- Charles Fourier's eighteenth-century Harmonia, a commune actualized in Europe and the United States

- Theodor Hertzka's *Freiland*, a worker-managed nation built on the communist models of Karl Marx and Friedrich Engels

- Étienne Cabet's collective units along the Seine River in *Voyage en Icarie* (1840)

- Edward Bulwer-Lytton's technologically advanced subterranean city of Vril-Ya in *The Coming Race* (1871)

- Metropolis, the capital city in Samuel Butler's *Erewhon* (1872), a clever dystopia masked by the speaker's tedious boosterism

- George Orwell's war-plagued Oceania in *1984* (1949)

- Lois Lowry's *The Giver* (1993), a children's dystopia much like Ayn Rand's *Anthem* (1937) in its oppressive rule of citizens and the minutiae of their lives

Laid-back retreats like François Rabelais's Abbey of Thélème and Ernest Callenbach's recycled haven in *Ecotopia* (1975) dominate visionary works by a variety of authors, from L. Frank Baum's vision of Emerald City, Samuel Taylor Coleridge's brief glimpse of Xanadu, and Voltaire's remote Eldorado to the utopian and dystopian cityscapes of William Morris, Edward Bellamy, Yevgeny Zamyatin, Marge Piercy, William Dean Howells, and Ray Bradbury.

As early as Lycurgus's plans for Sparta and Merlin's creation of Camelot, a chivalric retreat where King Arthur could build his idealized justice center, utopian city planning has prioritized the orderly governance of a controlled population. In the most prohibitive settings, the cadres of knights, police, spies, commissioners, priests, or border patrols maintain an essential stasis—a limited number of choices and a daily plan that varies little in style and content from every other day. Johann Andreae's *Christianopolis* (1619), a benevolent seventeenth-century theocracy, epitomizes the medieval walled city. Christianopolis flourishes on the basis of a benign dictatorship that rules over a system of concentric rings about a central stronghold at the heart of a symmetrical network of streets. Similarly altruistic in intent but deterministic in structure is Fra Tomaso Campanella's *Città del Sole* (1602), a subdued, heavily regimented municipality of sun worshipers who take pride in all forms of work, the focal point of urban life. These early examples of planned and controlled colonization perch blissfully among the less sanguine dystopias of twentieth-century fiction; however, regardless of purported bliss, each has its overtones of potential dissent over nagging human issues, especially the treatment of criminals, the intrusion of outsiders, freedom of religion and speech, distribution of wealth, and the socialization of children and youth.

One of the least enticing planned cities is the rigid, futuristic colony in Ayn Rand's fable, *Anthem* (1937), where limited education, barracks, and primitive technology deny the people a say in where they live, with whom they mate, and who is assigned to a careful sweeping of streets, cleaning of sewers, removal of refuse, or sowing of grain. The authoritarian committee that holds the reins of power in this fable resembles the control of a similar but more technologically advanced urban center in Aldous Huxley's *Brave New World* (1932), where human behaviors and individuality are stifled by laboratory eugenics, brainwashing through hypnopaedia, and designer fetuses cloned and conditioned to suit the city's needs rather than their own inclinations. Huxley equips his dystopia with a rare feature—a museum-like control model of life before authoritarian control. On the reservation of Malpais near Santa Fe, New Mexico, tourists can escape the conveyor-belt schematics of London to stroll among the aborigines and gawk at a snake dance and pueblo squalor, a strong contrast to the drug-ruled lives of a populace engineered from conception to the crematory.

Bleaker than the early–twentieth-century dystopias is Gilead in *The Handmaid's Tale* (1985) by Margaret Atwood, an oppressive fascist-conservative New England city that parcels out fertile handmaids to the elite. Gilead's physical layout arises from the need to rehabilitate, brainwash, and place breeders in homes of the wealthy. The rest of the city—public execution arenas, markets, residences, prayer boutiques, and checkpoints—epitomizes the siege mentality of an infertile race stunted by nuclear war, venereal disease, and pollution, and bent on protecting the limited pool of remaining healthy breeders. Parallel to simple home tasks—tending tulip beds, serving trays of lunch, and walking to the meat market to stock the larder—run the vans and staff cars that transport people to hangings, birthings, required monthly gynecological examinations, reassignments to other childless couples, and interrogations. Atwood's juxtaposition of mundane chores with hellish religious fanaticism exposes the principles that guide Gilead's history. From the beginning of totalitarianism into later stages of expulsion of traitors and manipulation of women—who serve the state in rigid tutorial roles, domestic tasks, militaristic guard posts, cleanup squads in radioactive colonies, or sleazy nightclubs/brothels—Gilead spotlights the negative side of city planning, which equates population control with coercion and potential execution.

Not all planned cities dismay as thoroughly as Atwood's Gilead. In James Hilton's *Lost Horizon* (1933), a hidden community in the remote Himalayan peaks of Tibet thrives under the enlightened dictatorship of Father Perrault, a liberal holy man. He withdraws from city government, letting the cycles of nature determine the lifestyle of newcomers who either wander into Shangri-La or are coerced into residence. The effects of temperate climate, blended decor and artistry from a variety of world cultures, Western plumbing and other comfortable amenities, and peace outside the world turmoil impelling nations toward World War II draw both the contemplative Hugh Conway and doers like Miss Brinklow, an obsessive missionary. A little bit of heaven on Earth, Shangri-La entices Miss Brinklow and haunts the memory of Hugh Conway, who gives up the enclosed community by guiding a disgruntled pair to China, then spends the rest of his life searching for his Himalayan utopia. (Andreae 1955; Atwood 1972; Bacon 1905; Butler 1968; Cabet 1973; Callenbach 1975; Campanella 1955; Fourier 1972; Hertzka 1972; Hilton 1993; Lowry 1993; More 1968; Plutarch 1971b; Rand 1946; Tennyson 1989)

See also Anthem; *Brave New World;* Camelot; *Christianopolis; La Città del Sole;* classism; *Ecotopia;* Eldorado; Emerald City; *Erewhon;* eugenics; Freiland; Gilead; *The Giver; The Handmaid's Tale;* Hertzka, Theodor; hypnopaedia; *Lost Horizon; The New Atlantis;* Shangri-La; theocracy; *Utopia; Voyage en Icarie;* Xanadu.

CIVITAS SOLIS

See *La Città del Sole.*

DE CIVITATE DEI

St. Augustine of Hippo began this theocratic masterwork in A.D. 413 and completed it in 426, the era in which the Roman Empire collapsed, leaving its citizens vulnerable to invasion from without, and ethical depletion and corruption from within. Impelled by the horror of the Visigoths' sack of Rome in 410, Augustine visualized an escape from earthly strife and the cyclical ups and downs that formed the human cosmology. To Augustine, the Bible promises a godly respite that beckons to those who live by biblical teachings. In his five-part, 22-book utopia, he calls on scripture—particularly Genesis, the Old Testament prophets, Psalms, and Paul's letters—to uphold Christian interpretations of past, present, and future events: the corruption and fall of Rome, Christianity's advancement over paganism, divine justice, providence, the afterlife, the failure of polytheism, creation, humanity's free choice between good and evil, original sin, and a contrast of the cities of God and man. He leads to a deterministic coda: the punishment due the unrighteous cities and the lasting happiness guaranteed to those who live in the city of God.

Although caught up in praise of human ingenuity, skill, artistry, and military might, in Book 22 Augustine makes plain his condemnation of Rome's graft and idolatry, which sprang from debased political leaders and manipulative, power-hungry priests. In wickedness and venality, Rome, Augustine's model of the *civitas terrena* (earthly city), evolves into an abysmally soulless, decadent civilization. Augustine remarks that the city of Mammon "has made for herself, according to her heart's desire, false gods out of any sources at all, even out of human beings, that she might adore them with sacrifices." With the fervor of Jeremiah, Daniel, and the other vehement prophets of the Old Testament, Augustine lays the blame for the decline on Rome itself, a world power that willingly indulges its carnal desires and persecutes the innocent. He thunders that the last judgment will result in "its appointed end—an end which will have no end."

In unequivocal didacticism, Augustine contrasts the lost and the saved. He fashions a graphic picture of a spiritual city that rejects the degradation of earthly habits and turns away from temptation. Unlike the city of Earth, the city of God, "living like a wayfarer in this world, makes no false gods for herself. On the contrary, she herself is made by the true God that she may be herself a true sacrifice to Him." Like the serenity of Eden before the fall, he returns to a historical era unhampered by greed, lust, and sin, a time when temperance, prudence, justice, fortitude, and love rule human relations. This godly municipality was not made by human plan or worldly wisdom. As Augustus describes it at the end of Book 3, the blissful city is a place where a resplendent deity will receive adequate reverence, a place that "has as its goal that reward of all holiness whether in the society of saints on earth or in that of angels of heaven, which is that God may be all in all."

In Books 19–21, St. Augustine outlines the hierarchy of human associations, beginning with the home and city and spreading outward to the world. In rolling hyperbole and with the oratorical gusto of a master preacher, he declares that "the sons of Adam" are beset with a host of mortal frailties:

> . . . heartaches, troubles, griefs, and fears; such insane joys in discord, strife, and war; such wrath and plots of enemies, deceivers, sycophants; such fraud and theft and robbery; such perfidy and pride, envy and ambition; homicide and murder, cruelty and savagery, lawlessness and lust; all the shameless passions of the impure—fornication and adultery, incest and unnatural sins, rape and countless other uncleannesses too nasty to be mentioned; the sins against religion—sacrilege and heresy, blasphemy and perjury; the iniquities against our neighbor—calumnies and cheating, lies and false witness, violence to persons and property; the injustices of the courts and the innumerable other miseries and maladies that fill the world.

Against the engulfing tide of sin, a single weak individual has but one hope—an unwavering faith in God and a willingness to serve and defend Him. Earnest faith, according to Augustine, is the unfailing tie that secures the penitent soul to heaven. At the end of the millennium, he promises that the faithful will know resurrection of the body and will earn lasting peace and freedom from all adversity.

Augustine presages that those who please God will see with the heart's eyes and will know a depth of beauty and glory beyond earthly imagination.

An illustration from a fifteenth century French manuscript of St. Augustine's *De Civitate Dei*, or *City of God*, shows death resulting from temptation.

In the New Jerusalem, the redeemed will share with angels and ranks of saints a "house of the New Testament," a lustrous, glorious edifice studded with precious jewels, a permanent haven that will never fall to ruin. In the confines of a hall dedicated to Christian faith, charity, and freedom from earthly temptation, the redeemed Christian "shall rest and see, see and love, love and praise— for this is to be the end without the end of all our living, that Kingdom without end, the real goal of our present life." (Augustine 1981; Bechtel 1981; Bogan 1984; Boorstin 1992; Burke 1984; Gibb and Montgomery 1980; Gilson 1983; Johnson 1968; Lawless 1987; Negley and Patrick 1952; O'Daly 1987)

See also asceticism; Augustine, St.; didacticism; heaven; religion; theocracy.

 # CLAIRVOYANCE

Clairvoyance is the ability to gaze into the future to learn future events. Unlike clairaudience, which presents sounds from the future, or telepathy, which provides awareness of others' thoughts and which channels current speech and thought into other people's minds, clairvoyance is restricted to viewing, a useful form of divination or extrasensory perception (ESP). A straightforward account of a shaman's introduction to the future is the 12-day vision of 9-year-old Black Elk, an Oglala Sioux holy man who begins with clairaudience and proceeds to an expansive heavenly vision. Black Elk visualizes a conference of "grandfathers" among the clouds. The sixth to speak lays a heavy onus on so small a priest as Black Elk: "My boy, have courage, for my power shall be yours, and you shall need it, for your nation on the earth will have great troubles."

Black Elk's complex vision of the encroachment of white settlers depicts the unity of his people in terms of a circle, the center of which is a ceremonial stake that grows into a blossoming tree. Over four roads, his people travel to their campsite. On the fourth ascent, they suffer famine; the holy tree dies. The circle fragments, creating an omen that, to an animistic priest, equates with the end of the world. Back through the clouds Black Elk travels on a mighty horse to his earthly body, which lies inert in his family's tepee. No longer an ordinary boy, he languishes because the vision has singled him out for greatness. Looking back on the trance later, he recalls that he was too young to understand the disturbing ramifications of the vision. Throughout his years of service as healer and prophet, he undergoes dramatic visitations, which are meant to return his energies to helping the Sioux cope with change.

In Chapter 22 of John G. Neihardt's *Black Elk Speaks* (1932), the famed healer and sage dances with his tribe, who weep and pray for a return of the old ways, now impossible because of the destruction of the buffalo herds. He slips out of his body and floats across a ridge to "a beautiful land where many, many people were camping in a great circle. I could see that they were happy and had plenty." The drying meat, clean air, and green pasturage renews Black Elk's hopes. An unidentified man indicates that Black Elk has reached the land of his dead father, but says that Black Elk must return to Earth to finish his mission—to comfort those few who survive the Battle of Wounded Knee. No longer a child, Black Elk faces an existential truth: His tribe is at the end of its dream. Burdened with existential thoughts of his nation's extermination, he returns to the specter of the broken circle: "The nation's hoop is broken and scattered. There is no center any longer, and the sacred tree is dead."

Less dramatic than Black Elk's impetus to strengthen his tribe is the motivating force that leads the unnamed speaker of William Morris's *News from Nowhere* (1890) into a waking dream (possibly clairvoyant). It carries him away from the dust and despair of the Industrial Revolution into a bucolic farm scene where workers join to harvest grain. Perhaps the author intends to prophesy the birth of socialism or predict a mass denunciation of Victorian features such as crowded cities, dank coal mines, and smoke-belching factories. By expecting less, the characters live simple rural lives dependent on agrarian toil. Whatever the reason for this detailed dreamscape, the speaker reluctantly parts with the idyll that carries him by boat from Hammersmith to less populous regions where workers enjoy one another's company and the shared fatigue of non-competitive outdoor labor.

In a third example, clairvoyance colors the mood of fleeing rabbits in Chapter 28 of Richard Adams's *Watership Down* (1972). Following a brush with a man armed with a shotgun, the animals sniff for signs of danger. Fiver, the visionary who began the exodus by warning his brother of impending doom, speaks words that elude the earth-centered philosophy of his brother:

> Well, there's another place—another country, isn't there? We go there when we sleep; at other times, too; and when we die. El-ahrairah [the rabbit deity] comes and goes between the two as he wants, I suppose, but I could never quite make that out, from the tales.

Fiver adds that some members of the warren assume that the other country is a placid haven, but that he is not so sure the place is safe. Enigmatically, he asks, "And where are we really—there or here?" The existential question stymies his warrenmates, who lack his gift of second sight and his ability to look beyond earthly life to an altered state in the life beyond death.

One of the strongest antiwar uses of clairvoyance occurs in James Hilton's utopian novel *Lost Horizon* (1933), a work that links outsiders with the timeless beauties of Shangri-La, a Tibetan monastery. Father Perrault, the Himalayan city's high lama, is a fragile holy man who lives well beyond 100 years. Capable of telepathy and clairvoyance, Perrault sips a soothing tea made from the *tangatse* berry and looks ahead to "doom that gathers around on every side," a time when he will need a successor. In Chapter 8 he claims to have foreseen World War I, a time when "all the loveliest things were transient and perishable, and that war, lust, and brutality might some day crush them until there were no more left in the world." His ability to coordinate information about past wars, present needs, and future conflicts on land and sea leads him to select Hugh "Glory" Conway as a likely spiritual leader. Optimistically, Father Perrault adds, "Then, my son, when the strong have devoured each other, the Christian ethic may at last be fulfilled, and the meek shall inherit the earth." (Adams 1972; Hilton 1933; Morris 1968a; Neihardt 1961)

See also Black Elk; Conway, Hugh; *Lost Horizon; News from Nowhere;* Perrault, Father; prophecy; Shangri-La; *Watership Down.*

CLARKE, ARTHUR C.

An unusual blend of scientist, inventor, and futurist, Clarke is also a prolific writer of sci-fi thrillers, nonfiction, screenplays, speeches, and speculative fiction, including these:

- *Childhood's End* (1953), his early masterpiece and most hopeful futuristic philosophy

- *2001: A Space Odyssey* (1968), which was made into an award-winning movie written by Clarke and Stanley Kubrick

- The sequel, *2010: Odyssey Two* (1982), a lesser work that attempts to clarify obscurities in *2001*

The son of Nora Willis and farmer Charles Wright Clarke, Arthur Charles Clarke was born December 16, 1917, in Minehead, Somerset, England. His interest in science began in childhood, when he used a homemade telescope to map the moon. At age 13, he focused on outer-space communication and travel after coming across a wrinkled science-fiction magazine. In his late teens, he read H. G. Wells's novels and began emulating them with his own fiction. Because he lacked money for tuition, he worked as an auditor for the British treasury and spent most of his spare time meeting fellow space-travel fans and science-fiction writers.

While maintaining private experiments and membership in the British Interplanetary Society, Clarke attended King's College in London; he graduated with honors and a B.S. degree in mathematics and physics from the University of London. Early in his career, he developed a sideline interest—underwater photography. During World War II, he served the Royal Air Force as an editor and technical officer in charge of an experimental radar project. In 1945 he earned honors for inventing a communications satellite that was not completed until April 1965, when the Early Bird satellite system was launched into space. He returned to the University of London in 1949 to study astronomy and edit *Science Abstracts.* By 1951 he committed himself to freelance writing of fiction and nonfiction and, in a class with Jules Verne, Michael Crichton, Carl Sagan, and Isaac Asimov, became one of the world's top popularizers of speculative science.

Clarke married Marilyn Mayfield in 1953 and settled in Colombo, Sri Lanka, to write, study undersea exploration and photography, and lead ocean-floor safaris with his partner, Mike Wilson. Clarke continued to write, invent, and develop ideas for astronautics and aeronautics, which have kept his name at the forefront of space exploration, and to propose feasible methods of communicating with extraterrestrial life. Recognition of his scientific acumen has also come from the Marconi International Fellowship commission, Franklin Institute, and Physical Research Laboratory of Ahmedabad, India; in addition, he received a fellowship from his alma mater, King's College.

An early proponent of the use of earth-orbiting communication links, Clarke has lectured widely and, from the 1940s to the present, produced articles for *Life, Holiday, Horizon, Vogue, Playboy, Wireless World,* and the *New York Times.* His first novel, *Prelude to Space* (1951), was followed by several decades of productive writing, particularly *Rendezvous with Rama* (1973) and *The Fountains of Paradise* (1979). In 1968 his work with Stanley Kubrick on the movie *2001: A Space Odyssey* earned an Oscar. Clarke authored a 13-week television series, *Arthur C. Clarke's Mysterious World* (1980; released on video in 1989), and its sequel, *Arthur C. Clarke's World of Strange Powers,* which brought recognition from scientists and the public.

Clarke is a member of the Academy of Astronautics and the Royal Astronomical Society, and is past president of the British Interplanetary Society. His awards include the 1961 UNESCO Kalinga Prize, the title of Grand Master from the Science Fiction Writers of America, and the Bradford Washburn Award, a Westhinghouse tribute for science writing, and recognition from *Hugo, Nebula, Jupiter,* and *Galaxy* magazines and the John W. Campbell Foundation, all for *Rendezvous with Rama.* One of his most prized honors was on-air assistance of Walter Cronkite's coverage of the Apollo moon shots on CBS. (Bernstein 1969; Clarke 1953; Clarke 1990; Rabkin 1979; Slusser 1977a; Sullivan 1992)

See also Childhood's End; classism; Karellen; speculative fiction; Wells, H. G.

 # CLASSISM

A severe separation of people into rigid work details, classes, or castes determined by heritage, birth, wealth, intelligence, work, status, or possessions, classism is an integral theme in utopian literature, permeating numerous works:

- a hierarchy of snobbish, isolationist birds over humankind in Aristophanes's satiric comedy *The Birds* (414 B.C.)

- an aristocratic perfecting of the prototypically well-schooled, well-mannered man of the world in Castiglione's *The Courtier* (1528)

- the winnowing out of lesser mortals from the beautiful people who enjoy the Abbey of Thélème in Rabelais's *Gargantua and Pantagruel* (1562)

- H. G. Wells's stark contrast between effete Earth-dwellers and their carnivorous alter egos who subsist in dark underground lairs in his futuristic novel *The Time Machine* (1895)

- the medieval demarcation between lord and serf in Mark Twain's *A Connecticut Yankee in King Arthur's Court* (1886)

- the sexist American territory visited by Aristides Homos, an emissary from Altruria sent to study other governmental systems in William Dean

Howells's *Traveler from Altruria* (1872) and its sequel, *Through the Eye of the Needle* (1907)

- Jack London's prediction of a Marxist-style workers' revolt against a plutocratic coterie of professionals and inheritors of wealth in *The Iron Heel* (1907)

- a rigid separation of ruling bureaucracy, office drones, and unschooled proles in George Orwell's scathingly dystopic *1984* (1949)

- the five-stage factory-engineered cosmos peopled with a staggered stratification of IQ in castes conditioned to be Alphas, Betas, Gammas, and the lowest, Deltas and Epsilons, in Aldous Huxley's *Brave New World* (1932)

- an arbitrary assignment to squadrons of manual laborers in Ayn Rand's fable, *Anthem* (1937)

- the system of Overlords that controls Earth in a benign thralldom for half a century in Arthur C. Clarke's *Childhood's End* (1953)

- a Brahman's departure from his caste on an exploratory self-examination in Hermann Hesse's pseudobiography of Buddha, *Siddhartha* (1951)

- a natural antipathy between staid English citizens and rapacious teen gangs in Anthony Burgess's imaginative *A Clockwork Orange* (1962)

- the delineation of women as Wives, Daughters, Marthas, Econo-Wives, Aunts, and Handmaids in Margaret Atwood's *The Handmaid's Tale* (1985)

- the killing of excess people in each echelon of 50 citizens in Lois Lowry's *The Giver* (1993)

Although these novels separate people by a variety of modes—lifestyle, birth, heritage, education, conduct, or purpose—the concept of increased national value to one and enslavement to another remains the delineating factor in theme and characterization.

The social scene in Mark Twain's fantasy novel reconstructs a historical reality—the strict hierarchy of medieval Europe that was founded on the concept of the divine right of kings. In Chapter 29, Hank Morgan, the Time Traveller from the future who journeys incognito with King Arthur among the serf caste, must prepare the king with a crude haircut and lessons in humility. Hank recognizes in Arthur an abhorrent, ingrained superiority. Because Hank admires the king, he forgives him for acting on the prevailing attitude of noblesse oblige and for looking "as humble as the leaning tower at Pisa":

> He was born so, educated so, his veins were full of ancestral blood that was rotten with this sort of unconscious brutality, brought down by inheritance from a long procession of hearts that had each done its share toward poisoning the stream.

Through reason and discreet commentary, Hank educates Arthur in abandoning the status quo for serfs and in genuine compassion and concern for one nameless family of undereducated, underfed, plague-ridden victims of lord and church.

Later utopian works champion a similar interest in humanitarianism and civil rights. In Orwell's *1984*, the lowest class—called proles, a shortened form of the word proletarians—remains free of society's strictures because they perform the lowest level of work in Oceania and offer the least vulnerability to brainwashing and manipulation. Set apart in ghettos from the professional and ruling classes, the proles perpetuate an existence that mimics the nearly defunct London that Oceania has attempted to destroy. Similarly, Aldous Huxley's *Brave New World* (1932) sets against a backdrop of pleasure-sogged futurism the equivalent of reservation savages who, like undereducated proles, survive in poverty and ignorance in Malpais, a New Mexican compound. Because of their bizarre rituals and passé mores and behavior, the savages become tourist attractions for the Alpha-plus elite, the only utopians allowed a view of the raw life that is now forbidden in the mechanized world-state. Most titillating to visitors is their perpetuation of vivaparous reproduction. Because Huxley's dystopia has replaced human sex with conveyor-belt reproductive factories, workers now stamp the in vitro fetus with its class before decanting, and socialize the infant to accept a predetermined caste.

Ayn Rand's *Anthem*, a less detailed version of a divided but no less rigid society than those created by Twain, Orwell, and Huxley, places young people in lowly jobs such as street sweeper or farm menial, and isolates them in kibbutz-style dormitories. To maintain their satisfaction at a minimal level of attainment, the governing councils provide brainwashing assemblies, which resemble the solidarity meetings and hypnopaedia of *Brave New World* and Hate Week in *1984*. Escape for Rand's main characters takes them away from society to complete isolation in the forest, where class is no longer a viable subject. Introduced to the pronoun I, the prototypical Adam and Eve begin a family and relearn the values that inspired early human beings to think for themselves.

In an extreme form of dystopian classism, H. G. Wells's *The Time Machine* creates so sharp a division in England's future between the privileged Eloi and the dronelike Morlocks that the latter live underground, reek like earthworms, and, because of their intolerance for light, venture to the surface of Earth only at night. As Darwin predicted in his concept of survival of the fittest, the Morlocks grow strong in their daily struggle and terrify the gentle, helpless Eloi, whose only weapon against these dark subterraneans is fire. Because of the Morlocks' foul smell, bedraggled appearance, and Neanderthal behavior, the Time Traveller recoils from them and their cannibalism and treachery. In remaining too long among them, he loses Weena, the guardian Eloi who guides him through the idyllic world; he stays too long in the forest and is consumed by the atavistic throwbacks.

In his mindlessly violent dystopian London, Anthony Burgess takes the class system one step further, toward anarchy. His juvenile delinquents, who prey on aged or helpless English citizens in *A Clockwork Orange*, demonstrate a predatory form of class revolt against the effete middle class, with whom the gang has nothing in common. Amoral to the point of bestiality, these roving bands of uncouth, uncivilized teenage boys grow so devoid of purpose that they prey on one another and victimize their leader, Alex.

In a similar schism of privileged aristocrats and gutter society, Hermann Hesse utilizes the theme of classism in a more familiar form. In a theocratic version of classism, his *Siddhartha* focuses on the title character, who is the son of a Brahmin, the intellectual elite of a Hindu world that has survived India's metamorphosis from colony to sovereign nation. To connect with some spiritual meaning that will enliven his depressed life, Siddhartha abandons his patrimony, joins with his best friend, and enters a commune of holy men who seek answers to religious questions. By the end of his long inward journey from sensuality to transcendent acceptance, Siddhartha travels so far beyond India's rigid caste structure that he bears little resemblance to his earlier self. In study and emulation of all facets of human destiny, he reaches nirvana, the divine haven produced by merging his spirit with the universal oversoul.

A modern dystopia that has earned Margaret Atwood a place in the genre, *The Handmaid's Tale* skewers a religious classism that places fundamentalists over sinful homosexuals, divorcées, and the aged in a doomed attempt to compensate for failing fertility. Following nuclear war, as more women and men lose their powers to reproduce, the ruling class conceives of an antifemale method of acquiring converts. By subjugating fertile females to the will of a childless ruling-class family, society perpetuates both its species and the grim fascism that turns womb culture into a pseudo-ritual. Young women who undergo stringent conditioning are meted out to childless couples, are fed like fattening hogs, and participate in mating ceremonies intended to produce the next generation of Gilead's citizens. If the "walking wombs" give birth to viable children, they surrender their maternity but maintain a degree of honor that places them outside the ruling class and above the breeders who await a chance to conceive. (Burgess 1962; Castiglione 1976; Clarke 1953; Hesse 1951; Howells 1907; Howells 1957; Huxley 1932; Orwell 1949; Rand 1946; Twain 1963; Wells 1964)

See also Alex; *Anthem*; bestiality; *The Birds*; *Brave New World*; *Childhood's End*; *A Connecticut Yankee in King Arthur's Court*; *The Courtier*; Eloi; *The Giver*; humanitarianism; *The Iron Heel*; *Lost Horizon*; Morlocks; *1984*; nirvana; Siddhartha; *Siddhartha*; *Through the Eye of the Needle*; *The Time Machine*; *A Traveler from Altruria*; Weena; women in utopia.

A CLOCKWORK ORANGE

This slangy, unsettling, and violently dystopic novel was written by Anthony Burgess in 1962 and filmed by Stanley Kubrick in 1971. The pessimistic vision of a world order severely distorted by amoral punks who haunt the night touches on numerous subjects common to the dystopian genre, e.g., brainwashing, social engineering, loss of individual freedoms, and suspect uses of technology. This generation's bleak modus operandi is replete with varied forms of terrorism—theft, rape, beatings, and murder of vulnerable targets. Fleshed out with criminal fantasies, Alex's group acts out the need to combat the failing family unit and to glorify the general dissipation and destruction of social mores. Critical and public response to Burgess's cruel, chaotic, and highly controversial cosmos, as well as to the movie version, remains mixed. Nonetheless, the film earned kudos from William Burroughs and Roald Dahl, as well as two Academy Award nominations, for best film and for Stanley Kubrick's direction.

Prefiguring punk and grunge movements of the 1980s and 1990s, the story is told to unidentified "brothers" by 15-year-old Alex, who has served time in reform school. The action spotlights an English gang composed of Alex, Pete, Georgie, and Dim, an aimless, ambitionless quartet who hang out at a bar called the Duke of New York. The teenagers terrorize the streets in random, impersonal attacks arising from boredom and spiritual emptiness. The gang targets Slouse's shop on Attlee Avenue; they assault the owners, empty the till, and steal cigarettes. The boys return to their base, establish an alibi, and feign innocence to the police. Later, they rough up a derelict.

At the Municipal Power Plant, they encounter Billyboy and his five gang members. Alex's band takes on the challenge and, swinging chains and striking with knives, routs the opposing gang. Before the police arrive, the foursome steal a car outside the Filmdrome in Priestley Place and drive to a village. By deceiving the woman who answers the door, they gain entrance to her home, maul her and her husband, and rend his humanistic book, entitled "A Clockwork Orange." A sentence from the work stands out in Alex's mind:

> The attempt to impose upon man, a creature of growth and capable of sweetness, to ooze juicily at the last round the bearded lips of God, to attempt to impose, I say, laws and conditions appropriate to a mechanical creation, against this I raise my sword-pen—

With the hapless author's utopian concept left in shreds, Alex joins his buddies and rides back to their "milkbar" in town. After a brief set-to with Dim, Alex departs for home and relaxes with classical music by Bach and Mozart.

A realistic factor in Burgess's dystopic miasma is the absence of parental discipline. Alex's father, who exercises little influence over the youth's activities, reports a dream in which Alex falls victim to the gang. In the next major crime scene, Alex's father's dream comes true. During an attack on a residence, Georgie, Pete, and Dim victimize an elderly woman. They arrange for Alex to be arrested and to face the full weight of the consequences, a prison sentence for murder.

In Burgess's depiction, prison puts Alex in close contact with more thugs. He learns that Georgie has died while burglarizing a house. In Part 2, the prison program insists on compliance, yet prisoners continue to savage one another. Following the bashing of his cellmate, Alex agrees to be the "trailblazer" by undergoing Ludovico's Technique, an experimental treatment similar to B. F. Skinner's behavior modification, which is intended to alter Alex's viciousness into submission to law and civility. As planned, Brodsky and Branom, the prison doctors, administer the drug and force Alex to watch horror films, a melange

Alex, protagonist of *A Clockwork Orange,* raises his glass as he sits with companions in the Korova Milkbar. The scene is from director Stanley Kubrick's 1971 film version of the Anthony Burgess novel.

of loathsome violence, torture, and war. The gruesome images terrify him; he pleads in vain to be set free from the experiment. As planned, Alex evolves into a seemingly Christian youth and gains release from prison on the basis of his altered behavior.

Burgess juggles the street milieu as a test of Alex's rehabilitation. In the third segment of *A Clockwork Orange,* Alex resumes his life in a changed world: London has achieved a utopian serenity. Streets are no longer havens for teenage thugs; even the walls are spared graffiti. He returns to his family and laments that their lodger, Joe, has taken his place. Alex walks the streets, enters a public library, and reads from the Bible. He is so filled with despair that he contemplates suicide. The author he had assaulted recognizes him and offers emotional support.

Because Ludovico's Technique appears to have transformed a hellish society into a model city, the authorities employ the brainwashing system broadly and effectively. Billyboy and Dim serve as police and apply their former cruelties to Alex, who is no longer able to commit brutal acts. Disheartened, Alex wanders the streets in search of home. The author, F. Alexander, welcomes him with food, warmth, and a bed. During the night, Alex locates and reads a copy of "A Clockwork Orange." The next morning, Alexander telephones people from "the Party" who can help Alex. The combination of classical music and a pamphlet advocating the overthrow of the government drive Alex to leap from a window. He recovers from his injuries in the hospital, where he receives a visit from his parents. From newspaper stories Alex learns that he is the subject of a rebellion against the government's brainwashing program. The novel concludes on an ambiguous note. F. Alexander learns that Alex took part in the attack that killed his wife.

Burgess's conclusion leaves the reader with a mixed set of dystopic images. Alex awakens in the hospital and finds himself tied to the bed. His saviors explain that he has been duped into a false program. Ultimately, Alex defeats behavior modification and takes solace from classical music. In the original English version of the novel, an additional chapter concludes the action with a skip in time, which shows Alex as a mature man haunted by guilt and fantasizing a return to childhood and innocence. The American version, shortened by this redeeming, optimistic chapter, concludes with Alex's delight in Beethoven's *Ninth Symphony* and the mindless violence of his teenage years. (Aggler 1986; Bloom 1987a; Burgess 1962; Coale 1981; Dix 1971; Mathews 1978; Morris 1971)

See also Alex; Burgess, Anthony; dystopia; futurism; Ludovico's Technique; technology.

CLOUDCUCKOOLAND, OR LAND OF COCKAIGNE

The English translation of the Greek *Nephelococcygia,* this manmade city for all species of birds is the setting and focus of Aristophanes's *The Birds* (414 B.C.). Created by Pisthetairos (Greek for Friend-Persuader), a street-smart utopian, Cloudcuckooland rises on a stretch of desert, a walled-off piece of heaven above Attica's Plain of Phlegra. The construction takes place in rapid order as 30,000 cranes ferry stones for foundations and 10,000 storks make bricks. Formed by the squaring of a circle, the bird realm is centered by a public square; avenues radiate outward like spokes. In Cloudcuckooland, birds usurp the powers of the Greek gods Zeus and Herakles by intercepting the rich fragrance arising from sacrificial altars and starving the gods. To assure serenity, the birds also eject such petty, meddling earthlings and potential immigrants as Cinesias the poetaster, a street preacher, an unctuous priest, a professional snoop, a lobbyist, and Meton, a noted astronomer.

Aristophanes's utopia is devoid of political connivance, taxes, greed, interest-peddling, and strong-arm governments; although suspenseful and comic in nature, it serves the author's satiric purpose: to expose the absurdity of Athens's expensive expedition to Sicily in 415 B.C. By mirroring earthly discontent at high taxes and pork-barrel politics, *The Birds* contains a germ of critical truth among a series of belly laughs at Herakles's hunger pangs and actors decked out in feathers and beaks. Paralleling the decline of late-fifth-century Athens during its treasury-depleting rivalry with Sparta, Cloudcuckooland extends a welcome to two world-weary Athenians who can no longer tolerate the pettiness of local politics or the undermining of their native deme. The story ends on a typically Greek note: compromise between gods and men and a bride for

Pisthetairos, Basileia (Greek for Sovereignty), who is Zeus's daughter and the maker of lightning.

So serious was the breakdown of Athenian might and civil integrity that Aristophanes's satire brought immediate theme recognition to audiences who themselves rebuked the city-state's faults. Preoccupied with epidemics, refugees, a second Peloponnesian cataclysm, and threats to national security, government leaders floundered amid assaults on personal freedoms and traditions, especially worship. Thus, Cloudcuckooland, which was built by a genuinely cooperative effort, symbolizes the escape that Aristophanes's contemporaries longed for—an orderly Eden, a safe harbor from adversaries, and a positive environment in which to enjoy simple pleasures. To celebrate their carefree birdland, the citizens host a joyous reception for Pisthetairos, who graciously receives the scepter of Zeus along with his daughter Basileia in marriage as a good-will gesture. (Aristophanes 1993; Feder 1986; Gassner and Quinn 1969; Howatson 1991; Lord 1963; Manguel and Guadalupi 1987; Prideaux 1953; Snodgrass 1988a; Spatz 1978; Ussher 1979)

See also Aristophanes; *The Birds;* city planning; disillusion; escapism; fantasy.

 # COLLECTIVISM

A synonym for communism or kibbutz-style living, collectivism is a social theory based on shared labor and public ownership of property, commerce, and utilities. To maintain its hold over society, collectivism—like the liberal system found in several utopian social experiments—sets up rigid laws to control or delete individual rights and freedoms. For example:

- Gerrard Winstanley's visionary *The Law of Freedom* (1652), an early experimental text calling for equality and communes as a means of upgrading the lowest standards of living

- Charles Fourier's Harmonia and other communes in his phalanx system, originated in 1808

- Étienne Cabet's *Voyage en Icarie* (1840) and in his Icarian Movement of the mid-1800s

- Theodor Hertzka's worker-run commune described in *Freiland* (1889), a displacement of free thought and action by substituting a political and economic regime that places the common good above individual needs

According to dedicated visionaries, under the most stringent form of collectivism, the capitalist state—rife with exploitation, nepotism, profiteering, and cynicism—self-destructs, making way for the mandate of a unified proletariat, or working class.

On the opposite end of the continuum from the fantasy and laissez-faire of Fourier or Cabet reside the most serious, iron-fisted collectivists, Karl Marx and Friedrich Engels. Historically, Marx, a tireless activist for organized working-class revolt, accepted exile from Germany and emigrated to England to study arcane documents on economics, finance, and government, which he found in the British Museum library. His detailed notes, filling a 2,500-page, four-volume masterwork, were left at his death for the editing and systematizing of Friedrich Engels, his friend and collaborator. As revealed in *The Communist Manifesto* (1848), the contention of both Marx and Engels was the inevitability of a working-class revolt against overlords, the aristocracy, and capitalists, and the spontaneous birth of a universal collectivism.

In literature, varying degrees of collectivism are often the concept on which authors ground their utopias. Sir Thomas More's *Utopia* (1516), the prototypical utopian treatise, bases its notion of perfection on an equalized social system where all citizens share from a community store, earn a common wage, and enjoy a society devoid of poverty. By eradicating money and private ownership of land and business, More's Utopians eliminate snobbery, luxury, and elitism. However, a significant difference separates Utopia from the totalitarian Marxists of the twentieth century: More's Utopia depends on the democratic election of a prince and magistrates. His improved world also lacks state control of religion, the insidious element in Mark Twain's *A Connecticut Yankee in King Arthur's Court* (1886), a dystopian fantasy that reexamines the social and moral underpinnings of medieval England.

An unconvincingly optimistic view of collectivism, William Morris's *News from Nowhere* (1890) supplants the grim, smoky, brick-shrouded visage of industrialism in nineteenth-century London with a pastoral utopia glimpsed by a visitor from the past. The visitor follows Dick, the leader of a group of grain reapers, upriver by boat to a bucolic setting where food, work, relaxation, and loyalties demonstrate the positive side of group ownership. According to Hammond, a social historian, in the absence of wealthy or intellectual parasites, the new working class welcomes the uplift of self-esteem and the contentment they receive from such manual tasks as cutting grain and tying sheaves. A disciple of the new wave, Hammond declares:

> People flocked into the country villages, and, so to say, flung themselves upon the freed land like a wild beast upon his prey; and in a very little time the villages of England were more populous than they had been since the fourteenth century, and were growing fast.

The resurgence of rural values and cottage industry uproots the degrading miseries of factory work, which often blinded or maimed the unwary, clogged the air and waterways with pollutants, and wearied child workers, who were far too young for the responsibility of overseeing dangerous machinery and completing a full day's work. Freed from acquisitiveness and the monstrously parasitic mercantile class, Morris's utopian England revives pride in handicrafts, learns to savor a day's toil, and comes to appreciate unity in labor.

In contrast to bucolic serenity, a merciless, overpowering juggernaut of collectivism fuels Jack London's *The Iron Heel* (1907). The fictional prophet, Ernest Everhard, berates the well-fed, complacent oligarchy for its lack of concern for the downtrodden and for malicious concealment of unfair monopolies. The emergence of a homeless, hopeless underclass strengthens the Iron Heel, an ominous metaphor for rebellion. The truth of Everhard's accusations and the trampling of opposition come at the cost of careers, fortunes, peace, and lives. Everhard himself expends his energies to the breaking point, leaving his wife Avis to carry on his work through a phalanx of underground anarchists. Perhaps the purest Marxism to be found in utopian fiction, *The Iron Heel* strips the abstract notion of revolution of all its romance in scenes of terror and revenge.

A counterview of collectivism activates the twentieth century's most influential and acclaimed literary dystopias. The focus of three dystopian novels by Ayn Rand—*Anthem* (1937), *The Fountainhead* (1943), and *Atlas Shrugged* (1957)—collectivism epitomizes the dreary world of institutionalized learning, inefficient bureaucracies, governmental tyranny, and regimented lifestyles. In Rand's *Anthem* and in Aldous Huxley's *Brave New World* (1932), characters grow up in managed child-care centers, have no choice of vocation, and endure codes of uniformity engineered to exterminate volition and individuality. Thrust into a state without options or horizons, Rand's protagonist, Equality 7-2521, defeats collectivism by escaping into nature and the past, where he and his mate move into a deserted house, re-create the nuclear family, and learn to appreciate the meaning of "I," symbolic of initiative and individualism. With less success in withdrawing from the hurly-burly of a technologically managed society, Huxley's John the Savage grows disillusioned as he tries to comprehend hedonism, a strict caste system, and drug-dimmed thinking. Ultimately, he attempts to flee society and purify himself of the Brave New World's hedonism. The collapse of his good intentions forces him to suicide.

The extremes of these fictional works imply that the worth of collectivism lies somewhere in the middle. Certainly not a panacea for society's ills, a communistic approach to work and profit can redeem people who live on the fringe, e.g., the handicapped, poor, feebleminded, and refugees. Taken to the opposing limit, however, Rand and Huxley's collective nightmares reach their goals through classism, coercion, punishment, and tyranny. With chilling dystopic logic, *Anthem* and *Brave New World* prove that, without a wholehearted consensus, a modicum of personal freedom, and genuine equality in education, worship, and opportunities, citizens become prisoners with collectivist overlords as their jailers. (Cabet 1973; Fourier 1972; Hertzka 1972; London 1982; Marx 1992; Marx and Engels 1985; More 1963b; Morris 1968b; Rand 1946; Twain 1963)

See also *Anthem*; *Brave New World*; classism; *The Communist Manifesto*; *A Connecticut Yankee in King Arthur's Court*; *Das Kapital*; disillusion; Equality 7-2521; escapism; Everhard, Avis Cunningham; Everhard, Ernest; *Freiland*; *The Iron Heel*; *News from Nowhere*; pastoral; *Utopia*; *Voyage en Icarie*.

THE COMING RACE

Edward Bulwer-Lytton's innovative utopian fantasy was written in 1871 as a thinly veiled prophecy of earthly doom resulting from corruption and human failings. Set below the earth in an imaginative society of winged beings, the story follows the unnamed American protagonist down a rope lowered into a mine shaft to Vril-Ya, a crimefree wonderland discovered by an English mining engineer. The engineer falls to his death, leaving the American alone and terrified of what lies on the lighted path before him.

Lytton draws on lush fantasies to embellish his utopia. The road leads the American past massive buildings decked with Corinthian columns and jeweled walls. Strange and alluring, the air smells sweet and echoes with the songs of exotic birds. A silent figure stands ready to greet and escort the American to a private residence. In this sensual, indolent paradise, the American adventurer learns about the skyless utopia after he follows his guide into a residence where robots attend the family. An elevator lifts him rapidly to a lavish upper chamber where Taë, a 12-year-old boy, breathes against the stranger's forehead and relieves him of pain and anxiety. The family welcomes their visitor to dinner, which consists of unknown foods. At the host's touch on the controls of an elevator, the group again rises to an upstairs chamber filled with books. From the balcony the visitor watches winged beings perform a choreographed air show.

Following a convention of romantic fiction, Lytton complicates the plot with a boy-girl attraction. The host's daughter, Zee, a brilliant philosopher who belongs to the College of Sages, becomes the American's instructor. While her father observes and shakes his head in doubt, the stranger replies to questions about the world above, known to the underground society only in ancient myths. The host makes his visitor pledge to tell no one of the underground society. Zee reveals the uniqueness of Vril-Ya. She introduces him to the wonders of a land powered by *vril*, an electrical force so necessary to the nation that citizens worship the deity who created it. Taë also answers questions, but Zee forbids him to ask about the civilization on the earth's surface.

Lytton hinges the success of his utopia on the sine qua non—the powerful, liquid *vril*. According to Vril-Yan traditions as revealed in Chapter 9, the first underground settlers, the barbaric Ana, were escaping the flood that covered the earth in Noah's time. As they moved deeper into recesses and caverns, they lost touch with the light, but not with their talents:

> The fugitives had carried with them the knowledge of the arts they had practised above ground—arts of culture and civilization. Their earliest want must have been that of supplying below the earth the light they had lost above it; and at no time, even in the traditional period, do the races . . . seem to have been unacquainted with the art of extracting light from gases, or manganese, or petroleum.

The discovery of *vril* enables the subterranean society to destroy, replenish, heal, and preserve. The application of this substance to mining, lighting, and engineering raises their standard of living.

At the time of the novel, the 12,000 families of Vril-Ya enjoy harmony and pure communism. They live crime-free under a mild government administered by magistrates. Countering the threat from reptiles and prehistoric animals is left to young boys, who hunt and kill predators without mercy. Children pursue whatever studies they like and emigrate to outlying colonies without permission from their parents. Marriages are renewable at the end of three years, but generally survive in mutual harmony, as demonstrated by their motto: "No happiness without order, no order without authority, no authority without unity."

Avoiding a frequent stumbling block for utopists, Lytton approaches personal faith in a vague manner. Vril-Yans consider religion a private matter. They withdraw to pray alone or with their children. In opposition to a time when people on Earth argued about the nature of God and evolved an orthodox style of worship, Vril-Yans have ceased studying disruptive "theological speculations." They refer to the supreme being as "the All-Wise, the All-Good, the All-Powerful," who displays the strength, benevolence, and wisdom of the Creator.

A multiracial, crossbred nation blended from the various escapees from Earth's surface, the people grow indolent, enjoy their repose, and frequently walk about town without their wings. They travel by airboats, rid their bodies of impurities with steam baths, and practice aromatherapy as a means of relaxation and naturopathic healing. To assure health, they abstain from alcohol, eat sparingly, and at times bathe with a small amount of rejuvenating *vril*. Their manners and demeanor stress courtesy and contentment.

To relieve his underground utopia of too easy a life, Lytton injects a negative element. This peaceful, even-tempered race must cope with the negative side of *vril*, which is capable of mass destruction. Lytton describes their *vril*-powered military acumen as formidable:

> War between the *vril*-discoverers ceased, for they brought the art of destruction to such perfection as to annul all superiority in numbers, discipline, or military skill. The fire lodged in the hollow of a rod directed by the hand of a child could shatter the strongest fortress or cleave its way from the van to the rear of an embattled host. If army met army, and both had command of this agency, it could be but the annihilation of each.

Instead of making conventional armaments, which they don't need, Vril-Yans apply technology to agricultural innovations, using machines and robots to end drudgery. Precious stones are so common that they adorn simple tools. Thus, without warfare, the commune spreads as a result of the congeniality, generosity, ingenuity, and unity of its people.

The visitor spends much time with Zee and Taë. The boy walks into the wild with the American and saves him from a fierce reptile by one zap of *vril*. The visitor puts on Taë's wings and, like the mythic Icarus, discovers

> I was the servant of the wings; the wings were not my servants—they were beyond my control; and when by a violent strain of muscle . . . I curbed their gyrations and brought them near to the body, it seemed as if I lost the sustaining power stored in them.

In jaunts with Zee, the two suspend flight to equalize their powers. The obvious attraction between Zee and the guest leads the Vril-Yan Commissioner of

Light, Aph-Lin, to observe that such a union would adulterate the race with carnivore traits. Aph-Lin's objection ends with a blunt threat directed at Zee: "If you yield, you will become a cinder."

The romantic motif leads to the timeworn tableau of lovers thrust apart by society. Threatened by the nation's limitless power and his tormenting, forbidden love for Zee, the visitor grows desperate to escape. In Chapter 28, he returns to the shaft by which he entered and finds it blocked. Guided by Taë, he expresses fear of death. Taë indicates that Zee has placed him in danger, but that he will intercede with his father, the supreme ruler, who has sent Zee with a *vril* staff to kill the visitor with a quick, painless blow. The visitor pleads for a chance to escape; Taë points out that Aph-Lin has authorized that the shaft be filled with boulders. Taë is so moved by the visitor's fear of death that he offers to share the experience with him by committing suicide. On the grounds of faith in God, he rationalizes, "The All-Good is no less there than here. Where is He not?" The visitor objects with a standard Christian precept: The God who gives life should choose the time and place to take it away.

In Chapter 29 the visitor reunites with Zee, who risks her life and her citizenship in Vril-Ya by making a new cleft through which the visitor can flee upward to the surface of Earth. During the escape, Zee commands the visitor to hold onto her winged form as she flies upward through the chasm to an occupied gallery in the mine. Weeping at the loss of her love, Zee willingly sacrifices love for her beloved's welfare: "Farewell for ever. Thou wilt not let me go into thy world—thou canst never return to mine." Before the chasm recloses, like a swan she flies back to her sunless, moonless home. The visitor returns to human society and contracts a fatal disease. He thinks wistfully of Zee, his winged savior, yet prays that the coming race will not destroy humankind while he lives. (Bulwer-Lytton 1979; Flower 1973; Manguel and Guadalupi 1987; Mumford 1959)

See also Bulwer-Lytton, Edward; fantasy; speculative fiction; technology; Vril-Ya; women in utopia.

THE COMMANDER

He is the gray-haired, stoop-shouldered head of security in the fundamentalist Republic of Gilead, a suburb of Boston in Margaret Atwood's dystopian fable *The Handmaid's Tale* (1985). Ostensibly a decent, compliant soldier, the Commander follows the prescribed mating ritual designed to provide Gilead with children during a period of declining birthrate. At monthly rituals he reads from the Bible, which is kept in a locked cabinet in the sitting room, and escorts Wife Serena and the unnamed Handmaid (called Offred, for "Of Fred," as were earlier breeders assigned to the Commander) to a chaste upstairs bedroom for prescribed copulation. At one of Offred's monthly physical examinations, the doctor suggests that the Commander may be sterile, a condition that afflicts many survivors of nuclear contamination.

Atwood contrasts a perfunctory side of the Commander with the needful lover and bon vivant. A fatherly man at home, the Commander dispatches his chauffeur to deliver a clandestine message to Offred asking that she visit the Commander's private den. Initially, the illicit visitation proves harmless. The Commander requests a game of Scrabble and a meaningful kiss. He complies with Offred's request for hand lotion and information about the outside world, and savors the sight of her hands stroking moisturizer on rough skin. On a festive occasion, he offers her a sequined and feathered costume, high heels, and makeup, cloaks her from observation, and escorts her by private car to Jezebel's, a shady nightclub. As though squiring a paid escort, he offers her a drink and describes the purpose of prostitution in Gilead where, theoretically, immoral practices no longer exist.

Atwood drains the nightclub fantasy of its allure by closing in on the expected conclusion—seduction in a motel. The Commander leads Offred to a room for the type of copulation that people once took for granted—the casual sexual union of consenting adults. Without his uniform, he appears shrunken and old. Appalled at a situation that requires her to act the part of call girl, Offred performs her part without passion or meaning. After police officials apprehend her for supposedly revealing state secrets, the Commander objects to her arrest without a warrant. Evidence gathered centuries later identifies him as Frederick Waterford and reveals that he was executed for harboring a subversive. (Atwood 1972; *Contemporary Authors* 1989; *Contemporary Literary Criticism* 1987; Davidson 1986; Dreifus 1992; Hammer 1990; Ingersoll 1991; McCombs 1988; *Major Twentieth-Century Writers* 1990; Van Spanckeren and Castro 1988)

See also Atwood, Margaret; city planning; *The Handmaid's Tale*; Lydia, Aunt; materialism; Offred; Serena Joy; speculative fiction; technology; women in utopia.

 # COMMUNISM

See collectivism.

 # *THE COMMUNIST MANIFESTO*

The formalized platform of scientific socialism mandated in 1847 by the League of the Just, a secret society inspired by philosopher Karl Marx, the *Manifesto* represented a compelling vision for a socialist state resulting from the violent overthrow of oppressive aristocracy by the proletariat, or working class. Published in 1848 in London during Marx's self-imposed exile from Germany, this 40-page statement of principle was composed in collaboration with Friedrich Engels. Requiring six weeks of intense writing and revision, the final draft appeared as the *Manifest der Kommunistischen Partei*.

As an outgrowth of local ferment, the *Manifesto* embodies Marx's study of untutored workers in Germany and France, and supplants the inchoate ravings of a disgruntled, landless underclass with a sophisticated polemic predicting that capitalism would self-destruct. He enumerates immediate, specific steps to end bondage. Among his demands are a progressive taxation system, usurpation of hereditary fiefdoms, a universal education system for all classes, free markets, and a classless society. A treasured document to communist nations, this slim tract, organized into four chapters, is the most explosive economic statement of its time.

The acme of Marx's monomania, Chapter 1, which opens with the declaration that previous history is the "history of class struggle," focuses on the problems that workers face in a socioeconomic milieu run by and for the benefit of a small, arrogant landed gentry. Marx and Engels compare the state of affairs to slavery, which they link with less civilized regimes in ancient times. By controlling the means of economic production, capitalistic monopolies exacerbate their constant tension with workers, who have no way but anarchy to express frustration at the unfair distribution of goods and power. This dynamic of proletarians jostling factory owners for a greater share of the wealth produces the energy by which revolutions take shape and alter the status quo.

To offset a constant state of class war, Marx and Engels propose a dramatic alteration of the economy into a classless society in which no one owns land or factories. From the equalization of social status, they anticipate a collapse of oppression and class struggle and the rise of communism, a new and equitable system of distribution. The premise of Marx and Engel's shift from private ownership to collectivism requires working-class bureaucracies to replace the exploitive bourgeois and to manage both labor and service.

In Chapter 2 of the *Manifesto,* Marx and Engels develop the strategies by which the idealized "ruling proletariat" can function to best advantage. The third chapter contrasts other socialist and communistic philosophies and pinpoints their weaknesses. The final segment builds up to communism's most virulent statement of purpose: The only method of dislodging corrupt ruling classes and replacing them with the deserving working class is through violence. The authors conclude with a rallying cry heard around the world: "Workers have nothing to lose but their chains. They have the world to gain. Workers everywhere, unite!"

After publication, this startlingly militant strategy quickly moved from the original German to French, Polish, Danish, Swedish, English, Russian, and Chinese, and on to minor languages, eventually numbering 100. By the middle of the nineteenth century, social and economic theorists were immersed in debate over the implications of dramatic social change that Marx predicted would create a Brotherhood of Man. Marx himself abandoned his original platform and disbanded his Communist League, but a century later the *Manifesto* remained philosophically and politically influential, even though the practical application of Marxist communism had peaked. (Carver 1991; Johnson 1968; Magill 1958; Marx 1992; Marx and Engels 1985; Worsley 1982)

See also collectivism; *Das Kapital;* Engels, Friedrich; Marx, Karl; slavery.

CONDITIONING

Defined as a manipulation of human tissue and/or thought processes to produce predictable, orthodox behavior, conditioning is systematized in B. F. Skinner's *Walden Two* (1948). The long-term goal of controlled human action is social stasis—a negation of spontaneity and will sometimes eradicated through drugs, hypnosis, confinement, or torture. As a theme of utopian literature, and often diabolical in nature, conditioning is the keystone to the classic dystopian novels as well as such lesser known works as David Karp's *One* (1953) and Marge Piercy's *Woman on the Edge of Time* (1976). In both of these minor treasures, psychologists reduce helpless protagonists to an amenable acquiescence. The novels epitomize a satanic subversion of Skinnerian mind manipulations through which the state assures control of even a hint of rebellion, creativity, or individuality. By halting the dynamics of a living, changing society, proponents of a conditioned utopia produce a closed system in which there are no surprises, improvements, or growth. Such control of behavior roots out emotion and individuality as it stamps out progress.

An understanding of conditioning is the open sesame to interpreting dystopian fiction. Demonstrated by Anthony Burgess's *A Clockwork Orange* (1962), the extinction of destructiveness in Alex, a teenage criminal capable of random intimidation, assault, theft, houliganism, and murder, results from Ludovico's Technique, a regimen of programmed torment that takes place in the laboratory of a prison doctor. To achieve the transformation, the conditioning manager pairs a selected behavior with pain to cause the organism to cease the offending behavior; a parallel application of pleasure encourages positive behavior and therefore increases the likelihood of repetition. The guinea pig—former gangster Alex—rejects random violence in favor of classical music, a nonviolent form of emotion.

In Aldous Huxley's *Brave New World* (1932), conditioning takes the form of a parody of human creation. The Social Predestination Room and the Neo-Pavlovian Conditioning Rooms at London's futuristic hatchery promote social stability by Bokanovsky's Process, or cloning, and by depriving embryos of oxygen and realigning chemicals in the developing fetus. After the infants are decanted from their fetal containers, they are reared in dormitory-style childcare centers and further disposed to a planned lifestyle by such scientific manipulations as the application of electric shock, e.g., to connect reading and the enjoyment of nature with pain. The second stage of conditioning is hypnopaedia, or sleep teaching. As toddlers sleep, their minds absorb repeated slogans: "Civilization is sterilization," "A gramme is better than a damn," and "Cleanliness is next to Fordliness," for example. These carefully instilled homilies encourage universal acceptance of the lifestyle of one of five social castes: Alphas, or intellectuals; Betas, or technicians; Gammas, who serve as drones; and the most robotic levels, Deltas and the stunted, semimoronic Epsilons. In later childhood, troops of children pass through terminal wards of the Park Lane Hospital for "death condition day," when they shed their fear of dying.

Huxley's nightmarish system does not end with childhood. Throughout their lives, conditioned citizens reaffirm their commitment to the common goal. By supplanting religious worship with the Solidarity Service, they merge separate identities with a nebulous deity, a god surrogate. When tension or trauma threatens the expected placidity, the state provides *soma,* a euphoria-producing soporific available in numerous forms, from pills to vapor to ice cream sundaes. Drugged into a witless acquiescence, the conditioned Utopian avoids rebellion, fear, anxiety, and other negative emotions that threaten unity and productivity.

Huxley's hypnopaedia pales before the heinous conditioning in George Orwell's *1984* (1949), Ayn Rand's *Anthem* (1937), and Margaret Atwood's *The Handmaid's Tale* (1985). In Orwell's dystopia, a regimented form of brainwashing occurs during Hate Week, an annual exercise in mass hysteria that focuses negative emotions on a common enemy chosen by the state. The extinction of rebellion, which minions of Big Brother force on protagonist Winston Smith, moves beyond propaganda to terrorism using individual phobias, which for Winston is exposure to rats. Similarly, Ayn Rand's *Anthem* treats controlled work groups to alternating sessions of menial labor and group solidarity lectures. At the proper time, wielders of power determine which citizens may mate. If controversy arises among dissenters, their tongues are cut out and they are burned at the stake as warnings to the populace that sheeplike passivity is less dangerous than revolt. In like manner, Margaret Atwood's sadistic system, the modus operandi of *The Handmaid's Tale,* employs matrons with cattle prods to instill in female victims the precepts of a new—and desperately underpopulated—society governed by the religious right. By the time the young women have completed their training, they are ready to serve childless families as breeders. Rebels are hanged or dismembered for disobedience; postmenopausal women are remanded to radioactive hinterlands. Handmaids who wither from confinement and fear of barrenness commit suicide in despair at their powerlessness. Such a creation of utopia from volitionless citizens demonstrates the root cause of dystopia—the eradication of the human role in society by a tyrannic, theocratic, or sadistic hierarchy. (Atwood 1972; Burgess 1962; Carpenter 1985; Karp 1953; Modgil 1987; Piercy 1976; Proctor and Weeks 1991; Rand 1946; Skinner 1968; Skinner 1976; Skinner 1993)

See also Alex; *Anthem;* Bokanovsky's Process; *Brave New World; A Clockwork Orange;* The Commander; *The Handmaid's Tale;* hypnopaedia; Ludovico's Technique; Lydia, Aunt; *1984;* Offred; *soma;* theocracy; *Walden Two; Woman on the Edge of Time;* women in utopia.

 # CONFUCIUS

A master teacher and sage known in China as K'ung fu-tzu, Confucius lost his Chinese identity when his name was westernized in the seventeenth century into the Latinate spelling. Confucius is the ceremonial name of Ch'iu Chungni, who lived in Lu in the Shandong province from 551–479 B.C. Few reliable details remain of his life. A tall man with a noticeable bulge on his forehead, he grew up fatherless and poor. He was strong, persistent, and resilient, and worked for an aristocrat as supervisor of livestock and silos. He appears to have married, for his disciples refer to a daughter, a son who died young, and a grandson, Tzu Su, who became a disciple.

Developing his scholastic skills, Confucius at first served as minister to an influential ruler. In Book II, verse 4 of his *Analects* (second century A.D.), Confucius summarized his academic growth:

> At 15, I set my heart on learning. At 30, I was firmly established. At 40, I had no more doubts. At 50, I knew the will of Heaven. At 60, I was ready to listen. At 70, I could follow my heart's desire without transgressing what was right.

At age 50 he either resigned or lost his job and, like Socrates and Jesus, became an itinerant teacher. He traveled with at least three disciples—Jan Ch'iu, Tzu-lu, and Yen Hui, his favorite—and spent the next 13 years instructing the sons of influential men of the knight class in ritual, music, horsemanship, archery, literature, and mathematics. Believing that learning belongs to all classes, he accepted both the rich and poor who came for instruction. One tally credits him with a life total of 3,000 pupils.

Confucius accepted a post in his home country and spent his last five years editing traditional Chinese lore, including the *Book of Songs,* earning for himself the revered title of Grand Master K'ung. At his death, his remains received ceremonial honors in the K'unglin cemetery near the Su River in Ch'ufu. Confucius's admirers stressed that he aspired only to the transmission of truth, self-respect, integrity, and dignity in an era that had lost its sense of decorum and ethics. He summarized his philosophy in capsule form by asking that students resist evil. His goal was the establishment of genteel, humanistic behavior as a contrast to the egregiously pompous, unprincipled titled gentry. For China, he hoped to halt four cruelties: capital punishment, torment, oppression, and petty bureaucracy. As he summarizes his attempts at social reform in Book XVIII, verse 6, "If the Way [Tao] prevailed under Heaven, I should not be trying to alter things."

Confucius was apparently modest and unassuming, claiming to love the past and to pursue a greater understanding of history. He had no inkling of the power and influence his teachings would generate in the coming millennia. His students revered him like a father; his birth date, September 28, was selected as National Teacher's Day. After a hostile government ordered the Confucian texts destroyed during the first century A.D., one adherent hid them in the walls of his house, which has since become a shrine. For centuries, Chinese schoolchildren memorized his words as a standard portion of their training. The texts also appeared on civil-service examinations for those seeking government posts. Currently, all 2,000 counties in China have Confucian temples.

As happened with the oral teachings of Christ, Buddha, and Socrates, Confucius's disciples, particularly Mencius and Hsun Tzu, collected his aphorisms into an anthology known as *The Analects of Confucius.* A loose compilation of his doctrines, many of them contradict one another. The work gained such value among Chinese readers that it became a pivotal text among world religions, on a par with the Talmud, Koran, Proverbs, and Plato's *Dialogues.* Confucius's philosophies eventually displaced Taoism and spread through the Orient to Korea, Japan, Indochina, and the Western Hemisphere. (Confucius 1992; Pelikan 1992a; Schwartz 1985; Thompson et al. 1991; Waley 1992)

See also *The Analects of Confucius;* asceticism; Buddhism; heaven; Koran; Lao Tzu; Plato; *The Republic;* Tao; *Tao Te Ching; Timaeus.*

 # *A CONNECTICUT YANKEE IN KING ARTHUR'S COURT*

In Mark Twain's 1886 dystopian satire, the framework novel opens on a voluble stranger who points out an anomaly to a visitor to Warwick Castle: a bullet hole in a suit of chain mail dating to the time of King Arthur. The narrator, who claims to be Hank Morgan of Hartford, Connecticut, alleges that he worked at the Colt Arms factory. After Hercules, a neighborhood bully, clouts him over the head in a fight, Hank collapses in the year 1879 and regains consciousness in Camelot on June 19, 528.

Twain's description of Camelot and its residents and visitors strays from the mystic lore of medieval poets. The elaborate dress, confusing idiom, and illogical superstitions of local English people convince Hank that he is talking with circus performers or lunatics escaped from an asylum. Clarence, a young attendant, guides him to a banquet hall to appear before King Arthur, Queen Guinevere, Sir Lancelot, Sir Kay, Sir Galahad, and Merlin, Arthur's magus. The feasting halts as participants question the newcomer, stripped naked and embarrassed; offhandedly they condemn him to burn at the stake. Hank insists that he has the power to stop the sun in the sky, a feat he performs during an eclipse. The deception saves him from immolation and raises him to a position of power.

Twain's syncretic utopian fantasy is a zany blend of medieval squalor and subservience and the optimism and worship of technological progress that marked the nineteenth century. Under the title of The Boss, Hank imports American technology and attempts to smarten up the amenities of the Middle Ages. The discharge of explosives, an unheard-of power, establishes his place as top magician, but falls short of displacing his most dangerous enemy, the church. He sets out to systemize patenting and the military, open a democratic school system and a telegraph and telephone service, remap the kingdom, and launch a newspaper. In his rise to power, he creates two significant enemies— Merlin, a disgruntled rival as chief magician, and Sir Sagramor, a vindictive knight.

Twain moves his protagonist around the kingdom by calling on the convention of knight-errantry. The king dispatches Hank to rescue a maiden from a trio of ogres. In the company of her loquacious sister Sandy, he sets out in armor on horseback and endures his guide's run-on narrative. Hank's venture

A nattily dressed, twentieth-century Hank Morgan, called Hank Martin and played by Bing Crosby in the 1948 movie version of Mark Twain's *A Connecticut Yankee in King Arthur's Court*, tours King Arthur's realm with Sir Clarence, played by William Bendix.

into the countryside reveals a repressive monarchy that allows feudal lords, the church, and Arthur's sister, Morgan le Fay, to squelch civil rights. Arthur joins Hank on a tour dressed in commoners' garb. Along the way, they witness the joviality of a band of pilgrims and the miseries of slaves under the overseer's whip. At the home of smallpox victims, Arthur takes pity on those who openly despise the king's neglect of cottage-class people. He earns Hank's regard for tenderly uniting a dying mother with her moribund daughter.

Twain makes an inept attempt to restate the logic of medieval economics. Posing as a bailiff, Hank outlines for a blacksmith and other tradespeople the financial system of nineteenth-century Hartford. The people rebel against his visionary philosophies, and sell him and Arthur to slave dealers. Hank extricates his arms from manacles and telephones Clarence that he and the king are condemned to hang. The resolution of this dire situation is Twain at his funniest: At the crucial moment, Lancelot leads 500 knights on bicycles to the rescue.

Obviously, Twain cannot allow Hank an easy berth as court innovator and reshaper of Camelot. His roving complete, Hank returns to the castle where Sir Sagramor, bolstered by Merlin, carries on his crusade against The Boss. Sir Sag and Hank face off in the lists. Hank outmaneuvers Sir Sag's lance with a lariat until Merlin steals it. To contend against nine knights, Hank overwhelms the medieval audience by shooting his opponents off their mounts.

Twain's love of children surfaces in the novel's denouement. At home again, Hank, who has deserted his Connecticut fiancée, Puss Flanagan, and married the affable Sandy, learns that croup endangers the life of his daughter, Hello-Central. Launcelot endears himself to the family by sitting up at night and keeping the steam kettle stoked to ease the child's labored breathing. A doctor sends Hank, Sandy, and Hello-Central on an extended sea voyage. Underneath his instructions lurks a church plot to keep Hank out of the way while authorities override his progressive schools, private ownership of property, demotion of the aristocracy, and other futuristic ideas.

The resolution of the plot pits Hank against the toughest obstacle—the church. Against an interdict, Hank and Clarence set up a stronghold to ward off the insidious Mordred, who undercuts Arthur's authority and dignity by pressing for action on Sir Launcelot's infatuation with Queen Guinevere. In Chapter 43, in his self-deprecating vernacular, Hank mourns:

> Ah, what a donkey I was! . . . The Church, the nobles, and the gentry then turned one grand, all-disapproving frown upon them and shriveled them into sheep! From that moment the sheep had begun to gather to the fold—that is to say, the camps—and offer their valueless lives and their valuable wool to the "righteous cause."

The resultant war pits the might of the kingdom in a wasteful battle for power. Mordred fells Arthur in battle. Ecclesiastical minions maneuver The Boss, Clarence, and 52 assistants into a cave.

In the ensuing slaughter, Hank halts an attack by 30,000 knights with dynamite, electric fence, and Gatling gun. The rebels' loss turns into victory as a ring of decaying bodies immures Hank and his staff and spreads contagion to their cave. After Hank is wounded and falls victim to Merlin's black magic, Clarence continues the handwritten account of the siege. Merlin's spell puts Hank into a deep sleep, which ends at Warwick Castle, where the visitor encounters him. Nearing death, Hank picks at the coverlet, shouts commands to his workers, and calls to his wife. Thirteen centuries away from Hartford and the arms factory, he dies. (Budd 1983; Hoffman 1988; Kesterson 1979; Twain 1963)

See also Arthur; Camelot; classism; fantasy; humanitarianism; *Idylls of the King*; Morgan, Hank; syncretism; technology; theocracy; Twain, Mark; women in utopia.

 # CONWAY, HUGH

The protagonist of James Hilton's 1933 fantasy classic, *Lost Horizon,* advances to the status of head lama because of his strength of character and an impressive variety of talents and interests. A semiautobiographical creation of the author, Conway is an English scholar known for his wit, impeccable literary taste, impressive keyboard performances, and mountain-climbing treks. At school he is nicknamed Glory for winning awards in the fields of competitive sports, theater, music, and academics. He continues his penchant for winning with a Distinguished Service Order award for his role in World War I. As a decorated veteran and an expert in Chinese, French, and Hindustani, Conway lectures at Oxford before launching a ten-year career up the consular ladder.

Hilton contrasts jittery, less able personae with Conway's laissez-faire attitude toward peril. His insouciance allows him to sleep during a skyjacking from India over the Himalayas, a bumpy, mysterious flight that terrifies fellow passengers. Employing a nonconfrontational approach to danger, Conway applies his energies to questions he can attempt to answer: where the plane is flying, how high, by whom, and for what reason. After a second landing, a Tibetan entourage appears and a polite Chinese leader offers shelter. Conway draws on his understanding of Orientals and courteously abstains from demanding information or immediate return. By this blend of consular tact and reason, he avoids violence and mental and emotional unrest.

At this point, Hilton seems to have created a character worthy of admiration. An even-tempered, contemplative man, Conway demonstrates the Greek concept of the balanced individual who perfects both physical and intellectual realms. As such, he becomes the focus of the search for a leader for Shangri-La, the serene Tibetan lamasery where inhabitants extend their life spans through peaceful contemplation and the consumption of a local sedative plant, the berries of which are made into a tea. For Conway, the lure of utopia is peace. He identifies in Shangri-La an absence of the hard-edged ambition common to a mechanized world and a respite from fanatics who foment their zealotry to the detriment of world peace.

The stereotypical loner, Conway cultivates few intimates, yet leaves his mark on people around him, most of whom admire his sagacity, brilliance, sensitivity, pragmatism, and cool control. With hysterics and complainers he maintains a tolerance and patience that endear him to two other outsiders, a fundamentalist missionary and an American embezzler fleeing the law under temporary cover of an alias. In the estimation of Father Perrault, Shangri-La's dying high lama, such balance of passion and pure reason is necessary for the measured growth of the remote monastery, which lacks the regenerative powers of a normal community.

The failure of Conway's wisdom lies in his attempt to suppress his love for an attractive Chinese novice and in his empathy for a pair of lovers who need his assistance in escaping Shangri-La. By lending his strength and know-how to the couple, he destroys his ambition of leading the utopian community into the mid-twentieth century. Like the legendary Wandering Jew, Conway epitomizes an idealist questing for the unattainable. Following an odyssey that takes him about the Eastern Hemisphere, he pursues Shangri-La, the land that brought his spirit peace and hope for a similar global harmony. (Hilton 1933; Kunitz 1942; *Something about the Author* 1984)

See also asceticism; escapism; Hilton, James; *Lost Horizon;* Perrault, Father; Shangri-La; women in utopia.

THE COURTIER

Castiglione's *Il Libro del cortegiano,* or *The Courtier* (1528), is one of the sixteenth century's most popular handbooks on behavior. A repository of the highest political, social, and ethical values, *The Courtier* serves as a manual to those aspiring to the zenith of Renaissance cultivation. So noteworthy is Castiglione's perfect courtier that a syntopic version of the book appeared in 1587, paralleling the original Italian manuscript with English and French translations.

As the epitome of education and inspiration for an upper-class gentleman, Castiglione's handbook is the outgrowth of a series of fictional dialogues that supposedly occur over a four-day period in 1507 at the court of Elisabetta Gonzaga in Urbino. Contributing to the discussion of the ideal Renaissance noble are Giuliano de Medici, Ludovico di Canossa, Bernardo Accolti, Gaspar Pallovicin Pietro Bembo, Ottaviano and Federico Fregoso, Alphonso Ariosto, and Bernardo Bibbiena. The stylized exchange of information and witty repartee moves realistically from subject to subject, and interpolates such minor topics as the most refined Italian dialect, the nature of women, and the purpose of humor. Castiglione graces his self-possessed, unassuming model with well-turned limbs; skill in riding, boxing, and shooting; and ease in the salons of the literati and courts of power.

A sophisticated, urbane treatise, *The Courtier* focuses on the ideal male aristocrat, whose modesty, sincerity, and honor make him the center of attention. In the introduction to Sir Thomas Hoby's English translation, Castiglione's hypothetical courtier is described as "a storehouse of most necessary implements for the conversation, use, and training-up of man's life with courtly demeanors." As an ornament and adviser to his liege, the courtier allies with people of similar refinement, ethical purity, and spirituality. Although not necessarily a noble by birth, he attains Castiglione's standards of propriety by imitating the prestigious families of Renaissance Italy.

In Book I, Castiglione emphasizes that his courtier cannot degenerate into foppishness or egotistic self-absorption. As a warrior, he demonstrates through energetic application of skills

> . . . his conquering of places impregnable, his sodein readiness in setting forward to geve battail, his putting to flight sundry times with a small number very great and puissant armies, and never sustained loss in any conflict.

Balancing the brutal exigencies of war, the courtier cultivates sports, music, and dancing; subtlety of imagination; knowledge of current events; and skill in debate.

Castiglione breaks up the list of requisites for a gentleman by lacing the dialogue with differences of opinion. Ludovico and Gaspar raise the issue of social class. Ludovico insists that the perfect gentleman must be born to gentility and respond nobly to the family's high level of attainment, which becomes "a clear lamp that sheweth forth and bringeth into light works both good and bad." Thus, an aristocratic birth ensures the courtier "wit and a comely shape of person and countenance, but also a certain grace." Gaspar counters that nobility is not a requirement of gentility. Rather, he credits luck with providing the model man with the right mix of personality traits and opportunities to display them to advantage.

A strength of Castiglione's fiction is an emphasis on details. The conversation turns to the particulars of activities. Ludovico names as essentials to the courtier the skills of riding, managing spirited horses, running "at the ring and at tilt," fighting at barriers, "running at bull," and throwing both darts and spears. Rounding out so athletic a personality, the courtier should demonstrate scholarship and speak and write clearly and knowledgeably without affectation. Without bragging, he should assert wise judgment and prudence.

Book IV turns to the matters of virtue and morality. Pietro Bembo declaims at length on the ability to love and to value beauty. He follows the Platonic paradigm, which requires that the viewer remain in control of the senses by applying reason to the worth of beauty. Bembo expands on the source of beauty, which is God. Thus, true beauty is a divine gift, a "sign of the inward goodness." To use the gift to best advantage, the wise gentleman pleases and reveres his beloved and accommodates her pleasures. He is discreet in his affairs and avoids disservice to his beloved's family. In all ways, the loving courtier applies control and appreciation to his lovemaking to enable both parties to savor the spiritual and sensual enjoyments that God intended.

Castiglione's graceful prose reveals an earthly ideal—the perfect man existing in idyllic circumstance. Neither too humble nor too proud, this supreme figure of Renaissance charm, knowledge, and self-control displays the goal of the Italian intelligentsia, a humanist coterie driven to refine learning and develop the human spirit to perfection. Obviously male-centered in his discourse, Castiglione conceives the best in personality and behavior, a figure capable of excellence under any circumstance. (Ady 1908; Castiglione 1976; Hanning and Rosand 1983; Hornstein et al. 1973; Mack 1962; Rollins and Baker 1954)

See also Castiglione, Baldessar; classism; materialism; women in utopia.

CREATION, MYTHIC

The earth's beginnings are a standard motif in mythic literature, particularly in Hesiod's *Works and Days* (eighth century B.C.), Plato's *Timaeus* (fifth century B.C.), and Ovid's *Metamorphoses* (A.D. 8). According to the Greek version, God and Nature interpose order on chaos and create heaven, earth, air, and sea. Having supplied the earth with rivers, shores, mountains, valleys, woods, springs, meadows, and plains, the Creator adds stars above, fish in the sea, birds in the air, and four-footed animals on land. To populate the earth with a nobler species, the Titan Prometheus takes handfuls of earth, blends them with water, and shapes man to look like the gods. To remind man of his place in the scheme of things, Prometheus makes him walk on two legs so that he can raise his eyes from the ground to the stars.

Creation myths in general contain an element of chance. In the Greek myth, the creative power assigns Prometheus's brother Epimetheus the task of

Scenes from Genesis in a fifteenth-century manuscript show events in the first book of the Old Testament such as Adam naming the animals, upper left, Eve being created from Adam's rib, upper center, and eating an apple, center.

equipping animals and humanity with self-preservation, as exemplified by wisdom, speed, strength, and courage. Epimetheus begins parceling out gifts: To the eagle he gives talons; to the tortoise a tough, domed carapace; to others, wings, fur, fins, and fangs. Because man appears at the end of the line, the profligate Titan, who had used up his divine gifts, has no natural protection to bestow. Prometheus takes the initiative to fly to heaven and snatch fire for man to use as weapon, heat, light, and source of the arts.

The power play between heaven's dictator and the earthly creators erupts into a no-win situation for Prometheus. Zeus determines to punish him for presumption. For stealing fire, Zeus creates Pandora, the first woman, who is endowed with beauty, persuasion, music, and other gifts. When Epimetheus accepts Pandora into his home, he leaves unsealed a jar of evils. Overly blessed with curiosity, Pandora lifts the lid and releases on humankind all the troubles, ills, diseases, and curses that doom humanity to misery. Prometheus claps the lid on the jar just in time to save hope, which nearly escapes along with the evils.

The setting of this embellished myth is the golden age, an idyllic time of righteousness and truth. Humanity lives in harmony with nature and has no need of police protection, weapons, or fortifications. Without breaking the sod or scattering seed, farmers take advantage of perpetual spring and harvest what they need without saving up grain for hard times. The rivers brim with milk, wine, and honey. The gods force on humankind a greater challenge by ending the idyllic age and replacing it with the age of silver: a time when spring gives way to summer, fall, and winter; when humankind must build shelters against the cold; and when grain will no longer grow without cultivation and sowing of seed.

In the pessimistic Greek cosmology, humanity is always mindful of the treasured times past but, powerless to change its ways, continues on the downward spiral. Earthly mores move farther from the utopian past in the third age, the age of bronze. People grow testier of spirit and threaten one another with violence, but it is not until the iron age that their enmity breaks out in war, the depths of human depravity. Crafters who once carved religious statues and temple friezes devote themselves to the making of ores into weapons and the hewing of timbers for battleships. Greed causes dissension as landowners grab for the most arable and best-watered lands. As Hesiod's *Works and Days* describes the ignoble human value system:

> The evil man will harm the better man, speaking against him unjustly and he will swear an oath besides. Envy, shrill and ugly and with evil delight, will attend all men in their woe.

Strife arises among nations, civil wars plague communities, and relatives rise up against their own kin in blood feuds. The earth becomes so despicable that even the gods abandon it and return to the serenity of Mount Olympus.

Unlike the Sumerian creation myth, which parallels and influences the Old Testament book of Genesis, the Greek version presents a carefully staged decline to explain why humankind deserves to lose an earthly utopia. In contrast to the religious ramifications of the symbolic Mesopotamian Adam and Eve, who are expelled from Eden for a single infraction of Yahweh's laws, the Greek creation myth focuses on generations rather than individuals. At the height of evil, however, the two myths converge in a similar ablution of human taint— in the Greek world, Deucalion survives the flood; in Genesis, Noah and his family play a similar role as the first and only family on a freshly washed land. (*Bulfinch's Mythology* 1964; Grimal 1991; Guerber 1921; Hamilton 1942; Hesiod 1973; Howatson 1991; Johnson 1968; Metzger and Coogan 1993; Morford and Lenardon 1977; Snodgrass 1988a; Snodgrass 1988b)

See also Adam; *Back to Methuselah;* Eden; Eve; Genesis; golden age; Hesiod; Ovid; paradise; *Paradise Lost;* pastoral; *Timaeus;* women in utopia.

A CRYSTAL AGE

The setting of this matriarchal utopian novel is a subdued, sexless society envisioned in 1887 by W. H. Hudson, author of the naturalistic idyll *Green Mansions* (1904). *A Crystal Age* takes place in a pastoral setting reminiscent of northern Scotland. Beyond the Elf Mountains in a nebulous, fictional country, Smith, a botanist, is collecting specimen plants. His arrival in an unusual land occurs through a fall of some 40 feet into a ravine. The area has no roads, and ancient buildings rise out of the earth like monoliths.

Hudson outlines the journey in first-person narrative with simplistic, pastoral details. In Chapter 1 the people who greet the botanist form a funeral procession. They dress in brightly colored hip-length kilts, knee hose, and loose-fitting shoes. Smith is immediately drawn to Yoletta, a delicate young girl with beautiful green eyes who appears to be in her mid-teens. She weeps for her beloved and grieves that she will never see him again.

The group cremates the enshrouded corpse in the grave and wishes the soul a pleasant journey back to the earth mother. The old man concludes, "not until she has made the sweet grass and flowers grow again on this spot, scorched and made desolate with fire, shall our hearts be healed of their wound and forget their grief." At the end of the interment, Smith introduces himself. An old man, the group's white-bearded patriarch and judge, insults Smith's "uncouth garments" and speech and claims to know nothing about England, Queen Victoria, Darwin, or a long list of notables from Homer to Bismarck and Voltaire that the outsider mentions, nor has he experience with cities or house construction. Their buildings all date from early times and are revered as national monuments.

The group escorts Smith to a magnificent stone manor house adorned with a lustrous portrait of Mistrelde, a matriarch who lived 400 years earlier and to whom Yoletta bears a strong resemblance. The family assembles in the dining room, where small birds skip about. The foods served at their evening meal reflect the bucolic setting—brown bread, dried fruit, milk, endive, crushed nuts, and honey. At dinner, Smith indicates that he would like to buy clothing in the local style. To himself he notes that a short costume like the others wear would display his fine legs and impress Yoletta. The old man is confused by references to money and suggests that a year's labor at felling trees or plowing would cover the cost of a suit of clothes.

In Chapter 5, which is set in the family room, everyone seems to take up some activity to occupy the remainder of the evening. Yoletta stitches with wool yarn; Smith tries to read an illuminated manuscript, but cannot decipher the letters. The old man interrupts the quiet with a soothing recitation on death that suggests a syncretism of the Christian god and animism:

> It is natural to grieve for those that die, because light and knowledge and love and joy are no longer theirs; but they grieve not any more, being now asleep on the lap of the Universal Mother, the bride of the Father, who is with us, sharing our sorrow, which was his first; but it dims not his everlasting brightness; and his desire and our glory is that we should always and in all things resemble him.

The speaker concludes that human habitation in a house parallels God's dwelling on Earth. He reminds his audience that a former generation defiled human life by excesses and drunkenness and were killed and eaten by worms.

As in William Morris's *News from Nowhere* (1890), Hudson depicts a people attempting to distance themselves from a shameful past. Admonishing all to remember the folly of the old regime, the speaker urges his hearers to follow God's ways so that they may live in "his everlasting mansion." His words reflect the imagery of Hesiod's *Works and Days* (eighth century B.C.), David's more didactic Psalms, Christ's parables, Confucius's analects, or the aphorisms of Marcus Aurelius:

> For the house is the image of the world, and we that live and labor in it are the image of our Father who made the world; and, like him, we labor to make for ourselves a worthy habitation, which shall not shame our teacher.

The speaker reminds his listeners that all human knowledge and skill become vanity if they are not put into the service of the heavenly Father.

Like Gulliver, Candide, Robinson Crusoe, and other fictional visitors to utopias, Smith learns more about his unusual find by asking questions and observing local traditions and behaviors. A decade of every life span is given to wandering the land and visiting each home, where wayfarers are welcomed. Far to the south, travelers come to the wilderness of Coradine, where "the stupendous columns of green glass uphold the roof of the House of Coradine." The mythic quality of this far dwelling is enhanced by the description of a deified matron in a bronze chariot drawn across the fields by bulls with gold horns.

Unused to asceticism, Smith disdains the straw pallet and pillow and suffers a miserable night, which is interrupted by a prowling house dog. The next morning, the patriarch and his brood enjoy communal bathing in the nearby stream. Carrying a basket of breakfast foods, Smith follows directions to a field, whistles for plow horses, and begins breaking up the sod with amazing ease. When the horses stop work and remove their harness, Smith deduces that his workday is finished. Returning to the house, Smith senses hostility as he is ushered into the chamber of justice. The old man accuses him of lying about being able to read and sentences him to 60 days of exile. Smith counters by taking up his pen and writing in English, which the old man has never seen. He apologizes for the misunderstanding and assigns Yoletta to teach Smith the local language. That evening, the group again gathers and sings to music from revolving spheres.

By Chapter 10, Smith has earned two suits of clothing, one for work and one for leisure. He exults in his simple rural life free from the cares of cities. On a rigorous hike with Yoletta, he kisses her hand and puzzles over her declaration that she is 31 years old and the patriarch, who is her father, is 198. Yoletta grows somber when she divulges that Chastel, her ailing mother, lives in the mother's room. Smith visits Chastel, who is mildly irked that he has waited so long to present himself to the all-important mother. In embarrassment and confusion, he flees to the woods for solace.

At this point, Hudson focuses on the keystone of local philosophy: The nation is matriarchal. Each residence features a mother's room, with dormitory cells for the other residents. In the evenings, Smith calls on Chastel—a name made up from "chaste"—and discerns from her blunt lectures that he must give up the vices of his island home, although she never names the most offensive of his habits. During the season of the autumnal rainbow lilies, Yoletta comes before her father, who judges her for tearing a book. She is confined to her room on bread and water for 30 days. Her absence ends Smith's talks with Chastel and sets him on a downward spiral of depression and fasting.

The author's depiction of a change of heart from hedonism to labor and service for the common good places the protagonist in self-imposed isolation. Each day, Smith carries his ax to the forest to cut wood. In Chapter 14, the old man interrupts him and explains his country's attitude toward balancing work with rest and enjoyment of nature:

> We give ourselves wholly to her then, and she refreshes us; the splendor fades, but the wealth it brings to the soul remains to gladden us. That must be a dull spirit that cannot suspend its toil when the sun is setting in glory, or the violet rainbow appears on the cloud . . . while it lasts, all labor, except that which is pressing and necessary, is unseemly, and an offense to the Father of the world.

Guessing Smith's motivation for withdrawing to the woodlot, the old man reveals that Yoletta has left seclusion to walk in the wild and ease her solitude. In vain, Smith hurries to catch up with her.

As an example of the excesses of his former life, Hudson employs Smith's yearning for Yoletta. Unrequited passion, hunger, and loneliness weaken Smith, who is bedridden with fever. For days he lies on his pallet, then creeps about the house as strength returns. The old man passes judgment on Smith for overtaxing his strength and neglecting to eat during Yoletta's exile. He sentences Smith to 13 days' exile; Chastel, his ministering "good angel," intervenes and grants a reprieve. Smith slips into a dreamy indolence and spends his days in her chamber.

Chastel attempts to relieve Smith's longing for physical union with Yoletta. For weeks, Chastel lingers on her couch in much pain, often wracked with headache and speaking in a frail whisper. Smith studies a book called *Renewal of the Family* and learns that only the chosen woman may assume the mother's role and breed children. He realizes that his ill-fated love for Yoletta is forbidden. In the niche beside the book is a vial of yellow liquid with an inscription urging the depressed to drink and be cured. Too late, Smith realizes that one taste condemns him to death, which is the antidote to uncontrolled passion.

For all its descriptions of nature and concord, Hudson's limp utopia lapses into a sentimental deathbed tableau. The differences between Smith and Yoletta seem obvious enough, yet, like Hugh Conway in James Hilton's *Lost Horizon* (1933), he must test them to the fatal limit before understanding society's disdain for sexuality and its rigid control of procreation. The chief weakness of *A Crystal Age* is Hudson's lavish euphemisms for lust and intercourse. The frail substructure of utopian philosophy carries little weight beyond its message of abstemious diet, rest, work, mutual respect, and frequent communion with nature. Locked into a tight stasis, the milieu of Yoletta, Chastel, and the old man becomes a museum piece devoid of normal human urges. (Hilton 1933; Hudson 1917; Kunitz 1942; Manguel and Guadalupi 1987; Miller 1990; Morris 1968a; Ronner 1986)

See also asceticism; Candide; Conway, Hugh; Gulliver, Lemuel; Hesiod; *Lost Horizon; News from Nowhere;* pastoral; *Robinson Crusoe;* syncretism; utopia; women in utopia.

 D-503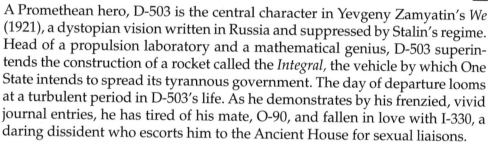

A Promethean hero, D-503 is the central character in Yevgeny Zamyatin's *We* (1921), a dystopian vision written in Russia and suppressed by Stalin's regime. Head of a propulsion laboratory and a mathematical genius, D-503 superintends the construction of a rocket called the *Integral,* the vehicle by which One State intends to spread its tyrannous government. The day of departure looms at a turbulent period in D-503's life. As he demonstrates by his frenzied, vivid journal entries, he has tired of his mate, O-90, and fallen in love with I-330, a daring dissident who escorts him to the Ancient House for sexual liaisons.

In Chapter 20, D-503 depicts the rebellion of a repressed human spirit as he studies his own reactions to emotion and treads the outer rim of legality by deviating from state laws. At the crux of his revolt lies his realistic view of history:

> Human history ascends in circles, like an aero. The circles differ—some are golden, some bloody. But all are equally divided into three hundred and sixty degrees. And the movement is from zero—onward, to ten, twenty, two hundred, three hundred and sixty degrees—back to zero. . . . We started from zero to the right, we have returned to it from the left.

The image of a hovering zero makes him think of Christopher Columbus and a symbolic circumnavigation of the globe. His imaginary expedition arrives at One State, "a pale blue mass, sparks, rainbows, suns, hundreds of suns, billions of rainbows," yet D-503 cannot shake the suspicion that he may be only a short distance from "the black side of the crag."

A suffering Christ figure anticipating crucifixion and resurrection, D-503 achieves martyrdom by confessing all to the Benefactor who rules One State, and by cutting ties with I-330. After D-503 is treated for an acute case of imagination, or soul, he embraces robotic compliance with state law and is unable to relate to his early writings. In Chapter 27, he describes virtual autism in brief, negative sense impressions: "Empty streets, an alien, wild city, an incessant, triumphant chorus of bird cries, the end of the world." In the final chapter, like Revelation in the Bible, the apocalypse produces "chaos, roaring, corpses, beasts, and—unfortunately—a considerable group of numbers who have betrayed Reason." In the same predicament as Karel Capek's Mr. Alquist in *R. U. R.*

(1920), Winston Smith in George Orwell's *1984* (1949), and, to a lesser degree, Connie Ramos in Marge Piercy's *Woman on the Edge of Time* (1976), D-503 opts for a heroic attempt to set right a utopia gone sour. By resurrecting humanistic values, he jeopardizes prestige, self, and sanity for the good of the state. (Grigson 1963; Kunitz 1942; Russell 1994; Shane 1968; Zamyatin 1992)

See also Alquist, Mr.; *1984*; O-90; *R. U. R.*; Smith, Winston; technology; *We*; *Woman on the Edge of Time.*

DANTE ALIGHIERI

Italy's master poet, he is the prototypical Renaissance man, father of the Italian language, and author of the *Divina Commedia*, or *The Divine Comedy* (1320). Dante (short for Durante) Alighieri was born to a notable but impecunious house in Florence in May 1265, an era of protracted civil strife and ruthless power grabs. Orphaned in his youth by first the death of his mother Bella and later the demise of his father, moneylender Alighiero, Dante showed scholarly promise. Under the mentorship of poets Guido Cavalcanti and Brunetto Latini he studied painting, philosophy, theology, music, rhetoric, and the classics of Aristotle, Boethius, Cicero, Augustine, and Aquinas. Dante graduated from the University of Bologna at age 23 and began obligatory military service, in which he distinguished himself as a horseman and fighter at Campaldino and Capronas.

Prominent in Dante's life was his unconsummated longing for a childhood sweetheart, Beatrice (pronounced "bay-uh-TREE-chay"); her father, banker Folco Portinari, pledged her to Simone, a banking magnate of the influential Bardi family. Her unexpected death in 1290 plunged Dante into severe depression, which he turned to literary use by penning an autobiographical chivalric verse cycle in 1294 entitled *La vita nuova* (The new life), a collection of poems that blend Beatrice's earthly virtues with the transcendent love of the Virgin Mary. For two years he withdrew to the Franciscan monastery of Santa Croce and immersed himself in the philosophies of Aquinas and Aristotle. Deprived of his ideal wife, he followed the political dictates of his ambitious family and wed the prestigious but meddlesome Gemma, daughter of Manetto Donati. So desiccated was Dante's family life that he never refers to Gemma in print, yet the couple produced sons Jacopo, Giovanni, and Pietro and a daughter Antonia, who entered a noviate under the name Sister Beatrice.

Member of a pharmacy guild and the Guelphs (the papal party that controlled the city-state of Florence), Dante rose in political prominence during his thirties by serving as a committeeman, prior or magistrate, and ambassador to San Gimignano and Rome. In 1302 a shift in the power structure denigrated Dante with charges of impiety by an attempt to buy a state office. Bereft of his savings and deprived of future offices and rights of inheritance, he and his sons were banished on pain of public immolation if they returned. Spiritually broken and penniless, he wandered Verona, Lucca, Padua, and possibly Paris and Oxford to whatever patrons took an interest in his work. During the

Italian poets Dante Alighieri, left, with Francesco Petrarch in a fourteenth-century painting

next 13 years, he championed vernacular language (the forerunner of modern Italian) and initiated and abandoned *The Banquet,* a poorly organized encyclopedic treatise on philosophy, and *The Illustrious Vernacular,* a scholarly examination of rhetoric. At age 50 he finished *On Monarchy* and, like John Milton, focused on a sonorous religious epic, *The Divine Comedy.*

About this time, Florence granted the poet a dishonorable amnesty, which he rejected, thereby adopting permanent exile. In 1320 he settled in Ravenna and, along with Gemma and daughter Antonia, lived out his exile with Guido Novello da Polenta, under whose patronage he completed *The Divine Comedy,* a graphic geography of the afterlife extending over 14,233 lines and caustically subtitled "The Comedy of Dante Alighieri, Florentine by Citizenship, Not by Morals." The classical and biblical research and composition of his masterpiece comprised 14 years of his life. Dante explains in his dedication to Can Grande della Scala of Verona, the last in a series of patrons, that the classical term *commedia* refers to a plot that begins in hell and rises by degrees of anticipation and happiness to *Paradiso,* the Christian's goal.

The success of his 100-canto poem, which was published in stages, established his place among Italy's literati but did not earn him retribution with petty authorities in his hometown. To stem Florentine hostilities with Ravenna, he served as legate to Venice in 1321. While working as a teacher to aspiring writers, he died of malaria at Ravenna on September 13, 1321, and was interred in the local Franciscan monastery. His son Jacopo was enlisted to complete the final 13 cantos, which were missing from the manuscript. Legend describes Jacopo as following his father's wraith to a wall safe, where the final pages lay moldering.

For Dante's masterly blend of classical subjects in vernacular language he has been called the father of modern literature. Eager to court the renown of their deceased black sheep, Florentine officials worked through Pope Leo X and a Vatican commission to exhume his remains for honorable burial in a tomb designed by Michelangelo to be erected in his homeland. Their attempts failed; Dante remains in his eastern Italian crypt. Fortunately for world literature, his works circulated widely and were admired and imitated by Christian and pagan alike. Rediscovered during the Romantic Age by Samuel Taylor Coleridge, Victor Hugo, and Henry Wadsworth Longfellow, Dante rose to prominence on a par with Virgil and Shakespeare. (Anderson 1989; Bloom 1986b; Boorstin 1992; Collins 1989; Dante Alighieri 1968; Dante Alighieri 1982; Mack 1962)

See also Divina Commedia; heaven; religion; theocracy; women in utopia.

 # *DAS KAPITAL*

Karl Marx wrote this monument of nineteenth-century economic theory, which is a painstakingly detailed history of capitalism, an indictment of social determinism, and the major source of strategy and justification for communism. Volume 1, an introduction to scientific socialism, was published in 1867. Marx collected the remaining material from his years of study at the British Museum, along with voluminous writings, discussion and conjecture with fellow radicals and economic theorists, and pages of notes, correspondence, paradigms, maps, and amplification, which he left in a collection at his death. In 1887 and 1895, Marx's collaborator and lifelong friend, Friedrich Engels, completed the second and third volumes as a means of preserving Marxism and furthering the cause of world revolution and the emergence of a classless society. *Das Kapital* remains the meatiest, most profound statement of economic idealism to emerge from the late nineteenth and early twentieth centuries.

The focus of Marx's strongly leftist philosophy is labor, the source from which capitalism draws its wealth and power. He theorizes that workers remain powerless and exploited so long as *haute bourgeois* parasites grow fat, complacent, and arrogant at the expense of the proletariat. Crucial to Marx's motivation are the sufferings of the working class, which go unnoticed and unaddressed. In Parts III and IV, Marx's formulaic view of the capitalist monopoly stresses surplus value or profit, which is the difference between the worker's wage and the true value of the product or service. In Marxist theory, managerial forces work against the laborer by encouraging competition and labor-saving devices, lowering wages, and depriving the worker of a fair share. Because profiteers own land, factories, and mines, they monopolize the productivity of the world market. In a buyer's market, the devalued worker sells labor at the going rate—usually at a loss—as a means of survival. If workers demand raises, they risk being replaced by the pool of labor agitating for jobs. Thus, both the privileged and the unemployed pressure the workers, who are caught in the middle of an endless cycle of work and struggle. The upshot of a one-sided and exploitative distribution of the world's wealth results in slavery, oppression, dangerous work conditions, child labor, and stress on families from self-destructive escapism in the form of alcohol and drug addiction.

Marx's *Das Kapital* offers an explanation of the cycles of good times, inflation, bankruptcy, and depression. He predicts that, as the working class grows larger and the pool of investors shrinks, the workers will grow powerful, organized, and savvy enough to rebel against their bourgeois overlords. Because the labor force holds the key to the entrepreneur's wealth, a strike at a crucial moment of a factory's history can place the investors in a tenuous position. When workers realize their strength, they can use their leverage to topple unscrupulous employers. Thus, capitalism, by its greed, arrogance, and miscalculation, is in imminent danger of destroying itself.

From Marx's observation of the workers' plight and his intense study of data, charts, and international trends in business and land ownership, he was able to assess future "laws of motion." His paradigm states that an expanded economy will lead to a fall in profits. Lower profits force business leaders to tinker with the manufacturing process, increase efficiency, and invent new technology. Consequently, the business world dooms itself to a constant pattern of boom and bust. In good times, big business overwhelms and devours small competitors, often driving down the price of mergers through underhanded manipulation of the market.

The only resolution to the problems of unstable capital, Marx declares, is a violent overthrow of capitalism and a replacement of social and economic inequities with a fairer arrangement—a classless world order and an end to war, which Marx typifies as a power play rooted in bourgeois self-interest but fought by men at the bottom of the social ladder. The utopian ramifications of his strategy found strong support in Russia, Cuba, and China, while the governments of France, England, Germany, and the United States countered with claims that capitalism is a fair and equitable reward for those who work hard, dream up new products, and risk their money in the establishment of new markets. In no country was there a total realization of Marx's paradigm.

A significant contention of Marx's theories is his belief that economics alone determines the degree of human contentment. Capitalists refused to accept his devaluation of religion, nationalism, pride, and individualism. Although the collapse of Tsarist Russia in 1917 and the rise of Soviet communism reflects little of what *Das Kapital* predicts, Marx and Engels did successfully enlighten historians and philosophers concerning the significance of economics in human affairs. Marx's closing sentences indicate a humanitarian concern for the people at the bottom of the production ladder. If they kowtow to the moneyed class, they suffer "the expropriation of the mass of the people by a few usurpers." However, if workers overthrow affluent capitalists, they deprive the wealthy of their hoard and free the masses from economic and political bondage. In simple terms, Marx prefers the latter case as the least violent and fairest way to distribute the world's wealth. (*Atlas of Communism* 1991; Carver 1991; Heilbroner 1989; Marx 1992; Marx and Engels 1985; Worsley 1982)

See also collectivism; *The Communist Manifesto*; Engels, Friedrich; escapism; humanitarianism; Marx, Karl.

DEFOE, DANIEL

A vigorous, opinionated journalist, pamphleteer, historian, poet, and novelist, Defoe is the prodigious author of 560 titles, including *Robinson Crusoe* (1719), a classic adventure tale and touchstone for writers of the "deserted island" subgenre of utopian literature. A product of the post-Commonwealth era, Defoe (who altered his surname from that of his father, James Foe, a butcher and candler) was born in 1660 or 1661 in St. Giles, London. He attended Morton's Academy and received sufficient grounding in Latin and Greek masters as well as history, geography, and modern languages to feed a lifetime of detailed writing.

Defoe spent many years as a stereotypical English tradesman, working at first in the hosiery business. He married Mary Tuffley and became a devoted family man, fathering the first of his seven children before involving himself in the swirl of rebellion and Whig-versus-Tory political intrigue that marked his age. Before his first business failed, he sailed to Portugal and Spain, a worthy practicum to supply information about the sailor's life at sea and in port. His second venture in imported wines and the tile trade earned him enough to retire £17,000 in debts and to secure a house in Tilbury and moderate ease for his family.

Never one to conceal his political loyalties, Defoe studied social betterment by compiling plans to lessen the load on debtors. In a gesture of good will to all citizens, he envisioned upgraded mental institutions, female academies, transportation systems, a humane system of slavery, and military training. He wrote of these innovations in his *Essay on Projects* (1697), which influenced Benjamin Franklin, one of Defoe's admirers. Defoe actively supported William of Orange and wrote satire and anti–Church of England propaganda. Before joining the spy network of the British government, Defoe suffered the pillory three times, was fined, and spent a year in Newgate Prison for his outspoken support of nonconformism, as described in *The Shortest Way with Dissenters* (1702). In a quirky gesture of defiance, he issued an audacious, richly satiric broadside, *Hymn to the Pillory* (1702). Like two-termers Miguel de Cervantes and John Bunyan, Defoe returned to jail for a subsequent charge of libeling Lord Annesley, whom he exposed as a traitorous Jacobite.

Defoe founded a thrice-weekly news and trade journal, *The Review*, in 1704. In his sixties he began composing novels, beginning with a best-seller, *The Life and Strange Surprising Adventures of Robinson Crusoe*—his masterwork—which he based on the five-year marooning of Scotsman Alexander Selkirk on the island of Juan Fernandez, an island cluster 400 miles west of Valparaiso, Chile. Crusoe's adventures epitomize the growth of the English novel from Renaissance romanticism to unembellished reportage, which became the author's trademark. Defoe wrote two sequels to the novel, but never approximated the quality of the first. However, the impetus of public acclaim and financial reward kept him writing novels at a furious rate. From *Captain Singleton* (1720), a novel on piracy, Defoe advanced to his picaresque *Moll Flanders* (1722), *Roxana* (1724), and his finest historical fiction, *Journal of the Plague Year* (1722). While in hiding from political adversaries and writing under the pseudonym of Andrew Moreton, Defoe died April 26, 1731, in Moorfields. (Baugh 1948; Bloom 1987b; Defoe 1963; Lovett and Hughes 1932; Richetti 1987; Whitten 1974)

See also didacticism; humanitarianism; materialism; naturalism; religion; *Robinson Crusoe*.

"DES CANNIBALES"

In this utopian essay, Michel de Montaigne details a Brazilian haven explored by Villegaignon in 1557 called Antarctic France. Montaigne compares the island utopia to Atlantis, as mentioned in Plato's *Timaeus* (fifth century B.C.). Montaigne is so caught up in the naturalism of his subject that he regrets that Lycurgus and Plato did not visit to learn that an earthly paradise could mimic the poet's conception of a golden age. In the essay, Montaigne claims that earlier writers are "incapable of imagining so pure and native a simplicity, as that which we see by experience; nor could they have believed that human society could have been maintained with so little human artifice and solder."

According to the speaker's ignorant servant, who lived a decade or more in the New World, the region is a vast land richly endowed by nature. He concludes:

> *Les lois naturelles les gouvernent encore, fort peu abatardies par les notres; mais c'est en telle pureté, qu'il me prend quelquefois deplaisir que la connaissance n'en soit venue plus tot, du temps où il y avait des hommes qui en eussent su mieux juger que nous.*
> [The laws of nature rule them still; they are scarcely corrupted by our own governance. But their civilization is so unsullied that I am annoyed that they were not known previously at a time that would have appreciated them better than we do now.]

Montaigne exonerates this land of the charge of barbarism by divesting himself of ethnocentrism and noting that unknown places are often mislabeled as wild or savage because the observer misinterprets traditions.

The Edenic beauty of this haven lies in the fact that it is governed by nature, simplicity, and purity, and is populated by "Viri a diis recentes," or people recently come from their creator. In a moderate climate at the edge of the sea and shadowed by mountains a hundred leagues away, inhabitants know little disease; they need no mathematics, science, literature, government, slavery, classism, legalities, munipalities, work, clothing, agriculture, metals, or alcohol. As with Herman Melville's indolent Polynesian tableaus in *Typee* (1846) and *Omoo* (1847), Montaigne's delight in primitivism departs from puritanic disdain of natives who do without clothing. More to the point is their lack of terms for "falsehood, treachery, dissimulation, avarice, envy, detraction, pardon." So pristine is the site that the people epitomize Seneca's "men newly created by the hands of God."

Similar to the Iroquois in longhouses, the cannibals live in A-frame bark buildings a hundred yards long, constructed to house 200–300 residents. Like whalers and other seafarers, they sleep in cotton hammocks, with men and women separate. Cooks prepare both fish and meat by boiling, broiling, grilling, or roasting, and form a flat, sweet-tasting bread for the people's one meal each day. Dining follows a sermon on valiant men and the worth of women, a recurrent text that one elder delivers to the assembled family. The remainder of the day, residents drink a pungent, lukewarm, burgundy-colored beverage made from roots and soothing to the digestive tract. An active people, these natives spend their time dancing and playing hollow cane flutes. The men enjoy bow hunting; women spend time preparing the national beverage. In grooming, they prefer a full-body shave, which is accomplished with a wooden or stone razor.

Priests who reside in the mountains provide visions of the future and spiritual guidance, especially in matters of patriotism and affection toward wives. The natives believe that the soul survives the body and dwells in a heaven to the east. Those who displease the gods reside in the west. The natives perpetually war with their neighbors on the other side of the mountains. Nude except for bow and arrow or wooden sword, each warrior engages in bloody mayhem, climaxing in the beheading of enemy prisoners and the cooking and eating of the carcass as a symbolic vengeance. During the months in which prisoners await execution, they appear uplifted by their fate and jeer at their captors. In this polygamous society, the most distinguished braves marry the most wives. The women exhort their men to take more wives as proof of valor.

The essayist summarizes with an injunction to the reader to suspend judgment on cannibals before evaluating this culture's practices. Montaigne notes that cannibalism, for all its barbarity, excels in civilization the European custom of torture, which is sometimes used "under the cloak of piety and religion." He admires the cannibals for nobility and generosity, and for their appreciation of nature. Unlike the uncharitable Europeans, to the cannibals all are family and no one among them goes hungry. (Johnson 1968; Mack 1962; Melville 1964; Melville 1968; Montaigne 1893b; White 1955)

See also clairvoyance; golden age; heaven; *The Life of Lycurgus;* Montaigne, Michel Eyquem de; naturalism; *Omoo; Timaeus; Typee;* women in utopia.

 # DIDACTICISM

This term indicates an instructive purpose and/or tone of a literary work. As demonstrated by the Bible, Koran (610), and Confucius's *Analects* (second century A.D.), didacticism, by definition, appears consistently in literature that describes a perfect world and its attainment. A lengthy list of utopists—Hesiod, Plato, Virgil, Lao Tzu, St. Augustine, Dante Alighieri, Baldessar Castiglione, John Bunyun, Daniel Defoe, John Milton, Karl Marx, Edward Bellamy, Alfred Tennyson, Thomas Carlyle, Black Elk, Aldous Huxley, James Hilton, George Orwell, Ayn Rand, Anthony Burgess, Margaret Atwood, P. D. James, and Marge Piercy—composed works meant to guide, moralize, indoctrinate, inculcate an attitude, or elucidate a point of view. A large body of early utopian fare is anchored in didactic religious lore or mysticism:

- Hesiod, a contemporary of Homer, tied his *Works and Days* and *Theogony* (eighth century B.C.) to the golden age and the steady decline of humanity and the parallel climb of violence and war.

- Augustine, from his eyewitness account of Rome's collapse during barbarian raids, set before Christians his *De Civitate Dei* (A.D. 426), a strict, orthodox biblical lesson in how to avoid sin and gain admittance to heaven.

- Dante Alighieri, the Renaissance master, composed his *Divina Commedia* (1320) as an exposé of political venality and personal moral decay.

- In similar vein, John Bunyan's *Pilgrim's Progress* (1678) offers detailed allegorical re-creation of the path to heaven and the enticements and dangers that inhibit the struggling Christian from reaching the goal.

- Less stringent than these moralistic doctrines is the Taoist verse of Lao Tzu from the third century B.C. These esoteric maxims encourage the meditative, nonconfrontational mindset of a soul at peace with the universe.

- More earthly than mystical is Plato's *Republic* (fifth century B.C.), a tutorial treatise that, by painstaking application of logic, leads to the inspiration and benign rule of the philosopher-king.

- Sir Thomas More, who participates in his utopia as a character, wrote *Utopia* (1516) to chide England and other parts of Europe for glaring faults—in particular, religious controversy, devaluation of farm laborers, unhealthful eating habits, and a disconcerting slide into crime and bawdy, unprincipled public behavior.

- During the late Italian Renaissance, Baldessar Castiglione's *The Courtier* (1528) adapted Plato's classist stance and dialogue format in formulating a curriculum for the aspiring courtier. Castiglione's manual expresses the basic route a young man must take to succeed in the multiple realms of court service, e.g., horsemanship, courtesy, scholarship, and self-control.

- Thomas Carlyle's *Past and Present* (1843), ostensibly a reflective narrative on the Middle Ages, loses perspective and lashes out at reprehensible acts of industrialists, who were the giants of the Victorian era. To Carlyle, the possibility of technocracy in England required the raw-edged rhetoric of repeated digressions contrasting bucolic garden labors with the stench and smoke of fortress-sized factories.

- In America's transcendental era, Henry David Thoreau composed *Walden* (1854), a contemplative homesteader's text on how to subsist in the wild. His intentions were less didactic than illustrative of a personal experiment in getting to know himself without interference from society and its blatant materialism.

For a variety of reasons, Hesiod, Lao Tzu, Plato, Castiglione, Bunyan, Carlyle, and Thoreau intended that readers draw on their texts for illumination and guidance to produce the best in behavior and to achieve a maximum of personal satisfaction.

Directed both to the mind and the spirit is prophetic or predictive didacticism, an essential of dystopian literature. The speculative wing of dystopian fiction—Edward Bulwer-Lytton's *The Coming Race* (1871), William Morris's *News from Nowhere* (1890), Jack London's *Iron Heel* (1907), Karel Capek's *R. U. R.* (1920), Yevgeny Zamyatin's *We* (1921), and Margaret Atwood's *The Handmaid's Tale* (1985)—adopts the form of the jeremiad. These dystopian works profess the alarmist position—a warning of changes in the world order that presage despotism, pollution, anarchy, or an irremediable slide into global collapse. (Atwood 1972; Augustine 1958; Bunyan 1896; Capek and Capek 1961; Carlyle 1977; Castiglione 1976; Confucius 1992; Cuddon 1979; Dante Alighieri 1968; Hesiod 1966; Hesiod 1973; Holman 1981; London 1982a; More 1963; Plato 1955; *Tao Te Ching* 1988; Thoreau 1965)

DIDEROT, DENIS

One of the eighteenth century's most able, enlightened, energetic, and tolerant minds, Diderot produced *Supplement aux Voyages de Bougainville,* or *Supplement to Bougainville's "Voyages"* (1772), a utopist work of the "island paradise" subgenre. A native of Langres, Champagne, in eastern France, Diderot was born October 5, 1713, in humble circumstances. His father, a knife-maker, managed to provide him with a worthy education. A product of Louis-le-Grande, a Jesuit college, and the Jansenist Collège d'Harcourt, Diderot completed a master's degree. To his father's dismay, he created a rift in the relationship with his family by rejecting a career in the professions and worked ten years for a book dealer. In 1753 he married a laundress, Anne Toinette Champion, the daughter of a textile manufacturer, and fathered Angélique, his only child to survive him. Their unsuitable mating caused Diderot to go his own way rather than tolerate daily unhappiness. Living the bohemian ideal in Paris's Latin Quarter, in 1755 he formed a long-lived alliance with his mistress, Sophie Volland, with whom he carried on a lively correspondence.

Because of the pleasing blend of Diderot's brilliance and good nature, he traveled widely to visit friends, wrote pamphlets, and attended notable salons to share in current events and speculative conversations. He came under the influence of the great thinkers, deists, and theatrical personalities of his day—Catherine the Great of Russia, the Grimm brothers, actor David Garrick, dramatist Johann Goethe, and Jean-Jacques Rousseau, a French philosopher. Because of Diderot's working-class upbringing, he injected into his writing and discourse beliefs in the commoner and freedom from aristocracy and classism.

Lauded for his wide knowledge of books and his respect for virtue and genius, Diderot wrote novels, plays, essays, critiques, and reviews. His most important work began as a translation of a contemporary encyclopedia by Ephraim Chambers. Diderot appended over 100 original essays on religion, science, fine arts, drama, and philosophy to the 20-volume work, entitled *Encyclopédie, ou Dictionnaire Raisonné des Sciences, des Arts et des Mètiers.* The completed work, for which Jean D'Alembert shared some of the editing duties, was published in 1751 under Diderot's name and survived numerous expansions and editions. The open-mindedness of Diderot's opinions churned up a storm of protest from conventional and conservative elements, especially the church, which accused him of being anti-Christian. In 1759 niggling complaints to bureaucrats caused Diderot to lose his publishing license. Broken in spirit by censors and hounded by lawsuits, Diderot died of stroke July 30, 1784, in Paris and was buried in the Church of St. Roch alongside the playwright

Pierre Corneille. (Bishop 1965; Diderot 1972; Fellows 1989; Gassner and Quinn 1969; Hornstein et al. 1973; Wilson 1972)

See also escapism; naturalism; *Supplement aux Voyages de Bougainville.*

 # DISILLUSION

A common theme in dystopian literature, disillusion arises from overblown expectations of ease, luxury, escape, unforeseen threats to life or liberty, or failed fantasy, as demonstrated by a number of characters:

- Lemuel Gulliver, naive protagonist and world traveler in Jonathan Swift's *Gulliver's Travels* (1727)

- Offred, the central breeder and escapee from Gilead in Margaret Atwood's *The Handmaid's Tale* (1985)

- the unnamed speaker and observer of anarchy in the streets in Doris Lessing's *Memoirs of a Survivor* (1974)

- Equality 7-2521 and Liberty 5-3000, the Adam and Eve of Ayn Rand's *Anthem* (1937)

- Winston Smith, hapless pawn of bureaucracy and victim of prison torment in George Orwell's *1984* (1949)

- gangster Alex, the focus of Anthony Burgess's *A Clockwork Orange* (1962)

- the overworked domestic animals in George Orwell's *Animal Farm* (1945) who despair of finishing the windmill, which is touted to save them work

- the disenchanted boys on an idyllic South Sea island in William Golding's *Lord of the Flies* (1954)

- the title character in Lois Lowry's *The Giver* (1993), a grieving old man who hesitates to train a successor for a life of heartbreak

On the whole, disillusion with outsized promises of a perfect world leads characters away from prophetic dreams and demagogues' glittering speeches to the application of dogma to everyday functions, e.g., the study of Karl Marx and Friedrich Engels's collectivist theories as contrasted with the realism of world communism. Usually, the disparity between promise and delivery results in a shortfall for society. Consequently, such characters as Aldous Huxley's John the Savage, George Orwell's Winston Smith, and Yevgeny Zamyatin's D-503 suffer a catastrophic collapse of belief systems and the ensuing malaise. The devastation by loss of faith causes the Savage to escape through suicide; for Smith, release follows capitulation to Big Brother, the symbolic head of Oceania. D-503, a cautious genius, lapses into physical decline before rousting himself from self-absorption and attempting to save a doomed race. In similar manner, William Golding's Ralph tries to flee his peers, who have become atavistic hunters on the Edenic Pacific island; Burgess's Alex allows himself to be indoctrinated as prison guinea pig in an experiment meant to rid him of the urge to ravage the city in senseless gang-style destruction; and Lois Lowry's Jonas pedals his bike into the bleak landscape to save one infant from extermination.

In an internalized form, disillusion is also a natural offshoot of the idealistic demands of a perfectionist, as demonstrated by the title character in Hermann Hesse's *Siddhartha* (1951). Having grown up in luxury, Siddhartha discovers the empty heart and soulless outlook of the jaded Brahman caste. In flight from his father's isolated milieu, he rids himself of worldly encumbrances and ultimately locates in his spirit the answer to disillusion in a righteous merger with God. Unlike Swift's Gulliver, who pushes himself so far from the norm that he can never be satisfied with anything human, Siddhartha welcomes the myriad faces of humanity in the stream of people who pass his hut at the riverside. In a single kiss of affirmation from Govinda, a fellow seeker, Siddhartha counters his former disillusion with a universal form of love. (Atwood 1972; Burgess 1962; Golding 1954; Hesse 1951; Lessing 1988; Lowry 1993; Orwell 1949; Rand 1946; Swift 1958)

See also Alex; *Animal Farm; Anthem; A Clockwork Orange; The Giver;* Gulliver, Lemuel; *Gulliver's Travels, The Handmaid's Tale;* John; *Lord of the Flies; Memoirs of a Survivor; 1984;* Siddhartha; *Siddhartha.*

DIVINA COMMEDIA

Dante Alighieri's grand, epic masterwork of the Italian Renaissance was begun in 1308 and ostensibly completed in 1320, a year before his death. Filled with figurative and literal trinities, the literary epic consists of an introductory canto and three segments, which are in turn made up of 33 cantos. Written in first person, Dante's 14,233-line *Divina Commedia* details the soul's journey from the lower reaches of hell upward through nine levels of lessening forms of torment and into Purgatory, the second stage of his poem. From this antechamber to heaven, the soul continues its quest for Paradise, the serene abode of the blessed. The underlying philosophy draws on the poet's extensive self-education in classicism, mythology, and biblical lore, and envisions Florence and all Christendom in ages to come. Replete with Dante's distaste for Vatican venality and nepotism and for Italy's turbulent back-stabbing politics, the work serves as a moral handbook of the early Renaissance.

The title indicates a work that uses the common language to achieve a satisfactory end. The poet, a key figure in the journey motif, follows Virgil, Rome's epic poet, who precedes the character Dante through hellish scenarios and out again into starlight. Composed in everyday Italian, *The Divine Comedy* employs terza rima—a tightly controlled three-line stanza featuring interlocking rhyme, i.e., aba, bcb, cdc. The poet's intense imagery and skillful versification perplexes the modern translator, who must retain the vigor and lyrical flow of Italian in the transfer of thought to the target language.

- *The Inferno*, arranged by degree of unrighteousness or violation of God's laws, delineates tortuous recompense for sin. Dante's hell contains the vilest villains plus assorted heretics, liars, miscreants, criminals, cheats, sybarites, and atheists. The path leads downward to Satan from the least culpable—Homer, the enlightened pagan, alongside Virgil, Horace, Lucian, Ovid, Plato, Aristotle, and Socrates, who dwell in the upper circle, or Limbo, the abode of the unbaptized.

  Opening in A.D. 1300 on Easter Friday, Dante loses his way in the murky Wood of Error and faces a she-wolf, lion, and leopard, an allegorical triad of worldly temptations. The 35-year-old pilgrim encounters his literary idol, Virgil, whom the Virgin Mary, St. Lucy, and Beatrice send to lead him through his descent to the lowest of hell's nine circles. Over the entrance, a discouraging inscription warns: "Abandon all hope, ye who enter here." The duo advance into a dismal landscape and, with assistance from Charon the boatman, cross Acheron, one of the four rivers that course through the mythical hell of Homer. On the far side, they confront the five strata that encircle the realm of Dis, or Hades, god of the Underworld and husband of Proserpina. At this stage of their descent, the journeymen enter Limbo and observe the least reprehensible of Hell's unrighteous—the unbaptized, who died outside the pale of the church.

  Circling lower into dire regions ruled by the judge Minos, one of the three justices in classical depictions of Hades, Dante and Virgil watch gales sweep over the lustful in imitation of lives controlled by passion. Below these sufferers in a mucky sty repose the gluttonous, guarded by Cerberus, the three-headed hellhound. Beyond, in the fourth and fifth tiers, the avaricious and profligate, like Sisyphus, shove boulders at one another in perpetual contest. Along the foul Stygian marshland on hell's bottom, circles six through nine house the violent—heretics, killers, and suicides—depicted as pathetic trees tormented by metal-clawed harpies. Beyond the bloody shores of Phlegethon, centaurs stand watch over despots, including Attila the Hun and Alexander the Great.

  Circle seven constrains usurers, blasphemers, and sodomites in smoldering graves under a deluge of fire over the desert plain. On this level, Dante speaks briefly with his former teacher, Brunetto Latini, who predicts the poet's eventual greatness. Beyond a cataract is the final and most despicable pair of circles, reserved for cheats, squanderers of ecclesiastic wealth, panderers, seers (including the Greek Teiresias), hypocrites, counterfeiters, alchemists, and plotters, who inhabit loathsome ditches. Encased in numbing ice in the frozen lake of Cocytus under the supervision of giants and Titans, Lucifer, who was once God's light-bringer, devours three earthly traitors: Judas Iscariot, Brutus, and Cassius. At this point in his tour, a baleful Dante follows Virgil by secret passage along Satan's flank and the center of gravity to the Southern Hemisphere of Earth, arriving at 7:30 A.M. on Easter morning.

- *Purgatory:* opposite hell lies the mountain of Purgatory, where Dante continues in the steps of Virgil, his guide. Through seven levels of purification for the deadly sins of pride, envy, wrath, sloth, greed, gluttony, and lust to the Garden of Eden at the top, the duo again witness a hierarchy of sins that must be expiated through penance. At each tier, sinners unburden themselves of whatever amount of culpability they carry from their earthly lives. The length of their stay is determined by the extent of wrong in their past. Like the purified sinners who have climbed through the gauntlet of terraces, Dante arrives at the top, where Virgil vanishes.

  To Dante's delight and amazement, a woman appears who bears strong resemblance to Proserpina or Venus. She promises to alleviate his "mind's thirst" at the stream at the crest of the hill, where nature is endowed by God's blessing. In Canto 28, the guide welcomes the wanderer to a haven:

  > Nor do I think my words shall less be prized
  > By thee, that they exceed my promises.
  > They who in old time dreaming poetized
  > Of the felicity of the Age of Gold
  > On Helicon perchance this place agonized.
  > Innocent here was man's first root of old;
  > Here blooms perpetual Spring, all fruits bound:
  > This is the nectar whereof each hath told.

At ease in her company, Dante relaxes and turns his attention fully to her words.

  Led by Beatrice, his idealized love, Dante approaches the goal: Heaven, the third segment of the poet's cosmology. Ahead she points out "a sudden splendor" so bright it resembles lightning. An entourage of 24 elders walking in pairs and adorned with white lilies sing songs of blessing. The spectacle taxes Dante's ability to describe it. He urges, "read Ezekiel, who describes so rich a vision in his prophecies." A gleaming chariot advances, around which three female dancers, robed in red, white, and green, form a ring. A fourth, decked in purple, precedes two aged men and one old man "with piercing visage," thus comprising seven figures, a significant number in biblical numerology reflecting the number of days the Creator worked to make the universe.

- *Paradise.* With Beatrice in the lead, Dante navigates the concentric circles separating the planets—Mercury, Venus, the Sun, Mars, Jupiter, Saturn— and fixed stars up to the *Primum Mobile,* or Prime Mover, the founding force that energizes the universe. Each ring corresponds to a virtue or area of knowledge that is epitomized by the elect of God. Along the way, Dante encounters the great mentors, leaders of godly militia, pious legislators, saints, and angels. At the Empyrean level, Dante again changes guides as Beatrice remains behind.

Giovanni de Paolo, a fifteenth-century Italian, illustrated a scene from *Divina Commedia*, or *The Divine Comedy*, by Dante Alighieri.

Under the care of Bernard of Clairvaux (1090–1153), a mystic and saint, the pilgrim achieves a vision of the Trinity. In Book 27, at a distance he hears heavenly voices raised in the unified song of Paradise:

> Glory to the Father, to the Son, and to
> The Holy Ghost . . .
> And that sweet song intoxicated me.
> What I saw was like a universe in smiles.

Overwhelmed by joy, love, peace, and security, in Book 30 Dante views a light shaped like a gold stream "painted with the marvels of the spring." The flowers along the bank sparkle like rubies set in gold. Straight ahead lies the heavenly court; the sublime vision melts his heart. With the wisdom gained from his tedious, terrifying trek through hell and Purgatory, Dante looks back on the unified whole of the cosmos, a revolving wheel powered by God's love.

(Anderson 1989; Bloom 1986b; Boorstin 1983; Boorstin 1992; Collins 1989; Dante Alighieri 1968; Dante Alighieri 1982; Johnson 1968; Mack 1962)

See also baptism; Dante Alighieri; didacticism; Eden; heaven; religion; Virgil; women in utopia.

 # DON QUIXOTE

Cervantes's fictional idealist is the central character of Spain's epic episodic novel *El Ingenioso Hidalgo Don Quixote de la Mancha* (1615). In Part I, Chapter 1, Señor Alonso Quixano, at age 50 a devoted reader of romances and dreamer of dreams, is so entranced by chivalric lore that he sells arable land to buy books, most of them written by his favorite romance writer, Amadis of Gaul. To deck himself in a fantasy of knight-errantry, he alters his name to Don Quixote, dresses in odd pieces of his great-grandfather's armor, and sets out on his rawboned nag Rozinante as the champion of right. Knighted by an innkeeper, he frees a young man from bondage and is battered by a vicious muleteer. His neighbor, Pedro Alonso, rescues the deluded romantic from the roadside and escorts him home, where Alonso's niece Antonia and the housekeeper dress his wounds.

Cervantes depicts his hero as rapt and entranced by romantic lore to the point of monomania. Against all obstacles, Don Quixote persists in his calling as knight-errant by joining with Sancho Panza, a peasant farmer, and searching for more adventures. Don Quixote jousts with windmills, fights with an innkeeper over a kindly barmaid, and launches a siege against a torchlight funeral cortege. In a benevolent act, he frees Ginés de Pasamonte from a coffle of galley slaves. The felon repays him by beating him and stealing Dapple, Sancho's mule.

Whatever the earthly woe, Don Quixote transcends its barbs by wrapping himself in visions of the ideal woman. Wandering toward the Sierra Moreno, he mourns for his lost love, Dulcinea, to whom Sancho hurries with a message. He is intercepted en route by Don Quixote's friends, Nicholas the barber and the local curate, who intend to lure the old man back to his home. Don Quixote continues to embroil himself in the unrequited loves and deceptions of scoundrels, rogues, and ne'er-do-wells. Against a background of deceit and violence, he maintains his belief in chivalry and his faith in Dulcinea, his fair maiden. As he rededicates himself to the quest, he insists that the knight, before engaging in some great feat of arms, shall

> . . . behold his lady in front of him and shall turn his eyes toward her, gently and lovingly, as if beseeching her favor and protection . . . and even though no one hears him, he is obliged to utter certain words between his teeth, commending himself to her with all his heart.

With this shimmering vision before him, Don Quixote, like Dante illuminated by the presence of Beatrice, presses on, not in the least daunted by recurrent disasters.

The author creates numerous opportunities for the old don to realign his idealism with reality; Don Quixote evades them all. In one instance, Samson Carrasco, a clerk sent by the old man's housekeeper, assists Don Quixote by playing a role in his delusions. Pressing on, Don Quixote and Sancho arrive at the island of Barataria on July 21, 1614. The duke and duchess, who intend to mock the wayfarers, experience a change of heart and sympathize with Don Quixote's struggles against evil. They award Sancho a governorship; he attempts to rule, then abandons the role, partly in disgust and partly because of homesickness for his family.

Cervantes ends the episodic journey with the aged knight's denunciation of the false philosophy that inspired him. Returned to La Mancha, Don Quixote recuperates. He contracts a lethal fever, then returns to normalcy and renounces the false persona of the knight-errant and the folly and deception of romance literature. In Part II, Chapter 16, he writes:

> My judgment is now clear and unfettered, and that dark cloud of ignorance has disappeared, which the continual reading of those detestable books of knight-errantry had cast over my understanding.

After composing a will, the old man dies. Samson, seeking to immortalize the nobility, altruism, and charity of his friend, writes that Don Quixote "reck'd the world of little prize, and was a bugbear in men's eyes; but had the fortune in his age to live a fool and die a sage."

The enduring theme of Don Quixote's exploits is his adherence to the ideals of chivalry, particularly justice and innocence. As both benefactor and victim of a cruel world, he maintains his exuberance and challenges all comers, whatever the size, number, or menace. He proclaims in Part II, Chapter 1:

> But our depraved times do not deserve to enjoy so great a blessing as did those in which knights errant undertook and carried on their shoulders the defence of kingdoms, the protection of damsels, the succour of orphans and wards, the chastisement of the proud, and the rewarding of the humble.

The only reward Don Quixote needs to complete his perfect world is the opportunity and privilege of bowing at the feet of his beloved, saintly Dulcinea, the mythic and unattainable lady of his dreams. At the end of his failed quest, the self-sacrificing don looks beyond drubbings and pratfalls, a lost ear and ruined armor, unseatings, ridicule, and robberies to his most painful shortcoming—the failure to help others.

Readers and critics alike have identified with Cervantes's visionary anti-hero and his delusions. The humor and pathos of Don Quixote's missions lie not in his accomplishments but in his influence. A repository of gentlemanly virtues consistent with the title character in Baldessar Castiglione's Renaissance handbook *The Courtier* (1528), Don Quixote proclaims his creed in Part II, Chapter 17:

> I know well the meaning of valor: namely, a virtue that lies between the two extremes of cowardice on the one hand and temerity on the other. It is, nonetheless, better for the brave man to carry his bravery to the point of rashness than for him to sink into cowardice.

Flawed, but at heart right-thinking, Don Quixote satisfies some human need to believe in a code of behavior and a purity of purpose that transcends the ugliness, squalor, greed, sacrilege, rapacity, and treachery of the real world. Because the old man clings to an impossible standard of gentility derived from a lifelong study of his romances, he epitomizes the seeker of truth who dedicates a doomed quest to the transcendent ideal that lives in his mind and heart and on the pages of his favorite books. Undaunted by failure and uplifted by Sancho, Don Quixote maintains a classic outlook that survives in those who read and emulate his fictional adventures. (Bloom 1986b; Byron 1988;

Don Quixote's companion, Sancho Panza, finds the idealist and his horse on their backs, victims of tilting at a windmill. French artist Gustave Doré illustrated an 1863 edition of *El Ingenioso Hidalgo Don Quixote de la Mancha* by Cervantes.

Castiglione 1976; Cervantes 1957; Duran 1974; Gilman 1989; Mack 1962; Nabokov 1984; Predmore 1990; Riley 1986; Russell 1985)

See also Cervantes Saavedra, Miguel de; *The Courtier;* Dulcinea del Toboso; fantasy; idealism; Sancho Panza; women in utopia.

 DOROTHY

A fresh, innocent, spunky child with the average ability to get into mischief, Dorothy is the central character and heroine in L. Frank Baum's *The Wonderful Wizard of Oz* (1900), a classic utopian children's fantasy. Like Alice in Wonderland and the Darling children of Barrie's *Peter Pan* (1904), Dorothy, a disillusioned Kansas farm girl who lives with Aunt Em and Uncle Henry, takes her dog Toto and leaves home. The motivation of her flight is discontent with midwestern rural life. With no warning of potential disaster, the two are whirled away in a tornado and deposited near the imaginary city of Oz.

For good reason, Dorothy displays hospitality and sympathy to other characters who share her search for a better life. She invites them to journey with her to the Wizard in the Emerald City, where she hopes to gain directions back to her home in Kansas. Dorothy's compassion leads her to befriend a Scarecrow, Tin Woodman, and Lion, who participate in the many adventures on the way to the palace of the Emerald City, the lair of the witch of the east, and the home of Glinda, the good witch of the south. During these fearsome wanderings, Dorothy reveals the kind heart and stout courage that make her a heroine. At length, Dorothy uses her magic silver slippers to return home, leaving behind each of her companions in a kingdom suited to them. (Baum 1983; Baum and MacFall 1961; Bewley 1970; Manguel and Guadalupi 1987; Mannix 1964; Snodgrass 1992; Snow 1954; Wagenknecht 1968)

See also Baum, L. Frank; Emerald City; escapism; fantasy; Oz; women in utopia; Wizard of Oz; *The Wonderful Wizard of Oz*.

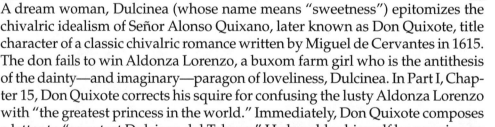 DULCINEA DEL TOBOSO

A dream woman, Dulcinea (whose name means "sweetness") epitomizes the chivalric idealism of Señor Alonso Quixano, later known as Don Quixote, title character of a classic chivalric romance written by Miguel de Cervantes in 1615. The don fails to win Aldonza Lorenzo, a buxom farm girl who is the antithesis of the dainty—and imaginary—paragon of loveliness, Dulcinea. In Part I, Chapter 15, Don Quixote corrects his squire for confusing the lusty Aldonza Lorenzo with "the greatest princess in the world." Immediately, Don Quixote composes a letter to "sweetest Dulcinea del Toboso." He humbles himself by penning an ornate rhapsody at the end: "Should it be thy pleasure to favour me, I am thine. If not, do what thou wilt, for by ending my life I shall satisfy both thy cruelty and my desires." Sancho remarks that the letter is the finest he has ever heard.

In contrast to the shallow, down-at-the-heels, out-at-the-elbow noblewomen, promiscuous serving girls, and gossipy, trivial peasants Don Quixote and Sancho encounter on their odyssey, Dulcinea remains a spiritual vision of chastity and unattainability, never appearing in the flesh. As lofty a mirage as a chance sighting of the Madonna, she is therefore incapable of negating her symbolic role as inspiration for a champion. Dulcinea is a personification of the idolized maiden of the Middle Ages and, like the Virgin Mary, Dante's

Beatrice, and Elaine, the Lily Maid of Astolat from Arthurian lore, she impels Don Quixote to acts of faith, bravery, self-sacrifice, and love. In her honor, the deluded old knight-errant, like the hypothetical court figure in Baldessar Castiglione's Renaissance classic *The Courtier* (1528), holds to the lofty goal of perfect courtly behavior and unswerving dedication. (Bloom 1986; Byron 1988; Castiglione 1976; Cervantes 1957; Duran 1974; Gilman 1989; Nabokov 1984; Predmore 1990; Riley 1986; Russell 1985)

See also The Courtier; Dante Alighieri; *Divina Commedia;* Don Quixote; fantasy; idealism; Sancho Panza; women in utopia.

 # DYSTOPIA

A literary and/or philosophical "bad place," anti-utopia, or hell on Earth, dystopia is the negative side of the perfect world, a haven corrupted by the misapplication of principles or theories or from deliberate tyranny, power-mongering, sadism, or subversion of human rights. Although the writer of dystopian literature may frame a haven, plot the perfect escape from ennui or coercion, or anticipate an otherworldly nirvana as in, for example, Happy Valley in Samuel Johnson's "Rasselas, Prince of Abissinia" (1759), eventually the edifice crumbles into spiritual emptiness, despair, tyranny, disillusion, loss, or chaos. Usually, the literary style departs from straightforward depiction toward parody, fable, fantasy, or satire, as demonstrated by Jonathan Swift's *Gulliver's Travels* (1727), Ray Bradbury's "There Will Come Soft Rains" (1950), William Golding's *Lord of the Flies* (1954), Doris Lessing's *Memoirs of a Survivor* (1974), and Lois Lowry's *The Giver* (1993).

The most influential examples in English literature are Aldous Huxley's *Brave New World* (1932), James Hilton's *Lost Horizon* (1933), Ayn Rand's *Anthem* (1937), and George Orwell's *Animal Farm* (1945) and *1984* (1949). The dystopic point of view in each case was a natural outgrowth of the grim totalitarianism that strangled Europe and radiated outward to Africa and the South Pacific following World War I and extending beyond World War II. From the failure of Nazism, fascism, and Stalinism evolved a readership for dystopian literature, which expresses widespread disaffection for collectivism, the annihilation of freedom, and terror of nuclear war. Other examples of nineteenth- and twentieth-century dystopian literature cover works from a variety of sources: Yevgeny Zamyatin's *We* (1921), Herman Melville's *Typee* (1846), Samuel Butler's *Erewhon* (1872), Ray Bradbury's *Fahrenheit 451* (1951), Anthony Burgess's *A Clockwork Orange* (1962), Marge Piercy's *Woman on the Edge of Time* (1976), Margaret Atwood's *The Handmaid's Tale* (1985), and P. D. James's *The Children of Men* (1993). (Connelly 1986; Cuddon 1979; Holman 1981; Johnson 1968; Oldsey and Browne 1986)

See also collectivism; disillusion; escapism; fantasy; totalitarianism; utopia; women in utopia.

 ECLOGUES

See Bucolics.

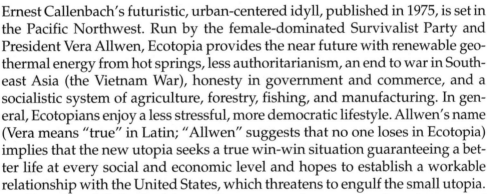 ECOTOPIA

Ernest Callenbach's futuristic, urban-centered idyll, published in 1975, is set in the Pacific Northwest. Run by the female-dominated Survivalist Party and President Vera Allwen, Ecotopia provides the near future with renewable geothermal energy from hot springs, less authoritarianism, an end to war in Southeast Asia (the Vietnam War), honesty in government and commerce, and a socialistic system of agriculture, forestry, fishing, and manufacturing. In general, Ecotopians enjoy a less stressful, more democratic lifestyle. Allwen's name (Vera means "true" in Latin; "Allwen" suggests that no one loses in Ecotopia) implies that the new utopia seeks a true win-win situation guaranteeing a better life at every social and economic level and hopes to establish a workable relationship with the United States, which threatens to engulf the small utopia.

The plot of Callenbach's novel centers on the two-month assignment of William Weston, a young, impressionable reporter for the *New York Times-Post*, to Ecotopia, an exclusive stretch of land north of Nevada that is independent of the United States. Having withdrawn from the 50 states in 1980, the Ecotopia of spring 1999 amazes Weston with its self-sufficiency, pragmatism, and successful recycling program, which permeates every human activity. He travels northwest from Reno to San Francisco aboard the Sierra Express, which is equipped with beanbags so passengers can lean back, smoke marijuana, and enjoy the beauties of nature. By cab, he penetrates security lines to a livable land that has not communicated directly with the rest of the United States in nearly two decades.

On arrival, Weston locates relics of the hippie generation—ragbag fashions, gypsy skirts, and patches clipped from natural fibers—and finds the same laid-back attitude toward bureaucracy, personal freedom, and human rights. He undergoes stringent border-patrol perusal, then enters a friendly microcosm where people take time to explain the improvements wrought by such antipollution measures as Ecotopia's unusual system of forestry and forest refuges. In San Francisco, Ecotopia's capital, wide walkways, free bicycles, and public-service trams replace traffic-clogged streets. Underground streams are rerouted to the surface; buskers and food vendors lend an air of street festivity to ordinary daily commerce. People who once lived on the fringe now live in the cities, and skyscrapers have been recycled into apartment buildings. Cable communication still exists, but programming centers on public information and education rather than mindless entertainment. Schools require direct student involvement in nature instead of passive acceptance of lectures and memorization of rules. A better informed, healthier populace throngs the streets and enjoys the people-friendly city.

Weston acclimates quickly to a spartan hotel room with hotplate and teapot and to the picturephones that assist him in communication. He is less enthusiastic about a deer carcass that hunters flaunt, or the matter-of-fact attitude of women toward casual sex and the honest expression of jealousy, rage, security, and desire. Sewage recycled into fertilizer has improved land productivity to the point that farming must be suppressed to halt surpluses. Renewable sources such as bone, shell, fur, and ivory supplant plastics and other synthetics created from petrochemicals. Factories still produce parts, which workers assemble by hand in a pleasant, stressfree atmosphere. Consumers demand do-it-yourself projects and partially completed products to assemble at home. Humanity rather than technology stands at the core of city services. When people have doubts, they ask themselves how the Indians would have settled problems.

An overwhelmingly antiestablishment feeling pervades Callenbach's call for more emotion, more human interaction, and less bureaucracy and structure, particularly in science, education, and invention. Deeply immersed in the philosophy of the 1970s counterculture, his characters explain the prevailing sentiment, as with Bert's comment in the May 8 entry in Weston's notes:

> [W]e don't have to be stable. The system provides the stability, and we can be erratic within it. I mean we don't try to be perfect, we just try to be okay on the average—which means adding up a bunch of ups and downs. But it means giving up any notions of progress.

Other changes in human affairs epitomize Callenbach's distaste for racial integration and crime, drifting or unstable human relationships, and competitive sports.

- Black communities withdraw to their own ghettos, universally known as Soul City.

- Victimless crimes such as prostitution are banished from the law books; true felons and those guilty of white-collar crimes (influence peddling, graft, embezzlement) work in labor camps, where conjugal visits are encouraged as a means of rehabilitation.

- Couples in Ecotopia have reason to love and commit to one another and to enjoy hiking, cross-country skiing, and camping, activities that emphasize togetherness.

- Private retreats have been turned into public parks. Dams have been dynamited to return human participation in white-water rafting and salmon runs. War games siphon off negative emotions.

Reproduction in Ecotopia focuses on overpopulation around the globe. Weston learns firsthand from Marissa Brightcloud, a forest dweller who becomes his lover, that Ecotopian women expect an even give-and-take in courtship, intercourse, and free expression. Female-controlled contraceptives and abortions stabilize the growth of population, and women dominate the family. Weston tries to draw citizens into discussions of eugenics, gene splicing, and cloning, but finds them unwilling to comment on biotechnology. A positive side of female equality is the intuitive professionalism of nurses, who use primary nurse care, massage, psychological comforts, and sexual arousal as a means of curing ailments.

The main character of Callenbach's utopia undergoes an extensive change of heart during his two months in Ecotopia. His loyalties sway back and forth between Ecotopia and his children in New York; his intense personal commitment to Marissa and her Edenic commune lead him to despair. At the request of President Allwen, Marissa's brother Ben orchestrates a benign kidnap to the hot springs. Under house arrest, Weston bathes in steaming saunas while he fights his mental battles over the direction taken by Ecotopia and its impact on the environment and on his own spirit. In an overly romanticized conclusion, he rejects the white-shirt-and-tie mentality of the East Coast milieu. In place of high-powered journalism, he chooses to commit himself spiritually and patriotically to Marissa and Ecotopia. He hopes that the U.S. president will authorize a diplomatic pass so that his children can join him. (Callenbach 1975; Callenbach 1981a; Callenbach 1981b; Callenbach 1990; *Contemporary Authors* 1988)

See also baptism; Callenbach, Ernest; city planning; naturalism; technology; women in utopia.

 # EDEN

A Hebrew synonym for the Persian concept of Paradise, the word derives from the Akkadian *edinu* and the Sumerian *Eden*, or plain. An early model of the verdant garden utopias is the earthly Sanskrit garden, Shambhala or Shambalah, described as a secluded Tibetan nook, which may have served as a model for the Shangri-La of James Hilton's *Lost Horizon* (1933). Perhaps the most common form of utopia, those in Edenic lore are often set in pastoral or idyllic locales, and are initially free of normal human strife, fluctuations of weather, and other vicissitudes of life and nature. Many are located on islands, in hidden valleys, or in out-of-the-way or unexplained spots such as the South Seas home of William Golding's survivors in *Lord of the Flies* (1954), the South American jungle of W. H. Hudson's lush setting in *Green Mansions* (1904), the classic landscape of H. G. Wells's Eloi in *The Time Machine* (1895), and Denis Diderot's *Supplement to Bougainville's "Voyages"* (1772).

Adam and Eve exist in an Eden envisioned by Dutch painter Hieronymus Bosch (1450–1516) in *Garden of Earthly Delights*.

By definition, Eden is an uncomplicated utopia. In an emotional vacuum exclusive of the complications of sexual passion or the necessity for human reproduction, the Edenic utopias exist in a fantasy stasis, unlike their satiric, antipastoral, or graphically asocial counterparts, particularly the antihuman Houyhnhnm-land of Book 4 in Jonathan Swift's *Gulliver's Travels* (1727), Ayn Rand's arbitrarily mated pairs in *Anthem* (1937), and *We* (1921), the suppressed Russian dystopia of Yevgeny Zamyatin. Genesis, a creation myth attributed to the Yahwist, an unknown Old Testament writer who wrote the J text, one of the literary strands from which the canon version derives, around 950 B.C., follows the Mesopotamian tradition in describing Eden as the home of the first male and female. The Hebrew Eden, meaning "delight," parallels a cultivated Mesopotamian oasis, enclosed park, or garden spot east of Israel in the midst of wilderness, possibly in modern-day Iraq. Eden is described in the pictorial cosmology or primeval history of Genesis, the opening book of the Pentateuch, which scholars link to Babylonian creation narratives. The idyllic garden is the cradle of the first human inhabitants, who led innocent, unsophisticated, uncomplicated lives in service to the Almighty.

In the first three chapters of the myth, an all-powerful deity hovers over a murky abyss and sets about reshaping nothingness into an orderly, productive framework. Bound in numerology, the story sets this action in a period of seven days. On day one, God—called *Elohim*, the patriarchal Creator who exists as a spirit—creates light as a contrast to darkness. The second day, he forms the firmament; the third day, he creates arable land as the antithesis of water, thus establishing a green habitat in which land animals, birds, and humankind can survive. This tripartite utopia reappears in Deuteronomy 5, a crucial chapter in which God presents Moses with the Ten Commandments. In Genesis 1:8, God restates the arrangement of matter as heaven above, Earth in the center, and waters beneath the earth, the menacing liquid chaos that later in Genesis overwhelms Earth's surface and drowns all but God's chosen family, their patriarch Noah, and an ark full of animals.

In the King James version of the story of Eden, God names his dry land "Earth" and the waters "seas." Having proclaimed them good, on the second day, as described in Genesis 1:11, he sets in motion the perfect, self-regenerating garden:

> Let the earth bring forth grass, the herb yielding seed, and the fruit tree yielding fruit after his kind, whose seed is in itself, upon the earth: and it was so.

To establish growing seasons, on the fourth day God makes evening and morning, seasons, days, and years, which are governed by the movements of heavenly bodies. By the fifth day, God's garden is ready for flying and swimming creatures. The next day, he adds beasts and cattle, the last stage of preparation for man and woman, the superintendents of the garden. By the seventh day, God is content with his earthly Paradise and blesses a day of rest.

In Genesis 2:7, the poet appends a second description in which God—called *Yahweh*, the sovereign lord—forms man in his image "of the dust of the ground, and [breathes] into his nostrils the breath of life; and man became a living soul."

In the paean to Adam, who walked with God and enjoyed immortality, the singer of Psalm 8 exalts the first man as "a little lower than the angels" and graced "with glory and honor." The poet lauds Adam's role in Paradise as a "dominion over the works of thy hands" as well as over "the beasts of the field, the birds of the air, and the fish of the sea, whatever passes along the paths of the sea."

Depicted as God's earthly agent, this noble caretaker derives the name Adam from the Hebrew 'adamah, or earth; the shortened form 'adam means man. He preceded the planting of God's utopia and received a splendid garden "eastward in Eden." The myth does not name the fruit trees by species, but the creator plants "every tree that is pleasant to the sight and good for food; the tree of life also in the midst of the garden, and the tree of knowledge of good and evil." In this detailed version of creation, God supplies Eden with four rivers—Pison, Gihon, Hiddekel, and Euphrates—as well as gold, bdellium (the resin called myrrh in the New Testament), and onyx, a semiprecious ebony stone. The Creator puts Adam in charge of tending this garden, but forbids on pain of death that he eat of the tree of knowledge of good and evil. To lighten the burden of work and loneliness, God makes animals and birds, which Adam names. Then God puts Adam into a trance, removes one of his ribs, and shapes it into a woman, or helpmeet, who provides the gardener with companionship. (The Sumerian version calls her "the lady of the rib"; the Hebrew calls her Eve, or life.) The two exist in harmony and without clothing, for they feel no shame of their bodies.

This dramatic, prototypic myth is concluded in Genesis 3, which accounts for the existence of evil. One of the creatures, a serpent of the field, tempts the woman to eat from the forbidden tree by convincing her that God has lied to Adam to conceal a hidden power. The serpent contends that if the two garden-dwellers eat of the tree of the knowledge of good and evil, they will themselves become deities. After the woman yields to the sophistry of the deceptive serpent, she and Adam, doomed by their act of hubris and rebellion, grow ashamed of their nakedness and cover their genitals.

Nemesis in Old Testament lore is swift and sure. In retribution for this disobedience of God's direct order, the guilt-ridden creatures are sentenced in reverse order. First, the proud, insinuating serpent receives appropriate demotion: It has to crawl on its belly and live in the dust, ever an adversary of humankind. God proclaims to Eve the second punishment, which is to bear children and undergo the rule of her husband. Adam, whom God chastens for his overweening ambition, is to suffer the gardener's hardship of unrelenting toil and stubborn soil that harbors thorns and thistles. God commands him: "In the sweat of thy face shalt thou eat bread, till thou return unto the ground; for out of it wast thou taken: for dust thou art, and unto dust shalt thou return." Finally, God denies the first couple access to the tree of life and condemns them to spiritual death, followed at the end of their days with physical death. The story ends in disunity, a jangle of misunderstanding between a beneficent heavenly sovereign and his disobedient first family. Earth no longer cooperates with the gardener; the serpent never returns to a harmonious biological scheme, which is the basis of the biblical utopia. God drives the original gardeners out of Eden, where a flaming sword wards off a second transgression against the Almighty's commandments.

Later biblical references enhance the picture of Eden. The prophet Ezekiel, who flourished about 600 B.C., describes a jewel-encrusted haven and a dazzling shimmer of color and beauty that reflects a similar passage in Gilgamesh, an Akkadian myth dating to 3000 B.C. In Chapter 28, verses 13–14, God speaks to Ezekiel of a glittering "garden of God" where, before the fall, man was covered with jewels:

> . . . sardius, topaz, and the diamond, the beryl, the onyx, and the jasper, the sapphire, the emerald, and the carbuncle, and gold: the workmanship of thy tabrets and of thy pipes was prepared in thee in the day that thou wast created.

Ezekiel reminds humankind that God created people as the "anointed [cherubs]" who inhabited God's sacred mountain. Ezekiel blames the sinful human heart for destroying utopian bliss by defiling Eden's perfection.

The last book of the New Testament, Revelation 22, achieves closure with the utopian myth of Genesis. At the end of a powerful and at times terrifying vision of the face-off between good and evil and the restructuring of Earth, the narrator looks back to the idyll that Adam and Eve once possessed. Poetic lines call forth "a pure river of water of life, clear as crystal." Revelation 22:2 recalls the tree of life, a regenerative female image, which "yielded her fruit every month: and the leaves of the tree were for the healing of the nations." Paralleling the disunity of the human fall from grace, the final lines of Revelation anticipate bliss in the heavenly tree and waters of life.

A similar description of Eden and its first denizens appears in Book 7 of the Koran, the sacred text of Islam. The scenario in which God's commandment is broken depicts Satan corrupting Adam and Eve simultaneously by simplistic guile: He claims to be their friend, thus seducing them into disobedience against God's law. In verses 23–24, the couple plead for mercy, but God remains adamant and orders: "Go one the enemy of the other, and live on the earth for a time ordained, and fend for yourselves." As with Genesis, this nonnegotiable sin tests God's patience with his creatures, whom he no longer treats as divine wards.

In Book 35 the writer returns to the glories of Paradise, created by an almighty hand intent on rewarding the virtuous. In verse 35 the blessings of Eden pour forth at the end of life: "They will enter the gardens of Eden, where they will be adorned with bracelets of gold and pearls, and of silk will be their garments." At the end of worthy lives, the blessed know "mansions of eternal rest, where there is no labor for us, nor does weariness come upon us." For the wicked, a fiery hell does not consume, but continually torments. The exact parameters of these idyllic and woeful abodes remain known only to God, who alone can attest to the sincere penance of the human heart. Moreover, Book 56 indicates heavenly rewards awaiting the worthy on the Day of Judgment: gold couches, perpetual youth, beakers filled to overflowing, dainties and delicacies to eat, and pleasant companions.

Much of the detail of these ancient accounts of Eden colors John Milton's 12-book *Paradise Lost* (1667), an English epic composed in the Puritan tradition. The dramatic plot details Satan's dismay at falling from heaven into an infernal burning lake filled with such demonic companions as Beelzebub, Mammon, and Dagon. Satan's corruption of Adam and Eve and their loss of Eden, where they had served as sole garden-keepers, achieves his goal to get even with God by spoiling the perfect garden. The despair of the first couple's departure from the entrance guarded by flaming swords, from which the first couple make their solitary way, completes the final lines. (Alexander and Alexander 1973; Anderson 1966; Eliade 1986; Hooke 1963; Johnson 1968; Holy Bible 1958; Mays 1988; Miller 1970; Pelikan 1992b; Rabkin 1983 et al.; Shepard 1990)

See also Adam; Avalon; *Back to Methuselah;* creation, mythic; Elysian Fields; Eve; Genesis; Gilgamesh; golden age; heaven; Koran; *Paradise Lost; Paradise Regained; Timaeus;* Valhalla.

ELDORADO

A fabled New World city paved with Incan gold, Eldorado is an imaginative product of European interest in exploring Mayan and Incan civilizations in search of treasure. According to fifteenth- through seventeenth-century lore, Eldorado is comprised of realms supposedly inhabited by the Noble Savage, a fictionalized utopian aborigine, in perfect worlds common to the writings of utopists Michel de Montaigne and Denis Diderot. As presaged by Richard Hakluyt's *Voyages* (1582) and Ponce de Leon's search for the Seven Cities of Gold and the Fountain of Youth, Eldorado so enflamed European fancy that it spawned reams of legends about the Caribbean isles, which were supposedly populated by gentle natives who lived off the progeny of nature and the teeming seas and who never worked, fought, suffered, or died of illness.

The sixteenth-century search for Eldorado appears frequently in literature, notably Chapters 17 and 18 of Voltaire's *Candide* (1759), in which a peripatetic hero and his valet Cacambo flee from Paraguayan pursuers, float away in an abandoned canoe, and "recommend [themselves] to Providence." After wrecking on the reefs downriver, they climb ashore at a mysterious city vaguely situated beneath "inaccessible mountains." The terrain bodes well, with its lacing of roads covered with carriages drawn by red sheep and bearing handsome people. Jewels and ore are so commonplace that children use them as markers for games; natives laugh at Candide's admiration of their value.

Throughout the breakneck episodes, Voltaire maintains the naïveté of his protagonist, Candide. At first he draws all the wrong conclusions about the profusion and availability of wealth, which he concludes belongs to the royal family. With the inept logic he learned from his tutor, he muses, "It is probably the country where all goes well, for there must obviously be some such place." Signs of a pleasant atmosphere include cheerful music, robust activity, and the smell of cooking. At the inn he is served several sugar-based drinks along with

... four soups each garnished with two parrots, a boiled condor that weighed two hundred pounds, two roast monkeys of excellent flavor, three hundred colibri hummingbirds on one platter and six hundred other hummingbirds on another; exquisite stews, delicious pastries; all this on platters of a sort of rock crystal.

Candide rouses the staff's mirth by paying with gold pieces, which Eldoradans disdain as worthless. The host clarifies his policy: "All the hostelries established for the convenience of commerce are paid for by the government." Candide and his valet conclude that this wonderfully hospitable country must be unknown to the outside world, "for there absolutely must be one of that sort."

While injecting a satiric jab against church corruption for the reader's sake, Voltaire also makes the sojourn in Eldorado into a learning experience for Candide. During a month's residency, he learns from an elderly retiree that the country was founded by Incas and that the people remain innocent of the value of their gold because they have no contact with the "rapacity of the nations of Europe." To maintain religious equilibrium, all Eldoradans are priests and thus have no monks to proselytize hapless victims. During a visit to the king, Candide and his servant are dressed in robes of hummingbird down, escorted to the throne room, and welcomed with kisses. A tour of Eldorado reveals lofty public buildings, colonnades, squares, the Palace of Sciences, and flavored and perfumed fountains, but no courts or prisons. At the end of a month of luxury and royal welcome, despite dissuasion from the king, Candide concludes that he must depart Eldorado. He tells his valet:

If we stay here, we shall be no different from anybody else; but if we go back to the old world with a mere twelve sheep laden with Eldorado stones, we shall be richer than all the kings of Europe put together.

Devoted to a work ethic and to his lady, whom he must seek in Cayenne, Candide returns, lifted by an ingenious hoist over the treacherous mountain passes, to civilization beyond Eldorado.

Candide is not the only utopian vision of the legendary city of gold. In 1849 American romantic poet Edgar Allan Poe devoted four stanzas to "Eldorado," to which a brightly clad knight journeys. The seeker grows too old to travel and despairs of finding the mysterious city. As his strength ebbs, he encounters a "pilgrim shadow." To the knight's question about the location of Eldorado, the shadow replies, "Over the mountains of the moon, down the valley of the shadow ride, boldly ride . . . if you seek Eldorado!" Other writers demystified the legends of a mythic city of gold. In "Un Voyage à Cythère," a lyric poem by Charles Baudelaire, a contemporary of Poe and ardent admirer of his fanciful verse, the speaker degrades the once-dreamed-of city of gold to a *"pauvre terre"*—"a country famous in song, banal Eldorado of all the old bachelors. Look! after all, it is a poor land!" (Bernstein 1983; Johnson 1968; Poe 1962; Thompson et al. 1991; Voltaire 1961)

See also Candide; city planning; idealism; satire; women in utopia.

ELOI

Eloi are the effete, insubstantial inhabitants of England 8,000 years in the future who welcome the unnamed Time Traveller of H. G. Wells's dystopic science-fiction novel *The Time Machine* (1895). Only four feet high and as chubby of limb as roly-poly babies, these gentle, flaccid beings are denuded of body hair, dressed in unisex robes and sandals, and speak in short, cooing sentences. To the Traveller's dismay, when he needs to extract information about his lost time machine, the Eloi quickly lose their train of thought, as though years of neglect have deprived them of powers of concentration. The Traveller notes that they resemble Dresden china figurines:

> Their hair, which was uniformly curly, came to a sharp end at the neck and cheek; there was not the faintest suggestion of it on the face, and their ears were singularly minute. The mouths were small, with bright red, rather thin lips, and the little chins ran to a point.

In this golden age of the future, Wells's deliberate diminution of the Eloi widens the gap between them and their alter egos, the grossly bestial Morlocks.

In Chapter 4 the Eloi, adorned with flowers and chatting amiably, invite the Time Traveller to a banquet hall, where they share meals composed solely of fruit and converse gaily while he studies them more closely:

> In costume, and in all the differences of texture and bearing that now mark off the sexes from each other, these people of the future were alike. . . . I felt that this close resemblance of the sexes was after all what one would expect; for the strength of a man and the softness of a woman, the institution of the family, and the differentiation of occupations are mere militant necessities of an age of physical force.

The Traveller concludes that exposure to constant violence and fear has reduced the birthrate and narrowed the sexual characteristics of the Eloi, as well as sapped them of courage. After dining, the Eloi huddle together for sleep on the hall's marble floors away from the depradations of their antithesis, the savage meat-eating Morlocks, who live in subterranean caves and roam the landscape by night to sniff out prey.

Shortly after his arrival, the Traveller acquires a female Eloi, Weena, as a knowledgable companion after he rescues her from drowning. Although her strength is limited, Weena manages to introduce the Traveller to much of her society's beliefs and activities by guiding him through a deserted museum. He observes the danger of a Morlock attack in dark corners of the building, which he illuminates with burning camphor. In the rough-and-tumble of a Morlock attack during a forest fire, the Time Traveller loses his precious guide Weena. Ominously, he concludes that the Eloi are "mere fatted cattle" for their malicious natural enemies. (Geduld 1987; Parrinder 1986; Wells 1964)

See also bestiality; classism; golden age; Morlocks; technology; *The Time Machine*; Weena; Wells, H. G.; women in utopia.

ELYSIAN FIELDS, OR ELYSIUM

A classic form of paradise, the Elysian Fields are the eternal isles of the blessed, according to lines 167–173 of Hesiod's *Works and Days* (eighth century B.C.), Book 4 of Homer's *Odyssey* (eighth century B.C.), and Book 2 of Pindar's *Olympian Odes* (fifth century B.C.). In the latter, the plain of Elysium suffers no foul weather or strong wind, but revitalizes itself each day in a refreshing sea breeze and produces fragrant, verdant spring bowers. The idea may have derived from Minoan descriptions of the afterlife, which separated the Underworld from the land of bliss. Described in two euphoric stanzas from Aristophanes's *The Frogs* (405 B.C.), Elysium suggests an Edenic or pastoral haven:

> . . . the fields of roses
> The flowery meadow lands,
> E'en as our will disposes
> This loveliest of bands.
> Beside us go the Muses blest
> Uniting us in song and jest.
>
> The sun to us is giving
> Alone his gladsome ray,
> For holy was our living,
> We have been taught the Way;
> Did citizen or stranger call
> We had a welcome for them all.

This serene abode, vaguely situated far to the west of the Mediterranean world under the rule of the Underworld judge Rhadamanthys or the Titan god Cronus, welcomed the virtuous and departed heroes for a restful sojourn and a taste of glory as a reward for valor, skill in weaponry and strategy, and patriotism. Still in possession of their former identities, the blessed enjoyed contests of strength, music, and banquets.

Other descriptions place the Elysian Fields elsewhere. In the third book of Pausanias's writings, the isle of the blessed, also known as the White Island in the Black Sea at the delta of the Danube River, lay beyond the Bosporus far to the northeast of Greece. Among the souls enjoying its delights were Cadmus and Harmonia, Achilles, Patroclus, Antilochus, Ajax the Great, Ajax the Lesser, and Menelaus and Helen. Adonis, condemned to six months' exile, spent his time in Elysium, then returned to Earth in early spring to spread green vegetation for the delight of Venus, his beloved.

Roman lore brings the Elysian Fields closer to the Judeo-Christian concept of heaven or the afterlife. In Virgil's *Aeneid* (19 B.C.), the Blessed Fields impart health and eternal life to those who have earned blessings. A bucolic way station located in the Underworld, Elysium stood apart from Tartarus, the place of punishment. Before reaching this spot, Aeneas followed the Cumaean Sibyl past Lake Avernus and the Fields of Mourning to the Secluded Fields and the Fields of the Blessed. As envisioned by Virgil, the Elysian Fields lay in a deep valley that offered the souls of the dead temporary respite from life before metempsychosis (rebirth in human or bestial form). Before this transformation, souls drank of the river Lethe, forgot their past lives, and journeyed back to Earth for a subsequent existence. Basing this recycling of spirits on early Orphic hymns and the writings of Pythagoras and Plato, Virgil may have adapted the concept of transmigration of souls to accommodate his glorification of Augustus's line by linking Rome's male heroes to the mythic warriors of Greece. (Durant 1939; Fischer 1968; Grant 1962; Guerber 1921; Hesiod 1973; Howatson 1991; Morford and Lenardon 1977; Seltman 1960; Tripp 1970; Virgil 1950)

See also Aeneid; Aristophanes; heaven; Hesiod; women in utopia.

 # EMERALD CITY

A symbol of fulfillment and hope, the Emerald City is the focal point of power and the source of rescue in L. Frank Baum's utopian children's fantasy *The Wonderful Wizard of Oz* (1900). On approach, Dorothy and her companions—a cowardly Lion, a Scarecrow, and a Tin Woodman—spot a green glow that grows brighter as they follow the Yellow Brick Road to the city wall. At a large gate studded with emeralds, Dorothy pushes the bell and the gate swings open. Inside, they find a high arched room and more emerald-studded walls. They are greeted by the Guardian of the Gates, a greenish Munchkin-sized man clothed in green, who warns them of the power of the terrible Great Wizard. To endure the brightness of the glowing city, the visitors don spectacles, which the Guardian produces from a large box. On the tour, they marvel at green marble houses and pavement joined by rows of emeralds and green glass windows. So powerful is the emerald glow that the sun's rays are also green, the color of hope.

Baum links his moralistic story with such delightful details as a preponderance of green in the Emerald City. The shops are filled with green goods and clothes. In place of horse-drawn conveyances, people use pushcarts. In the center of the city, a green-uniformed, green-bearded soldier guards the palace. No more than one visitor per day can see the Great Wizard, who terrifies everyone with his power. While awaiting their audience, Dorothy and her fellow travelers stay in comfortable green guest chambers perfumed with green fountains and supplied with green beds, clothing, and books.

Baum's deliberate connection of the Emerald City with Oz's humbuggery reaches its climax after Dorothy is granted an audience with the wizard. As she approaches the throne, she marvels at an impressive audience room rising loftily to an arched roof; a bright light sets off twinkling jewels. The Great Wizard's green marble throne dominates the center of the room. On it is seated a giant hairless head from which issues a voice saying, "I am Oz, the Great and Terrible." On a subsequent audience with the Scarecrow, Oz takes the form of a bejeweled, winged lady. The third day, Oz presents himself as a great beast that resembles a combination of elephant, rhinoceros, and monster, with five arms, five legs, and woolly hair. At the fourth audience, the wizard appears as a glowing ball of fire.

At this point, Baum ends the magic with some straight talk from Oz himself, who became the wizard by a series of accidents. After Oz reveals his deception through fakery, hauteur, and ventriloquism, the Emerald City ironically passes into the hands of the Scarecrow, an unlikely next ruler. Oz floats away beneath a silken hot-air balloon, leaving behind a grieving populace. The impression of majesty, control, and glitter, which were accomplished through theatrical trickery and the use of special glasses, proves that the power of the Emerald City is illusory. By freeing Dorothy from the hocus-pocus of the wizard on his throne, Oz sets in motion the change of attitude that prepares Dorothy for her abrupt reawakening in her own bed in Kansas. (Baum 1983; Baum and MacFall 1961; Bewley 1970; Manguel and Guadalupi 1987; Mannix 1964; Snodgrass 1992; Snow 1954; Wagenknecht 1968)

See also city planning; Dorothy; fantasy; Oz; Wizard of Oz; women in utopia; *The Wonderful Wizard of Oz*.

EMILY

Emily is the compelling urchin in Doris Lessing's dream-state dystopia described in *The Memoirs of a Survivor* (1974). Thrust on the anonymous speaker as a deserving foster child, Emily degenerates from clean, fussy little Miss Priss to pushy straw boss of a gang of street delinquents. At first she clings to a stray cat named Hugo, who eases the pain of a disrupted life and offers a frail bit of security. At the dissolution of a friendship with Janet White, a neighbor in the apartment house, Emily turns to roving bands in the street.

Lessing demonstrates the destructive power of random evil in the corruption of Emily, an unlikely convert to anarchy. An ill-advised sexual liaison with Gerald, Lessing's altruistic leader and rescuer of street children, impels Emily to greater involvement in crime, even the sacking of her foster parent's flat. Emily's interest in little-girl clothes turns to a symbolic desire for raw, amorphous, fur garments suggesting the atavistic state of her contemporaries. When the speaker searches for Emily and finds her in Gerald's heatless, comfortless dwelling, Emily lolls on skins like a Neanderthal bride held captive by the most repulsive inducements.

In the dystopian style of Anthony Burgess's *A Clockwork Orange* (1962) and Margaret Atwood's *The Handmaid's Tale* (1985), Lessing reaches a nebulous, joyless conclusion. The protagonist's departure from this anchorless dystopia is a gradual acquiescence to the threat of aimlessness, random crime, and defeat. The speaker accompanies Emily, Gerald, and the cat on a flight to the forest. Pathless and goalless in their failed civilization, the trio forms a semisolid family unit headed by Emily, whose strength of purpose will not allow her to sacrifice herself among the young hoodlums who cling to life on the streets. (Bloom 1986c; Dembo and Pratt 1993; Fishburn 1985; Knapp 1984; Lessing 1988; Myles 1990; Sprague 1986)

See also dystopia; *Memoirs of a Survivor*; women in utopia.

ENGELS, FRIEDRICH

A German social philosopher, economic analyst, and idealist, Engels collaborated with Karl Marx, the father of communism and author of *The Communist Manifesto* (1848). Born November 28, 1820, in Barmen, Prussia, Engels was the son of a cloth manufacturer whose plants in Westphalia, Germany, and Manchester, England, made him wealthy. Yet, from 1842, when Engels was dispatched to England to learn his father's business, he felt out of place among bluebloods and was drawn to a group of young radicals who called themselves "The Free." An advocate of socialism, he strongly supported the overthrow of capitalism, which he believed strangled the proletariat. At age 24 he met Karl Marx, whose opinions so paralleled his that the two formed a lifelong friendship grounded in ideology. Their first published work, *Die deutsche Ideologie,* illustrates their harmonious relationship, with Marx providing the fire and Engels the pragmatism and style.

Whether working in Belgium, studying proletarian demands in Germany, or agitating for reform in England, Engels and Marx remained true to the ideal of an end to the arrogant, overmoneyed aristocracy and the formation of an idyllic worldwide classless state. They wrote together, sometimes publishing under Marx's name alone. A separation of Engels's ideas is virtually impossible, but the clear, incisive writing style is uniquely his, as are views on the role of the military in revolution and the necessity for international cooperation. On his own he published *Conditions of the Working Class in England* (1845) and other articles and monographs that clarify Marxism. In 1847 Engels was instrumental in founding the Communist League. In 1848, he and Marx published a short document that became the catechism of nineteenth- and early-twentieth-century communism—*Manifest der kommunistischen Partei,* or *The Communist Manifesto.* Due to the failure of the European socialist coalition, Engels returned to the family business, which he managed until 1869. The financial success of the textile industry enabled him to support Marx, who depended on his meager earnings from freelance journalism to support his wife and five children.

Unlike his collaborator, Engels lived out a satisfying, successful life. At age 44 he married Elizabeth Burns. Six years later he retired, settled in London, and devoted his energies to social reform. After Marx's death, Engels kept up their ideal—writing, speaking, championing unions, and uniting socialists as a means of setting up a working-class society. In his mid-sixties Engels took over Marx's incomplete *Das Kapital* and published Volumes 2 and 3. A steadfast socialist to the end, Engels died August 5, 1895, and named the three surviving Marx children his heirs. (Carver 1991; Johnson 1968; Magill 1958; Marx 1992; Marx and Engles 1985; Rigby 1992; Worsley 1982)

See also collectivism; *The Communist Manifesto; Das Kapital;* Marx, Karl.

 # EPOPS

The king of fowl in Aristophanes's satire *The Birds* (414 B.C.), Epops's name means "all-seeing." He was once Tereus, husband of Procne and despoiler of her sister Philomela; as punishment for his sin, Zeus transformed him into a bird. In the cloud kingdom above the earth and below heaven, Epops is the ruler of birds when Euelpides and Pisthetairos depart from Athens in search of a respite from petty governmental meddling, wasteful spending from the public treasury, and crumbling moral values. By maneuvering the naive Epops into accepting a plan to build an extraterrestrial haven, Pisthetairos addresses the bird population and achieves a winged haven, Cloudcuckooland.

Aristophanes uses Epops as a comic character to contrast his manipulators. His pliant personality becomes a tool of the protagonist, Pisthetairos, who skillfully creates a demand for a walled utopian city and entices birds to build it out of stone and brick. Cloudcuckooland is safe from such earthly nuisances as building inspectors, poets, influence peddlers, and scheming politicians. With Epops's assistance, Pisthetairos realizes the dream of a simple, peaceful community out of bounds to war, demagogues, and bureaucracy, and beyond the reach of Zeus's tyranny. (Aristophanes 1993; Feder 1986; Gassner and Quinn 1969; Hornstein et al. 1973; Howatson 1991; Lord 1963; Manguel and Guadalupi 1987; Prideaux 1953; Snodgrass 1988a; Spatz 1978; Ussher 1979)

See also Aristophanes; *The Birds*; city planning; Cloudcuckooland; disillusion; escapism; fantasy.

 # EQUALITY 7-2521

The disillusioned, defiant protagonist of *Anthem* (1937), Ayn Rand's dystopian novella, Equality 7-2521 reflects the critical qualities of two Greek mythic heroes: Prometheus, the defier of Zeus and benefactor of humankind, and Daedalus, the state-controlled inventor who knew more about the dark secrets of Crete's royal family than they dared risk to public knowledge. To the brainy, inquiring Equality 7-2521, being different from others is a constant burden. In Chapter 1, referring to himself by the pronoun "we," the first-person plural that he terms "the word of serfdom," the 21-year-old speaker confesses: "We were born with a curse. It has always driven us to thoughts which are forbidden." Like bright, freethinking children everywhere, he is isolated in his genius, longs to be a scholar, and wistfully characterizes himself as "not like our brothers."

Rand uses Equality 7-2521 to demonstrate her disdain for tyranny because of its lethal opposition to individuality. Like the embryos engineered in a laboratory in Aldous Huxley's *Brave New World* (1932), Equality 7-2521 is the human product of a regressive, repressive state program of eugenics that breeds children selectively. He was nurtured in a mass-produced child-care system that sleeps a hundred children together in a dormitory. From age five, Equality 7-2521 trained at the Home of the Students under an unsatisfactory mishmash of collectivist slogans masquerading as education, e.g., "We are nothing. Mankind is all." Even then, he recalls, "we were lashed more often than all the other children."

The coming to knowledge for Equality 7-2521 occurred nine years earlier at the public immolation of a tortured, tongueless martyr. Even as he was dying, the saint flashed an unmistakable eye-to-eye message. In Chapter 12 the protagonist, who was only nine years old at the time, surmises that

> ... the saint of the pyre had seen the future when he chose me as his heir, as the heir of all the saints and all the martyrs who came before him and who died for the same cause, for the same word, no matter what name they gave to their cause and their truth.

"The cause" is the single unspoken word "ego," which Equality 7-2521 cannot guess until he flees the despotic city. In his memory, the martyr's hopeful gaze transcends verbal communication by transmitting joy and pride, which become the protagonist's patrimony.

Naive to the malignant forms of power and the potential harm he could do to the system, Equality 7-2521 longs to be a scholar and later reflects, "We wished to know about all the things which make the earth around us." What he fails to grasp is the danger of a single iconoclast among a nation of sheep. If so intelligent a mind surmised the fragility of his oppressors and broadcast the futuristic society's loss of the breakthroughs of past times—electric lights, medicine, astronomy, automobiles, rail travel, and engines—the drive for learning could spread to all levels of society and topple the despotism that remands him to daily toil at the City Cesspool.

From his nighttime tinkerings with a magnet and pilfered or discarded lab equipment, Equality 7-2521 holes up in an abandoned subway station and builds an electric generator. With all his clandestine diary-writing, he lacks the words to express his yearning for a more fulfilling, challenging job than street sweeper, which the hierarchy chose for him. He suspects that there are fascinating scientific laws to learn and apply and a variety of behaviors and pastimes to broaden his knowledge of self and bolster his self-esteem. After suffering imprisonment for his rebellion, he maintains a strong altruism and intends to share his invention with humanity.

Rand deliberately sets her protagonist on dangerous turf. Equality 7-2521's naïveté about the state's cold, repressive inner workings leaves him open to torture, rejection, questioning by the World Council, and possible execution at the stake. Exhilarated by freedom and nature, after his escape he roams the Uncharted Forest and joins with Liberty 5-3000, his Golden One, to create the beginnings of a family. He discovers pride, skepticism, laughter, and sexual freedom; in Chapter 11, like a disciple of René Descartes, he rejoices, "I am. I think. I will."

From this point on, Rand opens her hero to normal human happiness. In Chapter 12, the contemplative Equality 7-2521 extends his education with intense reading from a library of old masters. He looks forward to the birth of a son and plans to open a commune to "fellow-builders . . . all the men and the women whose spirit has not been killed within them and who suffer under the yoke of their brothers." A symbol of the resurrection of individuality, Equality 7-2521 rejects all forms of control—religion, monarchy, classism, collectivism, and racism. A man free of historic fetters, he exemplifies Rand's enthusiasm for human rights and self-actualization by planning a new center of learning, "the capital of a world where each man will be free to exist for his own sake." In place of a sonorous "amen," he concludes with his new watchword: "ЕGO." (Binswanger 1988; *Contemporary Literary Criticism* 1987; Den Uyl and Rasmussen 1984; Gladstein 1984)

See also Anthem; collectivisim; conditioning; disillusion; futurism; Liberty 5-3000; technology; totalitarianism; *We;* women in utopia.

EREWHON

Samuel Butler's antitechnocratic, dystopic twist on Thomas More's *Utopia* (1516) was published in 1872. *Erewhon* is an anagram of Nowhere, which in turn alludes to Sir Thomas More's coinage of the name *Utopia* from the Greek *ou* for "no" or "not" and *topos* for "place." The novel, written in first person, is set in 1868 in an undesignated pastoral locale far from contact with other nations but bearing a distinct hint of the England of Butler's time. The sparsely populated 800-mile beach offers good harbors, which eventually draw settlers to its expansive sheep farms, reflecting Butler's years of raising sheep in New Zealand.

The adventurous narrator climbs the alpinelike slopes and encounters a native chieftain and herder named Chowbok, an ugly, grinning aborigine who retires to his hut for an evening of grog. The speaker sets out to explore the terrain with Chowbok as guide. Their relationship falters; the speaker continues without his guide. He makes his way inland to a town, where he is placed under house arrest in a building filled with rusty machine parts. In panic, he realizes that he has been incarcerated for wearing a watch, an item of contraband that intrigues and repulses locals.

The jailer sets the speaker to learning the local language. He complies partly out of curiosity and partly out of interest in Yram, the jailer's daughter, who brings him blankets and hot whiskey and water as treatment for his head cold. He gains his release and finds himself the center of interest. Blindfolded, he walks under heavy guard to Erewhon, a metropolis graced by palatial turrets and ramparts, where he lives in the household of Mr. and Mrs. Nosnibor. Mr. Nosnibor is under the care of the local straightener, an official who cures him of the crime of embezzlement by correcting his flawed value systems, and Nosnibor is restored to social functioning.

To illustrate utopia's finer points, Butler sets his protagonist on a peripatetic perusal of Erewhon. Making frequent forays about town, the speaker studies the court system, which condemns people for illness but not for felonies. In Chapter 12 he observes:

> The judge was fully persuaded that the infliction of pain upon the weak and sickly was the only means of preventing weakness and sickliness from spreading, and that ten times the suffering now inflicted upon the accused was eventually warded off from others by the present apparent severity.

In this way, Erewhonians replace medicine with a regressive penal system that attempts to repair faulty character, as demonstrated by stealing, deceiving, and other crimes, which are treated like diseases.

Ruled by a king, Erewhonians enjoy a harmonious lifestyle made more pleasing by their inherent courtesy. At first charmed by this courteous, comely people, the outsider experiences doubt as he perceives their falseness. They maintain surface harmony by feigning agreement, but privately shelter their personal differences. Paralleling their personal duplicity are their hypocritical attitudes toward banking and religion; each Erewhonian pursues a public front and a private reality. Offsetting a worship system based on the allegorical representation of love, hope, justice, and fear, Erewhonians secretly worship the goddess Ydgrun, whom the priests abominate. Their devotion to Ydgrun has evolved into high and low church, a dichotomy that reveals Butler's satiric jab at England's religion, which parallels the Lilliputian set-to between big endians and little endians in Jonathan Swift's *Gulliver's Travels* (1727).

Other aspects of Butler's dystopia undermine the façade of perfection. The educational system centers on Colleges of Unreason, where students learn hypothetics. As the speaker observes in Chapter 21:

> Life, they urge, would be intolerable if men were to be guided in all they did by reason and reason only. Reason betrays men into the drawing of hard and fast lines, and to the defining by language—language being like the sun, which tears and scorches.

To offset a tyranny of rationality, Erewhonians choose the mean rather than the extremes, and follow illogic as a method of preserving rationality from the dangers of overapplication.

A nation of Luddites, Erewhonians have survived for centuries without technology, which they destroyed on the advice of a seer who believed that machines threatened to replace humankind. In Chapter 24 the speaker, applying Darwin's concept of natural selection, attempts to follow the logic of widespread sabotage of technology:

> The lower animals progress because they struggle with one another; the weaker die, the stronger breed and transmit their strength. The machines being of themselves unable to struggle, have got man to do their struggling for them: as long as he fulfils this function duly, all goes well with him—at least he thinks so; but the moment he fails to do his best for the advance of machinery by encouraging the good and destroying the bad, he is left behind in the race of competition. . . .

To repel future menace, government officials outlaw innovation and sanction only the spade, scythe, and horse-drawn wagon. Human beings are classed by horsepower as well as by kind, species, variety, and subclass.

Chapter 26 concludes the speaker's intense study of Erewhon and its distaste for machines. Disenchanted with the exotic land, he describes how the old prophet turns the people against eating meats because the slaughter of animals violates animal rights. To escape the lunacy of this pseudo-utopia, the speaker requests permission from the queen to launch an air balloon. The king concurs without realizing that his guest intends to depart Erewhon for good.

Like a romantic novelist intent on creating a cliff-hanger, Butler stresses the human ties that force the traveler into a dilemma. Back at the Nosnibor house, he confides in his beloved Arowhena and plans for her to join him in an early morning flight. In a slow ascent, the two shiver with cold as they wait for air currents to take them across the mountain to the plains and over the sea. Suspense builds while they await their doom. In darkness, they call out toward a massive shape and are rescued by the crew of the *Principe Umberto,* an Italian vessel loaded with guano (bat droppings), surely one of Butler's most pungent jests. The escapees transfer to an English ship bound from Melbourne to London.

While plotting to guide a gunboat back to Erewhon to convert the people to a more amenable way of thinking, the speaker encounters Reverend William Habakkuk. He turns out to be the drunken shepherd Chowbok, who delivers an unintelligible speech. The speaker is so dismayed by Chowbok's appearance that he decides to visit and proselytize him to the English way of thinking. Thus, Butler winds down his adventure to an anticlimactic dialectic through which the speaker attempts to restructure and redeem a pseudoperfect world. (Butler 1968; Cannan 1925; De Lange 1925; L. Holt 1989; Jeffers 1981; Manguel and Guadalupi 1987; Rattray 1974)

See also Butler, Samuel; pastoral; religion; satire; technology; *Utopia;* women in utopia.

 # ESCAPISM

An integral theme in utopian and dystopian literature, escapism is demonstrated by numerous scenes in utopian fiction by flight, temporary retreat, island hopping, and mental transcendence through drugs, hypnosis, out-of-body experience, trance, hedonistic debauchery, and extended sleep. Overall, escapism can take the form of physical freedom through numerous retreats:

- the enjoyment of nature
- autonomy or self-fulfillment
- avoidance of adult responsibilities
- meditation and an improved knowledge of the self
- emotional and spiritual rejection of tyranny
- idealized innocence
- travel from the known to the unknown
- immersion in the past
- indulgence in creativity and the expansion of innate capacities

All of these momentary departures allow individuals to elude tyranny, confinement, authoritarianism, boredom, or some other insidious form of enslavement.

Encouraged by Jean-Jacques Rousseau's *Social Contract* (1762), a paean to the joy of living in the wild and learning from nature, escapist writers tend to emphasize the right of freedom from religious, economic, and political constraints. In Rousseau's canon, one maxim stands out: "Man is born free, and everywhere he is in chains." This unconscionable state of affairs has influenced numerous scenarios in European literature:

- Lao Tzu's *Tao Te Ching* (third century B.C.) encouraged a withdrawal into the self through contemplation of "the Way," a mystical Oriental submersion into meditation and peace.

- Disgruntled Athenians withdraw from a public muddle to the freedom of Cloudcuckooland in Aristophanes's *The Birds* (414 B.C.).

- Two pairs of lovers withdraw from family alienation to the Edenic forest of Arden in Shakespeare's *As You Like It* (1599).

- Lemuel Gulliver abandons family and homeland during his travels in Jonathan Swift's *Gulliver's Travels* (1727); he returns a fusty old misanthrope so disillusioned by his observations that he can no longer tolerate his own family.

- An enlightened encyclopedist and social critic, Denis Diderot, contemplates a pleasant idyll on an island paradise in his *Supplement aux Voyages de Bougainville* (1772).

- W. H. Hudson's Smith escapes unhappiness and social pressures by plowing and woodchopping in *A Crystal Age* (1887).

- The Darling children are wafted away on fairy dust to Neverland in J. M. Barrie's classic play *Peter Pan* (1904).

- Father Perrault, high lama of Shangri-La, avoids the mounting world cataclysm as he sips *tangatse* berry tea and practices clairvoyance and levitation in James Hilton's *Lost Horizon* (1932).

- Siddhartha, title character in Hermann Hesse's historical fiction (1951), focuses on the stream of humanity that, like the flowing river, never ceases passing his hut.

- A terrified warren of rabbits departs for a peaceful lawn and an opportunity to live a normal rabbit life in Richard Adams's *Watership Down* (1972).

- Jonas, a receiver-in-training, pedals across a bridge and into snowy no-man's land to avoid an oppressive and murderous tyranny in Lois Lowry's *The Giver* (1993).

Additional names and settings from utopian literature summon more escapes: Hank Morgan's therapeutic ocean voyage to relieve his child of croup, Gargantua's Abbey of Thélème and the residents who prefer the delights within to the world without, Don Quixote's romantic fantasies that relieve him from the tedium of home and substitute dreams of gallantry, Candide's retreat from a venal world to his Turkish garden, Samuel Taylor Coleridge's poetic Xanadu, and the whirling dervishes of Sufism. For whatever reason and by whatever manner, each character accepts some degree of risk to search for release from the tensions and responsibilities that weary, terrify, bore, or dismay.

American literature contains noteworthy examples of escapism in the writings of Henry David Thoreau, Herman Melville, Mark Twain, and J. D. Salinger. Thoreau's retreat from society in *Walden* (1854) takes him beyond the materialism and narrow provincialism of New England to a pleasant sylvan cabin on Walden Pond, where he enjoys solitude, note-taking, and contemplation of his garden and the seasons. In contrast, Herman Melville's South Seas rambles carry his autobiographical character Tommo far afield from New England and even farther from petty deckside strictures to the gentle, unencumbered lifestyle of Polynesia, as seen on a first viewing of island paradise in *Typee* (1846) and its sequel, *Omoo* (1847).

Created two decades after the Civil War, Huck Finn seeks a respite from child abuse, civilizing females, and the encumbrances of the eastern United States in Mark Twain's *Adventures of Huckleberry Finn* (1884). At the end of Huck's picaresque journey, he determines to evade the stifling influence of the eastern Mississippi shore and "light out for the Territory," the loosely structured American Indian enclave left free of codified law and only remotely touched by religion, government, and family values. A similar yearning occurs in J. D. Salinger's *The Catcher in the Rye* (1951), in which the emotionally damaged protagonist, Holden Caulfield, wishes to found a community in an unspecified spot out west where innocence, like an endangered species, can be preserved and guarded.

A uniquely chilling antitechnologic fable is Ray Bradbury's *Fahrenheit 451* (1953), which typifies escapism from totalitarian control through reading and multidimensional video entertainment. Bradbury's pitiless examination of Mildred Montag, the main character's emotionally stunted wife, exonerates Guy for his lack of commitment to marriage. Against the setting of a war-ravaged society, she drives her beetle car rapidly into the night, hitting rabbits and dogs in her path without stopping. At home she idly puffs cigarettes while following the phantasms who people the wall-screens that fill her life with a pseudofamily. After her betrayal of Montag and hasty departure from his life, he observes a bomb blast in Los Angeles that probably has incinerated her instantly. Montag realizes that he feels no grief or pity at her going because of his delight in intellectual and physical freedom.

Unlike Guy's near celibacy in a doomed marriage, flight in George Orwell's *1984* (1949) takes the protagonist, Winston Smith, away from Oceania through pleasant trysts with his lover in a room over an antique shop. Winston flees an oppressive government that crushes individuality by installing a relentless spy system. The antique shop's symbolism of a romanticized past suggests that existence in a dystopian society forces Winston to grasp at such remnants from history as a paperweight. His frequent return visits enable him to endure the psychic pain of meaninglessness and manipulation by Big Brother, symbolic overlord of the state police. As a consequence of Winston's daring violations of Oceana's law, the room to which he retreats is the site of his arrest for Thoughtcrime, or rebellion against the state. The leader of the arrest team is Charrington, the owner of the antique shop, which turns out to be a trap for people like Winston who resist totalitarianism.

Another English utopian novel, Aldous Huxley's *Brave New World* (1932), epitomizes hedonistic escape from emotion through numerous technological advances such as Obstacle Golf, feelie-palaces, Violent Passion Surrogates, Pregnancy Substitutes, sex-hormone chewing gum, Orgy-Porgies, Solidarity Services, the Super-Vox-Wurlitzeriana music machine, piped-in fragrances, and *soma*, the drug that allows residents of his Brave New World to stabilize their passions and avoid pain. So common is the avoidance of discomfort that Lenina Crowne, a central character, wears a *soma*-dispensing belt to keep sedatives at hand for any situation. Tranquilized by the drug, Lenina and her date, who have just flown over a crematorium, forget old age and death and enjoy an evening of dancing to the ether-music of Calvin Stopes and His Sixteen Sexaphonists. Another escape from the Brave New World is open only to the country's elite Alpha-pluses. Their vacations to the Savage Reservation of Malpais in Santa Fe, New Mexico, bring them in contact with primitive Zuñi locals, who copulate in the old style, perform snake dances, and take pleasure in mescal, a natural hallucinogen that relieves them of the poverty and misery of the New Mexican desert.

Similarly, Equality 7-2521 and Liberty 5-3000 in Ayn Rand's *Anthem* (1937) flee a despotic kibbutz to exult in nature and personal freedom. Unlike Huxley's vacationers, however, Rand's central characters opt for exile rather than a brief getaway. In the Uncharted Forest they learn more about their inner drives and preferences by hunting birds and cooking them, dressing themselves in brightly colored attire, conceiving a child, and reading books from a library that reflect a past time of freedom. By discovering individuality, the couple abandon the "we" of convergent thinking that fettered their former lives and come to recognize the power of "I."

Poetry also embodies the utopian penchant for escapism. Two Victorian poets—Alfred Tennyson and Robert Louis Stevenson—depict a gentle escapism in verse. Tennyson's poem "The Lotus-Eaters" (1832) carries Homer's mariners into a well-defined land where residents yield to the soft, welcoming arms of nature. Sedated by a soporific fruit that grows nearby, the newcomers slip away in vision and spirit, and recline near the beach in a drug-lulled state. With wispy recollections of home in their numbed memories, they sink into the clouded state of forgetfulness. In like fashion, Stevenson's speaker in "The Land of Nod," which is included in his poetry anthology *A Child's Garden of Verses* (1885), retreats from home each night to a realm of dreams. Similar to Tennyson's sleepy haven, streams and mountains comprise the topography of an escapist landscape that intrigues the dreamer with fragile details of food, sights, and enchanting music. (Bradbury 1953; Holman 1981; Huxley 1932; Lao

Tzu 1993; Lowry 1993; Melville 1964; Melville 1968; Orwell 1949; Rand 1946; Stephens et al. 1949; Thoreau 1965)

See also The Abbey of Thélème; *Anthem; Brave New World;* collectivism; Don Quixote; Equality 7-2521; *Fahrenheit 451;* Huxley, Aldous; Lao Tzu; Liberty 5-3000; Lotus-Eaters; Montag, Guy; *1984; Omoo;* Smith, Winston; *soma;* sufism; *Tao Te Ching;* totalitarianism; *Typee; Walden;* Xanadu.

EUGENICS

Eugenics is the application of advanced science and technology to the selection of traits to be produced in the next generation. Because reproduction often obtrudes into or inhibits the creation of a perfect world, utopian writers have evolved a number of eugenic systems intended to control population in size, sex, strength, race, malleability, and intelligence. One of the first documented efforts to control population and produce the best in future citizens is found in Plutarch's *Life of Lycurgus* (first century A.D.). Not wholly appealing to modern parents, Lycurgus's decision to examine newborns and either let them live or expose them in the wild preserves a practice that continued into ancient Rome and is reputed to prevail in modern China and India.

Fictional eugenics varies from Fra Tomaso Campanella's mild regulations governing mating and reproduction to Aldous Huxley's conveyor-belt system, which deletes entirely the womb, human contact with the fetus, and potential accidents or variance in nutrition. In Campanella's *La Città del Sole* (1602), Prince Mor, one of a trio of officials, controls the population of the idyllic Sun City by studying science and educating citizens in basic principles of breeding, e.g., pairing tall with short, and thin with stout, to even the chances of producing a child closer to the standardized model. More stringent than Campanella's system is that of H. G. Wells's *A Modern Utopia* (1905), in which conception is meant to supply society with a clear division of four castes, the top being the samurai. Ayn Rand's *Anthem* (1937) depicts a closed society in which mating is allowed once annually between couples paired by the state. An equally limited system of reproduction exists in William Morris's *News from Nowhere* (1890), in which pregnancy and birth are the province of the house matriarch of an extended clan. In this arrangement, other fertile women under the same roof must remain barren for life because their reproductive pool is not needed.

As cruel as Rand's and Morris's limited procreation plans may sound, it is Aldous Huxley's Central London Hatchery and Conditioning Centre and Bokanovsky's Process in *Brave New World* (1932) that push technology into the godlike position of creating designer embryos on assembly lines. By adjusting the chemicals in which fetuses grow, laboratory technicians control the intelligence of beings who may be cloned into a phalanx of duplicates. By harvesting a single ovary, technicians create 150 batches of identical fetuses, resulting in citizens who match like gloves. The breezy flow of a Fordian conveyor line moves without a hitch:

> Whizz and then, click! the lift-hatches flew open; the bottle-liner had only to reach out a hand, take the flap, insert, smooth-down, and before the lined bottle had had time to travel out of reach along the endless band, whizz click!

The control of Huxley's technical wizardry contrasts the unpredictable visit to the Zuñi reservation, where Indian women breast-feed without shame and Linda shocks the Brave New World vacationers with memories of viviparous, random reproduction. (Campanella 1955; Huxley 1932; Morris 1968a; Plutarch 1971a; Rand 1946; Wells 1967)

See also *Anthem*; Bokanovsky's Process; *Brave New World*; *La Città del Sole*; *The Life of Lycurgus*; *News from Nowhere*; Plutarch; technology.

EVE

In Hebrew and Islamic lore and in John Milton's *Paradise Lost* (1667) and George Bernard Shaw's *Back to Methuselah* (1921), Eve is the protypical woman and the second human being whom Yahweh, or God, creates from the rib of Adam, her mate and fellow garden-keeper. At first innocent of the nearness of evil, she lives in a perfect haven filled with a variety of fruit trees, herbs, plants, animals, birds, and fish. A vulnerable candidate for deception, Eve falls victim to the subtlety of Satan in the form of a serpent, a symbol of treachery and a perversion of godliness. The serpent tricks her by convincing her that anyone tasting of the forbidden tree of knowledge will become godlike.

At the serpent's urging, Eve falls prey to specious logic, disobeys God's rule, and eats the forbidden fruit, then shares it with her husband. For her sin, she suffers greatly multiplied sorrow and a life of subjugation to her husband, whom she seduced into transgressing God's commandments by eating from the same stock of fruit. Her lifetime sentence prefigures woman's subjugation by man and her travail and pain in childbirth. Like her husband, Eve is forced out of Eden, the paradise she was intended to share in unending servitude to the Creator. (Alexander and Alexander 1973; Anderson 1966; Chase 1955; Johnson 1968; Holy Bible 1958; Mays 1988; Pelikan 1992c)

See also Adam; Alquist, Mr.; *Back to Methuselah*; creation, mythic; Eden; golden age; *Paradise Lost*; *Paradise Regained*; *R. U. R.*; *Timaeus*; women in utopia.

EVERHARD, AVIS CUNNINGHAM

Avis is the journal voice of Jack London's *The Iron Heel* (1907), a socialist dystopian novel set in the United States in the first quarter of the twentieth century. Like her mate Ernest, Avis Cunningham Everhard bears a symbolic name; her given name is Latin for "bird," her maiden name reflects guile, and her husband's surname is a monument to the couple's resourceful strength. At the outset, Avis is an astute but pampered daddy's girl who admires her father, a college professor. To Avis's delight and edification, he fills their home with a

Eve samples forbidden fruit in the painting *Eve* by Lucas Cranach the Elder.

variety of strong-minded visitors. During the Cunninghams' evening salons, she meets her father's pet project, Ernest Everhard, a savvy, outspoken socialist.

London appears to use Avis as devil's advocate by making her skeptical of Ernest's prophetic message. Avis takes some convincing to believe that Everhard is right in predicting a takeover of the country by a disgruntled proletariat who will throw off oppression and replace the professional class with workers. By the time of their marriage, Avis, who has shrugged off the trappings of privilege and adopted the socialist cause, echoes Ernest's socialist credo. A Cassandra in her own right, she attempts to warn the entrenched church and middle class that they occupy a tenuous position beneath the plutocratic Iron Heel.

After Everhard is elected to the House of Representatives, Avis's admiration mounts for her husband's tireless efforts on behalf of workers. By the onset of the economic waterloo, she appears unruffled by the violence of the oligarchs in their attempts to crush revolting bands of proletarians. Only at the impact of an assassin's bomb on the floor of Congress while Ernest is speaking does she lose control and crumple to the floor.

London, who is not known for championing feminism, endows the fictional Avis Everhard with wit and nerve. After Ernest's trial and imprisonment for sedition, Avis maintains her idealism and supports as fully as a field operative the dream of wresting power from the oligarchs and elevating the proletariat to its rightful place. During the news blackout following the demise of the publishing industry and the post office, Avis steals away to California and lives incognito, practicing daily her husband's suggestion that she cast off her former posture, voice, mannerisms, dress, hairstyle, and other identifying characteristics. By the time the couple reunite, her disguise is so effective that she fools Everhard into what he terms a "polygamous marriage" to both Avis and her assumed identity.

The worst of street warfare, which occurs five years after Everhard's election to Congress, fails to dismay Avis. She remains on the front lines, supports her comrades, and observes the most fearful of debacles, which maims and kills many of her fellow agents. At one point, she joins her husband on a rooftop; his arms about her provide her weary frame a suitable and reassuring prop. At the sudden conclusion of her journal, Avis remains strong in her belief in a working-class majority. (Beauchamp 1984; Hedrick 1982; London 1982b; Lundquist 1987; Perry 1981; Sinclair 1983; Stone 1978)

See also collectivism; Everhard, Ernest; *The Iron Heel;* London, Jack; women in utopia.

EVERHARD, ERNEST

Bearing a symbolic name indicating his sincerity and toughness, Everhard is the handsome, black-eyed socialist hero of Jack London's *The Iron Heel* (1907), a dystopian novel warning of the rise of an American oligarchy sufficiently strong and determined to stamp out a working-class revolt. Described symbolically as poorly outfitted in a dark, ill-fitting suit, Everhard stands at five feet nine inches and offers strangers a firm hand. His oxlike biceps and neck muscles bulge against his clothes as though embodying his bold thoughts and fierce energy. He unashamedly stares with interest at Avis, the daughter of Professor Cunningham.

London's depiction of his protagonist filters through the first-person diary entries of Ernest's wife. In retrospect, Avis casts her unrefined lover in the role of aristocrat in the enemy's camp, a Nietzschean "blond beast," an Aryan superman. Her father encounters Everhard standing on a soapbox addressing an audience of workers. Labeling him a "born expositor and teacher," Avis's father takes pleasure in his future son-in-law's ability to stymie the sophism of a clutch of clergy. A former mill worker and farrier, Everhard springs from a long line of proletarian Americans. Self-educated in German and French, he escaped an unsuitable apprenticeship that began at age ten by working as translator for a Chicago publisher of scientific and philosophical works.

The author imbues Everhard with his share of faults. After immersing himself in the data of labor, Ernest grows irritatingly cocksure that his view of the coming Iron Heel is correct and unavoidable. Knowingly, he lords his prediction over his interrogators and affirms his belief in the working class. During the worst of the oligarchy's backlash, he is elected by overwhelming affirmation to a seat in the House of Representatives. At a critical moment in the economic turmoil that follows the election, he stands stoically before Congress to warn of treachery. At that moment, an anonymous assassin sidelines Everhard by hurling a bomb at his feet.

Unfazed by violence and personal injury, which he had prophesied while addressing guests at the Cunningham home, Everhard survives and is tried and found guilty of sedition. During his years in jail, he continues to write letters to his wife and to support the workers' revolution. In 1915 he rejoins Avis in her California hiding place near their enemy's vacation home. He admires his wife for her spunk and creativity in changing her appearance to avoid detection by adversaries.

Eventually, Everhard must rejoin the fray, which threatens to collapse into a meaningless hand-to-hand street scrap. The churning, roiling mobs that clash in Chicago draw him from his hiding place. He fights with a losing front in an effort to turn the uneducated, undisciplined "people of the abyss" from total chaos. The clarity of his characterization grows murky in the smoke of street fights and subterfuge. At one point, Avis perceives him solely as the pressure of an arm around her. The story ends with a noble portrait of socialists fighting the money- and power-grabbers who threaten the revival of the United States. (Beauchamp 1984; Hedrick 1982; London 1982b; Lundquist 1987; Perry 1981; Sinclair 1983; Stone 1978)

See also classism; collectivism; Everhard, Avis Cunningham; *The Iron Heel;* London, Jack.

THE FABLE OF THE BEES

An eighteenth-century allegory depicting "private vices [as] public benefits," *The Fable of the Bees: Or, Private Vices, Public Benefits* (1714) is a 408-line poem depicting Bernard de Mandeville's belief that moral weakness is inevitable to humanity. In Mandeville's vision, the only way that utopia will evolve is through a restructuring of human nature. Originally published as *The Grumbling Hive: Or, Knaves Turn'd Honest* (1705), 19 years later this lengthy piece of doggerel resurfaced as *The Fable of the Bees*, a lively bit of controversy meant to stir readers from shallow complacency to a more sophisticated understanding of vice.

In the tyrannical world of the hive, the bees live "in Luxury and Ease" while subscribing to monarchy rather than the less dependable democracy. As a microcosm of human life, the hive, symbolizing a small town, abstains from "Engines, Labourers, Ships, Castles, Arms, Artificers, Craft, Science, Shop, or Instrument." Rebel bees overthrow the cohesiveness of the hive and begin to emulate humankind by taking up human foibles and vices. Their number include entrepreneurs, lawyers, physicians, priests, soldiers, and kings. Fairness, as symbolized by the stereotypical blindfolded woman holding up the scales of justice, at length gives way to bribery, vice, and cunning deceptions. The cause of so great a change in the bees' social order is avarice, "that damn'd ill-natur'd baneful Vice."

Mandeville's vigorous parody pretends to vilify the domination of hive life by hypocrisy, laziness, and profligacy, all of which appear to encourage decline. In actuality, the theme of this often misread poem is the necessity of vice, which serves the community and civilization through the utilitarian virtue of self-interest. The hive grows so depleted of willing laborers that disaster seems inevitable, but the faithful one-tenth stand their ground and defeat their enemies. Many thousands die in the conflict, but the rest, determined to "avoid Extravagance," fly "into a hollow Tree, Blest with Content and Honesty." (Crane 1932; Johnson 1968; Magnusson 1990; Mandeville 1989)

See also allegory; Mandeville, Bernard de.

FAHRENHEIT 451

Ray Bradbury's California Gold Medal–winning anti-utopian classic appeared as "The Fireman" in Horace Gold's *Galaxy Science Fiction* in February 1951. After 20 days of concerted typing and editing on a rental typewriter in the basement of the Los Angeles Public Library, Bradbury produced the manuscript in novel form in 1953 as *Fahrenheit 451*, perhaps his best-loved work. A post-Hiroshima apocalyptic vision of technological mayhem, the novel lauds an individual survivor of a hostile twenty-fourth-century dystopia. Ironically, 34 years after the novel's publication, it was banned in a Florida high school on the grounds of offensive language. Almost immediately, parents, teachers, students, and civil libertarians insisted that it be reinstated.

The story line of *Fahrenheit 451* focuses on Guy Montag, a ten-year veteran book burner whose helmet displays the number 451, the temperature at which paper ignites. The fire company follows Beatty, a cynical fire captain who scorns literature as a breeding ground of human discontent because it promotes independent thinking, nostalgia, and hope for the future. The Los Angeles of Montag's day soaks up drugs while coexisting with perpetual nuclear clashes, repression, apathy, brutality, and routine exterminations of citizens. Outwardly posing as a devout disciple of the status quo, he secretly stashes books behind his front hall grille to feed his desire to learn.

Bradbury brings together two most unlikely soulmates in a chance encounter. After midnight Guy, reeking of kerosene, strolls from work to the subway and down the sidewalk to his house. He meets Clarisse McClellan, a passionate 17-year-old neighbor who rhapsodizes over roses, dandelions, butterflies, and the man in the moon. Simplistically, she asks if he is happy. Marriage to Mildred, a vapid, emotionless, media-centered wife, leaves him unfulfilled and exasperated; Guy is intrigued by the girl's candor and accepts Clarisse as a friend. On an adult plane, he wonders why people have stopped caring for one another.

That same evening, Guy discovers that Mildred has thoughtlessly swallowed 30 or 40 sedative pills. In their cold, moonlit bedroom, Montag summons a medical team composed of impersonal technicians who pump Mildred's stomach and purify her blood. The disquieting near-death experience causes him to turn to books for answers to humanity's loss of compassion. While performing his duty as fireman, he encounters Mrs. Blake, a spirited, elderly bibliophile who sets fire to herself with a single kitchen match rather than surrender her freedom to the menacing company of book-burners. Numbed by her courageous display of martyrdom, Guy returns home to a dismal report—four days earlier, Clarisse was hit by a car; her family quietly moved away.

Guy's spiritual malaise infects his body. Suffering fever and chills, he stays home to recover and receives a visit from Beatty, an ominous figure who suspects that Guy suffers from career stress. To make conversation, Beatty relates the history of fire fighting. The tension between the two men mounts after Mildred plumps her husband's pillow during his conversation with the chief and discovers a hidden book. Guy asks about the McClellans; Beatty replies that the authorities have long suspected them, even before they moved from Chicago, and concludes that Clarisse is better off dead. As he departs, Beatty implies that Guy should rid himself of his books by the next day.

After Beatty leaves, Guy is pushed into a dilemma and vows to quit his job. Without Clarisse, Guy has fallen back on Mildred as a source of strength and values clarification, so he reveals to her his cache of 20 books. At this dramatic moment, Mildred recoils at the menacing door voice, which indicates an unspecified caller, possibly a spy looking for books. Fear separates her from her role as supporter. With Clarisse's noble spirit as his guide, Montag searches his contraband collection for an explanation of his society's repressive inhumanity. While Guy sinks into literature, Mildred retreats into the soap opera world of wall-screen television. The couple ceases to communicate.

Bradbury offsets the loss of Guy's teenage friend with the wisdom of an elderly bibliophile. Desperate for support and affirmation, Montag rides the subway to the residence of Faber, a retired English professor whom he once encountered in the park. Bearing a Bible, Guy shares Faber's enthusiasm for books. The two men conspire to confiscate and reprint great literature and to incriminate the book-burners with their own technique—by planting books in their homes and alerting the authorities. To maintain secret communication,

Three firemen in François Truffaut's *Fahrenheit 451*, the 1967 film version of Ray Bradbury's 1953 novel, ransack a house for books to be burned.

Faber provides a clever electronic hearing device, which he invented to restore Guy's equilibrium with the "still small voice" of reason.

Bradbury depicts Guy as being on a spiritual high from the brief contact with Faber. On Guy's return to Mildred and her four-screen madhouse, he antagonizes her women friends—Mrs. Phelps and Mrs. Bowles—by reading poetry to them, a daring act that suggests his flirtation with certain death. Fearful that the fire company will burn their house, Mildred pretends that fire fighters are allowed books once a year. She urges Guy to read them a meaningful bit of verse. At his recitation of Matthew Arnold's "Dover Beach," Mrs. Phelps breaks into tears. Guy forces the women out of the house.

Although Guy avoids returning to work, the inevitable clash of philosophies forces him back to the fire station. With Faber's transmitter pressing him on, Guy relinquishes a contraband book to Beatty, who is embroiled in an after-hours card game, symbolic of the intrusion of chance into Guy's reclamation. In a direct face-off, Beatty cites classical sources in an attempt to outwit Guy, who continues to follow Faber's whispered directions. The fire alarm ends the discussion; Beatty drives the Salamander to the Montag house, the fire department's next target.

Bradbury's dissolution of the Montag marriage leads to overconfidence and murder. Guy squirts kerosene on his own residence and watches the frenetic dance of the burning books. Suitcase in hand, Mildred, who summoned the squad, runs toward a beetle-taxi and out of Guy's life. Beatty arrests Guy and strikes his head, knocking the tiny device out of his ear. Because Beatty threatens Faber, Guy turns his flamethrower on the captain and his mechanical watchdog:

> . . . one continuous pulse of liquid fire . . . like a great mouthful of spittle banging a redhot stove, bubbling and frothing as if salt had been poured over a monstrous black snail to cause a terrible liquefaction and a boiling over of yellow foam.

The ghastly execution frees Guy from the danger of immediate arrest. However, before the dog disintegrates, it injects a numbing stream into Montag's leg.

Guy prepares to flee and rescues four books alongside his garden fence. He escapes surveillance by police helicopters, plants incriminating evidence at a fire fighter's home, reports the presence of the books to the authorities, and escapes to Faber's house. Faber offers a suitcase full of dirty clothes to throw the watchdog off the scent and dispatches Guy to the river. The refreshing dip, like a Christian baptism, renews Montag's energy and vision. No longer despairing, he travels along the railroad tracks toward a mysterious "winking eye," senses Clarisse has walked the same way, and encounters a band of bibliophiles and their leader, Granger, clustered around a camp fire.

The end of the past is violent and abrupt. Via portable television, Guy observes as duplicitous authorities execute an innocent man whom they claim to be Guy as a means of placating fearful citizens. A nuclear attack obliterates Los Angeles, obviously killing Mildred and many innocent victims. In sympathetic company, Guy, like Lot departing the destruction of Sodom and Gomorrah, turns his gaze from the city. He discovers that volunteers preserve classic ideas by memorizing titles that might otherwise disappear. Anticipating that Faber will contact him from St. Louis, Guy merges with a new society of individuals who devote themselves to freedom of thought.

Long a classic on book lists, *Fahrenheit 451* presents a reasonable balance between dystopic unrest and the promise of a new start. Bolstered by his baptism in the river that divides the paranoid past with the promise of a new beginning for literature, Guy loses his fireman's scent and eludes the mechanical tracker. Turning from nuclear fire, he reaches his hands to a simple camp fire, a symbol of the spiritual glow that keeps learning alive. In Bradbury's telling, Guy's defiance of despotism comes at a price—the loss of his job, Clarisse, Mildred, his secret library, and his home—yet the risk is worth the break from spiritual stagnation and constant fear of reprisal. The land ahead, although surely not a utopia, awaits with the promise of normal human endeavors and enlightenment, which book-lovers share by adopting the personae of books. (Bradbury 1953; Bradbury 1975; Breit 1956; Clareson 1976; Indick 1989; Johnson 1968; Johnson 1978; Knight 1967; Mogen 1986; Slusser 1977a)

See also Beatty, Captain; Bradbury, Ray; Montag, Guy; technology; "There Will Come Soft Rains"; women in utopia.

FANTASY

Fantasy is a capricious, fanciful, imaginative style or work of literature that delights in whimsy, inventiveness, and an escape from reality. Like speculative fiction and beast fable, fantasy comprises a subgenre of both utopian and science-fiction literature. A prevalent conceit or vehicle for utopists, fantasy may toss the reader by unusual transportation—a dream, a blow on the head, a violent outburst of nature, a fall into a chasm, or a trance—into an unexpected milieu; for example:

- In L. Frank Baum's *The Wonderful Wizard of Oz* (1900), Dorothy and her dog Toto are whirled by a cyclone from a Kansas farm to the Land of Oz, where Dorothy and her pals seek help from the Wizard, who lives in the Emerald City where everything is green, and who escapes his trumped-up throne and overrated power by boarding a hot-air balloon.

- Buoyed by pixie dust from their London nursery, the three Darling children navigate through the air to Neverland in J. M. Barrie's *Peter Pan* (1904), an escapist fantasy that lauds childhood fancy over the stuffy strictures of adulthood.

- In pursuit of a talking rabbit, Alice of Lewis Carroll's *Alice in Wonderland* (1865) rushes headlong into a steep rabbit hole leading her to Wonderland and its bizarre coterie of rats, caterpillar, turtles, lizard, and unusual humans, including a complete range of court personae clustered about the King and Queen of Hearts. In the sequel, *Through the*

Looking Glass (1872), Alice makes a more complex change of settings by reversing her image and penetrating a parlor mirror.

In these instances, fantasy transports the characters to three fanciful settings: a fairyland replete with undersized people and a witch who can be dissolved in water; a seaside children's society in constant battle with a crocodile, pirates, and Indians; and an unpredictable realm ruled by the Queen of Hearts and guarded by a deck of anthropomorphic playing cards, who do Her Majesty's bidding lest she scream her ominous command: "Off with their heads." These three children's stories, which depart from the more serious concerns and purposes of adult-level utopian literature, contain the enchanting trappings of adventure flung out of the ordinary world and into a playground that contains just enough tension and/or danger to make the plot interesting. On a separate plane, the authors use their momentary connection with young readers to satirize some of the mundane, pedestrian faults of real life—notably, books without pictures, stuffy rules about bedtime and eating all the vegetables on the plate, complete control by adults, and growing up to accept pictureless books, authoritarianism in all aspects of life, and even stuffier rules than in childhood.

Utopists also produce fantasy on the adult level. The most famous Renaissance escape into whimsy, Miguel de Cervantes's *Don Quixote* (1615), remains a tremendously popular, influential romance that takes a deluded old knight-errant dressed in outdated scraps of armor through the countryside of Spain in search of Dulcinea, his idealized lady. The fantasy that fuels the don's dreams departs from standard expeditionary motivation, for Don Quixote seeks to right wrongs and reestablish good deeds, courtesy, virtue, and right behavior in a place and time overrun by brigands, faithless clergy, deceivers, and venal innkeepers, barmaids, governors, and journeymen. Along the way to his imaginary perfect world, Don Quixote leaves a trail of wise aphorisms as guides to those who would follow him. In Chapter 51 he advises Sancho to "reverence God, for therein lies wisdom," a suggestion that springs from the Catholic environment of Renaissance Spain. Don Quixote's second maxim derives from classical Greece: "You are to bear in mind who you are and seek to know yourself, which is the most difficult knowledge to acquire that can be imagined." To these he adds injunctions to be humble, guard against the wrong kind of pride, and prefer truth to arbitrary laws and regulations. By virtue of these widespread sprinklings of the don's personal beliefs, Cervantes's novel transcends a picaresque fantasy and achieves a noble thematic framework worthy of a classic.

Other utopists have applied Cervantes's method to their own blends of fantasy and idealism. In Mark Twain's satiric *A Connecticut Yankee in King Arthur's Court* (1886), a blow to the skull precipitates the unlikely departure of factory hand Hank Morgan from his own time and place backward into the chivalric era. Hank's residency among King Arthur's subjects distorts the usual view of Camelot, a romantic setting indigenous to English lore. Similar to Twain's method of creating satire, in François Rabelais's *Gargantua and Pantagruel* (1562), the author ignores conventional restrictions on time, place, theme, and action by moving his family of giants about a shifting canvas capable of accommodating the cast of characters in a castle, abbey, drawing room, classroom, marketplace, or law court. So too does Jonathan Swift create four books of adventure on the seas in his *Gulliver's Travels* (1727). Swift's first two books illustrate the author's didactic purpose by moving from Lilliput, a land of minuscule people, to that of the Brobdingnags, a land of giants: These contrasting settings and characters offer the "gullible traveler" a pair of reverse images, each of which calls attention to human character flaws. In the first book, Gulliver concludes that human beings, with their petty, pointless religious wars, court posturings, and nit-picking laws, behave abominably. In Book 2, no less abominable are the giants, whose callousness creates a dystopic nightmare of cruelty and victimization for a visitor who is barely finger-length in comparison to his hosts.

Other fanciful settings and characters in adult fantasy invite the protagonist and the reader to examine life on new and sometimes quirky terms. Spanning the centuries, these utopian and dystopian studies take on zany, outlandish trappings:

- In Aristophanes's *The Birds* (414 B.C.), the characters acquire beaks and feathers in their haste to depart Athens and settle in Cloudcuckooland with the peace-loving Epops, king of birdland.

- Edward Bulwer-Lytton, author of *The Coming Race* (1871), creates a mysterious force, *vril*, that powers an underground city, heals the sick, and doubles as a weapon.

- In *The Time Machine* (1895), author H. G. Wells envisions a bicycle-shaped contraption capable of spinning its unnamed inventor into the near and distant future, where a dystopic world has declined to a desiccated wasteland lit by a pallid sunset and washed by a lifeless sea.

- George Bernard Shaw's five-act drama *Back to Methuselah* (1921) begins in the Garden of Eden with Adam and Eve, then carries his study of the prototypical human couple 30,000 years in the future.

- Karel Capek's *R. U. R.* (1920) concocts a world overrun by humanoids, which result from the experiments of one scientist, Dr. Rossum, and from a single factory on a remote island.

- An ominous beast fable, Richard Adams's *Watership Down* (1972) typifies the violence, coercion, and concentration-camp atmosphere of a hostile rabbit tribe that lures less savvy rabbits into servitude until the hero, Hazel, spearheads an escape and flight to a green, flower-strewn haven.

Some works are not easily delineated by the subgenre of fantasy utopia or dystopia or by science fiction. *Orlando* (1928), Virginia Woolf's tour de force novel picturing four cycles of reincarnation, pays tribute to women by liberating Orlando, born a man in the Elizabethan era and not set free of male domination until the Victorian Age, when she finds herself reborn as a female. With the luxury of "neither [fighting] her age, nor [submitting] to it; she was of it, yet remained herself. Now, therefore, she could write, and write she did. She wrote. She wrote. She wrote." Woolf's pleasure in Orlando's introduction to "Life, Life, Life!" depicts the character as strolling in the country, observing sparrows on limbs, and enjoying nature, a permanent condition of Earth that will continue after her completion of the current life. Overall, these titles vary on a continuum of fantasy to reality and realism to utopianism, e.g., *Alice in Wonderland,* which bears few identifiable dystopian elements but displays a remarkable command of imagination. (Adams 1972; Barrie 1981; Baum 1983; Bulwer-Lytton 1979; Cervantes 1957; Cuddon 1979; Hollister 1982; Holman 1981; Swift 1958; Twain 1963; Woolf 1928)

See also The Coming Race; A Connecticut Yankee in King Arthur's Court; disillusion; Don Quixote; escapism; futurism; *Gargantua and Pantagruel; Gulliver's Travels;* Peter Pan; *Watership Down; The Wonderful Wizard of Oz.*

❊ FOURIER, (FRANÇOIS-MARIE-) CHARLES ❊

Traveler and utopian socialist, Charles Fourier is the author of heavily detailed writings: *Théorie des Quatre Mouvements* (1808), a two-volume *Traité de l'association domestique agricole* (1822), a two-volume *Le Nouveau Monde industriel et sociétaire* (1829), and *Le Nouveau Monde Amoureux,* published posthumously in 1967. Born April 7, 1772 to a linen seller in Besançon, France, Fourier rejected his father's hopes that he settle into the draper's profession. Instead, Fourier worked in Lyons as a petty bureaucrat while inventing a socialist dream world, which he named Harmonia. He lost his wealth and property in the French Revolution, and in 1793 came so close to an appointment with the guillotine that he shuddered at the notion of revolt in any form.

A forerunner of the communistic writings of Karl Marx and Friedrich Engels, Fourier's treatises anticipated a series of communes, or phalansteries, devoid of the competitiveness inherent in capitalism. Believing that the earth responded to eight-stage cycles of 40,000 years of good times and a corresponding period of hard times, Fourier noted that the periods of confusion, savagery, patriarchy, and barbarity had already passed. He cataloged 12 passions and evolved a complex system of 810 personality types that must be fulfilled if civilization is to reach its height. He prophesied an earthly harmony, a golden age in which animals would cohabit in peace and human life would extend to 144 years.

Fourier's utopianism leans toward an evaluation and appreciation of human passions, instincts, and tendencies. Unlike lockstep utopias that require a single motivation or response, his perfect world, like the Israeli kibbutz or the hippie commune, uses his systemized study of passion in a complex and harmonized interaction. He sets population limits at 1,500–1,800 citizens of a predetermined mix of personalities and intends that they live in dormitories in a phalanx on a square league of turf laid out in arable fields, vineyards, orchards, and forests. Sufficing apart from neighbors, the self-contained phalanx requires a diverse terrain such as the cities of Halle, Brussels, or Lausanne.

In adulation of Fourier's accomplishment, critics laud his attention to detail and his clear schematics. At the center of his Harmonia stands a vast hall with three wings to govern material, social, and intellectual concerns. Rooms cover a variety of needs; there are workshops, museums, libraries, ateliers, refectories, salons, and reception rooms. One segment of the palace houses a temple devoted to the arts and gymnastics. At the far end is the Temple of Unityism to honor human cooperation amid diversity. Above all looms an imposing tower to serve as a communications center for signaling outlying phalanxes.

Charles Fourier

Citizens of Fourier's utopia avoid the burden of housekeeping by dining in public halls and by sending their children to vocational schools. This system frees women of drudgery so that they can participate in local governance. In exchange for work, each person receives lodging, food, clothes, entertainment, and profit sharing, i.e., a portion of the public treasury equivalent to the amount of stock the associationist holds in the common endeavor. Thus, the nation fosters ambition and individuality by allowing some options above the level of a strict commune.

Fourier's closed communities require a rigid factory system to supply each phalanx with goods and services. To relieve the tedium inherent in mechanized labor, workers rotate jobs. Like a massive labor union and wholesale cooperative, the phalanx governs itself and its productivity, and passes directly to shareholders the trade items it manufactures. Like a fine-tuned industrial army, Fourier's phalanx mobilizes its resources, both human and material, to build public works projects, replant depleted forests, irrigate fields, and drain bogs. In balance, Fourier provides one of the most generous of child-care plans, allowing for liberalized play, equestrian training, and a variety of musical instruments.

Before perfecting his associationist scheme and before redeeming his socialism from widespread ridicule, Fourier died in Paris on October 10, 1837. Despite his shortcomings as a utopist, he provided a paradigm reflecting individual differences and the role of ambition in productivity. His vision of worker colonies influenced the foundation of five short-lived American communes—Brook Farm, Oneida, New Icaria, the North American Phalanx, and Trumbull—and a steel factory in Guise, France. Followers Albert Brisbane and Victor Considérant expanded the Fourier model and searched for volunteers to populate communes. However, without the monomania of Fourier and his lengthy lists of details, the dream of harmonized phalanxes died with the founder. (Fourier 1972; Heilbroner 1989; Mumford 1959)

See also city planning; collectivism; Engels, Friedrich; golden age; Marx, Karl; technology.

 # FREILAND

Freiland is a visionary socialist utopia created by Austrian economist and civic planner Theodor Hertzka. Much of Hertzka's idyll reflects the goals of Karl Marx and Friedrich Engels, the designers of twentieth-century communism. Hertzka calls for an international free society, a commune or kibbutz of workers governed by central committees who apportion profits to all who take part. Composed in two stages—*Freiland: A Social Anticipation* (1890) and *A Visit to Freiland, or the New Paradise Regained* (1894)—Hertzka's work proposes a control on the runaway ills spawned by the Industrial Revolution. Five laws form the basis of Freiland's success: a right to land, support of indigents and the elderly, assistance to women and children, representation in government for all citizens over age 25, and a separation of governmental powers into legislative and executive branches.

On a study of Edendale, Freiland's capital, the fictional visitor views the university, bank, administration hall, libraries, theaters, and an arts academy. In addition, the city supports warehouses, schools, and other civic buildings. The visitor tours the Central Statistical Bureau, which keeps open books listing workers and their earnings. Strict right of public information prevents private deals and monopolies. Hertzka notes: "The prices at which goods are bought and sold, the net profits and the number of workmen, must be communicated at intervals which are fixed according to the judgment of the central office." Consequently, all have an equal opportunity to profit from community effort.

Hertzka concerns himself with welfare and promises a relief from the intense, onerous labor common to Europe's Industrial Revolution. Workers enjoy up to ten weeks of vacation per year, and are encouraged to find jobs that suit their temperaments and talents. Some choose small business, others opt for partnerships, but the majority vie for posts in large firms that supply work, housing, catering, and servants. Companies apply for a capital pool made up of taxes on individual wealth. This system hinders the growth of a shareholding elite whose profiteering deprives the working class.

At the Edendale Engine and Railway Manufacturing Company, the visitor learns the rules that govern private enterprise. Any applicant is eligible for a job. Presaging worker-owned experiments of the twentieth century, the staff receive a dividend based on their share of labor, which is calculated in hours. Losses and liquidation follow the same system of shared risk. Management's salary is determined by a called meeting of the company's general assembly, composed of stockholders or proxies. Before dividends are determined, the company treasurer must repay capital investment and pay state tax. Plans for expansion derive from the work of elected officials and a five-member inspection team.

The purpose of Hertzka's classless paradigm is, like Karl Marx's *Das Kapital* (1867), the equalization of enterprise, although by means other than revolution or totalitarianism. In Freiland, any entrepreneur can demand land and capital to underwrite either industrial or agricultural pursuits. Beyond its financial base, Freiland allots each family a private dwelling with garden. Zoning restrictions govern where and how building is to take place and how paved streets, canals, tramways, aqueducts, and other public works fit into the overall city plan. A sanitation department uses a vacuum system to rid streets of refuse. The obsession with mechanistic details of economics and logistics robs this utopia of life force—an interest in human participation. (Hertzka 1972; Mumford 1959; Negley and Patrick 1952)

See also city planning; *Das Kapital*; Hertzka, Theodor; Marx, Karl; technology.

FUTURISM, OR FUTUROLOGY

Futurism includes a literary prediction of probable trends, discoveries or medical breakthroughs, global weaknesses or readjustments, or the applications of scientific advancements and inventions on social systems—for instance, birth control, DNA manipulation, remote-control laser surgery, bionic replacement of human organs, or an expansion of alternative power sources to replace depleted pools of fossil fuels. Strongly connected with demographics, world power shifts, empowerment for women and other oppressed groups, and forecasting as a result of the fearful destruction of World War II and the menace of nuclear and biological weaponry, futurism remains viable in two realms:

- **Science fantasy** refers to an intriguing, sometimes diabolical exploitation of gadgetry, e.g., the rockets of Yevgeny Zamyatin's *We* (1921), mechanical workers found in Isaac Asimov's *I, Robot* (1950), and the control of nature, as with the use of *vril*, a plentiful ore that can fuel the city of Vril-Ya or cut down an enemy in Edward Bulwer-Lytton's *The Coming Race* (1871).

- **Speculative fiction,** by means of a thorough study of current knowledge, predicates which themes and theories will next uplift, streamline, dismay, or devastate humankind. Whether idealist or pragmatist, the speculator may hope to stem panic or prepare for significant changes in climate, housing, food distribution, national tensions, wars, depressions, drugs, or such natural disasters as dying animal species, virulent strains of common diseases, a warming planet, melting polar ice caps, or the greenhouse effect. Doris Lessing's study of anarchy in *Memoirs of a Survivor* (1974) illustrates her view of one of the future's greatest threats: the decline of urban living and the rise of a new dark age permeated with roving gangs of teenage vandals and rapists, scavengers looking for food, collapsing city bureaucracies, and related dangers.

Other examples of futurism predate this modern trend toward prediction and permeate the utopian genre with a materialistic delight in things:

- In H. G. Wells's *Time Machine* (1895), the unnamed Time Traveller, who maintains a home workshop and experiments with time travel, makes a lengthy voyage into the future aboard a poorly described conveyance resembling a bicycle and operated by levers.

- As anticipated by George Orwell's *1984* (1949), Ray Bradbury's *Fahrenheit 451* (1953), and Lois Lowry's *The Giver* (1993), telescreens and other communication and spying devices in residences and public buildings create societies dependent on their relationship with the electronic media and/or governments dependent on knowing the private thoughts and actions of each citizen.

- In the laboratory and hatchery in Aldous Huxley's *Brave New World* (1932), a future London society devoted to eugenics, conditioning, and hypnopaedia quells rogue passions by supplying citizens with *soma*, a tranquilizer that can be sprayed in a mist to quiet a mob or easily accessed from a cartridge belt worn on the daily uniform.

- The ambiguity of the One World concept requiring adoption of a global language, constitution, and governmental superstructure dominates the action of Arthur C. Clarke's *Childhood's End* (1953), a futuristic golden age replaced by a higher level of evolution, reducing differentiation in humans and replacing them with inert pupae, or cocoons. Clarke leaves the question of ethics to the reader, who must decide whether so great a degree of future change is truly utopian or just another form of coercion or regression.

Not all futurism resides in the world of improved science or technology. Two examples are the futurism in William Morris's *News from Nowhere* (1890) and Ayn Rand's *Anthem* (1937). Morris's novel depicts a time when a benign matriarchal system controls population and citizens abandon construction and revere houses built in the former age. In Rand's dystopia, the political situation chooses to suppress former technological advances and keep people occupied by assigning them supervised manual labor resembling the work of a press-gang. An indomitable curiosity surfaces in a street sweeper, Equality 7-2521, an amateur science buff who hides in the underground housing of an abandoned subway system to study iron rails, discarded glass laboratory equipment, and the construction of a primitive battery. Thus, the futurism of Rand's dystopia shuts citizens away from knowledge and the use of labor-saving devices, and suppresses their knowledge of incandescent lighting, sophisticated uses for glass, generators, motors, and other advantages of life in an earlier, more technologically sophisticated age.

Much of the success of futurism resides in the creation of believable characters. One of the pitiable creatures to survive a robot takeover, Alquist of Rossum's Universal Robots in Karel Capek's play *R. U. R.* (1920) slaves under the insensitive governance of a robot cabal and attempts to retrieve an earlier formulation for protoplasm so that humanity can continue on Earth. In Jack London's *Iron Heel* (1907), the position of Ernest Everhard epitomizes the powerful Marxist voice that unsettles the ruling professional class by predictions of a hostile takeover by the underclass. In Marge Piercy's *Woman on the Edge of Time* (1976), Connie Ramos, a patient being treated for schizophrenia, escapes by telepathic communication to a fragile society of the future. In each case, the well-turned character with idiosyncrasies intact proves its value to a fictional work that, without a reasonable cast, would resemble dry, unpalatable bombast or insubstantial theory. (Bradbury 1953; Bradbury 1990b; Capek and Capek 1961; Clarke 1953; Coates and Jarratt 1989; Lessing 1988; London 1982a; Morris 1968a; Orwell 1949; Piercy 1976; Rand 1946; Wells 1964; Zamyatin 1972)

See also Alquist, Mr.; *Anthem; Brave New World; Childhood's End; Fahrenheit 451;* fantasy; *The Iron Heel;* materialism; *Memoirs of a Survivor; News from Nowhere; 1984; R. U. R.;* speculative fiction; *The Time Machine; We; Woman on the Edge of Time.*

GARETH

Gareth is a young and idealistic would-be knight in Alfred Tennyson's *Idylls of the King*, a modification of medieval versions of the Arthur legends. In the second canto, Gareth, the last of the three sons of Lot and Bellicent, longs to escape his overprotective mother and seek his fortunes in Camelot, home base of King Arthur's court and the fabled Round Table. Gareth yearns to grow up, join brothers Gawain and Modred as the king's knight, and make a name for himself. To that end, he promises his mother that he will disguise his aristocratic name and work as a kitchen vassal until he can earn a worthy reputation. His mother wants him to remain in Arthur's kitchen because she believes Gareth will be safer scouring pots than riding into danger.

To justify to his mother that the dream outweighs the risk, Gareth exults in the boastful, boyish idealism that predates actual manhood:

> Man am I grown, a man's work must I do.
> Follow the deer? follow the Christ, the King,
> Live pure, speak true, right wrong, follow the King—
> Else, wherefore born?

Gareth's romanticized version of knight-errantry almost outdistances the original ethical grounding that Arthur intended for his city, its hard-fighting warrior-police, and the realm's chivalric code. By the time Gareth arrives at Camelot's gate, he is so dazzled by expectation and belief in local lore that he does not hesitate to lie to the gatekeeper to assure a role for himself on Arthur's staff.

Gareth is not disappointed. In Tennyson's Christianized setting of Arthurian lore, Arthur comports himself like a radiant deity, with morality, fairness, and beneficence, the virtues that lure young men like Gareth to join his knights. Gareth asks to remain anonymous and requests a year's service in the kitchen; Arthur agrees to his terms. Faithful to his word, Gareth the thrall performs menial service—turning meat on a spit, fetching water from the well, and chopping wood. As his hands perform each task, his ears endure the chaffing of Kay, the foul-tempered, bullying scullery supervisor.

Tennyson lauds Gareth's attention to humble duties and carries him nearer the justice center so that the boy can petition for a military patrol. During the daily press at Arthur's throne for justice for the weak and vulnerable, Gareth accepts a boon requested by Lynette, a disdainful maiden whose sister Lyonors is the prisoner of four loathsome knights in Castle Perilous. To prove his readiness, Gareth promises:

> My King, for hardihood I can promise thee.
> For uttermost obedience make demand
> Of whom ye gave me to, the seneschal,
> No mellow master of the meats and drinks!

Arthur rewards the boy's spunk with a gift of full equipage: war horse, shield, spear, and casque. Gareth's fellow kitchen workers cheer him on toward his ambition of serving the king.

Tennyson presents a second, more vitriolic male-female set-to: No longer arguing with his mother, Gareth finds himself thoroughly castigated and scorned when Lynette disdains Arthur's assignment of an underling to the case. From the outset, Lynette spurns Gareth because he is of low status and smells of kitchen grease, and because she had requested the best of Arthur's warriors—Sir Lancelot. On the ride out from Camelot, she sulks and complains. After Gareth proves able and true to his quest, she lessens her objections but continues to keep her distance. In the final scene, Gareth confronts a fearful triad issuing from gaudy tents: the living symbols of morning, noon, and evening. Behind them comes a skeletal death's head—the knight whom Gareth must overcome if he wants to restore Lyonors's liberty.

The episode of Gareth and the death-dealing knight epitomizes the too-neat allegory, the weakness of Tennyson's Victorian version of more vigorous and less tidy medieval legends. The first three knights, representing the three ages of man, sport the colors of morning, noontide, and evening. Gareth unmasks the fierce but silent fourth warrior, the bony skeleton of night, who is a mere lad under the trickery of his costume. To round out the tale with appropriate romance, Tennyson features Gareth freeing Lyonors and returning in triumph to honor his king. In one version, Gareth marries Lyonors. A second version weds him to Lynette. (Ashe 1987; Dixon 1974; Lacy 1986; Tennyson 1989; Twain 1963)

See also allegory; Arthur; Camelot; classism; *Idylls of the King;* Tennyson, Alfred.

GARGANTUA AND PANTAGRUEL

Gargantua and Pantagruel is an ebullient, witty, five-part satiric novel or comic epic about a family of giants. This episodic tale—dedicated to sots and syphilitics, cranked out on the underground press and banned by the Sorbonne for lewdness—was begun in 1532 and concluded with a questionable addendum in 1562, nine years after the death of the author, François Rabelais. So convoluted is the novel's blend of extravagant good humor, insatiable curiosity, and worldly wisdom that the author urged his readers to suck meaning from its pages like marrow from bones and to peel away the exterior layers like outer skins from an onion. Known by its enemies as an earthy, bacchic debauch and by its champions as a refreshingly untamed departure from dry dogma and rigorous pedantry, *Gargantua and Pantagruel* is subtitled "The Grand and Inestimable Chronicles of the Great and Enormous Giant Gargantua," who, with mate Badebec, produced the rollicking Pantagruel, the "Ever-Thirsty," grandson of Grandgousier, the king of Utopia.

Rabelais spares no ladylike prudes in his description of the lusty, priapic protagonist. Gargantua is born with an oversized phallus and prophetic words in his mouth: "I want drink! Bring me drink!" After extensive home tutoring, he studies Gothic calligraphy at the University of Paris, joins forces with his pal Panurge, and keeps up a steady enmity against the Dipsodes, or "Thirsty Ones." The book contains a loose stream-of-consciousness retelling of the quixotic adventures of two giants—father and son—and their retinue through a surrealistic melange of brawls, travels, and discoveries. In mock epic form, the episodic novel leads the pair to the Underworld and parodies ecclesiastical excesses, war and politics, and the medieval education system.

Rabelais employs visionary style in Chapters 52–57 of Book I, *The Abbey of Thélème,* an epicurean vignette the author intends as a gift to the endearing Frère Jean. The Abbey is a closed sybaritic community that overturns the usual rules of "chastity, poverty, and obedience," instead encouraging marriage, wealth, enjoyment, and personal freedom by following the precept of "do as you will." The inmates, who come from a privileged background of education and gentility, possess instincts for virtue, courtesy, and honor. Like the perfect Renaissance knight in Castiglione's *The Courtier* (1528), they are educated to "read, write, sing, play upon several musical instruments, speak five or six languages, and readily compose in them all, both in verse and prose." Encompassing the Renaissance spirit of sampling at will from life and learning, *The Abbey of Thélème* asserts the individual's right to throw off the yoke of scholasticism and civil authoritarianism in order to develop and express personal tastes. At the idealized court of Thélème, a local intelligentsia relishes a deformalized internal order free of clerical restraints, servitude, punishment, cumbersome laws, politics, taxation, and popery.

The story is set in a splendid château in the Loire Valley, where Gargantua rewards a monk, Frère Jean des Entomeures, for helping him in battle by naming him the abbot of Thélème. Called in French L'Abbaye de Thélème, from the Greek word *thelema* (meaning desire or will), the retreat operates contrary to the ascetic strictures usually associated with monastic life, i.e., poverty, self-denial, obedience, and chastity. The goal of the commune of Thélème reflects the height of Renaissance interests: a pleasurable absorption in learning, enjoyment, luxury, and beauty. Inhabitants—"jollie Friars and Nuns"—Rabelais describes as

> . . . lively, jovial, handsome, brisk, gay, witty, frolicsome, cheerful, merry, frisky, spruce, jocund, courteous furtherers of trade, and in a word, all worthy gentle blades . . . ladies of high birth, delicious, stately, charming, full of mirth,

ingenious, lovely, miniard, proper, fair. Magnetic, graceful, splendid, pleasant, rare, obliging, sprightly, virtuous, young, salacious, kind, neat, quick, feat, bright, compt, ripe, choice, dear, precious, alluring, courtly, comely, fine, compleat, wise, personable, ravishing, and sweet.

These Thélèmites reside under the benign rule of a wealthy patron who provides servants to do menial chores and artisans to supply gold, jewels, embroidery, clothing, and tapestries. Each resident accesses the freedom to expand mind and body to attain perfection, whether or not utility is served.

Key to liberty is the Abbey's lack of a wall. Rabelais insists that too stout a confinement produces "a store of murmur, envy, and mutual conspiracy." Adding to individual freedom is the absence of timepieces so that inmates expend no energy following precise schedules, which typify overregulated convent life. Gargantua declares, "the greatest loss of time that I know is to count the hours, what good comes of it?" Activity, he insists, should be guided by "judgment and discretion" rather than the tolling of a bell. Therefore, "None did awake them, none did offer to constrain them to eat, drink, nor to do any other thing."

Daily life at the Abbey consists of purposeful and pleasurable activity such as hawking, riding, swimming, dramatic performances, tilting, and hunting. Sumptuous garb brightens the residents, who desport themselves in Europe's latest styles cut from lavish fabrics and sewn with embellishments. Pairing of lords and ladies produces life mates who later marry and continue their "good devotion and amity" in the world beyond Thélème. Their marriages demonstrate the ideal of lifetime devotion, "in no less vigor and fervency than at the very day of their wedding."

Rabelais formulates his religious commune on a belief that people, if given the opportunity, live honorably and decently without the constant intervention of the moralistic clergy. Boldly ignoring the Catholic doctrine of original sin, he puts his faith in natural goodness. Going one step further, Rabelais lays the blame for human debauchery and evil on church doctrine, which, he claims, furthers suspicions that humankind cannot escape innate depravity. Defying the self-fulfilling prophecy that evil humanity will always follow evil, Rabelais's Gargantua proves the premise wrong by producing a lively, jovial atmosphere in which to thrive and be happy. (Bishop 1965; Boorstin 1992; Lewis 1969; Mack 1962; Manguel and Guadalupi 1987; Pollard 1970; Putnam 1993; Rabelais 1955; Screech 1980)

See also The Abbey of Thélème; asceticism; classism; *The Courtier;* fantasy; utopia.

 # GENESIS

A primeval history, Genesis is the first book of the Jewish Pentateuch, also called the Mosaic Books or the Old Testament, which existed in oral lore an indeterminate amount of time before it was arranged in narrative form around 950 B.C. Genesis covers the beginning of time up to the life of Joseph, the prophet who was sold into slavery and transported to Egypt. A memorable opening passage narrates an account of creation and Eden, the mythic home of Adam and Eve, where humanity first learned to follow the laws of their god, live and work as a couple, till the soil and tend plants, and use language in the naming of the living things around them. Embodied in the first family's actions is the universal paradigm of God's grace in contrast with human beauty and frailty, even the story of the first murder, which Cain—Adam and Eve's firstborn—commits against his brother Abel.

As opposed to similar creation lore of other nations—for instance, the animistic tales of American aborigines, whose primeval ancestors, according to the Kiowa version, crawled through a hollow log to be born, and the Greek story of the gold, silver, bronze, and iron ages as narrated in Hesiod's *Works and Days* (eighth century B.C.) and Ovid's *Metamorphoses* (A.D. 8)—Genesis is intrinsically eastern Mediterranean in style and dates to the developing civilization of nomadic Jews, or Israelites. The book is predicated on the premise that Yahweh, or the supreme God, established a fertile garden filled with earthly delights created for the pleasure of the first human being, a male, and relieved the man's loneliness and burden by providing the second human, a female. The story of the Garden of Eden, symbolic of bounty and blessing, takes a utopian form, and parallels or resets similar accounts in Babylonian, Sumerian, and Egyptian lore.

As delineated in Aristotle's *Poetics* (fifth century B.C.), the dramatic saga of Adam and Eve and their offspring contains the elements of pure Greek tragedy:

- unity of time, place, and action

- *hamartia,* or epic flaw, in Eve, who disobeyed God, and Adam, who allowed his love for Eve to entice him into a similar state of unrighteousness

- the intervention of fate; in this case, the paradox of the fortunate fall that precedes the coming of Christ to redeem the sinful human race

- *catastrophe,* as demonstrated by the serpent's success in suborning Eve through specious logic and guile

- a limited cast of *dramatis personae,* or characters—God, Adam, Eve, and the serpent

- spectacle arousing the audience to pity and fear, which Aristotle contended was a necessary adjunct to piety in that it served as a catharsis for harmful emotions

- *nemesis,* the divine retribution inherent in an act that exacts its own punishment, i.e., expulsion from the garden and a burdensome future of tilling the soil and giving birth to the following generation of Earth-dwellers.

Most poignant in the promise contained in Genesis is dramatic tension caused by the irrevocable loss of its beauty and delight through human frailty, as demonstrated by the inhabitants' temptation and subsequent disobedience of an angry, omnipotent god. Because the story contains the conventions of utopian

Incipit liber bresith qd nos genesis dicimus

In principio creauit deus celu et terram. Terra autem erat inanis et vacua: et tenebre erant super facie abissi: et spiritus dni ferebatur super aquas. Dixitq; deus. Fiat lux. Et facta e lux. Et vidit deus lucem qp esset bona: et diuisit lucem a tenebris. appellauitq; lucem diem et tenebras nocte. Factu q; e vespere et mane dies vnus. Dixit quoq; deus. Fiat firmamentu in medio aquaru: et diuidat aquas ab aquis. Et fecit deus firmamentu: diuisitq; aquas que erant sub firmamento ab hijs que erant super firmamentum: et factum est ita. Vocauitq; deus firmamentu celu: et factum est vespere et mane dies secundus. Dixit vero deus. Congregentur aque que sub celo sunt in locum vnu et appareat arida. Et factum est ita. Et vocauit deus aridam terram: congregationesq; aquaru appellauit maria. Et vidit deus qp esset bonu: et ait. Germinet terra herbam virentem et facientem semen: et lignu pomiferu faciens fructum iuxta genus suu: cuius semen in semetipo sit super terram. Et factum est ita. Et protulit terra herbam virentem et facientem semen iuxta genus suu: lignumq; faciens fructu et habes vnu qdq; sementem scdm speciem sua. Et vidit deus qp esset bonu: et factu est vespere et mane dies tercius. Dixitq; aut deus. Fiant luminaria in firmameto celi et diuidant diem ac nocte: et sint i signa et tepora et dies et annos: ut luceant in firmameto celi et illuminet terra. Et factu est ita. Fecitq; deus duo luminaria magna: luminare maius ut pesset diei et luminare min9 ut pesset nocti: et stellas. et posuit eas i firmameto celi ut lucerent sup terram: et

pessent diei ac nocti: et diuiderent lucem ac tenebras. Et vidit deus qp esset bonu: et factu e vespere et mane dies quart9. Dixit etiam deus. Producant aque reptile anime viuentis et volatile sup terram: sub firmameto celi. Creauitq; deus cete grandia. et omne anima viuete atq; motabilem qua produxerant aque in species suas: et omne volatile secundu genus suu. Et vidit deus qp esset bonu: benedixitq; ei dicens. Crescite et multiplicamini. et replete aquas maris: auesq; multiplicentur super terram. Et factu e vespere et mane dies quitus. Dixit quoq; deus. Producat terra anima viuentem in genere suo: iumenta et reptilia et bestias terre secundu species suas. Factu e ita. Et fecit deus bestias terre iuxta species suas: iumenta et omne reptile terre in genere suo. Et vidit deus qp esset bonu: et ait. Faciam9 hominem ad ymagine et similitudine nostra. et psit piscibz maris et volatilibz celi et bestijs vniuerseq; terre: omniq; reptili qd mouet i terra. Et creauit deus hominem ad ymagine et similitudine suam: ad ymaginem dei creauit illu: masculu et femina creauit eos. Benedixitq; illi deus. et ait. Crescite et multiplicamini et replete terram. et subiicite eam: et dominamini piscibus maris et volatilibus celi: et vniuersis animatibus que mouetur sup terra. Dixitq; deus. Ecce dedi vobis omne herbam afferentem semen sup terram. et vniuersa ligna que habet i semetipis semete generis sui: ut sint vobis i escam et cuctis aiantibus terre. omniq; volucri celi et vniuersis q mouetur in terra. et i quibus e anima viues: ut habeat ad vescendu. Et factu est ita. Viditq; deus cuncta que fecerat: et erant valde bona.

A 5.

A page from Genesis, the first book of the Old Testament, relates in Latin the story of creation; from a Bible printed by Gutenberg & Fust in about 1455.

literature, it has served as a touchstone to writers of numerous pastoral and utopian works, particularly *Paradise Lost* (1667), by England's epic poet, John Milton; Karel Capek's *R. U. R.* (1920); and George Bernard Shaw's five-act drama, *Back to Methuselah* (1921). (Alexander and Alexander 1973; Anderson 1966; Boorstin 1992; Holy Bible 1958; Mays 1988; Metzger and Coogan 1993) .

See also Adam; *Back to Methuselah;* Eden; Eve; Gilgamesh; golden age; *Paradise Lost;* pastoral; *R. U. R.;* theocracy; women in utopia.

GHAZALI

Mystic Islamic theologian and contemplative poet revered by Sufists, Ghazali was born Abu Hamid Mohammed ibn Mohammed at Tus-al-Ghazali (or Algazel in Latin) in 1058 near Meshed on Iran's northeast boundary. Ghazali spoke Persian, but joined his brother in Arabic classes in Tus, Gurgan, and Nishapur, where he studied under al-Mulk, the great theologian of his time. At age 33, Ghazali assumed a professorship in law at Nizamiya College, Baghdad, and wrote books and articles on law, theology, philosophy, and mysticism as well as autobiographies, *The Confession of Al Ghazali* and *Deliverance from Error.* His most notable polemic, *The Inconsistency of the Philosophers,* energetically refuted neo-Platonism, a syncretic blend of Christianity, oriental philosophy, and Plato's idealism. In 1096, wracked by skepticism, he abandoned the material world in search of the ascetic life of the Sufi, an Islamic mystic.

Ghazali claimed to have been visited by Allah in the form of a speech impediment, an affliction that humbled him in anticipation of greater uses for his talents. By way of explanation, Ghazali explained his conversion as an epiphany—a divine light that God shone into the inner chambers of his heart to illuminate the path to knowledge. Before seeking monastic lodging and withdrawing from worldly pleasures, he journeyed to Damascus, Jerusalem, and Mecca, and lived an ascetic hermitage. A changed man, he returned to college teaching until 1110, then retired a second time to Tus to live out his last months. Upon Ghazali's death on December 18, 1111, he was proclaimed the *mujaddid,* or reviver of the faith, an honorarium based on the extensive mystical essays he composed in his Sufist treatise *The Niche of Lights.* More significant to the ordinary Muslim was his *Revival of the Religious Sciences* and *The Alchemy of Happiness,* two celebrations of an uncomplicated dedication to faith. Some admirers placed him second in influence after Mohammed. (Burckhardt 1969; Ghazali 1964; Idries Shah 1964; Nicholson 1950; Schimmel 1975; Schimmel 1982; Waley 1993)

See also asceticism; Koran; Sufism; syncretism.

GILEAD

Austere and scrupulously clean, Gilead is a futuristic version of a Boston suburb in a theocratic society ruled by fundamentalist Christians in Margaret

Atwood's dystopian *The Handmaid's Tale* (1985). A grim, sanctimonious patriarchy, Gilead suffers from a faltering economy, confiscation of credit cards,
draconian laws, curtailed education for women, and a hovering unease marked
by controlled distribution of food, clothing, and other supplies; forced labor;
roadblocks; and public display of executed bodies on hooks. Upper-class men
are allowed to marry; working-class men like chauffeurs and guards receive
no mating privileges. Nonwhites are resettled on farms in National Homeland
One in North Dakota; dissidents from out-of-favor religious sects and unyield-
ing Jews are remanded to distant settlements. Barren females, Unwomen, and
old women are dispatched to the Colonies.

The managed community, like a greenswarded, citywide concentration
camp, counters heresy and rebellion by stamping out violence, lawyers, infan-
ticide, promiscuity, and freedom of thought. Varying in commitment from
dazed, dutiful automata to rabid fanatics, citizens mechanically go about the
business of serving the state. Shopping takes Handmaids through barricades
and passport checks to stores with biblical names: Milk and Honey for dairy
products, eggs, and fruit; All Flesh for meat and poultry; Lilies of the Field for
habits; and Soul Scrolls for automated prayers. Display of food tokens and
Identipasses legitimizes shopping trips.

In the rigidly ordered society of Gilead, the streets are segmented by frequent checkpoints operated by jackbooted storm troopers (euphemistically
named Angels of Light), killers who round up and exterminate apostates. Behavior is superintended by roving police vans adorned with eyes. Spies called
Eyes report to the hierarchy of elders the misdoings of any rebel, homosexual,
abortionist, priest, or other transgressor. While men continue competitive roles
in society and enjoy football and clandestine trips to a nightclub called Jezebel's,
women function as noncitizens who are forbidden to smoke, drink alcohol,
read, study, or testify in court. This blatant double standard in Gilead results
from a fear of human extinction, a result of raging venereal disease, nuclear
war, and toxic pollution that robs people of fertility. As the birthrate falls below replacement level, potential mothers become a natural resource to be
guarded and nurtured so long as their wombs serve the state.

Atwood stresses the hidden meanings and double entendres implicit in
sweetly righteous catchphrases. In response to their uterus-centered existence,
women greet one another with the standard exchanges "Blessed be the fruit"
and "May the Lord open." At parting, each piously intones, "Under His eye."
Surrogate mothers, an elite corps of breeders called Handmaids, produce offspring for childless officials; for failure to conceive, they are remanded to radioactive wastelands. Trained at the Rachel and Leah Re-education Center by
sadistic Aunts armed with cattle prods and whistles, the Handmaids are conditioned to despise the narcissism, pornography, rape, easy sex, and prostitution of the 1980s—a godless, amoral era that ended after the U.S. president and
members of Congress were assassinated, the Constitution suspended, and citizens' rights obliterated.

Fearful of its recent past, Gilead, once the home of America's Puritan ancestors, allows cemeteries and museums to remain, but shuts out remnants of

the 1980s—jogging suits, running shoes, makeup, high-heeled and miniskirted clotheshorses, second marriages, date rape, strident feminists, open homosexuality, and singles bars. In the place of perpetual tension between political forces, the republic substitutes a bland, predictable daily existence lacking in children and devoid of autonomy, entertainment, education, and normal male-female interaction. The study group that reflects on Gilead exists two centuries later, when the United States' brush with fundamentalist concentration camps proves an anomaly alongside other puritanical aberrations in the nation's past. (Atwood 1972; *Contemporary Authors* 1989; *Contemporary Literary Criticism* 1987; Davidson 1986; Dreifus 1992; Hammer 1990; Ingersoll 1991; McCombs 1988; *Major Twentieth-Century Writers* 1990; Van Spanckeren and Castro 1988)

See also Atwood, Margaret; The Commander; *The Handmaid's Tale;* Lydia, Aunt; Offred; Serena Joy; technology; theocracy; women in utopia.

GILGAMESH

Gilgamesh is the king of Uruk and epic hero of Akkadian lore dating to 3000 B.C. and recorded on 12 tablets about 1200 B.C. Like Ovid's Orpheus, Virgil's Aeneas, Homer's Odysseus, and Dante on a guided tour of hell, purgatory, and heaven, Gilgamesh explores the Underworld in search of answers to his questions about life and death. A Babylonian demigod and king of Uruk (now Erech) on the Euphrates River, Gilgamesh suffers the loss of Enkidu, his closest friend and hunting companion. To alleviate his spiritual torment, Gilgamesh accepts the challenge of the Scorpion Monster and enters the netherworld on a symbolic quest of life's most guarded secrets. Parting the portals at the base of a mountain, he traverses 12 leagues of palpable darkness so terrifying that no mortal has dared to breach the gates. Companionless, he suffers hyperventilation, hysterical weeping, and overwhelming fear. Running toward the glimmers at the end of the tunnel, he escapes and turns his face to the sun's rays, then searches for Utnapishtim, the only being who can answer his questions about death.

Gilgamesh's universal right of passage contains the epic conventions of confrontation with the inexplicable mysteries of death. From the bowels of the foul mountain passage, Gilgamesh emerges unharmed. He has reenacted human birth to become two-thirds mortal and reaps the rewards reserved for the bold. He wanders a sparkling, Edenic spot where:

> The fruit and foliage of the trees were all
> The colors of the jewels of the world,
> Carnelian and lapis lazuli,
> Jasper, rubies, agate, and hematite,
> Emerald, and all the other gems the earth
> Has yielded for the delight and pleasure of kings.

Beyond this paradise lies the sea and the tavern of Siduri, the alewife who shuts and bolts the door to the wanderer in an effort to dissuade Gilgamesh from seeking answers.

At Siduri's prompting, Gilgamesh recounts his deeds with Enkidu in the cedar forest and verbalizes the eternal fear: "Must I die too?" Siduri tries to ease his mind with earthly pleasures—a bath, food, drink, revelry, sexual release, rest—but Gilgamesh is not deterred by these temporary distractions. The search takes on new terrors as Gilgamesh faces Urshànabi, the only boatman who can ferry the wanderer across the waters of death, which are fatal to touch. Gilgamesh must cut 120 poles to propel himself to the distant shore and Utnapishtim's abode.

Like Dante, Gilgamesh completes his mission, however dire the consequences. He traverses the sea and wanders an unknown land. He fails the challenge of remaining awake, a symbolic test proving that sleep, like death, is irresistible to humans. Utnapishtim pities Gilgamesh enough to relate a secret—he can retain his youth if he locates a magic herb at the bottom of the ocean. However, a serpent steals the plant, sheds its skin, and slithers away, leaving Gilgamesh without hope.

An interpolated episode from Sumerian lore depicts Gilgamesh's meeting with Inanna. She offers him a ritual drum and drumstick, which he unintentionally drops into a hole that opens on the Underworld. He reunites with the spirit of Enkidu, which bursts through the hole like a puff of wind. Enkidu's exacting description of the netherworld ends so graphically that Gilgamesh has no illusions about the body's mortality, which must yield to worms and fall to dust.

An appended segment, badly garbled, answers Gilgamesh's questions about reward and punishment in the afterlife. For the fathers of many sons, the afterlife offers rewards commensurate with the number of male children sired. The father of six sons rejoices in his rich life. The father of seven sits on a throne and enjoys music. The drowned man lies on a couch and is comforted with pure water. The warrior is mourned by parents and wife. And in harmony with much of ancient lore, the most pathetic—"he whose corpse was thrown away unburied"—wanders eternally, while he who has no family to mourn him subsists on a diet of garbage. The poem breaks off here, leaving scholars to wonder whether Gilgamesh satisfies his curiosity and returns to his kingdom by the Euphrates. (Cavendish 1970; Ferry 1992; Hooke 1963; McDannell 1994; Metzger and Coogan 1993)

See also Aeneas; *Aeneid;* disillusion; *Divina Commedia;* heaven; women in utopia.

 # THE GIVER

When Lois Lowry's *The Giver* (1993) won the Newbery Award for the best of children's literature in 1994, the announcement brought thunderous approval from readers, parents, teachers, and librarians who welcomed the dystopian fable for its clarity, allegorical purity, and narrative control. Critics place it among the great dystopic works: Madeleine L'Engle's *A Wrinkle in Time,* George

Orwell's *1984*, Ayn Rand's *Anthem*, and Ray Bradbury's *Fahrenheit 451*. Responding to questions about the novel's ambiguous ending, Lowry said in her acceptance speech, "Those of you who hoped that I would stand here tonight and reveal the 'true' ending, the 'right' interpretation of the ending, will be disappointed. There isn't one. There's a right one for each of us, and it depends on our own beliefs, our own hopes."

The Giver is a masterly blend of *bildungsroman*, passing of the scepter, journey motif, and an anti-utopianism that counters heartless rationality, eugenics, mandated drugs, euthanasia, totalitarianism, and ominous topographical and emotional blandness. Shortly before the December celebration of his twelfth year, Jonas, the protagonist, grows restless and concerned because graduation at the Ceremony of Twelve will determine his life's work. In a controlled community where social intercourse requires formal apologies for any question or infraction, food is delivered by truck, births are maintained at 50 per year, the elderly and sick infants are euthanized, and rules require the sharing of dreams and feelings with family, Jonas tries to adhere to regulations. In his home, he takes meals with his adoptive parents and adopted sister, eight-year-old Lily. He wears a simple tunic and, since his ninth birthday, has ridden a state-issued bicycle to school and to his volunteer work at the House of the Old, where he bathes and tends inmates. Under a special dispensation that allows a sickly baby boy to live a trial year, Jonas's father, a Nurturer, brings home an infant named Gabriel. Like all children in this totalitarian environment, the baby cuddles with his assigned "comfort object," a stuffed hippo. Both Lily and Jonas enjoy playing with Gabe, who thrives, babbles, and learns to walk.

Jonas is a perceptive, sympathetic boy who realizes that Asher, his best friend, is unlikely to fare well in a career because he is often tardy, playful, garrulous, and forgetful. During playtime, Jonas tosses him an apple and realizes that it alters in mid-air in a new and unexpected fashion, one for which he has no scientific explanation. Another change that disorients Jonas is a budding sexual interest in Fiona, which his parents label normal "Stirrings." Knowingly, Jonas's mother, a worker at the justice center, explains that all people develop sexual feelings, which they counteract with a daily pill.

At the annual ceremony ranking children by age, 50 per level, parents and other citizens anticipate the most significant group—Jonas's group, the twelves, who await assignment. Asher naively comments, "If you don't fit in, you can apply for Elsewhere and be released." Back at the auditorium, the numbered children receive their assignments in order, but the Chief Elder passes over Jonas, number 19, and continues with 20 through 50. She returns to Jonas and proclaims him the next Receiver of Memory, a momentous honor and responsibility. Requisite to the job are intelligence, integrity, courage, wisdom, and clairvoyance. The community chants its approval. The unique position has remained unfilled for a decade while the decision makers looked for a likely candidate. Later, Jonas learns that the last trainee, Rosemary, had asked to released and had become an unperson whose name was never mentioned in public or passed to another baby.

At the Annex of the House of the Old, Jonas meets his master, The Receiver. The unique position of Receiver-in-training exempts Jonas from the rules on questions, rudeness, medication, release, and lying, but imposes strict confidentiality. He may read from a large book collection, which the aged Receiver places at his disposal, and may ask any question. During their first sessions, The Receiver demonstrates how Jonas will assume responsibility for a significant part of human experience: The Receiver lays his hands on Jonas's bare back and passes into his memory a sled ride in snow and a bask in the sun. During the first transmission, Jonas learns new concepts—snow, hill, sled, runners, sun, sunburn. At the end of the transfer, the perceptions no longer exist in The Receiver; Jonas is the only possessor for all time.

As Jonas searches for answers to the problems of a controlled society and the lonely job of The Receiver, his master, whom he calls The Giver, gradually introduces a mix of delight and suffering. Jonas learns that the shreds of perception he experienced while tossing the apple to Asher were a flirtation with color, which ordinary humanity has lost. Balanced against the joy of the color red plus family, love, birthdays, music, and holidays come cold, hunger, pain, fear, war, and death. On some days, The Giver, a spouseless recluse, is too overcome with alienation and suffering to instruct Jonas, who has figured out for himself that the euphemisms concerning "release" merely cover up murder of the sick, unacceptable, rebellious, and old. As the boy and his mentor grow close in their endeavor to pass on human experience, The Giver confesses the truth about Jonas's predecessor, Rosemary, who balked at the psychic pain of Receivership and chose suicide. The Giver, who watched by monitor as the girl killed herself, confesses that Rosemary was his daughter.

Jonas grows so distraught that he spends the night with The Giver. Because society has stripped itself of feeling and compassion, the pair conspire to redeem their community from their mechanical, dehumanized lives. As they plan Jonas's flight to Elsewhere, their hopes grow that they can easily fool the watchers and bring about wholeness by rounding out the robotic community existence with warmth, holidays, family, grandparents, individuality, and love. The night before Jonas is to hide his bicycle for the escape, his father reports that Gabriel is still crying at night and must be euthanized the next morning. At dusk, Jonas abandons The Giver's plan, seats Gabriel in a child carrier, and pedals his bike across the bridge and into the unknown. They elude searchers and planes with heat-seeking devices by flattening themselves on the ground to chill their flesh. After days of pedaling and foraging for food, Jonas reaches a snowy hill and, clutching Gabe, abandons the bike and sleds toward hope. Ahead he hears music and imagines that the same sound arises from the dreary land behind him. (Babbitt 1993; *Children's Literature Review* 1984; Cooper 1993; Corsaro 1994; *Dictionary of Literary Biography* 1987; Lorrain 1994; Lowry 1993; Miller 1990; Ray 1993; Ross 1984; *Something about the Author* 1984; *Something about the Author Autobiography Series* 1986; Veronica 1993)

See also allegory; city planning; classism; disillusion; escapism; futurism; Lowry, Lois; totalitarianism.

GOLDEN AGE

In classical mythology, the golden age, which Homer declares graced the earth a thousand years before the Trojan War, was a refined, carefree, idyllic era akin to the biblical notion of Eden or the Babylonian Paradise. The time span paralleled the sovereignty of Cronus, the almighty deity of Greek lore. Hesiod, a devout poet who farmed a rough tract of land in Ascra, Boeotia, around 700 B.C., describes this nostalgic haven beginning in line 90 of his *Works and Days*: "The bounteous earth beareth honey-sweet fruit fresh thrice a year." Beyond the waters of the Atlantic Ocean, this otherworldly land contained no harsh weather. Its topography stretched forth a fertile plain, where mankind, living without female companionship, enjoyed an unending celebration of life. Death released the spirit without pain and restored it to Earth as a benevolent spirit.

Unburdened by worry, disease, hunger, exploitation, or strife, the people of the golden age lived guiltless and forever youthful. Hesiod emphasizes that, during the period before Pandora emptied the jar of human miseries, humankind was

> Free from all evils, free from laborious work,
> And free from
> All wearying sickness that bring
> Their fates down on men.

In subsequent verses beginning with line 110, Hesiod caresses the memory of Cronus's reign:

> They lived as if they were gods,
> Their hearts free from all sorrow,
> By themselves, and without hard work or pain;
> No miserable
> Old Age came their way; their hands, their feet,
> Did not alter.
> They took their pleasure in festivals,
> And lived without troubles.
> When they died, it was as if they fell asleep.
> All goods
> Were theirs.

This era of blessing and abundance enjoyed perpetual spring and barrier-free relations between neighbors. It extended beyond the Titan hierarchy and into the reign of Zeus, who slew his atavistic father and established the rule of the Olympian gods.

Roman settings of the golden age myth in Catullus's *Peleus and Thetis* (ca. 55 B.C.), Virgil's *Fourth Eclogue* (38 B.C.), the epodes of Horace (30 B.C.), and Book 1 of Ovid's *Metamorphoses* (A.D. 8) depict an Italian location where God and humankind coexist in harmony. In Virgil's lines, when Janus arrived at Janiculum, the spot he founded on the Tiber River,

Saturn fled before victorious Jove,
Driven down and banished from the realms above.
He, by just laws, embodied all the train,
Who roamed the hills, and drew them to the plain;
There fixed, and Latium called the new abode,
Whose friendly shores concealed the latent god.
These realms, in peace, the monarch long controlled,
And blessed the nations with an age of gold.

Living off vegetables and fruits, the golden-agers refrained from murder and theft and improved their culture by heeding Saturn (the Roman equivalent of Cronus), who invented the sickle, the traditional tool for harvesting grain.

Unlike Virgil's account, in lines 89–110 of the *Metamorphoses*, Ovid's description of a golden earthly utopia stresses negatives. People did not fear punishment or threats nor petition a judge for mercy. No one felled native pines to make boats; no one traveled. Commenting on city planning and militarism, Ovid adds:

> Not yet were cities begirt with steep moats; there were no trumpets of straight, no horns of curving brass, no swords or helmets. There was no need at all of armed men, for nations, secure from war's alarms, passed the years in gentle peace.

The hunter-gatherer stage of humanity relieved men of the need for plows and hoes. The earth voluntarily grew grain; milk and nectar flowed in streams, and green oak trees exuded honey.

This blessed era of peace preceded a progressive deterioration in human behavior, leading to the ages of silver, bronze, and iron. Wistful Romans resurrected an annual re-creation of the golden age in Saturnalia, December 17-23, a week-long holiday requiring peace, an end of slavery and capital punishment, feasting, and gift-giving. Later writers drew on the classical lore of the golden age, which is found in Thomas Carew's "Upon My Lord Chief Justice," Geoffrey Chaucer's "The Former Age," John Keats's "Endymion," Christopher Marlowe's "Hero and Leander," William Shakespeare's *The Tempest*, Percy Shelley's *Prometheus Unbound*, Edmund Spenser's *Faerie Queene*, and William Wordsworth's "Vernal Ode." A twentieth-century novel, Arthur C. Clarke's *Childhood's End* (1953), utilizes a golden age as the second of his three-book speculative novel. In Clarke's structuring of utopia, the bittersweet decline of the golden age presages an alarming alteration in human shape, motion, and ego. His premise leaves the reader to ponder how closely heaven on Earth compares to hell on Earth. (*Catullus* 1893; Clarke 1953; Durant 1939; Graves 1968; Grimal 1991; Guerber 1921; Hamilton 1942; Hesiod 1973; Howatson 1991; Lattimore 1973; Morford and Lenardon 1977; Ovid 1977; Pennick 1992; Radice 1984; Rosenberg 1992; Smith 1984; Snodgrass 1988a; Snodgrass 1988b; Virgil 1950)

See also Avalon; *Childhood's End;* Clarke, Arthur C.; creation, mythic; Eden; Hesiod; Ovid; *Paradise Lost;* Saturnalia; *The Tempest;* Valhalla; Virgil.

GOLDING, WILLIAM

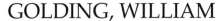

The author of *Lord of the Flies* (1954), one of the most riveting, perplexing dystopias in young-adult literature, William Gerald Golding was a native of Newquay, Cornwall, in southwestern England. Born September 19, 1911, his parents were Alex A. Golding, of a long family line of teachers, and Mildred A. Golding, an active feminist who campaigned for the vote for women. By age seven Golding was a literary prodigy at Marlborough Grammar School who filled odd hours with the beginnings of a 20-volume autobiography. In 1935 he enrolled at Brasenose College, Oxford, as a science major, but changed direction and completed a degree in Old English literature. He worked briefly at a settlement house, and began teaching philosophy and English at Bishop Wordsworth's academy in Salisbury, Wiltshire. He married Ann Brookfield and sired two children, David and Judith. Much of Golding's career involved him in local theatricals as director, writer, actor, and stage manager. At the age of 29 he entered the British navy and studied rocketry. He served in numerous military capacities, commanded a rocket ship in the North Atlantic, and was decorated for heroism at the D-Day landing in Normandy, France.

Nine years after the war, Golding vented some of his skepticism about war and its origins in human depravity in an unprecedented naturalistic novel, *Lord of the Flies*. A controversial *bildungsroman* or rites-of-passage novel favored on both sides of the Atlantic, the work has been labeled an allegory, fable, or doomsday parable. *Lord of the Flies* draws on the boys' adventure sept of the young-adult canon, calling on conventions and situations, e.g., bullying, one-upmanship, curiosity, boasting, and feats of daring, from Edgar Rice Borroughs's Tarzan novels, Jules Verne's science fiction, and Robert Louis Stevenson's *Treasure Island* and *Kidnapped*, as well as survival themes from Daniel Defoe's *Robinson Crusoe* (1719) and the cold, probing, satiric eye of Jonathan Swift's *Gulliver's Travels* (1727). To critics who question the novel's overpowering strands of atavism and despair, Golding's essay "On the Crest of the Wave" supplies a personal explanation: "I am by nature an optimist; but a defective logic—or a logic which I sometimes hope desperately is defective—makes a pessimist of me."

Sometimes challenging J. D. Salinger for the title of "novelist of the fifties," Golding published *The Inheritors* (1955), *Pincher Martin* (1956), *The Brass Butterfly* (1958), *Free Fall* (1959), *The Spire* (1964), *Pyramid* (1967), and others, which lack the philosophical validity of the initial success. After earning an M.A. from Oxford in 1960, Golding served as writer-in-residence at Hollins College and earned numerous honorary university degrees—from Bristol, Warwick, Oxford, Sussex, and the Sorbonne. In 1990 a color film of *Lord of the Flies* received mixed reviews, but was better received than the black-and-white version in 1963. In 1980 Golding returned to notoriety with *Darkness Visible,* winner of the James Tait Black prize, and *Rites of Passage,* which won him the Booker McConnell Prize. Three years later he became the first Englishman since Churchill to receive the Nobel Prize. The committee lauded his works for ease, thematic integrity, and "deep strata of ambiguity and complication." Five years after being knighted, he died of a heart attack in Perranarworthal, England, on June 19, 1993. (Baker 1988; Carey 1987; Gindin 1988; Golding 1954; Johnson 1968; Johnston 1980; Kinkead-Weeks and Gregor 1984; Snodgrass 1990; Subbarao 1987)

See also disillusion; Eden; *Lord of the Flies*; Merridew, Jack; naturalism; Piggy; Ralph.

 # GREEN MANSIONS

See Hudson, W. H.; utopia.

 # GULLIVER, LEMUEL

A native of Redriff, Nottinghamshire, England, Lemuel Gulliver serves as antihero of Jonathan Swift's satiric, semi-utopian *Gulliver's Travels* (1727). Like John the Savage of Aldous Huxley's *Brave New World* (1932), Gulliver maintains high standards without learning how to apply them to realistic situations. He attends Emmanuel College, Cambridge, but does not complete a degree. To set himself up in a profession, he studies under a surgeon, attends lectures in Leyden, and attempts to earn a living in medicine. He marries Mary Burton Gulliver and opens a medical practice in Old Jury, but never prospers. To aid his family, he works briefly as ship's surgeon on the *Swallow*.

On May 4, 1699, Gulliver goes to sea aboard the *Antelope* as ship's surgeon and sails from Bristol to the East Indies. He ventures into remarkable societies where ideologies contrast sharply with the worlds he has known and emulated. An ingenuous, sheltered observer, Lemuel peers down on tiny Lilliputians performing trivial rope stunts and leaping over sticks before their emperor, involving themselves in petty squabbles such as which end of an egg should be cracked first, and confining their children in public nurseries apart from their parents. His second voyage reverses his adventures by allying him with gross giants, the Brobdingnags, whose magnified human qualities disgust and alienate the observer from his hosts.

Gulliver's third and fourth encounters stand much closer to the heart of Swift's criticisms of human behavior. Reported as incisively as the first half of his sea adventures, the encounters with Laputa and the land of the Houyhnhnms intensify the guileless sailor's inability to maintain perspective. Withdrawing to a stable on his return to Redriff, Gulliver mourns his bestial qualities, thus immobilizing himself from taking action against illogic or from appreciating his better nature. A disconcertingly simple-witted booby, Gulliver distances himself from his wife and children and is so demoralized by his adventures that he is unable to cope with even the smell of his human family.

At first castigated and reviled as a misanthropic narrator, Gulliver evolved into a parody after critics surmised the source of his name—a portmanteau word, or merger of "gullible" and "traveler." When critics ceased to jeer at his irrationality and overreaction to adversity, they began to value Swift's refined gift for irony and parody in creating so naive a character. At length, the reading public delighted in Gulliver for opening their eyes to the irrationality of a fusty old hermit. He has since become a standard figure in young-adult literature, often re-created on a simpler level in cartoons and children's stories. (Drabble 1985; Harrison et al. 1967; Hornstein et al.1973; Johnson 1968; Magill 1958; Manguel and Guadalupi 1987; Pollard 1970; Quintana 1958; Swift 1958; Woods et al. 1947)

See also Brobdingnags; disillusion; escapism; fantasy; *Gulliver's Travels;* Laputa; Lilliput; satire; Swift, Jonathan.

GULLIVER'S TRAVELS

Jonathan Swift's masterly satire applies utopian and anti-utopian precepts to the correction of society's ills. Published in 1727, the work was an immediate success and has maintained an uncontested position as the greatest satire in English literature. Achieving what the "gullible traveler" assumes to be utopia in the horse-land of the Houyhnhnms, Gulliver loses his objectivity, deserts his family, and moves into the stable to live with horses, whom his distorted value system now prefers above humanity.

Book I

Begun on 4 May 1699, the *Swallow's* voyage from Bristol, England, around Africa's horn to the East Indies ends disastrously. Shipwrecked by collision with a boulder northwest of Van Diemen's Land on November 5, Lemuel Gulliver sets out in a punt that overturns. He swims ashore and sleeps for nine hours. On awakening, he realizes that he is bound hand and foot—a captive in Lilliput, a land ruled by people only six inches high. Drugged into stupor, Gulliver is transported by flatcar at great physical hardship to his conquerors, who install him nearer the royal palace. There he gains the citizens' respect and is allowed to rove and to question Reldresal, an imperial private secretary who serves as Gulliver's liaison officer.

The Lilliputians—a petty, minuscule folk—are marked by peculiarities, as in slanting their writing from corner to corner, believing the world to be flat, and burying their dead feet-upward so that they will stand upright on the day of resurrection. In court trials of state crime, if the defendant is proved innocent, the state executes the accuser. The legal system also dispenses rewards for good behavior by naming worthy citizens Snilpalls, or Legals. To acquire honors, Lilliputians dance on ropes or leap over sticks, thus earning wisps of thread from Emperor Golbasto.

Lilliput's children are highly valued. Parents produce only the number of offspring they intend to support; Lilliputian parents expect no gratitude from their offspring. Like the children in Plutarch's *Life of Lycurgus* (first century

A.D.), Aldous Huxley's *Brave New World* (1932), and Ayn Rand's *Anthem* (1937), young Lilliputians attend public nurseries and learn to accept a rigid social station, for which they are indoctrinated. Upper-class males attend rigorous schools that teach moral values. Lower-class males and females also receive education commensurate with their needs. The bottom caste is left illiterate.

In Chapter 6 Swift explores the utopian qualities of Lilliput. The courts maintain order by enacting strong laws against treason and false testimony. To assure the best in government, the nation demands a high standard of ethics and religiosity from its bureaucracy. Swift's stratification of Lilliput into a three-layered social order echoes Plato's concepts in *The Republic* (fifth century B.C.). Yet, for all the idealism of the Platonic concept, the Lilliputian spirit never rises above its petty infighting, cruelties, jockeying for court positions, and envy.

The emperor grants his guest freedom but requires certain compromises, notably that the giant man will enter town by the road and take care not to squash Lilliputians. Gulliver must vow to aid in fights with the enemy, carry urgent messages, and survey the kingdom in exchange for enough food to sustain 1,728 locals. Gulliver accepts these strictures and ventures into Mildendo, Lilliput's capital. He reaches the breaking point, however, during the Lilliputian war with Blefuscu. Towing warships like model boats in a pond, he ends the miniature sea battle and is rewarded with the title of Nardac.

The pose as war hero ends with strained relations between Gulliver and the emperor and a near escape from blinding. After Gulliver refuses to loot Blefuscu on behalf of the emperor of Lilliput, he earns the spite of Flimnap, the imperial treasurer, and Skyresh Bolgolam, head of the navy, and is charged with treason. A more embarrassing gaffe is Gulliver's decision to save the palace from fire by urinating on the flames. The empress expresses her contempt and anger for this pubic display of Gulliver's privates. The emperor ends the contretemps by extending a pardon.

Gulliver's tribulations grow more absurd, more laughable. The burden of feeding so large a guest leads Flimnap to suggest ousting the giant, whom he suspects of flirting with his wife. The emperor rejects suggestions of capital punishment and proposes putting out Gulliver's eyes as a more humane punishment for insubordination. On learning of the danger he faces from court plotting, Gulliver wades across to Blefuscu, where he takes refuge. The first adventure ends in Chapter 8 while the militaristic nitter natter between Lilliput and Blefuscu continues. Gulliver maintains his autonomy by locating a beached boat. He repairs it, collects 300 miniature sheep and 100 oxen to slaughter, and departs on September 24, 1701. On September 26, he locates a passing English merchant vessel and returns to England. The only reward he gains from his four months at sea is a lucrative sideshow of Lilliputian animals.

Book II

A restless Gulliver boards the *Adventure* on June 20, 1702, and sets sail from Liverpool toward Surat. For the duration of the winter, the ship is grounded at the Cape of Good Hope for repairs. Captain John Nicholas comes down with ague; his illness holds up the voyage until March. The crew sets out again; in June, a storm at sea ends Gulliver's second voyage, also bound for the East Indies. During a search for water, Gulliver separates from the crew, who hurry away from oversized pursuers. On a 6,000-mile-long volcanic peninsula in the northwestern Pacific, he is marooned among the Brobdingnags, a nation of 60-foot giants. In vain he hides among stalks of grain, where a farmer rescues him from the ungentle hands of children.

As caretaker for Gulliver, Swift creates Glumdalclitch, a nine-year-old farm girl and one of the author's most endearing characters. Glumdalclitch watches over her charge until the farmer can put him on display. By market day, Gulliver has learned enough of the native tongue to understand what his captors and viewers think of him. The farmer earns a sizable income from displaying his homunculus, who suffers from the rigors of trying to keep up with giants and from the undignified capers he must perform to earn his keeper's living.

In the coming scenes, the theme of greed predominates. The queen learns of the farmer's freakish miniature man and purchases him, retaining Glumdalclitch as Gulliver's attendant. The Brobdingnagian philosopher-king, who attempts to rule by wise and compassionate laws, dismays Gulliver by failing to quell the grossness and cruelty of his oversized race. Gulliver entertains at court by telling sea adventures and survives the frequent plots of the queen's dwarf, who tries to drown his competition in a cream pitcher.

In Chapter 6 the king listens to Gulliver's description of England and deprecates its history. To Gulliver, English exploits are noble, but to the king's discerning values, there are too many uprisings and too much violence. Hearing of a nation so embroiled in treachery, mean-spiritedness, court intrigue, and insanity leads him to conclude that the English are disreputable vermin. In contrast to a nation that employs gunpowder, the king lauds the Brobdingnagian values, morality, and penchant for verse and mathematics.

As in Book I, Gulliver's patience wears thin. He tolerates a court role for two years, but secretly pines for home and family. As a reward for his congeniality, the queen makes him a traveling coach and transports him to the seashore. An eagle snatches up the conveyance and carries it far out to sea before dropping it. The intervention of English sailors aboard the *New-Holland* saves him from drowning. They ferry him safely home to England and his wife and daughter by June 3, 1706. Gulliver's wife complains that these adventures should come to an end, but he doubts that he can override destiny.

Book III

For a time, Gulliver insists that he has had enough of roving; then he grows bored with home. To escape, he joins the *Hopewell* two months later, and on August 5, 1706, sails for China. Following a severe gale the ship is commandeered by Japanese pirates, who set Gulliver adrift in a canoe. He nears some islands and camps under an overhanging crag. Setting out from home base, he explores other islands in the group and subsists on birds' eggs.

Just as Gulliver loses heart with his predicament, the flying island of Laputa appears above him. At his gesture of need, the Laputans lower a seat and raise him with pullies to their island, which functions and maneuvers through the manipulation of a lodestone, or magnet. The Laputans are a people with many peculiarities, such as holding their heads tilted so one eye can gaze up and the other down. As students of science and mathematics, they apply their skills to forcible control of the Balnibarbi, an earthbound nation on which they drop rocks. If the surface of Balnibarbi were not so irregular, they would land the entire island on the citizens below and crush them.

Gulliver requests a visit to Balnibarbi and is befriended by the ruler, Munodi. In Lagado, the country's capital, Gulliver comes upon ruined farmsteads and cities. The people explain that project leaders at the academy create unworkable plans, such as grinding ice into gunpowder, breeding naked sheep, and building houses from the roof down to the foundation. These extremes of illogic destroy people and habitations. Gulliver moves on to Maldonada, capital of Glubbdubdrib, an island governed by a sorcerer capable of recalling the dead to life. To satisfy his curiosity about historical figures, Gulliver has the magician restore Alexander, Hannibal, Julius Caesar, Pompey, Aristotle, and Homer so he can interview them. The theme of evil forms a single strand as the historical parade passes by.

Arriving at the island of Luggnagg, Gulliver engages an interpreter; through him Gulliver learns that 1,500 residents called Struldbruggs are immortal. He welcomes the thought of living forever until he realizes that the sufferings of old age create insurmountable problems for the deathless Luggnaggians, who grow weak, fretful, and sad. Through the intervention of the king of Luggnagg, Gulliver ends a three-month stay by boarding the *Glanguenstald* on May 7 and pressing on to Japan to take passage on the *Amboyna* for Amsterdam. By April 10, 1710, Gulliver arrives safely home after an absence of five and a half years.

Book IV

For five months Gulliver lives in harmony with his family. In September 1710 he takes control of the *Adventure,* a ship that calls into the port of Barbados in the Leeward Islands to hire replacements for crewmen who have died of fever. Along the way to Madagascar, he learns that the new mariners are brigands. They overpower Gulliver, then set him adrift in a longboat. He arrives at a land populated by foul-smelling, tailless beasts.

In this polarized society, a race of horse-creatures known as Houyhnhnms revile and segregate the Yahoos, a distasteful race of humanoids. The horse-people rescue Gulliver from a Yahoo attack. The Houyhnhnms live in a self-styled utopia, a land of health and happiness, by demonstrating the extreme of Plato's concept of reason. The Yahoos, who epitomize passion, mimic the side of human nature that bestializes and perverts behavior. Because Gulliver is wearing clothing, the Houyhnhnms seem unaware at first that he bears a strong resemblance to the Yahoos.

Lilliputians, small in body and in mind, tie down Lemuel Gulliver, the antihero of Jonathan Swift's *Gulliver's Travels.*

Happy at last to find a people he can admire and emulate, Gulliver embraces the philosophy of the Houyhnhnms because they approach life with wisdom and logic and behave judiciously. By learning the local language and locating food to supplement the horse diet of oats, he studies the beauties of this ideal land, and is particularly interested by their lack of a word for "falsehood." As he grows more enamored of their noble nature, the Houyhnhnms begin to suspect that his gloves, vest, pants, and shoes conceal a loathed Yahoo.

Thus, in this idyllic setting, Swift refuses Gulliver the haven he has sought in four voyages. Unable to suppress the bestial side of his nature, he offends the Houyhnhnms by relating that Englishmen ride on horses' backs and often war on neighboring nations. Gulliver's mild-mannered host compliments his guest, but is horrified at such historical motifs as hunger, violence, wine-bibbing, greed, and graft. In contrast to the illogic of England, the Houyhnhnms display virtue and reason in their choice of mates, who are selected on the basis of color, strength, beauty, and a sincere effort to upgrade the race. By cultivating temperance, hard work, exercise, and cleanliness, the Houyhnhnms have arrived at a state of sturdy resilience, which Gulliver admires.

At the climax of Book IV, the Houyhnhnm assembly meets to debate a long-standing question—whether Yahoos should be tolerated or exterminated. During this period, Gulliver grows more at home among the philosophical horse-people, but the Houyhnhnms fear that he may betray them to the ravening Yahoos, with whom he has much in common. Like the biblical Adam,

Gulliver is forced out of his Eden by decree. He swoons at the news that he must depart; however, he concurs with their logic.

Swift seems to enjoy the conclusion of the idyll and the complete disorder in the protagonist's rationality and sense of proportion. Gulliver is so distraught over losing his utopian ideal that, after many tears and grievous leave-taking of his host, on February 15, 1715, he departs in a crude canoe covered with Yahoo skins and fitted with sails from the same source. His friend, the Sorrel Nag, weeps: "Take care of thy self, gentle Yahoo." Borne by Portuguese ship to Lisbon on November 5, 1715, and two weeks later from there to England, he is greeted by his wife, who feared that her husband had died.

Gulliver lambastes himself for copulating with his wife, who resembles a female Yahoo and has given birth during his absence to another child. He is so traumatized by the tremendous difference between Yahoos and Houyhnhnms that he disdains food touched by human hands and abandons his family. He purchases two stallions with the intention of teaching them the Houyhnhnm language and spends his evenings in conversation with them. Unable to bear human contact, he stops his nose with herbs to ward off the repulsive Yahoo smell of his wife and shuns all humankind. (Drabble 1985; Harrison et al. 1967; Hornstein et al. 1973; Johnson 1968; Magill 1958; Manguel and Guadalupi 1987; Pollard 1970; Quintana 1958; Swift 1958; Woods et al. 1947)

See also bestiality; Brobdingnags; disillusion; escapism; fantasy; Houyhnhnms; Laputa; Gulliver, Lemuel; Lilliput; satire; Swift, Jonathan.

THE HANDMAID'S TALE

Margaret Atwood's misogynist nightmare, published in Canada in 1985 and filmed by Cinecom in 1990, is a bold, chilling dystopia that speculates on where and how contemporary society is likely to derail and destroy itself. The novel is set in the late-twentieth-century Republic of Gilead, a futuristic military compound outside Boston. Against a backdrop of indistinct sectarian religious wars, Gilead is ruled by authoritarian fundamentalist Christians—enemies of homosexuals, dissidents, adulterers, divorcées, Baptists, Presbyterians, Catholics, Jews, Jehovah's Witnesses, and Quakers. Following a presidential assassination, the murder of members of Congress, the suspension of constitutional rights, and nuclear war, the story's conclusion looks back from a twenty-second-century perspective on a temporary tableau of chaos, as described in taped narratives by a female bondswoman known only as Offred.

Reflecting real episodes of violence, censorship, archconservatism, and antifemale measures throughout Canada, the United States, Iran, Romania, and Russia, *The Handmaid's Tale* focuses on ultra–right-wing sexist coercion. Gilead's uncompromising theocracy imprisons women in a tight servitude under arbitrary labels: Wives, Widows, Daughters, housemaids, amazons (Marthas), workers (Econowives), indoctrinators (Aunts), Unwomen, and breeders (Handmaids). The atmosphere is so tainted by toxins that many women have become barren or have borne freakish offspring, known as "shredders." The few women who retain fertility in second marriages and illegal liaisons are torn from husbands and lovers and rationed out as Handmaids to breed children for the elite echelon, the Commanders of the Faithful. The remaining female population scuttles about under the eye of a repressive patriarchal regime mouthing platitudes about the family, performing public prayers and executions, and rejoicing at the birth of healthy babies.

Atwood's politico-orthodox hierarchy is supported by a female-controlled internment center—the Rachel and Leah Re-education Center, or Red Center—set up in an abandoned high school gymnasium and run by the schoolmarmish Aunt Lydia and her cattle prod–brandishing coterie, who winnow out racial minorities and brainwash fertile white breeders into compliance with mandated matings. A seemingly benign bondage requires Handmaids to dress in white wimples and shapeless red habits, hose, and gloves that contrast the color-coded female hierarchy: white for virginal Daughters, blue for Wives, black for Widows, khaki for Aunts, dull green for Marthas, and red, green, and blue stripes for working-class Econowives.

Under the discipline of a Martha, or household guard, and the tight-lipped care of Rita and Cora (the Commander's suspicious, short-tempered servants), one Handmaid, 33-year-old Offred, lives in a seemingly pleasant late-Victorian home, where she copulates with the Commander during her fertile periods. Immured in a chaste upstairs cell without reading material, television, cosmetics, cigarettes, tea, or coffee, Offred prepares her body for motherhood. In Chapter 11 she goes to the doctor and repulses his offer to impregnate her to spare her an ignoble death for failure to conceive. Her mind returns to the cry of Rachel, Jacob's barren wife in the book of Genesis: "Give me children, or else I die."

Atwood highlights enmity among different levels of women by pitting Offred against Serena Joy, the Commander's wife. A former evangelist and singer, Serena Joy limps arthritically about her garden and glowers at Offred, who replaces a previous Handmaid who hanged herself. Each month Serena supervises a loveless, ritual intercourse intended to provide the family with a child. In the sitting room, with the entire staff present, the Commander reads from scripture, a privilege forbidden to women of any status. Upstairs in a canopied bed he mounts Offred, who lies supine between the spread thighs of the Commander's wife. Offred appears to comply with the perverse procedures, while secretly courting the Commander during illicit night visits and simultaneously conducting an affair with Nick, the Commander's macho chauffeur. Offred's attachment to the Commander arises from her yen for news of the outside world, especially the whereabouts of her mother, husband, and daughter.

The dreary, repetitive cycle of grocery shopping with Ofglen, readying her body for pregnancy, Prayvaganzas, Salvagings, and birthings locks Offred in a circumscribed lifestyle that revolves around her menstrual cycle, the proof that her monthly matings have yet to bring sperm and egg together. Her survival hinges on being able to produce a child within three years. A momentous break in the monotony comes with the impending birth of Ofwarren's baby. A gathering of panting, chanting Handmaids welcomes baby Angela, who is immediately placed in the hands of Warren's wife. Offred returns home from the excursion in a turmoil of emotion and falls asleep. After a "date" with Commander Fred, she retires to her room to cower in the closet as she represses hysteria.

At the novel's climax, events press Offred to desperation. At a Salvaging, all of Gilead's women, including Ofglen and Offred, participate, serving as executioners of rebels, adulterers, and dissidents. Offred is repulsed by Ofglen's apparent enjoyment and by Ofwarren's retreat into madness. After Ofglen's arrest, Offred panics that Ofglen will implicate her in the conspiracies of Mayday, an underground rebel network. As Offred returns to the Commander's door, she is met by Serena Joy, whose possession of a sequined costume

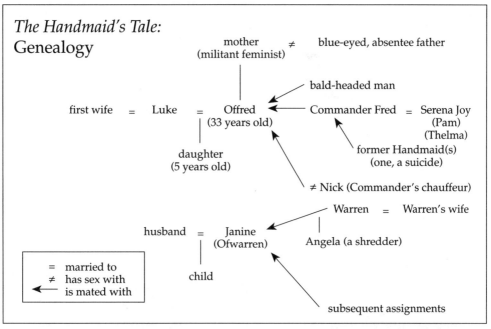

The Handmaid's Tale:
Genealogy

mother   ≠   blue-eyed, absentee father
(militant feminist)

                                                    bald-headed man

first wife   =   Luke   =   Offred   ◄───   Commander Fred   =   Serena Joy
                              (33 years old)   (Pam)
                                                                             (Thelma)

                    daughter   former Handmaid(s)
                    (5 years old)   (one, a suicide)

                                            ≠ Nick (Commander's chauffeur)

                                                    Warren   =   Warren's wife

            husband   =   Janine
                            (Ofwarren)   Angela (a shredder)

        ┌─────────────────────────┐
        │ =   married to   │
        │ ≠   has sex with   │   child
        │ ◄── is mated with   │
        └─────────────────────────┘

                                            subsequent assignments

indicates that she knows of Offred's clandestine "dates" with the Commander. These outings take her to Jezebel's, an old-time night spot where Offred reunites with Moira, a rebellious Handmaid who escaped from the Red Center to Salem before being captured.

Offred's mind hastily picks over an unappealing set of alternatives. Repulsed by contemplation of fire, suicide, escape to Nick, pleading for the Commander's mercy, flight, or murder of Serena Joy, Offred is interrupted by Nick, who bursts into her room and insists that she accompany two unidentified men in a police van. As Offred is ostensibly arrested for revealing state secrets, the Commander objects to the lack of a search warrant. Her captors ignore him and thrust Offred into the van.

Atwood concludes the novel with an insider's twist—a rapid flight to the future to gain a brief glimpse at the past. On June 25, 2195, the Twelfth Symposium studying Gileadean history convenes at the University of Denay, Nunavit. Professor Pieixoto explains how researchers unearthed 30 recycled cassette tapes from a way station in Bangor, Maine, assembled them into chronological order, and transcribed the journal on paper. The female narrator's description of her life as a Handmaid during Gilead's early period suggests that she was the concubine of Commander Frederick Waterford, a highly placed official who was killed during a purge of liberals for harboring a subversive. Pieixoto surmises that Offred escaped on the "Underground Frailroad" to Bangor, where Quakers often arranged escape to Canada or England. He concludes that Offred, out of fear of retaliation against her family, may have lived out her life in seclusion.

Critics responded with a mix of praise and censure for Atwood's dire fable and its too witty, too detached conclusion. Some declare her premise—that the United States could be easily commandeered by right-wing, misogynist fascists—an unlikely scenario. Others lament the dearth of character information on male characters, particularly Nick, the Commander, Pieixoto, and Luke. Most critics find the work historically possible, exacting, and so charged with warning that they proclaim it a feminist *1984* and a dystopian classic on a par with those of Aldous Huxley and George Orwell. (Atwood 1972; *Contemporary Authors* 1989; *Contemporary Literary Criticism* 1987; Davidson 1986; Dreifus 1992; Hammer 1990; Ingersoll 1991; McCombs 1988; *Major Twentieth-Century Writers* 1990; Van Spanckeren and Castro 1988)

See also Atwood, Margaret; *La Citté del Sole;* city planning; The Commander; conditioning; didacticism; disillusion; Gilead; Lydia, Aunt; Offred; technology; theocracy; women in utopia.

HAPPY VALLEY

Happy Valley is the utopian setting in Samuel Johnson's "Rasselas, Prince of Abissinia" (1759). The home of the Ethiopian prince is an isolated dell enclosed by mountains so remote that it can be reached only through a rocky cavern, which is obscured by woods and protected by an ancient iron gate manipulated by mechanical closures. Fed by mountain streams, the valley—similar to

Oliver Goldsmith's *Asem* (1759), William Morris's bucolic setting for *News from Nowhere* (1890), and James Hilton's Valley of the Blue Moon in *Lost Horizon* (1933)—grows green and productive. In this Eden, nature produces flowers, spices, fruit, and animals, both wild and domesticated. Johnson embellishes his utopia with colorful diversions. During the emperor's annual eight-day visits to the royal children, residents work tirelessly to entertain and amuse, and musicians and dancers compete for the opportunity to perform. Those who bore Happy Valley's citizens are banished and replaced by more innovative performers. The result of this fierce competition is an upward spiral in the lavishness of the annual fete.

The author's ingenious architecture parallels other mesmerizing utopias—Shangri-La, the Emerald City, Oceana, Atlantis, Cloudcuckooland, Vril-Ya, and the palace of Kublai Khan. A gargantuan stone-roofed royal residence with numerous inner courts hovers 30 paces above the lake. Like Daedalus's Labyrinth of the Cretan Minotaur in Greek mythology, the passages wind so intricately that only the oldest wardens know the building's inner secrets. Within inner chambers and alcoves, princes immure their treasures behind marble until the kingdom lapses into need. To record the location of each cache, princes keep a tally in a secret book that is stored in a tower and accessed only by the emperor and the heir apparent.

Like residents of Hesiod's golden age, the privileged lords and ladies who enjoy François Rabelais's Abbey of Thélème, and Baldessar Castiglione's lavish salons of the Italian Renaissance, princes and princesses repose in splendor and delight. Their attendants are attuned to every need, from the aroma of the garden and fine dining to total security of the palace. To assure Happy Valley's future, royal tutors dwell on the chaos and discord that lie beyond the imperial compound. Entertainers sing of the joys of Happy Valley, where sybaritic pleasures become the focus of each day. In a blessed milieu free from strife and want, developing princelings learn to value luxury and to pity those shut out of "this seat of tranquility." (Boswell 1981; Boulton 1978; Engell 1985; Goldsmith 1992; Johnson 1968; Johnson 1982; Magill 1958; Nath 1987)

See also The Abbey of Thélème; *Asem, an Eastern Tale*; golden age; Hesiod; *Lost Horizon*; naturalism; *News from Nowhere*; "Rasselas, Prince of Abissinia."

HARRINGTON, SIR JAMES

Harrington was an Elizabethan jurist, royal staff member, utopian, and the author of *The Commonwealth of Oceana* (1656), which proposes an eradication of England's social ills through improvement of the economy and an end to unlimited powers and terms of office. A contemporary of John Milton, Harrington was born in Upton, Northamptonshire, on January 3, 1611, to a privileged and highly refined family. He read widely and completed a law degree at Trinity College, Oxford. He served in the army in Holland, traveled Scandinavia, and studied the romance languages in Belgium, France, and Italy. On each leg of his journeys, he made copious notes on the achievement of stability through law and republican institutions.

In 1646 Harrington entered the service of King Charles I as equerry. He attempted to ameliorate the deteriorating relationship between Puritans and Royalists and, as a personal supporter of the king, was present at Charles's beheading three years later. Harrington's failure to offset civil war produced a deep depression, which he countered through private study of Latin classics, history, and politics. He published anonymously *The Commonwealth of Oceana*, a thinly veiled proposal for an idealized replacement for monarchy with a government based on reason and temperance. Conceptualizing on Aristotle's notions of the use of property as power, he created a fictional land where rulers and landed gentry were forbidden to subjugate the landless class. The treatise displeased Oliver Cromwell, England's Lord Protector, who had it impounded.

In 1659 Harrington formed the Rota Club as a means of promulgating his vision of a fair and just government. His publication of "The Rota: The Principles of Government" in 1660 calls for a balanced democracy evolving from popular assembly. Five years after the appearance of *The Commonwealth of Oceana* came the Glorious Restoration: The Puritans were deposed, the English monarchy reestablished, and Charles II enthroned. As a potential antimonarchist, Harrington was imprisoned for conspiring against Charles II and for threatening English constitutional law. During his incarceration, he went insane and was never brought to trial. He died September 7, 1677 in Westminster, London. Thomas Jefferson and Theodore Roosevelt studied Harrington's utopian theories, which directly influenced the American Constitution with its stress on balanced powers, bicameral legislation, secret ballot, the electoral college, direct vote by the people on each law, agrarianism, rotation of political appointments and offices, and antitrust laws. (Downs 1977; Harrington 1992; Johnson 1968; Magnusson 1990; Negley and Patrick 1952; Tawney 1993)

See also Milton, John; Oceana.

HAZEL

Hazel is a pragmatic, resilient, and unassuming leader of a band of terrified rabbits in Richard Adams's naturalistic beast fable *Watership Down* (1972). Level-headed but not particularly heroic, Hazel thrives in the role of epic rescuer by believing in his friends, trusting his second-in-command, making careful alliances, and remaining true to the search for a peaceable kingdom. At the head of Hazel's list of needs stands the prime requirement for existence—a warren where rabbits are not menaced by humans, dogs, tyrants, poisoned gas, guns, or bulldozers. He takes seriously the clairvoyance of his little brother Fiver, a prophet who senses that the pack must seek a new home immediately or suffer some unnamed doom. Against the rebuff of a pompous council of ruling-class rabbits, Hazel goes with his instinct and sticks to the minority opinion. In Chapter 3 he replies deliberately to the curious, "Fiver and I will be leaving the warren tonight. . . . I don't know exactly where we shall go, but we'll take anyone who's ready to come with us."

Hazel's honest description of the impromptu expedition convinces a small band of followers. On the six-mile journey from Sandleford Warren to Watership Down, he encourages group loyalty and delegates individual responsibility. His nondirective method enables him to work with others to come up with innovative methods of overcoming such obstacles as a bridge, a boat trip, and the pickets who guard a rabbit concentration camp. In moments of fear, he consults his inner stock of myth and belief in rabbit gods and an idealized hereafter. The animal equivalent of the impeccably honest, loyal, and god-fearing Aeneas, Hazel risks his life to free some caged rabbits from slaughter and to provide enough does to assure future litters of young.

Part of the novel demonstrates Hazel's fearlessness in facing potentially disastrous obstacles, notably fences, hasps, guard dogs, and a human with a shotgun, who disables Hazel with a blast to the thigh. Near death at a foul-smelling drain, Hazel lies stupefied from the pain in his leg until his brother finds him. Rescued and rejuvenated by the free-ranging haven his clan takes possession of, Hazel slowly recovers and pushes himself to greater acts of courage and cunning. In the end, he lives out his three years and more, and slips painlessly away from his body to a spiritual reward—a haven where rabbits run fast and leap high. (Adams 1972; *Contemporary Authors* 1981; *Contemporary Literary Criticism* 1976; Gilman 1974; Prescott 1974; Smith 1974)

See also allegory; bestiality; clairvoyance; fantasy; humanitarianism; naturalism; prophecy; synergy; *Watership Down*.

HEAVEN

Heaven is paradise, the resting place of righteous souls, a nonphysical nirvana, an unconscious merger with nature, or the home of the blessed in the Babylonian, Persian, Greek, Roman, Chinese, Hindu, Norse, Celtic, Polynesian, Balinese, Native American, Christian, Mormon, and Islamic afterlife. These otherworldly utopias are variously described in religious and epic texts as a pleasurable garden, a temporary abode of transmigrating souls, a permanent repository of spirits or demigods enjoying various degrees of contentment, a great hall for feasting and remembering conquests and war trophies to the most valiant, a conference hall for gods and goddesses, or a gradual incorporeal immersion with the most high, whether Yahweh, Rama, Vishnu, Allah, Shamash, the shining Devas, or Manitou. Most beneficent of these multinational idyllic afterlives are the various descriptions of isles of the blessed, which house with honor specific residents:

- national and military heroes
- the elect or chosen, i.e., the god's favorites, who are foredestined to attain heaven

- those who have earned grace or salvation for good works or acts of contrition

- those who sire sons

- those whose families attend to the ritual task of mourning

The least complicated of heavens is the Persian afterlife, a goal of worshipers as early as 550 B.C. Described in Zarathushtra's Zenda-Vesta, a collection of Zoroastrian lore, it is a final resting place on high for the righteous who survive an apocalyptic battle between good and evil. A bit more complicated in outlook is the Finnish *Kalevala*, a syncretized text dating from Elias Lönnrot's 1835 collection of stories and evolved from ancient lore overlaid with Christian influence. The *Kalevala*'s sparse depiction of the afterlife features Tuoni, a distant, blazing headland on the isle of Manala, or land of the dead, from which no voyager returns. The hero Väinämöinen, like Odysseus, Orpheus, and Aeneas in Mediterranean myth, dares breach the divide between living and dead in order to learn a hundred magic incantations. A girl rows Väinämöinen across and chastises him for trying to enter the land of the dead while he still enjoys life. Väinämöinen persists and spends the night wide-eyed on heaven's soft bed. By morning, he has acquired the magic words he needs to repeat in order to escape. Safely ashore among the living, he decrees that Jumala, the sky god, should never again let a living being enter the timeless afterlife, which holds for the wicked a dismal eternity of "burning boulders and [bed] covers woven of Tuoni's hissing serpents."

In the lore of some nations, heaven is more fully delineated than in the diminished views of the Zoroastrian scripture or the Finns' *Kalevala*. Typically, heaven is characterized as the ultimate goal of a tripartite cosmos. Unlike either hell, the permanent abode of the damned, or Earth, the home of mortals, heaven crowns a complex and interrelated triad. It is linked to light and blessing, a star-sprinkled firmament far above the gloomy, demonic netherworld reserved for the unworthy, doubters, apostates, evildoers, and blasphemers. Such graphic theological utopias form a major touchstone for writers like Hesiod, Ovid, Virgil, Plato, Cicero, St. Augustine, John Milton, John Bunyan, Johann Goethe, and Dante Alighieri, who draw on traditional religious visions as a basis for utopias grounded in godliness and inspiring to the righteous.

Heaven: God's Home

A constant in the religious and philosophical visions of humanity, heaven grew out of a need for beneficence, which originally attached to sunlight with its warming, healing, fructifying effect on earthly flora and fauna. Most often, heaven, as described by the Greek myth of Phaethon, the doomed son of Hyperion, was an anthropomorphic human dwelling, a palace where the sun lived, high in the sky or beyond the horizon. The pervasive concept of heaven as the supernal abode of a god or gods is similar in form and purpose in many cultural traditions:

- the Native American happy hunting grounds
- the ancient Chinese T'ien
- the "house of the Lord" that the poet-king David describes in Psalm 23
- the Norse Valhalla, a many-doored banquet hall designed to seat 800 war heroes
- the Islamic paradise tended by subservient houris
- King Arthur's floating isle of Avalon with its cadre of handmaidens
- the Roman Elysian Fields
- Gilgamesh's passage through a land decked in jewels
- the conference hall of Bayu, father of Bhima, the Balinese epic hero. In Bhima's eyes, heaven is an artistic oasis where gods and artisans are equals. There, stonemasons and wood-carvers decorate buildings, and souls of the wise enjoy all forms of beauty.

On the whole, the idea of freedom from Earth and relaxation or ease in a vast, resplendent setting satisfies the human need to look beyond a coffin, small rectangle of sod, cold headstone, or crematory fire that marks the end of human life.

To the ancient Egyptians heaven lay to the west, where sunset and darkness emulated the demise of the body. A sun-bright ladder led up to the Egyptian afterlife, where dutifully preserved bodies continued their earthly lives in the presence of Osiris. By extension, a firm grasp on light, a symbol of truth, was the soul's method of attaining eternal life. According to Chapter 98 of *The Book of the Dead* (fifteenth century B.C.), to reach heaven, the soul had to emulate Osiris and, ray by ray, scale the ladder that Ra extended from the sun to Earth. This challenging task was a heaven-blessed fleeing of Earth's miseries to a single access—the eastern portal—which was guarded by *cynocephali,* or dog-headed apes, and angels known as the spirits of light. An anthropomorphized version of the myth described the metaphoric ladder of heaven as the arms of god, which reached down to the blessed and lifted them to eternal rest.

The faithful in Egypt attended to earthbound affairs while living, but kept an eye to the future. The wealthiest and most prestigious accumulated vast sums to pay for quality mummification to preserve the *khat,* the physical remains. Egyptians believed that they would one day reenact the transformation of Osiris, the dismembered god, and rise to live again. In the linen wrappings of the body of Thothmes III, a lengthy address to Osiris avers:

> Homage to thee, O my father Osiris, thy flesh suffered no decay, there were no worms in thee, thou didst not crumble away, thou didst not wither away, thou didst not become corruption and worms; and . . . I shall possess my flesh for ever and ever, I shall not decay, I shall not crumble away, I shall not wither away, I shall not become corruption. (Budge 1960)

The residence of this resurrected *sahu,* or spirit, was the tomb, which was fitted out with the necessities of life, i.e., shelter, food, wine, weapons, slaves, clothing, chariots, boats, and favorite animals. The storage of so full an equipage for eternity was often re-created in miniature or symbolic form, drawn on wall friezes, or formed into ritual statuary.

To assure that the dead reached their destination, mourners placed ceremonial ladders in tombs or painted them on frescoes. Other symbols served as talismans: the twin-headed guardian cobra, the sun disk, a beetle, and the head of a hawk in flight. In affirmation of a spiritual life beyond Earth, the soul chants, "I am the plant of life which grows through the ribs of Osiris" (*The Book of the Dead*). By allying the *sahu*'s resurgent hope for eternal life, the speaker compares the newly risen body to a frail tendril of greenery sprouting and twining through the corpse of the resurrected god like ivy on a trellis.

In its new form, the *sahu* could rise to heaven, the palace of Anu, and mingle with the gods. Perpetually freed of earthly fetters, the spirit had a double, the *ka*, which was first explained by Nestor L'Hôte in 1840. In an expanded version written in 1878 for the members of the Congress of Lyons, France (Budge 1960), M. Maspero surmised that

> . . . *le* ka *est une sorte de double de la personne humaine d'une matière moins grossière que la matière dont est formé le corps, mais qu'il fallait nourrir et entretenir comme le corps lui-même; ce double vivait dans le tombeau des offrandes qu'on faisait aux fêtes canoniques.* . . . [The *ka* is a kind of twin image composed of less substantial tissue than that of a human body, but which must be nourished and sustained as though it were flesh; this double lives in a tomb and survives on offerings made during holy festivals. . . .]

Similarly described in Sudanese lore, the concept of the double called for priests to nourish, pray for, and attend the invisible, incorporeal spirit, which did no harm if properly placated.

According to the minutely detailed lore of *The Book of the Dead*, to reach the Egyptian heaven, the spirit passed through a slab of sky that rested on four pillars, which symbolized the four winds and the four children of Horus. In contrast to an upper haven, there existed a dark earthly realm called the *Tuat*. Similar to Dante's purgatory, the *Tuat* extended over a somber, shadowy desert pitted with smoldering fires through which the soul made its passage. For the punishment of the wicked, a staff of executioners burned undeserving souls or hacked them to pieces. Also, monsters and serpents loomed in the distance and preyed on souls that ventured too near an encircling river.

Counter to the Christian view of heaven, the Egyptian afterlife contained a contiguous realm, with the borders of no-man's-land touching on the land of the blessed. At a distance lay Osiris's court in the Field of Reeds, from which the god, the "Lord of Souls," ruled his kingdom, attended by a staff of 36 guards. At each of the 12 portals, three doorkeepers kept watch and announced the name of each newcomer. Those who passed through the twelfth gate lived with Ra, the sun god, ate at the divine table, and dressed in brilliant raiment. This idyllic life of privilege continued only so long as earthly mourners gave gifts to Osiris.

As characterized in Babylonian, Norse, Greek, and Roman epic, essay, and oratory, other ancient afterlives are stereotypically male-centered resting places designed to honor warriors and heroes. These havens are sometimes staffed by female or sexually neutral couriers and handmaidens such as the Valkyries, angels and archangels, and Houris. In Norse lore, a nine-layered male heaven is known by a variety of names: light-bringer, twin-lit, clouded-brightness, wind-dark, rich-wetter, and wide-embracer. In the "Gylfaginning," the first collection of *Edda,* or Icelandic lore (A.D. 1056), the holiest council of the gods sprang from Yggdrasil, a great ash tree that shelters the earth and spreads across the sky. Beneath one of the roots, the well of Mimir the giant flows with sweet rivulets of wisdom and intelligence. Odin—the creator, All-Father, All-Knowing, and bringer of light—was so desirous of the blessings of heaven that he traded one eye for a drink at Mimir's well.

Mortals wishing to attain the Norse heaven were instructed to cross the red stripe in the rainbow and enter a variety of beautiful mansions, which the gods protected. In one distinguished hall near Yggdrasil lived three maidens— Weird, Verdandi, and Skuld—who, like the Greek fates, shaped destiny according to their whim. Less intrusive in human fate were other accesses to the afterlife: Alfheim, where the light and dark elves lived; Breidablik, known for its beauty; Glitnir, the most splendid of resting places, which had walls and pillars of gold and a silver roof; and Valhalla, residence of Odin and his wife Frigga and the most famous of Norse havens, which offered an unending feast of roast boar and mead to the brave who died in battle and whom Odin adopted as foster sons. Each day the warrior wraiths reenacted their bold deeds, died again, and were reborn. In contrast to this vivid military idyll was Gimle, chief among the Norse pleasure palaces, the only heavenly home slated to survive the end of time. In it lived the righteous in delight and harmony for all ages.

In the writings of Plato, Hesiod, Cicero, and Virgil, heaven was a privilege attained by good works, piety, or heroic deeds. In Book X of Plato's *Republic* (fifth century B.C.), the soul netted rewards in the afterlife for acts of goodness, mercy, and compassion performed on Earth. In the "Myth of Er," Plato explained that heaven was separated from the Underworld by judges who dispatched souls either to a great chasm below Earth or to a corresponding chasm in the sky. After the worst of souls wandered for a millennium to expiate their crimes, they appeared before the three sisters—Lachesis, Atropos, and Clotho. These tailors fit the souls for new lives, which the spirits entered by drinking from Lethe, the River of Forgetfulness, so that they could be born afresh with no memory of past lives.

Cicero, Rome's consummate moralist and essayist, used Plato's favorite format, the dialogue, to describe a timeless world in "The Dream of Scipio," part of *De Republica* (51 B.C.). While serving as a military tribune under the consul Manius Manilius, Cicero conversed in depth with a vision of Publius Cornelius Scipio, one of Rome's most illustrious military leaders and consul in 218 B.C. The essay relates how, despairing of life on Earth and lost in his dream, Cicero is ripe for a philosophical discussion of the afterlife. Scipio obliges with a discourse on the Milky Way, harmony of the spheres, and the realms that exist beyond the petty struggles of humanity.

In Scipio's cosmology, the death of the body is of minor consequence—a mere dot on the extended canvas of the universe. He advises his friend to realize that humanity exists in the energy of the godlike soul:

> Know then that you are divine, for that is divine which throbs with life, feels, remembers, foresees, which rules, controls, and makes to move the body over which it has been placed in charge, as over this universe rules that supreme God; so this mortal body is made to move by a deathless soul within.

Scipio's logic assures Cicero that anything set in motion by the prime mover (God) is fated to last forever, so long as God decrees. The souls that suffer most in the transition to the afterlife are those who have debauched and shamed themselves with sensual delights. Scipio frees Cicero of fear by assuring him that a noble life conducted with probity and reverence for life has no need to fear the heaven that lies amid glorious harmony that synchronizes the planets.

Heaven in Epic Literature

In ancient epics, the composition of heaven was variously depicted as air, water or other precipitate, finely woven muslin or damask, or skin or hide. In Psalm 104:1–5, David, the Hebrew psalmist and founder of a unified Israel, followed this tradition by noting that God, or Yahweh,

> ... coverest thyself with light as with a garment; who stretchest out the heavens like a curtain, who layeth the beams of his chambers in the water; who maketh the clouds his chariot; who walketh upon the wings of the wind; who maketh his angels spirits; his ministers a flaming fire; who laid the foundations of the earth, that it should not be removed for ever.

Metaphorically, otherworldly commentary of this type often characterized heaven as a body wrap, blanket, veil, or ceremonial robe for the sky god. More solid heavenly foundations included polished metal, precious stone, or a glass mirror, as described in Job 37:18, Homer's *Iliad* (eighth century B.C.), and the Finnish *Kalevala*. In Middle Eastern lore, heaven was stratified in as few as three and as many as seven layers, as claimed by Islamic writings, which list pure silver, yellow gold, pearl, white gold, blended silver, ruby, and garnet as its elements. In ancient Egyptian lore, the vault of heaven rests on four ceremonial uprights. Such tangible materials and verifiable shapes gave concrete images to minds that were unable to grasp an abstract heaven.

A less complicated heaven, the description of Elysium in Homer's *Odyssey* (eighth century B.C.), falls into the category of a gentle respite. In support of Menelaus, Homer's wearied warrior and voyager, the author speaks of a universal need for succor at the end of a toilsome life. In Book IV Menelaus is to be honored in the afterlife with a seat near Rhadamanthos, the Underworld judge,

> ... where all existence is a dream of ease. Snowfall is never known there, neither long frost of winter, nor torrential rain, but only mild and lulling airs from Ocean bearing refreshment for the souls of men—the West Wind always blowing.

Rich with suggestion, this description of atmosphere symbolizes the frosty chill Menelaus endured after losing a loving wife and the torrential rain of weapons from the Trojans, whom Menelaus battled to retrieve his lovely Helen.

Basing his writing on Homer's, Virgil wrote his literary epic of Rome, the *Aeneid* (19 B.C.), focusing on a more palpable land where Pluto and Proserpina and their judges supervised the transmigration of souls. While visiting the Elysian Fields, Aeneas describes the transmutation of beings yet to be born— the illustrious leaders who await rebirth in the Roman Empire. (Note that the yet-to-be-born heroes magnify the royal genealogy of Augustus, Rome's empire-founder, who hired Virgil to ennoble his newly established line of emperors by composing a literary epic for Rome linked to Homer's epics.)

Somewhat similar to Virgil's cosmology, the oldest literary expression of immortality arises from the Celtic belief in the Otherworld, a divine land that reflected Elysium because it served as a way station for souls on their way to reincarnation. Mentioned by Sotion of Alexandria and Clement of Alexandria, the Celtic abode of the dead provided a reprieve from suffering and guilt. On October 31, or Halloween, originally called the night of the dead or Feast of Samhain, the Otherworld materialized out of invisibility so that worshipers could celebrate their future destination. As the portals of the afterlife swung open, the deceased (prefiguring Halloween pranksters) earned the right to avenge wrongs done them by victimizing people still alive on Earth.

In addition to afterworlds where spirits come and go in frequent communion with Earth, the Celts also designated places of eternal rest:

- One of the most beloved and anticipated is the Land of Life, or Tir-na-nóg, a fairyland where the famed Ossian, Fingal's son, joined mortals in a happy afterlife.

- Another version was the Land of Promise, or *Inis-Manann*, currently known as the Isle of Man, where the sea god Mac Lir ruled over residents in peace and joy.

- A third Celtic haven was the House of Donn, an island off Ireland's southwest coast, the realm of Bilé and Donn. To populate this realm, Ogma, a minor deity, served as selector of souls to be transported for permanent residency. Only the boldest mortals breached the forbidding isle.

Most significant in Irish lore were Cúchulainn, the Irish incarnation of Achilles, and Cúchulainn's party, who braved the afterlife to fight ravaging sea serpents. On a less dire mission, Oisín, or Ossian, rode his magic steed to the afterlife to languish for 300 years in the arms of Niamh, a sea nymph. At length he grew tired of Paradise and his lovely companion, and was allowed to return to Ireland. Like Arthur and Merlin in English fiction, the lore of Oisín and Cúchulainn permeates much of Irish literature, particularly the poetry of William Butler Yeats and Seamus Heaney.

Heaven in Judeo-Christian Scripture

In contrast to the more fearful, less beneficent punishment centers and exclusive, male-centered havens of Homer, Virgil, and the Egyptians and Celts, the

Judeo-Christian heaven, as opposed to the hell or abyss of *sheol* that supposedly exists under the earth, is a clearly delineated haven. The Hebrews of the fifth century B.C. described a vision of ineffable light and joy, a paradise that parallels the afterlife of the Zoroastrians of Persia. This Hebrew haven exists in the sky and, together with the earth and hell, forms the whole of creation. Passage to heaven fulfills a godly covenant and rewards the blessed, who dwell among ranks of angels, archangels, saints, and the Almighty, who reigns supreme. A brief glimpse of heaven appears in Genesis 28:12–15 when Jacob has a vision of a ladder and angels moving up and down the rungs in attendance on God. God speaks directly to Jacob, promising guidance during his assigned task: fathering a great nation. In verse 17 Jacob mutters to himself, "How dreadful is this place! this is none other but the house of God, and this is the gate of heaven."

Unlike Jacob's dream, Moses' open-eyed experience with God is more dramatic. In Exodus 19:18–20, speaking in resonant, trumpetlike tones, God departs heaven and descends to Mount Sinai long enough to confer directly with Moses, who is to charge the Israelites to obey holy law. He warns Moses that only he and his brother Aaron are allowed on this sacred ground, because the divine presence might overwhelm mere mortals. A similar comment on heaven occurs in I Kings 8:27,43, when David comments that God's glory exceeds the confines of heaven. Psalm 139:8–10 repeats David's assurance that God dwells in a heaven above Earth, to which both Enoch and Elijah are lifted (Genesis 5:24, II Kings 2:1–12). Elijah's passage, as described in II Kings 2:11, augments the glory of his transformation as a fiery chariot drawn by blazing steeds descends and returns to heaven in a whirlwind.

In the Judeo-Christian tradition, heaven, or paradise, exists on Earth in Eden at the end of the first six days of creation. Recorded in Genesis 2, the Old Testament concept of heaven brings together fruitful plants and abundant species of animals in a blameless, balanced environment—a serene abode where land, water, and sky form an agreeable, nurturing resting place for humankind. By extension, an afterlife for the soul floating free of its earthly body beyond the stars resituates heaven in the upper air, a place of bliss. Here the righteous are transfigured into sublime oneness with God. In Deuteronomy 26:15 the author describes the afterlife as God's "holy habitation," a place of light and spiritual nurturance. In Isaiah's predictions of the triumph of God's kingdom, Israel is fated to know a new age—a serene, deathless existence based on divinity, pardon, and fulfillment of ancient prophecies.

When added to the 39 books of the canon Old Testament, Christian doctrine, as propounded in the 27 books of the New Testament, augments the importance of heaven for the redeemed. Its location is skyward, where Christ, who triumphs over death, turns his eyes (Mark 7:41; John 17:1) and toward which he ascends (Luke 24:51). In John 14:1–3, one of the most commonly read passages at Christian funerals promises a home to the redeemed. The dramatic setting contains the personal warmth of what Martin Buber calls an I-thou experience. To Peter, who despairs that his master must leave the earth, Christ comforts:

Let not your heart be troubled; ye believe in God, believe also in me. In my Father's house are many mansions: if it were not so, I would have told you. I go to prepare a place for you. And if I go and prepare a place for you, I will come again, and receive you unto myself; that where I am, there ye may be also.

According to Luke 20:34–36, the human concept of earthly bliss among loved ones is replaced with an angelic state. In Romans 8:38–39, such an appealing end to earthly life convinces Paul of its permanence, which

> . . . neither death, nor life, nor angels, nor principalities, nor powers, nor things present, nor things to come. Nor height nor depth, nor any other creature, shall be able to separate us from the love of God, which is in Christ Jesus our Lord.

Although vague in its physical description, the strength of Paul's commitment, repeated in Ephesians 4:10, suggests an epiphany—a heavenly experience of the soul, which actualizes God's covenant that humankind will one day become one with love. In I Thessalonians 4:14–17, Paul makes his most dramatic promise: The dead who died in the faith will respond to a trumpet call and the archangel's voice, and will live eternally above Earth with the Lord.

As the offspring of God, those who enter heaven achieve all desires. In John 6:38, the gospel writer notes that Christ descended from heaven, a blessed place to which he returned. Explained in Mark 16:19, heaven is the sovereign abode of the Almighty, where Christ enters the upper atmosphere and sits at God's right hand. As ruler of heaven, Christ remains in power in the upper reaches until his return, which is characterized in Matthew 24:30 as a resplendent, triumphal reentry of "the Son of man coming in the clouds of heaven with power and great glory."

New Testament writers removed heaven from a geographical cosmology to a spiritual, metaphysical plane populated by angels and presided over by identifiable beings: the archangel Gabriel and other seraphs, three of whom—Raphael, Michael, and Uriel—are called by name. In Luke 23, while facing death by crucifixion, Christ promises paradise to the repentant thief. According to John 3:5, this celestial resting place is available to all who accept a watery and spiritual baptism. In the development of church dogma, this tangible "place" evolved into a transcendent oneness with God, an intangible submergence of the soul with a deity similar to that of oriental cosmology. In the lyrical vision in Revelation 19, the opening of heaven will reveal a military panorama—mounted armies clothed in white and God identified by an effulgent banner proclaiming "King of Kings and Lord of Lords."

A literary offshoot of this biblical heaven is the Renaissance heaven that Dante Alighieri's *Divine Comedy* (1320) called *Paradiso*, where the souls of the blessed enjoy cosmic communion with the divine, and which Johann Goethe's *Faust* (1808) builds around a sublime deity both vast and unknowable whose "essence none can say." Likewise, heaven is the goal of the suffering slaves in Harriet Beecher's Stowe's *Uncle Tom's Cabin* (1852), an overwritten melodrama that President Abraham Lincoln credited with contributing to the Civil War. In Chapter 26, as Little Eva passes over the divisions between Earth and heaven,

"Earth was past, and earthly pain; but so solemn, so mysterious, was the triumphant brightness of [her] face, that it checked even the sobs of sorrow." To a question about what she was experiencing, Eva replies "O! love,—joy,—peace!" and expires in blessed calm. Her loved ones anticipate that she is with Christ and will return on the day of the Second Coming, when heaven shall triumph over evil.

Heaven in Islam, Buddhism, and Hinduism

In other faiths, the concept of a perfect world or ultimate reward for goodness or faith reveals itself in sacred writings. According to the Koran, the dead who have remained faithful will undergo resurrection and judgment. If earthly behavior proves merit, the faithful will cross the bridge of al-Aaraf and know an otherworldly union with the Almighty, who promises satisfaction of all earthly appetites. The lyricism of the Islamic paradise details physical pleasure, which,

> . . . for the godfearing is a fair resort, Gardens of Eden, whereof the gates are open to them, wherein they recline, and wherein they call for fruits abundant, and sweet potions. . . . [surah 37]

In surah 38:50–54, Mohammed stresses: "This is what you were promised for the Day of Reckoning; this is Our provision, unto which there is no end." A more sublime aspect of this graphic afterlife is that pictured by al-Ghazali and the Sufists, a sect who believed that immersion in God transcends or replaces the human element with a disembodied oneness with the divine. Whether concrete or abstract, Islamic heaven vivifies a single dwelling for the righteous and reassurance that Allah will remain with his elect for eternity.

Amid the joy and bliss of entering the afterlife, Muslims unite with Allah only after touring hell, or *gehenna*, where infidels, having tumbled from the bridge because of their transgressions against Allah, suffer everlasting torment, "wherein they are roasted—an evil cradling! All this; so let them taste it—boiling water and pus, and other torments of the like kind coupled together" (surah 38:56–58). This unending agony is not without hope. For those whose souls are salvageable, purification leads to a restoration of the soul and a second chance at Paradise.

Other world religions provide substantially more complicated views of heaven and how to attain it. The holy texts of Buddhism—which have existed for thousands of years in various forms in Japan, Korea, and China—picture a reflective paradise, or pure land, where the doer of good deeds rejoices in the fruits of a virtuous life. On a wheel of experience that constantly rotates, human souls pass in and out of heaven as they return to Earth for rebirth. To achieve the most desirable state, the devout seek enlightenment as an escape from sensuality. In Buddhist teachings, the *kamalokas*, the lower realms of heaven, or nirvana, satisfy carnal desire. Above these sensual layers are the *rupalokas*, 16 purifying increments that gradually withdraw the soul from sensate fulfillment to spiritual envelopment until the soul, like unbound energy, becomes one with the universe.

The Buddhist cosmology includes Himavant, one of the stages of heaven that leads to nirvana. This nineteenth century Burmese representation shows a heaven populated by gods, elephants, and lions.

By meditation and discipline, the seeker strips the body of its earthly yearnings and enters whatever heavenly realm suits the soul's level of attainment. Compassion, the most liberating of virtues, releases the soul from the wheel and grants eternal salvation. The highest four levels, or *arupalokas*, contain the most ephemeral of states, in which there exists neither structure nor volition. Thus extracted from longing, will, or sensual ties, the soul enjoys a transcendent state indescribable in human terms. Similar to the Hindu concept of Vishnu's heaven, or *nirvana*, Buddhism anticipates a glorious reward free of mortal fears, disease, pain, and death.

The Chinese version of Buddhism maintains a unique emphasis on the *Tao*, or path, which the first line of the *Tao Te Ching* describes as the nameless fount of all things. *Tao* resembles nature's phenomena—the seasons, heavenly bodies, and human growth stages—but is composed of pure energy. Thus, the *Tao* is shapeless matter that is beyond the ability of the human mind to picture. Paradoxically, by not seeking heaven, the quiet, contemplative, undemonstrative Taoist finds the heart's desire by letting ambitions fall away and clearing the mind of distractions.

As described by T'an-luan, a sixth-century Chinese Taoist, the soul must follow the path of truth to the Pure Land, where the body knows no pain and exults in a vibrant garden decked with jewels and glorified in unearthly music. A more recent Chinese variant, as described in the four books of Confucius (555–479 B.C.), offers a less definitive heaven and concentrates on egalitarianism, the divine right of the emperor as God's emissary, and ancestor worship, all forms of piety that focus on the living, on universal order, and on those who have already entered heaven and await the intercessory prayers of succeeding generations still on Earth. The spiritual bases that undergird the Confucian heaven—love, justice, reverence, and wisdom—transcend mortal comforts and concentrate on the tranquillity of the soul.

A much later version of Taoism stresses a form of record-keeping—the tally of good against evil. As delineated in *The Book of Rewards and Punishments by the Great Supreme*, a much later version of Taoism written during the Sung dynasty (960–1279), the attainment of eternal rest required that the faithful pay for their evil deeds:

> The Great Supreme says: Misfortune and fortune have no door; men themselves incur or win them; recompense follows virtue and vice, as the shadow follows substance. (Jurji 1946)

People who conducted themselves without regard for goodness violated "the way." Their lives were shortened and filled with sorrow. The accounting was exact—12 years for large faults, 100 days for smaller infractions. If the weight of sin followed them to their graves, the punishment fell on their children, who were forced to suffer punishment in the Underworld before entering heaven.

In its emphasis on earthly experiences and spiritual refinements, the Hindu paradise, as defined by the *Rigveda*, a collection of lore dating from 1500–1200 B.C., requires purification of the flesh by the fires of Agni, intermediary agent of the deceased. In imitation of the first human casualty, Yama, all the faithful must avoid Maya, the veil of illusion, and perform a sufficient number of sacrifices, offerings, and rituals to redeem the soul from wrongdoing. After death, these righteous pass upward to the stars, the kingdom of Varuna, the sky god. In the presence of the divine Vishnu, the supreme Indian god, souls live forever.

With the evolution of Hinduism from the sixth to first centuries B.C., a less direct method of attaining heaven contrasted the simplicity of Christian worship. Hinduism resulted from a blend of scriptural eras: the *Upanishads*, a series of verses or hymns advising seekers of God to follow the path of the devout, and the *Bhagavadgita*, or *Song of the Lord*, a Sanskrit dialogue written in the second century B.C. as part of the *Mahabharata*, the Indian epic begun two centuries earlier. According to this involved mystical cosmos, human souls, which Hindus consider to be deathless, enter into a cycle of lives, earthly demises, and reincarnations. Thus, heaven becomes a multilevel way station for the soul on its journey to final rest, or nirvana. At the concluding entry into the afterlife, having earned its reward from multiple human experiences, the migrating soul attains eternal repose and unites with Krishna, the supreme God.

As with Greek and Roman concepts of paradise, male military heroes receive special dispensation. In the closing lines of the *Mahabharata*, heaven lays a short drive away from the battlefield, where glorious warriors pass into permanent glory. Driven in a flower-decked chariot, the slain Bhishma, a blameless hero, reunites with family members and sits beside Drona, who becomes the hero's heavenly tutor. Along the airy heights walk other mighty men of war who have gained eternity by shedding their mortality, passing through heaven's gate, and claiming a celestial abode. The epic promises that kindness, gentle words, and endurance presage a better life and sanctified future for all earthly beings.

Mormonism

The philosophy of the Church of Latter-day Saints is a uniquely American extension and augmentation of Christianity. According to *The Book of Mormon* (1830), revealed by the angel Moroni, translated and expounded on by Joseph Smith, and in part influenced by the writings of Emanuel Swedenborg, a Swedish mystic, God intends to redeem all humankind, including pagans and infants. The shape and nature of so broad a heaven is richly detailed in the revelations of leaders of the faith of Latter-day Saints. As described in II Nephi 8:11:

> . . . the redeemed of the Lord shall return, and come with singing unto Zion; and everlasting joy and holiness shall be upon their heads; and they shall obtain gladness and joy; sorrow and mourning shall flee away.

As with New Testament descriptions, the prophet Nephi foresees a transcendent haven where earthly pain no longer troubles the spirit.

Both before and after life, the soul remains permanent. Alma 11:43–45 promises that spirit and body will coalesce into perfection, "both limb and joint shall be restored to its proper frame, even as we now are at this time." Thus readied to meet the Most High, the soul awaits arraignment and judgment. In Enos 1:27, the prophet remarks,

> And I rejoice in the day when my mortal self shall put on immortality, and shall stand before him; then shall I see his face with pleasure, and he will say unto me: Come unto me, ye blessed, there is a place prepared for you in the mansions of my Father.

This union with the Almighty reflects similar beliefs of Christians, who dwell on the transcendental aspects of heaven rather than graphic details.

A later testimony broadens the Mormon concept of heaven. In III Nephi 28:13–15, a personal revelation of heaven proclaims that three Nephites received the touch of Jesus and witnessed the opening of the heavens. Like Elisha in the Old Testament, "they were caught up into heaven, and saw and heard unspeakable things." Forbidden to reveal the joys of eternity, they were transfigured from flesh to "an immortal state," which allied their senses more closely with God.

According to more recent scriptural interpretation, after a period of amnesia during life on Earth, the redeemed soul departs the physical realm and reestablishes itself in a three-tiered celestial glory. In its new stage of existence, the soul remains in a perfectable state until the resurrection of Christ. During this preheavenly state, missionaries and teachers continue broadening the individual's understanding of God. The dead are still redeemable and thus candidates for heavenly glory if a living believer undergoes a proxy baptism.

The Mormon afterlife is blessed by the intensification of love between mates and families. The unique concept of celestial marriage or spiritual wifehood, which derives from Joseph Smith's *Revelation on the Eternity of the Marriage Covenant, Including Plurality of Wives,* countenances multiple marriages between a man and two or more women. Originally, the purpose of Smith's dictum was the spread of Mormonism through large families of believers, who would then become missionaries to increase the outreach of salvation. In current interpretation these unions, usually serial rather than polygamous, presage a celestial meeting in heaven, where the husband and his wives and children enjoy an eternal bond countenanced by God's grace and blessing.

Until the millennium, or end of time, the Mormon faithful continue their search for godliness. At the supreme moment, their writings predict that the earth will transform itself into a celestial home where the faithful will at last earn their rewards and "happiness, which is called paradise, a state of rest, a state of peace, where they shall rest from all their troubles and from all care, and sorrow." (Alma 40:12) The highest-ranking Mormons anticipate equality with Christ as just recompense for orthodox beliefs and their attention to duty. Marriage performed in the temple establishes an undying community of families who will live in harmony, righteousness, and peace and continue to produce offspring.

Native American Cosmology

No single written body of Native American literature contains the multiple views of a blessed haven that colored the oral traditions of most early tribes. An English version of Native American lore comes from the paintings of George Catlin and the writings of Mary Eastman and H. R. Schoolcraft, whose studies of the Algonquin nation inspired the American epic *The Song of Hiawatha* (1855), written by poet Henry Wadsworth Longfellow. Hiawatha, a Woods Indian who is both culture hero and prophet of the Iroquois on Lake Superior, dwells in an idyllic state with his Dakota bride, Minnehaha. Unified by the beneficent forces of nature, he lives a gladsome life of happiness, peace, and plenty. He brings progress to the primitive natives by teaching them to grow corn, heal themselves with herbs, and write their thoughts in pictographs.

In Book 19 Longfellow turns from romanticized earthly lore to a legendary heaven, the home of Gitche Manito, the almighty master of life. Longfellow describes visitors from the Blessed Islands, also called the land of the hereafter and the kingdom of Ponemah, a mystic land where the much-mourned singer Chibiabos dwells after his death. At first Hiawatha and Nokomis, his grandmother, ignore the pale, haggard wraiths who glide in and out among the shadows. Then Hiawatha grows so distressed by their plaintive cries that he addresses his pale guests and asks why they grieve. The gentle voices reply that they are the ghosts of former Indians who have come to warn Hiawatha that tears and calls from the living are troubling to the dead. The ghosts refer to this lamentation as "useless sorrow," a deterrent to the implied peace of the afterlife. The voices insist that they need no wampum, furs, pots, or kettles to weigh down the souls for the four-day journey to the Blessed Islands. Requiring only fire for purification, the departed pass from earthly cares, taking with them Minnehaha, Hiawatha's beloved, who dies of fever during a great famine.

In Book 23 Longfellow focuses on Hiawatha and his preparations for departure from life to the Blessed Islands. He divests himself of grief and sits expectantly outdoors on a summer day, both palms turned upward as though anticipating a gift from Manito. Canoes arrive bearing the black-robed prophet, who tells Hiawatha about a place to the west where others have accepted the message of Christ. After serious words of farewell to his people and to nature, he floats outward and upward in a birch canoe, his conveyance to "the glory of the sunset."

This indistinct Iroquois vision of a sorrowless haven that syncretizes with the Christian heaven contrasts the despair of Black Elk, an early-twentieth-century holy man of the Oglala Sioux whose vision of a failed paradise appears in his dictated autobiography *Black Elk Speaks* (1932), as translated from the Sioux language and recorded by John G. Neihardt on the Pine Ridge Reservation near Lincoln, Nebraska. Considered the only Plains Indian bible, *Black Elk Speaks* is an outgrowth of the messianic lore of Native Americans, i.e., the Ghost Dance and the influence of the prophet Wovoka, who predicted the nearness of a heaven on Earth, when souls would rise from the dead and resume a peaceful Indian community living as one with nature. History defeated Wovoka's message in the late nineteenth century, when rapidly Americanized customs and beliefs rationalized genocide, the near extinction of the buffalo, the spread of fences around pasturage, and murderous plots by white settlers and soldiers.

With the aid of two interpreters, Flying Hawk and Black Elk's son Ben, and Neihardt's daughter Enid, a stenographer, Neihardt preserved Black Elk's memoirs of a vision he had at age five. The vision recurred throughout his youth as reminders of halcyon days when the Sioux lived in close communion with and dependence on the migratory pattern of the buffalo across the Midwest. The haven that Black Elk foresees is the plains of his childhood, a golden age when living things prospered in rhythm with nature and when Indians respected the earth as a mother, giver of life. As the seer reports in Chapter 3, "And as I looked ahead, the people changed into elks and bison and all four-footed beings and even into fowls, all walking in a sacred manner on the good red road together." Symbolic of that era is the Lakota concept of the sacred hoop, the circle that has no end and no beginning and which appears in the cyclic movement of the sun and astral bodies, the changing of the seasons, the circle of tepees, and the shape of the tepee. Yet, Black Elk's haven begins to sicken and die as outsiders threaten the earth and break the sacred unity that undergirds Sioux theology.

On further study of the gods' revelation, Black Elk, like the Greek seer Teiresias, experienced the ebbing of his human vision as his power vision turned inward to accommodate thoughts and prayers. In *Black Elk Speaks,* he looks out on a perfect day colored by contrasting tones of natural beauty, which he views from the highest mountain. His mysticism weaves a spiritual vision of the "Other World" with the outdoors, which he reports as "the shape of all shapes as they must live together like one being." And the Sioux hoop blends with

> . . . many hoops that made one circle, wide as daylight and as starlight, and in the center grew one mighty flowering tree to shelter all the children of one mother and one father. And I saw that it was holy.

After planting a magic herb, the seer marvels at the rainbow-doored "tepee of the Six Grandfathers," over which flying things hover and in which animals and humankind rejoice.

The greening earth becomes a blessed haven sanctified by the union of all living things into a single power, which Black Elk's contemporaries saw as a vast animistic deity. In innocence, Black Elk recalls that this beatific vision promised prosperity for the Oglala Sioux, whom he hoped to preserve and strengthen. As he grew older, however, he gave up his idyll because nature mourned the changing of the old ways and the demise of a dream after a substantial defeat—the 1890 massacre at Wounded Knee, which ended the Ghost Dance and robbed his people of hope. (Abbott et al. 1969; Anderson 1966; Boorstin 1992; Brewer 1899; Budge 1960; *Bullfinch's Mythology* 1964; Cavendish 1970; Cavendish 1980; Clark 1959; Cross 1957; Deram 1968; Dutt 1910; Eliade 1987; Ellis 1991; Evans 1817; Faraday 1902; Ferry 1992; Hastings 1951; Holy Bible 1958; Hooke 1963; Jurji 1946; *Kalevala* 1950; Leeming 1990; Longellow 1992; Lurker 1980; McDannell 1994; Mack 1962; Mullen 1966; Neihardt 1961; Pelikan 1992b; Pelikan 1992c; Picard 1964; Plato 1955; Pucci 1992; Quinn 1987; Roberts 1985; Smith 1971; Smith 1982; Stowe 1958; Sturluson 1987; Virgil 1950)

See also *Aeneid;* asceticism; Avalon; baptism; Black Elk; *The Book of Mormon;* Celestial City; *De Civitate Dei;* Confucius; *Divina Commedia;* Eden; Elysian Fields; Ghazali; Gilgamesh; Hesiod; Koran; *Pilgrim's Progress; The Republic;* Sufism; Tao; *Tao Te Ching;* Valhalla.

HERTZKA (OR HERZKA), THEODOR

This Austrian economist and utopist (1845–1924) published a pair of visionary works—*Freiland: A Social Anticipation* (1890) and *A Visit to Freiland, or the New Paradise Regained* (1894). From 1872–1879, he edited Vienna's *Neue Freie Presse,* moved to the *Wiener Allgemeine Zeitung* in 1879, and edited a third journal, *Zeitschrift für Staats- und Volkswirtschaft* in 1889. In 1890 Hertzka stirred interest in an economic utopia with the publication of *Freiland,* which appeared in most European languages and quickly ran through ten editions. Hertzka based his theories on Adam Smith's *Wealth of Nations* (1776), and like Charles Fourier, Bronson Alcott, Étienne Cabet, Joseph Smith, and other social experimenters in communal living, attempted to combine social and civic planning with individuality. Much like the vision of a proletarian state in the writings of Karl

Marx and Friedrich Engels but more social than political, Hertzka's delicate balance of human initiative and the intransigent demands of industry resulted in the ideal of the cooperative state, where maximum productivity would sustain a controlled population.

Hertzka's work produced a fervor among his followers for communes. Spin-offs from *Freiland*'s economic utopia include a magazine, European and American planned cities, and the failed vision of an African colony after Freelanders organized societies to band together and purchase an appropriate parcel of land in British East Africa. The sheer weight of idealistic anticipation toppled the pragmatic needs of construction and implementation, smashing the dream of creating an Eden in the wild. (Heilbroner 1989; Hertzka 1972; Mumford 1959; Negley and Patrick 1952)

See also Cabet, Étienne; city planning; Engels, Friedrich; Freiland; idealism; Marx, Karl; Smith, Joseph, Jr.

 # HESIOD

An ascetic Greek poet and moralist, Hesiod wrote *Works and Days, The Shield of Herakles,* and *Theogony* (eighth century B.C.), three notable paeans to Greek mythology. He is most famous for composing a verse tribute to creation and the golden age, a time when humankind lived godly lives free of war, dissension, and disease. In line 122 of *Works and Days,* Hesiod glorifies Greece's earliest inhabitants as "pure and blessed spirits" who "watch over mortal men and defend them from evil."

Hesiod was born in Boeotia near Mt. Helicon around 800 B.C. The son of a commercial shipper, he grew up in Cyme, Aeolia, a shore village in Asia Minor. In adulthood he moved away from his brother Perses, who cheated him out of his inheritance. Showing no bitterness or urge for retribution, Hesiod farmed and raised sheep in Ascra near Thespiae. As a means of rehabilitating Perses, Hesiod dedicated to him *Works and Days,* a poetic text rich in piety and ethics, as an admonition against greed and duplicity.

Neither rich nor famous, Hesiod reputedly was a poor bachelor, although he is credited with two sons, Perses and Hesiod. The poet won a prize for verse in Euboea, yet remained anchored in pragmatism and husbandry, expecting a day's earnings for a day's labor. He produced the *Theogony* in the epic style and meter of Homer (Herodotus the historian claimed that Hesiod was a contemporary of Homer). Unlike other utopists and dreamers, Hesiod was an unassuming man given to puritanic tastes; he never let notoriety deter his daily work, never lost respect for the land and its demands on the farmer. Tradition links him with a violent death because of an alleged slight to a woman in a grove sacred to Zeus in Nemea. Supposedly murdered by her kin, his body, which was hurled into the sea, received a poet's funeral—recovery by a cadre of mournful dolphins who returned it to shore for burial. Despite this lurid tale, Hesiod remained Greece's most respected didactic verse writer because he produced a clear, spare, readable anthology of Greek myth, wisdom, and folklore. His influence on later poets sets him apart from lesser versifiers. (*Bulfinch's Mythology* 1964; Grimal 1991; Guerber 1921; Hamilton 1942; Hesiod 1973; Howatson 1991; Johnson 1968; Morford and Lenardon 1977; Snodgrass 1988a)

See also asceticism; creation, mythic; didacticism; Genesis; golden age; naturalism.

 # HESSE, HERMANN

This German-Swiss pacifist and mystic is the author of *Siddhartha* (1922; trans. 1951), a fictionalized biography of Gautama Buddha. Hesse's mystical novel found favor among Western college students in the 1960s; his readers elevated him to cult status, perhaps because his own search for peace resulted from a renunciation of his family's rigid Calvinism. The son of Johannes Hesse, a highly respected Lutheran missionary to India, Hesse was born July 2, 1877 in Calw, Germany. As the son and grandson of devout men, Hesse grew up among books and discussions of Protestantism and Eastern mysticism. A brilliant student, he preferred self-directed study in his grandfather's library to the confines of a repressive, stultifying classroom.

Early in his youth, Hesse wrestled with his frustrations and decided to become a writer. To the consternation of his household, he abandoned the Maulbronn Seminary, where he had been studying theology, and in 1894 worked in a clock factory. The next year, he gave up clock making and apprenticed himself to a bookbinder in Tubingen, Germany. At the age of 27 he married Maria Bernoulli and sired a son, Martin. At home in Gaienhofen, Hesse began to write philosophical articles and published *Beneath the Wheel* (1906), a semiautobiographic novel.

Seriously undermined by family illness, a desk job at the German embassy in Bern, and Germany's militarism, which exterminated his wife's family, Hesse suffered a physical and emotional collapse in 1916. He moved to Lucerne and entered a rehabilitation center. Under the care of Dr. Joseph Lang, a Jungian psychologist, he began working out the plots of his next works: *Demian* (1919), *Siddhartha* (1922), *Steppenwolf* (1927), *Death and the Lover* (1932), *Journey to the East* (1932), and *The Glass Bead Game* (1943). Three decades after his nervous breakdown, he received the Nobel Prize for literature.

Much disturbed by World War II, death camps, and the rise of the military-industrial complex, Hesse developed a distaste for nationalism and Nazism and permanently withdrew from German society to self-imposed exile in Switzerland. He was living with his third wife, Ninon Ausländer, in his villa at Montanola when he died on August 9, 1962. Youth in many parts of the world displayed an uncommon homage to the German writer because of his individualism and deliberate rebellion against the governmental and educational establishment. Some of his readers, themselves youthful rebels like Siddhartha, turned to Eastern mysticism, meditation, and Buddhism as an escape from the oppressive atmosphere of the modern competitive world. (Antosik 1978; Baumer 1969; Field 1970; Fleissner 1972; Hesse 1951; Mileck 1958; Rose 1965)

See also asceticism; Buddhism; classism; heaven; nirvana; Siddhartha; *Siddhartha.*

HILTON, JAMES

One of the early twentieth century's most creative utopian writers, James Hilton (September 9, 1900–December 21, 1954) intrigued the reading public with his 1933 realistic fantasy adventure *Lost Horizon,* which earned him the Hawthornden Prize, an annual literary award accorded a young English writer of imaginative literature. The novel provided the English language with the term Shangri-La, a synonym for an idyllic escape from stress and war, a visionary nirvana or remote haven free of the turmoil that besets normal human life. Hilton was a gifted storyteller blessed with understated charm and wide-ranging talents, but he longed to be a musician like Hugh Conway, the hero of his novel. After his educator father settled in London, Hilton attended Leys School, Cambridge, and dreamed of becoming a concert pianist, although his talents directed him toward literature. Near the end of World War I, he joined the ROTC, but never served on a battlefield. Nevertheless, this brief military experience influenced both his thinking and writing.

At the age of 17, Hilton began submitting articles to the *Manchester Guardian.* Two years later, as he entered a third year at Christ College, Cambridge, with a double major in history and English literature, he published *Catherine Herself,* his first novel. To establish a regular income while he wrote unprofitable novels, he penned a biweekly column for Dublin's *Irish Independent;* as a monetary supplement, he also lectured at Cambridge, wrote book reviews, and published under the pseudonym Glen Trevor. In the fourteenth year of his career, Hilton's second novel, *And Now Good-bye,* brought critical acclaim but slender income. His next three titles—*Murder at School* (1932), *Contango* (1932), and *Rage in Heaven* (1933)—did little to advance his career. It was not until 1933 that *Lost Horizon* established Hilton's mastery, although the work did not immediately achieve public recognition.

In December of that same year, Hilton neared the deadline for a contract with the *British Weekly,* a liberal Christian magazine. Following an early morning jaunt on his bicycle, he ended a spell of writer's block and in four days produced *Good-bye Mr. Chips.* The second edition featured pen-and-ink drawings. Ultimately appearing as stage drama, novella, television drama, two movies, a drama, and a musical, the novel received an immediate reprint in the *Atlantic Monthly* and gained worldwide recognition. From this rise in Hilton's literary merit came a renewed interest in *Lost Horizon.* More novels followed—*Knight without Armour* (1933), *We Are Not Alone* (1937), *To You Mr. Chips* (1938), *Random Harvest* (1941), *So Well Remembered* (1945), and *Time and Time Again* (1953). Only *Random Harvest,* the story of a World War I veteran's postwar trauma, met with success; on film, it earned five Academy Award nominations, including best script.

James Hilton, 1950

Hilton became a naturalized American citizen in 1948, and moved to Long Beach, California, in the mid-1930s with his wife, Alice Helen Brown, whom he divorced in 1937. During his five-year marriage to second wife Galine Kopineck, whom he wed in 1940, he earned fame as a radio talk-show personality, novelist, essayist, and Hollywood screenwriter. In 1942 he won an Oscar for his most notable screenplay, *Mrs. Miniver.* He achieved temporal notoriety for his wit and charm, continental tastes in theater and entertaining, and a love of music, contemporary fiction, hiking, and mountain climbing. These specialized interests found their way into the characterization of Hugh Conway, the autobiographical hero of *Lost Horizon.* While working daily in his Los Angeles garage apartment, Hilton fought a lengthy battle with cancer and died at Seaside Hospital at the age of 54. (Eagle and Carnell 1992; Ehrlich and Carruth 1982; Hilton 1933; Kunitz 1942; *Something about the Author* 1984)

See also asceticism; Buddhism; clairvoyance; Conway, Hugh; disillusion; escapism; idealism; *Lost Horizon;* materialism; Perrault, Father; prophecy; Shangri-La; syncretism.

HOH

Hoh is the supreme ruler and metaphysical priest of Fra Tomaso Campanella's *Città del Sole* (The city of the sun) (1602), which imitates the Platonic concept of the philosopher-king. According to the dictates of natural science, Hoh rules by virtue of his command of mathematics, science, and philosophy. His staff consists of three princes—Pon, Sin, and Mor—whose knowledge in particular fields assists in such serious policy making as correction of criminals, mating of appropriate couples, and education for the young. Campanella insists that the best governance derives not from the medieval learning of rote passages devoid of experience with the natural world, but from "intellects prompt and expert in every branch of knowledge and suitable for the consideration of natural objects."

Just such a Renaissance man, Hoh governs his commune for the benefit of all by applying scientific principles, overseeing military might and fortifications, and requiring universal education based on observations of natural phenomena. In an official capacity, Hoh hears confessions, offers lengthy morning prayers to the four directions, extends pardons, and sacrifices to God, yet keeps to himself the name of individual perpetrators. For those who choose to set an example of their recovery from sin, there is a state ritual that requires the altar table to be drawn by pullies to the top of the temple dome. After a lengthy fasting and return to the floor below, the sinner usually becomes one of Hoh's priests. Thus, Hoh's role is a blend of Merlin, Arthur's engineer and magus, and Baldessar Castiglione's courtier, the educated Renaissance man of affairs whose well-rounded experiences, scholarship, and refined background make him the ideal upper-class gentleman. (Campanella 1955; Manguel and Guadalupi 1987; Negley and Patrick 1952)

See also Castiglione, Baldessar; *La Città del Sole; The Courtier;* philosopher-king; Plato.

HOMOS, ARISTIDES

International ambassador and Christian, Homos is the central observer during the summer of 1893 in William Dean Howells's *Traveler from Altruria* (1894). After his first journey to the United States, he marries Eveleth, the correspondent who reports *Through the Eye of the Needle* (1907). A bearded, tanned, and vigorous male, Homos is middle-aged, gentle-eyed, and average in height. Coming from Altruria, a balmy utopia based on an unspecified ocean isle, he at first appears delighted with train travel and hotel accommodations in the United States. However, in Chapter 1 he alarms his host by rushing to the aid of a servant girl laden with a heavy tray. Homos's comment prefaces more altruistic observations:

> She is, as you said, a perfect lady, and she graces her work, as I am sure she would grace any exigency, and I see now what the spirit of your country must be from such an expression of it.

The host's reply that ignorant immigrants fill most summer jobs puzzles Homos, a Christian who expects total equality and equal respect for all types of labor.

Sprinklings of cynicism continue to stymie Homos, who can't justify to himself the American attitude that women are born to servitude, that apartments reject families with children or dogs, or that professional gentlemen or entrepreneurs are the only citizens to whom travel and leisure are available. The host privately labels Homos naive. In Chapter 6 Homos expresses disdain for the "incivism," or discourtesy, of unequal distribution between poor and rich: In his country, such a contrast represents "bad citizenship."

In *Through the Eye of the Needle,* Homos becomes a secondary character as his American wife, Eveleth, describes her transformation from American hedonism to Altrurian asceticism. Homos continues to live by his Christian principles and displays courtesy and tact to Mr. Thrall, whose yacht is wrecked near one of Altruria's beaches. Homos makes no attempt to coerce Thrall and his family to the Altrurian philosophy but, like the Good Samaritan in one of Christ's parables, visits and commiserates with their plight. (Bennett 1973; Cowie 1951; Escholtz 1975; Howells 1907; Howells 1957; Parrington 1964)

See also asceticism; classism; synergy; technology; *Through the Eye of the Needle; A Traveler from Altruria;* women in utopia.

 # HOUYHNHNMS

Houyhnhnms are a superior, untainted race of horses who dominate the fourth book of Jonathan Swift's *Gulliver's Travels* (1727). Dependent on reason as their guiding strength, they live on an unnamed island south of Africa near Madagascar between the Atlantic and Indian oceans. According to the fictional Lemuel Gulliver, a well-traveled ship's doctor, in Chapter 1 the courteous horses inspect him with their hooves, but restrain themselves from abusing or upsetting him. Because of their courtesy, he forms an immediate opinion of their character:

> Upon the whole, the Behaviour of these Animals was so orderly and rational, so acute and judicious, that I at last concluded, they must be Magicians, who had thus metamorphosed themselves upon some Design; and seeing a Stranger in the Way, were resolved to divert themselves with him . . .

The Houyhnhnms welcome Gulliver, even though they fear that he might be a Yahoo. They invite him into a clean dwelling and lodge him in an exterior shed between the main house and stables, promising him privacy. Situated where he can view the magnificent steeds and their slaves—the hairy, foul-odored, depraved Yahoos—Gulliver develops a strong attraction for the Houyhnhnm way of life while concealing the fact that he resembles the horses' enemies, the Yahoos.

To advance his satire, Swift makes good use of "horse sense," the overly prim, opinionated, class-conscious manners of the Houyhnhnms, whose name—pronounced hwih' nuhmz—means "perfection of nature." The Houyhnhnms live an eighteenth-century ideal of polite conversation, temperate behavior, and sensible vegetarian diet. Their use of hooves parallels the human ease with hands and fingers. Speaking a language similar to Dutch, the horses indicate that they have no understanding of terms such as lying, evil, government, the science of law, power, religious wars, or punishment, concepts that Gulliver introduces to them. The horses maintain a state so close to Adam before his expulsion from paradise that they fail to comprehend the information that Gulliver deems important. They are also bemused by his insistence on wearing clothes, which Houyhnhnms consider a subversion of nature.

In the exchange between the newcomer and the Houyhnhnms, the horses demonstrate their natural inclinations toward truth, charity, gentility, care of the body, respect for others, and responsibility for their offspring. They read no books, but compose oral verse based on tradition. Their healers use herbs to treat cuts and bruises, and are shocked by Gulliver's descriptions of the abominable English diet and the spread of venereal disease; in contrast, Houyhnhnms thrive on a controlled diet of oats and enjoy a life span that reaches into the seventies. When they die, their remains receive dignified interment without mournful ceremony.

The Houyhnhnms have no knowledge of iron tools and rely on flint implements for the cutting of hay. They have grown adept at carpentry and can build a home, plastered with clay, for Gulliver. Instinctively they seek morality in mating, family life, and decision making. By juxtaposition and excess, in Chapter 10 Swift turns into parody Gulliver's praise of their natural urge to right living:

> I wanted no Fence against Fraud or Oppression: Here was neither Physician to destroy my Body, nor lawyer to ruin my Fortune: No Informer to watch my Words and Actions, or forge Accusations against me for Hire; Here were no Gibers, Censurers, Backbiters, Pickpockets, Highwaymen, House-breakers,

> Attorneys, Bawds, Buffoons, Gamesters, Politicians, Wits, Spleneticks, tedious Talkers, Controvertists, Ravishers, Murderers, Robbers, Virtuosos: no Leaders or Followers of Party and Faction; no Encouragers to Vice, by Seducement or Examples: No Dungeon, Axes, Gibbets, Whipping-posts, or Pillories; No cheating Shopkeepers or Mechanicks: No pride, Vanity or Affectation: No Fops, Bullies, Drunkards, strolling Whores, or Poxes: No ranting, lewd, expensive Wives: No stupid, proud Pedants: No importunate, overbearing, quarrelsome, noisy, roaring, empty, conceited, swearing Companions: No Scoundrels raised from the Dust upon the Merit of their Vices; or Nobility thrown into it on account of their Virtues: No Lords, Fiddlers, Judges or Dancing-masters.

Indubitably, Gulliver is drawn to this land governed by wonderfully noble, reasonable beasts, although he is spiritually needled by concealment of his Yahoo nature. To carry off his charade, he must act like a Houyhnhnm, even though the horses lack intellectual depth, enslave the Yahoos, and treat them with open contempt. On his arrival home in England, Gulliver lives apart from his family's human smell, spends his time talking with horses in the barn, and devotes himself to publishing his journals about the Houyhnhnm philosophy. (Drabble 1985; Harrison et al. 1967; Hornstein et al. 1973; Johnson 1968; Magill 1958; Manguel and Guadalupi 1987; Pollard 1970; Swift 1958; Woods et al. 1947)

See also bestiality; Brobdingnags; disillusion; escapism; fantasy; Gulliver, Lemuel; *Gulliver's Travels;* Laputa; Lilliput; satire; Swift, Jonathan.

 # HOWELLS, WILLIAM DEAN

A Christian visionary, editor, and fastidious, straightforward novelist, his works rivaled the popularity of Bret Harte, Henry James, Sarah Orne Jewett, and Mark Twain. One of his era's most prolific and influential novelists, Howells's canon leans toward passionless social commentary, as displayed by his two-stage utopian study—*A Traveler from Altruria* (1894) and its sequel, *Through the Eye of the Needle* (1907)—which concentrates more on morality, correct behavior, and an escape from poverty than on municipalities, politics, or economics. Howells was an idealist who sought a spiritual, egalitarian, and rather mundane society; his fictional Altruria illustrates his preference for peace over war and equal rights for women and nonwhites. By writing two books on the subject of his utopia, he displayed the observations and interests of a late-nineteenth-century idealist, abolitionist, and Luddite. His disaffection for machines condemns his fictional characters to extensive manual labor. In addition, in working toward communal attitudes and intrinsic compensations, he overlooked such integral aspects of social order as currency and banking.

The son of a newspaper owner, Howells was born March 1, 1837, in Martins Ferry, Ohio. Like Mark Twain, he learned the printer's trade; like Abraham Lincoln, he taught himself through home study and extensive reading. In 1847 his family resettled in Dayton. When the family newspaper failed, the Howells moved to a shack on the Little Miami River, cleared ground, farmed the land,

William Dean Howells

and reclaimed a pair of run-down mills for the manufacture of paper. Howells later recaptured his youthful labors in *My Year in a Log Cabin* (1893). At age 14 he supplemented the meager family income by typesetting for the *Ohio State Journal* in Columbus. By 1859 he had advanced from printer to writer, the fount of his lengthy career.

During the Civil War, Howells earned an embassy post in Venice. At the end of his appointment, he edited the *Atlantic Monthly, Cosmopolitan,* and *Harper's Monthly.* This period saw the death of his terminally ill daughter Winifred, but proved most conducive to his style and content, particularly his masterpiece, *The Rise of Silas Lapham* (1885). An added incentive to his string of six social commentaries, written from 1888–1907 and including *A Traveler from Altruria* and *Through the Eye of the Needle,* was a severe economic depression that reduced 4 million workers to begging in the streets. In all, he produced travelogues, propaganda, psychological and social studies, historical fiction, and dramatic fiction. A sincere man of principle, Howells suffered for his outspoken liberalism and was out of favor with critics and the reading public when he died May 11, 1920. (Bennett 1973; Cowie 1951; Escholtz 1975; Howells 1907; Howells 1957; Parrington 1964)

See also asceticism; classism; Homos, Aristides; synergy; technology; *Through the Eye of the Needle; A Traveler from Altruria;* women in utopia.

HUDSON, W. H.

A naturalist, Hudson is the introspective author of *Green Mansions* (1904) and *A Crystal Age* (1887). The first is a romantic escape novel set in the rain forest of Guayana on the Atlantic and Caribbean coasts in northeastern South America; the second is a utopian fantasy about a sexless matriarchy somewhere in Scotland. William Henry Hudson was born the sixth of seven children to distinguished New England gentry, Daniel and Katherine Kimball Hudson, in Quilnes outside Buenos Aires, Argentina, on August 4, 1841. An unsettled youth from an expatriate American farm family, Hudson helped tend sheep; because of his absence from home, he received little schooling or discipline. He was devoutly attached to bird-watching on the pampas; however, a rheumatic heart condition brought on by working cattle in a blizzard ended his dreams of working outdoors. As a compromise to illness, he studied Charles Darwin's *Origin of Species* and wrote romances, short stories, and nature lore for Argentine and British publications.

At the age of 33, Hudson traveled to London to make a new life. He married Emily Wingreave, who was little more than Hudson's nurse and the housekeeper at their two boarding houses, and cultivated a lengthy friendship with Joseph Conrad. Hudson's prolific writings, which fill 25 volumes, brought only a modest income, but caught the attention of critics, who admired his utopian novel *A Crystal Age,* in which a matriarchal society profits from longevity and the loss of libido. Later works displayed Hudson's knowledge of ornithology, travel, and his experience in the South American jungle. His most famous work,

Green Mansions, brought monetary rewards as well as recognition in Europe, the United States, and South America. Hudson found a suitable home in Penzance on the Cornish shore and wrote scholarly critiques of the poetry of John Keats and Friedrich von Schiller. Growing stronger by bicycling and walking, he composed a profusion of bird lore and nostalgic memoirs of his childhood. He died in his sleep from heart disease August 18, 1922.

A lasting monument to the mystical beauty of *Green Mansions* stands in Hyde Park—Jacob Epstein's sculpture of Rima, the elusive forest heroine whose death devastates her lover Abel and causes him to rejoin civilization. The final words of the novel speak Abel's despair:

> That is my philosophy still: prayers, austerities, good works—they avail nothing, and there is no intercession, and outside of the soul there is no forgiveness in heaven or earth for sin. Nevertheless there is a way, which every soul can find out for itself—even the most rebellious, the most darkened with crime and tormented by remorse. In that way I have walked.

Like Abel, Hudson endured frustration and weakness and vented his anguish against hunters who endangered South American wildlife and helped deplete the world's bird population.

The glamour of *Green Mansions* remained alive 37 years after Hudson's death. In 1959 MGM made a movie of the romantic plot set against an exotic backdrop; it was directed by Mel Ferrer and starred Anthony Perkins as Alec and Audrey Hepburn as Rima. Although Ferrer hired novelist Dorothy Kingsley to write the script and Hispanic composer Hector Villa-Lobos to create the musical score, the movie failed to capture the escapism, otherworldliness, and compassion of the novel. (Hudson n.d.; Hudson 1917; Kunitz 1942; Manguel and Guadalupi 1987; Miller 1990; Ronner 1986)

See also A Crystal Age; escapism; naturalism; utopia.

HUMANITARIANISM

A point of view taken by notable utopian writers in their works, humanitarianism is particularly demonstrated in Sir Thomas More's *Utopia* (1516). The narrative's central intelligence, Raphael Hythloday, disdains the plight of beggars, wounded war veterans, and farmers dispossessed by landlords who prefer to use open land for pasturage than for crops. Likewise, the people kidnapped and flown to Shangri-La in James Hilton's *Lost Horizon* (1933) demonstrate escapism from a troubled world as well as altruism toward the residents of Blue Moon Valley. At first, Miss Brinklow, a missionary, intends to accept a brief tenure in Shangri-La to work in God's service, learn the language, and proselytize for her religion. In her description of the unorthodox flight from India, it was Divine Providence that offered her an opportunity to preach to the Tibetans. After acclimating herself to a syncretic religious commune, she abandons her orthodoxy and decides to stay.

Other utopian works depend on the theme of humanitarianism as a balance to less altruistic motivations:

- Hesiod devotes his pious, didactic *Works and Days* (eighth century B.C.) to his brother Perses, who cheated him of his patrimony.

- Daniel Defoe's *Robinson Crusoe* (1719) bases its themes on Crusoe's Christian beliefs and his willingness to rescue a victim who is about to be slaughtered and eaten by cannibals.

- Zee, the love interest in Edward Bulwer-Lytton's *The Coming Race* (1871), risks her position in family and society to fly her beloved upward through rubble to a shaft that will return him forever to earth, thereby ending their relationship.

- William Dean Howells's pair of utopian novels—*A Traveler from Altruria* (1872) and its sequel, *Through the Eye of the Needle* (1907)—demonstrate the antique Christian virtues of Aristides Homos, an ambassador from a distant utopian island who cannot ignore the classism and sexism of American communities.

- Hermann Hesse's *Siddhartha* (1951) reaches its self-fulfilling conclusion in the main character's ability to flee a Brahmin's privileged life and build a satisfying career out of meditation and the operation of a ferry, on which he meets travelers of all classes and physical and mental conditions.

- Jonas, the Receiver-in-training in Lois Lowry's *The Giver* (1993), risks capture and execution to rescue an unwanted toddler.

Other utopian and dystopian works highlight such moments of humanitarianism as Karl Marx and Friedrich Engel's desire to free workers of their chains in the final lines of *The Communist Manifesto* (1848); Arthur C. Clarke's rapid end to poverty, ignorance, war, disease, and superstition in *Childhood's End* (1953); and Theo's compassion for a woman drowned in a ritual killing of the elderly in P. D. James's *The Children of Men* (1993).

More than a highlight is Mark Twain's concern for the excessive separation of classes in England's medieval period in *A Connecticut Yankee in King Arthur's Court* (1886). For commercial reasons, Twain's protagonist, Hank Morgan (also known as The Boss), makes an effort at restructuring Camelot by supplying technical know-how to raise the standard of living for the lowest serf. In the most altruistic segment—Chapter 29, "The Smallpox Hut"—Twain places Hank and King Arthur in disguise at the hovel of a family stricken by smallpox. The woman's comments about upper-class opportunists and the coldhearted church skewer Arthur, whom she does not recognize as nobility, much less as regent. Gently, lovingly, Arthur performs his Good Samaritan's duty by opening shutters to fresh air. Hank realizes the danger that pestilence places on the king, but Arthur replies, "It were shame that a king should know fear, and shame that belted knight should withhold his hand where be such as need succor. Peace, I will not go."

The scene intensifies with Arthur's climb into the loft, where the woman's husband lies dead. He descends with a slender 15-year-old girl in his arms.

Half-conscious as she nears death, she lies near her mother and moves her lips in an attempt to speak. Hank is so moved at Arthur's gracious gesture that he exclaims in admiration:

> Here was heroism at its last and loftiest possibility, its utmost summit; this was challenging death in the open field unarmed, with all the odds against the challenger, no reward set upon the contest, and no admiring world in silks and cloth of gold to gaze and applaud; and yet the king's bearing was as serenely brave as it had always been in those cheaper contests where knight meets knight in equal fight and clothed in protecting steel. He was great, now; sublimely great.

Hank applies a sensible approach to bringing out the best in Arthur. By subjecting the king to the inequities of life for medieval serfs, Hank fills a void that separates king from subjects as surely as a moat distances a castle from outlying farms.

In contrast to Twain's chivalric era, an unusual approach to the humanitarian spirit permeates *Watership Down* (1972), Richard Adams's twentieth-century beast fable about rabbits who trust their instincts and escape a doom-laden warren that is soon exterminated of rabbits and bulldozed. Hazel, the spiritual spokesman for the refugees, sets up a home on a pleasant, sunny grassland, but cannot luxuriate in peace after a friendly kestrel flies him over the rabbit cages on Nuthanger Farm. At the risk of a farm dog, prowling tomcat, and the farmer's shotgun, Hazel releases the cowed, domesticated rabbits from certain death. The effort proves reciprocal: While Hazel heals from a near-fatal gunshot wound to his leg, the warren prospers by the addition of does to its mostly male residents. (Adams 1972; Bulwer-Lytton 1979; Clarke 1953; Defoe 1963; Hesiod 1973; Hesse 1951; Hilton 1933; James 1958; Marx and Engels 1985; More n.d.; Twain 1963)

See also Arthur; Camelot; *Childhood's End; The Children of Men; The Communist Manifesto; A Connecticut Yankee in King Arthur's Court;* Engels, Friedrich; Gareth; *The Giver;* Hazel; Hesiod; Hythloday, Raphael; *Lost Horizon;* Marx, Karl; Morgan, Hank; *Robinson Crusoe;* Shangri-La; *Siddhartha; Utopia; Watership Down.*

 # HUXLEY, ALDOUS

A brilliant, articulate English social satirist, Huxley is the author of the classic dystopian novel *Brave New World* (1932) and its sequel, *Brave New World Revisited* (1958). Huxley was a native of Godalming, Surrey, born July 26, 1894, to a notable family of scientists, artists, and literati including his grandfather, essayist Thomas Henry Huxley, and a granduncle, poet Matthew Arnold. He was the third son of Julia Francis Arnold and Leonard Huxley, a poet and editor; his brother Julian was a noted biologist.

A series of momentous events highlighted Huxley's youth with both promise and loss. At age 14, the year he entered Eton on scholarship, his mother died. In 1911 a loss of vision from keratitis and a need for braille ended his

Aldous Huxley, 1962

ambitions for a career in medicine. After he regained partial sight, the brush with blindness influenced his decision to pursue a degree in literature and philology from Balliol College, Oxford. During his second year, his brother Trev committed suicide. Huxley joined a literary society, came under the influence of D. H. Lawrence and T. S. Eliot, and in 1916 published *The Burning Wheel*, a verse collection. During World War I, he took a post on Eton's faculty.

For the remainder of his life, Huxley valued sight and tried to understand in depth by "seeing" beneath surface details. His first serious collection of verse, *Defeat of Youth*, introduced a theme that permeated the creative output of the 1920s—the malaise that gripped survivors of the war years, labeled by Gertrude Stein as "the lost generation." Prevented from serving on the front line during World War I, Huxley contented himself with clerking for a military office, and in 1919 married Maria Nys, who fled Belgium during the worst of the trench warfare that devastated her country. The Huxleys remained great traveling companions throughout their marriage, touring Central America, India, and much of Italy; they also spent some years in Provence at their second home. In 1937 they settled with their son Matthew in California, where Huxley sought a respite from despair at the defeat of pacifism.

About the time of Huxley's marriage, he began submitting articles to *Athenaeum*, a British literary review, and served as theater critic for the *Westminster Gazette*. In 1920 he published *Limbo*, a collection of short fiction, and *Leda and Other Poems*, a sequel to *The Burning Wheel* and *Jonah* (1917), companion volumes of symbolist verse. Huxley settled on satiric fiction, essays, and drama around 1921. Beginning with the blasé *Antic Hay* (1923), his novels reached their height of artistry in *Point Counter Point* (1928). He developed a hypercritical eye for social criticism, as demonstrated by his masterwork, *Brave New World*, a scathing condemnation of perverted technology, materialism, orgiastic escapism, prenatal conditioning, hypnopaedia or sleep-teaching, amoral sexual liaisons, and selective breeding. He followed with three collections of essays and *Eyeless in Gaza* (1936), an autobiographical novel about the pacifist movement.

While writing for Hollywood moviemakers in 1940, Huxley altered his original style and direction. He scripted several versions of *Pride and Prejudice* and the biography of Marie Curie. His attraction toward Taoism, Brahmanism, and other forms of Eastern mysticism revealed a changed man in *The Perennial Philosophy* (1945). To learn more about mind-altering drugs, he experimented with mescaline and LSD, which became the impetus for *The Doors of Perception* (1954). Following the death of his first wife, in 1956 he married Laurel Archer.

During the decade that preceded his death from cancer on November 22, 1963, Huxley published *Brave New World Revisited*, a discussion of his classic dystopia, and *Island* (1962), a utopian novel set on an isolated, oil-rich Indonesian archipelago. In a pacifist Buddhist environment, the personae of *Island* eliminate hunger and disease, overpopulation, excesses of government and the media, the military, and prisons. Overall, Huxley's life's work earned significant critical attention plus election to the British Royal Society of Literature and an honorary doctorate from the University of California. Many critics consider him one of the most significant utopists and literary savants of his day.

(Baker 1990; Bedford 1985; Holmes 1970; Huxley 1932; Huxley 1989; Magill 1958; Nance 1988; Negley and Patrick 1952; Watts 1969)

See also Brave New World; *Brave New World Revisited;* city planning; classism; conditioning; escapism; eugenics; hypnopaedia; John; Linda; Malthus, Thomas; Marx, Karl; materialism; Tao; technology; women in utopia.

HYPNOPAEDIA

A type of conditioning that employs sleep-teaching of toddlers as a means of mass indoctrination, Aldous Huxley's *Brave New World* (1932) accomplishes it at the nursery level in public child-care centers. Tiny microphones repeat into each sleeping child's ear the simplistic slogans that encourage acquiescence to a preordained lifestyle in one of five social castes—Alpha, Beta, Gamma, Delta, or Epsilon. Coupled with electric shock, lockstep training, and monotone uniforms, hypnopaedia succeeds as a useful adjunct to the rigid classism of Huxley's dystopia. In the author's words in Chapter 2:

> Roses and electric shocks, the khaki of Deltas and a whiff of asafoetida—wedded indissolubly before the child can speak. But wordless conditioning is crude and wholesale; cannot bring home the finer distinctions, cannot inculcate the more complex courses of behaviour. For that there must be words, but words without reasoning. In brief, hypnopaedia.

The sight of toddlers listening through earphones as they sleep suggests the exploitation and manipulation of Huxley's dystopia, where the minds of each echelon of society are forced into a rigid, predetermined doctrine. To a Brave New World, a controlled classism means controlled behavior, where there are no surprises, no abrupt deviations from the norm to unsettle the balance.

After 26 years Huxley returned to the theme of subtle methods of coercion in a prosaic sequel, *Brave New World Revisited* (1958). In "Brainwashing," the author warns that future generations must stay on the alert for such insidious forms of thought control as Pavlovian conditioning, which could endanger individuality and freedom. In Chapter 9 he warns that subliminal projection persuades the subconscious, as demonstrated by mass advertising. Chapter 10 speaks directly to hypnopaedia as a moralizing and socializing mechanism. He concludes that education should link indissolubly with liberty, tolerance, and cooperation. To safeguard individuality, Huxley insists that future nations must labor to rescue freedom from any form of tyranny or suppression that might endanger it. (Baker 1990; Bedford 1985; Holmes 1970; Huxley 1932; Huxley 1989; Nance 1988; Negley and Patrick 1952; Watts 1969)

See also Brave New World; *Brave New World Revisited;* classism; conditioning; escapism; John; Linda; Malthus, Thomas; Marx, Karl; technology.

HYTHLODAY, RAPHAEL

A fictional character in Sir Thomas More's visionary treatise *Utopia* (1516), Hythloday is an experienced voyager who sailed with Italian cartographer

Amerigo Vespucci and, for five years, visited the island of Utopia. More becomes a character in his work, joining Peter Giles in an informal encounter with the fictional Hythloday in Bruges, Belgium, and engaging Hythloday in a discussion of European social weaknesses. Hythloday uses as a touchstone his visits to a perfect world, the island of Utopia, where money and private property do not exist, competition and crime are virtually nonexistent, and no privileged class lives in luxury at the expense of underlings. As an observer, he recounts in orderly fashion the interconnected customs, laws, productivity, and life rhythms of this unidentified microcosm. An obvious savant on the subject of human communities, he expresses keen insight into the question of moral decay and governmental inefficiency and waste, particularly the execution of felons who might be rehabilitated and their experiences put to good use. Hythloday remarks on the public disgrace caused by the nation's abandoning disabled war veterans to scavenge the countryside for food and resort to thievery to stay alive.

An idealist of noble proportions, Hythloday advocates a small, well-ordered society in which the rulers enrich the people rather than themselves. He would supplant a social system in which wasteful nobles do no work but spend their idle hours consuming the best of the nation's goods and resorting to prostitutes, gambling, sports, and drunkenness for diversion of their boredom. To assure Utopians a sound future, he taught a few intellectuals the Greek language and presented them his personal library, comprised of titles by poets and philosophers (Aristotle, Homer, Plato, and Sophocles), historians (Herodotus, Thucydides, and Plutarch), and healers (Galen and Hippocrates). To promote literacy, Hythloday instructed the people in printing and book production. Before departing, he introduced Christian teachings and baptized converts.

For Hythloday, the work ethic creates the greatest good by putting all hands to work and rewarding each in accordance with individual productivity. Such an evenhanded system, he concludes, would greatly enhance life in Europe. He notes enthusiastically, "Would that all nations would adopt the rule of the Utopians!" He agrees with More that Plato's advocacy of the philosopher-king is a sound basis for government, but Hythloday rejects the urging of his fellows to enter civil service as an adviser. To his way of thinking, the position would be a thankless task calling for unpopular counsel that, in all likelihood, would languish for lack of support. (Chambers 1935; Donner 1969; Johnson 1968; Logan 1983; More 1963a; Negley and Patrick 1952; Nelson 1968; Rollins and Baker 1954; White 1955)

See also baptism; idealism; More, Sir Thomas; philosopher-king; Plato; *Utopia*.

 ICARA

Icara is an idealistic capital city of the republic of Icaria in Étienne Cabet's visionary novel *Voyage en Icarie* (1840). Icara, which was built by architects who studied the most beautiful cities in the world, mirrors the Paris that grew up on both banks of the Seine River. Halved by the waters, the city boasts a straightened channel carved out to allow oceangoing ships. In the center of Icara lies an island formed by encircling tributaries. Like Paris's L'Ile de la Cité, this focal point serves as a tourist treat, complete with palace, terraced garden, and imposing monument. In the distance stretches a fringe of public buildings and quays.

The communal arrangement of Icara, a model of collectivism and urban planning, supports 60 units, each equipped with school, medical and worship centers, shops, and parks. The placement of 50 parallel boulevards at right angles to 50 avenues expedites traffic. Residential centers contain 15 homes and gardens per block with a civic center at the heart of the cluster and two more flanking the ends. Icarians attend to scrupulous cleanliness and enjoy covered sidewalks, street lamps, and public transportation. On the perimeter cluster hospitals, stables, abattoirs, and factories, which are built alongside canals and on rail lines for maximum efficiency and minimum noise, odor, and inconvenience to citizens. Icarians work a seven-hour day in summer and a six-hour day in winter. (Cabet 1973; Johnson 1974; Manguel and Guadalupi 1987; Mumford 1959; Piotrowski 1935)

See also Cabet, Étienne; city planning; collectivism; Icaria; *Voyage en Icarie.*

 ICARIA

An idealistic republic designed by visionary Étienne Cabet for the Mediterranean coast, Icaria reflects the European-style city planning of post-Napoleonic France. Icaria, with its circular capital Icara, is the focal point of Cabet's utopian novel *Voyage en Icarie* (1840). Opposite the city of Marvols to the west, Icaria lies on the eastern leg of a double peninsula. Although it lacks both border patrols and customs officials, Icaria is a closed community allowing no tourism except visits from study groups wishing to spread its socialistic life-style. (Cabet 1973; Johnson 1974; Maguel and Guadalupi 1987; Mumford 1959; Piotrowski 1935)

See also Cabet, Étienne; city planning; collectivism; Icara; *Voyage en Icarie.*

 # IDEALISM

Idealism is dedication to a high degree of productivity or achievement, and denial of impediments and unforeseen obstacles to the completion of unrealistic plans for advancement, contentment, self-fulfillment, or reward. Central to utopian thought, idealism is an elusive quality that can either make or break the observer or dreamer. On the positive side, these examples of utopian longings and schemes demonstrate the uplifting nature of perfectionism, at least in the early stages:

- The chivalric age initiated a cycle of works lauding the legendary King Arthur and his stronghold, Camelot, a city allegedly built out of music by Merlin the magician. Because of its promise of justice and an end of random violence and power struggles, writers from Sir Thomas Malory to Alfred Tennyson, Mark Twain, John Steinbeck, and Mary Stewart have set fictional works in the fabled realm of Camelot.

- In Baldessar Castiglione's *The Courtier* (1528), expectations of the creation of an effective, self-contained young gentleman cause the writer to study methods of dressing, educating, training, and inculcating likely candidates with all the manners and assets necessary for a useful life among nobles and royalty at a court in Renaissance Italy.

- The layout of Étienne Cabet's *Voyage en Icarie* (1840) produces a series of planned communes along the Seine River that are intended to display the best in collectivism and self-sufficiency.

- Likewise, the prediction of a classless state engineered by an uprising of the proletariat in *The Communist Manifesto* (1848) demonstrates on paper the height of the economic vision of Karl Marx and Friedrich Engels.

- Similar in tone and method is Jack London's *The Iron Heel* (1907), a novelized version of the inchoate longings and anarchy in the streets when the working class begins to act on its yearning for equal distribution of wealth and an end to privilege and class distinctions.

Implicit in each of these idealistic visions is the unforeseen snag, the breaking point that was never factored into the original plan, e.g., the collapse of Arthur's Round Table following severe disillusion among knights and a war instigated by Arthur's nephew Modred, or the insufficient ambition or leadership among unionized workers to initiate and carry through class warfare.

On the downside of dreams of a perfected social order, a strong canon of dystopias catalogs the negative aspects of hopes held higher than humankind is capable of achieving. Works and characters exhibiting impossible dreams that are doomed from the outset include:

- Voltaire's *Candide* (1759), a classic novel featuring the frenetic travels of a naive young dreamer from Europe to South America and back to Europe in search of Cunégonde, his lady fair. At length, she ages and loses her beauty before he can rescue her. Ultimately, Candide learns to settle for less than the best by establishing a homestead in Turkey, where he contents himself while tending his garden, a microcosm he is capable of controlling.

- More intensely disappointed and disillusioned than Candide is his English predecessor, Jonathan Swift's Gulliver, protagonist of *Gulliver's Travels* (1727). Gulliver's discontent at home and longing for sea adventures leads him through a dismal series of near disasters and returns him home to his wife and children after a particularly painful departure from a land ruled by a race of horses. However, Gulliver's arrival on English shores exacerbates his admiration for horses and his distaste for humankind, his own species.

- Also plagued with the dreamer's curse is Miguel de Cervantes's Don Quixote, the epitome of literature's visionary, who is best known for tilting at windmills. Dressed in ragtag heroic finery and mounted on an undistinguished nag, the aged don looks beyond realistic detail to the image of idealistic womanhood, his Dulcinea del Toboso. Although the female impetus for his crusade is nonexistent, Don Quixote manages to clutch to his heart the values of a knight-errant and to accomplish worthy deeds in a milieu rife with crime, squalor, venality, and cynicism. Throughout the Renaissance and into the current era, Don Quixote, mounted on Rozinante and followed by squire Sancho Panza, has become a universal symbol of adaptation. The ideal, which never materializes through all the drubbings and humiliations brought on by Don Quixote's quest, remains alive in its proper locale, a heart that refuses to accept less than the best in human behavior and who redoubles efforts at each defeat to focus on a distant gleam.

(Cabet 1973; Castiglione 1976; Cervantes 1957; Johnson 1968; Marx and Engels 1985; Swift 1958; Voltaire 1961)

See also Cabet, Étienne; *Candide;* Castiglione, Baldessar; Cervantes Saavedra, Miguel de; *The Communist Manifesto; The Courtier;* Don Quixote; Dulcinea del Toboso; Engels, Friedrich; *Gulliver's Travels;* Marx, Karl; Sancho Panza; Swift, Jonathan; Tennyson, Alfred; Twain, Mark; Voltaire, François; *Voyage en Icarie.*

IDYLLS OF THE KING

This progressive compilation of precise, rhythmic epic poems was based on Sir Thomas Malory's Arthurian lore and composed by Alfred Tennyson, poet laureate of England during the Victorian era. Tennyson's overview of the chivalric age, published in 1888, exhibits the author's absorption in the utopian principles undergirding Camelot, seat of King Arthur's knights and their council, the famed Round Table. The doomed kingdom, which collapses as a result of Queen Guinevere's adultery with Sir Lancelot, Arthur's friend and lead knight, destroys a visionary plan for control, peace, and prosperity. Arthur, the philosopher-king who employs Merlin's skills to engineer a workable statecraft, misdiagnoses jealousy, the internal cancer that erodes his authority and demoralizes his supporters.

Following an effusive dedication to Tennyson's living model (Prince Albert, Queen Victoria's consort, who died in 1861), the poet launches into "The Coming of Arthur," the romantic tale of the feisty, idealistic Arthur, who rises to England's throne against strong opposition. Under a cloud of ignoble birth, Arthur, illegitimate son of King Uther and Queen Ygraine of Cornwall, convinces Leodogran to pledge his daughter Guinevere in marriage. The canto ends in pomp and glory: Arthur marries his queen, defeats pagan adversaries, and establishes Camelot.

Canto 2 tells of the yearnings of Gareth, Gawain's youngest brother, who accepts the lowest of court chores, "kitchen vassalage," in exchange for nearness to the king. As Arthur dispenses justice to all petitioners, Gareth puts himself in line for a quest and rides out to free Lady Lyonors from Castle Perilous. Gareth's doughty persistence in the face of four mounted and armed challengers demonstrates the spirit of the Arthurian knight who accepts impossible odds because he trusts in the ethical standards for which the Round Table stands.

The third and fourth Cantos, "The Marriage of Geraint" and "Geraint and Enid," the romance of a knight and his lady, foretell the slow spread of decay through Arthur's haven as Guinevere's lust for Lancelot weakens the moral fiber of Camelot. The fifth segment, "Balin and Balan," describes Arthur's governance. In disguise, he confronts two insidious malcontents who intend to subvert the knights of the royal staff. Although the duo lack the clout to undermine Arthur's control, additional trouble for his visionary kingdom crops up in the sixth Canto, "Merlin and Vivien," in which a conniving virago deceives the weary old magus into revealing the source of his magic spell. In Book 7, Lancelot complicates his relationship with Guinevere by fighting in the lists while wearing a love gift from Lady Elaine of Astolat. The knight departs without marrying Elaine, who dies of grief. Now doubly weighted with guilt, Lancelot is further compromised, thereby weakening Arthur's kingdom with additional misgivings.

Canto 8, "The Holy Grail," departs from Camelot and introduces Galahad's search for Christ's communion cup. The vision of a celestial city and the chalice floating in air precedes Galahad's disappearance. Percivale, who shared the knight's epiphany, returns to Camelot, a dismal contrast to perfection. Because the Round Table is seriously depleted of military might and Arthur has lost his idealism, Percivale concludes that the kingdom will crumble.

In the ninth segment, "Pelleas and Ettarre," the young Pelleas, who joins a new generation of Round Table knights, falls prey to the advancing corruption that leaves Camelot a "black nest of rats." The tenth Canto, "The Last Tournament," details a similar note of doom in the despair of Dagonet, Arthur's court jester. The final segments, "Guinevere" and "The Passing of Arthur," bring Camelot and the dream to its shattered end. Modred, Arthur's nephew, divulges the sin that most of the realm has long suspected: the adulterous bedroom scene of Lancelot and Guinevere.

Too late, Arthur returns to Camelot to fight for his realm and his dream. With Lancelot fled to France and Guinevere in retreat at a convent, the king perceives the ebb of his fortunes, which depended on moral vision from his two best friends. Forced into civil war against former comrades, the weary Arthur falls on the battlefield and is borne away on a kingly barge. Disillusioned by multiple losses, Sir Bedivere, Arthur's most trusted ally, laments the broken dream:

> Ah, my Lord Arthur, whither shall I go?
> Where shall I hide my forehead and my eyes?
> For now I see the true old times are dead,
> When every morning brought a noble chance,
> And every chance brought out a noble knight.

Arthur's reply acknowledges Camelot's demise: "The old order changeth, yielding place to new, and god fulfils himself in many ways." The moribund king bids Bedevere to pray. As the barge glides into the sunrise, Bedevere detects a distant echo of victory as though a city were welcoming a victorious monarch. (Albright 1986; Rosenberg 1973; Stephens et al. 1949; Tennyson 1989)

See also Arthur; Avalon; Camelot; city planning; *A Connecticut Yankee in King Arthur's Court*; escapism; Gareth; humanitarianism; Morgan, Hank; philosopher-king; Twain, Mark; women in utopia.

 # INFERNO

See Divina Commedia.

 # THE IRON HEEL

This futuristic sociological fiction, written in 1907, was based on Jack London's notion of a utopian effort crushed by fascism. Written from a 700-year perspective, like that of Margaret Atwood's *The Handmaid's Tale* (1985), the work consists of a manuscript set in the 1910s written by Avis Cunningham Everhard, devoted wife of Ernest Everhard, a socialist martyr whose theories smack of hard-line Marxism. Described in the foreword as a "personal document" lacking perspective and objectivity, *The Iron Heel* opens on the meeting with Avis and her hero-mate, a man who foresaw the descent of crushing oppression against rebellious proletarians.

In the summer following Everhard's assassination, Avis Cunningham comments that he forfeited his life for revolution. She reflects on a dinner in February 1912, when she met her future husband at a gathering of the clergy in her home in San Francisco. He engages Dr. Hammerfield in a dialectic concerning mistreatment and exploitation of the working class. Tactlessly, he implies that Hammerfield misidentifies sincerity as truth. As Everhard insists in Chapter 1, "You do not know the real world in which you live." Comparing twentieth-century capitalistic do-gooders to an Indian shaman making incantations "in the primeval forest ten thousand years ago," Everhard challenges the twisted logic that permits exploitation of workers to persist. Calling the clergy "metaphysicians," he persists in citing examples of a lack of humanity and concludes with a simple test of social theory: "Will it work? Will you trust your life to it?"

London's novel rests on a single bet: that the proletariat has no need of society's indulgent, parasitic upper crust. Everhard dismays his audience by predicting that the working class will thrive without the oligarchy that browbeats it. Hammerfield refuses to endure further explosions of insolence, but Bishop Morehouse, intrigued by the certitude of the lively young activist, returns some days later to the Cunningham veranda for tea and more discussion. Avis, who has read Everhard's writings, accuses him of fomenting class hatred. He counters by emphasizing the world's state of "class struggle," a more precise statement of the antipathy between workers and the privileged class.

In the face of another transportation strike, Everhard accuses the Bishop of pig-ethics, an anti-Christian disinterest in the plight of workers, particularly female and child laborers. Avis challenges Everhard to prove his data. He bests her by describing her gown, food, and home as dripping with the blood of underpaid workers. After she sees herself as an oligarchic obstruction to equality, Avis weeps. Everhard points out Jackson, a one-armed man passing by who was maimed by a machine at Sierra Mills. The company fought his damage suit and won. By interviewing Colonel Ingram and two stockholders, Avis corroborates Everhard's claim that Jackson was a victim of overwork and deserved better from the company.

London stokes Everhard for even greater confrontations with plutocrats. After Avis and Everhard become lovers, in Chapter 5 they meet on a Tuesday evening with the Philomath Club, where "Ernest bearded the masters in their lair." Facing off against Colonel Van Gilbert, a stuffy, self-congratulatory aristocrat, Everhard speaks quietly of his working-class background, from millhand to farrier, and of his admiration for revolutionaries, who extended faith in humanity, idealism, unselfishness, even martyrdom. The voice of Mr. Wickson interrupts with a sneer of "Utopian."

Everhard picks up the pace of his soliloquy by exploiting his disillusion with upper-class oppressors, especially those cloaked in a semblance of genteel Christianity while simultaneously shooting strikers. Everhard classes his idealistic world as an "arid desert of commercialism," a dystopian comeuppance that he failed to foresee. Both bored and dismayed, he abandons crass capitalists and, claiming that the United States's population of rebels amounts to a million and a half, realigns himself with assorted revolutionaries. At this critical point in his diatribe, Everhard charges capitalists with deliberate concealment of census figures that would reveal 3 million child laborers. Such duplicity proves that capitalists have reached the nadir of their commercial empire. Soon, he predicts, revolutionaries will wipe out a predatory entrepreneurial class, "fat with power and possession, drunken with success." He defies his listeners to halt the momentum of the revolution that will make them obsolete.

Colonel Van Gilbert retorts that Everhard's words are the infantile ravings of a fanatic. Everhard challenges him item by item, reducing him to a puddle of self-indulgence, greed, and arrogance. For three hours the battle rages between the outraged Philomaths and Everhard over the matter of poverty and disenfranchisement of the working class. The only quiet voice at the gathering belongs to Wickson, who proposes that his fellow members "hunt the bear" and crush the opposition.

In Chapter 7 the propaganda machinery cranks up first with heartfelt words from Bishop Morehouse, who presides over a convention in San Francisco. He relates his own attempt to emulate Christ by uplifting the lowly whom his carriage passed in the streets. Supported by Bishop Dickinson, who concurs with Morehouse on the need for greater altruism among the clergy, Morehouse uges the impassive audience to open their hearts to "the Master's lambs." Two dissenting conventioneers quietly lead Morehouse from the dais. Everhard correctly predicts that the morning paper will report that the bishop has collapsed from strain.

London balances dialectic with intensification of action in the next scene, in which Everhard runs for Congress. He comes in contact with the scum of the entrepreneurial class, the big marketers who conspire to shut out smaller businesses. Everhard predicts that the elite will allow their own atavism to destroy them when workers rise up against their affluence and disregard for fair market ethics. He also cites national law introduced to the House on July 30, 1902, that provides for a militia to crush such uprisings.

London's showdown is stoked with fireworks. To a banquet hall filled with spluttering, excuse-making moneymen, Everhard explains why socialism is inevitable. He outlines simple paradigms of the influence of capital, especially on the Third World. Citing Karl Marx's concept of surplus value, Everhard enlightens his audience, who panic and wonder how to halt so certain a death knell for the middle class. Everhard retorts that they are caught inevitably between millstones.

Everhard continues his tirade by naming the nation's three classes: the plutocrats, in particular the railroad magnates, who possess billions; the struggling middle class; and the wage-earners, the lowest and most downtrodden rung of society's ladder. In his estimation, the wealthy can withdraw into their bank accounts and labor can risk the nothing that forms its patrimony. Ultimately, the citizens most in jeopardy from such a squeeze play are those in the middle: farmers, manufacturers, and lesser businessmen. In the face of his hearers' consternation, Everhard wishes that they understood more about evolution and sociology.

London orchestrates the falling action with the novelist's flair for contrast. The collapse begins much as Everhard predicts. First Mr. Cunningham loses his job at the university. Publishing houses refuse to print the dire situation in which truth is trapped. The post office escalates the situation by labeling a proletarian newsletter, *The Appeal to Reason,* a seditious propaganda rag. The formation of Black Hundreds mobilizes the reactionary right, who give the Iron Heel its rationale for calling out the militia. Wages fall; factories stand idle; Wall Street reels; strikers capitulate to the will of capitalism. The result is the collapse of the market economy.

The mood of laborers grows ugly. By the summer of 1912, when Everhard runs for office, the plutocrats have bought up deflated shares of stock, thus bringing the middle class to its knees. Scoffers at Everhard's predictions eat their words. As he prepares to marry Avis, her father falls under the full force of the Iron Heel and is arrested for attempted assault. His family is ruined, their house repossessed for mortgage default. At a pivotal point in Everhard's struggles on behalf of the working class, Avis lauds his sincere acts of altruism. He overworks mind and body translating articles for socialist publishers, campaigning, and stretching his meager income to meet his debts. His sole pleasure is the joy of home and wife.

During the worst of the economic fray, Bishop Morehouse, gaunt with the pressures of loss and humiliation, disappears. Avis encounters him at a butcher shop, where he drops a sack of potatoes intended as a gift for a poor seamstress. The bishop and Avis visit the woman, who mourns the sufferings of her hungry children. Avis learns that the woman is one of many in the neighborhood who work for a pittance to keep their families from hunger. In Chapter 12 Everhard is touched by the bishop's humility and his devotion to easing the sufferings of the poor, to whom he devotes his life savings. Reacquainted with a Christlike love for the downtrodden, the bishop walks rather than ride in a carriage and lives in humble dwellings. His face alight with joy, he concludes, "It is the Master's work." A week later, Everhard reads an item in the newspaper indicating that the bishop's enemies have confined him to the Napa Asylum.

After Everhard's election by landslide vote in 1912, the Hearst publishing empire falls, bringing down its adjunct, the Democratic Party. Hard times create turmoil in all venues of society, from farm to bank to church. That miserable winter, the oligarchy presses for war with Germany. The United States falters without newspapers or mail. By January 1913 the oligarchs bow to pressure from the strongest unions. Violence expresses the workers' vitriol against the oligarchs, who are persecuted and ostracized. The world market blames the United States for global depression. Rampant racism ignites centuries-old hatreds and suspicions. Mass mayhem becomes so prevalent that Indian tribes predict the coming of a messiah.

London's observations of national idiosyncrasies pack the novel with believable detail. As Everhard moves Avis to Washington at the beginning of his first term of office, the nation is wracked by the work of provocateurs hired by the oligarchy to inflame a peasant revolt. The militia scrambles to suppress grange uprisings. Socialists employ counteragents to infiltrate and undermine the oligarchy. In Chapter 17, at a showdown in the House of Representatives, Everhard takes a new tack by stating to the oligarchs, "You have no souls to be influenced. You are spineless, flaccid things." The Iron Heel retorts in kind with catcalls and cries of "anarchist" and "sedition." Everhard suspects an assassination plot. As an explosion halts his stand, he sinks, warning his constituents to take no action against the counterrevolutionaries. Avis never learns who hurled the bomb.

Near the end of his influence over events, Everhard survives and is tried for sedition; Avis goes to prison for complicity. On her release, she attempts to shake off the agents of the Iron Heel and disappear on the West Coast. Hiding only a quarter-mile from Wickson's vacation home, Avis lives with a companion for 19 years without being discovered. From prison, Everhard advises his wife to change herself physically and materially. About this time, Avis's father disappears. She buoys her flagging zeal by hard work for the revolution. In 1915 socialist agents free 51 congressmen from jail, along with 300 revolution leaders. Avis and Everhard reunite.

The couple thrill to relaxing moments in sight of Wickson's property. At an underground rendezvous, the Everhards encounter Philip, Wickson's son, and take him prisoner. Eventually, Philip joins the revolt, which grows bloodier and more mercenary. The aristocrats evolve a tight network of self-protection and shut out any contamination from "the beast," which is their name for the revolution. Everhard chafes at his confinement. In January 1917 he returns to the outside world to serve as provocateur against the Iron Heel. Aided by Mexican and Canadian comrades, the anarchists blow up fuel dumps, ammunition storehouses, bridges, and other segments of the infrastructure that supports the oligarchy. The supreme achievement occurs in Chicago, where fires consume buildings after anarchists destroy the water mains.

The fighting grows uglier. The socialists quail at the magnitude of antiproletarianism. Like the storming of the Bastille during the French Revolution, "the people of the abyss," a seething, leaderless peasant mob, rages out of control and sweeps Avis along in its path. The anarchists use hot-air balloons as a means of quelling violence. In the turmoil of bombs, fallen comrades, and the rubble that comprises all that's left of Chicago, Avis reunites with Everhard. The revolutionary front shrinks in number as many die in the fray or are executed. Avis's journal halts in midsentence.

Jack London's ruse of an incomplete manuscript, a plot device later employed in Margaret Atwood's *The Handmaid's Tale* (1985), leaves the reader to guess London's purpose in so stirring, suspenseful, and idealistic a war scenario. He draws on much of the era's labor history and the backlash of railroad and oil magnates, who sensed the danger implicit in a powerful working class. Ironically, London was never lauded for his socialistic treatises and earned his greatest accolades for adventure stories of the outback and the instinctive call of nature, the controlling themes of *Call of the Wild* and *White Fang*. *The Iron Heel* lost its audience in the mounting nationalistic cohesion prefacing World War II and the financially accommodating Eisenhower years, which saw an unprecedented upsurge in working-class ambitions and middle-class wealth.

(Beauchamp 1984; Hedrick 1982; London 1982a; Lundquist 1987; Perry 1981; Sinclair 1983; Stone 1978)

See also Atwood, Margaret; classism; collectivism; *The Communist Manifesto; Das Kapital;* didacticism; Engels, Friedrich; Everhard, Avis Cunningham; Everhard, Ernest; *The Handmaid's Tale;* London, Jack; Marx, Karl; women in utopia.

JAMES, P. D.

James is the author of the bleakly dystopian novel *The Children of Men* (1993), a Book-of-the-Month Club featured selection. Known primarily for her murder mysteries, especially *Cover Her Face* (1962), which introduced her clever persona, Commander Adam Dalgliesh of Scotland Yard, James followed with *Unnatural Causes* (1967), *An Unsuitable Job for a Woman* (1972), *Death of an Expert Witness* (1977), *Innocent Blood* (1980), and *A Taste for Death* (1986). In addition, she contributed to various anthologies of mystery stories. These works repeat her motif of ratiocination or application of logic, but the focus shifts from Dalgliesh to Cordelia Gray, a 22-year-old detective, and eventually to Kate Miskin, a second female sleuth. James's thrillers have found success in print and in film and television screenplays of her fiction, which are popular in the United States and England.

The author was born Phylliss Dorothy James in Oxford, England, on August 3, 1920, to Dorothy May Hone and Sidney Victor James, a revenue agent. She graduated from Cambridge Girls' High School. Prior to World War II, she participated in the Festival Theater of Cambridge; during the war she volunteered as a Red Cross attendant and a clerk in the Ministry of food, and served as administrative aide to the North West Regional Hospital Board. In 1942 she married Dr. Ernest Conner Bantry White, a physician and the father of James's daughter Jane. In 1964 Dr. White suffered schizophrenia and died.

James's work in criminal investigation and forensic medicine has enriched her popular murder mysteries, which she began writing in longhand in 1966. A former employee of the British Civil Service from 1949 to 1979, James has worked in the home office of the Police and Criminal Law Service and has served as magistrate at the Department of Home Affairs and as an official of the BBC. Her awards include the Crime Writers Association prize in 1967 and a title, Baroness James of Holland Park, which she received in 1991. She currently resides in Oxford and London. (*Contemporary Literary Criticism* 1981b; Finn 1993; Hughes 1992; James 1993; Reading 1992; Siebenheller 1991; Symons 1992; Wangerin 1993; Wynn 1977)

See also The Children of Men; dystopia; eugenics; women in utopia.

JERUSALEM DELIVERED

This 20-book romantic epic of the Italian Renaissance is composed in tight ottava rima and rigid epic standards under the title *La Gerusalemme liberata*, or *Jerusalem Delivered* (1581). Poet Torquato Tasso, drawing on Virgil's *Aeneid* (19 B.C.) but catering to Catholic censors, embroiders an idealized picture of the Crusades with utopian details of pleasant bowers in a pastoral haven. Set in 1099, the plot features a chivalric hero, Godfrey of Bouillon, who departs on the first crusade against the infidel Saracens. With the aid of Armida the magician, Godfrey defeats Satan's plan to capture the holy city of Jerusalem. An allegorical battle between good and evil, the epic poem—similar in style to Dante's *The Divine Comedy* (1320) and in theme to John Bunyan's *Pilgrim's Progress* (1678)—employs Christian and pagan motifs, sorcery, chivalric knights, and winsome maidens. (Boulting 1969; Johnson 1968; Magill 1958; Tasso 1987)

See also Aeneid; allegory; Bunyan, John; Milton, John; *Paradise Lost; Pilgrim's Progress;* Satan; Tasso, Torquato; Virgil.

 # JOHN

The stern, doomed antihero of Aldous Huxley's *Brave New World* is the antithesis of the state-run assembly-line birth center, which divides embryos into five rigid classes. Conditioned from infancy to find contentment in a single stratum of utopian existence, the citizens of Huxley's *Brave New World* are in contrast to John, a blond savage. His mother Linda bore him vivaporously 25 years earlier in Malpais, New Mexico, on a Zuñi reservation after separating from his father, Tomakin, the Director of Hatcheries. Isolated from the Indians, who despise his promiscuous, drug-abusing mother, John discovers *The Complete Works of William Shakespeare,* which Linda's lover Popé brings as a gift. Like a monk reading the Bible, John is profoundly influenced by the passion and nobility of Shakespearean drama. He adopts an Elizabethan worldview that values honesty, spirituality, and emotion, all of which have long been eradicated in Huxley's futuristic utopia.

Ill-equipped socially and educationally to cope with the sterile, blasé utopian society, John nonetheless looks forward to the transoceanic rocket trip that carries him to London. He recoils from his mother's overindulgence in *soma;* the bestial mass of gammas, deltas, and epsilons conditioned to carry out menial labor; and the blatant eroticism in entertainment and social behavior. Least tolerable to John is his perpetual exhibition as the Savage, a freak of the outer rim brought to London and managed like a sideshow.

Ironically, John suffers more alienation in the promised land of utopia than had consumed him on the reservation:

> At Malpais he had suffered because they had shut him out from the communal activities of the pueblo; in civilized London he was suffering because he could never escape from those communal activities, never be quietly alone.

Utopia's promiscuity and inanity distress him so thoroughly that he is unable to love Lenina, the woman to whom he is torturously attracted. Because John deems physical intimacy a mysterious and sacred life element, he rejects Lenina's immodesty and licentiousness. He longs to be worthy of her so that she will return his affection and respect, but he fails to comprehend that Lenina, with her amoral utopian conditioning, is oblivious to his idealized notion of love.

Huxley uses John's frustrations as an adjunct to Linda's pathetic attempts to elude death. The intensity of John's love and loyalty appears in an abortive deathbed scene in which he tries to dissuade his mother from technological escapism and a dependence on drugs, which sap her energies and hasten physical collapse. He has suffered since childhood because of his mother's exile among Zuñi natives, and his anguish continues at her outcast state in utopia. In a fit of pique, he tries to organize a rebellion among hospital workers against the drug *soma*, precipitates a riot by tossing drugs out the window, and is arrested.

In the novel's tense ideological face-off between Mustapha Mond, the World Controller, and the savage, John states his antipathy to a managed utopia: "But I don't want comfort. I want God, I want poetry, I want real danger, I want freedom, I want goodness. I want sin." His attempts to gain love and truth through suffering seem misguided, inappropriate, even foolish in a society where love and truth no longer exist and suffering has been obliterated. Mond respects John, but he disdains the savage's predilection for pain, isolation, melodrama, and tragedy.

Stubbornly upholding a fatal idealism, John maintains his primitive values of an extinct world and ultimately dies of them. To end his existence as a classless freak in a rigidly stratified society, he tries to create a third alternative: a hermit's cell at an abandoned lighthouse, where he purges himself with mustard and lacerates his flesh with a flail. When voyeurs violate his peace, John chooses death as a final refuge from disillusion. Despairing over his inability to rise above social depravity, he hangs himself. In death, his pendant body swings aimlessly like a symbolic compass arrow, emblematic of utopia's directionless slide into self-indulgence and moral atrophy. (Bedford 1985; Holmes 1970; Huxley 1932; Huxley 1989; Magill 1958; Nance 1988; Negley and Patrick 1952; Snodgrass 1990; Watts 1969)

See also *Brave New World*; *Brave New World Revisited*; classism; conditioning; disillusion; escapism; eugenics; futurism; Huxley, Aldous; hypnopaedia; John; Linda; prophecy; *soma*; women in utopia.

JOHNSON, DR. SAMUEL

One of England's finest literary minds, Samuel Johnson was a veritable whirlwind—moralist, poet, lexicographer, playwright, critic, conversationalist, and author of an oriental utopian fable, "Rasselas, Prince of Abissinia" (1759). Johnson was born in poverty on September 18, 1709, in Lichfield, England, and suffered from weak eyesight and scrofula, a lymphatic disorder. His father,

Samuel Johnson as painted by his friend Sir Joshua Reynolds in 1756

Michael Johnson, a book dealer, managed to finance his son's education at the local grammar school and to augment the boy's learning with books from his shop. Johnson attended Oxford briefly and founded his own short-lived academy.

At the age of 28, Johnson moved to London and lived with actor David Garrick while working as a translator and freelance writer. Johnson's wife, Elizabeth Porter Johnson, was twice his age, and remained his devoted companion until her death in 1752. By 1755 Dr. Johnson had escaped poverty by publishing his two-volume *Dictionary of the English Language.* Surrounded by friends, fellow writers, and artists, including Oliver Goldsmith, Sir Joshua Reynolds, and Edmund Burke, he formed a literary circle that raised his image to guru. With the completion of "Rasselas, Prince of Abissinia," which he subtitled "The Choice of a Life," Johnson contributed his rational overview of the seventeenth-century mindset. Grounded in reason with a strong tinge of Christian philosophy, the fable, which echoes the conclusions of Voltaire's *Candide,* also published in 1759, follows its protagonist through a seeker's journey of worldly wisdom and concludes that the needs of the soul far outrank the frivolities of the world of fashion and sensual delights.

Johnson published a weekly journal, *The Rambler,* and its sequel, *The Idler,* as well as *The Lives of the English Poets* (1781). In his sixties he traversed Scotland on horseback and wrote a travelogue, *Journey to the Western Islands of Scotland* (1775). Neurotic, lonely, and fearful of death, he died on December 13, 1784, and was buried in Westminster Abbey among England's most distinguished literati. (Boswell 1981; Boulton 1978; Engell 1985; Johnson 1982; Lovett and Hughes 1932; Magill 1958; Nath 1987)

See also *Candide;* Happy Valley; "Rasselas, Prince of Abissinia"; Voltaire, François.

 # JOURNEY TO ICARIA

See *Voyage en Icarie.*

KARELLEN

Karellen is the ambiguous alien authority figure who serves as intermediary between Earth-dwellers and the spaceships that hover over it in Arthur C. Clarke's *Childhood's End* (1953). A benign overlord hovering a few centimeters above the ground in his "metallic bubble," Supervisor Karellen holds weekly conferences in a one-room spacecar with his earthly counterpart, Rikki Stormgren, secretary-general of the United Nations. On the sixth day of Earth's capture, Karellen speaks in clear English over every radio frequency. His message is unequivocal: Earth must yield to a greater intellectual force. Shielded from view aboard the fleet flagship, Karellen maintains his distance until 50 years pass and he completes his mission of readying Earth for the next stage of human evolution.

A beneficial aspect of Karellen's assignment as supervisor is his calm, non-threatening voice; some earthly analysts believe he uses a voice synthesizer to hide his monstrous form and sound. On a first-name basis with the secretary-general, Karellen discusses the threat of Alexander Wainwright and the Freedom League, and avoids direct questions that might divulge the reason for Earth's disempowerment. In Part 1, Chapter 2, in a moderate set-to with Stormgren, Karellen complains: "I wish people would stop thinking of me as a dictator, and remember I'm only a civil servant trying to administer a colonial policy in whose shaping I had no hand." He defuses a potential argument by denying that he is a robot and by laughing about a political cartoon in the *Chicago Tribune* that depicts him as a centipede.

To questions of trust and concerns raised by Wainwright, the leading dissenter, Karellen makes a strong defense of reason over domination by a righteous hierarchy:

> You will find men like him in all the world's religions. They know that we represent reason and science, and, however confident they may be in their beliefs, they fear that we will overthrow their gods. Not necessarily through any deliberate act, but in a subtler fashion. Science can destroy religion by ignoring it as well as by disproving its tenets.

To legitimize his statement—and, parenthetically, to affirm his knowledge of human conditions on Earth with respect to religion—Karellen cites as examples the demise of Zeus, Thor, Mohammed, and Moses, who once were worshiped and/or propitiated by earthly followers. Acting as agent for a greater authority, Karellen promises to gain permission from headquarters to divulge more of the aliens' plans for Earth.

Because he is straightforward in these and other matters, Karellen gains the trust of the characters and the reader. In Part 3, Chapter 20, Karellen returns to radio frequencies to explain the first century of Earth's domination by residents of Carina. He explains that the purpose in overtaking Earth and pacifying it was humanitarian: to save earthlings from their pell-mell rush toward self-destruction. Like a chiding father, Karellen reminds his naughty listeners that they are guilty of stockpiling "deadly toys," the nuclear gadgetry that threatened a global plunge into ruin. He expands on humanity's threat by alluding to the greater dangers inherent in paraphysics, a "telepathic cancer, a malignant mentality which in its inevitable dissolution would have poisoned other and greater minds." As a guardian angel, Karellen has held back the human race until its wisdom superseded its menace.

In the final stages of Earth's destruction, Karellen remains in touch with Jan Rodricks, who teases his own sanity by pondering how he came to leave Earth and travel to Carina. Paranoia engulfs Jan as he demands an answer to the enigma: Did he cleverly evade Karellen and the others, or did he fall into their neat plan to preserve one human observer and commentator on Earth's last gasp? The point of view shifts to Karellen, whose admiration for Earth's people suggests an altruist capable of saluting the noble but dying breed of earthlings. His nostalgia implies that he had come to love, trust, and admire them. He becomes so rapt in the final scene that his fellow Carinians leave him musing at the telescreen.

The nature of Karellen and the emissaries from Carina piques the curiosity of critics and readers. Some believe the central character is a Mephistophelian demon deceiving Earth by a gentle despotism and by pseudo-utopic improvements to their lives. Others perceive an affirmation of God, the Overmind that absorbs creation's energy by disabling human limbs and minds and by overriding the powers of the mind and senses. The emergent role of Karellen rings from the sound of his name and his country—he is a caring figure, yet he is a tool in the hands of a higher authority. Although Stormgren, Rodricks, and the Greggson children may have become *carus* (the Latin word for "dear"), Karellen is a company man. He does as he is told. Like the weak Homo sapiens who withers to a halt on his control screen, Karellen himself is but a glimmer in the cosmos. (Bernstein 1969; Clarke 1953; Clarke 1990; Rabkin 1979; Slusser 1977b; Sullivan 1992)

See also Childhood's End; Clarke, Arthur C.; classism; futurism; golden age; humanitarianism; religion; science fiction; speculative fiction; utopia.

 # KARMA

Karma is a Sanskrit theological term indicating a permanent stasis in the force generated by human actions. The positive or negative energy of the actions, which are never the result of blind chance or fate, determines a soul's span of revolutions on the unstoppable cycle of life, death, and rebirth, as revealed in the *Bhagavad Gita* (The Song of the Lord) (second century B.C.), a compendium of India's Sanskrit heritage. Unlike nirvana, a merging of the soul with the universe, karma epitomizes the plight of seekers who try to live by Hindu or Buddhist law in order to attain permanent release from earthly ties. Temporarily reprieved from karma to visit a twofold afterlife, the dead encounter either punishment for evil deeds or divine bliss for goodness. For this reason, karma is of pivotal concern to Buddhists and Hindus, who expect justice to reward social responsibility and religious piety. The concept of divine justice varies from text to text and generally includes a formal hearing, where the deceased's earthly deeds are scrutinized by a judge or panel of judges. Those who fail to measure up to standards are recycled in a new incarnation.

In this subsequent chance to obtain reward, the soul begins again, condemned to suffer for past sins that lie beyond memory. For this reason, karma helps human beings to understand the inequities of life, which reflect former flaws of character or illicit acts and beliefs. When the seeker reaches karma, or the ideal stopping place, either through virtuous living or by a divine stroke of *bhakti*, or divine mercy, the joys of paradise and life among the gods reward virtue.

In Hermann Hesse's *Siddhartha* (1922), the title character grows weary of hedonism and deserts his mistress to locate a permanent happiness. At his residence with the ferryman, Siddhartha observes the motion of the river and compares its constant flow to the stream of people who cross it. Late in his life, Siddhartha deduces that the stream, like human history, is a blend of all the events and passions that have ever been or ever will be. He meditates and sinks into blissful repose from his understanding of karma and his immersion in love. (Andrews 1992; *Bhagavad Gita* 1992; Hall 1991; Hesse 1951; Pappu and Rao 1987; Van Pelt 1975)

See also asceticism; Buddhism; heaven; Hesse, Hermann; kismet; nirvana; Siddhartha; *Siddhartha.*

 # KISMET

The Anglicized form for the Arabic word *qismah*, kismet is the philosophical concept of fate or destiny, a chance encounter between events and innocent bystanders. Equal to the Greek *moira* and the Latin *fatum*, kismet accounts for the prosperity or failure of an individual, village, or nation, often because of some cataclysm of nature such as fire, lightning, hurricane, flood, earthquake, or tidal wave. A momentous aspect in Norse, Egyptian, Greek, Roman, and Arabic lore, kismet also permeates the stoic philosophy of Marcus Aurelius as well as Taoism, which fosters an acquiescence to mortal joys and sorrows. In each of these examples, human will plays no part in events, which are often cruelly imposed upon the godly or whimsically profitable to the least deserving of scamps.

In literature, kismet appears in counterpoint to the concept of heaven, which is not achieved through luck or fortune. An opposing explanation of history as random or chance events appears in Karl Marx's *Das Kapital* (1867). Karma, a belief in the control of a higher power, is reflected by the Hindu philosophy in Hermann Hesse's *Siddhartha* (1922) and the Christian outlook by Dante Alighieri's *Divine Comedy* (1320), John Bunyan's *Pilgrim's Progress* (1678), and John Milton's *Paradise Lost* (1667). Events of the moment are interpreted as the result of improprieties and sins either committed earlier in a lifetime or left over from a former life or lives. In the Hindu and Buddhist views, for the soul to experience nirvana, or oneness with the universe, these wrongs must be exonerated. The Christian view requires acts of contrition and faith, such as baptism and public confession, to earn God's grace and free the soul of sin. (Anderson 1966; Budge 1960; *Bulfinch's Mythology* 1964; Cavendish 1970; Cavendish 1980; Clark 1959; Cross 1957; Dutt 1910; Eliade 1986; Hastings 1951; Holy Bible 1958; Hooke 1963; Jurji 1946)

See also Buddhism; Bunyan, John; Dante Alighieri; *Divina Commedia*; heaven; Hesse, Hermann; Lao Tzu; Marx, Karl; Milton, John; nirvana; *Paradise Lost*; *Pilgrim's Progress*; Siddhartha; *Siddhartha*; Tao.

KORAN

Koran is the Anglicized spelling of the Arabic *Qur'an*, the sacred text of Islam, comprised of 114 surahs, or chapters. Composed by Mohammed (570–632), a caravan master, the Koran contains revelations delivered by Gabriel from God, or Allah, around A.D. 610. In 622 dissidents forced Mohammed to escape Mecca, his hometown (now part of Saudi Arabia), and move west to Medina, where he was revered as a teacher and moralist. In the decades following his death, Mohammed's followers formed a cohesive religious sect as well as a powerful political union of Arabs, often referred to as the Nation of Islam.

The Koran, which was influenced by the Bible, the Talmud, and the Zoroastrian Zenda-Vesta, was collected into a single written text. Today it is valued as a repository of traditional and godly truth, which the devout apply to daily life and to political and theological questions that puzzle or threaten. The theme of submission impels Muslims to prepare themselves for *jihad*, a holy war that is the ultimate battle between good and evil and to repel Satan, who lures the righteous away from their divine duty.

In Alex Haley's *The Autobiography of Malcolm X* (1965), the reading of the Koran plays a significant role in the conversion of Malcolm Little, a petty thief condemned to jail. After parole, the main character departs from street crime and impure living and adopts asceticism and devotion to family. He follows the example of the prophet Elijah Muhammad and changes his name to Malcolm X. Faithful to the dictates of the Koran to pray and seek righteousness, Malcolm X makes a pilgrimage to Mecca and observes a greater truth than the black Islamic movement of the United States. He determines that the acceptance of all seekers of holy inspiration requires a universal brotherhood, which he is at-

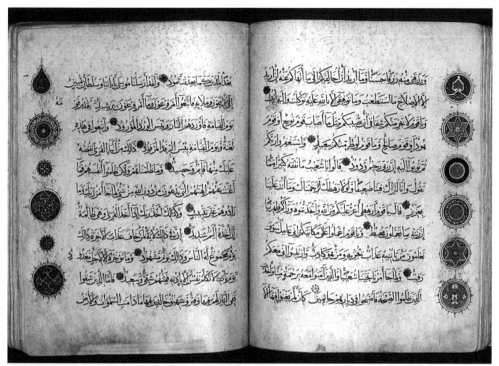

Pages of a Koran, or, in Arabic, *Qur'an*

tempting to organize at the time of his assassination. (Cavendish 1970; Cavendish 1980; Eliade 1986; Haley 1965; Hastings 1951; Hooke 1963; Jurji 1946; Koran 1992)

See also asceticism; Black Muslims; Eden; heaven; Malcolm X; Sufism.

"KUBLA KHAN"

This unfinished tribute to the notable Mongol hero is described by Samuel Taylor Coleridge's tantalizing verse fragment "Kubla Khan: Or, a Vision in a Dream" (1798). Resembling Uruk in *Gilgamesh* (1200 B.C.) or Camelot in Arthurian lore, the poetic Xanadu was the fabled home of Kublai Khan (1215–1294). Symbolic of the height of the Mongol empire during China's Yuan dynasty, Kublai Khan received training and grooming for leadership and succeeded his militarist father, Tolui. After his mother's death, Kublai Khan adopted Buddhism as a state religion to halt religious infighting.

Throughout his turbulent career as Mongol chief, Kublai Khan found no earthly respite from war and fought off numerous attempts to unseat or assassinate him. He extended the Mongol empire across Asia and into the southern peninsula of Vietnam, Burma, and Campuchea. Basically anti-Chinese, he encouraged free trade with his adversaries and founded a courier system for mail delivery. A symbol of his opulent reign includes Shang-tu, his summer residence, which Coleridge immortalized as Xanadu. In old age he suffered

In a vision once I saw:
It was an Abyssinian Maid,
And on her Dulcimer she play'd
Singing of Mount Amara.
Could I revive within me
Her Symphony & Song,
To such a deep delight 'twould win me,
That with Music loud and long
I would build that Dome in Air,
That sunny Dome! those Caves of Ice!
And all, who heard, should see them there,
And all should cry, Beware! Beware!
His flashing Eyes! his floating Hair!
Weave a circle round him thrice,
And close your Eyes in holy dread.
For He on Honey-dew hath fed
And drank the Milk of Paradise.———

This fragment with a good deal more, not
recoverable, composed, in a sort of Reverie, brought
on by two grains of Opium, taken to check a
dysentery, at a Farm House between Porlock &
Linton, a quarter of a mile from Culbone Church,
in the fall of the year, 1797.———
                                    S. T. Coleridge

Sent by M.ʳ Southey, as an
Autograph of Coleridge.

The last lines of Samuel Taylor Coleridge's manuscript of "Kubla Khan," with his note that he had written it in 1797 "in a sort of reverie brought on by two grains of opium, taken to check a dysentery"

the loss of his wife and successor, Chen-chin. As a refuge from sad memories, he indulged himself in luxury and died from the resulting obesity, gout, and alcoholism.

Coleridge's 54-line mystical, poetic tribute to Kublai Khan, said to have resulted from an opium-produced dream that was interrupted before the poet could capture all of its sensual intimacies, depicts the yearnings of a bright but frustrated English romantic who also wrote *The Rime of the Ancient Mariner* and *Christabel*. The idyllic bliss of the Khan's "stately pleasure-dome" alongside the sacred river Alph typified for critics and readers of Coleridge's day the height of romanticism and escapism. Graphically described as a walled enclosure with watchtowers and ten miles of arable land, Xanadu blossoms with fragrant trees, sunny gardens, and icy caverns. As a maiden plucks the dulcimer, the poet records a vision of her performance. The final lines ward off too great a trust in utopian pleasures, which belong only to Khan himself. The poet, who "on honey-dew hath fed, and drunk the milk of Paradise," tempers his earthly delight with rumors of war and the flow of the river to a "sunless sea," both images of destruction and flux. (Coleridge 1948; Dille 1969; Hornstein et al. 1973; Magill 1958; Willey 1973)

See also asceticism; Buddhism; Camelot; escapism; Gilgamesh.

LAND OF COCKAIGNE

See Cloudcuckooland.

LAO TZU

Lao Tzu was a noted Chinese sage and the founder of Taoism, a mystical faith that permeates the Orient, particularly China. Sources place Lao Tzu in the Honan province as early as the sixth century B.C., although more recent evidence suggests that he lived at least three centuries later and was not, as was formerly supposed, a contemporary of Confucius. Lao Tzu composed the *Tao Te Ching* (Way of life), a brief religious and ethical manual urging followers to seek contentment through virtue. The philosopher's life is shrouded in mystery and farfetched legends. According to predominant lore, his mother conceived him in 662 B.C. while watching a comet. His gestation extended to September of 604 B.C., when she leaned against a plum tree in Ch'u Jen and gave birth. When he learned to talk, the child named himself Li, which is Chinese for plum, and Erh, or ear. However, after his hair turned white, people called him Old Sir or Master or Lao Tzu.

Lao Tzu grew up in Loyang, the imperial capital, where he worked as secretary and archivist at the Chou palace. He despaired of the decadent Chou dynasty, and in his 160th year, mounted on a black ox, he departed from Loyang via the Han-Ku Pass to the Middle Kingdom near the Gobi Desert. The guardian of the pass, Yin Hsi, anticipated the arrival of the great wise man and asked that he write a book. Drawing on traditional Chinese lore dating to Huang Ti in 2600 B.C., in one night Lao Tzu composed on a bamboo parchment the 5,000 cryptic verses of the *Tao Te Ching*. His style tends toward the elusive, thought-provoking image or comparison, as demonstrated by the fourteenth aphorism:

> We look at Tao and do not see it;
> Its name is The Invisible.
> We listen to it and do not hear it;
> Its name is The Inaudible.
> We touch it and do not find it;
> Its name is The Subtle.

By spurring readers to thought, Lao intended to increase the world's goodness one individual at a time and to prepare followers for the afterlife, or merger with the Tao. He grew disillusioned after accepting his inability to convert the Chinese from violence and acquisitiveness to forbearance and resilience. Lao Tzu disappeared into western China near the Himalayan Mountains of Tibet. His conjectural death date is placed at 503 B.C. (Blofeld 1973; Cleary 1991; Hornstein et al. 1973; Kaltenmark 1969; LaFargue 1992; Lao Tzu 1993; Lau 1963; Mitchell 1988; Welch 1958)

See also Confucius; heaven; karma; Tao; *Tao Te Ching*.

 # LAPUTA

A 10,000-acre floating island in the Indian Ocean off Australia's west coast in Jonathan Swift's *Gulliver's Travels* (1727), Laputa hovers above the land of the Balnibarbi. The island is 7,837 yards wide and 300 yards thick; catch basins are used to store rainwater and ropes are lowered to haul up supplies. Ranging outward are mezzanines and connecting stairs. In the center of the land, a passageway leads to the Flandona Gagnole, an underground cave where astronomers use astrolabe, sextant, telescope, and quadrant to view the heavens. A centralized lodestone 6 by 3 yards manipulates the island and holds it in balance above the earth. During wars, the king can maneuver Laputa over landmasses, shut out sunlight and rain, and drop stones on adversaries.

Featuring figures dressed in robes covered with mathematical and musical symbols, Book II, Chapter 2 describes the Laputans' curious posture: "Their Heads were all reclined either to the Right, or the Left; one of their Eyes turned inward, and the other directly up to the Zenith." Often, the distracted Laputans trip on an obstruction or fall down a hill. They maintain so keen an interest in the clouds and in their inner selves that body servants, called Flappers, must strike them on the ear or mouth with a pebble-filled inflated bladder to return the dreamer's attention to a conversation.

The unimaginative male Laputan mindset tends toward elevated abstractions—mathematics, music, and changes in the stars—and away from such common or everyday concerns as clothing, sex, or the comforts of home. Female Laputans—even the royal ladies—protest their husbands' disinclination for romance and eagerly depart the island to settle for a lessened lifestyle among the Balnibarbi, who relieve the women's sexual tensions and their boredom with the obsessed male Laputans. In Book III, Chapter 2, Gulliver reports one succulent bit of gossip about the prime minister's wife; she deserted her family and, claiming ill health, fled to Lagado, the main city of the continent of Balnibarbi, where

> . . . she was found in an obscure Eating-house all in Rags, having pawned her Cloths to maintain an old deformed Footman, who beat her every Day, and in whose Company she was taken much against her will.

The woman suffered no reproach on her return to Laputa, but again bribed her way back to Lagado and disappeared. Gulliver fails to comprehend the reason for Laputan women's defections, but credits the prime minister's wife's bizarre flight to the universal "Caprices of Womankind," which are not limited to any race or nation. (Drabble 1985; Harrison et al. 1967; Hornstein et al. 1973; Manguel and Guadalupi 1987; Pollard 1970; Swift 1958; Woods et al. 1947)

See also Brobdingnags; fantasy; Gulliver, Lemuel; *Gulliver's Travels*; Houyhnhnms; Lilliput; satire; Swift, Jonathan; women in utopia.

LESSING, DORIS

Pacifist, poet, and playwright, Lessing is the author of *Memoirs of a Survivor* (1974), a strangely detached, dystopic reaction to a barren human landscape in a dying metropolis ravaged by homeless, hungry, and violent youth gangs. Born Doris May Tayler to planter Alfred Cook and Emily Maude McVeagh Tayler in Kermanshah, Iran, on October 22, 1919, Lessing lived on a farm in Salisbury, Southern Rhodesia, from 1924–1949, where her father also served as an army captain and financier. Largely self-educated, she attended a Catholic convent school and girls' academy, ending her formal studies in 1933. She read widely from American and European classics and began writing in her teens. During her years in Africa, she was twice married—first to Frank Charles Wisdom, father of her son John and daughter Jean, then to Gottfried Anton Lessing, father of Peter, her second son. She worked as a governess, office clerk, telephone operator, and transcriber for Southern Rhodesia's Parliamentary Commissioner before close observation of a dying colonial empire pushed her to the political left. She legitimized her ethical stance through activism in Black Power politics, humanitarian causes, and communism, which she repudiated in 1956. Her outspoken criticism of Rhodesia's racist regime led to the revocation of her passport and permanent exile from Rhodesia.

In 1949 Lessing moved to England, a serene climate conducive to reflection and writing. Resettled in London with her three children, Lessing developed fiction and fantasy into compelling and complex assessments of female disenfranchisement. After writing a first novel, *The Grass Is Singing* (1950), and a short fiction collection, *This Was the Old Chief's Country* (1951), she published a hard-edged fictional tetralogy on violence—*A Proper Marriage* (1954), *Ripple from the Storm* (1958), *Landlocked* (1965), and *The Four-Gated City* (1969). Introducing utopian concepts to her work, Lessing launched a strident call for the empowerment of women in *Memoirs of a Survivor*. The novel depicts the life of Martha Quest in a placid, ideal metropolis doomed to collapse because of political corruption and societal forces. Her scenes of senseless violence echo some of the social angst of Anthony Burgess's *A Clockwork Orange* (1962) and presage the antifeminist oppression of Margaret Atwood's *The Handmaid's Tale* (1985). (Bloom 1986c; Dembo and Pratt 1993; Fishburn 1985; Knapp 1984; Lessing 1988; Myles 1990; Sprague 1986)

LIBERTY 5-3000

The 17-year-old mate of Equality 7-2521, the protagonist in Ayn Rand's dystopian fable *Anthem* (1937), Liberty 5-3000 works at dray labor similar in simplicity and drudgery to her mate's street sweeping, but more evocative of her adult role, which the author implies by connecting agricultural work with fecundity and motherhood. A sower of seeds, Liberty 5-3000 dresses in a white tunic and plants the black furrows of a plowed field. After Equality 7-2521 demonstrates his attraction to her mane of golden hair, dark eyes, and straight posture, Liberty 5-3000 risks imprisonment, torture, and execution by following his footprints across the plain as he flees into the Uncharted Forest. In an oath derived from the book of Ruth in the Old Testament, Liberty 5-3000 vows, "we shall follow you wherever you go." In the face of danger, death, and damnation, Liberty 5-3000 pledges fealty to her mate and, like a cringing serf, bows her head and begs not to be sent away.

Ayn Rand's disposition of the "Golden One" epitomizes the author's disaffection for feminism and the prejudicial incarceration of women into the role of wives, servants, and mothers. Just as Liberty 5-3000 is forced to sow seeds in the regimented city, a similar life awaits her in the abandoned house in the Uncharted Forest, where she demonstrates no more imagination than the witless Pandora of Greek mythology or the gullible Eve in the Garden of Eden. For Rand, casting Liberty 5-3000 as a shallow clotheshorse drawn to color and fabric and as a contented pregnant mate to the more cerebral Equality 7-2521 defines the spiritual and emotional gap that, in Rand's opinion, divides men and women. Freed by her own initiative, as her ironic name implies, Liberty 5-3000 slips easily and contentedly into the position of handmaiden, capitulating to the aspirations of her lord and master, Equality 7-2521.

Even more degrading to the female protagonist is the couple's longing for a son. Rand seems content in her philosophy of determinism for the male half of the world's population and continued bondage for females. Rand excludes a coming-of-knowledge for Liberty 5-3000 and apportions no work of importance beyond mindless domestic tasks, obedience to her contemplative mate, and procreation. In Chapter 12, as Equality 7-2521 looks beyond his life span to the achievements of his sons and chosen comrades, he foresees "the freedom of Man. For his rights. For his life. For his honor." In a work that splits hairs over the designation of the plural pronoun for a single being, Rand regresses from champion of individuality to enslaver of women. (Binswanger 1988; *Contemporary Literary Criticism* 1987; Den Uyl and Rasmussen 1984; Gladstein 1984; Rand 1946; Snodgrass 1990)

See also Atwood, Margaret; *Brave New World*; conditioning; disillusion; Equality 7-2521; eugenics; futurism; *The Handmaid's Tale*; Huxley, Aldous; technology; totalitarianism; *We*; women in utopia; Zamyatin, Yevgeny.

THE LIFE OF LYCURGUS

This biography of Lycurgus is one of a lengthy collection of biographies of notable Greeks and Romans written by Plutarch, prolific Mediterranean observer, essayist, and encyclopedist of the late first century A.D. Plutarch opens his study with a lengthy conjecture about the ninth century B.C., the time in which Lycurgus lived in and ruled Sparta, and concludes that there are more alternate versions than can be accommodated. King Lycurgus succeeded his older brother Polydectes, then yielded the throne after controversy arose following the posthumous birth of Polydectes's male heir. In self-exile, Lycurgus studied the laws in Crete, collected Homer's works in Asia, and made similar examinations of Egypt, other parts of Africa, Spain, and the Indies, "just as physicians compare bodies that are weak and sickly with the healthy and robust."

In time the Spartans grew weary of monarchs who abused their power and sought Lycurgus's return. He complied, organized 30 armed citizens to seize power, and fervidly sought to put Sparta on a hierarchical diet to rid it of excess bureaucracy. The oracle at Delphi promised that he would succeed and would make his commonwealth known worldwide for excellence of governance. According to the Rhetra, or grand covenant, Lycurgus's oral laws were never committed to paper so that people would memorize and preserve them through use rather than by external enforcement or lip service.

With the aid of mature advisers, Lycurgus created two kings and a senate of 28 with power equal to the throne as a means of mediating between democracy and absolute monarchy. To assist in legislation, a popular assembly met outdoors without prior debate to ratify or veto each bill. The role of Lycurgus's counselor was a plum position sought by men over age 60, and Lycurgus filled vacancies with the strongest, swiftest, and wisest rather than the most influential or prestigious. On election day, contenders marched past the reviewing stands. Locked out of sight of the proceedings, electors gauged the shouts of onlookers and selected the most popular. Followers formed an entourage behind the winners and, moving in a procession to the temples, sang praises to the new senators. The day ended, Greek fashion, in a triumphal feast.

The second stage of Lycurgus's improvements in the state was the reapproportionment of land and the furtherance of homogeneity among the classes. To end poverty, envy, arrogance, luxury, and crime, he divided Laconia into 30,000 shares, each share producing 70 bushels of grain; to reward husbandry, he based allotment on merit. So pleasing was the harvest that he noted how all Laconia resembled "one family estate justly divided among a number of brothers." To even the distribution of portable property, he recalled gold and silver coins and replaced them with an unwieldy iron coinage, which was too bulky for extensive stores. Not only did he control miserliness, but also fear of theft and bribery.

The control of wealth brought a peripheral benefit in that itinerant traders, artisans, teachers, whoremongers, smiths, and jewelers ceased to visit Laconia. In time, luxury "wasted away" and a more functional form of crafting replaced the merely decorative with useful objects—cups, plates, utensils, chairs, tables, and beds. To fend off a future rise in affluence, the law required that ceilings, gates, and doors should be plain-hewn with ax and saw. Thus, a simple home demanded simple furnishings, another aspect of Lycurgus's long-range plan to simplify Spartan lifestyles. Lycurgus's pragmatism eventually produced a pride in humble design, austerity, and utility that proved more beneficial and more soul-satisfying than the uncontrolled system prevailing before his election.

The third stage of Lycurgus's innovations was the sharing of meals, except when citizens cooked a thanksgiving offering for the altar or returned from the hunt with fresh game. To halt sybarites from luxuriating at banquet tables and weakening their bodies with overindulgence in food or beverage, bathing, and nap-taking, he created public tables and forced all to eat, 15 to a table, in the presence of other citizens. No one was allowed to carry food into private homes lest they be condemned for daintiness and effeminacy. A riot of the disgruntled wealthy led to stone-throwing. Lycurgus fled the marketplace too late to avoid Alcander, who thrust a spear into his eye. Lycurgus took Alcander as his personal challenge, brought him into his home, and forced him to serve at table. By example, Lycurgus instilled such virtue in the youth that Alcander became the king's staunchest supporter. A second improvement growing out of senseless violence pleased Lycurgus even more: The senate banned weapons from public assembly.

From the simple manipulation of public meals, Lycurgus pioneered numerous innovations, notably the concept of wholesale buying in bulk quantities and the creation of an inviting, peaceful atmosphere. Public repasts caused a need for a community warehouse for meal, wine, cheese, and figs, and a treasury to buy fish and meat. In addition to the creation of a centralized supply house and perpetual inventory, diners gained an extra benefit from the captive audience of children, who came in contact with statesmen and learned gentility and refinement by imitating their elders. An outgrowth of Lycurgus's socialization was a damper on warmongering, which the homebody Spartans considered self-defeating.

To bolster the family, Lycurgus regulated marriage and designed a curriculum for women of "wrestling, running, throwing the quoit, and casting the dart" so that they might strengthen their bodies and have an easier time in childbirth. He added nudity to toughen them and arranged coed processions, singing, dancing, and feasting, which concluded with a show of patriotism, a spiritual boost of self-esteem and nationalism. The unremarkable sight of naked bodies reduced immodesty and brought a greater attention to health, strength, and noble actions. As an inducement to bachelors, the processions ridiculed those who held back from matrimony.

Lycurgus's insistence on healthful practices for females also strengthened families. Brides approached the altar in ripe, robust maidenhood. After the ritual abduction of the bride, a wedding director sheared the girl's hair, dressed her in man's clothing, and left her in a darkened room on a mattress. The groom left the dinner table and, clad in ordinary dress, approached his mate; he consummated their union, then returned to the men's quarters for sleep. This parceling out of time together kept relationships fresh and ardent. In addition,

Lycurgus countenanced extramarital relations, particularly between single men and married women. In cases of old men marrying maidens, custom allowed the husband to select a substitute breeder to sire children.

Lycurgus's communal society valued children as the property of the commonwealth. His eugenic system encouraged the best alliance of mates, just as husbandry mated the most promising mares and studs to breed the strongest, most resilient product. By removing the aspect of jealousy and possessiveness, the king also banished adultery, which played no part in a natural society. A commission of elders at the Lesche, or treasury, examined each child and determined whether it should live or be exposed at Apothetae, a chasm in the earth near Mount Taygetus. To condition children's flesh, mothers bathed them in wine and allowed them freedom from the swaddling cloths with which other countries tethered the young. Lycurgus believed that unconstrained children developed no peevishness, ill humor, or fear of the dark. So well received were his precepts of early childhood nurturance that Greeks valued Spartan nurses above other nationalities.

Learning, like breeding, demonstrated Lycurgus's interest in upgrading the average Spartan in terms of imagination, intelligence, and behavior. Instead of studying at home under tutors, which was the custom among the privileged in the ancient world, seven-year-old Spartans entered companies and classes, lived in dormitories, and elected a 20-year-old captain to help them develop obedience. The elders observed the formation of character, taught them reading and writing, and concentrated on hardening the children to pain and the vicissitudes of weather. Like an extreme version of boot-camp recruits, the children wore their hair cropped and lived naked and shoeless.

Apparently Lycurgus was correct in his assumptions concerning childrearing. By age 12, Sparta's tempered youth spoke little, sang lustily, had no interest in effeminate unguents and emollients, bonded with lovers, and lived in small bands. Their elders attended them, supervised their out-of-classroom hours, and encouraged a right attitude toward duty. An elected official superintended the formation of companies under captains, who dispatched boys to forage for firewood and food. In battle, military authorities relaxed their hold, so that Spartan men found battle a respite from daily rigor rather than a hardship. In peacetime, soldiers lived in a bivouac atmosphere, used hirelings as plowmen, and spent their days feasting, parading, hunting, conversing, and exercising.

To maintain an even temperament, Lycurgus discouraged superstition and an excess of emotion. He established burial plots within the city walls and encouraged survivors to think of death as natural. Before corpses were interred, family members adorned them with olive leaves and scarlet shrouds. No markers named the deceased. After 11 days, mourners sacrificed to Ceres, goddess of grain and fertility. In place of superfluous honors to the dead, Lycurgus looked to Sparta's future and championed virtue in the living.

To solidify the Lacedaemonian lifestyle, Lycurgus forbade travel or intermingling with outsiders, except for the purchase of foreign slaves, who were a necessary adjunct to Sparta's well-run bureaucratic machinery. In Plutarch's opinion, Lycurgus "was as careful to save his city from the infection of foreign bad habits, as men usually are to prevent the introduction of a pestilence." Plutarch implies disapproval of the habit of assassinating Helots or of hazing by forcing them to drink or parading them before the Spartans as models of base behavior. This difference of opinion reveals that Plutarch is capable of admiring Lycurgus without accepting *in toto* the stringent laws of Sparta.

Plutarch lauds Lycurgus's freedom from greed and self-aggrandizement by detailing his departure from home. To cement his bond with law and discipline, Lycurgus swore his senators and two kings to fealty and set out on a journey. At Delphi he received word from Apollo that the Spartan legal system was an excellent method of preserving the people's health and prosperity. To complete his example as worthy public servant, Lycurgus starved himself to death. As he expected, martyrdom suited the Lacedaemonian outlook and helped to extend the life span and purity of Lycurgan law. Spartans, who worshiped their late king like a god, observed his laws unchanged and unaugmented for 500 years. Plutarch marvels that they remained "free-minded, self-dependent, and temperate."

The overall effect of Plutarch's biography leaves in question how Lycurgus managed a strong-arm takeover of the Spartans, reduced them to virtual robotic obedience to his radical laws, and still achieved near-godhood as the embodiment of Plato's "philosopher-king." Certainly life in Laconia was not pleasant for Helots or slaves, whom his racist, classist system reviled and murdered at will. Nor were women glorified above the level of kept women and baby machines. So worthless were females in Lycurgus's grand scheme that he failed to mention how young girls were trained for their civic role. In a state where free men were forbidden to travel, handicapped or weak babies were left for wild animals to dismember, and slaves were murdered for sport, the dark testimony of Plutarch's admiration leaves doubt about both Lycurgus and his biographer. (Johnson 1968; Plutarch 1971a; Negley and Patrick 1952; Snodgrass 1988b; Warner 1971)

See also classism; eugenics; philosopher-king; Plutarch; slavery; women in utopia.

LILLIPUT

The home of a disproportionately small race of people, Lilliput is the setting of Book I of Jonathan Swift's *Gulliver's Travels* (1727). This self-absorbed empire is ruled by natives only six inches tall, and outfitted with animals, plants, and trees of equivalent smallness. In barbed commentary on the nation's pettiness Swift smirks, "Nature hath adapted the eyes of the Lilliputians to all objects proper for their view. They see with great exactness, but at no great distance."

Lilliputians, whose name adds to the English language a worthy synonym for diminution, inconsequentiality, and small-mindedness, contrast most of society in their denigration of the family. In Swift's commentary, "considering the miseries of human life," Lilliputian children have no reason to thank their parents for begetting them. Because of the profligacy of the parents' lustful union, the state does not trust them to rear their young past the age of 20 months. Instead, each town provides state nurseries, each programmed to suit a particular social class and financed by tax levies against the family, which the emperor's staff assesses and collects.

Swift's description echoes elements of the Spartan upbringing for boys described by Plutarch's *Life of Lycurgus* (first century A.D.). In the Nurseries for Males of Noble or Eminent Birth, boys are dressed and fed simply, and are brought up to respect "principles of honor, justice, courage, modesty, clemency, religion, and love of their country." To maintain the boys' aristocratic self-assurance, they are waited on by attendants and are not required to speak to menials. The boys receive the constant attention of professors who supervise the semiannual visit of parents, who are allowed to kill their children at the beginning or end of the session. In general, male children are protected from coddling, treats, and gifts.

Whatever Lilliput's intentions for males, its stereotypical plan to turn females into wives and mothers incorporates a form of sexism still found in patriarchal countries like Saudi Arabia and Pakistan. Girls' nurseries for children of the elite offer quality upbringing. Small girls are dressed by maids, who are supervised by professors to halt the practice of terrifying the young with scary stories. Any foolhardy chambermaid who transgresses the rules is publicly whipped, imprisoned for a year, and banished to some desolate part of Lilliput. Like young men, girls grow up to be bold, forthright citizens, and they learn from birth to disdain ornamentation. They also share with males a demanding curriculum of physical education and sufficient studies to make each a "reasonable and agreeable companion" to her husband. At age 12, the girls are ready for matrimony.

The lack of egalitarianism in Lilliput, like Aldous Huxley's hatchery and conveyor-belt system in *Brave New World* (1932) and the coercion of young workers into menial jobs in Ayn Rand's *Anthem* (1937) and in Lois Lowrys *The Giver* (1993), widens the gap between classes. Nurseries for people of common rank provide instruction commensurate with the needs of the class, including apprenticeships for future tradesmen, who leave school at age seven. In addition to tuition, working-class parents also forfeit to the government a portion of their incomes as an appropriate reminder that begetting children places a responsibility on each family. These funds are held in escrow for the children's needs and use.

Swift's satire spotlights the demeaning attitudes of Lilliput toward farmers and unskilled workers. The bottom rung of society is excluded from public nurseries and education of any kind. These "cottagers and laborers," another name for the agricultural class, rear their own children and are "of little consequence to the public." Intent on eddifying the upper levels of society, Lilliput is nonetheless attentive to physical needs among the lowest caste and thus maintains public hospitals for the sick and infirm as a control on public begging. (Drabble 1985; Harrison et al. 1967; Hornstein et al. 1973; Maguel and Guadalupi 1987; Pollard 1970; Swift 1958; Woods et al. 1947)

LINDA

Linda is a former Beta-level technician and the cast-off lover of the Director of Hatcheries and Conditioning in Aldous Huxley's *Brave New World* (1932). At age 19 Linda followed the director from England to Santa Fe, New Mexico, and became separated from him at the Malpais reservation. He returned to London, leaving her to fend for herself among primitive Zuñi Indians to whom utopian society was unknown. She gave birth to John, her noble son, in the old way—viviparous reproduction—which the Brave New World had replaced with a factory system of in vitro fertilization, eugenic monitoring, and decanting.

Huxley's interest in Linda implies a sympathy with her life as a castaway and social pariah. An outsider in two worlds, Linda once attempted to instruct natives in the principles she retains from her utopian conditioning. Unfit for the primitive, monogamous Indian reservation, she submerged a wounded ego in the consumption of mescal and peyote and in sexual debauchery with willing husbands. The resulting uproar from their angry wives spilled over into John's memories of his mother, causing him low self-esteem, introversion, and self-accusatory martyrdom.

Huxley uses Linda's downward spiral as a commentary on dystopia and a prophecy of her son's wretched demise. After Bernard Marx transports Linda and John to London, she sinks into a moribund state amid the futuristic, mind-engaging trappings that form Huxley's Brave New World. Withdrawn into electronic sense stimulation and life-threatening doses of *soma* at the Park Lane Hospital for the Dying, at age 44 Linda lies in a semistupor—bloated, unfocused, and imbecilic, singing nursery rhymes and dreaming of Popé, her Zuñi lover. A paroxysm throws her into respiratory arrest, leaving John to grieve and blame himself for her ignoble death. (Bedford 1985; Holmes 1970; Huxley 1932; Nance 1988; Negley and Patrick 1952; Watts 1969)

See also *Brave New World; Brave New World Revisited;* conditioning; escapism; eugenics; Huxley, Aldous; hypnopaedia; John; *soma;* women in utopia.

"LOCKSLEY HALL"

A dystopian elegy published by Alfred Tennyson in 1842, "Locksley Hall" details the despair of a young man disappointed in his love for his cousin Amy. The poem, written in rhymed couplets, concludes with a dismal vision as the speaker looks to the future as "far as human eye could see." Similar to the technological wizardry foretold by Jules Verne's speculative fiction, the speaker anticipates air travel as "the heavens fill with commerce, argosies of magic sails," and the use of airships to drop "a ghastly dew" of bombs. At the end of a mighty struggle, he predicts the rise of a "Federation of the world," a prefiguration of the League of Nations, and a time of peace reminiscent of Hesiod's golden age or the Arthurian Camelot.

In 1886 Tennyson published a second look at Locksley Hall with "Locksley Hall Sixty Years After." Disillusioned by hopes come to nothing and the loss of Amy, his love of 60 years ago, the crotchety grandfather assesses the dystopic scene with passions roused to rhetorical questions and contempt for human folly, addressing his grandson Leonard in lines 171–174:

> Warless? when her tens of thousands, and her thousand millions, then—
> All her harvest all too narrow—who can fancy warless men?
> Warless? war will die out late then. Will it ever? late or soon?
> Can it, till this outworn earth be dead as yon dead world the moon?

The speaker blames his godless generation for the carnage that decimates England and France, and takes no comfort from either nature or technological advancement.

A diametric opposite to the idealism of *Idylls of the King*, Tennyson's disillusioned tone suggests a depressing atmosphere laden with withered anticipations for a worthy heir to replace the aged grandfather. To return his grandson to the idealism of past times, the speaker urges that the boy seek a nobler, more altruistic goal: "Follow you the star that lights a desert pathway . . . till you see the Highest Human Nature is divine." At age 80 the speaker relinquishes title to Locksley Hall with an oversimplified, hackneyed bit of advice: "Follow Light, and do the Right." His spleen emptied of its bitter contents, the grandfather says no more. The nebulous reference to "right" leaves to Leonard's interpretation the morals that should guide him and protect Locksley Hall from further deterioration and dishonor. (Abrams 1968; Albright 1986; Tennyson 1949a)

See also Arthur; Camelot; disillusion; golden age; *Idylls of the King*; *Looking Backward*, 2000–1887; Lotus-Eaters; prophecy; technology; Tennyson, Alfred.

LONDON, JACK

London is considered one of the United States's finest writers of naturalistic novels, nonfiction books, stories, essays, and social criticism, including the dystopic collectivist novel *The Iron Heel* (1907). Born in San Francisco, California, on January 13, 1876, John "Jack" Griffith was the illegitimate son of Flora Wellman, a psychic, and astrologer William Henry Chaney, who left his suicidal mistress with orders to seek an abortion. Adopted at age five by his stepfather, John London, this timorous, frail, and introspective boy grew up on a ranch near Colma, California. He read Rudyard Kipling and other adventurers, and longed to rid himself of poverty. In adolescence he quit school and, discontent, delinquent, and unemployed, combed the slums of Oakland's waterfront in search of his biological father. With assistance from the director of the Oakland Public Library, he completed his education by reading the classics.

Gradually, Jack London pulled himself out of the spiritual miasma that threatened to turn him into a sour, cynical criminal. He abandoned membership in a gang of thieves and worked as an oyster-bay patroller. At age 17 he sailed the Pacific, applying his experiences to his novel *The Sea Wolf* (1904). In his late teens, he acted on altruistic yearnings by joining Coxey's industrial army to protest poverty. Even with the best of intentions, his association with homeless men brought him to grief in Niagara Falls, New York, when he was arrested for vagrancy in 1894.

The next year, London obtained his high school diploma and drifted through a variety of jobs—newspaper carrier, longshoreman, coal-stoker, canner, jute mill operator, and laundryman. An Oakland barman, impressed with London's keen intellect, loaned him the money to enroll at the University of California at Berkeley, where he studied philosophy. London stood out from the rest of the student body with his unkempt appearance and his extensive knowledge of *The Communist Manifesto* (1848), Karl Marx, Friedrich Engels, Friedrich Nietzsche, Charles Darwin, and social philosopher Herbert Spencer. Already a believer in collectivism, at the age of 20 London became a socialist. He was arrested for anticapitalist oratory in the town square, and in 1901 and 1905 ran unsuccessfully for mayor of Oakland. During these formative years, he prospected for gold in the Yukon. Sick with scurvy, he returned to California to write his first novel, *Daughter of the Snows* (1900), and adventure tales for the *Overland Monthly* and the *Atlantic Monthly*.

Settled for the first time in his life, London married Bessie Maddern, the stereotypical clinging vine, and fathered two daughters. When the marriage foundered, he toured England and wrote *The People of the Abyss* (1903), a sociological study of slum life. His outlook improved with marriage to Charmian "Mate" Kittredge, his beloved soulmate, with whom he shared Beauty Ranch in Glen Ellen, California. In hopes of acquiring the capital to finance an extensive ranching operation, he began writing his masterpiece, *The Call of the Wild* (1903), followed by *The Sea Wolf* (1904), *White Fang* (1904), the autobiographical *Martin Eden* (1909), *Burning Daylight* (1910), and *The Valley of the Moon* (1913). To supplement his meager income, he lectured and wrote for local newspapers.

In tandem with his bent for fiction, London continued to ponder the social significance of working-class people in England and across the United States. For altruistic reasons he produced *The War of the Classes* (1905), *The Iron Heel* (1907), *Revolution and Other Essays* (1910), and *John Barleycorn* (1913), all serious sociological commentaries on substance abuse, class warfare, unemployment, substandard housing, and poverty. Knowing firsthand about illegitimacy, alcoholism, and opiates (which he took to assuage kidney and back pain), he commiserated with the downtrodden and hoped to alleviate their misery by educating capitalist overlords, whom he openly repudiated. From a two-year trek about the South Pacific in the *Snark*, a homemade ketch, he derived an article about life in a leper colony, which he visited in Hawaii. In 1913 London's financial difficulties worsened after an arsonist torched his house. On November 21, 1916, he died of an accidental overdose of morphine, which he used to stem chronic back pain. Two years after his death, his survivors published his

Jack London, about 1914

dystopian novelette, *The Red One.* (Beauchamp 1984; Hedrick 1982; London 1982a; Lundquist 1987; Perry 1981; Sinclair 1983; Stone 1978)

    See also classism; collectivism; *The Communist Manifesto;* didacticism; Engels, Friedrich; futurism; *The Iron Heel;* Marx, Karl; prophecy.

 # LONGFELLOW, HENRY WADSWORTH

One of the nineteenth century's greatest and most popular writers, Longfellow was an American epic poet, teacher, and author of *The Song of Hiawatha* (1855), an adapted version of Iroquois lore taken from the sociological studies of H. R Schoolcraft, the portraits and landscapes painted by George Catlin, and of the 1849 novel *Dacotah*, by Mary H. Eastman. Born a lawyer's son on February 27, 1807, Longfellow grew up in upper-class surroundings in Portland, Maine. The area suited his romantic outlook and gave him ample opportunity to study Native American traditions. After earning honors for work in modern languages at Bowdoin College, he spent 1826–1829 studying in Europe. On his return to the United States, he wrote essays for the *North American Review.*

His middle years brought contentment and fame as well as tragedy. He married Mary Potter, began concentrating on poetic technique, and at age 28 taught at Bowdoin College. He was awarded a professorship in literature at Harvard University. During a second journey to Europe in 1836, his wife died in Amsterdam. Longfellow resumed his teaching career, polished several translations of French and Spanish verse, and published *Voices in the Night* (1838), his first poetry collection. Subsequent publications include *Hyperion* (1838), *Ballads and Other Poems* (1841), *The Belfry of Bruges* (1847), and his best-selling verse romance, *Evangeline* (1848).

The security of his reputation as a master poet gave Longfellow the courage to resign his professorship in 1854 and work full-time on poetry. His completion of *The Song of Hiawatha* preceded two of his greatest works, *The Courtship*

Henry Wadsworth Longfellow

of Miles Standish (1855) and *Tales of the Wayside Inn* (1863). During this period of literary productivity and public acclaim, he married Frances Appleton, who was burned to death in 1861. Grieved by his loss and by the outbreak of the Civil War, Longfellow worked at original verse and a translation of Dante's Italian epic, *The Divine Comedy* (1320). He received accolades from both sides of the Atlantic, visited Queen Victoria, and was acclaimed as a gentleman scholar of the highest merit. He died at his home in Cambridge, Massachusetts, on March 24, 1882.

Longfellow's view of an Iroquois golden age and an afterlife blend animism, epic lore, and the Christian concept of heaven. Termed the Indian *Edda,* the stylistic details of *The Song of Hiawatha* echo serious study of European epics, particularly the Finnish *Kalevala,* Homer's *Iliad* and *Odyssey,* Virgil's *Aeneid,* and Torquato Tasso's *Jerusalem Delivered* (1581). The serenity of the earthly Indian idyll, set on Iron River, Wisconsin, describes a time of Native American progress and harmony, yet is freighted with prophecy of the eventual loss of land and power to European settlers. Based on oral tradition, *The Song of Hiawatha* was a favorite of children and adults for half a century. (Dexter 1972; Kennedy 1972; Longfellow 1992; Wagenknecht 1968; Williams 1964)

See also *Aeneid;* Dante Alighieri; *Divina Commedia;* golden age; heaven; Homer; prophecy; syncretism; Virgil.

LOOKING BACKWARD, 2000–1887

Edward Bellamy published this speculative novel, the most successful American world vision, in 1887. Bellamy's protagonist, the 30-year-old upper-class neophyte Julian West, suffers from insomnia, which he combats by sequestering himself in the silence of a concrete-walled cell and consulting hypnotist Pillsbury, a doctor dedicated to questionable standards. After dinner with fiancée Edith Bartlett and her father, West departs from the late-nineteenth-century milieu in a hypnotic state. His residence burns while he is asleep in his basement chamber. Julian is hurled into the year 2000 and, like a latter-day Rip Van Winkle, is not immediately found by searchers, who assume that he died in the fire.

In Chapter 3 Julian West—like the speaker in William Morris's *News from Nowhere* (1890), H. G. Wells's Time Traveller in *The Time Machine* (1895), and Mark Twain's Hank Morgan in *A Connecticut Yankee in King Arthur's Court* (1886)—awakens in an unexpected time warp. He has entered the year 2000 and feels out of sync with the Boston of the future. The impressive architecture of a once-familiar city tempts West to believe that he has journeyed a thousand years forward rather than only 113 years. Dr. Leete, the gentle retired physician who attends West during his initial shock, helps him to accept the mental and emotional wrenching that whirls his befuddled brain to the brink of insanity.

Through fictional characters and action, Bellamy dabbles in prognostication in the areas of city planning, travel, entertainment, and education. West recognizes the river and harbor of the Boston he once knew and marvels that thoroughfares are canopied to protect inhabitants from inclement weather and too much sun. Home sound systems produce lectures, sermons, and instructional programs. Relaxation and family life answer to rules of the commune. In the style of Lycurgus's Sparta, families dine in private rooms of public refectories and are served by a catering staff.

Hospitality takes the edge off West's unfamiliarity with the future Boston. Welcomed into the home of Leete and his daughter Edith, West listens to their description of an impersonal, futuristic society that resembles an orderly laborers' army, headed by an American president elected by a gerontocracy of voters over 45 years of age. The Boston of the second millennium, an all-electric city that survives the economic turmoil of strikes and labor disputes of West's time, possesses imposing architecture, pleasant parks, and a balanced community in which no one rises above the average standard of living.

Boston's militaristic government has overthrown the dysfunctional free-enterprise system, and now controls public institutions and industry without the need to resort to law enforcers, attorneys, financiers, soldiers, or clerks. Lacking paper money, Bostonians use a federally funded bank card that doles out a regular yearly allowance of $4,000. This controlled, egalitarian system allows individuals to spend for whatever pleases them, but never more than any other citizen's base worth. People who prove incapable of managing their personal finances receive government supervision as a means of ending hunger and profligacy. West visits a government-run emporium and examines a huge array of samples and clerks waiting to take his order, which is dispatched from a centralized stockpile. By the time the orderer returns home, the item has already arrived.

To stabilize the Boston of A.D. 2000, the government requires education in the arts and professions until the age of 21, when workers enter a three-year hitch in the "industrial army." In a style reminiscent of Fra Tomaso Campanella's *La Città del Sole* (1602), students sample a variety of vocations and trades until they locate work that suits their talents. If they score low on government ability tests, counselors encourage them to try another profession. Workers who refuse to comply with the system are jailed and fed bread and water, a suitable deterrent to apathy or shirking.

In a socialistic setting approximating Karl Marx and Friedrich Engel's vision of the classless society, all work carries equal prestige and remunerative value. There are no privileged few, no overpaid managerial class, and no sexism or slavery delegating dreary jobs to women, nonwhites, or an overburdened subclass. The most oppressive jobs are made palatable by a reduction in hours. Every worker's salary is deposited directly into the National Bank. After 24 years of public service, workers retire, with both male and female citizens receiving equal pensions for their labors. The only alternative is retirement at age 33 on half the usual income.

In Dr. Leete's home library, West rereads Tennyson's doom-filled "Locksley Hall," a prophetic poem popular in the previous century, and realizes that the poet's vision of air power and global alliances has come true. According to Edith, because of the efficacy of public education in skills and tastes, culture and work create a balance in Boston. Art flourishes. Libraries continue to stock English classics; readers admire Dickens for his foresight in condemning the oppressive nineteenth-century form of capitalism. An unusual dispensation allows writers to earn royalties for their publications in the usual manner, i.e., the sale of books is credited to individual accounts. Likewise, journals and newspapers are capitalistic endeavors, but publishers must repay the government for the loss of their service to industry.

As with other utopias, the Boston of A.D. 2000 is a dream world that suffers no anarchy and subsists in harmony and peace. Women make up a separate but equal part of the industrial army. They may choose to bear children or opt for a career. Older citizens, who have mustered out with honor, can indulge in hobbies, support athletic teams, or travel on funds transferred from the National Bank. As a whole, the people profit from technological innovations powered by electricity and such work-saving inventions as free laundry service and full programs of music available by telephone in all homes. As Dr. Leete notes in Chapter 11, "The broad shoulders of the nation . . . bear now like a feather the burden that broke the backs of the women of your day."

Dr. Leete also comments on the negative side of human nature. Social engineering treats crime as a mental dysfunction. Law-breaking lessens because money is removed as an enticement. Boards of education and medicine are devoid of the competitive rush for privilege, prestige, and monetary success that marred the nineteenth century. Headed by the president's advisers, the bureaucracies of the second millennium improve the quality of life by applying earnest altruism for the good of all. To assure fairness, a special women's rights clause empowers a single female representative with veto power.

After the first Sunday's sermon, West sinks into depression and loneliness, which Edith relieves by confessing the secret she has been hiding—her love for him from the day of his arrival. The connection between Edith Leete and Edith Bartlett, her great-grandmother, explains this affective link with West. Steeped in the romantic lines of her grandmother's correspondence, Edith Leete had been awaiting a mate like the writer of those antique love letters. Her profession of love demonstrates a new openness in women, who no longer play the simple-witted coquettes of the previous century; now they speak directly to the men who appeal to them.

West sleeps well that night and is awakened the next morning by Sawyer, his servant. The surroundings attest to a cruel reality; West's three-day visit to A.D. 2000 was a dream. In Chapter 28, he reads a newspaper dated May 31, 1887 and learns of the "impending war between France and Germany." From his historical perspective, the news is traumatic. He turns over in his thoughts the "unmistakable touch of fatuous self-complacency" characteristic of the 1880s.

Fully aware of the headlines' implications, West mutters ominously about the final line, "the moral grandeur of nineteenth-century civilization." To West, there is no doubt that news of the coming carnage in Europe belies "a bit of cynicism worthy of Mephistopheles, and yet of all whose eyes it had met this morning I was, perhaps, the only one who perceived the cynicism." Like Shakespeare's doomed Macbeth, West totters under the burden of knowing the future. He falls prey to disillusion and nostalgia for the future Boston, "a city whose people fared all alike as children of one family and were one another's keepers in all things." He returns to Washington Street and laments the noise, squalor, unemployment, poverty, and jangle of competition. Boston is "the land of Ishmael, where every man's hand was against each and the hand of each against every other."

After a day of wandering, West stops at Edith's house and joins the family for dinner. His plaintive cries for the poor leave his fellow diners speechless. He attempts to express what his dream has taught him, that "the labor of men . . . was the fertilizing stream which alone rendered earth habitable." The women isolate him by turning aside from his discourteous babblings. There are cries of "Madman!" "Pestilent fellow!" "Fanatic!" "Enemy of society!" Mr. Bartlett tosses him out.

By a fictional sleight of hand, Bellamy returns West to the Boston of the future, where he awakens suddenly in his bed at Dr. Leete's house. In the garden below, Edith Leete gathers flowers. West realizes that he has truly leapt through time and may enjoy the anguish-free life of A.D. 2000 without fear that he will be returned to the past. Somewhat guilt-ridden at the shambles he leaves in the Boston of 1887, he prostrates himself before Edith and weeps with joy. In a brief postscript, Bellamy summarizes optimistically, "the Golden Age lies before us and not behind us, and is not far away. Our children will surely see it, and we, too, who are already men and women, if we deserve it by our faith and by our works."

As the best-received utopian novel in the United States, Bellamy's *Looking Backward* holds its place on high school and college reading lists for the social sciences and challenges the popularity of such twentieth-century works as B. F. Skinner's *Walden Two* (1948) and Ayn Rand's *Anthem* (1937). A populist triumph, the work spawned 150 nationalist organizations that sought to allay democratic squeamishness at the thought of adapting to socialism and monopolies. By alluding to the ease with which capitalism could transfer power to a scaled-down government, Bellamy smoothed the way for his readers to avoid the pitfalls inherent in Marxism and to anticipate the equality found in socialism. Paramount to his visionary state is the demise of drudgery; the end of poverty, sexism, and elitism; and a cultivation of all talents.

Critics cite a telling weakness in his altruistic model society: the lack of checks and balances on the president, who could easily mutate into a dictator. An additional drain on Bellamy's future is the hierarchy of officials needed to manage an equal distribution of goods and services. Although well plotted, the romantic notions of *Looking Backward* fall short of a thorough accounting of the disappearance of greed, cruelty, disease, and war, which he blames on "the barbaric industrial and social system, which has come down to us from savage antiquity, undetermined by the modern humane spirit, riddled by the criticism of economic science." An outright plan of optimism, Bellamy predicates *Looking Backward* on the belief that human beings are capable of utopia. (Bellamy 1960; Bowman 1958; Johnson 1968; Mumford 1959; Patai 1988)

LORD OF THE FLIES

One of the most repellent, fiercely barbaric of twentieth-century dystopian novels, *Lord of the Flies* was published by William Golding in 1954. The novel belongs to a particular subclass of island utopias similar to Daniel Defoe's *Robinson Crusoe* (1719), Herman Melville's *Typee* (1846) and *Omoo* (1847), and William Dean Howells's *Traveler from Altruria* (1872) and *Through the Eye of the Needle* (1907). Written in rebuttal to Robert Michael Ballantyne's euphoric novel *The Coral Island* (1857), *Lord of the Flies* follows a plane crash on an exotic island setting with the creation of a hell on Earth, where young male survivors maul one another for power, sacrifice the weak, and cavort in ritual worship of a fly-encrusted pig's head. Beginning as well-bred English choirboys, the children deteriorate into compassionless savages bent on cruelty, revenge, and power.

The story opens near a lagoon on an unspecified coral island. Shaped like a boat, the balmy island suggests numerous interpretations—a microcosm, Eden, Noah's ark, or the vulva of the earth mother, through which is born a generation devoted to evil. The sheltered lagoon, a re-creation of the amnion and chorion in which an embryo floats before its birth, warms and reassures the children like tepid bathwater. Against the backdrop of Pacific blue, the spot of land is heavily textured with rocks, slopes, and pink crags. At the far end, a second island resembles the battlements of a fort. The most pleasant aspects of Golding's island refuge are butterflies, birds, ripe fruit, warm sand, and candle-shaped flowers deep in the gloom. In contrast to the solidity of coral blocks, the shoreside palms crawl with green creepers that resemble snaky coils, the symbolic serpent of Eden.

Amid the splendors of their idyllic isle, the traumatized evacuees stroll in partial awareness of their brush with death. The "long scar" in Chapter 1, caused by the thrust of metal on sand, represents an intrusion on nature and the ultimate loss of innocence as the children cope with a lack of supervision in an otherwise perfect world. The most noteworthy characters are 12-year-old Ralph, a tall, contemplative lad, and the obese, asthmatic Piggy, his literary foil, who blows on a conch shell to call the others to assembly. The pair set up a simplistic democracy, and Ralph is elected leader. Along with Jack Merridew, the chapter chorister, and Simon, Ralph climbs to the island's vantage point to establish what he already expects—they are marooned on an otherwise unpopulated island.

Golding's blameless setting lulls the children into a comfortable respite from lessons, rules, and adult tyranny. A child's fantasy, the island is sheltered by a coral reef lying perhaps a mile out and parallel to what they now consider their private beach. In an image emblematic of an impotent god, Golding comments that "the coral was scribbled in the sea as though a giant had bent down to reproduce the shape of the island in a flowing chalk line but tired before he had finished." Freed from restrictive clothing, the boys dive and swim, lie in the sun, climb rocks, and explore the jungle. One unnamed child disturbs the complacency of the others with reports of a fearful beast. Ralph restores the fiesta of optimism by insisting that the group keep a fire going on the highest elevation to signal rescue vessels. After the fire gets out of hand, Ralph discovers that the anonymous child has vanished.

Golding builds to a conflict by enlarging on the character of Jack Merridew. Jack tends to bully the young and weak; over several weeks, he tires of Ralph's supremacy and evades rules by arming himself with a sharpened stick and stalking a wild pig through the undergrowth. The other children build shelters from palm fronds, play, and enjoy the beach atmosphere. Jack intensifies his absorption in hunting by painting red, black, and white marks on his face. When others join his band, they lose interest in tending the fire, which, like a beacon of hope and illumination, goes out.

The inevitable conflict between contemplative and vigorous leaders occurs when Jack and his stalkers return with a fresh kill. Ralph and Piggy complain that the hunters have neglected the signal fire. Jack lashes out at Piggy and breaks one lens of his glasses, a symbolic weakening of Piggy's insight into the castaways' plight. Ralph attempts to restore order, but realizes that control over the boys has grown too slack. The group's discussion of order drifts to another sighting of a dangerous night creature: the skeletal remains of a downed pilot. The children break into a frenetic dance and chant. That night, twins Samneric awaken by the signal fire and spot the dangling remains of the dead man still harnessed to the wispy ropes of his parachute.

The strongest of the children—Ralph, Jack, and Roger—climb to the spot and investigate. The grisly scene alarms them and they flee to the relative safety of the shore. The children's innocence departs like the tide. As Golding describes the ominous, animistic hellishness in Chapter 6:

> . . . it seemed like the breathing of some stupendous creature. Slowly the waters sank among the rocks, revealing pink tables of granite, strange growths of coral, polyp, and weed. Down, down, the waters went, whispering like the wind among the heads of the forest. . . . Then the sleeping leviathan breathed out, the waters rose, the weed streamed, and the water boiled over the table rock with a roar.

Order breaks up as hunters depart with Jack and fire-watchers desert their post. When Jack triumphs with a slaughtered sow, he sets up a stick to display the totemic, fly-decked head, a primitive deity that menaces young imaginations. Not yet cowed by the unknown, the children dine on roast pork. Simon, the mystic of the group, steals away to study the danger that lurks in the jungle. He sets free the tangle of cords and allows the parachutist to drift down to a watery burial in the receding tide. Simon rejoins the feast at a pivotal moment, when primitive death urges grip the island braves and cause them to overwhelm and kill him. His corpse, like that of the parachutist, washes away with the tide.

The falling action hinges on Ralph's skill at running the gauntlet. The next day, he languishes in regret at the group's uncontrollable savagery. Jack's followers steal Piggy's glasses; Ralph attempts to recover them. In the struggle, Roger unseats a boulder that strikes Piggy and crushes his skull as he tumbles to the rocks below. Their blood thirst inflamed by a human kill, the hunters pursue Ralph, unintentionally setting fire to the jungle. In Chapter 12 Ralph flees like a denless beast:

> He forgot his wounds, his hunger and thirst, and became fear; hopeless fear on flying feet, rushing through the forest toward the open beach. Spots jumped before his eyes and turned into red circles that expanded quickly till they passed out of sight. . . . Then he was down, rolling over and over in the warm sand, crouching with an arm to ward off, trying to cry for mercy.

He happens upon a British naval officer, who has seen the fire and come to investigate. Rescued at last, Ralph blubbers about Piggy, his dead friend, as the other boys assemble and weep their own trauma and shame.

In contrast to the loveliness of the boat-shaped coral island, the deteriorating action of *Lord of the Flies* conflicts with the idyll of fresh bananas and coconuts, sun, surf, sand, and a lagoon as warm as bathwater and as comforting as the prenatal chorion and amnion. From isolated bliss to the intense hunt for human prey, the novel sinks into an ignoble fray with Ralph as target. Just as Ralph and Piggy had insisted, the cleansing fire draws adults to the scene; however, there is little likelihood that naval officers can restore badly maimed innocence. Like the island, which was scarred by the descending fuselage, the children bear their own scars left by willful torture and murder. Innate evil is a force that overrides their better natures, unmasking a darkness of heart that openly, vigorously, and vaingloriously attacks and kills Simon and Piggy.

As didactic allegory, Golding's novel merits admiration for his deft disclosure of a killer strand woven into the human soul. The fly-specked beasthead chortles, "Fancy thinking the Beast was something you could hunt and kill!" Piggy the child dies like the woods pig, both slaughtered to appease an inner demon in Jack's killer band. Unbridled jealousy, vengeance, cruelty, and malice in what were once unsullied children competes with the external milieu—the atomic war from which they were originally fleeing. The microcosm of the unnamed island mirrors society's indigenous barbarism, which is parent to anarchy and social and individual disintegration. (Baker 1988; Carey 1987; Gindin 1988; Golding 1954; Johnston 1980; Kinkead-Weeks and Gregor 1984; Snodgrass 1990; Subbarao 1987)

See also allegory; didacticism; Eden; Golding, William; Merridew, Jack; Piggy; Ralph.

 # LOST HORIZON

James Hilton's realistic utopian fantasy novel draws on the post–World War I disillusionment that followed the birth of trench warfare, mustard gas, aerial dogfights, and machine guns. Written in 1933 in the tense in-between years that presaged World War II, *Lost Horizon* turned from dependence on mechanization to a quieter, less stressful existence based on the consumption of the *tangatse* berry, which characters consume in restful cups of tea.

A framework novel set in the spring of 1932 after an evening together at Berlin's Templehof Airdrome, *Lost Horizon* jumps ahead to the reflections of former school chums. Sanders, an English pilot, relates how on May 20 of the previous year a mutual acquaintance—Hugh "Glory" Conway, a 37-year-old British consul and former Oxford lecturer in oriental history—was kidnapped in a skyjacking at Baskul, India. Flown aboard a maharajah's plane to Peshawar, Conway had intended to escape an Indian rebellion. As an addendum to Sanders's narration, Rutherford, a fiction writer, invites him to his hotel and finishes the story of Conway's misadventure in Baskul with a surprise conclusion: While vacationing in China the previous fall, Rutherford met Conway, who was recuperating from amnesia at a Chung Kiang mission infirmary. Two weeks later, while sailing by Japanese liner bound from Shanghai to San Francisco, Rutherford heard Conway play an unpublished Chopin étude that he claimed to have learned from one of Chopin's students.

According to Rutherford, from late evening until ten the next morning, Conway, whose memory returns, relates his adventure in an Asian utopia known as Shangri-La. He slips away from Rutherford in Honolulu, joins the crew of a banana boat bound for Fiji, then pushes west for Bangkok, Kashmir, and beyond. Three months later, Conway posts a manuscript from Bangkok to Rutherford with the rest of his tale. According to the text, Talu, a Tibetan convert and the maharajah's pilot, kidnaps four Caucasian passengers: Conway; Miss Roberta Brinklow, a member of the conservative Eastern Mission; an American named Henry Barnard, who is traveling under the alias Chalmers Bryant to avoid capture for embezzlement; and Captain Charles Mallinson, a 24-year-old member of the British consulate.

Ostensibly, the story follows a believable topographical expedition. The plane flies an erratic north-by-northeast course, lands for refueling in mid-afternoon, then resumes passage over hazardous peaks; high altitude causes the passengers discomfort. Mallinson becomes agitated after discovering that Talu carries a pistol and is taking them toward an unknown destination. Conway, a mature, self-contained man, occupies his time in composing pleas for help in a variety of Eastern languages in hopes of dropping the messages from the plane to attract rescuers. He refuses to speculate on the outcome of the flight.

Awakened from sleep at 1:30 A.M. during an awkward landing, Mallinson attempts to disarm Talu, who is unconscious. The group examines the pilot; Conway deduces that the extreme altitude has precipitated a heart attack. Miss Brinklow revives Talu with brandy. Uncertainty and bitter winds create a miserable night; the survivors wonder how they will stay alive in such intolerable conditions. Conway calculates that Talu has landed near Kuen-Lun in the western Himalayas. The next morning the pilot dies, leaving the foursome with no food, a damaged plane, no fuel, and scant information about a nearby lamasery called Shangri-La.

James Hilton's 1933 novel, *Lost Horizon,* was filmed in 1937 with Frank Capra directing. Hugh Conway, played by Ronald Colman, leads a class as a Shangri-La resident, played by Jane Wyatt, looks on.

Hilton builds character studies as the passengers quibble over whether to take Talu's advice or return on foot to Peshar. A party of 12 strangers clothed in yak skin and escorting a hooded sedan chair arrives from the monastery. A blue-robed Chinese man named Chang, who leads the group and speaks English, provides wine and delectable tropical mangoes from a hamper. At Conway's direction, the passengers rope themselves together and, while Chang sleeps in his chair, ascend the icy slope to Shangri-La, a refreshingly temperate mountain retreat. In the shadow of a 28,000-foot crag called Karakal, or Blue Moon, the foursome delight in modern plumbing, central heating, and a pleasant layout of verdant gardens, courts, and Chinese motifs.

At first, the rescue seems fortuitous. Chang plays host by offering data about the monastery and by indulging hopes for a quick return to India. With polite evasion, Chang avoids a full explanation of how the valley was modernized. Miss Brinklow, who looks forward to a mission post, plans to request ministers from headquarters to convert Shangri-La's residents. Barnard, a folksy Texan, contents himself in the isolated lamasery, but Mallinson, an overly ambitious sort, chafes to return to his job and girlfriend. Conway observes the situation and assumes that the group was expected and possibly sedated on their first night. He conceals his fluency in oriental languages. With tact and courtesy, Chang relieves the group's anxiety by indicating that they may leave at will, although the icy passes threaten their safety. He suggests that they plan their return in two months, when the supply train arrives. The prospect of delay annoys Mallinson, who discerns that the lamasery's maps make no mention of Shangri-La.

Conway, a skilled logician, watches the rites honoring Talu and concludes that the group is under surveillance. Undisturbed by Chang's partial answers about why his party set out to meet the plane, Conway admires Lo-Tsen, a young Manchu harpsichordist who appears to be the only female initiate at the lamasery, and peruses the well-stocked music collection and library, where newspaper files are inexplicably outdated. As the visitors acclimate themselves to the altitude, they grow less fretful. The temporary peace is disrupted after Mallinson discloses that Barnard is wanted for fraud. Barnard excuses a questionable reputation by blaming his notoriety on miscalculations of the stock market rather than outright deception.

Hilton presses toward the commune's motivation when Conway receives a late-night invitation to join the high lama. In a dim, overwarm chamber, a frail old man introduces himself as Father Perrault, a wandering Capuchin monk who in 1719 stumbled on Shangri-La while seeking an obscure religious sect. At the Valley of the Blue Moon, lamas nursed the weary traveler to health and lengthened his life with *tangatse*, a medicinal berry, which Conway sips in a delicate tea. With the aid of Henschell, an Austrian arrival, the priest had attempted to Christianize the Asians; he evolved a benign autocracy grounded on the principles of moderation and peace. To supply the dwindling population of lamas, Perrault derived a plan to steal the maharajah's plane and escort its passengers to Shangri-La.

To convince Conway that the lamasery's ideals are preferable to the mayhem of the outside world, Perrault describes how longevity will give new converts an opportunity to refine sensual appreciation, create strong friendships, study, and refresh and renew their spirits with solitude and contemplation. Conway, the most likely of the four, is especially suited for the slow savoring of life's goodness because he expended his negative passions during the war. Perrault concludes that life in the outside world hovers on the brink of destruction and that those who blend into Shangri-La's contemplative lifestyle may be the only survivors of future calamity. Conway concurs, and bows to the fragile old priest, then takes his leave to ponder Perrault's offer.

With Chang's assistance, Conway considers a five-year apprenticeship to purge his passions and savor the lengthy initiation, culminating seven decades later in ordination. He subdues a surface attraction to Lo-Tsen and visits regularly with Perrault, who thinks of Conway as a potential successor. Chang divulges the fact that Lo-Tsen was a Chinese princess whose bearers lost their way to Kashgar, where she was to marry a Turkish ruler. In time, her striving to return to the outside world ended and she succumbed to the timeless contemplation expected of an initiate. Gradually, Brinklow and Barnard quell their urge to leave the lamasery. Brinklow studies the Tibetan language; Barnard plots an increase in profits earned by the valley's gold miners, whose ores are traded for books, oriental treasures, and other amenities. Mallinson remains the only passenger who longs to return to his former life. Perrault warns that a single holdout will challenge Conway when he succeeds to the post of high lama.

The night of Perrault's death sets the idyllic story into its inevitable decline. Mallinson reveals to Conway a love for Lo-Tsen. The two plan to escape Shangri-La via porters, who wait five miles beyond the gates to guide them. Conway tells Mallinson the whole story of Father Perrault and the life-extending drug. Mallinson labels the story an unmistakable fiction, and prefers to see the lamasery destroyed. He sets out with the porters, then returns that same evening in fear of the icy pass. By shaking Conway's belief in Perrault's story, Mallinson convinces him to accompany the expedition to Tatsien-Fu, 1,100 miles east on the Tibet-China border. As the trio depart, Conway realizes how deeply Lo-Tsen loves Mallinson.

Hilton's epilogue returns to the framework, composed at Woodford Green in April 1933, with a reunion of the unnamed speaker and Rutherford in Delhi at a viceregal dinner party. Rutherford goes to the speaker's hotel room to tell of his search for Conway over 1,000 miles of Asia—as far as northern China and upper Siam. Rutherford lists the clues he follows: consignment shipments, the pianist Briac, the location of Karakal, and the whereabouts of Barnard. One detail surfaces from his painstaking investigation—a doctor reports that on October 5, 1931, an aged Chinese woman led Conway to the doctor's mission. The frail woman—quite possibly Lo-Tsen herself—died soon afterward. Departing on February 3, Conway evidently resumed his search for Shangri-La. The speaker wonders if Conway will ever relocate the lamasery.

Lost Horizon forms the basis of Frank Capra's 1937 black-and-white film, which earned Academy Award nominations for best picture, Dmitri Tiomkin's musical score, and H. B. Warner's performance. The film also highlighted Ronald Colman for his portrayal of Hugh Conway. In 1979 a remake of the movie cut to the bare plot by excising the philosophical discussions of Conway and Father Perrault. A lesser remake by Ross Hunter in 1972 added color and the music of Hal David and Burt Bacharach, but a skilled cast—Sally Kellerman, Liv Ullman, Peter Finch, George Kennedy, Michael York, Olivia Hussey, John Gielgud, and Charles Boyer—could not rescue an ill-founded attempt to turn *Lost Horizon* into a musical. (*Halliwell's Film Guide* 1989; Hilton 1933; Perkins et al. 1991)

See also asceticism; Buddhism; Conway, Hugh; escapism; Hilton, James; Perrault, Father; Shangri-La; syncretism; vision; women in utopia.

 # LOTUS-EATERS

The Lotus-Eaters are a cult of drug users who figure in a minor episode in Homer's *Odyssey* (eighth century B.C.). In Book IX, lines 83–104, Odysseus narrates to King Alcinous his epic wanderings. He describes an escape from the Ciconians and a rapid nine-day rowing past the island of Cythera to the country of the Lotus-Eaters. On a landfall unidentifiable by the poet's description, the foray brought Odysseus's weary mariners to an inland commune where residents devour a flowering plant. At first Odysseus dispatches a pair of men to reconnoiter. When they and a messenger encounter the Lotus-Eaters, they learn that the Greeks, by eating the "honey-sweet fruit of lotus," sink into a gentle insouciance, the prevailing indolence of the realm. Outsiders who fall under the spell of the lotus fruit lose all drive to return home. Their muscles no longer strive at the oars of Odysseus's fleet, nor do their ambitions impel them toward family, duty to the gods, or patriotic obligation.

Homer puts his hero squarely in charge of an investigation. When Odysseus retrieves his seamen, he forces them to the rowing benches and ignores the men's grief at contact with ships that will separate them from the succulent, Lethean fruit. Historians have connected this minor episode with a North African harbor community, which Ernle Bradford identifies as Jerba, a spot where locals cultivate and consume a soporific poppy or possibly a buckthorn fruit (the sloe or Zizyphus lotus). For Odysseus's men, a casual consumption of narcotics quickly dims yearnings for familiar faces, replacing them with a temporary pleasure in dreamland.

In 1832 Alfred Tennyson, England's poet laureate during the Victorian era, composed a 173-line, eight-stanzaed verse called "The Lotus-Eaters." An obvious embroidery of Homer's small episode, the poem describes the landfall as a place "in which it seemed always afternoon." The ephemeral nature of frail waterfalls and "wavering lights and shadows" entices weary rowers toward a bright beach and three snow-capped mountains, "a land where all things always seem'd the same!" Mild-eyed with melancholy, the inhabitants extend branches of lotus, heavy with flowers and fruit. The innocent partakers taste at their peril. Devoid of interest in duty, the Lotus-Eaters resemble the speaker's drowsy complacency in Robert Louis Stevenson's "Land of Nod": They hearken to the throb of their own hearts, sit on the sand, and drift in visions "of Fatherland, of child, and wife, and slave." Content with cool moss, ivy, dewy flowers, amaranth, moly, and poppy, they grow heavy-limbed and content with a dreamy tranquillity. In the distance, their eyes perceive purple hills, vines, and emerald-green water; their bodies sink into the sweet lull of warm air, and their ears, tuned inland, barely catch the pound of the surf.

These two passages bear an emotional and psychological resemblance. Like gods, Odysseus's men recline on gently rolling turf and expanses of asphodel. The bright-hued landscape spreads out in valleys and "golden houses, girdled with the gleaming world." To songs of toil, warfare, harvest, and endless malcontent, the Lotus-Eaters, like inhabitants of a golden age, rest in forgetful slumber. Tennyson's depiction replicates the motif of escapism: The Lotus-Eaters take sweet delight in withdrawing from an epic journey fraught with weapons and sea perils, fighting and dying, in a land where the good life is no farther away than overhead branches heavy with narcotic fruit. (Homer 1967; Mack 1962; Severy 1977; Stevenson 1989; Tennyson 1949c)

See also escapism; golden age; Tennyson, Alfred.

LOWRY, LOIS

A prolific writer of young adult fiction in a class with Madeleine L'Engle, Robert Cormier, Cynthia Rylant, Gary Paulsen, and M. E. Kerr, Lois Lowry tackles such esoteric or humanistic topics as survival, treachery, and loyalty to self. The middle child of dentist and former army officer Robert E. Hammersberg and Katharine Landis Hammersberg, Lois Hammersberg Lowry was born March 20, 1937, in Honolulu, Hawaii; she was four when Japanese bombers made their surprise attack on Pearl Harbor. Until the end of the war, she, her older sister Helen, and their mother took refuge at Lowry's grandmother's home near an Amish community in Pennsylvania. Lowry tended toward solitude; the love of a doting grandfather helped her tolerate the separation that splintered the family until their reunion in an American community in Tokyo in 1948. A later tragedy—Helen's death from cancer—struck in 1962 and influenced the creation of characters in *A Summer for Dying*, a novel about a young girl coping with the imminent death of her sister.

Lowry graduated from high school in New York City and attended Brown University from 1954 to 1956, married naval officer Donald Grey Lowry in 1956, and completed a bachelor's degree from the University of Southern Maine in 1972. As a military wife, she reared four children, settled and resettled in five states, then supported her husband while he completed Harvard Law School. The family leaning toward the military recurred during the Persian Gulf War, when Lowry's son flew fighter planes for the Air Force.

Working as a freelance magazine and fiction writer and photographer from 1972 to the present, Lowry has established a steady rhythm of publication, completing 21 books in 17 years along with photos, short fiction, and articles for *Downeast*, *Redbook*, and *Yankee*. She is divorced, lives in Boston, and maintains a summer residence in Sanbornton, New Hampshire. Three of her children are grown; she cares for an invalid daughter who suffers from a crippling nerve disease.

Through the fictional adventures of her tough, mischievous alter ego, Anastasia Krupnik, Lowry tackles the sensitive issues of coming of age. For her compassion and appreciation of young characters she won the Children's Book Committee Child Study Award (1987) and a Newbery Medal (1990) for *Number the Stars*, a suspenseful historical novel about Danish children coping with Hitler's anti-Semitic storm troopers during World War II. The second Newbery, won in 1994 for *The Giver* (1993), brought some dissension among a minority of librarians and teachers who consider its dystopic themes too grim for young readers. Other awards include an ALA Notable Book, American Book Award nomination, *Horn Book* award, Golden Kite award, National Jewish Libraries award, National Jewish Book award, and Sidney Taylor award. (Babbitt 1993; *Children's Literature Review* 1984; Cooper 1993; Corsaro 1994; *Dictionary of Literary Biography* 1987; Lorraine 1994; Lowry 1993; Miller 1990; Ray 1993; Ross 1984; *Something about the Author* 1993; *Something about the Author Autobiography Series* 1986; Veronica 1993; "Writer, Illustrator" 1990)

See also allegory; city planning; classism; disillusion; escapism; futurism; *The Giver*; totalitarianism.

 # LUDOVICO'S TECHNIQUE

An experimental form of brainwashing and behavior alteration, this fictional technique is accomplished by injections administered to hardened felons in Anthony Burgess's *A Clockwork Orange* (1962). In Book 2 Alex, a juvenile delinquent serving time for murder, accepts a treatment intended to rehabilitate his violence-prone personality. Under the influence of a drug, he sits in restraints and watches filmed sessions of torment, humiliation, Nazi atrocities, and other forms of physical menace. With his eyelids locked into an open position, he has no choice but to comply. The application of this theoretical method appears fruitful in Alex's case: His mind recoils at the very thought of violence. He pleads to be spared the horror show, but is dragged to the viewing chamber for his daily dose of brainwashing. The doctors, Brodsky and Branom, declare Alex a success. At the end of Book 2, Brodsky crows:

> He will be your true Christian . . . ready to turn the other cheek, ready to be crucified rather than crucify, sick to the very heart at the thought even of killing a fly.

He ends his outburst with cries of "Reclamation" and "Joy before the Angels of God." In counterpoint, the prison chaplain's ominous bass voice doubts that the method is valid because Alex functions from manipulation of his behavior rather than from any transformation of conscience. In the chaplain's words, "He ceases also to be a creature capable of moral choice." (Aggler 1986; Bloom 1987a; Burgess 1962; Coale 1981; Dix 1971; Mathews 1978; Morris 1971; Stinson 1991)

See also Alex; Burgess, Anthony; *A Clockwork Orange*; conditioning; technology.

 # LYCURGUS

See The Life of Lycurgus.

 # LYDIA, AUNT

Aunt Lydia is a khaki-clad, teacherly termagant in Margaret Atwood's dystopian *Handmaid's Tale* (1985). As the matron of a repressive indoctrination center and coordinator of public executions euphemistically labeled Salvagings, Aunt Lydia brainwashes young women into a handpicked cadre of breeders to provide fertile wombs for Commanders of the Fundamentalist Republic of Gilead. Alert, attentive, and armed with electric cattle prod and whistle, Aunt Lydia surveys the girls in the militaristic Rachel and Leah Reeducation Center, searching out the rebellious, disobedient, conniving, or immodest among the faithful. Mouthing a philosophy of either/or's, Aunt Lydia influences Offred, one of her pupils, through martinet-like repetition of such platitudes as "They also serve who only stand and wait," a citation from a sonnet by John Milton, ironically, a poetic treatise on blindness. The recurrence of these aphorisms and fragments of worldly wisdom testifies to Lydia's skill as an indoctrinator.

A wise but intimidating administrator, Aunt Lydia recognizes the hostile subtleties of the domestic situations into which she thrusts her futuristic breeders. There is inherent jealousy between Wife and Handmaid and a natural suspicion that calls for emotional control, understanding, and obedience on the part of Handmaids. Like her peers, Aunt Sara and Aunt Elizabeth, Aunt Lydia is named for a product—Lydia Pinkham, a vegetable and alcohol elixir that women of the early twentieth century took as a health restorative and tonic for "women's complaints." (In a similar vein, Sara and Elizabeth suggest Sara Lee desserts and Elizabeth Arden cosmetics.)

See also asceticism; Atwood, Margaret; The Commander; Gilead; *The Handmaid's Tale;* Offred; Serena Joy; women in utopia.

 # MALCOLM X

This charismatic, militant orator, black power leader, and philosopher is the focus of Alex Haley's *The Autobiography of Malcolm X* (1965), a detailed memoir of the Nation of Islam from the 1930s until 1965. Malcolm Little, born May 19, 1925, in Omaha, Nebraska, was the son of Louise Little and the Reverend Earl Little, a Baptist minister and follower of Marcus Garvey's idealistic back-to-Africa movement. Malcolm fled the Midwest after his father was murdered by the Black Legionaries, his mother placed in an asylum, and his ten siblings scattered among foster homes. Working the streets, nightclubs, and numbers parlors of Boston and Harlem, he sold drugs and bootleg whiskey and maintained ties with small-time criminals in the black underworld.

While serving a ten-year sentence in Charlestown State Prison for his leadership role in a burglary ring, Malcolm Little gave the impression of religious conversion by corresponding with Islamic leader Elijah Muhammad. The ruse eventually gave way to genuine religious fervor. Malcolm accepted the Nation of Islam's belief that whites are devils who are responsible for the evil in the world. He changed his surname from Little to X to represent the unknown factor in his genealogy since slave times. In 1952, paroled and rehabilitated into a fiery antiwhite proselytizer, he sought to change the outlook of his race by teaching them to look to themselves for betterment.

As early as 1955, Malcolm X heard rumors that Elijah Muhammad was violating principles of the Koran by cohabiting with two of his young secretaries, who claimed that Muhammad fathered their illegitimate children. Malcolm continued to support his mentor, but internalized a disturbing premonition that the Nation of Islam would one day require redirection. In 1964 he traveled to Mecca, Islam's holiest city, and merged his idealism with that of many Muslims from all races and nations. On his return to the United States, Malcolm X—renamed Al-Hajj, Malik Al-Shabazz—set up his own ministry, called Muslim Mosque, Inc. He also founded the Organization of Afro-American Unity and introduced pan-Africanism, an idyllic worldwide emergence of black interests and needs. In 1965 he began accepting white people as potential converts and was petitioning the United Nations to end racial oppression in the United States. Three black males attending his speech at the Audubon Theatre in Harlem executed him at the lectern.

Malcolm X's dream to further Islam in the United States as an antidote to racism remains alive in his books and speeches. Following Alex Haley's completion of Malcolm X's best-selling autobiography, collections of his speeches, interviews, and correspondence found favor with readers who believed that Malcolm X had introduced a worthy utopian dream of a multiracial society made one in purity, resourcefulness, and devotion to the teachings of Allah. These works include *Malcolm X Speeches: February 1965* (1992), *Malcolm X Speaks* (1990), *Malcolm X Talks to Young People* (1991), and *Malcolm X: The Last Speeches* (1989). (Breitman 1965; Breitman 1967; Carson 1991; Crenshaw 1991; Gallen 1992; Goldman 1979; Haley 1965; Kly 1986; Leader 1992; Wolfenstein 1990)

See also asceticism; *The Autobiography of Malcolm X;* Black Muslims; Koran; Sufism; utopia; women in utopia.

Malcolm X

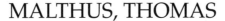

MALTHUS, THOMAS

British economist, demographer, and fellow at Jesus College, Cambridge, Thomas Malthus wrote *An Essay on the Principle of Population as It Affects the Future Improvement of Society, with Remarks on the Speculations of Mr. Godwin, M. Condorcet, and Other Writers* (1798). This slender anti-utopian pamphlet (published anonymously) warned that the population was growing geometrically and food was growing arithmetically, a technical way of announcing that the world's population would soon outdistance the food supply. Malthus envisioned famine stringent enough to trigger hoarding, black marketing, vice, riots, pestilence, misery, war, and planetary catastrophe.

Malthus was born February 14, 1766, in Dorking, Surrey. He grew up in suburban ease and studied at home, concentrating on mathematics and statistics. In 1797 he was ordained, but relinquished his parish in favor of friendship with the intelligentsia—Jean-Jacques Rousseau, the marquis de Condorcet, David Ricardo, and William Godwin. Malthus traveled northern and western Europe gathering material for *An Investigation of the Cause of the Present High Price of Provisions* (1802), an economic study of supply and demand.

An incisive writer, Malthus admonished the utopists and world havens of his era, including the pipe dreams of his father, Daniel Malthus. Central to Malthus's 50,000-word jeremiad are the need for daily food and the passion that provokes copulation. The dichotomy of needs results in a burgeoning population, but no more room on Earth for the growing of crops or housing of families. Malthus concludes:

> The best arguments for the perfectibility of man are drawn from a contemplation of the great progress that he has already made from the savage state. . . . But towards the extinction of the passion between the sexes, no progress whatever has hitherto been made.

Malthus feared that social tinkering only worsens the problem by uplifting the lower classes and encouraging them to produce more offspring.

A favorite source for nineteenth-century utopists, Malthus himself studied Benjamin Franklin and Thomas Paine. He influenced politicians, economists, philosophers, and writers, but his doom-laden prophecy set off a storm of outrage from social radicals and the clergy, who maintained that a benevolent god oversees the nutrition of his followers. In 1807 Malthus enlarged and expounded on his original theory in a 610-page version of his essay on population. With the publication of his fifth revision, he had reached three volumes comprising 1,000 pages.

Malthus lived a simple, uneventful life, marked in his late thirties by marriage, the siring of three children, and a 30-year teaching post at the East India Company's college at Haileybury, where he taught civil servants in three areas: economics, history, and political science. Malthus died December 23, 1834, at Haileybury near Bath, Hertfordshire.

Offshoots of the Malthusian theory include writings by James Bonar, Alfred Wallace, John Maynard Keynes, and Charles Darwin, the brilliant proponent of an evolutionary theory that sprang from a reading of Malthus in 1838. Against Malthus's personal abhorrence grew the birth control movement, labeled neo-Malthusianism or planned parenthood, which was sponsored in the 1920s by Malthusian Leagues. In *Brave New World* (1932), dystopian novelist Aldous Huxley draws on the mechanics of population control with the Malthusian belt, a cartridge belt worn by fertile women to halt conception. (Baugh 1948; Downs 1956; Huxley 1932; Malthus 1990; Peterson 1979; Turner 1986; Winch 1987)

See also Brave New World; futurism; Huxley, Aldous; prophecy.

MANDEVILLE, BERNARD DE

Eighteenth-century French parodist, translator, and pamphleteer, he expanded *The Grumbling Hive: Or, Knave Turn'd Honest* (1705) into *The Fable of the Bees: Or, Private Vices, Public Benefits* (1714), an ambiguous 408-line mock epic verse ostensibly detailing the decline of a hive that takes on human characteristics. Born in Dort, Holland, Mandeville (1670–1733) was educated at Leyden, a Dutch city on the Rhine River. He became a physician, lived in London, and married an Englishwoman. An outgrowth of his practice of medicine was his *Treatise of the Hypochondriack and Hysterick Passions* (1711), which he expanded in 1730.

Mandeville also wrote dialogues, verse, and philosophical musings. His radical tract, *The Virgin Unmasked* (1714), called for state-run brothels and the liberation and education of women. His *Free Thoughts on Religion, the Church and National Happiness* (1720) was a defense of deism; a later work, *An Enquiry into the Origin of Honour* (1732), examined the subject of self-esteem. He earned the respect of radicals of his time, including Benjamin Franklin. Critics, confused by his tongue-in-cheek doggerel or differing with his belief that luxury and affluence benefit mankind, refuted his verse. Alexander Pope made him the butt of satire and public humiliation, as did numerous other contemporaries. To these repudiations Mandeville replied in an apologia, *A Letter to Dion* (1732). However, a substantial number of voices—Daniel Defoe, Dr. Samuel Johnson, Robert Browning, and David Hume—acknowledged his ready wit, pungent satire, and subtlety. (Crane 1932; Drabble 1985; Johnson 1968; Magnusson 1990; Mandeville 1989)

See also The Fable of the Bees; synergy.

MARX, BERNARD

Marx is a central figure and a bit of comic relief in Aldous Huxley's *Brave New World* (1932). With his small, bent frame, depressive moods, and heretical anti-utopian tastes, he symbolizes the dystopian antihero who lacks compensatory virtues and character strength. Marx serves on the Psychology Bureau of a state hatchery, which engineers the intelligence levels of embryos. As the butt of staff jokes, he develops into a malcontent because he blames the state for his deformity, yet continues to live and work under its strictures because of the strength of his conditioning.

In a nation as conformist as Huxley's Brave New World, Marx is unable to conceal the traits and behaviors that set him apart from the masses. By preferring to walk and talk alone rather than enjoy sports or electronic entertainments with crowds, he dismays his date, Lenina Crowne, who considers him "Odd, odd, *odd.* " Her friend Fanny concludes that the rumors about Marx must be true—his blood-surrogate was contaminated with alcohol while his embryo was still in the bottle. Much of his behavior proves Lenina's allegations. He rejects a raspberry sundae laced with the sedative *soma* so he can remain nasty-tempered but sincere: "Not somebody else, however jolly." On a moonlit flight over the English Channel, he stops the helicopter and gazes on the scene below, terrifying Lenina with his desire to be an individual, to feel passion.

To impress his superiors and save himself from probable exile in Iceland, Marx transports Linda and John, a pair of savages from the Zuñi reservation in Malpais near Santa Fe, New Mexico. An opportunistic bent surfaces in his personality, marking him for destruction. Through the attention that John attracts, Marx enjoys temporary notoriety and takes delight and a small degree of prestige from his association with two freaks from the United States. Eventually, John refuses to play the sideshow role, thereby reducing the arrogant Marx to ignominy. For his role in corrupting John, His Fordship Mustapha Mond condemns Marx to exile on an island. Marx's loss of control indicates his downfall: He is carried out and subdued with *soma,* the drug he once spurned. (Bedford 1985; Holmes 1970; Hopper 1952; Huxley 1932; Nance 1988; Negley and Patrick 1952; Watts 1969)

See also Brave New World; conditioning; escapism; eugenics; Huxley, Aldous; hypnopaedia; John; Linda; *soma;* technology; totalitarianism.

MARX, KARL

The nineteenth century's most cogent economic theorist, Marx was a collectivist and the author of *The Communist Manifesto* (1848) and *Das Kapital* (1867). From his dedication to the goal of a homogeneous society, Marx earned the title of father of modern communism. Born in Trier, Germany, on May 5, 1818, Karl Heinrich Marx was the child of liberal, middle-class Jews who posed as Christians to avoid anti-Semitism. His father, an attorney, established a successful practice in Treves and anticipated that his son would join the firm. In Karl's late teens, he rejected law and studied history and philosophy at the University of Bonn, finishing his formal education at the University of Berlin in 1841. During these formative years, he identified with Hegelian religious skepticism. A brilliant, spontaneous polemicist, Marx chose for his doctoral study a contrast of the philosophies of Democritus and Epicurus.

After graduation Marx was unable to locate a teaching position because of his vigorous attacks on religion and monarchy. He reported for the *Rheinische*

Zeitung, a liberal Cologne newspaper; the post ended a year later when the German government halted anti-tsarist commentary. Resituated in Paris with his aristocratic Prussian-English wife, Jenny von Westphalen, Marx associated with like-thinking anarchists, particularly Friedrich Engels, and began evolving revolutionary notions about the rise of the working class. His first formal statement was *The Economic and Philosophical Manuscripts of 1844,* which remains unpublished.

In 1845 Marx emigrated to Brussels and continued formulation of communist doctrine, which appeared in print as *Manifest der Kommunisten,* or *The Communist Manifesto,* in 1848. During a period of instability in Italy, Germany, Czechoslovakia, and Austria, ferment among dissidents seemed to favor Marx's beliefs. He returned to Cologne to edit the *Neue Rheinische Zeitung,* but pressure from conservatives forced him once more to relocate. This time, he, Jenny, and their six children moved first to Paris, then to London, where he lived on a meager income as a freelance correspondent for the *New York Daily Tribune* while publishing more anti-tsarist tracts and, in 1867, his masterpiece, *Das Kapital.* This dismal period caused serious privations, e.g., the sheriff's confiscation of Marx's clothes and linens, the children's toys, even the baby's cradle.

Settled on Dean Street in Soho, Marx worked energetically from 1864 to 1872 as a political organizer of the First International Working Men's Association. During these eight years, his disciples attempted numerous coalitions and compromises before disunity ended their effectiveness. In his final years, Marx fought disillusion, poverty, and declining health from overwork and a series of infections. To maintain some income, he pawned his clothing, valuables, and heirlooms and pushed himself to work nine-hour days at the British Museum, where he examined mammoth stacks of documents on economics, on which he based calculations and predictions. His sons Guido and Edgar and daughter Franziska succumbed to poor nutrition and inadequate heat and medical care. Two years after the death of his loving, supportive wife, Marx died in London in 1883 and was interred in Highgate Cemetery. Only one of his children survived to adulthood. Engels completed Volume II of *Das Kapital* in 1885 and published a third volume in 1894. The last appeared in 1910, 15 years after Engels's death.

A visionary who remained rooted in history and tradition, Marx is associated with the most radical antiestablishment philosophy of the nineteenth century, which influenced such works as Jack London's vivid socialistic novel *The Iron Heel* (1907) and George Orwell's anticommunist beast fable *Animal Farm* (1945). After studying the whole of world history, Marx deduced that humanity progresses via revolutionary stages, each overthrowing the credo of its precedessor until the world arrives at perfection. Choosing as his target the faults of capitalism—particularly children working in mines, rampant tuberculosis among shift workers who contaminated others by sharing beds, and women harnessed to canal barges—Marx encouraged the burdened working class to rise up against the moneyed, privileged plutocracy and form a classless, communistic utopia. In a perfect world, Marx anticipated that humanity would live in peace, work together, and share the rewards without having to pay homage to a workfree and purely ornamental aristocracy.

Critics are divided as to whether Marx should be classified as a utopist, philosopher, or social agitator. Perhaps more than fiction writers, he and Engels pressed for the ideal society, which they foresaw translated from books and manifestos into an uprising of ordinary people against an entrenched landed gentry. However, after Russia shook off its tsarist regime in 1917 with the execution of Nicholas II and his family, the long-anticipated world revolution never materialized; Marx had underestimated the strengths and resilience of capitalism. Thus, the theoretical utopia of Marx, Engels, Jack London, and other hopeful socialist zealots failed to ignite the conflagration that was intended to sweep away the ruling classes and equalize all. (*Atlas of Communism* 1991; Carver 1991; Downs 1956; Lichtheim 1969; Marx 1992; Marx and Engels 1985; Worsley 1982)

See also *Animal Farm*; collectivism; *The Communist Manifesto*; *Das Kapital*; Engels, Friedrich; idealism; *The Iron Heel*; London, Jack; Orwell, George.

MATERIALISM

A form of escapism through purchase, display, and/or hoarding of goods, foodstuffs, services, and entertainments, materialism is a central motif of numerous utopian classics. Depicted both pro and con, it serves as a major theme and motivator in utopian and dystopian literature. Notable examples emphasize the worldliness of some utopists. Without pomp, inherited titles, and court frippery, Baldessar Castiglione could not have composed *The Courtier* (1528), a valued Renaissance handbook to appropriate behavior of the best-dressed, best-equipped, and best-educated of upper-class gentlemen. Likewise, lacking extravagance in dress, food, entertainment, and sport, François Rabelais could not have fleshed out the Abbey of Thélème, a richly profligate, self-indulgent getaway for elite monastics of both sexes in *Gargantua and Pantagruel* (1562). Samuel Johnson's "Rasselas, Prince of Abissinia" (1759), like Oliver Goldsmith's *Asem* (1759), creates enough luxury in Happy Valley and Abissinia to delight any voluptuary; and the tantalizing glimpse of Xanadu in Samuel Taylor Coleridge's "Kubla Khan" (1798) teases the sybarite with a dream scenario, an eastern paradise, and an escape from the ordinary.

In contrast to the excesses that adorn these utopias, consumerism can lie at the heart of dystopian unhappiness. The utopians of W. H. Hudson's sentimental romance *A Crystal Age* (1887) devote themselves to an ascetic form of communal living. The simple costumes, recycled residences, unadorned graves, and preference for hard manual labor, reading, and handicrafts solidify the nonacquisitive nature of the nation of Coradine (a derivative of the Latin *cor*, or heart). The Coradinians strive to avoid a consumer mentality by attending nightly lectures by their white-haired elder, who in Chapter 5 reminds them that they are survivors of a sinful, self-indulgent era. Their forebears died of an epidemic madness that "preyed on their bodies, and worms were bred in their corrupted flesh." He encourages his audience to avoid the vanities that lead to self-delusion.

Like the vices of Coradine's predecessors, a frenzied, sybaritic lifestyle forms the national character in Aldous Huxley's *Brave New World* (1932), where a drug-induced euphoria causes despairing citizens to escape tyranny in feelies (sensual movies), sexual orgies, obstacle golf, and vacations to overseas reservations. The novel's depiction of managed consumerism, which binds lower-class workers on a treadmill of create–consume–need–create more, reaches destructive proportions in the final scenes. John, the savage from the Zuñi reservation of Malpais near Santa Fe, New Mexico, escapes from isolation by reading Shakespeare's plays. In England he watches Linda, his aged mother, submerge herself in sounds, scents, tastes, drugs, and entertainments from a complex of electronic devices, and grieves that she is ebbing toward death in a cloud of meaningless self-anesthetism.

As an antidote to materialism, John attempts to cleanse himself of the amorality and soullessness of the acquisitive, thrill-seeking populace. The opportunistic Primo Mellon photographs John's masochism, indicated by knotted whip and juniper brambles, and sells the multisense cinema to the "feelies." London audiences, titillated by John's self-abuse, cluster tourist-fashion around his retreat in a deserted lighthouse in the Wye Valley. The lure of potential martyrdom exceeds the theatergoers' expectations. The media crush fuels a confrontation between John's urge to free himself of sin and the crowd's voyeurism. John's capitulation to carnality and drugs destroys his tattered spirit, causing him to hang himself. A defeated Christ figure, John represents materialism's corruption of the spirit. As his body swings freely, the symbolism of the lighthouse and its macabre pendulum points out the citizens' profound directionlessness.

Diametrically opposite of the Brave New World's plunge into artificial joys, pastimes, and distractions is the ascetic experience of Henry David Thoreau, author of *Walden* (1854), who deliberately removes himself from a burgeoning urban locale to live out a test of self-knowledge and self-improvement in the wild. Complaining of urban growth in Chapter 6, he grouses:

> We meet at the post-office, and at the sociable, and about the fireside every night; we live thick and are in each other's way, and stumble over one another, and I think that we thus lose some respect for one another.

To circumvent the intrusion of the marketplace on his solitude, he builds a hut and lives free of crowds, purchased food, ornamentation, the high cost of social intercourse, and things in general. During his absence from society he attends no sparkling formal dinners, buys no new cravats, and engages in no temporal conversations about fashion and self-conscious public display of wealth. Undismayed by his rustic, out-of-fashion retreat, in Chapter 18 he lampoons the fops and dilettantes of his day with his ready sense of the absurd: "A goose is a goose still, dress it as you will." In a burst of revolt, he pleads, "Rather than love, than money, than fame, give me truth." The wit, maturity, and self-sufficiency of Thoreau's anticonsumerism bolsters his self-respect by removing obstacles to a communion with nature.

Huxley's defiance of materialism and Thoreau's back-to-nature asceticism and self-abnegation underscore a basic truth of utopianism and literature in general: Utopists draw on their internal values to create a perfect external microcosm. A few model texts laud extravagant goods, jewels, rich foods, lavish entertainment, travel to exotic climes, and the tastes and pleasures that only the wealthy can aspire to or afford. On the whole, however, the utopian genre spurns affluence in favor of asceticism or self-denial, as shown by the actions of these characters:

- Siddhartha, the focus in Hermann Hesse's *Siddhartha* (1951), departs from Brahmin wealth in his family's home to serve humanity as wise philosopher, comforter, and ferryman.

- At the heart of François Rabelais's *Candide* (1759), the main character enjoys the pastoral simplicity of Eldorado, a homely wife and unusual mix of friends and servants in Turkey, and his garden.

- According to J. M. Barrie's play *Peter Pan* (1904), the three Darling children prefer the rough-and-tumble and unpredictability of Neverland over their well-stocked, well-controlled nursery in London.

- Contrasting the hedonism of Harlem street life, the home- and family-centered Muslim code of ethics inherent in Malcolm X's ministry arise from his devotion and study of the Koran, as described in Alex Haley's *The Autobiography of Malcolm X* (1965).

- From near drowning, the main character of Daniel Defoe's *Robinson Crusoe* (1719) accepts contentment with the bare essentials that he retrieves from the wrecked ship, and acquires patience in learning to improvise or do without.

- Michel de Montaigne's naturalistic islanders delight in an unstructured paradise in his fanciful essay "Des Cannibales" (1580).

- The epic hero of Miguel de Cervantes's *Don Quixote* (1615) replaces wealth with fantasy, decking in make-believe finery the simplest of inns, the humblest of servant girls, the least comely of horses.

- Herman Melville's Tommo in *Typee* (1846) recovers from his harrowing journey inland and welcomes a wholesome indolence in a swaying Polynesian hammock far from the money-mad, troubled cities of New England.

- Emmanuel Goldstein's book, in Book 2, Chapter 9 of George Orwell's *1984* (1949), explains why wars destroy "materials which might otherwise be used to make the masses too comfortable, and hence, in the long run, too intelligent."

- Lao Tzu's *Tao Te Ching* (third century B.C.) advises the seeker of contentment to free the body from sensuality and attain oneness with the sublime.

Against the consumerism that clogs cities with buyers and sellers, the mind set free of incessant malcontent and desire for more wealth, more splendor, more embellishment recognizes utopia in inner strength, good health, satisfying work, family, friendship, and the intrinsic beauties of nature. As exemplified by the experiences of Fiver and Hazel, protagonists of Richard Adams's beast fable *Watership Down* (1972), in their flight from a doomed warren, rabbits need little more than a safe place to sleep, green grass and lush clover, fresh water, and the camaraderie of like-minded companions. For courage, Hazel and his commune turn to the rabbit god and familiar myths, which help to coalesce the remaining animals into a contented society. (Adams 1972; Barrie 1981; Castiglione 1976; Cervantes 1957; Coleridge 1948; Goldsmith 1992; Haley 1965; Hudson 1917; Huxley 1932; Johnson 1982; Montaigne 1893b; Rabelais 1955; Thoreau 1965)

See also Adams, Richard; asceticism; *Asem, an Eastern Tale; The Autobiography of Malcolm X*; Barrie, Sir James Matthew; *Brave New World;* Candide; Castiglione, Baldessar; Cervantes Saavedra, Miguel de; *The Courtier; A Crystal Age;* Defoe, Daniel; "Des Cannibales"; Don Quixote; Eldorado; escapism; *Gargantua and Pantagruel;* Hazel; Hudson, W. H.; Huxley, Aldous; John; Johnson, Dr. Samuel; Koran; "Kubla Khan"; Lao Tzu; Linda; Malcolm X; Montaigne, Michel Eyquem de; naturalism; Neverland; pastoral; Peter Pan; Rabelais, François; "Rasselas, Prince of Abissinia"; *Robinson Crusoe; soma;* Tao; *Tao Te Ching;* Thoreau, Henry David; *Walden; Watership Down.*

 # MELVILLE, HERMAN

One of America's most revered novelists, Melville produced three stirring sea tales with utopian slants—*Typee* (1846), *Omoo* (1847), and, to a lesser degree, *Moby Dick* (1851). A standoffish man with dark moods and soul-plaguing doubts, Herman Melville was one of literature's most underappreciated geniuses. He was born in New York City on August 1, 1819, the third of eight children of Maria Gansevoort and Allan Melvill (spelled without the second e). Of illustrious pre–Revolutionary War stock, Melville nevertheless suffered from his father's emotional deficiencies, which broke the family and left Melville's mother to support her clan by moving them in with her parents. After graduating from Albany Classical School, Melville studied engineering and surveying at Lansingburgh Academy and worked briefly in banking and sales. His abysmal choice of careers reduced him to additional unappealing attempts at farming and teaching. By 1839 he realized that he was unsuited for the nine-to-five world and took a post as cabin boy on the *St. Lawrence*, which was bound for Liverpool.

Melville returned to New York with a deeper appreciation of British, American, and French classics, which he read at sea; he taught in Pittsfield and East Albany before returning to sea aboard the whaler *Acushnet* in 1841. In July 1842 Melville and fellow crewman Toby Greene jumped ship in Nukuheva, an island in the Marquesas, which impressed Melville as a true heaven on Earth—

Herman Melville

a gentle, hospitable civilization living in harmony with nature. The truants enjoyed an Edenic simplicity in sexual relationships, rested and conversed under rustling palms, and dined on fresh sea catches and fruit. Melville concluded that the mechanistic progress of New England bore little likeness to real happiness, free from factories and long workweeks, religious tyranny, and social hypocrisy.

Utopia faded for Melville after the men found evidence of feasting on human flesh; the idyll turned into a frightful confinement among the Typees, whom Melville and Greene discovered to be cannibals. After a few months of idleness, Melville fled aboard an Australian whaler, which mirrored the untenable conditions he had suffered aboard the *Acushnet*. Mutinous and risking further embroilment in capital offenses, he escaped to Papeete, Tahiti, in 1842. Working sporadically as a day laborer, he again fell in love with the gentle breezes and unhurried lifestyle of Polynesia.

After bumping about Pacific ports, in 1844 Melville returned to Boston and worked at odd jobs. Within two years he had captured his picaresque adventures in *Typee: A Peep at Polynesian Life,* a semiautobiographical dystopian novel that earned little income but introduced to the reading public the Marquesas Islands and a lifestyle that contrasted the Yankee diligence, acquisitiveness, and religious fervor of New England. The next year, he married Lizzie Shaw, settled in New York City, and completed *Omoo,* which replicated his success with descriptions of Tahiti. More travel romances entered his canon—*Redburn* (1848), *Mardi* (1849), and *White-Jacket* (1850).

By the mid-1800s Melville's family had grown to two sons and two daughters, and he was forced to seek a larger house, located outside Pittsfield, Massachusetts. His career took an unforeseen turn after he altered his focus from lighthearted sea tales to satire. Through his friendship with mentor Nathaniel Hawthorne, in 1851 he found the courage to defy public tastes and write his masterpiece, *Moby Dick.* The task depleted him physically and emotionally as a result of the research required for a thorough account of whaling and a daunting analysis of the sin-blighted soul of Captain Ahab. Melville's father-in-law believed that such fierce monomania would kill Melville or, at the least, leave him hopelessly deranged.

The publication of the savage, compelling *Moby Dick* provided world literature with a troubling glimpse of a human attempt to escape culpability, subdue nature, and profit from its treasures. In Chapter 111, Melville allows his sea romance a full range of romanticism:

> The same waves wash the moles of the new-built California towns, but yesterday planted by the recentest race of men and lave the faded but still gorgeous skirts of Asiatic lands, older than Abraham; while all between float milkyways of coral isles, and low-lying, endless, unknown Archipelagoes, and impenetrable Japans. Thus this mysterious divine Pacific zones the world's whole bulk about; makes all coasts one bay to it; seems the tide-beating heart of earth. Lifted by those eternal swells, you needs must own the seductive god, bowing your head to Pan.

Popular and critical rejection of such lyrical and philosophic probings led to Melville's physical decline. Although he published *Pierre* (1852), *Israel Potter* (1855), *The Piazza Tales* (1856), *The Confidence Man* (1857), and *Battle Pieces* (1866), he formed no new readership. Frustrated and broke, he collapsed and sought a rest cure. After touring Europe, the Middle East, and northern Africa, he returned to the sea with his brother Tom on a voyage to California.

The Civil War years brought added hardship. Melville found no work suited to his talents or needs, which demanded the support of his family as well as of his mother and sisters. The Navy rejected him for military service because of chronic rheumatism, sciatica, and diminished eyesight. The only job that appealed to him was deputy inspector of customs, a paltry assignment that filled his days for 20 years. In 1866 and 1869, the deaths of his sons—Malcolm by suicide and Stanwyx from tuberculosis—left Melville on the raw edge of despair. At age 67, he retired to seclusion and produced his most compellingly symbolic sea story, *Billy Budd*, a moralistic novella that he completed five months before his death from heart disease on September 28, 1891. Devoid of the romanticism of his early works, the manuscript delves into the nature of goodness and inherent evil and the capricious workings of justice. The book was neglected for 33 years, then published along with his correspondence, some sketches, and his journals. (Allen 1971; Bloom 1986d; Boorstin 1992; Bryant 1986; Hillway 1979; Melville 1961; Melville 1964; Melville 1968; Sealts 1982; Wolff 1987)

See also disillusion; escapism; naturalism; *Omoo*; technology; *Typee*.

 # MEMOIRS OF A SURVIVOR

This visionary dystopian fable was written in 1974 by Doris Lessing, one of Africa's most successful nonnative authors. A borderline success, *Memoirs of a Survivor* produced mixed reviews—from raves for its prophetic relevance to pans for its phantasmagoric dreamscapes and for inept character motivation. Like Margaret Atwood's *The Handmaid's Tale* (1985) and Anthony Burgess's *A Clockwork Orange* (1962), Lessing's semiautobiographical novel echoes violent action from a perusal of ominous events culled from the daily news.

Opening in a ground-floor, flea-ridden room, the plot depicts the observations of an unnamed female speaker who smokes, looks on the filth of a crumbling city, and chronicles the decay on the streets. For months, gangs rove the street, scribbling graffiti and leaving urine and excrement as their nonverbal comment on social conditions. The speaker becomes obsessed with her view of civil deterioration. She accepts 14-year-old Emily Mary Cartright as a foster child, who is thrust on her by "them," the faceless, nameless bureaucracy that carries on a semblance of control. The rented first-floor residence is ample for them both, but the fascist atmosphere reported by the media unnerves the speaker and pushes her toward resettling in less menacing surroundings. She attempts to supply Emily with clothing and allows the child to keep a cat named

Hugo. On occasion, the speaker makes a two- or three-day food-shopping trip to outlying areas and leaves Emily unattended.

Lessing uses materialism as a window on Emily's yearnings and emotional needs. As gangs loll on the streets, Emily turns to an aged sewing machine and creates outlandish costumes for herself. She gathers the courage to join the children outside the window. The speaker turns to her writing as an escape from the anarchy in the streets, which seems to reach in and grasp Emily body and soul. The speaker envisions a brief visit from Emily's parents with their infant son. Emily clings tightly to Hugo, the cat, but is unable to avoid her parents' visits. Her father tortures her with sadistic episodes of tickling. After Emily puts on her pajamas, the father follows her to bed; Emily pleads for her mother to stay and cuddle her, but the mother seems too bound up in her young son to defend Emily from pedophilia.

On the streets, Emily forms a relationship with Gerald, an older man who protects homeless children and forages to feed them. The speaker hears rumors about Gerald's seduction of young girls and worries that he will impregnate Emily. A little girl named June visits the apartment. The speaker is aware that pockets of these wayside waifs litter the city with their outdoor habitations; to maintain themselves, they steal food and cadge baths from private dwellings. The city bureaucracy ignores the privations of the homeless. The speaker considers herself a member of the conspiracy to overlook the poor.

Lessing motivates the aimless speaker by bringing crime from the outside into the apartment. On her return from scavenging, the speaker finds electrical appliances missing and Emily supervising her tribe in hauling them off. Because the speaker observes the theft, Emily directs her accomplices to return what they took. The speaker comments on the uselessness of electrical gadgets with no power to supply them. She helps Emily and the other gang members collect appliances from the whole building to sell.

The speaker digresses with a description of the Ryans, June's drunken parents—one Irish, one Polish—who are Catholics and the parents of 11 children. The sorry state of the Ryans' indiscriminate breeding and lackadaisical parenthood leads to pregnancy for their second oldest girl and subsequent dependence on the public dole. The speaker terms their insouciance "the way of the Ryans," a threat to civic responsibility. Accompanied by Emily, the speaker tours the chaos wrought by unmanaged and unmanageable street urchins. Emily grows jealous of Gerald's interest in another girl. Turning to her work, the speaker stops to define "it," the degeneration of civilization taking place outside her quarters. Growing out of the chaos is June's introduction to sex and the decline of her health. By the end of summer, more people join the roving street bands, and June disappears among them. Neighborhood householders grow more wary of the snarling, underfed population outside. In time, hunger drives the children into savagery and raids on residences.

Lessing causes the speaker to view danger and impending social collapse from Emily's point of view. After she takes part in the roiling fray, Emily is injured. She grows savage toward Hugo, who cries at her defection to gang behavior. She disappears. The speaker locates her in Gerald's lair and stares at her costume, sewn from a ragtag collection of fur. The two return to their rooms and discover Janet, Emily's former acquaintance, and her parents at the door. Luggage in hand, the trio attempts an unofficial flight from the city's anarchy to the north. The speaker tries to maintain her residence, but the building itself is moribund. The speaker purchases two buckets of water from a hard-eyed child vendor. Before she can return with them, a savage bully forces her to hand over half of her haul. She quickly safeguards the other bucket behind locked doors.

In view of the worsening circumstances, the speaker ponders taking Emily and the cat to a better locale, but can think of nowhere to go. The hungry street gangs menace Hugo and attack Gerald, who is too disheartened to fight back. Emily brings him into the apartment for first aid. He is aghast that his attackers are three- and four-year-old children, and declares that the little ones can be neither saved nor blamed. He follows Emily and Hugo into the forest as the walls of the apartment dissolve.

Analysts of Lessing's dismal, out-of-focus dystopia are hard-pressed for words to label Lessing's twist on fiction. The journalesque atmosphere and tone of *Memoirs of a Survivor* echo the dystopic hell of Anthony Burgess's *A Clockwork Orange*, a blend of reportage and surreal dreamscapes with the stark reality of roving, animalistic street bands. The speaker's bond with Emily, her unofficial charge, and with Emily's paramour, the Christlike Gerald, extends to the family cat, Hugo. As the situation worsens outside the speaker's apartment, Hugo becomes a symbol of civilization, a warm and caressable remembrance of a time when society could afford to keep a domestic pet. By the story's end, the departure of the loose-knit menage—bolstered by the word "survivor" from the title—seems the only escape from a random tyranny of child criminals. Their vagrancy, which has grown into murderous vandalism, leaves little hope that society will reestablish its balance and again attain the upright stance of Homo sapiens. (Bloom 1986; Dembo and Pratt 1993; Fishburn 1985; Knapp 1984; Lessing 1988; Myles 1990)

See also Atwood, Margaret; bestiality; Burgess, Anthony; *A Clockwork Orange*; *The Handmaid's Tale*; Lessing, Doris; women in utopia.

MERRIDEW, JACK

Jack is a bullying, power-mad leader of choirboys in William Golding's dystopic *Lord of the Flies* (1954), the literary foil to Ralph the peacemaker and Piggy the law-keeper. In a setting filled with the wholesomeness and abundance of the tropics, Jack stirs barbaric longings in a heretofore innocent group of boys. Intrigued by the promise of contact with the primeval forces of nature, they follow him into the jungle to kill pigs to supply meat to the settlement. The symbolic colors of Jack's red hair and black cloak suggest a Mephistophelian evil—a joy in intimidation, control of underlings, and gratuitous slaughter. Jack paints lines on his cheeks and surrounds himself with willing sycophants, whom he manipulates into a power struggle with Ralph against self-discipline, order, and logic.

Jack's satanic nature spouts from his mouth in brief infantile demands—"Give me a drink," "All sit down," "Come on! Dance!" and "Back! Back to the fort!" The depth of his depravity highlights Chapter 9 when he impels the boys to strike blindly at a sacrificial being, whom Golding conceals from full view as the boys obey their master. Amid cries of "Kill the beast! Cut his throat! Spill his blood! Do him in!" Jack blends into the clot of spear-wielding children who strike, bite, and tear the flesh of Simon, the visionary child who is the gentlest and most vulnerable of the island castaways. By the end of Jack's reign over the island, he recedes into his former self, "a little boy who wore the remains of an extraordinary black cap on his red hair." The damning evidence of his cruelties, Piggy's mangled spectacles, hangs from his waist in token of a fragile vision that failed. (Baker 1988; Carey 1987; Gindin 1988; Golding 1954; Johnston 1980; Kinkead-Weeks and Gregor 1984; Subbarao 1987)

See also allegory; bestiality; dystopia; Eden; Golding, William; *Lord of the Flies*; Piggy; Ralph.

A MIDSUMMER NIGHT'S DREAM

An ethereal, frolicsome Elizabethan court masque, William Shakespeare wrote this play between 1595 and 1596 to honor a royal wedding. This romantic comedy is composed of a tyrannical father, humorous mismatches, and enchantments suitable to madcap midsummer zaniness, set partly in a pastoral haven vaguely located "outside Athens." Woven into a fantasy about fairyland and its interplay with the human world is the mythic locale, introduced in Act II, Scene i. Oberon describes an outdoor scene in lines 254–257:

> I know a bank where the wild thyme blows,
> Where oxlips and the nodding violet grows,
> Quite over-canopied with luscious woodbine,
> With sweet musk-roses, and with eglantine.

The setting is so restful and dreamlike that Oberon's wife Titania, Queen of the Fairies, goes there to sleep, "lulled in these flowers with dances and delight." Still, for all her powers, nature lacks the full scope of utopian qualities and cannot protect Titania from a scheming, mean-spirited husband.

Like Titania, the dramatis personae of *A Midsummer Night's Dream*, both real and supernatural, come to the enchanted moonlit woods in search of rest, privacy, and respite from officious dicta, arguments, and obstacles to youthful amour. In Act II, Scene ii, lines 1–8, Titania speaks the characters' common need for peace as she settles for the night:

> Come, now a roundel and a fairy song;
> Then, for the third part of a minute, hence—
> Some to kill cankers in the musk-rose buds,
> Some war with reremice for their leathern wings,
> To make my small elves coats, and some keep back
> The clamorous owl, that nightly hoots and wonders

At our quaint spirits. Sing me now asleep.
Then to your offices, and let me rest.

Titania's edginess echoes that of the rest of the cast, who are beset by squabblings, jealousy, and confusion. They share a mutual purpose—hope for a resolution and release from a tedious jangle of human relationships. Unfortunately, nature is not an arbitrary truce zone immune to Oberon's trickery. In Titania's bower grows a magical plant that Oberon uses to bewitch and muddle the senses of his victims. Thus, like tossing a stone into a millpond, he spoils the natural world by setting off widening concentric circles of pettiness and vengeance.

As Shakespeare indicates, utopia's fulfillment depends on the absence of baseness and manipulation. In the words of Bottom, one of the comic characters, "Man is but an ass, if he go about to expound this dream" (IV, i, 212–213). When people invade the forest, strange and unforeseen events occur, hearts are broken, misunderstandings arise, and long-lived friendships teeter on a tenuous rim. The ambiguous setting, although embellished on the surface with flowers and benevolent rays of moonlight, accommodates both reconciliation and lurking evil—a potentially disruptive nightmare to two pairs of parted human lovers and to Oberon, an anthropomorphic deity who wars with his wife over a minor matter—the possession of an Indian servant boy, the child of a former handmaiden who served Titania.

Blending utopia and dystopia, Shakespeare replicates Eden, a self-contained microcosm that survives human whims and caprice. Oblivious to the characters' tiffs and spats, the enchanted wood maintains its neutrality and untamed loveliness. According to the demands of comedy, the players work out their farcical differences without nature's intervention by applying wit and compromise, and conclude hostilities. Through the magical workings of Puck, the mischievous fairy servant of Oberon, "Jack shall have Jill:/Naught shall go ill" (III, ii, 485–486). An echo of the "happily ever after" plot in Shakespeare's *As You Like It,* idealized matrimony settles the conflict; the characters restore normality and return to Athens. (Boyce 1990; Johnson 1968; Papp and Kirkland 1988; Sandler 1986; Shakespeare 1958; Shakespeare 1959)

See also As You Like It; Eden; Shakespeare, William.

 # MILTON, JOHN

Milton is England's Christian epic poet, one of the seventeenth century's boldest religious polemicists, and a major writer of world literature, including the profound *Paradise Lost* (1667) and its companion piece, *Paradise Regained* (1671). Born the middle of three children on December 9, 1608, to a virtuous Puritan mother, Sarah Jeffery, and her husband, a well-to-do law scribe and musician also named John Milton, he demonstrated a prodigious talent for the humanities by reading incessantly and composing verse in Italian, Latin, and English. His parents encouraged his literary skills by hiring the classical tutor Thomas Young and by sending Milton to St. Paul's School. A fastidious scholar proficient in Hebrew, Greek, and Latin and thoroughly acquainted with the Roman poets, Milton entered Christ's Church, Cambridge, at the age of 16. He finished an M.A. by June 1632, when he published his salute to Shakespeare, which served as a preface to the Second Folio.

Milton was deeply troubled by ecclesiastical tyranny and corruption; at first, tempted by both literary and religious leanings, he withdrew to Horton, the Miltons' family estate in Buckinghamshire outside Windsor, where he remained for six years in serious contemplation of his future. At length he abandoned his interest in the ministry and consecrated himself to humanistic scholarship. On trips to London to search for books, his choices demonstrated a serious intent toward balancing his education with historical, theological, mathematical, musical, and literary works.

After extending his reading list and imitating the classics in an original masque, *Comus* (1634), and *Lycidas* (1638), an elegy on the death of classmate Edward King, Milton traveled Europe for 15 months, during which time he visited Galileo and Barberini. At the height of political unrest in England, Milton returned to London to found a boys' school. His role in theological controversy spurred extensive pamphleteering—in particular, the polemical tract *Of Reformation Touching Church-Discipline in England* (1641), a prelude to his antipapist writings. In 1642 Milton married 17-year-old Mary Powell, but within months their union proved unsatisfactory, perhaps because of the intense seriousness of Milton's scholarly and political pursuits and his teenage bride's boredom with a tedious, middle-aged pedant. Following his separation from Mary, he published *The Doctrine and Discipline of Divorce* (1643), a subject in which he had a personal interest. The couple reunited and produced two daughters, Anne and Mary.

One of Milton's most eloquent libertarian orations is the *Areopagitica* (1644), a scholarly, ethical plea for freedom from censorship. The treatise and a subsequent tract, *Of the Tenure of Kings and Magistrates* (1649), grew out of rumblings that produced England's civil war, the rise of a contentious Puritan junta, and the beheading of Charles I. The success of Milton's argument for revolution brought him an appointment, Latin secretary to the Council of State. During this unstable period, he produced some of his most sensitive and least appreciated verse—"On the Morning of Christ's Nativity" and the paired tone poems "L'Allegro" and "Il Penseroso." Personal tragedies—the death of his infant son John and of his wife as a result of the birth of his daughter Deborah—left him with the custody of three girls and an increasing visual handicap. By this point, Milton faced a debilitating dilemma: a sincere religious calling to compose a Christian epic in English and the failure of his eyesight, which led inexorably to blindness by 1652. His most poignant statement of this test of faith permeates his famous sonnet, which begins: "When I consider how my light is spent . . . ."

Free from despair, Milton revived his ambitions after marriage to Katherine Woodcock in 1656. A cruel fate crushed his resurgence of hope: Katherine died two years later while giving birth to Milton's fourth daughter, who also died. He allied himself with professional office assistants, who served as researchers, scribes, and editors. In 1660, with the restoration of the monarchy and the

John Milton, his eyesight failing, is portrayed in Mikhaly Munkacy's painting *Blind Milton Dictating* Paradise Lost *to His Daughters.*

crowning of Charles II, he was briefly jailed in retaliation for his support of Oliver Cromwell, who had ruled England for a decade during the Commonwealth. This shift in England's power struggle ended Milton's public service.

Again buoyed by the will to utilize his considerable talent, in 1663 Milton married Elizabeth Minshull, the right woman for his needs. In domestic peace at last, he discarded plans for a lengthy work on King Arthur, engaged himself in scriptural study, and completed *Paradise Lost*, England's literary epic, which he wrote in blank verse. For ten years—during plague, the Great London Fire, and personal losses—Milton maintained his concentration and delineated the struggle between Satan and God and the loss of Eden, a verdant earthly paradise, by its mythic denizens, Adam and Eve. Joseph Addison proclaimed the work England's noblest expression of genius. Completed by the sequel *Paradise Regained,* which glorifies Christ as savior of the sinful world, Milton's work achieved a degree of literary sublimity surpassing Homer's epics. In his final years, the poet turned to the Old Testament love story, *Samson Agonistes* (1671), which he produced as tragedy.

Disillusioned by politics, plagued by gout, and restricted by blindness, Milton abandoned writing and, in his remaining three years, took refuge in oral readings, music, meditation, and gardening. He suffered family squabbles between his wife and her two stepdaughters, whom he threatened to disinherit. He became distraught with the girls' anti-intellectualism and Anne's speech impediment, and apprenticed them to a lace-maker; the girls retaliated with indiscreet, vitriolic attacks. Resettled east of London near Bunhill Fields, he enjoyed the devotion of his youngest daughter Deborah, the friendship of poet and collaborator Andrew Marvell, and the equanimity of his third wife. He died, possibly of systemic poisoning, on November 8, 1674. (Boorstin 1992; Enroth 1970; Harrison et al. 1967; Hornstein et al. 1973; Martz 1967; Milton 1957a; Parker 1958)

See also Adam; Eden; Eve; Genesis; heaven; *Paradise Lost; Paradise Regained;* Satan; women in utopia.

MOND, MUSTAPHA

Mond is a brilliant Alpha-Plus intellectual and the World Controller for Western Europe in Aldous Huxley's *Brave New World* (1932). His steely eyed swarthiness hints at sinister powers, and he spouts the party line on history while concealing forbidden books in his safe. The insidious duplicity of his control of law-breakers suggests the rot that corrupts the foundations of the Brave New World. To vivify an impromptu lecture downgrading homes and nuclear families, Mond overplays his hand by detailing more of the odor, heat, and "suffocating intimacies" than the audience is prepared to hear. Shifting his cadence, he is equally at home with hypnopaedic slogans, e.g., "Every one belongs to every one else."

Appreciating utopia's need for social stability, Mond reveals his callousness during an interrogation of John, Bernard Marx, and Helmholtz Watson, who are arrested during a riot of hospital workers and taken to the Controller's study. In the guise of host, in Chapter 16 Mond extols the virtues of utopia in a lengthy, slangy peroration:

> People are happy; they get what they want, and they never want what they can't get. They're well off; they're safe; they're never ill, they're not afraid of death; they're blissfully ignorant of passion and old age; they're plagued with no mothers or fathers; they've got no wives, or children, or lovers to feel strongly about; they're so conditioned that they practically can't help behaving as they ought to behave.

By restricting society, art, and science, by withdrawing God, and by substituting *soma* in place of true emotion, utopia stabilizes and prospers. Mond concludes in Chapter 17: "God isn't compatible with machinery and scientific medicine and universal happiness. You must make your choice."

To questions about his experiments with physics, this shameless opportunist acknowledges that he at one time flirted with such dangerous activities as cooking and scientific experimentation, but gave them up to avoid being exiled on an island. To the savage's inquiries about Shakespeare, Mond demonstrates a better-than-average understanding of literature and a belief in God, which utopians are forbidden. Yet, Mond is willing to pay the price and deny such spiritual pursuits as reading and worship if his abstinence will allow the nine other controllers to perpetuate their despotic stranglehold. (Bedford 1985; Holmes 1970; Huxley 1932; Nance 1988; Negley and Patrick 1952; Watts 1969)

MONTAG, GUY

Hero of Ray Bradbury's *Fahrenheit 451* (1953), Montag was at one time a gung ho fire fighter in a dystopian society that perverts the original purpose of a fire department by burning books along with the people who read them. At first he emulates the cynicism of the state and of his employer, Chief Beatty. Montag mollifies his inane wife Mildred by spending a third of his annual salary to install wall-to-wall telescreens. However, his surface professionalism proves to be a sham after a single event—one old woman striking a kitchen match—impels him to seek a mentor to enlighten his ignorance. Montag allies with Faber, a former professor he once met in the park. The literary foil of Montag's chief, Faber lives on society's fringe and supports the efforts of radicals who keep literature alive. To help Montag understand the importance of literature, Faber relates the myth of Antaeus, the giant who survived attack only so long as he remained in contact with the earth.

At the fire station, his ear equipped with Faber's two-way listening device, Montag chooses to face off against Beatty, lamely matching wits with a man

Guy Montag, right, played by Oskar Werner, torches books, which ignite at a temperature of 451 Fahrenheit, in the 1967 film version of Ray Bradbury's *Fahrenheit 451*.

who has read widely but has disregarded the humanistic themes of classic literature. Clinging to orthodoxy by a fragile tether, Montag snaps after Beatty attacks. The breaking point for Montag is the threat to the hapless Faber, whose only crime is a love and respect for books. Beatty's eyes widen as Guy flips the safety on a station-issue flamethrower and sets him afire.

Impassioned by Faber's trust in books as redeemers of society's repressed spirit, Montag implicates a fireman in sedition by hiding books in his home and sounding the alarm. A blend of idealist and activist, Montag accepts the challenge to build a more tolerant world by joining anarchists who become great books: They memorize them to keep them alive. He baptizes himself in the river that ends his relationship with the corruption of twenty-fourth-century Los Angeles. Like Christ emerging from the waters of the Jordan River, Montag arises to new life in the company of Granger and his band of rebels. (Bradbury 1953; Bradbury 1975; Bradbury 1990a; Breit 1956; Clareson 1976; Indick 1989; Johnson 1978; Knight 1967; Mogen 1986; Slusser 1977a)

See also baptism; Beatty, Captain; Bradbury, Ray; escapism; *Fahrenheit 451*; futurism; technology; "There Will Come Soft Rains"; women in utopia.

MONTAIGNE, MICHEL EYQUEM DE

Renaissance writer and the father of the modern essay, Montaigne wrote "Des Cannibales" (1580), which draws on both Platonic utopianism and the lure of the New World's Eldorado, peopled by noble savages. Montaigne was born February 28, 1533, at Castellan outside Périgord east of Bordeaux, France. He was the grandson of Ramon Eyquem and the eldest son of Antoinette de Lopez, a Spanish Jew, and Pierre Eyquem, a wealthy, somewhat pretentious trader and mayor of Périgord. Montaigne was the center of his family's attention, pampered in luxury. Only Latin was spoken in the household; he learned French as a second language and received home tutoring in the classics and German before studying law at the College of Guienne in Bordeaux and Toulouse. At age 24 he devoted himself to civil service as magistrate, courtier, adviser, and ambassador, but hated the hypocrisies and double-dealing of church, court, and marketplace.

During his years in the army of Francis I, Montaigne fought at the siege of Thonville in 1558. The next year, he met magistrate Étienne de la Boétie, his dearest friend and probable lover until Boétie's death in 1563. The loss ended a prolific correspondence and pleasurable conversation; to compensate, in 1572 Montaigne began writing his *Essais* and assuaged his grief by finding a suitable bride. At age 38 he and his wife, Françoise de la Chassaigne, left the political wranglings at court and the religious entanglements that precipitated the Saint Bartholomew's Massacre, and retired to the family château.

In seclusion, Montaigne studied literature, his first love, and slowly internalized the wisdom of Seneca, Cicero, Marcus Aurelius's *Meditations,* and Plutarch's *Lives* and *Moralia* (first century A.D.). From Seneca he learned that the first humans and their immediate descendents enjoyed a golden age by following nature and searching for a simplified form of goodness. Cicero's ora-

Europeans such as Montaigne idealized the inhabitants of the New World, thinking of them as "noble savages." Artist George Catlin published renderings of American Indians three centuries after Montaigne's idea of primitive naturalism in the New World.

tions taught him the value of structured logic. From Marcus Aurelius, Montaigne acquired the habit of anchoring essays to aphorism just as ministers tie exegesis to scripture. And from Plutarch he developed a keen compassion for human talents, foibles, and shortcomings.

A skeptic as well as a naturalist, Montaigne traveled Europe, read the thinkers of his day, and plunged into spirited dialectic, both in conversation and by letter to his many correspondents, particularly the lively Marie de Gournay, his one-woman fan club and possible mistress. From his eclectic browsing and vigorous study of logic and form grew a literary genre, the essay. His first two collections, *Essais* (1580), preceded a more polished third edition eight years later. His motto, *Que scay je* [That I may know], epitomized a questing, introspective intellect that perused, studied, weighed, and examined thoughts of all types. Montaigne died of kidney failure and serious throat infection on September 13, 1592, at his estate. Three years later, his widow and Gournay, bound by a mutual love for the deceased essayist, oversaw the fourth edition of his works.

A work both thought-provoking and titillating to readers of Montaigne is "Des Cannibales," a comparison of sixteenth-century Europe to the aborigines of South America, whom he admired for *"leur naiveté originelle."* In Montaigne's day, the New World Indian epitomized an era of primitive naturalism. Montaigne's essays show his admiration for the vigor and fullness of Indian civilization and its lack of contact with European decadence, cynicism, and worldliness. His expressive literary praise of the New World inspired William Shakespeare to apply equivalent idealism to passages in *The Tempest* (1611), which is set in Bermuda. (Bloom 1987d; Boorstin 1992; Hall 1972; Montaigne 1893b; White 1955)

See also "Des Cannibales"; Eldorado; naturalism; Shakespeare, William; *The Tempest.*

MORE, SIR THOMAS

Diplomat, principled theologian, hero, martyr, saint, and rational socialist, More wrote *Utopia* (1516), the prototypical world vision that coined the word "utopia" and spawned the utopian branch of literature. The eldest son of Judge John More, Thomas More was born on February 7, 1477, in London. He attended St. Antony's School; was tutored by John Morton, archbishop of Canterbury; and studied Greek, Latin, and logic at Canterbury College, Oxford. In 1494 More moved to London to study law at New Inn and Lincoln's Inn, and was admitted to the bar two years later. At age 22 he launched a careful study of St. Augustine's *De Civitate Dei*. Hesitant to challenge his father's plan for a law career, More nonetheless withdrew to Charterhouse to pray and meditate and to consider entering the priesthood. But after two years of cloistered life among Franciscan friars, he chose Christian laity over the priesthood. However, for the rest of his adult life he wore a hair shirt, prayed and meditated daily, and projected a pious, holy demeanor.

In 1505 More married Jane Colt, settled in Bucklersbury, and fathered three daughters and a son. A successful trial attorney and noted skeptic, he studied literature and formed a close friendship with Desiderius Erasmus, Rotterdam's influential humanist, who leased a residence in London and joined More in a translation of Lucian's *Dialogues* (1506). More's literary biography of Pico della Mirandola, published in 1506, gave proof of his literary potential. In 1511 he suffered a temporary setback after the death of his wife, who left him four children to rear. For practical reasons, only weeks after his first wife's death he married Alice Middleton.

In 1516, during a diplomatic journey to Bruges to negotiate a trade agreement for the crown, More enjoyed several weeks free of obligations. Through Erasmus, he met Peter Giles in Antwerp and formed a close and stimulating camaraderie. As a result, More initiated his Latin manuscript *Utopia*, an imaginative social and moral idyll that detailed the visit of Raphael Hythloday, a fictional mariner, to an imaginary island he called *Nusquama*, or "nowhere." As a character, More functions as a devil's advocate, arguing for private property against Hythloday's contention that pure communism assures a fairer distribution of goods. More blames a "conspiracy of the rich" for exploiting the poor while sating their hedonistic urges. Therefore, like Étienne Cabet, Karl Marx, Jack London, and W. H. Hudson, he concludes that property should belong to the state for equal distribution so that all humanity can live free of want and oppression.

Two years after completing *Utopia*, More began the *History of King Richard III*, which, though unfinished, is considered by critics a historical tour de force.

Sir Thomas More, painted by Hans Holbein, the Younger

A lover of religious and philosophical dialectic, More dabbled in controversy with the publication of his *Dialogue of Comfort against Tribulation* (1528) and other antiheretical tracts. At the age of 27 he served in Parliament and rose to the rank of undersheriff, master of requests, knight, privy councillor, undersecretary of the exchequer, speaker of the House, and in 1529, lord chancellor. Along the way, More's championship of humanism and the liberal theology of Martin Luther brought him the dual role of steward of Oxford and Cambridge. As a member of the staff of Henry VIII, he advised the king in theology, astronomy, geometry, and international politics; to the neglect of his family, he often spent a month in the royal household. However, More suspected the king of inconstancy and reserved judgment on his sincerity.

By taking sides against Henry in the scandal arising from the king's divorce of Catherine of Aragon and by refusing to attend the royal marriage to Anne Boleyn or her coronation, More jeopardized himself with a likely arrest and execution for treason. On April 17, 1534, his surmise proved true: The willful Henry imprisoned More in the Tower of London for rejecting the Act of Succession and Supremacy, an unprecedented legal document that replaced papal authority with Henry's sovereignty. More's wife pleaded with him to submit to the king's will, but More contended that duty to God and to principle superseded his allegiance to an earthly monarch.

On July 1, 1535, More was tried for denying the king's supremacy over the Church of England. Five days later, More faced the axman with a cheery exhortation: "Pluck up thy spirits, man, and be not afraid to do thine office." As an example to future challengers of Henry's authority, More was beheaded, his body buried, and his head displayed for public edification. Noted European humanists decried Henry's act as a violation of intellectual freedom. Erasmus named More the "man for all seasons," a compliment to his strength of character. Called by his biographer a "mirror of virtue," four centuries later, under Pope Pius XI, More was canonized by the Vatican. (Chambers 1935; Donner 1969; Logan 1983; More 1963a; Negley and Patrick 1952; Nelson 1968; Rollins and Baker 1954; White 1955)

See also Cabet, Étienne; city planning; *De Civitate Dei*; collectivism; Hudson, W. H.; Hythloday, Raphael; London, Jack; Marx, Karl; utopia; *Utopia*.

 # MORGAN, HANK

The protagonist of Mark Twain's dystopian historical novel, *A Connecticut Yankee in King Arthur's Court* (1886), Hank is an energetic New Englander. As a metal worker at the Colt Arms factory, Hank typifies the bustling enterprise and faith in progress common to the New World at the time of his inexplicable transfer from Hartford, Connecticut, to sixth-century Camelot. Bursting with pride in endeavor, he says in Chapter 8:

> I was no shadow of a king; I was the substance; the king himself was the shadow. My power was colossal; and it was not a mere name, as such things have gen-

erally been, it was the genuine article. I stood here, at the very spring and source of the second great period of the world's history; and could see the trickling stream of that history gather, and deepen and broaden, and roll its mighty tides down the far centuries; and I could note the upspringing of adventurers like myself in the shelter of its long array of thrones. . . . I was a Unique; and glad to know that that fact could not be dislodged or challenged for thirteen centuries and a half for sure.

As his words indicate, Hank is a pompous idealist and a sometime strutter; he brings about his downfall by attempting too much change in a medieval environment. Beset by callous monarchy, church treachery, and centuries of ignorance and superstition, he unseats himself by discounting the political clout of the envious courtiers and clergy.

Twain achieves a comic air with the creation of his protagonist, a whizbang optimist and man-of-all-trades. By wearing the guise of the magus, Hank (dubbed The Boss) sets up a progressive alliance of capitalistic workers, baseball teams, democratic schools, insurance agencies, improved transportation, newspapers, and industrial expansion. Faithful to the nineteenth-century ideal of universal betterment, Hank neglects the political structure that democratization replaces. The enmity of knights, church prelates, and Merlin the Magician erupts into medieval warfare, which defeats Hank's plans to raise the working class to nineteenth-century standards.

Twain's utopia founders and collapses for numerous reasons. According to Chapter 8, the Roman Catholic Church, ever looking toward its own power and aggrandizement, "in two or three little centuries had converted a nation of men to a nation of worms." With consummate skill, churchmen circumvent the wily Hank by striking at his weakest point—his love for his wife Sandy and his daughter, whimsically named Hello-Central. Ostensibly for beneficent reasons, the church dispatches the family on a sea voyage to restore the child's health after a bout of croup.

Part of the pathos of Hank's demise is a betrayal of honor and trust, virtues he expects from gentlefolk. Too late, Hank realizes the church's duplicity in getting him out of the way so that the holy hierarchy can usurp his power. A husband and father of the old school, he gladly sets aside national concerns and ferries wife and child to more healthful surroundings until Hello-Central can recover from life-threatening bronchitis. On his return, he realizes how cold malice has gathered strength and outmaneuvered his modern contrivances. A great blow to The Boss and the kingdom is the death of Arthur at the hands of his reprehensible nephew, Mordred.

Serious flaws stand in the way of Hank's modernized Camelot, not the least of which is egotism. More insidious is Hank's dependence on weaponry and gunpowder. In the end, he faces off against hosts of mailed and mounted knights and kills them with electrified fences. Camelot's end is swift and surprisingly detrimental to Hank. Ringed about by three tiers of decaying corpses, the victor lives out his final hours a virtual prisoner of his own cleverness. Put to sleep by the redoubtable Merlin, Hank hibernates into Twain's time and dies in Warwick Castle after passing a detailed journal to the narrator. Still clinging to his medieval mirage while breathing his last, Hank calls: "It is the king! The drawbridge, there! Man the battlements—turn out the—" and dies.

Twain's Hank—ever the brash, pushy optimist—never doubts that his brand of technological know-how will rescue him. To preserve his ideas, he scribbles feverishly in a diary as predators encircle his small band. In Chapter 43, he acknowledges:

> The Church, the nobles, and the gentry then turned one grand, all-disapproving frown upon them and shriveled them into sheep! From that moment the sheep had begun to gather to the fold—that is to say, the camps—and offer their valueless lives and their valuable wool to the "righteous cause."

In the final battle of the Sand Belt, the combined efforts of his workers produce a Pyrrhic victory. Thirty thousand knights—killed by Gatling gun, flood, and electric fences—lie rotting in a triple ring about his stronghold, shutting him in like a prisoner.

Clarence, The Boss's handpicked assistant and budding genius, takes up the narrative and describes how Sir Meliagraunce stirs long enough to stab Hank. Placed under a curse by Merlin, who slips into the cave disguised as a woman, Hank sleeps until the nineteenth century, when he communicates his fantastic experience in a handwritten manuscript. In his final moments at Warwick, the awakening Hank, too frail to last long, gasps out his disillusion:

> I thought that Clarence and I and a handful of my cadets fought and extermi-nated the whole chivalry of England! . . . Yes, I seemed to have flown back out of that age into this of ours, and then forward to it again, and was set down, a stranger and forlorn in that strange England, with an abyss of thirteen centu-ries yawning between me and you! between me and my home and my friends! between me and all that is dear to me, all that could make life worth the living! It was awful—awfuler than you can ever imagine. . . .

Still calling his minions to arms in the voice of a top sergeant, Hank lies on his deathbed in a confused state of hallucination. His mind clings to his wife, and he trusts his young corps of engineers to overcome the foe and renew his plans for a sixth-century utopia. His body, sunken under Merlin's spell and revived briefly in the nineteenth century, gradually slips away. (Budd 1983; Hoffman 1988; Kesterson 1979; Twain 1963)

See also Arthur; Camelot; classism; *A Connecticut Yankee in King Arthur's Court;* disillusion; fantasy; humanitarianism; idealism; technology; theocracy; Twain, Mark.

MORLOCKS

Morlocks are sallow, dehumanized beings who inhabit the dark subterranean expanse visited by H. G. Wells's Time Traveller in *The Time Machine* (1895). In overly dramatic contrast to the Eloi, the effete homunculi of the upper world, the luminous gray-red eyes of Morlocks peer over the rims of wells at the classic, lavish lifestyle of the privileged Eloi. Soft of body with "queer little ape-like" shapes, these bestial subhumans, similar to Jonathan Swift's Neanderthal Yahoos, exhibit colorless skin untouched by the sun and blond hair that extends down their spines. Like "human spiders," the Morlocks maneuver on all fours in the dark underground tunnels that form their environment.

Morlocks epitomize Wells's fears for a severe division of labor, which frees the Eloi from reponsibilities while heaping menial labor on the backs of the lesser class. Morlocks are incapable of leaving their underground work space in daylight because they have lost their adaptation to light. Similar to London's East-enders, the below-ground subsistence has reduced the Morlocks to a have-not status. Immured in a lightless, foul-smelling crawl space, they acclimate to the thrum of machines and grow oversized convex eyes that strain to focus. The Morlocks' subhuman shadow world affords only crude slabs of meat snatched from the Eloi, personalizing the post-Victorian era's disillusion with progress and limitless optimism, symbolized by Prince Albert's World's Fair at the Crystal Palace with its exposition of machinery and scientific innovations. Impeded by a widening gulf between classes, the Morlocks devolve into simple-witted cannibals, whom the Time Traveller compares to a "standing horse [pawing] with his foot." Such uncivilized beings become the threat that forces the Eloi "out of the ease and the sunshine" into a constant state of alert. (Costa 1985; Crossley 1986; Draper 1988; Negley and Patrick 1952; Smith 1988; Wells 1964)

See also Eloi; Swift, Jonathan; *The Time Machine*; Weena; Wells, H. G.

MORRIS, WILLIAM

Author of the ebullient, strongly collectivist utopian novel *News from Nowhere* (1890), Morris's skill as a designer, poet, translator, and craftsman overshadows his contribution to early socialism. He was born to a wealthy family on March 24, 1834, in Walthamstow outside London. He left public school and entered Marlborough College at age 13. Six years later, he enrolled at Exeter College, Oxford, and pursued a theology degree.

Exasperated with the shallow tastes of Victorian England, Morris gave up formal studies, apprenticed with an architect, and collaborated with the Victorian era's most gifted talents—Dante Gabriel Rossetti, George Street, Ford Madox Brown, Philip Webb, Edward Burne-Jones, and John Ruskin—on a Gothic Revival of the glories of the Middle Ages. A devout medievalist, Morris painted murals based on Arthurian legends and composed *The Defence of Guenevere and Other Poems* (1858). In 1859 he married his model, Jane Burden; however, her declining health ended her attempts to keep up with an energetic husband and his houseful of creative friends. During this period, Morris shared a London workshop with Burne-Jones and designed furniture. Morris decided to build a splendid brick manor at Bexley and form a coterie of craftsmen skilled in stained glass, woodworking, wood-carving, and embroidery and dedicated to restoring individualism and integrity to home design. In 1861 he achieved

William Morris

his goal with the foundation of Morris, Marshall, Faulkner & Company, and lived his happiest years with his wife and young daughters, Jenny and May.

Overwork brought on a severe bout of fatigue; in 1865 Morris returned to London to open a second workshop, where he began designing wallpaper and illuminated books. He wrote verse based on epic and myth, producing *The Life and Death of Jason* (1867) and the beautifully illustrated *Book of Verse* (1870). In 1871 Morris moved to an Oxfordshire estate, traveled to Iceland, and returned to study dyeing, fabric, carpets, and tapestry. In 1877 he began a series of lectures on his artistic projects and his intent to rescue historic properties from ruin.

In 1883 Morris joined a socialist federation and began touring industrial sites. His interest in the welfare of workers placed him in contact with other liberals, particularly George Bernard Shaw. When dissension splintered the core group, Morris launched his own socialist society. He began a study of typesetting and founded a journal, *The Commonweal,* then published two influential romances, *A Dream of John Ball* (1887) and *News from Nowhere.* Overly optimistic utopian propaganda for a futuristic society, the novels were based on the simpler economy of cottage industry. His most finely crafted books were his production of Chaucer's works. By 1896 Morris realized that he had expended his energies and was entering a fatal decline; he died on October 3. Although he made an impact on the emerging socialism of his time, he was better known for molding public taste in home furnishings than for literary models of collectivism. (Arnot 1976; Forman 1992; Morris 1968b; Thompson 1992)

See also Arthur; collectivism; Marx, Karl; *News from Nowhere;* prophecy; Shaw, George Bernard; speculative fiction; technology.

NAPOLEON

Napoleon is a despotic, Stalinesque pig in George Orwell's *Animal Farm* (1945). A fierce, secretive, taciturn Berkshire boar of 24 stone, Napoleon allows ambition to overrule principle. Cunning and self-serving, he deceives his rival, the ingenuous pig Snowball, and trains nine puppies to become a brass-collared hit squad as a means of assuring control. To the question of Sunday morning meetings, he bars future examples of wasted time and sets up a puppet committee of pigs, headed by himself. Lacking concrete plans for Animal Farm, Napoleon achieves political aims by subverting Snowball's plan to construct a windmill and by seizing psychological control through militant posturing, intimidation, and brainwashing.

Cowed by his audacity, the animals ask no questions; Boxer, a sycophantic horse, concludes dissension with the claim that "Napoleon is always right." Napoleon's presumption impels him toward greater atrocities. In Chapter 7 he kills three hens who disobey and slaughters sheep for minor offenses. In despotic style:

> They were all slain on the spot. And so the tale of confessions and executions went on, until there was a pile of corpses lying before Napoleon's feet and the air was heavy with the smell of blood, which had been unknown there since the expulsion of Jones.

This closemouthed conspiracy heightens Napoleon's bold power grabs and bloody public executions. As the old generation dies off and new animals take their place, the young, who have never known any other system, accept Napoleon's savagery as the norm.

In the end, Napoleon prevails by applying blitzkrieg tactics against the failed Snowball and blaming all setbacks on his former rival; he allies the pigs with Pilkington, a human neighbor who helps resurrect Manor Farm, the name by which Animal Farm was once known. Luxuriating in the farmhouse and partaking of whiskey, human beds and clothing, and the best farm produce, Napoleon subverts the Seven Commandments to his own ends. He appears in full strutting glory in Chapter 10, "majestically upright, casting haughty glances from side to side, and with his dogs gambolling round him. He carried a whip in his trotter." A formidable, greedy overlord, he overworks and underfeeds the animals, who lack his savvy in figuring out how to avoid exploitation. (Buitehuis and Nadel 1988; Crick 1980; Ferrell 1988; Gardner 1987; Orwell 1946; Reilly 1989)

See also *Animal Farm*; Orwell, George; Snowball; totalitarianism.

NATION OF ISLAM

See Black Muslims, Koran, Malcolm X.

NATURALISM

Naturalism is a biological realism, a blend of practicality and optimism that bases its expectations, ideals, and code of conduct on the example set by nature. Akin to mythic and pastoral verse, oriental oneness with primeval creation, and ancient fantasies of a golden age as balmy and blessed as Eden, naturalistic literature counters the drive toward mechanized living and city planning by emphasizing the value of accepting nature on its own terms, whether blissful, demanding, or menacing. French essayist Michel de Montaigne, author of "Des Cannibales" (1580), requires little fantasy and less structure in his utopian vision of the noble savage. Buoyed by the energy, purity, and opportunity in the Western Hemisphere, he lionizes the American Indian as a New World Adam who inhabits an unspoiled Eden. Montaigne's fervor reveals an anti-Christian bias—a belief that humankind is neither sinful nor in need of redemption. Rather, human beings are naturally good and capable of living in harmony with one another and nature. His essay, drawn from the Stoics—Plutarch, Virgil, and Seneca—repeats similar beliefs espoused in classical literature that the nation remaining closest to the earth and more in tune with simple pleasures enjoys the most idyllic life, the most hopeful outlook.

In utopian works composed after the sixteenth century, writers observe the tradition of respect for or worship of nature. In Daniel Defoe's *Robinson Crusoe* (1719), the marooned protagonist demonstrates clearly how right-mindedness turns potential catastrophe into easeful living. Cast away on an uninhabited island, Crusoe centers his efforts on the cycle of planting and harvesting, guarding against predators, and enjoying the bounty of his toil. Similar to Henry David Thoreau on Walden Pond, the fictional Robinson Crusoe takes pleasure in his island home and counters moments of loneliness by contemplating the order of nature and its random beauty. Following illness and a moment of panic, Crusoe writes in his journal on July 4, 1660:

> I saw here abundance of cocoa trees, orange and lemon and citron trees; but all wild and very few bearing any fruit, at least not then. However, the green limes that I gathered were not only pleasant to eat but very wholesome; and I mixed their juice afterwards with water, which made it very wholesome and very cool and refreshing.

Crusoe demonstrates perhaps the best attitude toward symbiosis—a pragmatic acceptance of what is offered, i.e., a natural defense against scurvy, and a cessation of longings for elements that fit other climates and places. Like the farmers in Hesiod's *Works and Days* (eighth century B.C.) and Virgil's *Bucolics* (42–37 B.C.), Crusoe lays up useful stores and congratulates himself on unforeseen bounty.

Like Daniel Defoe, other writers demonstrate right-thinking toward serendipity. In these accidental brushes with a heaven on Earth, their characters must adapt to circumstance as a method of accessing an unfamiliar utopia. In *Typee* (1846), Herman Melville relieves his stressed sailors, Tommo and Toby, of the tyranny aboard ship by transforming them into beach bums and visitors to Polynesian havens. In a nonchalant society, the two former sailors quickly learn the rhythm of the days and champion a tribe that takes seriously the art of napping and relaxing. The sequel, *Omoo* (1847), loosens the social ties and allows the men to gad about more of the South Seas paradise and to sample religion and work opportunities. In Chapter 42, on the entrancing island of Motoo-Otoo, the speaker loses himself in examining the unusual:

> Prickly branches down to a snow-white floor of sand, sprouting with flinty bulbs; and crawling among these are strange shapes:—some bristling with spikes, others clad in shining coats of mail, and here and there round forms all spangled with eyes.

In contrast to Melville's scientific study of the lagoon floor, Black Elk, a Native American seer, takes a more religious stance on the matter of human relations with nature. In his visionary autobiography *Black Elk Speaks* (1932), the visitations of spirits from the afterlife promise Black Elk that a new era of peace and unity with nature will return only after restored warriors from the past drive out white settlers and cavalry, enabling Native Americans to enjoy the outdoors without endangering or despoiling it.

Additional dreams of lifestyles set to the rhythms of the universe appear in varied utopian and dystopian texts:

- Both Greek and Roman poets feature details of a golden age when people lived in nature and did no work. These segments of Greek myth, derived from Hesiod's *Works and Days* (eighth century B.C.), Virgil's *Bucolics* (42–37 B.C.), and Book 1 of Ovid's *Metamorphoses* (A.D. 8), delight in a time when the soil voluntarily produced grain and the trees fruit. Ovid adds that honey flowed from oak trees and nectar and milk poured from streams.

- Sir Thomas More's *Utopia* (1516) respects agrarian pursuits and the bucolic lifestyle of Utopians, who produce wholesome food. To assure the best in farm training, families send representatives to annual city forums to study innovations in husbandry.

- In the eighteenth century, Samuel Johnson produced an extravagant setting and an indulgent lifestyle, both of which dismay the title character in

"Rasselas, Prince of Abissinia" (1759), who recognizes a nameless, lacerating ache and finds release in the playful interaction of a flock of sheep. Rasselas acts on instinct to escape the ideal life in Happy Valley and returns to his home in Abissinia to encounter reality.

- Ayn Rand's *Anthem* (1937) lures her protagonists from a structured, tyrannic collective to the freedom of wandering at will in the Uncharted Forest. There, Equality 7-2521 views his reflection in water for the first time and experiences pride in hunting birds for a meal.

- William Golding's island castaways in *Lord of the Flies* (1954) attempt to set up a makeshift society without the guidance of grown-ups. Their miscalculation reaches ecological chaos when fires rage across the green mountainside and, ironically, signal adults to rescue the children.

- W. H. Hudson, who grew up in the outdoor freedom of the South American pampas, returns to nature in *A Crystal Age* (1887) and *Green Mansions* (1904). In the matriarchy of his first utopian novel, Smith labors at the plow and, by chopping wood, vents frustrations that arise when he tries to adapt to a futuristic commune. *Green Mansions*, far more picturesque and alluring, intrigues the central character, Alex, with a mystic bird-woman named Rima, who temporarily draws him into her jungle bower.

- In a perusal of the work ethic as applied to nature, William Morris takes his protagonist to the English countryside at harvest time in his futuristic novel *News from Nowhere* (1890), a paean to collectivism and the non-competitive life of farm workers. As Morris describes the worryfree atmosphere in Chapter 24:

  > No one unburdened with very heavy anxieties could have felt otherwise than happy that morning; and it must be said that whatever anxieties might lie beneath the surface of things, we didn't seem to come across any of them.

  At the end of his dream escape from Hammersmith to the green fields of a future England, the speaker advises: "Go on living while you may, striving, with whatsoever pain and labour needs must be, to build up little by little the new day of fellowship, and rest, and happiness," which is his summary of a nation unhampered by the noise, filth, and coercion of industrialism.

These examples contain a variety of responses to nature while clearly opposing communes and planned cities, which are a staple in utopian settings. Perhaps the most naturalistic is Richard Adams's *Watership Down* (1972), a fitting habitat in which a band of rabbits can achieve oneness with flora and fauna. Less managed than the open range of Jonathan Swift's Houyhnhnms in Book 4 of *Gulliver's Travels* (1727) and less confining than Denis Diderot's idealized village in *Supplement aux Voyages de Bougainville* (1772), in Chapter 50 the meadow becomes Adams's animal Eden:

The sun sank below Ladle Hill and the autumn stars began to shine in the darkening east—Perseus and the Pleiades, Cassiopeia, faint Pisces and the great square of Pegasus. The wind freshened, and soon myriads of dry beech leaves were filling the ditches and hollows and blowing in gusts across the dark miles of open grass.

At the core of rabbit contentment is a simple diet of green growing things, a companionship with birds and other animals, and a knowledge that their heroic efforts have delivered them from a gory, undeserved annihilation by bulldozer, poison gas, or shotgun. In their dependence on nature and the cycle of the seasons, the animals thrive; the warren grows. (Adams 1972; Golding 1954; Hesiod 1973; Hudson n.d.; Hudson 1917; Johnson 1982; Melville 1964; Melville 1968; Montaigne 1893a; More 1963a; Morris 1968b; Neihardt 1961; Ovid 1977; Rand 1946; Swift 1958; Thoreau 1965; Virgil 1950)

See also Adams, Richard; *Anthem;* Black Elk; *Black Elk Speaks; Bucolics;* city planning; *A Crystal Age;* "Des Cannibales"; Eden; golden age; *Gulliver's Travels;* Hesiod; Houyhnhnms; Hudson, W. H.; *Lord of the Flies;* Melville, Herman; *News from Nowhere; Omoo;* Ovid; pastoral; "Rasselas, Prince of Abissinia"; *Supplement aux Vayages de Bougainville;* technology; *Typee; Utopia;* Virgil; *Watership Down.*

NEIHARDT, JOHN G.

See Black Elk, heaven.

NEVERLAND

Neverland is the island setting of James M. Barrie's children's classic, *Peter Pan* (1904). The title character lives in an imaginary land populated by lost boys who fall from their prams and remain unclaimed for seven days, or children who are invited guests, which is the case with Wendy, John, and Michael Darling. To Wendy's request for an address, Peter replies: "Second to the right and straight on till morning." After Tinker Bell the fairy sprinkles them with magic dust, Peter flies his friends to Neverland. He leads them through dark and light, cold and hot, across the sea. After "many moons," they reach an unspecified island bristling with the sun's golden arrows to mark the way.

The topography of Neverland is abundantly textured. On first sight, the children spot the mermaids' lagoon, where turtles bury eggs in the sand. They notice a broken-legged flamingo, a cave, and a wolf and her whelps in the underbrush. From the Piccaninny Indian camp, which lies across Mysterious River, smoke curls up over the residence of a tribe led by Chief Great Big Little Panther. In the treetops dwell the fairies, whose nests give off a faint glow. A pirate sleeps in the pampas. Peter and his guests are greeted by the wily crew of the pirate chief, Captain James Hook; Indians on the warpath; Peter's boys; and a large crocodile that ticks. Local enmity remains in a frequently interrupted stasis as Indians waylay boys and boys scrap with pirates.

Seating himself on a hot mushroom, the pirate Hook reveals the existence of a peculiar mushroom that is really a chimney guiding smoke from the boys' one-room underground home. After Wendy's collapse from an arrow wound inflicted by the Piccaninnies, the boys build her a brush house nearby. Wendy sings:

> I wish I had a pretty house,
> The littlest ever seen,
> With funny little red walls
> And roof of mossy green.

Emblematic of Neverland's ability to fulfill wishes, the rhyme describes exactly Wendy's temporary residence. One resident completes the edifice with a door knocker made from the sole of his shoe.

The placement of characters in this Victorian idyll is typically prim, typically sexist. Wendy rules the house, but sleeps outside; her brothers are fitted to tree limbs at night and slide into the underground home each morning, where a Never tree makes a daily attempt to sprout, serves briefly as a table, and is cut back after teatime. Mushrooms become stools at mealtime, when Wendy doles out local specialties—breadfruit, yams, coconuts, bananas, and papaw juice. Over an enormous fireplace Wendy stretches a clothesline. The boys use the rest of the space for play until 6:30 P.M., when their tilt-down bed takes up most of the space. All the boys except Michael sleep wedged into place like sardines. Because Michael is still young and vulnerable, he is lodged in a swinging basket. In a small bird cage–sized recess, Tinker Bell has a private, curtained-off apartment. Inside, her furniture consists of a Queen Mab sofa, Puss-in-Boots mirror, and bedspreads of fruit blossoms, which change with the seasons. In addition, Tinker Bell owns a few conversation pieces: a reversible pie-crust washstand, Charming the Sixth chest of drawers, carpet and rugs of the Margery and Robin period, and a Tiddlywinks chandelier.

Enjoyment of nature supplants more formalized styles of education. On lazy days the children swim and float in the lagoon and play games with the mermaids, who live below in coral caves and bat around the bubbles stirred up by storms. At times they sunbathe on Marooners' Rock, where the pirates Smee and Starkey imprison Tiger Lily, the Indian princess. Occasionally, the nest of the Never bird floats by. Roughhousing with the pirates, the boys dive into the lagoon to elude the crew of the brig *Jolly Roger*, Hook's ship, which is moored in Kidd Creek. (Barrie 1981; Darlington 1974; Maguel and Guadalupi 1987)

See also Barrie, Sir James Matthew; escapism; fantasy; Peter Pan.

 # THE NEW ATLANTIS

An unfinished utopian vision of a perfected England, *The New Atlantis* was composed by Francis Bacon about 1624 and published posthumously in 1627. Bacon was influenced by Plato's *Republic* (fifth century B.C.), Thomas More's

Utopia (1516), and possibly Johann Andreae's *Christianopolis* (1619). Like Fra Tomaso Campanella's *La Città del Sole* (1602), the story is set on an isolated Pacific isle about 5,600 miles in circumference. The speaker reaches the spot after a year's voyage from Peru to China and Japan. Sailing into cloudy weather in the South Sea, the crew stumble on a port that leads to a flat, woodsy land. A launch bearing eight citizens approaches the ship. The leader hands over a scroll marked with angels' wings and a cross. The message—written in Hebrew, Greek, Latin, and Spanish—offers food, water, first aid, and repairs, but warns that the ship must depart within 16 days. The launch returns to port, leaving a single servant to await a formal reply.

The puzzled crew replies in Spanish that they are well, but that their voyage has been fraught with hard sailing. They beg to land to seek treatment for the many on board who are ill. A second boat approaches bearing a leader dressed in a blue robe and turban, and an honor guard of 20 follows in a third craft. The leader signals for a parley; five crew members row out to the meeting. The leader demands an oath of Christianity. At six the next morning, six of the crew are allowed in and enter the strangers' house, which is constructed of blue brick and pierced with glass windows. The guide requires that the newcomers remain indoors for three days and sends servants with a meal of bread, meat, wine, ale, cider, and a fruit that resembles an orange, which the locals use as a nostrum against illness. The guide leaves medicines to heal the ailing crew members. The visitors rejoice that a miracle has brought them to a beneficent people.

The governor, who calls himself a priest, arrives the next day to grant the visitors a six-week pass and free room and board. The only injunction on their sojourn is a limit on their wanderings to a mile and a half beyond the city walls. At 10:00 A.M the next day, the same priest returns to welcome them to Bensalem, a closed community that limits visits as a means of guarding state secrets. A benign monarchy, Bensalem sprang from the foundations laid by the great-hearted King Solamona 19 centuries earlier—20 years after Christ's crucifixion—following the mysterious appearance of a column rising from the sea near the city of Renfusa on the island's east coast. A sage from the Society of Solomon's House abased himself before the pillar and prayed to God to reveal the secrets of creation. He bowed toward the pillar, which disintegrated, leaving behind a small cedar chest containing a Bible and a letter on parchment written by Bartholomew, one of Jesus' apostles.

Known from ancient times by sailors from Tyre, Phoenicia, Carthage, Egypt, China, and America for its magnificent temple, palace, and citadel, Bensalem exists apart from foreign influence or contamination by outsiders. A patriarchal nation, the country reveres monogamous marriage and chastity, and therefore displays no prostitution, polygamy, or bawdy behavior (which was common to the Europe of Bacon's day). According to Bacon, "marriage is ordained a remedy for unlawful concupiscence." To assure a stable mating, friends of unwed men and women observe the intended while he or she bathes in the pool of Adam and Eve. Some couples marry without parental consent, but they are not allowed to inherit a full portion of the family wealth.

Bacon believed that the application of inductive reason to natural phenomena could produce answers to most of the problems troubling humankind. Therefore, Bensalem credits its stability and innovation to technology, which springs from natural science. The focus of scientific experimentation lies at Solomon's House, the expansive secret society that fosters the nation's learning. The governor reveals to his visitors that a pair of ships sets sail every 12 years to study and collect foreign technology, books, abstracts, compilations of data, and instruments. The governor emphasizes that these expeditions are "not for gold, silver, or jewels, nor for silks, nor for spices, nor any other commodity of matter; but only for God's first creature, which was light."

After two crewmen partake of a family meal, they report that the paterfamilias, or Tirsan, hosts a ceremonial feast, which is paid for from public funds. On the feast day, the mother remains absent. The Tirsan sits on a raised chair festooned in ivy and canopied by his daughters in silver and silk. With remarkable pageantry of sons and daughters, the father receives from the king's herald a scroll or charter honoring the family. The group exclaims: "Happy are the people of Bensalem." The feast is accompanied by hymns praising Adam, Noah, and Abraham and by formal blessings on the children. The Tirsan concludes with gifts of jewels to guests. The feast climaxes in music and dancing. Organized into a commune, Bensalem prospers from the evenhandedness of its distribution of goods, relief of the poor, and law courts. The governor of Bensalem greets the speaker and explains the scientific nature of the nation. The focus of scientific endeavor covers a variety of fields, from transportation to underground refrigeration and synthetic food to metallurgy. In subterranean laboratories, alchemists make imitation ore and artificial metal. Half-mile-high towers occupied by hermits offer observation points for the study of weather and meteors. Salt and freshwater lakes provide fish and waterfowl and are also used for the study of vapor, desalinization, and wind and water power. Special fountains produce spas and a salutary elixir called water of paradise.

The Bensalemites work energetically toward life betterment. They study pharmacology from plants and animals and produce a variety of simples and drugs. Their workshops and factories make paper, linen, silk, dye, and other materials. Furnace operators experiment with dry and moist air as well as with insulation and convection and other types of heating. In "perspective-houses," scientists demonstrate light, radiation, and color, and create spectacles and microscopes. "Sound-houses" perform similar observations of tones. Perfumeries likewise imitate aromas; bakeries produce desserts, wine, milk, soup, and salad.

According to the governor, other developers study the secret of longevity, perpetual motion, herbs and grafting, agriculture, animal dissection, silkworms and bees, weaponry, ships, clocks, mathematical instruments, and spontaneous generation. From the collectors sent forth, twelve are "merchants of light," three are collectors of foreign-based experiments, three study mechanics, three are pioneer experimenters, and three compile tables and axioms. A final trio, called benefactors, search for practical applications to improve life. Other trios study nature, set up experimental laboratories, and interpret phenomena. In a pair of galleries, Bensalemites revere statues of Columbus and the inventors of sailing, guns, music, writing, printing, astronomy, metallurgy, glass, silk, wine, bread, and sugar. The citizens sing hymns and honor God for his benevolence. Prayers ask for greater enlightenment. The authorities make national tours to announce worthwhile inventions and to reveal prophecies of plagues, natural disasters, and other events that can be prevented and remedied by human intervention. The governor concludes with a blessing to the speaker and remarks, "We here are in God's bosom, a land unknown."

Critical acclaim for Renaissance utopias is mixed in regard to Francis Bacon. Some rate Bacon a poor third after Johann Andreae and Fra Tomaso Campanella. Others lambaste Bacon for emphasis on pointless details, particularly ceremonial garments and embellishments. These assertions are consistent with the lengthy descriptions of wide-sleeved robes, exquisite blues and golds, shoulder-length hair, and tedious rituals. (Bacon 1905; Berneri 1951; Manguel and Guadalupi 1987; Mumford 1959; Negley and Patrick 1952)

See also Andreae, Johann Valentin; Bacon, Francis; Campanella, Fra Tomaso; *Christianopolis; La Città del Sole*; technology.

NEWS FROM NOWHERE

Reputedly, William Morris launched this rural, antitechnological idyll as a riposte to Edward Bellamy's mechanistic utopian novel *Looking Backward* (1887). Published serially in *The Commonweal* in 1890 and in an illustrated volume the next year, *News from Nowhere or an Epoch of Rest* espouses Morris's enthusiasm for socialism and noncompetitive work. The novel is composed mostly of questions and exchanges among the protagonist; an amiable companion named Dick, a passionate lover of the earth; and Hammond, an elderly historian; it opens on a first-person speaker who lives in Hammersmith and awakens to a new world. Sensing that London has altered, he examines the building taking the place of his own residence, trying to learn the extent of change in the England he once knew. In Chapter 4, while walking with strangers, he comments:

> This whole mass of architecture . . . bore upon it the expression of such generosity and abundance of life that I was exhilarated to a pitch that I had never yet reached. I fairly chuckled for pleasure.

The prosperity of people around him stirs him to ask Dick, his companion from the future, how children are taught. Dick replies that they learn swimming, reading, writing, and foreign languages quite naturally without schools.

In Morris's structured utopia, markets still exist, but factories have given over to workshops, where artisans enjoy the creation of craft items. In Chapter 9 Dick accounts for this interest in happiness and productivity and for the longevity of the race:

> . . . you must know that we of these generations are strong and healthy of body, and live easily; we pass our lives in reasonable strife with nature, exercising not one side of ourselves only, but all sides, taking the keenest pleasure in all the life of the world.

Unburdened by alcohol consumption and tobacco, the people remain hand-some and active well beyond 100 years. A lack of sex discrimination has ended drudgery for housewives, and there are no poor or destitute citizens. There is no violence to call for legislation nor any law for courts to judge. People have grown open-minded and nonjudgmental of their neighbors. To relieve the op-pressiveness of the Industrial Revolution, the city planners of the future have pulled down dreary factories and encourage grass and open views of the sky.

In England, residents live in parishes or communes and decide for them-selves how their community should deal with internal matters such as the sal-vaging of an old bridge or the construction of a new one. To comprehend the amicable situation before him, in Chapter 14 the speaker asks how this degree of harmony came about. Dick replies that all people have meaningful work without outside coercion toward jobs they dislike.

Speaking through Dick, Morris presses his personal opinions in a thinly veiled diatribe against the capitalism of nineteenth-century England:

> It is clear from all that we hear and read, that in the last age of civilisation men had got into a vicious circle in the matter of production of wares . . . they could not free themselves from the toil of making real necessaries, they created in a never-ending series sham of artificial necessaries, which became, under the iron rule of the aforesaid World-Market, of equal importance to them with the real necessaries which supported life. By all this they burdened themselves with a prodigious mass of work merely for the sake of keeping their wretched system going.

To restore happiness, leisure, and amusement, socialism halted the need for new markets and the invention of so-called labor-saving devices, the double curse of capitalism. In place of these exploitive methods, people began to make by hand only what they needed.

At the heart of his commune, Morris anticipates Marxism's faith in a spon-taneous overthrow of capitalism. By Chapter 17 the questioner has learned what he needs to know about the change except for the prime question: How did the change take place between nineteenth-century capitalism and the fu-ture socialism? Hammond, an eyewitness, replies that the transformation re-quired enlightened socialists to displace the middle class. When the workers revolted in 1952, he saw the terrible battle that broke out in Trafalgar Square and the massive numbers of corpses disfigured by machine guns. In a matter of days, government toppled from the pressure of the newly roused working class.

On a lighter note, the visitor enjoys a visit with Clara and Dick, who look forward to rowing on the Thames and going haying. In Chapter 26, to the visitor's questions about the meaning of "easy-hard work," Dick congenially replies:

> I mean work that tires the muscles and hardens them and sends you pleas-antly weary to bed, but which isn't trying in other ways: doesn't harass you, in short. Such work is always pleasant if you don't overdo it.

In the clean atmosphere of Kelmscott, which features open countryside rid of university spires and railroad tracks, the speaker reflects on his enjoyment of a time freed from "struggle and tyranny of the rights of property, into the present rest and happiness of complete Communism."

The speaker reaches his journey's end in Chapter 30 and summarizes his perusal of the future and his condemnation of the errors and mismanagement common to the nineteenth century. The panorama of fields, clean river, woods, and stone buildings delights him so thoroughly that he expects it to melt into a dream, replaced by the

> . . . two or three spindle-legged back-bowed men and haggard, hollow-eyed, ill-favoured women, who once wore down the soil of this land with their heavy hopeless feet, from day to day, and season to season, and year to year.

While seated with Dick, Clara, and her friend Ellen, the speaker fades back into his dwelling in Hammersmith, where people are "engaged in making others live lives which are not their own." Far removed from the fellowship of the future, the dreamer hears Ellen's encouragement to prepare humanity for future improvements in living. He determines to turn his dream into an attainable goal.

The inverse of Mark Twain's *A Connecticut Yankee in King Arthur's Court* (1886), which pushes the observer from the nineteenth century into medieval England, Morris's utopia, like Edward Bellamy's *Looking Backward, 2000–1887* (1887), leaps ahead to a vibrant, promising future free of the coercion and spiritual malaise of the past. *News from Nowhere* exhibits a nostalgia for simplicity and shared labor. In Morris's ideal commune, citizens revert to a system of artistry that requires few machines and no managers. Living in small, sheltering communities, future workers require no factories and thus avoid England's late-nineteenth-century slums. Morris's speaker learns from the aged historian that revolution is capable of returning the industrial era to a less repressive, mechanistic economy. Led by disgruntled laborers who form unions and battle the entrenched management, a grass-roots effort echoes the siege at the Bastille during the French Revolution and prefigures anarchists' revolt against Tzar Nicholas II in precommunist Russia.

Overall, *News from Nowhere* falls short of noble aims. The speeches of his characters—like the puppet voices of Hythloday and Thomas More in *Utopia* (1516), the stodgy exchanges in Fra Thomaso Campanella's *La Città del Sole* (1602), and the stormy, posed confrontations in Jack London's *The Iron Heel* (1907)—resound like soapbox oratory rather than conversation. Another weakness in the novel's motivation is a clear accounting for the people's oneness in a love of manual labor. However, as a practical plan for restoring rural values and relieving workers of the tedium and health and safety hazards of the Victorian factory, the romance makes several strong points in favor of abandoning a burdensome central bureaucracy and unwieldy educational system and supplanting them with communes that breed happy, healthy, and productive workers. (Arnot 1976; Forman 1992; Morris 1968a; Thompson 1992)

See also La Città del Sole; collectivism; *The Iron Heel*; *Looking Backward, 2000–1887*; Marx, Karl; materialism; Morris, William; prophecy; speculative fiction; technology; *Utopia*.

1984

George Orwell's dystopian classic, arising from antitotalitarian fervor of the post–World War II era and influenced by Yevgeny Zamyatin's anti-Soviet *We* (1921), continues to merit critical praise for insight into the human drive for freedom. Published in 1949 within months of the author's death from tuberculosis, the novel was an instant best-seller. Orwell's grim warning of political encroachment via intellectual manipulation and subversion of truth remains a standard entry on young-adult book lists. It was the subject of a 1956 British film starring Michael Redgrave and Edmond O'Brien, and an American color remake in 1984, featuring Richard Burton and John Hurt. In the decades following Orwell's death, the reading public continues to find deep spiritual insight and psychological themes that warn of opportunism and insidious plots against individualism, as demonstrated by the German Reich, Castro's Cuba, Stalinist Russia's high command, and Serbian monomania in Bosnia.

In the opening scene of the novel, it is April 4, 1984, shortly before Hate Week. Winston Smith, a pensive, dyspeptic bureaucrat, resides in London, the capital of Oceania. A loner and Outer Party minion, he walks the kilometer from his office at the pyramidal Records Department of the Ministry of Truth, where three slogans—"War Is Peace," "Freedom Is Slavery," and "Ignorance Is Strength"—govern thought and squelch individuality. Dressed in blue overalls, the uniform of his class, he arrives at his eighth-floor flat in the Victory Mansions in a borough of what used to be known as London. Towering over the setting—a seedy apartment complex dating to the 1930s—and scattered about the city are giant likenesses of the ruling tyrant, a grim-eyed, mustachioed face that constantly warns: "Big Brother Is Watching You." The Thought Police—a fictional spy/strike force suggestive of Hitler's SS, the Iranian Savak, the American CIA, and communist Russia's KGB—patrol the neighborhood in a hovering helicopter.

Inside, Winston faces a two-way telescreen, by which a centralized spying network keeps tabs on his private life. Orwell stresses the onus of suspicion that demoralizes Winston, who could be executed or imprisoned at hard labor for the merest variance from Party rule. Asserting his individuality, he swallows a hasty glass of gin, conceals himself in an alcove to avoid the prying screen, and begins a diary with an entry on war cinema, which he inscribes in a blank book he bought at an antique store in the free-market section of Airstrip One, the neighborhood in which he lives. His actions constitute "thoughtcrime," Oceania's most heinous infraction of Big Brother's regime.

Orwell intensifies his study of individualism by zeroing in on an intelligent man's ambivalence toward Big Brother. Winston mulls over the frenzied "Two Minutes Hate," part of the morning routine by which the Inner Party directs hostilities toward a national enemy, Emmanuel Goldstein. Winston ponders the behavior of two fellow citizens, an attractive 27-year-old woman and O'Brien, a suspicious upper-level bureaucrat who gives the appearance of sedition. Encouraged that he is not alone in despising authoritarian control, Winston writes in capital letters "DOWN WITH BIG BROTHER" repeatedly over a half page. A knock at the door interrupts his noontime revery, filling him with the dread of arrest and vaporization.

Winston's visitor is the wife of Tom Parsons, his shallow coworker and father of a boy and girl who delight in spying on potential rebels and plead to be taken to hangings. At Comrade Parsons's request, Winston extracts a hair clog from the kitchen drain, then returns to his apartment to finish his journal entry and relive a dream he had seven years earlier in which O'Brien promised, "We shall meet in the place where there is no darkness." Although fearful that he will one day be executed for thoughtcrime, Winston believes that the dream is prophetic. As the 4:30 deadline nears, he pens: "To the future or to the past, to a time when thought is free . . . greetings!"

In dismal nightmares, Winston relives the virulent purge of the 1950s, a period of contained nuclear war during which his mother, father, and baby sister died. Although he was only ten, he holds himself responsible. To escape guilt, he imagines a romantic tryst with a lovely coworker in her late twenties. The shriek of sirens ends his fantasy with a summons to the Physical Jerks, a televised exercise ritual. As his body responds, his memory replays the bombing of Colchester. So deep is Winston in thought about Party lies and deception that the leader scolds him for failure to keep up. With effort, he stretches toward his toes.

Boredom and job dissatisfaction plague the protagonist, who occupies a windowless cubby opening onto a dismal passageway. On a regular workday, Winston excels at his job: rewriting current events according to the whim of Inner Party dicta. The most common subjects involve Oceania's incursions against Eastasia and Eurasia. Depending on the outcomes of these aggressions, Winston's job is to realign Big Brother's predictions with historical fact. As Winston restates a speech lauding Withers, a failed Party regular who was executed, he expunges Big Brother's inappropriate support for Withers with the name of a fictitious war hero.

Syme, a philologist and mindless Party sycophant, joins Winston at the ministry canteen. Syme prides himself on his destruction of works for the eleventh edition of Newspeak, an easily manipulated Partyese. Winston concludes that Syme, a regular at the Chestnut Tree Café, knows too much for his own good. In Winston's estimation, despite Syme's gung ho support of the Party, he will one day be vaporized. Tom Parsons arrives to solicit a voluntary donation. His mindless Party loyalty depresses Winston, as does the tasteless stew and sordid surroundings. In the midst of workday gloom, Winston catches the eye of his lovely dark-haired coworker and wonders if she is spying for the Party.

Orwell stresses the alienation that drives Winston to take chances. Winston confides to his journal his questionable manhood. He confesses that he has been celibate for the past two years and that he solicited a prostitute in a grubby cellar the year preceding his abandonment of sex. He recalls how Katharine, his witless loyalist wife, departed in 1973 as a result of their childlessness. Because the Party mates people of unlike interests as a means of restricting intimacy, Katharine and Winston never achieved satisfactory sexual union. Winston blames government oppressors for subverting normal human urges.

Winston's respect for Oceania's lower class parallels the basis of Marxism. For humanity to rescue itself, Winston concludes that the proles, or working class, who comprise 85 percent of the population, must revolt. Because of their menial worth to the Party, proles observe a lifestyle similar to the old ways, when humans mated out of passion and lived with more exuberance. Winston thinks about the capitalistic system that formerly governed Great Britain. By the mid-1960s, the Party purged textbooks and vaporized rebels; by 1970, Big Brother ruled Oceania. Opposing him is a single holdout—Emmanuel Goldstein, the anarchist who heads the Brotherhood, the Party's major rival.

The key to Winston's malaise is forbidden knowledge. He clings to a single shred of proof that the Party distorts truth: a photo of Jones, Aaronson, and Rutherford in New York ten years earlier, the time when they supposedly betrayed Party secrets in Eurasia. These three turncoats were allegedly brainwashed and released, but in actuality were executed. Winston's acknowledgment of deliberate Party falsification encourages him to add to his journal that "Freedom is freedom to say that two plus two make four. If that is granted, all else follows." He hopes that O'Brien will someday read his bold entries.

Following a rocket attack, Winston walks through the working-class sector and overhears proles discussing the Lottery. He follows an old man to a pub and asks him to describe the era of capitalism before Big Brother. The man recalls only the details of his everyday life. Disappointed, Winston returns to Mr. Charrington's antique shop where he had bought the journal. Winston spends four dollars for a glass paperweight containing a bit of coral. Charrington shows him upstairs to a room he once shared with his wife. To achieve privacy and freedom from telescreens, Winston decides to rent the room the next month. On leaving the shop, he sees his young coworker. He suspects that he is being followed and considers murdering her. Fearing torture and vaporization, he is too depressed to carry out the deed and returns to Victory Mansions.

At work, Winston assists the woman after she falls. When he helps her up, she places in his hand a crumpled note attesting to her love, which is a crime in Oceania. Winston is overjoyed with the prospect of meeting a fellow rebel against the Party. After abortive attempts to meet her, he joins her in the canteen and rèquests a rendezvous near the monument in Victory Square at 19 hours. While Asian prisoners are marched through the street, Winston and the unnamed woman secretly touch hands. She invites him to meet her the following Sunday.

Orwell makes a strong case for sexual satisfaction by supplying Winston with the first willing partner he has ever found. In a country setting on May 2, he plucks bluebells while waiting. She leads him to a fallen tree near a hillside and introduces herself as Julia. She acknowledges what Winston has suspected:

Winston Smith, portrayed by actor Edmond O'Brien in Michael Anderson's 1956 film of George Orwell's *1984*, runs past the visage of Big Brother, the everywhere presence in the utopian nation of Oceania. The film was followed in 1984 by a second, also British-made version, directed by Michael Radford.

She despises the Party and rebels by secretly meeting lovers. The pair defy authority by carrying on their affair in out-of-the-way places, once in a bombed-out bell tower. Julia, a former worker at Pornosec, first indulged in sex at age 16. Although she lacks Winston's idealism, she gets a thrill from cheating on Party strictures. Winston narrates his wretched past and confesses that his marriage was so unsatisfying he once thought of murdering Katharine, his ex-wife. Julia encourages him to enjoy all of life that he can.

At this point, Orwell moves Winston inexorably toward his doom from an obvious setup. The next month, Winston rents the room and continues the affair under the threat of arrest, torture, and execution. Julia sparkles in makeup and perfume and brings real sugar, coffee, tea, white bread, and jam for them to enjoy during their secret liaisons. The sight of a rat in their room terrifies Winston, who regains control of himself by looking into the glass paperweight. Before Hate Week, Winston grows tense from Syme's disappearance and the surge in prole fanaticism. In the safety of Charrington's room, Winston tries to discuss Oceania's war record, but Julia resists this line of conversation, which is too political for her interests. At the Ministry of Truth, O'Brien slips Winston his address; Winston envisions joining O'Brien in a coup against the Party.

Orwell meticulously explains Winston's psychological shortcomings. While spending time with Julia, Winston recalls living in a children's home in 1945 and regrets the loss of his family, especially his sister, from whom he stole chocolate. Winston assumes that his mother departed so that he would not have to care for her. He grows bitter at Oceania's oppressors and decides to join the Brotherhood, even if he and Julia are punished for rebellion. Daring to think for themselves as a result of the temporary high of sexual union, the couple promise to remain true, even if they are tortured in the Ministry of Truth.

At O'Brien's elegant flat, Winston is surprised to see him turn off the obligatory telescreen. O'Brien lifts a glass of wine in honor of Emmanuel Goldstein. Julia and Winston pledge fealty to the Brotherhood and vow to carry out destructive acts against the Party. O'Brien promises Winston a copy of Goldstein's book. Anticipating permanent separation, Julia and Winston exit O'Brien's home individually.

During a Hate Week assembly, an Inner Party leader manipulates the crowd to hate first Eastasia, then Eurasia. Winston spends the next week supplanting Eurasia with Eastasia in various texts. While awaiting Julia at the antique shop, he reads Goldstein's *Theory and Practice of Oligarchical Collectivism*, a three-part treatise refuting Party slogans. Winston later reads to Julia the Party's falsification of history and realizes the purpose of oppression—to provide employment and encourage the consumption of goods. Julia falls asleep before he reads the Party's purpose in overrunning Oceania. He feels better when he awakes and observes from the window a prole hanging up wash. Her energy proves to him that proles live a sensible lifestyle. As he ponders his class's purpose, he comments: "We are the dead." Julia echoes his statement, as does a voice from the telescreen. Winston destroys the framed picture that conceals the telescreen. Led by Mr. Charrington, Thought Police enter to arrest the couple.

The falling action moves inexorably toward Winston's ineffectual rebellion against tyranny. With no clues as to his punishment, Winston is parted from Julia and incarcerated in a windowless white cell in the Ministry of Love. Four prisoners join him: the poet Ampleforth; Tom Parsons, whose daughter betrays him; an unidentified starving man, who is taken to Room 101; and O'Brien. Winston discovers that the latter, pretending to be a brother rebel, actually exposed Winston and Julia by luring them into the Brotherhood. It exists only to trap unwary rebels.

For nine months Winston endures drugs, beatings, and questioning. O'Brien, who changes roles and becomes his interrogator, tries to convince him that two plus two equals five. Winston complies by confessing to crimes. Weary and disoriented, he sees four fingers as five. O'Brien tells Winston that Julia betrayed him and implies that Winston already knows what to expect in Room 101. During reintegration (brainwashing), O'Brien explains to Winston that "God is power."

Orwell honors his protagonist for his attempt to remain true to principle. Winston refuses to give in to mental manipulation and clings to a shred of his former principles—he has not betrayed Julia. After he recuperates and tries to reconcile his belief in O'Brien's illogic, he continues to dream of her. O'Brien punishes him for hating Big Brother by remanding him to Room 101, where he can expect to meet his worst fear. His head is plunged into a cage of rats. He begs O'Brien: "Do it to Julia! Do it to Julia! Not me!" The betrayal proves to O'Brien that Winston has broken. He gains release and faces an empty chessboard at the Chestnut Tree Café. Julia joins him and admits that she also betrayed their pledge. After her departure, Winston weeps in despair. An announcement of Oceania's victory elicits his love of Big Brother. (Alok 1989; Bloom 1987c; Brown 1976; Buitehuis and Nadel 1988; Calder 1987; Connelly 1986; Hynes 1974; Jenson 1984; Oldsey and Browne 1986; Orwell 1949; Stansky 1984)

See also bestiality; Big Brother; dystopia; Oceania; Orwell, George; Smith, Winston; speculative fiction; *We*; women in utopia; Zamyatin, Yevgeny.

NIRVANA

The Hindu concept of heaven, nirvana is the goal of an earthly cycle of births, deaths, and reincarnations. The merger of self with the universe, an achievement of godliness through acquiescence to the unending flow of suffering and joy, ultimately merges into pure energy, an abstract haven that contrasts with the Judeo-Christian belief in a concrete afterlife. In Hindu tradition, the unity of self with otherworldliness relieves the soul of the search for understanding and release. A transcendent state, nirvana is attained by the seeker only after wisdom and teaching prove futile and the seeker realizes the true simplicity of the divine. By locating the individual path to oneness with the universe, the seeker willingly drops the burdens of sensuality, pride, and emotion and welcomes the eternal truth. In this mystical cosmos, past, present, and future lose their meaning in the continual flow of events. Peace is a contentment with all phases of life, which are necessary experiences to the follower of Buddha.

In Hermann Hesse's *Siddhartha* (1951), the seeker allies his metaphor for nirvana with the flow of the river. Content at the humble home of the ferryman, Siddhartha watches the faces of passengers, who blend into a stream of all human lives that have ever been or ever will be. He is content at the riverside, where contemplation delivers him from worries, passions, and self-pity, and slips easily into bliss. Liberated from Earth's trappings, he snuffs out self and all its demands and fears. The letting go reduces dependence on impermanence and replaces it with a sublime tranquillity. (Cavendish 1970; Cavendish 1980; Dutt 1910; Eliade 1986; Fleissner 1972; Hastings 1951; Hesse 1951; Jurji 1946; McDannell 1994; Pelikan 1992b)

See also asceticism; Buddhism; heaven; Hesse, Hermann; karma; Siddhartha; *Siddhartha*.

 O-90

O-90 is the name of the naive, rosy-cheeked ingenue who loves a mathematician, D-503, in Yevgeny Zamyatin's *We* (1921). Unassuming and mediocre of thought, O-90 (nicknamed O) lacks the importance in D-503's life to earn much more than his casual dismissal in Chapter 2:

> Dear O! It always seems to me that she looks exactly like her name: about ten centimeters shorter than the Maternal Norm, and therefore carved in the round, all of her, with that pink O, her mouth, open to meet every word I say.

Paradoxically, to D-503, O is both baby and sexual release. She bypasses his mental competitiveness, serving his physical needs by acquiring pink coupons that entitle her to private liaisons. She relates to him physically because she lacks the intelligence to understand a man who thinks in numbers and formulas.

The couple's relationship withers after D-503 wearies of her and turns to I-330, an alluring, daring woman who flouts the rules and bedazzles her lover. In Chapter 18, undeceived by his excuses, O-90 presents a formal departure notice, which concludes optimistically,

> I need only two or three days to put together the pieces of me into some semblance of the former O-90, and then I will go and tell them myself that I withdraw my registration for you.

In Chapter 19 she begs D-503 to give her a child before they part permanently. Eyes closed, radiant, and smiling, she insists that pregnancy is her only goal. D-503's agreement to one last sexual encounter clears his mind of interest in O-90. After D-503 and I-330 have succumbed to the state dictator's machine, O-90 presents a tentative hope that the bit of humanity in the child's father may spark a rebellion against oppression. (Grigson 1963; Kunitz 1942; Russell 1994; Shane 1968; Zamyatin 1972)

See also D-503; totalitarianism; *We*; women in utopia; Zamyatin, Yevgeny.

 OCEANA

Oceana is an antiroyalist Elizabethan utopia created by Sir John Harrington in his *Commonwealth of Oceana* (1656). Harrington's republican idyll proposes an alternate to England's social ills through the eradication of monarchy and the application of fair economic principle. The political treatise reflects the turmoil preceding the English civil war, which overturned the monarchy and for 11 years imposed the rule of two Puritans—Oliver and Richard Cromwell—as Lord Protectors of the Commonwealth. Although a republican in spirit, Harrington regretted the decapitation of Charles I and later suffered an unjust imprisonment for alleged treason and support of Puritan regicides.

Oceana's strengths lie in a justly elected bicameral legislature and an even-handed distribution of property and seignory, or positions of power, including knights, burgesses, and ambassadors. By moving upper and lower classes toward a broad-based middle class, Harrington proposes to end despotism and the tyranny of land ownership. The imaginary state, divided into 50 shires governed by horse and foot soldiers, elects an elder—who is beyond the age of 30—to serve as parish deputy for a single term of one year. By passing the control to subsequent deputies annually, Harrington spreads the power base over most of the male population, who also elect a justice of the peace, juryman, captain, ensign, and constable.

The annual meeting of Oceana's deputies results in a national legislature, which debates public concerns. The ultimate will of the people results in fair laws and a sensible military headed by the roll-keeper, or census-taker. A parallel hierarchy rules the state church, which is required by law to be Christian but allows for any variance of worship. Likewise, the coordination of youth into a standing militia provides Oceana with sufficient foot and horse soldiers.

Harrington's intensely stratified paradigm reveals his bias toward a tight bureaucracy held accountable to the people through checks and balances. As with Plato's *Republic* (fifth century B.C.), his major weakness lies in making no specific statements concerning children, women, servants, or other noncombatants. Such disenfranchisement, springing from the prejudices of his age, exhibits the sexism of any patriarchal system that invests power and authority in able-bodied males. (Downs 1977; Harrington 1992; Magnusson 1990; Negley and Patrick 1952; Tawney 1993)

See also classism; Harrington, Sir James; Plato; *The Republic;* women in utopia.

 # OCEANIA

The repressively austere setting of George Orwell's *1984* is ostensibly the London of the mid-nineteenth century. Oceania suffers from a collapse of the world order and the rise of a bullying power broker named Big Brother. Society, an out-of-proportion pyramid broken into a tripartite class system, features a handful of Inner Party rulers at the top, a small Outer Party made up of powerless, manipulated bureaucrats, and a sea of proles, the drones who carry out menial tasks. Daily life, made tolerable by the regular consumption of Victory Gin, witnesses a melange of wretched images: constant shortages of shoes, chocolate, and cigarettes; party loyalists clad in dreary uniform coveralls; crumbling buildings; and private lives controlled by the ubiquitous, falsifying telescreen, which portrays history and current events in whatever light the Party deems necessary for maximum public control.

Because reality conforms to whatever lies the Newspeakers are currently peddling, paranoia is a perpetual state in Oceania. Thought Police brutalize at will by applying uncodified law and exacting the death penalty for any sign of opposition. Military parades remind citizens that international violence has become a way of life. Similarly, consumerism and godlessness sap human values. In Book 2, Chapter 5, Orwell comments on indistinct visions and sounds of violence:

> Late at night, when crowds of rowdy proles roamed the streets, the town had a curiously febrile air. The rocket bombs crashed oftener than ever, and sometimes in the far distance there were enormous explosions which no one could explain and about which there were wild rumors.

Winston explains to Julia that the bombings keep the gullible lower classes in line and make them more patriotic toward Oceania's military. Tinged by fear of annihilation, free-floating hostility, alienation, propaganda posters turning nonwhite faces into terrifying enemy soldiers, contempt for the working class, and tense moments of organized hate, life in Oceania forces characters like Winston Smith into desperate attempts to break free to celebrate their humanity. (Alok 1989; Bloom 1987c; Brown 1976; Buitehuis and Nadel 1988; Calder 1987; Connelly 1986; Hynes 1974; Jenson 1984; Oldsey and Browne 1986; Orwell 1949; Stansky 1984)

See also bestiality; Big Brother; classism; disillusion; Orwell, George; slavery; Smith, Winston; technology; totalitarianism.

 # "OF CANNIBALS"

See "Des Cannibales"

 # OFFRED

Offred is the unnamed central intelligence of Margaret Atwood's *The Handmaid's Tale* (1985), a sinister dystopian fantasy set in a future United States decimated by nuclear war, toxic pollutants, and fanatical totalitarianism. Modestly clad in a red wide-sleeved, ankle-length Mother Hubbard, gloves, and overdress topped by a winged wimple and undergirded by petticoat, red stockings, and white cotton bloomers, 33-year-old Offred serves Gilead as a Handmaid, or breeder. Named "Of Fred" for the aging Commander of the Faithful—later identified as Frederick Waterford, head of Gilead's security force, who services her in ritual matings—she replaces a predecessor, also named Offred, who killed herself rather than wait to be annihilated for inability to conceive. Offred is a chillingly matter-of-fact narrator who loses her job, financial control, and identity after her womb is commandeered by the state. She bargains to learn the fate of her husband Luke and her militant feminist mother; she schemes to escape and reunite with her daughter.

Under more normal circumstances, Atwood reveals Offred's strengths. On her first unauthorized "date" with the gray-haired Commander, Offred creeps downstairs to an off-limits hideaway for a game of Scrabble, at which she excels, although she is denied reading material and fears she will lose her literacy skills. Expecting perversion, possibly torture, she is surprised that he craves affection, a commodity long since banned in pious, repressive Gilead. In exchange, she asks for hand lotion and information about the outside world. The forbidden fruits of their dalliance include an out-of-date issue of *Vogue* magazine, chaste kisses, and a late-night foray to Jezebel's, a garish night spot staffed by whores and designed to improve trade relations with Arab and Japanese businessmen.

Offred is a literary foil to both her militant mother, who campaigns against pornography, and Moira, an irrepressible, witty, lesbian college friend who resurfaces during their days at the Rachel and Leah Re-education Center. Neither rebel nor Unwoman, Offred is a bright pseudocollaborator who skillfully works the system against itself. Aswirl in her brain are doubts about the future, fear for her loved ones, a controlled urge for suicide, concern that she is losing her smooth complexion, suspicions that her lover Nick may belong to a spy unit, and the maddening loss of humanity that deadens most of Gilead. She replays "reconstructions" of scenes in which Luke is shot during a break for the Canadian border, or imprisoned and tortured. Her dreams and thoughts turn frequently to her daughter, whom her captors removed from her custody on the day that Offred and Luke tried to cross into Canada on phony visas.

Although Offred is capable of thinking for herself, the structured ennui that trains her for the role of Handmaid and immures her in a chaste cell erodes her resolve. When Janine, a Handmaid-in-training, weeps at an afternoon testimonial, Offred joins the voices condemning Janine as the instigator of gang rape. Likewise, Offred is caught up in the cohesive effort of Handmaids to welcome Ofwarren's newborn daughter, Angela. The emotional event, one of the blessed birthings that does not produce a deformed infant, brings out tears and hysteria in Offred, who retires to her room to sleep. Later, Offred reports that Angela is a "shredder," deformed by Gilead's chemical and radioactive pollutants.

The end of the novel carries the reader two centuries into the future to 2195, out of range of proof that Offred, a diarist of 30 cassette tapes, was able to escape Gilead and reunite with her past. Professor Pieixoto, who studies the evidence and presents his views at a symposium of experts, assumes that she took the Underground Frailroad to Bangor, Maine, and found shelter with Quakers. He concludes that she emigrated to either Canada or England and lived in seclusion. (Atwood 1972; *Contemporary Authors* 1989; *Contemporary Literary Criticism* 1987; Davidson 1986; Dreifus 1992; Hammer 1990; Ingersoll 1991; McCombs 1988; *Major Twentieth-Century Writers* 1990; Van Spanckeren and Castro 1988)

OMOO

The second sea romance in the canon of Herman Melville, *Omoo* (1847) is the picaresque literary offshoot of a real voyage that the author made when he escaped the Marquesas Islands in July 1842. Having deserted the *Acushnet* four months earlier with comrade Toby Greene, Melville sought solace from sea duty among the Typees, a tribe of cannibals across the mountains from Nukuheva Bay. These adventures in a tropical paradise serve as the basis for the semiautobiographical dystopian novel *Typee* (1846).

The second stage of Melville's revolt against harsh naval justice and bad food takes him to Tahiti on the Australian whaler *Lucy Ann.* Separating from Toby, Melville tolerated the vagaries of shipboard justice, joined a budding mutiny, and served a few weeks in an English jail. Deserting a second time, he joined John Troy, the ship's doctor, for a jaunt in Papeete, the capital of Tahiti. His beach-bum existence required little work; when he ran short of cash, he found employment as a day laborer. The remainder of his time was spent in island pleasures. From these months in the Society Islands and gleanings from other sea tales, he composed his second adventure novel, *Omoo: A Narrative of Adventures in the South Seas,* a revealing commentary on American colonization and the resulting disease, press-gangs, and squalor that quickly depleted indigenous Polynesians of their innocence and breezy joie de vivre.

The protagonist, Herman Melville, a lackadaisical rover, departs from Nukuheva aboard an English whaler, the *Julia,* which stops in port long enough to fill shortages among the crew. Melville is expected to function as an ordinary seaman, but his leg injury, received while crossing the mountains beyond Nukuheva, impairs movement. Consequently, he relieves the tedium with chess games and books, and forms a strong bond with Dr. Long Ghost, the ship's doctor. The men endure a diet of hardtack and salt pork; conditions worsen, causing death to two crewmen from the vermin-infested hulk of the decaying *Julia.* After Captain Guy grows too ill to continue the voyage, the ship docks at Papeete, Tahiti.

Melville encourages his comrades to sign a round robin, an informal crew petition announcing intentions to defect, but the incompetent captain, who is wise to their disgruntlement, keeps the boat under sail in the harbor and goes ashore by longboat to seek medical care. Doctor Long Ghost, a good-natured peacemaker, maintains a semblance of order among the men, who pursue their plans to desert by maneuvering the *Julia* into the harbor. The crew dispatches the cook with a list of complaints to British authorities. They side with the captain.

To emphasize the sailors' reasons for departing a bad life and seeking something better, Herman Melville highlights the disenfranchisement of sailors. As the *Julia* is made ready for continuing its voyage under Jermin, the first mate, a Maori harpooner sabotages the ship. The mate attempts to bring the *Julia* to port. The crew are held accountable for insubordination, and are confined for five days to a French frigate. Reassigned to the *Julia,* they rebel and fall to "Capin Bob," a local guide and keeper of a native lockup dubbed the Hotel de Calabooza. The men are marched a mile beyond a village. At the beginning of Chapter 31, Melville remarks on the natural loveliness surrounding the jail:

> A mountain stream here flowed at the foot of a verdant slope; on one hand, it murmured along until the waters, spreading themselves upon a beach of small, sparkling shells, trickled into the sea; on the other, was a long defile, where the eye pursued a gleaming, sinuous thread, lost in shade and verdure.

In the distance, he spies at the top of a slope their destination: an oval native residence topped with white thatch.

In primitive surroundings, the crew are shackled to 20-foot boards by night. By day they are shepherded to a river for bathing and receive friendly visits from curious islanders. Prison meals consist of turnips, oranges, and bread-fruit, a native staple. Melville rhapsodizes:

> In many places the trees formed a dense shade, spreading overhead a dark, rustling vault, groined with boughs, and studded here and there with the rip-ened spheres, like gilded balls. In several places, the overladen branches were borne to the earth, hiding the trunk in a tent of foliage. Once fairly in the grove, we could see nothing else: it was oranges all round.

A gradual relaxation of confinement frees the men to receive local visitors and to traverse Broom Road, where they befriend natives and go "a-pleasuring."

Still adamant about punishing the mutineers, Consul Wilson dispatches a doctor to examine the inmates, who feign illness. The men's health is actually much improved; they reject medication, but drink up any elixir containing alcohol. Supercilious English missionaries supply them with religious tracts and pious brow-beating; French priests offer liquor and loaves of fresh bread. After three weeks of recuperation, Captain Guy recovers, hires a new crew, and departs on the *Julia.* The prisoners are released from the stocks and left to fend for themselves. They live off local produce, infringe on island hospitality, and steal from ships, whose willing crew members smuggle food from larders and galleys. Melville wearies of idleness and attends the English church. Delivered in pidgin English, the sermon is a thinly veiled attempt to exploit natives, and offends him because it patronizes Polynesian intelligence.

Melville learns that the nearby island of Imeeo offers work to day laborers. The Tahitians, in contrast, make little effort:

> Strolling among the trees of a morning, you came upon them napping on the shady side of a canoe hauled up among the bushes; lying under a tree smoking; or, more frequently still, gambling with pebbles. . . . Upon the whole, they were a merry, indigent, godless race.

Melville and the doctor interview with planters Shorty and Zeke. Traveling under the aliases of Peter and Paul, the two idlers steal a boat and approach the plantation to work. A few days of hoeing potatoes in the steamy, mosquito-infested fields convinces Melville and the doctor that the Tahitians are wise to avoid drudgery.

The duo journey to Tamai, a remote village. In Chapter 63, among natives unsullied by white culture, Melville observes local girls dancing in a traditional ceremony:

> ... they softly sway themselves, gradually quickening the movement, until at length, for a few passionate moments, with throbbing bosoms, and glowing cheeks, they abandon themselves to all the spirit of the dance, apparently lost to everything around.

Melville and Doctor Long Ghost consider taking up permanent residency among the natives. Two days later, the Tamaians inexplicably oust them.

Melville and his companion make a leisurely visit to Partoowye, home of Pomaree Vahinee I, queen of Tahiti, in hopes of obtaining court posts. After five weeks, Melville and the doctor gain entrance to the queen's hall through a kindly emissary. The queen, who is dining, shoos them away.

The men encounter a former ship's carpenter, who mentions the arrival of a whaler, the *Leviathan*. Melville and Doctor Long Ghost question the crew and learn that conditions are similar to those on the *Julia.* Returning to the *Leviathan,* Melville and his friend discover that the crew, eager to remain in port, had lied about the ship so the captain would be unable to hire enough men to depart. Melville and Doctor Long Ghost apply for berths. Melville conceals his role in mutiny aboard the *Julia* and is hired, but the captain rejects the doctor. The whaler departs for a year's cruise to Japan, leaving the doctor in Tahiti.

Lighter in tone but similar in thematic thrust to *Typee,* Melville exposes missionaries for exploiting natives and denounces the extermination of island laissez-faire in favor of rigid theocracy. His lackadaisical protagonist moves lazily and purposelessly through Tahiti in the style of a rover, which in Tahitian is *omoo.* From the point of view of the narrator, a ne'er-do-well rambler, the island utopia, which once knew no white intervention, has lost its idyllic qualities through contact with a motley pack of disease-ridden sailors, adventurers, beachcombers, land thieves, and suspect religious workers. From a critical standpoint, the good-humored tale of Melville's rovings possesses less philosophical import than does *Typee,* but his candid jibes at unscrupulous Bible-thumpers heighten the value of the novel as antitheocratic social criticism. (Allen 1971; Bloom 1986d; Bryant 1986; Hillway 1979; Melville 1964; Melville 1968; Sealts 1982; Wolff 1987)

See also disillusion; Eden; escapism; Melville, Herman; theocracy; *Typee.*

ORWELL, GEORGE

George Orwell is the pen name of anti-intellectual, antiaristocrat British propagandist, journalist, and fiction writer Eric Arthur Blair (June 25, 1903–January 21, 1950). He is best known for his nonconformist patriotism and for two dystopian novels, *1984* (1949) and *Animal Farm* (1945). His literary imperfect worlds provided the English language with the terms "Orwellian," "doublethink," "newspeak," and "Big Brother." Classed in the league of such masters as Jonathan Swift, Charles Dickens, and Rudyard Kipling, Orwell was clever at hooking readers with provocative opening lines; for example, "As I write, highly civilized human beings are flying overhead, trying to kill me" and "It was a bright cold day in April, and the clocks were striking thirteen."

Orwell's father, Eric Blair, Sr., served the Indian bureaucracy as a narcotics agent in Motihari, Bengal. Orwell grew miserably aware of British class consciousness (he considered his family "lower-upper-middle" class). At age four Orwell and his two sisters, Margaret and Avril, sailed for England, where he entered Eastbourne's St. Cyprian's Boys' School. Homesickness and ridicule of his portly frame robbed him of energy. Lethargic and lonely, he longed to return to India. Among the sons of elite families, he came to despise petty snobbery and favor-currying as well as picky rules (which he was frequently accused of breaking). Orwell took comfort in his studies, particularly languages and literature; his favorite authors were Swift and Kipling. He distinguished himself at age 11 by publishing a poem about the death of Field Marshal Kitchener, a British hero. A promising scholar, Orwell enrolled at a reduced rate to prepare for Wallington. In 1917 he won a scholarship to Eton.

A diligent reader and debater, during World War I Orwell preferred pacifist and socialist issues. Although labeled a leftist, he kept his distance from party politics. He chose a career in social service and rose to the rank of sergeant in the Burmese police, an assignment he obviously despised, as demonstrated by his much anthologized essay "Shooting an Elephant." By 1927 Orwell so disliked the racism implicit in police work under British imperialism that he quit and took up writing. While wandering France and Great Britain, he adopted the pen name George Orwell from an English river.

Influenced by Jack London's *The People of the Abyss* (1903), Orwell drifted through menial jobs in pub kitchens and slept in sheds and cheap hostels to study the low end of the working class. By 1933 these humbling experiences provided him material for *Down and Out in Paris and London* (1933). He published three unprofitable titles—*Burmese Days* (1934), *A Clergyman's Daughter* (1935), and *Keep the Aspidistra Flying* (1936)—over the next three years while teaching at Hawthorne High School for Boys in Hayes, Middlesex, and clerking in a bookshop. In 1936 Orwell wed Eileen O'Shaughnessy, a journalist and teacher. During the late 1930s the couple operated a pub and grocery in Wallington, Hertfordshire.

Jewish scholar Israel Gollancz, founder of the Left Book Club (an antifascist, anti-Nazi publishing house), financed Orwell's trip to a depressed industrial area in Manchester in the early months of 1937. Orwell kept a diary, and these writings evolved into *The Road to Wigan Pier* (1937), which expressed his political views on joblessness and other discouraging aspects faced by unskilled laborers. In his political commentary, he wrote that all avenues of society—work, finance, religion, education, marriage, and family—are political and that no one can avoid political issues. To Orwell, politics— with its basis in untruth,

George Orwell

evasion, foolishness, animosity, and schizophrenia—was untrustworthy and more than a shade dishonorable.

As Europe entered a troubled age, Orwell joined the P.O.U.M., a Marxist republican militia fighting Generalissimo Franco's fascism, and served as war correspondent. In June 1937, after five months at the Aragon front, Orwell caught a sniper's bullet in the throat. He recovered from paralysis and aphasia, and continued writing antifascist propaganda, but discovered that his beliefs were out of favor as communism gained power. Fearful of a purge led by communist hard-liners, he and his wife fled across the Pyrenees to France. They settled on a Hertfordshire farm, where Orwell raised hens and grew vegetables until Nazi bombings drove him out. As a result of their escape of imminent execution, Orwell channeled his intense anticommunism into *Homage to Catalonia.*

Orwell's socialistic beliefs gained strength and bolstered a significant phase in his literary career. He composed "As I Please," a literary column for the *London Tribune,* and published *Inside the Whale and Other Essays* (1940), *The Lion and the Unicorn: Socialism and the English Genius* (1940), and critiques and articles in other journals and newspapers. Shortly before World War II truncated this prolific phase, he published his first successful fiction, *Coming Up for Air* (1939), a novel about suburban stagnation. Abandoning his characteristic humanism after Axis powers overran Eastern Europe, he sought a commission in the army, but was declared ineligible because of consumptive lungs. He enlisted in the national militia, served the British Broadcasting Corporation as their Indian editor, and made antitotalitarian broadcasts overseas.

The most lucrative portion of Orwell's career began at the end of the war, when he wrote his classic Swiftian satire *Animal Farm,* an internationally best-selling novel incorporating his experiences at Wallington. So trenchant was his dystopian beast fable that it went unpublished for a year until Orwell could locate a company willing to tackle antiauthoritarianism. While polishing *Dickens, Dali, and Others: Studies in Popular Culture* in 1946, he suffered a worsening of his tuberculosis and the unexpected death of Eileen during a routine hysterectomy.

Although grief-stricken, terminally ill, and frequently bedfast, Orwell elected to keep his adopted infant, Richard. With the help of a sister, the family settled off Scotland's west coast at Barnhill on Jura, Argylls, a windswept, isolated island of the Inner Hebrides. He recognized the brevity of his time, and in January 1949, before hospitalization at a sanitarium in Gloucestershire, England, he completed *1984,* a dispirited dystopian novel that he originally intended to call *The Last Man in Europe.* During a brief rally in strength, he penned a harsh diatribe, *Such, Such Were the Joys,* detailing the atrocities of the English boarding school system. In a final attempt to reestablish life and health, he wed Sonia Mary Brownell in 1949. He made plans to retire to a Swiss sanitarium, but within months he collapsed, sick and exhausted from repeated lung hemorrhages. On his deathbed Orwell composed both his will and an understated epitaph:

Here Lies
Eric Arthur Blair
Born June 25th 1903
Died January 21st 1950

He asked that no biography be written about him. In a rural churchyard in the village of Sutton Courtenay, his remains lie buried near the end of an avenue of yews. *Shooting an Elephant and Other Essays* was published in late 1950, and *Such, Such Were the Joys* in 1953. His essays, polemics, and correspondence were gathered into four volumes and published in 1968. (Buitehuis and Nadel 1988; Crick 1980; Ferrell 1988; Gardner 1987; Reilly 1989)

See also *Animal Farm;* Big Brother; London, Jack; Napoleon; *1984;* prophecy; satire; Smith, Winston; Snowball; totalitarianism.

OVID

Ovid authored the *Metamorphoses* (A.D. 8), Book 1 of which contains the idyllic lore of Rome's creation and a carefree golden age, a reevaluation of the era described in Hesiod's *Works and Days* (eighth century B.C.). Born March 20, 43 B.C., Publius Ovidius Naso was a native of the Abruzzi Mountains. His parents were wealthy enough to send Ovid to Rome to study literature and grammar under two scholars. From his Italian tutelage, Ovid advanced to Athens and studied philosophy. Later, he traveled to the site of ancient Troy.

On his return to Rome, Ovid practiced law and delighted in composing his orations in verse. At age 19 he went into an emotional decline after the untimely death of his older brother. Abandoning trial law, Ovid devoted his talents to poetry, publishing his first collection in 20 B.C. He quickly found a patron and continued writing erotic verse, including the *Ars Amatoria* (1 B.C.), *Metamorphoses* (A.D. 8), *Heroides* (15 B.C.), *De Medicamine Faciei Feminae* (date unknown), *Fasti* (posthumous, A.D. 18), *Remedia Amoris* (A.D. 2), *Ibis* (date unknown), and *Halieutica* (date unknown).

Ovid's most remarkable writing reset Greek mythology into dizzyingly lush verse. Proclaimed a national treasure, he lived the charmed life of the local artist-in-residence, and influenced a coterie of contemporaries. He found contentment in marriage to Favia, his third wife, then lost all by quarreling with Emperor Augustus. In A.D. 8, Ovid sailed east to Tomis, a grim fishing village on the Black Sea. Whatever the cause of this royal rift, Ovid never recovered. Grim and despairing away from the glitter and buoyancy of Roman city life, the poet wrote *Epistulae ex Ponto* (posthumous, date unknown), as well as verse dedicated to Favia, friends, and Emperor Augustus. Ten years after abandoning all that he held dear, Ovid died in exile. (*Bulfinch's Mythology* 1964; Grimal 1991; Guerber 1921; Hamilton 1942; Hesiod 1973; Howatson 1991; Morford and Lenardon 1977; Ovid 1977; Snodgrass 1988b)

See also golden age; Hesiod; Virgil.

OZ

A whimsical, child-pleasing land, its center is the Emerald City, a green-tinged, allegorical utopia in L. Frank Baum's *The Wonderful Wizard of Oz* (1900). Ruled by four witches, two good and two evil, Oz is no longer tyrannized by the Witch of the East after Dorothy's whirling house lands on her, leaving only her feet sticking out. The corresponding Witch of the West, an evil sorceress, is balanced by the good witches of the north and south. Other territories added to Baum's growing series of Oz books include Munchkin country in the southeast, the Quadlings to the southwest, Winkie land in the east, and Gillikin to the north. On the perimeter lie great deserts, shifting sand, wastelands, and impassable terrain. The usual approach, preferred by the wizard and used by Dorothy in her arrival by cyclone, is by air across impermeable borders.

The anomalies of Oz suit a child's fantasy novel. The history of Oz centers on the arrival of a hot-air balloon labeled O. Z. and bearing the man who assumes the role of the Great Oz. The supreme ruler is a great wizard, whose centralized palace is the site of the most engaging part of the plot and of Dorothy's realignment of values. Dotted about the countryside that surrounds his palace are fertile grain fields, vegetable patches, and woods. Citizens are free of aging, sickness, and death. No one needs money; everyone divides time between work and frolicking. (Baum 1983; Baum and MacFall 1961; Bewley 1970; Manguel and Guadalupi 1987; Mannix 1964; Snodgrass 1992; Snow 1954; Wagenknecht 1968)

See also Baum, L. Frank; Dorothy; Emerald City; fantasy; Wizard of Oz; *The Wonderful Wizard of Oz.*

PANDEMONIUM

A literary capital of hell and the consummate gathering of evildoers in *Paradise Lost* (1667), the term was created by John Milton from Greek words meaning "all demons." Pandemonium was erected by Mulciber; like Satan and the denizens of the Christian Underworld, he was once an angel and had built towers in heaven. After falling from heaven, Mulciber joins Mammon, a demon who heads a contingent of fallen angels tunneling into a volcano in search of precious metals. Because Mammon perpetually studied the gold pavement when he lived in heaven, he continues to cast his eyes downward and locates the building material needed for Pandemonium. In Book I, lines 686–690, Milton characterizes Mammon's rapaciousness:

> . . . with impious hands
> Rifl'd the bowels of their mother Earth
> For Treasures better hid. Soon had his crew
> Op'n'd into the Hill a spacious wound
> And digg'd out ribs of Gold.

The release of ore causes molten metal to erupt in a strong exhalation, "as an Organ from one blast of wind to many a row of Pipes the sound-board breathes."

Like a Christian community, hell emulates sanctity. At the heart of Pandemonium rises a temple set with pilasters, Doric columns, bronze doors, porches, hall, throne, and gaudy cornices, friezes, and moldings. Its golden roof rivals the splendors of Babylon and Egypt, both pagan nations. Magic light fixtures adorn the exterior edge of the gables. This ostentatious gathering spot becomes the conference hall for Satan's allies—Astarte, Beelzebub, Belial, Dagon, Isis, Moloch, Orus, and Osiris—who sit on gold seats "in close recess and secret conclave." Book II, lines 1–505, records the speeches as Milton's hellish collection of miscreants plots a war on God by circumventing Adam and Eve, the garden-keepers of Paradise, God's new creation. When they complete their first session, they take a break for physical activity, music, boating, and discussion in the hollow abyss of hell. (Enroth 1970; Harrison et al. 1967; Hornstein et al. 1973; Hughes 1957; Martz 1967; Milton 1957a; Parker 1958)

See also Adam; Eden; Eve; heaven; Milton, John; *Paradise Lost; Paradise Regained;* theocracy.

PANGLOSS

The oracular sage and comic teacher of Voltaire's *Candide* (1759), Pangloss (whose name means "all tongue") resides in the home of Baron Thunder-ten-tronckh, a Westphalian aristocrat who hires him to instruct his daughter and Candide, a retainer who is possibly the son of the baron's sister. As a teacher of "metaphysico-theologo-cosmolo-nigology," he dispenses the Leibnitzian theory that "there is no effect without a cause." Doctor Pangloss's philosophy tends toward unquestioned optimism that "all that happens is for the best in the best of all possible worlds." Set against the tutor's lust for chambermaids, this unrealistic expectation of worldly goodness turns ludicrous as Voltaire molds the tale toward caustic satire of carnality, tyranny, ignorance, and a host of other human vices.

Pangloss demonstrates a remarkable resilience against venereal disease, penury, and torture, resurfacing twice during Candide's world travels. Although Pangloss loses an eye and an ear and narrowly escapes burning at the stake and subsequent dissection at a mortuary, he returns unharmed to support Candide with infusions of optimism, which forms the bulk of the hero's personal creed. In the final chapter, as Candide turns from wandering to tending his small garden patch, Pangloss acknowledges, "You are right . . . for when man was put in the Garden of Eden, he was put there *ut operaretur eum*, to work; which proves that man was not born for rest." Later, he rationalizes Candide's misfortunes as a fateful kismet and concludes, "if you had not lost all your sheep from the good country of Eldorado, you would not be here eating candied citrons and pistachios." (Andrews 1981; Ayer 1986; Gay 1988; Mason 1981; Richter and Ricardo 1980; Voltaire 1961)

See also Candide; *Candide*; escapism; kismet; satire; Voltaire, François.

PANTISOCRACY

A utopian commune or nation in which all people rule equally, the word is derived from the Greek for "equal rule." The egalitarian concept of pantisocracy belongs to an idealized time and place that suggests a museum showcase, as characterized in the pastoral lore of Hesiod, Virgil, and Ovid. Pantisocracy contrasts with less roseate systems of government that accommodate the needs of the populace and the exigencies of time and place; for example,

- gang-style rule in J. M. Barrie's fantasy play *Peter Pan* (1904), and the subverted terrorism in Anthony Burgess's *A Clockwork Orange* (1962) and Karel Capek's robot-run island in *R. U. R.* (1920)

- monarchic rule in the person of the philosopher-king in Plato's *Republic* (fifth century B.C.), Aristophanes's *The Birds* (414 B.C.), and Alfred Tennyson's *Idylls of the King* (1888)

- the benign despotism in Frank Baum's *The Wonderful Wizard of Oz* (1900), James Hilton's *Lost Horizon* (1933), Richard Adams's rabbit world in *Watership Down* (1972), and Daniel Defoe's *Robinson Crusoe* (1719)

- a subdued matriarchy that supports communal living and suppressed reproduction in W. H. Hudson's *A Crystal Age* (1887)

- the tyranny of Big Brother in George Orwell's *1984* (1949) and a book-burning state in Ray Bradbury's *Fahrenheit 451* (1953)

- the unsophisticated collectivism that upholds a frail ecosystem in Marge Piercy's *Woman on the Edge of Time* (1976)

- totalitarianism, the force that controls Ayn Rand's *Anthem* (1937) and P. D. James's *The Children of Men* (1993)

- technocracy, the science-driven system of Francis Bacon's *New Atlantis* (1627)

- theocracy, the god-centered rule in St. Augustine's *De Civitate Dei* (426) and Dante's *Divine Comedy* (1320), in John Bunyan's Celestial City, at the heart of *Pilgrim's Progress* (1678) and Joseph Smith's *Book of Mormon* (1830), and as an impetus to the Inquisition in Voltaire's *Candide* (1759) and to Brakelondia's success in Thomas Carlyle's *Past and Present* (1843)

- in Jack London's *The Iron Heel* (1907), the self-serving plutocracy, a self-centered oligarchy that devalues the proletariat, even though working-class people keep it afloat

- anarchy, the out-of-control system of survival that erodes the confidence of the unnamed diarist of Doris Lessing's *Memoirs of a Survivor* (1974)

- the benign, sybaritic theocracy at François Rabelais's Abbey of Thélème in *Gargantua and Pantagruel* (1562), where the guiding principle is "Do what you will"

Pantisocracy is a convention of simplistic pastoral havens where everyone shares in the care of flocks, or in the beast fable, which depicts a loose confederation of animals, notably in Richard Adams's *Watership Down* (1972). Although tinged with servitude by the enslavement of the Yahoos, pantisocracy also appears in the fictional land of the Houyhnhnms in Book 4 of Jonathan Swift's *Gulliver's Travels* (1727), where a general assembly sends out exhortations rather than dicta. A second model appears in the sharing of grain harvesting by English farm workers in William Morris's *News from Nowhere* (1890). As revealed in historian Hammond's commentary, government relies on neighborliness, and therefore lacks both violent acts and the criminal law to punish them. Morris's agrarian economy has much in common with Hesiod's golden age.

Pantisocracy may begin with the best intentions, then lose its balance and slide into a corrupt form of commune. In the first stages of the animals' ouster of Jones, the owner of Manor Farm in Chapter 1 of George Orwell's dystopic allegory *Animal Farm* (1945), the animals sing an anthem, "Beasts of England," that rejoices in their shared lot:

Bright will shine the fields of England,
Purer shall its waters be,
Sweeter yet shall blow its breezes
On the day that sets us free.

For that day we all must labour,
Though we die before it break;
Cows and horses, geese and turkeys,
All must toil for freedom's sake.

The painting of the Seven Commandments on the barn wall guarantees equality and concludes with the naive assumption that, under bestial rule, "all animals are equal." By the end of the fable, however, the greedy pig Napoleon has distorted the rule by making some animals more equal than others.

Historically, the idea of pantisocracy does not lend itself to human nature, even in Eden and heaven. In the mid-1800s, Karl Marx joined Friedrich Engels in writing *The Communist Manifesto* (1848), a plan for a worldwide workers' revolt against capitalism to create communism. Marx and Engels's idealized collective society elects its ruling committees to oversee workers without jeopardizing the proletarian notion of classlessness. For all its discussion of righting wrongs done the working class under capitalism and monarchy, the purest of Marxist ideals requires a layer of bureaucracy—an overseer class that regulates government, finance, education, the military, and domestic and international policy. (Carlyle 1977; Marx and Engels 1985; Morris 1968b; Orwell 1946; Swift 1958)

See also *Animal Farm;* Carlyle, Thomas; *The Communist Manifesto;* Eden; Engels, Friedrich; *Gulliver's Travels;* heaven; Hesiod; Houyhnhnms; Marx, Karl; Morris, William; Napoleon; *News from Nowhere; Past and Present;* pastoral; utopia; *Watership Down.*

PARADISE

See Avalon; *Divina Commedia;* Eden; heaven; nirvana; *Paradise Lost; Paradise Regained.*

PARADISE LOST

England's elegant, dramatic Christian epic was completed by John Milton in 1667; it is based on the biblical Garden of Eden, which is closed to Adam and Eve after their fall from grace. A monument to the English Renaissance, *Paradise Lost* remains unequaled in scope, control, and rhetorical excellence. From boyhood, Milton felt both a call to Puritanism and the stirrings of literary excellence. From his reading knowledge of Hebrew, Greek, and Latin came a syncretism of classical, Christian, and humanistic philosophy. The majestic sweep of Milton's masterwork contrasts the extremes of dystopia and utopia. The subject, the fall of humankind, depicts the struggle between good and evil, the alluring powers of hell, and the loss of Eden, God's earthly Paradise.

Milton laid out the technical and structural goals of his epic about the time that he became blind. The 12-book poem began with 10 books until Milton produced a second edition in 1674 in which Books 7 and 10 were split. The unrhymed iambic pentameter verse, seeking to explain God's ways to human-kind, opens in Book 1 with the classical argument, which seeks to study

> . . . man's first disobedience, and the fruit
> Of that forbidden tree, whose mortal taste
> Brought death into the world, and all our woe,
> With loss of Eden, till one greater Man
> restore us, and regain the blissful seat. . . .

In classical style, the poet calls on a supernatural muse, the Holy Spirit, to answer a single query: Who subverted God's righteous plan by tricking Adam and Eve and causing them to disobey?

The work, begun *in medias res* with a council of war, turns immediately to the villain by spotlighting Lucifer, the leader of a cosmic rebellion against God. In defeat, the snaky form of the fallen angel lies in coils on a sulfur-fed burning lake in the depths of hell. The indomitable spirit of Satan invigorates and re-charges him and his demonic band: He rationalizes that it is "better to reign in Hell, than serve in Heaven." Calling his minions—Mulciber, Moloch, Belial, Mammon, Dagon, Beelzebub, and the rest of his lieutenants—to aid him in the epic struggle, Satan vows to challenge the Almighty by seducing his newest, most innocent beings.

Milton's descriptions of Eden lend charm and delight to the serious, theo-cratic epic. In Book 4, line 209, Satan gets his first view of God's paradise, which is planted "east of Eden," growing in fertile soil all kinds of trees "of noblest kind for sight, smell, taste." The poet's diction creates a word garden of sen-sual delights—tumbling waters, fresh springs, sloped terrain, and golden sands. In its original design, Eden is capable of watering and supporting fruit-bearing plants and flocks in an everlasting springtime, from which nature "poured forth profuse on hill and dale and plain" the rural pleasures designed to de-light the first human couple and to serve as their permanent home.

The blissful garden and its keepers surprise Satan, who travels for a day through a creation that is new and strange to him. The most pleasing sights—the tall, valorous man and the soft, sweet, golden-haired woman—comprise a pure and simple sight of "spotless innocence," the target of Satan's enmity. Walking together on luxurious greens, the first couple enjoy a childlike guilt-lessness. Unaware of their nakedness, they sip from streams and peel and eat the plentiful fruit, then romp with the animals, which coexist in mutual accord.

Both Adam and his wife know their place in God's universe. When evening draws near, they prepare for sleep in anticipation of a busy day spent working the arbors and flowerbeds along the paths, which tangle in blithe profusion. Eve, who makes no attempt to overrule her master, looks forward to the sweet-breathed morning, decked with dew and early showers. Hand in hand the two retire to the bower God chooses for them, where hyacinths, crocuses, and vio-lets form an inviting mosaic. Before falling asleep, they contemplate "sky, air, earth and heaven" and the future generations of laborers they have been prom-ised to help tend the garden.

Satan himself reconnoiters the newly created garden by flying to Earth. He confesses, "for only in destroying I find ease to my relentless thoughts." He studies Adam, Eve, and their nemesis, the Tree of Knowledge, the fruit of which will condemn them eternally. Uriel sounds an alarm; Gabriel dispatches a pair of angels to shelter the human residents of Eden. But the intervention arrives too late. Appearing as a toad, Satan has already infiltrated Eve's night thoughts.

Book 5 opens with a hint of danger. Eve's hair is tangled from the tossing and turning that accompany her unsettling dreams; her cheek glows red. Adam awakens her and learns that she dreamed of the Tree of Knowledge. She rejoices that the passing phantasm ended when she woke up. More to the point, she exults in the fact that her disobedience of God's command was only a nightmare. Adam blames an overactive imagination for her distress and joins her in prayer to the "universal lord," whom they beg to scatter wayward thoughts and restore them to light.

Milton provides distinguished support of the first couple. Raphael visits Eden to comfort and uplift their fitful morning. After Eve prepares food for them, Adam asks the angel how Eden compares with Heaven. Raphael replies that Adam should accept his place in the chain of being, which commences with the lowest aspects of creation and spirals heavenward to the human soul, which is capable of reason. The angel warns Adam not to exceed earthly knowledge by attempting to unravel the complexity of creation. Adam replies that God has already warned of the forbidden fruit and, out of compassion for his gardener, created from his rib a woman to serve him as a helpmeet.

Raphael dominates Book 7 with an explanation of the shift of power in Heaven. After God expelled Satan and his henchmen, he set about a six-day creation of Earth. Gabriel prophesies that, if humankind remains faithful to God's decrees, Earth will blend into Heaven, "one kingdom, joy and union without end." The earth itself rose from chaos, over which God hovered like a winged spirit and brought forth light, firmament, a separation of land and water, heavenly planets, animals, and a single man, whom he endowed with a heart, voice, and eyes to use in devotion to the supreme Creator.

To the keenly attendant human pair, Raphael predicts that there may come a time when angels and human beings will live together, a time when corporeal reality will give way entirely to spirit. At the end of Book 7, this extensive discussion and tutelage points to a crucial concept: God gave humanity the substance and opportunity to be happy, but Adam and Eve are responsible for remaining obedient. In harmony with deity and nature, they must apply their powers over flora and fauna. Raphael concludes, "remember, and fear to transgress."

Book 8 recaps the story of Eve's creation. In line 261 Adam enjoys "hill, dale, and shady woods, and sunny plains, and liquid lapse of murmuring streams." Delighting his senses are birdcalls, the sight of creatures in their natural habitats, and the inviting fragrance of nature. He uses his physical powers to move through Eden, name its denizens, and rejoice in his humanity and privilege. God calls Adam by name and leads him up a mountain to a circular plain filled with trees, paths, and bowers. The sight of succulent fruit tempts Adam's appetite. He awakens from his trance to find the dream a reality. God exhorts him to take charge of Eden and to eat "freely with glad heart." God's only stricture is to forbid a taste of the Tree of Knowledge, which would make the transgressor subject to mortality. Otherwise, God encourages Adam to possess "all things that therein live, or live in sea, or air, beast, fish, and fowl."

Noting that nature is set up in living pairs of birds and animals, Adam hesitates to complain of solitude. The Almighty, not displeased by his comment, remarks,

> What next I bring shall please thee, be assur'd,
> Thy likeness, thy fit help, thy other self,
> Thy wish, exactly to thy heart's desire.

In line 459, as Adam sinks into sleep, the Creator moves to his side and extracts a rib, which he fashions into a lovely, fair-skinned creature endowed with sweetness of heart and a loving spirit. God delivers her to the "nuptial bower." In the background, heaven and the stars shine on the wedded couple, Earth congratulates them, birds rejoice, and gentle zephyrs whisper to the woods. The idyllic bridal scene, lighted by the evening star and blessed with love, brings about human bliss.

After Raphael leaves, in Book 9, shortly before dawn Satan takes the form of a mist and hides himself inside a serpent. The next morning, Adam and Eve go about their daily chores cultivating the garden. Although Adam counsels otherwise, Eve chooses to work apart from her mate, an act he interprets as a test of her goodness. Before they part, in line 373, he urges her to "rely on what thou hast of virtue, summon all, for God towards thee hath done his part, do thine." Thus, Milton sets the stage for the most crucial trial of Eden's mistress.

The hapless wife strays among myriad-colored roses, a fragrant spot that disarms her, rendering her vulnerable to lurking evil. Eve runs afoul of the snake, which appears nearby like a burnished tower, both pleasing and lovely. Burning with the heat of hell, Satan realizes that he will never know a world so sweet, so filled with grace, as Eden. In envy, he immediately sets about seducing Eve into violating God's injunction by enticing her to become a "goddess among gods, adored and served by angels numberless, thy daily train." He stokes her pride by worshiping her as "Sovran of creatures, universal dame" and entices her to increase her wisdom by eating the gold and ruddy fruit of the Tree of Knowledge.

At this pivotal point, Eve capitulates to temptation. After tasting the fruit, the "credulous mother . . . root of all our woe" eats greedily and promises to worship the tree each morning. To perpetuate her relationship with her husband, without whom she could not live, she prepares a defense of her sin by confessing her actions. Horrified, he regrets her imprudence but, out of love for Eve, who is "flesh of my flesh, bone of my bone," Adam defies God and samples the fruit. Nature trembles and thunder sounds in the sky; the pair copulate for the first time and shame themselves with animal lust. They fall asleep and suffer nightmares as high winds disturb Eden's quiet.

Obviously, God intended that Adam and Eve apply judgment and free will, because he sends no emissary to halt their indiscretions. The two angels who had watched over them wing back to God in Book 10 to report the transgression, which they made no effort to prevent. Christ, who is God's son, visits Eden to judge the sinners, now worthy of death. Beginning in line 163, his sentence is the identical harsh punishment detailed in Genesis: The serpent will always be humankind's enemy, Eve will serve her husband and bear children, and Adam will toil in the earth to raise food for his family. Now linked with sin and death into an unholy trinity, Satan celebrates his successful coup, then sinks among his coconspirators into a hissing, intertwined heap of reptiles. God completes retribution for the first sin by bringing foul weather to Earth, setting animals against one another, and putting husband and wife in perpetual discord. Shouldering responsibility for their waywardness, Adam and Eve suffer remorse and marital strife and consider killing themselves, but end in prayer for grace.

In Book 11 Milton sets up the logic of the Fortunate Fall, the event that triggers a need for God's son to come to Earth to redeem sinners. God sends Michael to evict the couple from Paradise, a loss that exacerbates their despair. While Eve sleeps, Michael leads Adam to a hill, from which he views the spot where Satan will tempt Christ. Michael predicts that Adam's children will commit murder and that war, oppression, flood, pestilence, and the many other forms of death will stalk the earth. The angel holds out a single hope—that the degrading human penchant for wickedness will result in the birth of Christ as a savior who shall "admonish and before them set the paths of righteousness."

Book 12 continues with prophecies of Old Testament events—in particular, the rise of Abraham, who will father a great nation, and the deliverance of the Mosaic law as a behavioral guide to humanity. Michael predicts the birth, ministry, and crucifixion of Christ and the Second Coming, which will transform Earth into a paradise even happier than Eden:

> O goodness infinite, goodness immense!
> That all this good of evil shall produce,
> And evil turn to good; more wonderful
> Than that which by creation first brought forth
> Light out of darkness!

Mollified, Adam and Eve clasp hands and depart from Paradise, their faces toward the flaming sword. Eyes overflowing with tears, they tread the lonely path from Eden.

Milton's purpose in creating an epic on a cosmic scope reflects his ambivalence toward using his considerable literary genius and intense religiosity for such mundane topics as King Arthur or the Holy Grail. Instead of temporal or national subject matter, Milton settled on the Fortunate Fall, a concept that accounts for the subversion of God's Paradise and for Satan's betrayal of Adam and Eve. To Milton, the subject of freedom of choice ranks supreme in the study of original sin. As a consequence of Satan's successful temptation, Adam and Eve, both guilty of pride and disobedience of a direct interdiction from the Almighty, depart the perfect kingdom, the Garden of Eden. (Enroth 1970; Harrison et al. 1967; Hornstein et al. 1973; Martz 1967; Milton 1957a; Parker 1958)

PARADISE REGAINED

The four-book sequel to John Milton's *Paradise Lost* (1667), England's literary epic, relies heavily on the book of Luke for source material. *Paradise Regained* (1671), a weaker version of its predecessor, is set in the first century A.D. and pits Christ against the master tempter. Satan responds accordingly and batters the Redeemer's faith with physical needs for food and drink, a lust for glory, and a weakening of faith that stirs both pride and an urge to retaliate against adversaries.

Book 1 depicts an invisible Satan observing while John the Baptist baptizes Jesus, son of Joseph, in the river Jordan. The news that Jesus is God's earthly offspring sets Satan against the heavenly plan to redeem humankind. He convenes his council in Pandemonium and plots a strategy that is destined to fail. In Heaven, God and His angels look into the future to a resounding victory over evil. God explains that

> . . . men hereafter, may discern
> From what consummate virtue I have chose
> This perfect man, by merit called my son,
> To earn salvation for the sons of men.

Assured of His prophecy, God declares that Christ will not fall victim to frustrations, terrors, and other "stratagems of hell."

Milton utilizes Satan as the alter ego of Christ, the central character. At Bethabara, Christ ponders the trial that awaits him in the desert. Mary, his mother, recaps his birth and the prophecies of greatness. The Holy Spirit leads Jesus into the pathless desert for a 40-day period of prayer and self-study. Satan's initial disguise as an aged shepherd fails to inveigle Jesus into changing stones into bread. At this stage of their ineluctable confrontation, Satan, the archfiend, reveals his true self and describes how he was driven into hell, "that hideous place," yet continues to move about the earth to admire excellence, goodness, and virtue.

Satan hides "anger and disdain" and continues his glib badinage with a lame cliché: "Hard are the ways of truth, and rough to walk, smooth on the tongue discoursed, pleasing to the ear." The half-truths make little impression on Jesus, who labels these fanciful statements lies from beginning to end. The book concludes with Christ bidding Satan "do as thou findest permission from above; thou canst not more." As night falls, Satan bows courteously and disappears as ominous wild beasts exit from the woods to roam the desert.

Milton opens Book 2 on serious concerns for the Messiah. Mary, Andrew, and Simon search in vain for him. Following a second meeting with his evil minions, Satan returns to the challenge of subverting Jesus' holy purpose. Belial suggests tempting Christ with "daughters of men the fairest found." Satan knows that Christ will not fall victim to the same enticements that Belial himself admires. Instead, Satan offers a banquet table covered with fish, fowl, and pastry; he tries money, power, a prestigious career, even freedom of the Jews from their Roman overlords. Jesus' pointed rejoinder strikes at the weakness in Satan's argument: Satan is pressing Jesus toward his ultimate destiny—an endless paradise, a fulfillment of the prophecies of the Old Testament.

Milton uses the strengths of his two characters to depict an allegorical clash between good and evil. At an impasse in the exchange between Christ and Satan, the third book opens with Satan pretending to be stymied. He advances the debate between good and evil with flattery and a call to action. To tempt Jesus with potential power bases, Satan escorts him to a mountain crest and points out the earthly realms of Parthia and Rome, the eastern and western extremes of the Semitic world. His goal unshaken by Satan's wily sophistry, Jesus spurns the offer.

Discounting defeat in the opening lines of Book 4, Satan transports God's son to Jerusalem, "the Imperial City." Still, the vision of earthly dominance holds no delight for Jesus, who anticipates coming to David's throne in fulfillment of Isaiah's prophecy. Satan's next ploy resembles his Faustian role; he offers Jesus command of all the erudition of the ancient world—all philosophy, oratory, and verse. Jesus counters with Hebrew lore, which he declares is more precious to God, whom it seeks to glorify. In line 560 Jesus counters, "Tempt not the Lord thy God." Because Jesus' methods outweigh Satan's specious arguments, Satan once more overestimates his persuasive ability and stumbles into ignominy.

At this point, the doctrine of the Fortunate Fall takes shape. Christ recognizes that Satan will never again attempt to subvert Paradise. Although Eden has failed,

> A fairer paradise is founded now
> For Adam and his chosen sons, whom thou
> A savior art come down to reinstall,
> Where they shall dwell secure.

A band of angels rejoices over Jesus' triumph and treats him to refreshment in a pleasing vale. Their tuneful victory songs precede Jesus' return to his mother, who has been concerned for his welfare. (Enroth 1970; Harrison et al. 1967; Hornstein et al. 1973; Martz 1967; Milton 1957a; Parker 1958)

See also Eden; heaven; Milton, John; *Paradise Lost*; theocracy; women in utopia.

PAST AND PRESENT

An anti-industrial diatribe by Victorian essayist and philosopher Thomas Carlyle, this stiffly didactic treatise deceptively poses as a nostalgic, roseate description of the glories of the Middle Ages. Published in 1843, *Past and Present* contrasts the unsettling qualities of the Industrial Revolution—hunger, paupers, workhouses, soullessness, atheism, rage, and coming chaos—with the control, religiosity, self-possession, and purpose of the feudal era. In Chapter 1 of Book II, Carlyle returns to the past through the writings of Jocelinus de Brakelonda, author of *Chronica Jocelini de Brakelonda, de rebus gestis Samsonis Abbatis Monasterii Sancti Edmundi: nunc primum typis mandata, curante Johanne Gage Rokewood* (The chronicles of Jocelin of Brakelond, concerning the deeds of Samson, abbot of the monastery of St. Edmund: for the first time in print, by the work of John Gage Rokewood). Composed in stilted "Monk-Latin," the book focuses on a cheerful, ingenuous, open-hearted narrator whose contentment, like that of Thoreau in *Walden* (1854) and Dick, the speaker in William Morris's *News from Nowhere* (1890), lies in what Carlyle terms a "wise simplicity." Carlyle laments that the benighted reader can hear but not address the "clear-smiling" prelate: "The good man, he cannot help it, nor can we." The hero of Jocelin's text is Samson, abbot of Bury St. Edmunds, an energetic worker who strives to apply wit and muscle to daily problems. Devoted to order, utility, and productivity, he prefigures the twentieth century's attempts to reuse and recycle. Powered by determination and a faith in the work ethic, Abbot Samson gradually upgrades the lapsed abbey into a center for justice based on individual input at all levels.

Concerning Samson's England of 1200, Carlyle extols an asceticism rich with joy, physical involvement, and spiritual replenishment. The cyclical organic virtues of serfdom's daily chores produce

> . . . a green solid place, that grew corn and several other things. The Sun shone on it; the vicissitude of seasons and human fortunes. Cloth was woven and worn; ditches were dug, furrow-fields ploughed, and houses built. Day by day all men and cattle rose to labour, and night by night returned home weary to their several lairs.

Carlyle calls the symmetry of this life "wondrous Dualism," a clear delineation "between Light and Dark; between joy and sorrow, between rest and toil,— between hope, hope reaching high as Heaven, and fear deep as very Hell." Indeed, a solid sense of place and purpose anchors the deep-souled serf in idyllic service to Earth, society, and God.

At the heart of Carlyle's paean to medievalism is Book III, including Chapter 4, "Happy," an essay exalting the noble task of cotton spinning. Carlyle remarks that "all dignity is painful; a life of ease is not for any man, nor for any god." A companion essay, Chapter 11, "Labour," resounds with Emersonian prose in a call to work and duty:

> Doubt, Desire, Sorrow, Remorse, Indignation, Despair itself, all these like helldogs lie beleaguering the soul of the poor dayworker, as of every man: but he bends himself with free valour against his task, and all these are stilled, all these shrink murmuring far off into their caves. The man is now a man. The blessed glow of Labour in him, is it not as purifying fire! . . .

Thus, the spinner and potter attain their contentment through toil, blessing themselves with "life-purpose." The inner contentment derived from such menial chores as draining swamps and cultivating meadows results in self-knowledge growing out of the motion of drudgery, which the author claims is "of a religious nature . . . a *brave* nature."

Springing from religious environs, *Past and Present* lauds the heaven-centered life, which awaits its earnings in the hereafter. Carlyle expands on the connection between work and worship by linking the expected return or wages with the reward of an afterlife. He comments, "On the whole, we do entirely agree with those old Monks, *Laborare est Orare*." To intensify his message, Carlyle contrasts the soul-satisfying labors of the cobbler and weaver with the uninspired, enervating toil of factory-driven industry, which he terms "bondage to Mammon . . . a tragic spectacle." By working for material purpose, nineteenth-century laborers serve an "imprisoned god, writhing unconsciously or consciously to escape out of Mammonism!" Urging that members of Parliament create a wageless work order, he expounds, "I would aid, constrain, encourage [the legislator] to effect more or less this blessed change."

With antidemocratic force, brow-beating, and bombast, Carlyle lashes out against the illusion of the democratic republic, a will-o'-the-wisp that lures the worker into a "May-game for men: in all times the lot of the dumb millions born to toil." Such idylls yield only mediocrity and despair, robbing the wage-earner of time to till a plot of ground in which to grow the family's vegetables. Exerting Calvinistic fervor, the author questions the foundations of liberty that deny the worker a true path—not to aimlessness, leisure, the illusory victory of the vote, and "other cob-webberies"—but to honest toil. (Buckler 1958; Carlyle 1977; Greene 1971; Hodgkins 1904; Mack 1962)

See also The Abbey of Thélème; asceticism; didacticism; humanitarianism; *News from Nowhere;* synergy; *Walden; Walden Two.*

PASTORAL

This innocent, rural literary motif is found in such varied sources as Eden in the book of Genesis, the Greek and Roman verse of Hesiod's *Works and Days* (eighth century B.C.), Theocritus's *Ecologues* (third century B.C.), and Virgil's *Bucolics* (42–37 B.C.); in the English Renaissance in William Shakespeare's *As You Like It* (1599) and *A Midsummer Night's Dream* (ca. 1595); in the American romantic era in Henry Wadsworth Longfellow's *The Song of Hiawatha* (1855); and in the outdoorsy grace and camaraderie of reapers in William Morris's *News from Nowhere* (1890). The pastoral, set in a simplified, rustic, and sometimes dull milieu outside the commercial, governmental, and military arena, possesses its own tensions and strivings. Its emotions pour from hearts smitten by love or loss; its stylized measures tend toward love song, lyric, and elegy, some of which are heightened by allegory.

Replete with singing contests, swains wooing their lasses, yearnings, deaths, and the rites and celebrations of nature, the stereotypes and primitivism inherent in pastoral literature contrast the less idealized themes and moods and more distinct conflicts and characterizations found in urbanized drama, history, and fiction. An idealized verse from Virgil's eighth eclogue reads like Hesiod's and Ovid's paeans to the golden age:

> Now even let the wolf flee unchased before the sheep; let gnarled oaks bear apples of gold: let the alder flower into narcissus, and rich amber ooze from tamarisk bark: yes, let screech-owls vie with swans, let Tityrus be Orpheus, Orpheus in the forest, Arion among the dolphin shoals.

Virgil's flowing lines, rich with mythological allusion, musical phraseology, Arcadian landscapes, and herbal lore, rely on a naturalism that approaches worship.

The utopian convention is strong in pastoral verse, epic, drama, and novel. In an unchanging golden age, shepherds and shepherdesses with stereotypical names like Daphne, Pollio, Phyllis, Amaryllis, Thalia, Corydon, and Chloe, and such identifiable mythic characters as Pan, Silenus, and Linus, sing, play the flute, and attend their flocks on rocky slopes, flower-strewn dells, and verdant pastures. The characters' soliloquies, as demonstrated by John Milton's *Lycidas* (1638) and Torquato Tasso's *Aminta* (1573), center on emotional trauma, camaraderie, unity, and honest expression of feelings. Consoled by the meadows and woodlands that form their Edenic microcosm, the winsome figures of pastoral literature take comfort in nature and in the cyclical verities of the stars, weather, animal life, and change of the seasons. (Cuddon 1979; Hesiod 1973; Holman 1981; Longfellow 1992; Milton 1957a; Morris 1968b; Shakespeare 1958; Shakespeare 1959; Snodgrass 1988a; Snodgrass 1988b; Virgil 1950)

See also allegory; Arcadia; Arden; *Bucolics*; Eden; Genesis; golden age; Hesiod; Longfellow, Henry Wadsworth; Milton, John; naturalism; *News from Nowhere*; Ovid; Tasso, Torquato; women in utopia.

PERRAULT, FATHER

Perrault is the Capuchin priest who heads a utopian monastery in James Hilton's *Lost Horizon* (1933), a devout wanderer who has serendipitously located the perfect world—a remote Tibetan lamasery known as Shangri-La. An intent orthodox Christian missionary dispatched by the Vatican, he departs Peking in 1719 with three companions to locate an isolated sect. Perrault's hardihood enables him to survive his fellows and, through the tender nursing of Shangri-La's priests, recover his health. By immersing himself in the temperate climate of Blue Moon Valley, he discovers the regenerative powers of the *tangatse* berry, which provides the longevity necessary for the gradual dissolution of worldly passions.

In time, Perrault ceases trying to convert the Tibetans to Christianity and evolves a benign autocracy syncretized from the best of world philosophies, including Buddhism, Taoism, and oriental mysticism. Following a philosophy reminiscent of Ovid's *in medio tutissimus ibis* ("you go safest in the middle"), Perrault leads his followers safely in the middle, neither excessively ascetic nor morally licentious. Under this gentle rule, Shangri-La evolves a beneficent atmosphere that encourages contemplation, reading, music, and deep friendship. Near the end of his phenomenal two-and-a-half-century life, he exists in a rarefied atmosphere of warmth and muted light and employs mental telepathy as a means of establishing oneness with the outside world.

As background for the novel, Perrault's mission spreads to other parts of the world in search of new converts. By continuing his dependence on *tangatse* and by studying yoga and Buddhism, he wills his body to cling to life until his assistant, Chang, can locate a suitable replacement. To Hugh Conway, the kidnapped ambassador who thrives under the high lama's benign house arrest, in Chapter 8 Father Perrault demystifies the structure and purpose of his Himalayan utopia:

> We are not workers of miracles; we have made no conquest of death or even of decay. All we have done and can sometimes do is to slacken the *tempo* of this brief interval that is called life. We do this by methods which are as simple here as they are impossible elsewhere; but make no mistake; the end awaits us all.

Perrault realizes that death will soon snuff out his physical being, and his soul will continue its search for the god-ordained absolute, more familiarly known as heaven. With the ease of a departing spirit, he exits his body and leaves his near-perfect world to Hugh Conway, his successor. (Eagle and Carnell 1992; Ehrlich and Carruth 1982; Hilton 1933; Kunitz 1942; *Something about the Author* 1984)

See also asceticism; Buddhism; *La Città del Sole;* clairvoyance; Conway, Hugh; escapism; Hilton, James; *Lost Horizon;* Shangri-La; syncretism; Tao.

 # PETER PAN

Peter Pan is the central character of a classic, internationally loved children's play written by James Matthew Barrie in 1904, which was recast as the novel *Peter and Wendy* in 1911, and again in play form in 1928. Symbolizing the human wish to cling to the verities and joys of childhood, Peter Pan is a leaf-clad gamin who flies between Earth and his utopian Neverland. He eavesdrops on nursery stories told to human children, then retells them to his gang of boys, whom he also entertains with tunes on the panpipes. The boys look to him for leadership in a world devoid of parents and human females, with the exception of Wendy, their honorary mother.

In Chapter 15, entitled "Hook or Me This Time," Peter responds to a pivotal question from his nemesis:

> "Pan, who and what are thou?" [Hook] cried huskily.

> "I'm youth, I'm joy," Peter answered at a venture, "I'm a little bird that has broken out of the egg."

Partly terrorized by thoughts of maturity, Peter rejects school and the "solemn things" that children must learn. To Mrs. Darling he speaks the brand of truth

J. M. Barrie's *Peter Pan* was first staged in London with actress Nina Boucicault as Peter in December 1904. In this scene, Peter is in the Darlings' nursery and is trying to reattach his shadow.

of which only the innocent are capable: "O Wendy's mother, if I was to wake up and feel there was a beard!"

At the end of Peter's adventure with John, Michael, and Wendy Darling, he returns them to the Kensington section of London to their parents, who have harbored terrible fears at their unexplained absence. Peter visits often to view them in their beds; he later teaches Wendy's daughter Jane. Although Peter remains his perpetually immature self (symbolized by his complete set of first teeth), the human children he captivates continue to change, passing from Jane to her daughter Margaret and succeeding generations, "so long as children are gay and innocent and heartless."

The stage version of *Peter Pan* has spawned music by Leonard Bernstein and numerous female leads in the part of Peter, notably Maude Adams, Eva Le Gallienne, Mary Martin, Veronica Lake, Mia Farrow, and Sandy Duncan. A demanding role, the flying boy-leader requires exacting acrobatics and timing as well as stage engineering of the flight harness. Walt Disney's animated *Peter Pan*, filmed in 1953, features the voices of Bobbie Driscoll as Peter and Hans Conreid as Hook. A favorite children's song to emerge from the film was "Never Smile at a Crocodile." A moderately successful 1991 reprise starred Dustin Hoffman, Robin Williams, and Julia Roberts. (Barrie 1981; Darlington 1974; Manguel and Guadalupi 1987)

See also Barrie, Sir James Matthew; escapism; fantasy; Neverland; women in utopia.

 # PHILOSOPHER-KING

The archetypical learned and humanistic ruler, the philosopher-king is Plato's ingenious solution to the usual pitfalls of earthly governance, which he places in the hands of a mature intellectual in his *Republic* (fifth century B.C.). Mirrored by Plutarch's father-figure, Lycurgus, who overran the Lacedaemonians to found a self-sustaining Greek utopia in *The Life of Lycurgus* (first century A.D.), Plato's notion of the enlightened despot places abiding trust in human nature and in the strength of virtue over vice. Typical of Greek attitudes, Plato gives no thought to investing these same qualities in a philosopher-queen.

The concept of the benign enlightened despot recurs in utopian lore, as with these examples:

- At the height of the Italian Renaisssance, Baldessar Castiglione suggests a similar method of developing an intelligent, rational, well-groomed, well-rounded man of government in *The Courtier* (1528).

- At the beginning of the seventeenth century, Fra Tomaso Campanella conceived of Hoh, the fictional leader of a triad of princes and the benign ruler of *La Città del Sole* (1602).

- Later dabblings on the subject of wise and compassionate leadership are personified in Hiawatha, mythic Indian hero of Henry Wadsworth Longfellow's Native American epic *The Song of Hiawatha* (1855).

- Father Perrault, the elderly mystic in James Hilton's *Lost Horizon* (1933), demonstrates isolated aspects of enlightenment, sobriety, respect for divinity, mysticism, self-control, and humanism in their dealings with subjects.

- The benevolent Hazel of Richard Adams's *Watership Down* (1972) leads by the lightest touch on his followers and shares their dangers.

Other utopias lean away from cerebral rulers toward remote or disinterested monarchy, as found in L. Frank Baum's children's classic, *The Wonderful Wizard of Oz* (1900), and Herman Melville's peaceful, self-indulgent Polynesian chiefs encountered in *Typee* (1846) and *Omoo* (1847). Few serious utopists picture a pantisocracy, a nation run by complete egalitarianism, which was the collectivist dream of Friedrich Engels and Karl Marx, the father of communism, and the ideal of Jack London, author of *The Iron Heel* (1907). Alfred Tennyson displays the talents and potential of a philosopher-king through the idealism of Arthur, ruler of Camelot, in *Idylls of the King* (1888), chiefly as a gesture from England's poet laureate to Prince Albert, the consort of Queen Victoria. Equally unrealistic is T. H. White's *Once and Future King* (1958), a reassessment of Arthurian lore with emphasis on magic, idealism, and undeserved tragedy at the collapse of Camelot. A less sanguine view of Arthur as the philosopher-king, Mark Twain's *A Connecticut Yankee in King Arthur's Court* (1886) reminds the reader that political power in the grasp of a philosophic, forgiving, but flawed king can lead to anarchy, which is the situation at the end of Arthur's reign. When Arthur accepts defeat and proposes no designated leader to supplant him, Camelot falls to ruin during a resurgence of greed, lawlessness, and revenge. (Adams 1972; Baum 1983; Campanella 1955; Castiglione 1976; Hilton 1933; Longfellow 1992; Melville 1964; Melville 1968; Rabkin et al. 1983; Tennyson 1989; White 1955; White 1965)

See also Arthur; Camelot; *La Città del Sole;* collectivism; *A Connecticut Yankee in King Arthur's Court; The Courtier;* Engels, Friedrich; Hoh; Houyhnhnms; *Idylls of the King; The Life of Lycurgus; Lost Horizon; Omoo;* pantisocracy; Plato; Plutarch; *The Republic; Typee; Watership Down; The Wonderful Wizard of Oz.*

 # PHOENIX

A one-of-a-kind bird from ancient Arabian, Turkish, and Egyptian lore, the phoenix is said by ancient historians, the Greek Herodotus and Roman Tacitus, to live for half a millennium, or 500 years, and by Jewish theologians to survive 1,000 years. As its life span ends, the phoenix sings a death song and climbs atop a fragrant pyre, where the sun's rays kindle the sparks that cause the bird's immolation. From gray ash springs a worm that grows into a new phoenix decked in gorgeous red, blue, gold, and purple feathers, symbolic of the indomitable, regenerated soul and the royal majesty of the mythic bird. In fourth-century verse by Claudian, the poet credits the bird with initiating new ethical and governmental principles after the sun's fire rejuvenates the bird's former vigor.

From medieval bestiaries, Christian apologists drew a close analogy between the rare phoenix and the resurrected Christ and his earthly kingdom, which is prophesied in the New Testament book of Revelation (A.D. 90–95). A symbol of resurrection and triumph over destruction, the phoenix decorates the walls of the City of the Sun, the setting of Fra Tomaso Campanella's *Città del Sole* (1602). Among architecture that also serves as emblematic education to city dwellers, the phoenix seems no more lauded than the geometric symbols or astrological signs that cover the inner rings around the citadel.

Surviving time, the phoenix colors the rhetorical images of modern writers. In Ray Bradbury's *Fahrenheit 451* (1953), the character Granger, who leads a band of rebels along the fringe of a twenty-fourth-century totalitarian society, recalls the mythical Phoenix, a "first cousin to Man" that embodies the human inclination toward such self-destructive passions as tyranny, repression, violence, or the "perverted science" of which Winston Churchill warned during Adolf Hitler's search for a self-propelled bomb. According to Granger, these negative forces balance human resilience. Granger extends the analogy to encompass his trust in the future—that humanity, unlike the Phoenix, will recognize

> . . . all the silly things we've done for a thousand years and as long as we know that and always have it around where we can see it, some day we'll stop making the funeral pyres and jumping in the middle of them.

With optimism in Guy Montag, his new convert, Granger anticipates an end to conflagration—a peace-loving era in which humankind can "build the biggest steamshovel in history and dig the biggest grave of all time and shove war in and cover it up." (Biederman 1992; Bradbury 1953; Campanella 1955; Cavendish 1970; Cirlot 1971; Holy Bible 1958)

See also Beatty, Captain; Bradbury, Ray; Campanella, Fra Tomaso; *La Città del Sole; Fahrenheit 451;* idealism; Montag, Guy; syncretism.

PIERCY, MARGE

Piercy is an outspoken radical activist, feminist poet, and author of the dystopic *Woman on the Edge of Time* (1976). A native of a poor black section of Detroit, Piercy was born March 31, 1936, to machinist Robert Piercy and Bert Bunnin Piercy. After completing a B.A. from the University of Michigan and an M.A. from Northwestern University in 1958, she taught creative writing to graduate students. During the 1960s and 1970s, she headed the radical Students for a Democratic Society and agitated to end the Vietnam War.

Piercy supported herself by working at menial jobs while learning the writer's craft. Her early work—two novels, *Small Changes* (1973) and her favorite, *Woman on the Edge of Time,* and a poetry collection, *The Moon Is Always Female* (1980)—speak her belief in civil rights and feminist causes, and the necessity for women to find both voice and vehicle to express their frustration with the injustice of second-class citizenship. Admired by Margaret Atwood, a Canadian dystopist and critic, Piercy pursues polemics and speculation in creating a limited glimpse of a world in which man and woman live in a cooperative effort to perpetuate life on Earth. (Buck 1992; *Contemporary Authors* 1984; *Contemporary Literary Criticism* 1981a; Piercy 1976; Walker and Hamner 1984)

See also Atwood, Margaret; speculative fiction; *Woman on the Edge of Time;* women in utopia.

PIGGY

A tragicomic figure in William Golding's demonic *Lord of the Flies* (1954), Piggy is a bespectacled fat boy, the favorite of his aunt, who owns a candy store. He protects himself from asthmatic attacks by avoiding the demanding physical activities common to boys his age. His wisdom, hypochondria, and lack of physical coordination suggest the shape, wisdom, and demeanor of Winston Churchill. Piggy is a natural follower, and willingly backs up Ralph, the island's fount of leadership, pragmatism, and control. A modern version of Prometheus, the fire-bringer of Greek mythology, Piggy applauds the concept of a perpetually tended fire to summon rescuers. He uses his eyeglasses to focus the sun's heat on kindling to generate a blaze.

Loyal in service and content with his spot as sergeant-at-arms, Piggy is unaware that his adversaries are capable of grisly horrors and a subversion of the majority. In Chapter 11 he clutches the pink conch shell, symbol of order. His chief flaw—naïveté—leads to the unforeseen attack from behind when Roger unearths a boulder and sends it spinning onto Piggy's body. Piggy's pathetic martyrdom becomes the central testimony to the hunters' savagery:

> The rock bounded twice and was lost in the forest. Piggy fell forty feet and landed on his back across the square red rock in the sea. His head opened and stuff came out and turned red. Piggy's arms and legs twitched a bit, like a pig's after it has been killed.

A bespectacled Piggy in the 1963 Peter Brook film version of William Golding's dystopian novel, *Lord of the Flies*, holds a conch shell trumpet as he faces the bully Jack.

Like the innocent Simon, the visionary of the group, Piggy recedes into nature, clasped in the breakers and drawn out to sea. With him goes the conch and the hope that order can prevail over dystopic anarchy and chaos. (Baker 1988; Carey 1987; Gindin 1988; Golding 1954; Johnston 1980; Kinkead-Weeks and Gregor 1984; Subbarao 1987)

See also allegory; Eden; Golding, William; *Lord of the Flies*; Merridew, Jack; Ralph.

PILGRIM'S PROGRESS

John Bunyan's vivid, mildly humorous, and highly valued Christian allegory and social satire was published in 1678. The episodic nature of Christian's adventures parallel human yearning for righteousness and the reward of heaven. At the same time, the opportunities for profligate, sybaritic, or heretical behaviors prefigure the punishment of hell for those who fail to follow a godly path. Influenced by vernacular English and biblical writings, the book was composed in the blended traditions of medieval dream lore and prison literature. It is a symbolic application of both Christian dogma and utopian concepts of the Promised Land, or New Jerusalem.

For the hero, paradise is a goal to be won by the long-suffering Christian sojourner after the completion of a trying pilgrimage through temptations and beyond death, which is symbolized by the Jordan River. Populated by such allegorical characters as Christian, Faithful, Despair, and Ignorance, the book adheres to the standard paradigm of allegory, which emphasizes symbolism over realism. The universal appeal of Bunyan's plainspoken journey far outdistanced his ambitions to convert nonbelievers. For three centuries the book influenced social theorists and theologians and found its way to the New World, where pioneers read episodes aloud by camp fire.

Set in the visionary genre, the adventures of Christian—a devout, plucky Everyman springing from Bunyan's personal experience—begin with a prophetic dream of doom that causes the tattered hero, laden with original sin, to tremble and cry, "What shall I do to be saved?"—a question that echoes the biblical query of a jailer to Paul and Silas (Acts 16:30). Evangelist comforts Christian, gives him a useful parchment scroll, and urges him to launch a perilous journey to Glory from the City of Destruction, which is about to be burned by heavenly fire. Before setting out, Christian attempts to spread an alarm, but residents ignore his warning of imminent danger. Leaving Christiana, his four children, and neighboring nay-sayers behind, he presses on toward salvation.

At the Slough of Despond, Christian falls under the influence of Obstinate and Pliable and nearly bogs down in a bottomless quagmire. Help gives him a hand out of the scummy waters, which engineers from the Celestial City have tried for two millennia to fill; Mr. Worldly Wiseman of Carnal City tempts him to despair of heaven and choose instead the village of Morality, Legality, and Civility. Evangelist convinces Christian that neither counselor is noteworthy and directs him to a wicket gate, which opens onto the road to Mount Zion.

The footpath passes the Interpreter's House, a palatial rest stop and distribution center for armor. Met by Good Will, Christian is advised to knock at the Interpreter's House, where he studies such Christian mysteries as Passion, Patience, and the Day of Judgment. Christian gains strength from the visit and, with a hearty laugh, easily eludes Hypocrisy and Formalist, residents of Vain-Glory.

Bunyan intensifies Christian's sufferings on the final leg of the pilgrimage. At the Hill of Difficulty, Christian labors on hands and knees up the grueling slope past the fear of death. At a gate of the House Beautiful, the Lord of the Hill assigns Discretion, Piety, Prudence, and Charity to assist Christian. He spends a peaceful night and tours an armory, where the faithful are outfitted with weapons, breastplates, prayer, and shoes that never need repair. Before he departs from his new friends, he arms himself with the sword and buckler of Christian Faith.

Bunyan's attempt at a parallel to Satan results in an original ogre—Apollyon, a towering, scaly backed fiend representing doubt. In the Valley of Humiliation, a rich pasture and country estate of the Lord of Celestial City, Christian squares off against the monster and suffers dart wounds in heart, hand, and foot, which he treats with poultices of leaves from the Tree of Life. He trudges on to the Valley of the Shadow of Death through a sickening stench and creeps beneath shadowing wings that obscure satyrs, dragons, and hobgoblins. Gladdened by the dawn, he reaches the far end of the valley and joins Faithful, a knowledgeable companion who helps Christian avoid vice.

In typical Puritan asceticism, Bunyan delivers a strong warning against worldliness and materialism, yet lightens his didacticism with bits of comic relief. Warned that the ancient town of Vanity Fair, Beelzebub's abode, lies ahead of Wilderness, Christian anticipates enticements that lure followers of Christ from a heavenly path. Because he and Faithful refuse to purchase tawdry goods of Luxurious, Having-Greedy, and Lechery, the two wayfarers face arrest, chains, and arraignment. At the court of Lord Hategood, three false witnesses—Envy, Superstition, and Pickthank—testify against them. A jury composed of Mr. Blind-man, Mr. No-good, Mr. Malice, Mr. Love-lust, Mr. Live-loose, Mr. Heady, Mr. High-mind, Mr. Enmity, Mr. Lyar, Mr. Cruelty, Mr. Hate-light, and Mr. Implacable sends Christian to jail; Faithful is slated for public torment, scourging, stoning, and burning at the stake. At his death, a waiting chariot carries his spirit to heaven. Allied with Hopeful, Christian escapes a host of double-dealers, including By-ends, Any-thing, Two-tongues, Turn-about, Fair-speech, Love-gain, Gripe-man, Money-love, Hold-the-World, and Smooth-man.

The climax of the pilgrimage occurs in dangerous terrain. Christian's euphoria meets with the most daunting challenge—a glimpse of the Delectable Mountains, a beneficent site for sheepherders where only the righteous may cross in safety. Nearby lies the Hill of Lucre, where a silver mine has enticed weaker sojourners from their goal; also, the salt pillar that was once Lot's wife stands like a sentinel. As a respite, Christian and Hopeful refresh themselves at the River of Life.

Rains threaten to bring a flood; a heavenly voice impels the wanderers back from By-path Meadow and the Plain of Ease to the highway. Wearied past travel, they spend the night near Doubting Castle, abode of the infamous Giant Despair. In punishment for trespass, he locks them in a dismal dungeon and beats and tortures them. Christian swoons from hunger and pain. After several days of ill-treatment, he suddenly recalls a key named Promise, which unlocks the cell and outer wall. To warn future victims, Christian and Hopeful erect a signpost, an altruistic gesture of support to all who seek union with God.

Arriving in the Delectable Mountains among the shepherds named Knowledge, Experience, Watchful, and Sincere, Christian and Faithful learn that one landmark, the Hill of Error, overlooks a deep abyss. At a distance, a segment of Mount Caution is populated by blind unfortunates who lost their vision at the hands of Giant Despair. Along the path yawns a shortcut to Hell, which entombs biblical hypocrites and villains like Esau, Judas, and Ananias. To lift their spirits, the sojourners climb Clear Hill to peer through a spyglass at the gates of the Celestial City. Along the way, the two journeymen pass the Country of Conceit and draw near Broad-way-gate and Dead-man's-lane, which prove the undoing of Little-Faith and the three brothers named Faint-heart, Mistrust, and Guilt. Stalked by Ignorance, Christian passes Atheist, who turns his back on Mount Zion and laughs at seekers of God's grace. Christian learns that Hopeful overcame sinful ways by praying repeatedly to Christ for forgiveness and guidance.

Although close enough to Celestial City to buoy his spirits, Bunyan forces Christian to face more dangers. A forest called the Enchanted Ground precedes Beulah, a sweet land echoing the calls of birds. So close are the men to the Celestial City that they grow weak with longing. They nearly drown in the deep, menacing River of Death, which extends no bridge to travelers. With a reminder from Hopeful that he must exert his faith, Christian holds his head above the torrents and fords roiling, treacherous waters. On the opposite shore, they abandon mortal garments.

Bunyan colors the falling action with details of heaven. Christian climbs a hill and reaches two resplendent attendants who await their entrance to the Celestial City, a utopian wonder of golden avenues and structures made of pearls and precious gems. Through the gate and up the slope they stroll without exertion, free for the first time of dismay and doubts in their anticipation of meeting angels and such just men as Abraham, Isaac, Jacob, and the prophets. If there exist just women, Bunyan omits their names from the list.

The pilgrims eagerly await the voice of God. Arrival at this long-sought Paradise sets off a clangor of bells, trumpets, choirs of angels, and shouts of joy. Angels escort Christian through the portals, which are inscribed with a message: "Blessed are they that do His commandments, that they may have right to the Tree of Life; and may enter in through the Gates into the City." Decked with gilt garlands, Christian receives a certificate of entrance as harps play and crowned figures walk about with palm branches in hand.

Bunyan stresses the vain hopes of those who complete the journey but lack the credentials required of a believer. In the distance, Christian spies Ignorance, who crosses the river with the aid of Vain-hope, a ferryman. Without a certificate, Ignorance knocks in vain at the portals and is tied up and cast into Hell as

Christian and Hopeful press on to God's ornate throne. At this point, Pilgrim awakens from his dream and appends four stanzas of advice to the reader to look deep among the metaphors of his allegory for the gold among the dross.

In the second part, Book II, Christian's wife experiences a similar dream enumerating her sins. Chastened, she gives up her old ways and adopts the name "Christiana." She receives a sweetly perfumed letter from her husband urging her to come to the Celestial City. Impelled by conscience and accompanied by her four sons—James, Samuel, Joseph, and Matthew—and friend Mercy, she sets out to reunite matrimonial bonds with her husband. She ignores the warnings of Mr. Sagacity and the meddling Mrs. Timorous, who frightens herself with embroidered tales of lions, demons, the Valley of the Shadow of Death, and Vanity Fair. More voices—Mrs. Light-mind, Mrs. Bats-eyes, Mrs Inconsiderate, and Mrs. Know-nothing—come to hear Christiana describe the route that will take her to her husband and Paradise.

At the Slough of Despond, Christiana contemplates the mud that hindered Christian. When dogs bark, she exits the gate and sings a hymn on her way past the wall of Devil's Garden. Her sons jeopardize her progress by eating from overhanging boughs heavy with fruit. With Reliever's help, she repents of past sins and presses on to the Interpreter's House, where she walks in his garden and eats at his table. Interpreter compares her to two virtuous women of the Bible, Naomi and Ruth. A serving woman provides white linen garments. With the aid of Mr. Greatheart, whom Interpreter dispatches as guide, the party moves on to House Beautiful and the Hill of Difficulty, the site of a spring where passing feet have polluted the waters. Christiana lets the dirt settle, then drinks an invigorating draft.

This portion of Bunyan's allegory threatens to overrun the proportion of symbol to action by overstating the dangers. Up the king's highway, Greatheart recites the adventures of Christian, which strengthen Christiana's resolve. At the Porter's Lodge, Greatheart prepares to return to his master and let Christiana and her sons fend for themselves. They ask to spend the night in the same room that Christian used. Matthew requires medical care for the green plums that he ate on the way. He is purged with the flesh and blood of Christ, a cleansing communion that allows him to sleep. The physician, old Mr. Skill, proffers a box of medicine to guard them from disease.

Bunyan persists in helping his heroine along by supplying constant male guidance. At Christiana's request, Mr. Greatheart returns to conduct them. He defeats Grim Bloody-man and supplies the group with wine, parched corn, pomegranates, figs, and raisins. They set out for the Valley of Humiliation, where Christiana sees a monument raised to honor her husband's battle with the monster Apollyon. Christiana and her sons survive illness, foul smells, snares, and menacing adversaries. A fierce battle between Mr. Greatheart and the Giant Maul ends with the giant's beheading. Mr. Honest greets them, salutes the family of Christian with good wishes, and listens to a summary of Christiana's adventures.

Bunyan provides a bit of relief from didacticism with a cozy evening of food, rest, and light entertainment. Gaius, a generous host, offers a substantial supper of wine, butter, honey, nuts, and apples. The boys retire, but Mercy, Christiana, Gaius, Mr. Honest, and Greatheart stay up all night to enjoy riddles and stories. The next morning, Christian's family approaches the cave of Giant Slay-good, who preys on travelers along the king's highway. Greatheart confronts the giant, then beheads him in retaliation for all the pilgrims the giant had killed. The group remains ten days at Gaius's house for the betrothal of Matthew to Mercy and James to Gaius's daughter Phoebe. Gaius serves a great departure feast and refuses to take money for his hospitality.

The betrothal scene exacerbates Bunyan's diminution of women. The group parts with an insubstantial companion, Mr. Feeble-mind, who takes up with Ready-to-Halt. The original coterie of pilgrims spends a night outside Vanity Fair under the protection of Mr. Mnason, who introduces Christiana to his neighbors, Mr. Contrite, Mr. Holy-man, Mr. Love-saint, Mr. Dare-not-lie, and Mr. Penitent. Before the pilgrims' company departs, Samuel is betrothed to Mr. Mnason's daughter Grace and Joseph to Grace's sister Martha.

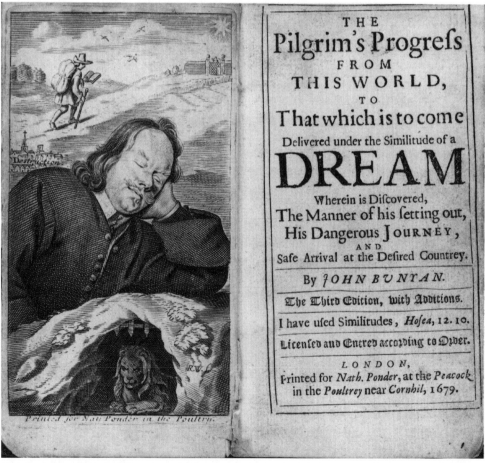

The frontispiece of the 1679 edition of *Pilgrim's Progress* shows author John Bunyan dreaming his Christian allegory.

From the river near the Delectable Mountains to the By-path Meadow, the group skirts robbers and demons. Leaving the women in the road, Christiana's sons, Mr. Honest, and Mr. Greatheart attack the Giant Despair of Doubting Castle. Mr. Greatheart beheads him; the group dismantles the castle. They continue toward three mountains—Marvel, Charity, and Innocent; local shepherds point out the forbidding entrance to Hell, where the moans and shrieks of the doomed pierce the air. The shepherds invite the pilgrims to the palace for dinner. Playing the stereotypical vain woman, Mercy covets a looking glass that hangs on the banquet-room wall. The shepherds grant her request and give jewelry to the other women as well.

At the Enchanted Ground, Greatheart leads the way through the Arbor. He consults a map to the Celestial City and guides them successfully past a mud pit to the right. Joining Stand-fast, they encounter Madame Bubble, a conniving sorcerer who claims to be Mistress of the World. To counter her evil gossip and deception, the pilgrims stand and sing a forceful hymn. Outside the king's gardens, children gather bouquets. Spices anoint the pilgrims' bodies to prepare them for the dark river that lies ahead. On the opposite shore of the River of Death, Christiana and her entourage arrive at a heavenly utopia, the Celestial City. They delight in sunlight and godliness. The scene unfolds into a progress of trumpeters, pipers, singers, players of harps, and chariots drawn by horses. Husband and wife are reunited; their sons and the four brides produce children to increase the church.

A triumph of episodic plotting, biblical citations and allusions, journey motif, allegory, and pictorial language, *Pilgrim's Progress* avoids heavy moralizing and concentrates on human skills, particularly cooperation, pragmatism, compassion, heroism, and determination. Just as Bunyan introduces it, the work abounds in the common dialect of a variety of personalities, both pious and ungodly. The clever depiction of pitfalls and meretricious encounters underscores the strengths of the hero, Christian, who gladly embraces assistance on his lengthy and terrifying journey to heaven. True to its time, this monument to the Puritan era denigrates women as helpless victims who survive on the fringes of their male rescuers and serve heaven as handmaids. (Baugh 1948; Bunyan 1896; Lindsay 1969; Manguel and Guadalupi 1987; Reason 1961)

See also allegory; Beulah Land; Bunyan, John; Celestial City; Christian; Christiana; Dante Alighieri; *Divina Commedia*; heaven; satire; women in utopia.

 # PISTHETAIROS

Pisthetairos is the central figure of Aristophanes's satire *The Birds* (414 B.C.), a mock-serious creation of heaven away from Earth. A facile manipulator and savvy city planner, Pisthetairos speaks for Aristophanes. He accompanies Euelpides, his fellow malcontent, on a journey away from Athens, away from earthly vice, to the kingdoms of Epops, a bird sovereign in the clouds. With Epops's assistance, Pisthetairos persuades a bird council to relinquish their rules against humans and allow the building of Cloudcuckooland, a walled city where birds and winged men can coexist in peace and harmony.

By power of will and judicious touches of diplomacy, Pisthetairos outmaneuvers the hostile birds and acquires birdhood. In pursuit of a more civil living arrangement, he honors his new wings by keeping his word and procuring sovereignty for birds, who are able to inhabit a city without dishonoring its democratic and altruistic underpinnings. A good-natured pitchman for a farfetched utopia, Pisthetairos concludes the play in upbeat form, newly wed to a wise bride and anticipating a fairer world where birds hold both the scepter of Zeus and sway over humankind. (Aristophanes 1993; Dearden 1976; Ehrenberg 1943; Henderson 1975; Lord 1963; Snodgrass 1988a; Spatz 1978; Ussher 1979)

See also Aristophanes; *The Birds;* city planning; Cloudcuckooland; Epops; fantasy; satire; women in utopia.

PLATO

A fourth-century B.C. Greek philosopher and author of numerous idealistic writings, notably *Timaeus, Critias,* and his masterwork, *The Republic,* Plato is the quintessential spokesman for Western thought. An Athenian citizen near the end of his deme's intellectual golden age, he earned immortality by recording the ideas of Socrates in a series of dialogues. Plato, whose name means "broad-shouldered," was born in 428 B.C., the son of Ariston and Perictione and an ornament to a distinguished family. His early training familiarized him with mathematics, literature, and music.

In his formative years Plato opted for a career in politics, but the unrest and corruption that followed Sparta's defeat of Athens in the Peloponnesian War altered his ambition. He made a formal break with government in 399 B.C., after his friend and teacher, Socrates, was imprisoned for impiety and forced to drink poisonous hemlock. Plato left Athens altogether, moved south to Megara, and stayed with Euclid, a fellow philosopher.

Plato remained single and devoted his life to research. Following a brief stint in the army from 395–394 B.C., he studied astronomy in Egypt and mathematics in Cyrene in North Africa, where he lived with his friend Theodorus. He ignored the strivings of Athenian despots and pursued an idealized world of order, a utopia managed by even-tempered logicians. In his mystical, harmonious cosmology, the good strive on Earth for recompense in the afterlife. Dismissing demagogues and scientists, he diagrammed a perfect society where petty power struggles and inflated honors have no worth.

Plato's utopianism brought him little temporal reward. On a tour of the Mediterranean in 388 B.C., he visited Dionysius I of Syracuse, who differed with his philosophy. Plato suffered degradation and deportation to Aegina, where he was exhibited for sale as a slave. Anniceris, a Cyrenian, paid the auctioneer's price and set him free. Plato once more departed alone, this time touring Tarentum in southern Italy, home of Archytas, a famed mathematician who convinced him that society would one day depend on mathematics.

In 387 B.C., Plato returned home to open an academy near Colonus, where he remained for 38 years. Over his door he inscribed a single dictum: "No one shall enter who knows no geometry." Students from all parts of the Mediterranean enrolled to study mathematics, logic, and astronomy. Twenty years later, Plato became embroiled in a contretemps between Dion and his father, Dionysius I. The virulence of their plotting forced Plato to flee for his life, leaving Eudoxus in charge of the school. On a visit to Sicily, Plato designed a governmental system for colonies. He was still working out the details at the time of his death, about 347 or 348 B.C.

Most significant to Plato's philosophy was a lifetime dedication to avenge Socrates, whom Athenian reactionaries executed for sacrilege. Plato's *Apology* casts Socrates in a speaking role, through which he vindicates his theories. Plato's 42 dialogues and 13 letters demonstrate his respect for reality, truth, and justice, which inspired later philosophies and established his position as a fount of Western idealism. The most influential of his dialectics, *The Republic*, details the ideal state and its ruler, the philosopher-king, who rules a model state by the exercise of knowledge, wisdom, and an appreciation of truth. (Hare 1982; Jordan 1981; Jowett 1937; Lodge 1956; Nettleship 1968; Plato 1937b; Rouse 1956; Snodgrass 1988a; Warner 1958)

See also city planning; idealism; philosopher-king; *The Republic*; *Timaeus*; utopia.

PLUTARCH

Plutarch was a significant contributor to Roman history and literature and the author of *The Life of Lycurgus* (first century A.D.), one of a series of paired biographies of notable Greek and Roman leaders. Lucius Mestrius Plutarchus was born to a wealthy family in A.D. 45 southwest of Athens in Chaeronea, Boeotia. Educated in astronomy, philosophy, and rhetoric under the best tutors in Smyrna and Athens, he developed into a civic-minded family man, the father of five; he performed priestly rituals at Apollo's temple at Delphi, ran for mayor, and served as magistrate and market commissioner. Plutarch was a learned world traveler, cultivating acquaintances in Egypt, Italy, and Asia Minor; at age 24 he served ten years as envoy to Rome.

Well-versed in Roman history and steeped in its literature, Plutarch acquired the savoir faire of a wise bilingual observer capable of critical comment on governments and societies foreign to his own background. On his return to Boeotia, he founded an academy and produced 300 titles, boasting an encyclopedic list of topics from child-rearing and anger to God's punishments, superstition, the man in the moon, and oracles. His two most famous works, *Moralia* and *Parallel Lives*, contrast the human foibles and strengths of notables ranging from Themistocles and Pericles to Cicero and Julius Caesar. As a purveyor of character, Plutarch earned acclaim from both Romans and Greeks and influenced the writing of later generations, especially William Shakespeare, whose *Julius Caesar* is a direct offshoot of Plutarch's biography. At Plutarch's death around A.D. 120 or 125, he was honored with a statue at Delphi, his second home. (Fuller 1959; Negley and Patrick 1952; Plutarch 1958; Plutarch 1971a; Snodgrass 1988b)

See also La Città del Sole; *The Life of Lycurgus;* Montaigne, Michel Eyquem de; philosopher-king.

PROMISED LAND

The Promised Land is an earthly haven described in Exodus, the second book of the Hebrew Pentateuch, or Old Testament. As a reward for faith and sacrifice, Yahweh (the name given to Moses' God) promises the Children of Israel a settled life, free of their historical nomadic insecurities. Under their first king, the poet David, and his successor, his wise son Solomon, these Semitic wanderers established a prosperous and glorious kingdom that eventually gave place to the sybaritic luxuries of their enemies, the Babylonians and Assyrians, whom they categorized as infidels. During this unsettled time, the prophets Amos, Hosea, Jeremiah, Isaiah, and Daniel created new utopias, visionary Edens that could be realized only through the drastic rededication of Jews to orthodoxy.

According to Isaiah's prophecy describing New Jerusalem (seventh century B.C.), an emerging monarchy, led by a Messiah who springs from the "rod of Jesse," will replace the imperfect world with a utopian kingdom. Delivering the strongest message to both Jews and Christians, the prophet envisions this peaceful world in Isaiah 11:5–7:

> And righteousness shall be the girdle of his loins and faithfulness the girdle of his reins. The wolf also shall dwell with the lamb, and the leopard shall lie down with the kid; and the calf and the young lion and the fatling together, and a little child shall lead them. And the cow and the bear shall feed; their young ones shall lie down together; and the lion shall eat straw like the ox.

Isaiah comments that this creation of a promised utopia will reunite Jews from Assyria, Egypt, Pathros, Cush, Elam, Shinar, Hamath, and the islands of the Mediterranean. These "dispersed of Judah" will come together from north, south, east, and west to cry out God's name and exalt it in a land watered by the "wells of salvation."

Isaiah returns to this prophetic perfect world in Chapters 34–35. He foresees that an angry god will destroy the Jews' adversaries and leave their corpses to rot. So gloriously triumphant is this utopian vision that Isaiah predicts Zion will survive on a day when "the heavens shall be rolled together as a scroll." In a horror of brimstone, pitch, and unending night, dragons, owls, wild beasts, and a satyr will join a vulture in usurping land once inhabited by the unworthy. For the faithful, Isaiah promises that God will arrive to rescue the deaf and blind, the mute, and the crippled. In place of the unholy realm that he destroys, God will open desert lands to fresh springs, which will water reeds and rushes. In Isaiah 35:8, the prophet calls this oasis the Way of Holiness, a refuge for the redeemed and the ransomed. He concludes jubilantly in verse 10, "They

shall obtain joy and gladness, and sorrow and sighing shall flee away."
(Alexander and Alexander 1973; Anderson 1966; Chase 1955; Holy Bible 1958;
Johnson 1968; Mays 1988; Pelikan 1992)

See also Celestial City; creation, mythic; Eden; Eve; heaven; *Paradise Lost;
Paradise Regained;* prophecy.

PROPHECY

Prophecy is the purpose and motif of the most compelling utopian literature.
Unlike speculative fiction, which warns of what might be, prophecy foretells
what will be, as found in Isaiah's Old Testament prediction of a Hebrew Messiah (seventh century B.C.), Virgil's foretelling of a messianic child in the *Bucolics*
(42–37 B.C.), and Alfred Tennyson's brief, bellicose vision of militaristic technology in "Locksley Hall" (1842). A distinctive voice foreseeing the possibilities of American democrary is the learned Parisian Alexis de Tocqueville
(1805–1859), a political analyst, historian, and logician. In his magnum opus,
De la démocratie en Amérique (1835), he defends a broad liberal stance and successfully depicts the future cataclysms that have tested and continue to perplex the United States. Prominent among his remarks are his pronouncements
against racism, which in his day envisioned the continued persecution and
near extinction of the Native American, and a coming battle over slavery, which
did not begin until two years after Tocqueville's death.

The direst fictional predictors of dystopian malaise or hellholes to come
occur in H. G. Wells's *The Time Machine* (1895), Jack London's *The Iron Heel*
(1907), Aldous Huxley's *Brave New World* (1932), George Orwell's *1984* (1949),
and Richard Adams's *Watership Down* (1972). Wells, the dystopian novelist of
the expiring Victorian world, presages a malaise that eclipses an era of unprecedented expansion and progress. As more of England's wealth accrues from
factories, the author predicts that Morlocks, or laborers, will be forced into
dehumanized environments. Like troglodytes, they will devolve into cannibalistic drones, blinded by underground habitats and suppressed and devalued for their lack of gentility and grace, which are epitomized by their antithesis,
the privileged Eloi. Fending for themselves in a spiritual wasteland by sucking
nourishment from Eloi bones, the primal Morlocks contrast the promise of the
prenuclear age, which Wells predicts in his perusal of machines that challenge
time and space, the last frontiers.

In *Brave New World,* Huxley speaks through a thinly veiled persona, that of
World Controller Mustapha Mond, to predict to his captive audience the dangers of eugenics, drugs, technology, inane entertainments, and other forms of
social control and engineering. In his introduction to dystopia, Huxley notes,
"I projected it six hundred years into the future. Today [1932] it seems quite
possible that the horror may be upon us within a single century." He concludes
that two alternatives lie at hand: either militarism or a vast totalitarianism,
"called into existence by the social chaos resulting from rapid technological
progress in general and the atomic revolution in particular. . . . "

Likewise, Orwell's *1984* sets a time limit, only 35 years after the publication of his novel. The insidious mind-controls of the Ministry of Truth and Thought Police reflect a fearful world-state that critics find alarmingly menacing. Like the baby-making factories of *Brave New World,* which have come true in scientific advancements such as cloning and DNA manipulation, Orwell's warnings about Newspeak and rewritten history bear a stark and terrifying resemblance to political scandals involving blatant distortion of fact and the selling of political candidates and policies via mass media, an insidious form of propaganda that is properly described as Orwellian. As Canadian philosopher Marshall McLuhan warned in the 1970s, a satisfied audience of television watchers can easily mistake acting and real life. Thus, Orwell's demoralized world-state seems less and less like fiction as modern journalism and advertising reflect the efficacy of current methods of deception and indoctrination.

Less political but no less predictive is the warning of tyranny in the rabbit concentration camp of Richard Adams's *Watership Down.* Although framed in the conventions of a beast fable, the story of Hazel and his band of rabbits focuses on prophetic dreams that launch a rapid exodus from certain death. The animals' escape hinges on a frail, undersized rabbit named Fiver, a furry Jeremiah whose brother trusts his frenzied, doom-ridden nightmares enough to challenge the complacent leadership of Sandleford Warren to flee to safer territory. In Chapter 1, on a peaceful day Fiver experiences a nameless, doom-laden dread—"something oppressive, like thunder." Fiver whimpers at the nearness of danger and cries out, "There isn't any danger here, at this moment. But it's coming—it's coming. Oh, Hazel, look! The field! It's covered with blood!" Fiver expands his vision with a description of the evil—a wire about his neck, which causes him to act out the pathetic writhings of imminent death, "kicking frantically as a rabbit does in a snare." The prophecy proves true, but not before Hazel and his followers depart on an adventure that yields an idyllic home on Watership Down.

Some examples of prophetic writings reveal an astounding knowledge of things to come and the writers' moral compulsion to spread the alarm. Major apocalyptic visions are contained in these works:

- Jack London, author of *The Iron Heel* (1907), indicates a trust in the architects of communism, Karl Marx and Friedrich Engels, who envisioned the violent emergence of a proletarian revolt against the extremes and repression of capitalists. London foresees a fictional society being overrun by workers who make their own utopia after creating an anarchic hell of extermination and cleansing. Through the eyes of activists Avis and Ernest Everhard, hand-to-hand street battles fought by disillusioned workers act out scenarios described in *The Communist Manifesto* (1848).

- Another work that foresees doom, James Hilton's *Lost Horizon* (1933) depicts Father Perrault as a withered high lama, who must kidnap a likely candidate to replace him to keep alive the syncretic philosophy of Shangri-La. In late-night conferences, Perrault corroborates the distancing of Hugh Conway from his role in World War I, which Perrault predicts will break anew into another world conflict.

- Similar desperation colors Marge Piercy's *Woman on the Edge of Time* (1976), a fictional account of present hopelessness for female schizophrenics and futuristic fear that the days of Earth are numbered. By time-traveling from one era to another, Connie Ramos, the protagonist, gains a broadened perspective of two states of powerlessness, one medically induced and the other the result of pollution, anarchy, and civilization's decline.

- P. D. James's *The Children of Men* (1993) warns of the loss of fertility that spells the end of the human race. The corresponding loss of reverence for life condemns the elderly to ritual drownings to spare society their upkeep. The smallest thread of hope attaches to the conclusion, in which Julian, a former activist for the underground, anticipates the birth of a child.

The variance in tone of prophetic literature depends on the author's determination to shock, dismay, or reassure. In Thomas Malthus's nineteenth-century premonitions of doom to an overburdened planet, the future holds outbreaks of violence and despair while the burgeoning human population depletes the supply of food and raw materials. Almost as grim, but not so all-encompassing, are *Black Elk Speaks* (1932), one holy man's overview of European destruction of Native American society, and Anthony Burgess's *A Clockwork Orange* (1962), a microcosm terrorized by a spiritually bankrupt gang led by Alex, a teenage Attila the Hun of the future, whose chief form of entertainment is victimizing the weak. Similarly, Doris Lessing's *Memoirs of a Survivor* (1974) lays out an even smaller microcosm—an apartment house and the surrounding streets of a decaying city beset by nomadic teenage gangs. The despair and bestiality of youthful characters presage the anarchy that follows urban disintegration.

Opposite the gloomy pictures of Malthus, Lessing, and Burgess is William Morris's *News from Nowhere* (1890), an unlikely socialist idyll in which a variety of Marx's vision produces an agrarian utopia where factories give way to cottage crafts and interdependent, rural work-gangs. Also intent on reassuring readers, American utopist Edward Bellamy, author of *Looking Backward, 2000–1887* (1887), foresees urban comforts such as piped-in music and sermons similar to modern cable television and a livable Boston where rational people attain a high level of civilization and defeat disease and social ills. (Adams 1972; Bellamy 1960; Burgess 1962; Hilton 1933; Holy Bible 1958; Huxley 1932; James 1958; Lessing 1988; London 1982; Malthus 1990; Marx 1992; Marx and Engels 1985; Morris 1968b; Neihardt 1961; Orwell 1949; Piercy 1976; Tennyson 1949a; Tocqueville 1969; Wells 1964)

See also Brave New World; Bucolics; The Children of Men; classism; *A Clockwork Orange;* Eloi; Engels, Friedrich; Hazel; *The Iron Heel;* "Locksley Hall";

London, Jack; *Looking Backward, 2000–1887;* Malthus, Thomas; Marx, Karl; *Memoirs of a Survivor;* Mond, Mustapha; Morlocks; *News from Nowhere; 1984;* Revelation; speculative fiction; technology; *The Time Machine; Watership Down;* women in utopia.

 # PURGATORY

See Divina Commedia.

RABELAIS, FRANÇOIS

A restless, daring French Renaissance savant, linguist, naturalist, and satirist, Rabelais wrote *Gargantua and Pantagruel* (1562). He extended Sir Thomas More's sixteenth-century concept of utopia by emphasizing a cornucopia of human sensual delights as an antidote to the dowdy, sour, uncompromising monasticism of the Middle Ages. In contrast to his contemporary John Calvin, the strict Presbyterian who governed sinful Genevans by theocratic fiat, Rabelais rejoiced in human goodness and jocularity. So cogent were his writings on freedom that they influenced Thomas Jefferson, who was well read in French literature, and other drafters of America's Declaration of Independence.

A native of La Devinière near Chinon in Touraine, Rabelais was born around 1494, although information about his youth suggests an earlier date. He entered Abbaye de Seuillé, a proscriptive Franciscan monastery that forbade the study of Greek classics. Under pressure from censorious prelates who disdained his tastes and radical notions and confiscated his texts, Rabelais transferred to Abbaye de Maillezais, a less repressive Benedictine order in Angiers. With the blessing of Pope Clement VII, there he could more freely study Greek, astronomy, medicine, and Hebrew and enter the priesthood. In 1526 Rabelais violated his vows by divesting himself of clerical robes, departing without permission, and living openly in Paris and Montpellier with a widow, who bore him two children.

At the Faculty of Medicine of Montpellier, Rabelais entered into a broad-based humanistic study of philosophy, medicine, anatomy, and law, his father's profession. Prominent in several fields, Rabelais graduated in 1537 and practiced law at the bar of Lyons. He heeded his literary muse by translating the Greek medical texts of Galen and Hippocrates for lesser students to read and by editing contemporary medical texts. He also attended as personal physician his patron, Cardinal Jean du Bellay, during his acute attacks of sciatica. On semiofficial business with the cardinal and later with the cardinal's brother, Guillaume Seigneur de Langey, Rabelais made several extended tours of Italy and lived in Turin, where he studied Arabic.

In 1532, under the anagrammatic pen name Alcofribas, Rabelais published the first segment of his five-part *Gargantua et Pantagruel,* a jolly burlesque.

François Rabelais

Growing out of a country squabble is a meandering, picaresque plot filled with puns, comic dialogues, parody, coinages, aphorism, riddles, misogyny, professional lore, political mockery, barroom jest, educational theory, rhyme, and utopian visions. Essentially, the work's erudition lies encased in coarse, scatological humor and centers on joie de vivre, appreciation of nature, and an open, benevolent trust in curiosity, knowledge, unbridled experimentation, and natural forms of worship. Rabelais risked apostasy in order to relieve medieval superstitions and ossification with an envigorating breath of Renaissance fresh air. Because of his liberal musings and ribaldry, he offended conservative elements and was forced to flee France.

With the intervention of Clement's successor, Pope Paul III, and still under du Bellay's protection, Rabelais returned to the Benedictine order in 1535 and took up serious hospital work and anatomy lectures. The climate menaced a joker and punster like Rabelais, who saw his printer Dolet burned at the stake for heresy in Paris in 1546. Rabelais advanced to a curacy and continued writing festive, episodic satire. Late in his life, still influenced by his motto *Rire est le propre de l'homme* ("Laughter is suitable to humankind"), he returned to Paris and was named curé of Meudon. His death on April 9, 1553, preceded the publication of a fifth segment of his satiric novel and a public outpouring of admiration for his buffoonery from Michel de Montaigne, Jean La Fontaine, Honorè de Balzac, Jonathan Swift, and Laurence Sterne, among others.

The success of *Gargantua and Pantagruel* supplied linguistics with a useful eponym. The term "Rabelaisian," a specific adjective, evolved from the satirist's surname and means robust, vigorous, extravagant, and naturalistic. Connotatively, "Rabelaisian" carries a hint of coarse, crude exhibitionism. The word appeared early in the nineteenth century as a modifier depicting any form of caricature or parody that pillories dogma, bigotry, cant, fundamentalism, pedantry, conformity, and other forms of narrow-mindedness. "Rabelaisian" eventually typified the Renaissance itself, with its exuberant embrace of life, earthly pastimes, humor, creativity, and learning. (Bishop 1965; Boorstin 1992; Lewis 1969; Mack 1962; Manguel and Guadalupi 1987; Pollard 1970; Putnam 1993; Rabelais 1955; Screech 1980)

See also The Abbey of Thélème; classism; escapism; fantasy; *Gargantua and Pantagruel*; Montaigne, Michel Eyquem de; More, Sir Thomas; satire; Swift, Jonathan; utopia; women in utopia.

RALPH

The intelligent, noble lawmaker and organizer in the opening chapters of William Golding's dystopic *Lord of the Flies* (1954), Ralph applies normal logic to the plane crash that isolates a group of English schoolboys on an Edenic island. Backed up by Piggy and the symbolic conch, Ralph demands order, cleanliness, and dedication to rescue, which he predicts will come if the boys keep a fire going to attract a passing ship. The innate wickedness of Jack Merridew, Ralph's nemesis, forces Ralph to flee an escalating level of savagery that costs Simon and Piggy their lives and transforms a band of former choristers into a ragged troop of assassins.

At the end of his sojourn on the island, Ralph is the first of the group to encounter rescuers. Unable to verbalize his dismay at the inhuman scenario that has burst into overt bestiality and threatened him with similar brutality, he is overwhelmed with the enormity of the hunters' intent and weeps incoherently, perhaps in terror of his brush with death. In the background, fire sterilizes and cleanses the island of potential evil. As described in the final paragraphs, Ralph succumbs to

> ... great, shuddering spasms of grief that seemed to wrench his whole body. His voice rose under the black smoke from the burning wreckage of the island; ... Ralph wept for the end of innocence, the darkness of man's heart, and the fall through the air of the true, wise friend called Piggy.

The adventuresome lad in Chapter 1 has lived through a terror capable of extinguishing all sparks of trust in human goodness. Before reaching his teens, he recognizes that all the safeguards in England and on the island cannot stave off the evil born in humanity. (Baker 1988; Carey 1987; Gindin 1988; Golding 1954; Johnston 1980; Kinkead-Weeks and Gregor 1984; Subbarao 1987)

See also allegory; bestiality; Eden; Golding, William; *Lord of the Flies*; Merridew, Jack; Piggy; Ralph.

RAMOS, CONNIE

A shortened form of Consuelo Camacho Ramos, this 35-year-old Mexican-American is the protagonist of Marge Piercy's *Woman on the Edge of Time* (1976), a searing exposé of psychological torment, inhumane incarceration, and experimental brain surgery to control psychosis. Separated from her husband Edward for three years and living on AFDC funds, Connie has one child, four-year-old Angelina, as well as a brother, Luis, and a niece, Dolly, a victimized prostitute. In Chapter 1, during Dolly's violent set-tos against her pimp, Connie intervenes and is battered. Luis remands her to Bellevue, a mental institution in New York.

Drugs, which are a determining factor in Huxley's *Brave New World* (1932) and, to a lesser extent, Alfred Tennyson's "The Lotus-Eaters" (1832), James Hilton's *Lost Horizon* (1933), Alex Haley's *The Autobiography of Malcolm X* (1965), and Margaret Atwood's *The Handmaid's Tale* (1985), dominate much of the characterization and motivation in Piercy's novel. Both the street variety and prescriptions of Thorazine befuddle Connie's wits until Luciente penetrates and guides her through future centuries to a twenty-second-century commune. At first skeptical, Connie identifies with Luciente's world, which battles the environmental damage caused by the profligate twentieth century. As her suspected hallucinations grow more violent, Dr. Redding and his staff opt to place tranquilizing metal implants in her skull and control her behavior as though changing channels on television.

The deft charactization of Connie blends barrio violence, retribution against a lifetime of poverty and cruel treatment, guilt from her failed mothering of Angelina, and escapism from hostility against mental illness, particularly female psychotics. The ambiguity of Luciente's future world leaves the reader with no clear definition of Connie's mental state. The utopian interpretation tantalizes with its pragmatic view of a wiser, less mechanistic time when surviving generations dwindle in number, return to nature, and battle the technological waste and poisons left over from the twentieth century. Whatever the reason for Luciente's incursion into the violent ward, the meetings with Connie offer a scrap of hope too elusive, too nebulous for long-term reassurance. Subsumed by swirling thoughts as the implants jangle her brain waves, Connie succumbs to her era's psychiatry, a mechanistic and drug-induced crazy-making that inadvertently defeats sanity and wholeness. (Buck 1992; *Contemporary Authors* 1984; *Contemporary Literary Criticism* 1981a; Piercy 1976; Walker and Hamner 1984)

See also conditioning; escapism; futurism; Piercy, Marge; prophecy; *Woman on the Edge of Time;* women in utopia.

RAND, AYN

Rand was a spirited Russian lecturer and the author of *Anthem* (1937), a dystopian fable honoring individualism, her favorite theme. The daughter of a St. Petersburg merchant, Alissa Rosenbaum Ayn Rand (February 2, 1905– March 5, 1982) displayed unusual intelligence in early childhood. After completing a history degree at the University of Leningrad, she escaped communism by emigrating to Chicago to live with her aunt, and in four years became a U.S. citizen. Rand moved to Hollywood and for 12 years worked as a movie extra and scriptwriter for De Mille Studios, RKO, Universal, Paramount, Hal Wallis, and MGM Pictures. In 1929, during the filming of *King of Kings,* the De Mille version of the life of Christ, she met and married fellow extra Frank O'Connor.

Rand's early fiction output includes *We the Living* (1936), *Anthem,* and *The Fountainhead* (1943), her best-selling novel, loosely based on the life and works of Frank Lloyd Wright. Rand adapted *The Fountainhead* into a turgid, symbol-ridden screenplay, which was filmed in 1949 and featured Raymond Massey, Gary Cooper, and Patricia Neal. In her mid-forties, Rand moved to New York to advance her literary career. An intensely motivated atheist and capitalist, she lectured on objectivism at Yale, Princeton, Columbia, Johns Hopkins, Harvard, MIT, and the U.S. Military Academy. In 1957 she published her magnum opus, *Atlas Shrugged,* the American manifesto of individualism. Later works—*The Romantic Manifesto* (1969), *The New Left* (1971), and a monthly journal, *The Objectivist* (1962–1971)—grew out of her preference for dramatic polemics and identifiable absolutes.

Rand's uncompromising stance favoring determinism and free will insists on a realistic acceptance of human failings. Championing the application of pure reason to the overthrow of dictators and despots who would enslave humanity, she makes an impassioned case against collectivism, which she believed endangered individuality, creativity, and basic human freedoms. Though stridently anticommunist, during the McCarthy era Rand lacked a popular audience because of her distaste for American society. Her limited awards are capped by an honorary doctorate from Lewis and Clark College in 1963. The next year, she donated her manuscripts and papers to the Library of Congress. Rand's protégés perpetuate her doctrines with lectures, newsletters, and an

Ayn Rand testifies before the U.S. House Subcommittee on Unamerican Activities in Washington, D.C., in 1947.

annual essay contest and scholarship. (Baker 1987; Buck 1992; O'Neill 1977; Rand 1946)

See also *Anthem;* collectivism; Equality 7-2521; eugenics; Liberty 5-3000; naturalism; prophecy; women in utopia.

"RASSELAS, PRINCE OF ABISSINIA"

A neoclassic oriental idyll written by Samuel Johnson in 1759, the poem expresses the anti-utopianism common to eighteenth-century rationalists, who disdained fantasy and raised systematic logic to the level of deism. Johnson's didactic poem, set in Ethiopia, details Happy Valley, a pastoral haven that deludes his readers into expecting a blissful, luxuriant Eden. Like Voltaire's Candide, Tennyson's Gareth, Anthony Burgess's Alex, and William Golding's Ralph, Rasselas allows youthful idealism to blind him to the truth of human nature—its imperfectability.

Rasselas escapes his father and sets out for Egypt with his sister Nekayah, her slave Pekuah, and the wise old Imlac. But Prince Rasselas grows moody and contemplative, and in the midst of dainties and entertainments, he abruptly withdraws to a woodsy bower to listen to bird songs and observe the leap of fish and the pasturing animals. A court sage follows him on his solitary stroll and overhears his internal musings on the causes of his discontent. The spy observes that Rasselas returns to court placated by his contemplation of life's inequities.

Johnson creates a scene in which Rasselas enters into a dialectic with a philosophic adversary. The sage Imlac, an aged tutor long in the prince's employ, questions him about his restlessness and dolor. The prince replies that "pleasure has ceased to please; I am lonely because I am miserable, and am unwilling to cloud with my presence the happiness of others." The sage remarks that Rasselas is an anomaly—the first royal inmate to complain of misery while contemplating unending pleasure and beauty. The prince answers that, even though he wants for nothing, he cannot name the cause of his complaint.

Rasselas's only clue derives from nature—the frolic of kids and lambs that chase one another in spontaneous, natural play. He envies their need to pursue or attain something. Longing for purpose like Alexander the Great, who wept because he had no more worlds to conquer, the spoiled prince begs, "give me something to desire." The sage replies that, if the prince were to view the world's miseries, he would value luxury and leisure. Rasselas looks within to disclose the personal philosophy that inhibits his pleasure: In order to perceive happiness, he must experience its antithesis. Echoing the oriental concept of yin and yang, the two needs are inseparable, one enlarging on the other.

Twenty months later, still consumed with the desire to know real humanity through pain, Rasselas fantasizes about the robbery of an orphaned virgin. Realizing that he is wasting valuable time, he spends four more months lamenting his benign imprisonment. He then turns his attention toward a plan of escaping Happy Valley's pleasant ennui and returning to Abissinia. In the same way that Voltaire's Candide takes comfort in tending his garden and Hermann Hesse's Siddhartha learns to value human suffering by working as a ferryman, Rasselas prepares himself for the real world and for the serendipitous glimpses of contentment that lie enfolded in ordinary human affairs. (Boswell 1981; Boulton 1978; Engell 1985; Johnson 1982; Nath 1987)

See also Alex; Burgess, Anthony; Candide; *Candide; A Clockwork Orange;* dystopia; Happy Valley; Hesse, Hermann; Johnson, Dr. Samuel; naturalism; Siddhartha; *Siddhartha;* Voltaire, François.

 # RELIGION

Religion is a central, arbitrary element in utopian and dystopian literature that may appear in the form of authoritarian theocracy, worship, belief in a higher power, myth, ritual, devotion through altruism, humanitarianism, meditation, trance, asceticism, or complete withdrawal from the world. In ancient writings, particularly the mythic creation in Genesis (ca. 950 B.C.), Isaiah's lyric prophecies (seventh century B.C.), Lao Tzu's collected sayings in the *Tao Te Ching* (third century B.C.), Confucius's *Analects* (second century A.D.), Hesiod's *Works and Days* and *Theogony* (eighth century B.C.), Virgil's *Aeneid* (19 B.C.), Ovid's *Metamorphoses* (A.D. 8), Revelation (A.D. 90–95), and St. Augustine's *De Civitate Dei* (A.D. 426), religion is a given: a definitive answer in matters of ethics and behavior, a foundation for life and family, an otherworldly afterlife, or the Tao, or path, amid worldliness and chaos. These sources of didactic advice are not to be questioned or neglected without dire consequence. The influence of bedrock belief systems permeates utopias most frequently where earthly governments or societies have disappointed by falling short of their promise or have capriciously assigned happiness, health, prestige, or treasure to only an undeserving few.

In flight from the godlessness of dystopian or sacrilegious settings are notable, memorable characters from a wide spectrum of literary periods and styles:

- Dante's extensive odyssey from the pit of hell to a union with archangels and God in *The Divine Comedy* (1320)

- newly baptized converts in Sir Thomas More's *Utopia* (1516)

- a uniform body of citizens living in harmony in Johann Andreae's *Christianopolis* (1619)

- the disobedience of John Milton's Adam and Eve in *Paradise Lost* (1667) and humankind's redemption through Jesus' temptation in *Paradise Regained* (1671)

- Pilgrim and his wife Christiana reaching Celestial City in John Bunyan's *Pilgrim's Progress* (1678)

- the reaffirmation of faith in a just, merciful, all-powerful god in Daniel Defoe's *Robinson Crusoe* (1719)

- the reverent central character in Henry Wadsworth Longfellow's mythic *The Song of Hiawatha* (1855)

The religious motif moves into the twentieth century with more visionaries, prophets, and holy seekers of God:

- the medicine man Black Elk describing and interpreting his visions of visits with four supernatural "Grandfathers" in *Black Elk Speaks* (1932)

- late-night discussions between the frail, ascetic high lama, Father Perrault, and his chosen successor, Hugh Conway, in James Hilton's *Lost Horizon* (1933)

- the making of a deity from mortal beginnings in Hermann Hesse's *Siddhartha* (1951)

- Malcolm X and his crises of faith after an Islamic pilgrimage in Alex Haley's *The Autobiography of Malcolm X* (1965)

Serving as corollaries to the lambent visions of an easeful afterlife depicted in the Bible, *The Book of the Dead* (fifteenth century B.C.), *The Book of Mormon* (1830), the Koran (610), and other religious or visionary works are the disturbing dystopias where religion is trivialized, subverted, or repressed:

- the heinous kangaroo courts and tortures springing from the Inquisition in Voltaire's *Candide* (1759)

- the minutia of religious lore in Lilliput, a land of little people in Jonathan Swift's *Gulliver's Travels* (1727)

- *vril*-worship in the ominous subterranean society of Vril-Ya in Edward Bulwer-Lytton's *The Coming Race* (1871)

- the hypocrisy of Samuel Butler's citizens in *Erewhon* (1872), who claim to worship the abstract deification of justice, hope, love, strength, and fear while secretly praying to the pagan goddess Ydgrun

- the crow's references to Sugar Candy Mountain in George Orwell's *Animal Farm* (1945)

- the suppression of the Bible in Ray Bradbury's *Fahrenheit 451* (1953)

The classic twentieth-century revolts against religion gained strength from the antigod, antichurch writings of Karl Marx and Friedrich Engels, whose collectivist philosophy permeates Jack London's *The Iron Heel* (1907). Outstanding among these rebel works is Aldous Huxley's *Brave New World* (1932), a pessimistic worldview that supplants God with the drug *soma*, materialism, eugenics, hypnopaedia, technology, and "Our Ford," the founder of the factory system that produces perfectly engineered embryos for five rigid social strata. In a more positive mode, Arthur Clarke's *Childhood's End* (1953) evolves a benevolent utopia over a 50-year period, during which education supplants ignorance and worshipers abandon superstition and evolve a "purified Buddhism."

Decades after Huxley's classic novel and Clarke's syncretism of world faiths into a more tolerant mysticism, Margaret Atwood wrote *The Handmaid's Tale* (1985), a terrifying perversion of biblical scripture set in Gilead, a fictional New England theocracy where fecund women are enslaved in a breeding program. In a chilling mockery of Christian ritual the breeder, or handmaid, attends a reading of scripture; then, veiled and gripped by her mistress's hands, lies symbolically between the thighs of the barren upper-class woman and is mounted by the man of the house, who is always a member of an elite class. Other subversions of righteousness in Gilead occur regularly as the survivors of nuclear disasters try to populate the earth by careful husbandry of fertility and by coercive propaganda, police-state spying, and recriminations. Rebels die on the hangman's rope in view of the obedient, who assist in springing the trap and adorn the ceremony with hymns, pious greetings, and appropriate aphorisms. (Adams 1972; Andreae 1955; Augustine 1981; Bellamy 1960; Bradbury 1953; Budge 1960; Bunyan 1896; Burgess 1962; Butler 1968; Campanella 1955; Clarke 1953; Dante Alighieri 1968; Defoe 1963; Golding 1954; Haley 1965; Hesiod 1966; Hesiod 1973; Hesse 1951; Hilton 1933; Huxley 1932; Longfellow 1992; Marx 1992; Marx and Engels 1985; Milton 1957a; More 1963a; Neihardt 1961; Orwell 1946; Swift 1958; Waley 1992)

See also *The Analects of Confucius; Animal Farm; The Autobiography of Malcolm X;* Beulah Land; Black Elk; *The Book of Mormon;* Buddhism; Celestial City; *Childhood's End; Christianopolis; De Civitate Dei; A Clockwork Orange; Divina Commedia; Erewhon; Fahrenheit 451;* Genesis; Gilead; *Gulliver's Travels; The Handmaid's Tale;* heaven; Hesiod; Koran; *Lost Horizon; Paradise Lost; Paradise Regained; Pilgrim's Progress;* Sermon on the Mount; *Siddhartha;* Swift, Jonathan; *Tao Te Ching;* theocracy; *Utopia.*

 # THE REPUBLIC

In a controlled, logical interconnection of ideas, *The Republic,* the Western world's most revered utopian work, collects Plato's thoughts on the ideal life and his conception of the work and influence of the philosopher-king.

Book I

Styled after his typical dialogues, the work opens on a holiday gathering of a dozen men at the home of Cephalus. The lead question arises between the host and Socrates, who disagree on the role of wealth in the attainment of happiness. Socrates disputes Cephalus's belief that a comfortable income increases the likelihood of contentment and morality. Cephalus deserts the disputation, leaving his son Polemarchus to debate the nature of justice. In his definition, acting in the right means "giving everyone his due." At Socrates's insistence, Polemarchus extends the definition to rewarding friends and attacking enemies.

Socrates deliberates on the matter of who is best equipped to execute Pole-marchus's axiom and concludes that the statement omits identification of friend and enemy. In Socrates's estimation, evil is never the right choice, whether applied to friend or enemy. Polemarchus concurs.

The style, which is heavily dependent on exacting definitions, draws strength from debate. In response to Thrasymachus, who intrudes on the discussion to demand a definition of justice, Socrates retains his composure and awaits input from other guests. Thrasymachus proposes that justice is what benefits the most powerful party, as exemplified by a ruler who codifies laws that benefit him. Socrates notes that despots often err in legislation by benefiting the citizenry while harming themselves. He pursues the matter with a counteraxiom: Rulers should accede in all matters to the good of the people rather than to personal aggrandizement or enrichment.

Thrasymachus cynically rejoins that only weaklings and fools believe that justice is virtuous. Such morality results from ignorance, fear of arrest, or dread of punishment for doing wrong. In contrast, strong people have no fear of tax evasion and embezzlement from the public treasury and consequently attain success that timid folk can never enjoy. Thrasymachus surmises that the best way to succeed is to cow the public through outright despotism. At the urging of other guests, Socrates rebuts Thrasymachus's paradigm supporting tyrants:

- First, responds Socrates, there is no proof that opportunists are more intelligent.

- Second, even criminals must rely on justice if they are to conspire successfully.

- Third, Socrates insists that, by its very nature, injustice does not allow people to live well or find contentment.

Book II

After a lull in conversation as the men return to their plates, Plato's brothers, Glaucon and Adeimantus, reopen the debate over which is preferable, the just or the unjust life. Glaucon faces off against Socrates's position that the just life is intrinsically good by contending that, originally, justice sprang from society's need to halt predators from stirring up a constant state of uproar. In essence, law and morality evolved not out of a mutual desire for goodness but out of mutual fear. To prove his case, Glaucon cites the example of a magic ring of invisibility that obscures both the lawful man and the criminal. Glaucon declares that both men, given the cloak of invisibility, would commit crimes because there would be no reason for them to avoid it. He concludes that the unjust who are clever enough to conceal their misdeeds live in seeming happiness among neighbors who never suspect them of injustice.

Glaucon's brother Adeimantus shores up his brother's point of view with a salient side note: He comments that parents teach their children to behave because the children will increase their social standing if they appear just. Thus, the children grow up following their parents' dictates in order to acquire a worthy reputation, rather than for virtue's sake. Adeimantus adds that theology proves that the unjust have little reason to fear retribution from the gods, because literature proves that the gods are vulnerable to bribery. Adeimantus ends by agreeing with Glaucon that a wealthy, powerful criminal who can act unjustly and still maintain a good reputation will thrive.

At Adeimantus's request, Socrates attempts to prove that a just life is preferable. He begins by explaining that people come together to form a community by dividing the labors of supplying food, building material, clothing, and other needs. A complex society also needs artists, servants, doctors, and the military. The presence of police in the community could prove menacing if officers have no love of wisdom. In Socrates's paradigm, education is the key to the formation of respectable soldiers. As a means of building character, educators must acquire the most positive material to teach their students. To establish a philosophic temperament, Socrates advocates that future peacekeepers be schooled in stories of gods and heroes. To train soldiers to risk their lives without fear of death, Greece must provide stories devoid of devious gods and a dismal Underworld, both of which can be found in Homer's verse. Socrates expounds more of his theories of education with examples of a healthful diet and proper physical training.

Book III

Turning to the matter of how the ideal state should be ruled, Socrates declares a need for two types of authorities: Officials, he insists, must be the best men—wise, experienced, intelligent, skilled, and public-spirited. The only way that such rulers can maintain their worth is to abstain from graft and deception. To ascertain a candidate's worth, the public must evaluate them in their younger years. Along with top leaders to rule and civil servants to carry out the law exists a class of merchants, professionals, builders, and farmers. To assure each trade class its autonomy, Socrates indicates that society must establish stability and harmony. To dissuade rulers from despotism and corruption, he proposes that they live communally and abstain from riches. To repay them for their vital role, the community must settle on a plan of remuneration in food, clothing, and necessities rather than cash.

Book IV

Adeimantus interjects a fault in Socrates's hypothetical rulers. Since neighboring governments may lavish wealth on their heads of state, how can the ideal state keep its rulers from being jealous? Socrates retorts that the ideal rulers will be content if they suppress discontent in the state. To assure the society a fair dispersal of goods, the state must resist creating haves and have-nots, otherwise only the upper class will gain luxuries and privileges. In the model state, Socrates adds, there is little need for laws since a well-educated citizenry will learn to behave well and to avoid excesses. To create the essential grounding, the state must demonstrate wisdom, courage, discipline, and justice, and must allot each citizen a single role to fill a particular need. If each citizen accepts these premises and performs an assigned task adequately, society will function harmoniously and well. By assigning rulers to do the thinking, enforcers to exercise emotions, and tradespeople to satisfy desires, the state delineates the role expected of each participant. When a stable government functions, justice reigns in the same way that a functioning body displays health.

Book V

Glaucon and Adeimantus press Socrates to extend his search for a definition of justice. Socrates replies that the internal order that controls the body and the state results in justice just as disorder produces injustice. So long as the passions accede to the rule of reason, goodness will result. He includes women in this paradigm by noting that they too have their place to fill and must be educated to serve the ideal state. Socrates includes a need for sexual fulfillment, child care, and a regulated system of eugenics:

- To assure the best offspring, the state should hold nuptial festivals and pair the best males and females for mating.

- To encourage acceptance of the state's choice, officials must convince participants that they concur in the choices.

Like Spartan infants in Plutarch's planned society described in *The Life of Lycurgus* (first century A.D.), the children who result from state marriages must be brought up kibbutz-style, expecting no knowledge of or affection from their biological parents. Instead, the nuclear family should give place to a state family, with each adult accepting responsibility for each child.

To Glaucon's doubts Socrates contends that only through dissolution of families can there be an end to jealousy. By directing loyalties to the state, citizens will have no need of private ownership and will share in the needs and responsibilities inherent in normal life. Further dissension among the guests leads Socrates to admit that his paradigm is a paper model, not a plan of action. Thus, the ideal state can never take form until rulers study philosophy. Diverted to a definition of philosophy, Socrates describes a love of wisdom and knowledge. True philosophers must be curious, open-minded, and truth-loving. By valuing ideal beauty rather than mere beautiful objects, the philosopher rises above the temporal level to achieve a sublime knowledge of truth. In so doing, the philosopher reaches the height of understanding.

Book VI

Socrates moves from identifying the philosopher to proving that a lover of truth should rule the model state. In order to administer the common good and set a worthy example, the philosopher is best suited for control because he disciplines his passions and avoids frivolity. Unmoved by wealth or prestige, the philosopher strives for the highest level of goodness. Lacking a fear of death, he rules bravely. Adeimantus reminds Socrates that, in real life, societies do not value philosophers. Socrates agrees that philosophers are often scorned, but he reminds Adeimantus that the fault lies in citizens who have not been trained to respect intelligence and wisdom. The current state of affairs finds politicians ruling the state and philosophers grown corrupt. Socrates blames a faulty environment for encouraging egotism rather than intrinsic rewards. He hopes that one day society may acquire a philosopher-king or develop a ruler into a well-rounded philosopher. The discussion turns to the nature of goodness, the virtue that enables the philosopher to value beauty and justice.

Book VII
To establish the four states of the mind, Socrates launches into his famous allegory, the cave parable. He describes a subterranean cave separated from the outside by a long entrance. Cave dwellers, who have been chained to the ground since infancy, can see one wall. Between these prisoners and the road passing by the cave is a fire. Limited in point of view, the cave dwellers come to think of shadows cast on the wall by the fire as reality. Several possibilities affect the cave dweller's responses:

- If a single cave dweller were freed and allowed to face the road beyond, he would suffer from stiffness and the glare of light on his eyes.

- If he were forced to accept the people on the road outside and abandon belief in the shadows he has viewed all his life, he would scorn reality and turn back to the shadows.

- If he were forced out the entrance into sunlight, he would grow fearful in the bright glare until his eyes accustomed themselves to the light.

- If he studied how heavenly bodies create shadows, he would perceive the importance of the sun, the creator of shadows.

In his enlightened state, the former prisoner would value his freedom and pity the cave dwellers he left behind. However, a return to the cave would require a new tolerance for gloom. The other prisoners would mock and deride him for leaving the cave and for being tricked by the outside world.

Socrates ends his parable and labels the parts of the model. The cave represents belief, daylight equals knowledge, and the sun goodness. By moving from belief to knowledge to goodness, the former prisoner suffers a necessary form of pain. At length, the prisoner values his coming to knowledge, even though his fellows in the cave ridicule his experience in moving from delusion to enlightenment. Similarly, the ruler who becomes a philosopher-king must make a passage from belief to understanding. At the end of his training, he must assist his lessers in rejecting shadows. The best method of producing such rulers, asserts Socrates, is an education grounded in solving problems by applying pure mathematics—arithmetic, plane geometry, solid geometry, astronomy, and harmonics. By mastering abstract logic, the student must learn dialectic, which explores reality in search of truth. If the pupil is intelligent, decent, courageous, and hard-working, he is a good candidate for a rigorous 30-year program of studies in literature, music, mathematics, martial arts, and logic. By age 35, the candidates who survive are ready to assume leadership roles.

Book VIII

At Glaucon's urging, Socrates returns to a differentiation of types of wrong. He names four kinds of failed societies: timocracy, oligarchy or plutocracy, democracy, and despotism or tyranny.

- Timocracy, a military state, arises when a ruler favors power over knowledge.

- In a worse scenario, the exaltation of money and property results in oligarchy.

- If a debtor nation revolts against property owners, a democracy will result in which citizens are equal in rank. Lacking the discipline of assigned roles, the democratic state suffers a weakened military and politicians who cater to a crass and demanding citizenry.

- As respect for authority degenerates, demagogues jockey for place in the people's favor. Resultant disharmony leads to revolution, with the most popular leader rising to power. To maintain his despotic role, he must cushion himself against the mob with a corrupt militia, whom he must bribe with funds extorted from the people.

Book IX

Socrates falls back on a study of the just individual, for whom tyranny is slavery. To be truly happy, the just man must control passions and desires. By choosing knowledge over emotion or desire, the just man experiences the height of pleasure, which surpasses such temporary satisfactions as food and drink. Because the content individual values knowledge over money, reputation, and carnal delights, he will lead a just and satisfying life.

Book X

Socrates adds comments about the arts, which create illusions by copying reality. He insists that the arts corrupt by moving an audience to emotional outbursts, which reveal a loss of self-discipline. Although he admits that he admires the epics of Homer, Socrates pronounces hymns to gods and heroes as the best models of art. Moreover, Socrates uses this postdialectic moment to assert that the rewards for goodness come in the afterlife. The soul, he claims, is immortal because no evil can destroy it. To illustrate the relationship between earthly life and heaven, he relates the myth of Er, a soldier who died in battle in Asia Minor and observed the choices of great heroes for a reincarnation. Orpheus, the singer, chose to be reborn as a swan; Ajax the bold wanted to be a lion. Agamemnon, the leader of Greek forces at Troy, preferred the life of an eagle. Odysseus, who had wandered the Mediterranean and recalled the troubles of his illustrious past, chose the simple life of an ordinary man. At the conclusion of the story, Socrates exhorts Glaucon to select a virtuous life that will be rewarded in heaven. (Hare 1982; Jordan 1981; Lodge 1956; Nettleship 1968; Plato 1955; Snodgrass 1988a; Warner 1958)

See also heaven; philosopher-king; Plato; women in utopia.

REVELATION

This visionary final book of the New Testament is attributed to St. John the Divine (not to be confused with John, the disciple of Christ) and dated A.D. 90–95, a period when the writer, once a prisoner of the Romans at hard labor in the quarries of Patmos, fled to Ephesus in Asia Minor. Composed during one of the frequent periods of Roman persecution of Christians, the text appears to censure the Roman custom of emperor worship—in this case, for Domitian (81–96). Written in the style of rigorous Old Testament prophets (Daniel, Ezekiel, Isaiah, and Jeremiah), this obscure, apocalyptic, and at times disjointed work seeks to comfort and revitalize the faith of disillusioned followers of Christ and churches afflicted by dissension and political turmoil or the temptation to return to pagan worship and altar sacrifices. Revelation has been described as a coded message written in magic numbers and broad symbols; it makes frequent references to the Old Testament prophecy of apocalypse, or the end of time, when good and evil will fight for control of creation and righteousness will overwhelm Earth. Because of its cosmic motif, Revelation is believed to be free of specific charges against the Roman Empire or incriminating references to the Seven Churches of Asia Minor—Ephesus, Smyrna, Pergamum, Thyatira, Sardis, Philadelphia, and Laodicea. With these words in hand, Christians could safely share their faith with others without fear of arrest for plotting a rebellion.

If read as a prophecy of the Second Coming of Christ, Revelation envisions relief from pagan overlords when the rapture, a power greater than Rome and all its legions, will without warning swoop down to Earth to rescue the righteous and the dead and set them before the throne of God to be judged. Historically, Revelation has both mystified and terrified the unwary reader because of its grandeur and whirling prophecy, filled with dire symbols and the promise of destruction—earthquakes, plagues, winds, floods—for evildoers and rewards for the faithful. John claims in Chapter 19 to have heard "a great voice of much people in heaven, saying, Alleluia; Salvation, and glory and honor, and power, unto the Lord our God." John warns those expecting God's grace to avoid false prophets, who may lead the chosen astray. John foresees an exalted figure appearing on a white horse in a cleft of heaven. With flaming eyes and crowned head, the figure leads a heavenly army dedicated to the "king of kings and lord of lords."

After the victorious deity presides over the chaining of Satan in an abyss, a thousand years of conflict between good and evil will result in a New Jerusalem. According to Chapter 21, this perfect world will shine with light and precious stones and stand surrounded by a high wall with 12 gates. Angels will enroll members of the Twelve Tribes of Israel. From God's throne will issue the water of life, replenishing the tree of life, a remnant of Eden, with 12 kinds of fruit and healing leaves. The creation of a New Jerusalem will mean an end of night, which symbolizes confusion, doubt, and oppression. John concludes that this glorious reign will have no end. (Alexander and Alexander 1973; Holy Bible 1958; Mays 1988; Metzger and Coogan 1993; Turner 1993)

See also Eden; Genesis; heaven; nirvana; *Paradise Regained;* prophecy; Satan.

ROBINSON CRUSOE

A utopian idyll and adventure story by Daniel Defoe, published in 1719, this fictionalized survival tale features a crucial theme in utopian literature: the relationship of humanity to God and nature. Composed in the first person, the book advocates moral behavior in a milieu completely devoid of religious or state influence and with no witnesses to embarrass a law-breaker. Literary historians credit Defoe with influencing the development of the documentary novel, which he fills with realistic details much as a journalist would cite facts and quote eyewitnesses in straight reportage. Authors who claim admiration for Defoe's literary innovations include Samuel Taylor Coleridge, Jean-Jacques Rousseau, and Karl Marx.

The title character, delineated by a lengthy genealogy, is the third son of a family from York. In Chapter 1, a prophetic statement delivered by his father advised:

> I might judge of the happiness of this state by this one thing, viz., that this was the state of life which all other people envied: that kings have frequently lamented the miserable consequences of being born to great things, and wished they had been placed in the middle of the two extremes, between the mean and the great; that the wise man gave his testimony to this as the just standard of true felicity, when he prayed to have neither poverty nor riches.

In 1651 Crusoe runs away from his parents and signs aboard a ship. His first voyage whets his tastes for greater adventures off Europe, Africa, South America, and the Caribbean.

Shipwrecked on a deserted island off Trinidad in the Caribbean on September 30, 1659, Crusoe collects supplies, stored goods, tools, and utensils to guarantee a minimal level of civilized living. Using a homemade raft, he ferries ashore bread, rice, cheese, dried goat meat, corn, and wine. He rescues a carpenter's chest, guns and ammunition, and two swords. Six subsequent trips to the vessel produce hatchets, a grindstone, nails, crowbars, bedding, and clothing. On the thirteenth day of his misadventure, he watches a storm wash away the remains of the wreckage.

A naturally talented survivalist, Crusoe cooks meals, plants a garden, builds a crude fortress and lookout station, and improvises a shelter, boat, and goat pens. In Chapter 7 he prioritizes his needs in four categories:

> . . . first, health and fresh water I just now mentioned; secondly, shelter from the heat of the sun; thirdly, security from ravenous creatures, whether man or beast; fourthly, a view to the sea, that if God sent any ship in sight, I might not lose any advantage for my deliverance.

Occasional bouts of melancholy yield to rationality and self-control. Crusoe determines that he is the only crewman to survive and that "all evils are to be considered with the good that is in them, and with what worse attends them." Into late fall, his journal carries him from despair to trust in God and self-reliance. By summer, he alters his outlook to joy in being alive.

The Wonderful
LIFE
And most Surprizing
ADVENTURES
OF
Robinson Crusoe,
OF YORK, *Mariner.*

CONTAINING

A Full and Particular Account how he lived
Eight and Twenty Years in an Uninhabited
Island, on the Coast of *America*; how his
Ship was lost in a Storm, and all his Compa-
nions were drowned; and how he only was
cast upon the Shore by the Wreck.

WITH

A True Relation how he was at last miracu-
lously preserved by Pirates.

Faithfully epitomized from the *Three Volumes,*
and adorned with *Cuts* suited to the most Remarkable Stories.

LONDON:
Printed for J. FULLER, at No. 6, *Ave-Maria
Lane.*

Frontispiece of *Robinson Crusoe* by Daniel Defoe

During his field labors, Crusoe plants and tends corn. In his journal, he notes that agriculture "began to affect me with seriousness, as long as I thought it had something miraculous in it." He turns to the Bible in search of deliverance. He concludes

> . . . how much more happy this life I now led was, with all its miserable circumstances, than the wicked, cursed, abominable life I led all the past part of my days; and now I changed both my sorrows and my joys; my very desires altered my affections . . . and my delights were perfectly new, from what they were at my coming, or indeed for the two years past.

Like a resurrected being, Crusoe rejoices in his blessings, which assure him survival in the wild through the intervention of Divine Providence. By the third year, Crusoe values utility in the things he can use; he spurns money, pomp, self-indulgence in food and drink, fashion, and the ostentatious frippery he left behind in England.

In Chapter 17, filled with solitude, trial and error, and reflection by the eleventh year, Crusoe is adept at navigating a canoe, raising grain for bread, and training a parrot to speak. He comes to think of his shelter, vineyard, and pasture as "my country seat . . . a tolerable plantation." His idyll alters after 24 years with the visit of cannibals to his shores and his rescue of Man Friday, his faithful servant and friend. With the recovery of a Spanish sailor and Friday's father, Crusoe revamps his thinking:

> First of all, the whole country was my own mere property, so that I had an undoubted right of dominion. Secondly, my people were perfectly subjected. I was absolute lord and lawgiver; they all owed their lives to me, and were ready to lay down their lives, if there had been occasion of it, for me.

Crusoe gains his freedom on December 19, 1686, when he quells a mutiny aboard a visiting freighter and sails with Friday to England. He finds little of his family left, but his investments in a Brazilian colony are still viable. In his sixties, Crusoe continues to manage his business and look forward to adventures.

Crusoe reflects a variation of the Renaissance utopia. Although Defoe may have intended the work to be read as allegory, it leans heavily toward the psychological novel in its frank examination of desolation and spiritual need. Because of his quarter-century of solitude and subsistence, the hero concludes that true contentment can be found through submission to God and the daily application of skills, common sense, ingenuity, optimism, and enterprise. This survivalist tale contrasts the workfree, carefree utopias that fail to take into consideration the needs to feel useful and to build self-esteem through achievement. Consequently, as a forerunner of Samuel Johnson's "Rasselas, Prince of Abissinia" (1759), Voltaire's *Candide* (1759), and William Morris's *News from Nowhere* (1890), Defoe's romantic idyll comes closer to realism than most utopian works, which seek to negate toil or responsibility by replacing them with indolence and hedonism. Unlike the indolent Tommo in Herman Melville's *Typee* (1846), Crusoe is no runaway to a Polynesian paradise. His vigor and resolution epitomize the Protestant work ethic, a mandate to be taken seriously and to be fulfilled through hard work. (Baugh 1948; Bloom 1987b; Defoe 1963; Lovett and Hughes 1932; Richetti 1987; Whitten 1974)

See also Candide; Defoe, Daniel; didacticism; humanitarianism; Johnson, Dr. Samuel; Marx, Karl; materialism; Melville, Herman; Morris, William; naturalism; *News from Nowhere;* "Rasselas, Prince of Abissinia"; *Typee;* Voltaire, François.

ROSSUM, OLD DR.

Old Dr. Rossum is a fictional physiologist, atheist, utopist, entrepreneur, and the founder of Rossum's Universal Robots, a factory on an unidentified island. His work, following his death, is the subject of a dystopian play, *R. U. R.* (1920), by Karel Capek. Before the opening of Act I, Rossum had come to the island to study sea animals. Begun in 1920 and ended in 1932, his experiments applied simulated protoplasm—the biological key to life—to the invention of mechanical humanoids, or artificial humans. One employee, Harry Domin, exults at the ego boost of so momentous a chemical reaction and cites Rossum's anecdotal remark from his notes:

> Nature has found only one method of organizing living matter. There is, however, another method, more simple, flexible and rapid, which has not yet occurred to nature at all. This second process by which life can be developed was discovered by me to-day.

Domin pictures Rossum as a "fearful materialist" who sought to supplant God and create his own beings. Actually, the purpose of Rossum's creations was the avoidance of drudgery for humankind. The factory's shareholders had a less lofty dream: reaping dividends. Rossum died in his laboratory and was succeeded by his son, young Dr. Rossum, who used engineering skills to streamline the factory's productivity. (Capek and Capek 1961; Dickinson 1943; Harkins 1962; Manguel and Guadalupi 1987; Massaryk 1938)

See also allegory; Alquist, Mr.; Capek, Karel; futurism; Rossum, Young Dr.; Rossum's Island; *R. U. R.;* speculative fiction; technology; women in utopia.

 # ROSSUM, YOUNG DR.

Young Dr. Rossum is a fictional engineer, student of anatomy, and simplifier of the robots built in his father's factory in the dystopian play *R. U. R.* (1920) by Karel Capek. An atheist, he lacks his father's reverent outlook and does not hesitate to give himself godlike airs. According to Domin, the fidgety young doctor claimed it "absurd to spend ten years making a man." He shut his father away in a lab and "let him fritter the time away with his monstrosities, while he himself started on the business from an engineer's point of view." Old Rossum cursed his son and his methods, which produced "two physiological horrors." A single reference to the old man's death suggests that young Rossum may have shoved his father into an early grave.

What old Dr. Rossum lacked in sangfroid, pragmatism, and entrepreneurial spirit, young Dr. Rossum possesses in excess. By cutting costs, overhauling human anatomy, and omitting unnecessary details, e.g., happiness and an enjoyment of music, young Dr. Rossum creates the first efficient robot, a scaled-down improvement over the more cumbersome mechanical humanoids designed by his father. By imitating old Dr. Rossum and playing God, young Dr. Rossum manufactures a soulless, intelligent, working prototype of superior robots 12 feet tall and capable of completing the tasks that shackle humankind to mind-numbing drudgery. (Capek and Capek 1961; Dickinson 1943; Harkins 1962; Manguel and Guadalupi 1987; Massaryk 1938)

See also allegory; Alquist, Mr.; Capek, Karel; futurism; Rossum, Old Dr.; Rossum's Island; *R. U. R.;* speculative fiction; technology; women in utopia.

 # ROSSUM'S ISLAND

Rossum's Island is the fictional setting of Karel Capek's dystopian play *R. U. R.* (1920), a mechanistic nightmare emerging from the technological wizardry of old Dr. Rossum and his hard-nosed son, young Dr. Rossum. On an island possibly located off the east coast of North America, the former Rossum, an inventor and marine biologist, synthesized protoplasm, the fertile tissue that gives life to cells. Young Rossum, his money-mad heir, sets up a factory to produce Rossum's Universal Robots, a race of servile 12-foot humanoids.

Capek's dark motif leaves no doubt of his fears for the world when technology moves faster than human ethics can control it. The isolated robot factory symbolizes the sugarcoating that hides an ominous, ill-advised, and unsuccessful venture. Decorated with cushioned sofa, leather chairs, and oriental rugs, the office area looks out on smokestacks and the manufacturing floor as though young Dr. Rossum had intended to separate the idealistic intent of robotics from the gritty air and pulsating rhythm of the stamping room. Adjacent to work areas are Rossum's living quarters, offices, and music room. The harbor beyond contains the inventor's link with the world, his three-ship fleet—the *Amelia, Ultimus,* and *Pennsylvania,* an evocative blend of words derived from love, finality, and an American state established by a believer in religious freedom. (Capek and Capek 1961; Dickinson 1943; Harkins 1962; Manguel and Guadalupi 1987; Massaryk 1938)

See also allegory; Alquist, Mr.; Capek, Karel; futurism; Rossum, Old Dr.; Rossum, Young Dr.; *R. U. R.;* speculative fiction; technology; women in utopia.

R. U. R.

Karel Capek's stark, biting satire on a mechanized dystopia where robots supplant human laborers and humans cease to reproduce is a modernistic de-creation myth, a twist on the familiar story of Adam and Eve in Genesis. Written in 1920, the play debuted the following year and received instant fame. Capek's imaginative island factory spawned a new term for humanoid—robot, the last word in his abbreviated title for Rossum's Universal Robots. A popular play in the mid-1900s, Capek's work has enjoyed frequent stage production and inclusion in high school and college anthologies.

Echoing the "isolated island subgenre" of utopian literature, e.g., Thomas More's *Utopia* (1516), Daniel Defoe's *Robinson Crusoe* (1719), Jonathan Swift's *Gulliver's Travels* (1727), and William Golding's *Lord of the Flies* (1954), the setting of *R. U. R.* is an unspecified island where mechanical beings cross over from nonhuman function into the human realm of thinking, feeling, and rebelling against their maker. The plot uses the convention of the distant, inaccessible, or uncharted microcosm, similar to Gulliver's Lilliput or Laputa or Francis Bacon's New Atlantis. At Rossum Universal Robots the founder, a physiologist, studied protoplasm, the material of life, and in 1932 synthesized it for use in humanoids. His product—mechanical drones—passes to his heir, young Dr. Rossum, a market-minded engineer who cranks out models for the purpose of alleviating human drudgery. As the play opens, a visitor named Helena Glory follows general manager Harry Domin through the plant and marvels at the lifelike qualities of Marius and Sulla, a pair of robots.

Capek uses this visit to draw the factory from obscurity to world scrutiny by a suspicious humanist. An agent of the Humanity League, Helena attempts to improve the robots' living conditions, which condemn them to a dreary, routine life devoid of beauty, relaxation, or camaraderie. She learns that the factory has encountered disturbing problems: Robots sometimes jump their traces and behave in unpredictable ways. These symptoms of rebellion lead to dismantlement of the offending robot in the stamping mill and recycling of usable parts into more amenable models. In her interviews with several robots, Helena hears their matter-of-fact descriptions of a colorless, hopeless situation and discerns that they lack the ambition or sensitivity to think beyond the workplace.

With no thought to the consequences, Domin humors Helena by allowing her to spark feeling in the robots, who number in the hundreds of thousands. Because he does not agree with her attempts to humanize or alleviate the tedium of the humanoids, he explains to her the role of well-designed servant machines, which the factory ships to buyers throughout the world to replace the weak human laborer. Although Domin admits that some models behave peculiarly by jerking spasmodically and grinding their teeth, he denies their rights to freedom. His staff is working on pain receptors as a means of monitoring these unforeseeable seizures. Helena concludes that robots are doing the unthinkable—evolving souls.

As often happens when humanists tackle pragmatic problems, Helena's idealism runs afoul of the profit motive, which is young Dr. Rossum's guiding principle. The management of Rossum's Universal Robots brags to Helena that manufactured items and farm produce are now cheaper because robots do most of the work. To the executives, progress in robotics equates to leisure for humanity; to Helena, widespread robots mean unemployment for human workers. One humanistic staff member—Mr. Alquist, who heads the works

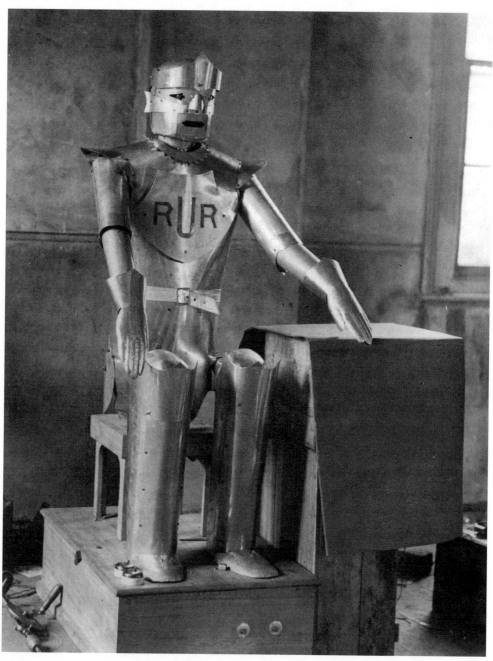

Karel Capek's 1920 play, *R. U. R.*, featured Rossum's Universal Robots, which inspired an English engineer to construct this robot to open the 1928 Model Engineers Exhibition in London.

department—sides with Helena. To Alquist, work and achievement are necessary for a satisfying life. However, because his lone voice carries only one vote, he makes no impact on the smug, profit-motivated managers. In a surprise announcement near the end of Act I, Domin proposes to Helena. Equally surprising is her acceptance.

As Act II opens a decade later, the executive staff tries to conceal from Helena the increase in customer complaints about disgruntled, erratic robots in settings all over the globe. These rebels face squadrons of robot soldiers, who carry out full-scale war against the mechanical militia. When Helena discovers this portentous state of affairs, she pleads in vain with Harry and the other managers to shut down the factory.

Helena's role as resident humanist has made little impact on the staff, which is composed of relentless capitalists. Still buoyant with the success of their product, all the managers except Alquist rely on a gunboat in the harbor to subdue fomenters of trouble in the warehouse. Alquist, the only staff member who retains faith in a higher being, prays that God will return humankind to supremacy over robots. His greatest fear is that human beings will cease bearing children, a situation suggested by disturbing news: a seven-day period with no reported births anywhere in the world.

Ironically, as human procreation declines, the robots take on human body functions. The plant physiologist, Dr. Gall, is the first to suspect that the brighter models are showing signs of nerve reaction and heart palpitations. He teeters on the brink of blaming technological godlessness for the world's untenable position after 30 years of unfair competition from robots:

> That's the awful part of it. You might almost think that nature was offended at the manufacture of the Robots. All the universities are sending in long petitions to restrict their production. Otherwise, they say, mankind will become extinct through lack of fertility.

The robots' development of extreme emotions supports his conclusion that the situation is growing critical, but complacent stockholders prefer counting their riches to solving long-range problems. Around the world, power-mongers are too dependent on a robotic military to request an end to production. Sensing doom, Gall alerts Helena to the danger of all-out war and urges her to save herself.

As though proving that Alexander Pope was correct in surmising that "a little learning is a dangerous thing," Capek indicates how far removed the staff is from the original laboratory work of old Dr. Rossum. The engineers have little insight into the situation except for their knowledge of how the robots are manufactured. The cocky Dr. Hallemeier, head of the Institute for Psychological Training of Robots, patronizes Helena as though soothing a fearful child:

> If the time-table holds good, human laws hold good; Divine laws hold good; the laws of the universe hold good; everything holds good that ought to hold good. The time-table is more significant than the gospel; more than Homer, more than the whole of Kant. The time-table is the most perfect product of the human mind. Madame Domin, I'll fill up my glass.

To free the world of being overrun, the staff plans to reveal the secret to each nation. Thus, like the building of the Tower of Babel in Genesis, the creation of different national models will impede communication and rebellion, and will halt the formation of a global unionization of robots. Domin underscores the naïveté of the plan by announcing plans to increase the manufacture of robots after the current difficulties are settled.

Capek freights his dramatic conclusion with fearful omens of catastrophe to the human race. The falling action thrusts the factory hierarchy into the first stage of disaster. When the mail boat reaches the island, it bears leaflets warning that the world union of robots should immediately kill every human on Earth. The robots apply capitalistic thinking to their revolt and justify their decision to rid the planet of the less profitable human race, whom they claim are mere parasites feeding off the stronger, more intelligent, more efficient race of humanoids. In the robot view, the world belongs to mechanical forces, not to human weaklings.

Capek does not belabor the clash of human manager against nuts-and-bolts robot. In Act III, the predicted battle between product and producer breaks out in the factory; the staff loses. Harry remains proud of his idealistic creation, which he hoped would equalize all humanity by ending poverty and halting class warfare between workers and management. He cannot account for the change in robots, who seem almost human in their responses and ambitions. Helena admits that she convinced Dr. Gall to equip robots with souls as a means of promoting understanding. The plan foundered after the robots developed human weaknesses.

A timely power play proves the uselessness of engineers. The staff weighs their options and concludes that they must persuade the robots to spare their makers, who possess the secret of robotics. Harry wipes sweat from his forehead as he admits to doubts:

> Perhaps we've been killed these hundred years and are only ghosts. It's as if I had been through all this before; as if I'd already had a mortal wound here in the throat.

He remains adamantly opposed to mediating with hostile robots; the others favor mediation, and cast dissenting votes. Arbitration breaks down after the staff learns that Helena has burned old Dr. Rossum's formula in an effort to entice parents around the world to bring forth more human children. At the end of Act III, the robots, led by Radius, triumph by slaying all humans except Alquist. Elated by momentary glory, Radius shouts, "The power of man has fallen! A new world has arisen: the Rule of the Robots! March!"

In the epilogue, Alquist, formerly a manager, resembles the humanoids because he now performs manual labor under their direction. Without human models, he is unable to re-create the formula or rescue the robots, who are dying out. At some point, he arrives at a solution to the world's dilemma: He dismantles Radius, a Christ figure who volunteers for dissection. The work unnerves Alquist, who prays: "O Lord, let not mankind perish from the earth." Meanwhile, Primus and Helena, a male and female pair of robots, fall in love.

As Alquist searches for the source of their romantic feelings, he discovers that the two humanoids are so committed that they refuse to part and would die for each other. Alquist deduces that the pair's intense emotion is the secret of life. From Primus and Helena—a symbolic "first man" and a manufactured duplicate of Helena Glory Domin—a new race will replenish the earth. Alquist blesses their union by his final instructions: "Go, Adam, go, Eve. The world is yours."

Although the play ends on a positive note, Capek's warning unsettles a world that grows increasingly dependent on sophisticated technology, which, as Helena deduces, takes jobs from human laborers. As speculative fiction, much like Aldous Huxley's *Brave New World* (1932), Ayn Rand's *Anthem* (1937), George Orwell's *1984* (1949), Margaret Atwood's *The Handmaid's Tale* (1985), and P. D. James's *The Children of Men* (1993), Capek predicts doom if human-kind continues exceeding its limitations by dabbling in the creation of an underrace. Paradoxically, he concludes his drama by refuting his premise that the soul cannot be duplicated by clever engineering. (Capek and Capek 1961; Dickinson 1943; Harkins 1962; Manguel and Guadalupi 1987; Massaryk 1938)

See also Adam; allegory; *Anthem; Brave New World;* Capek, Karel; Eve; futurism; Gulliver, Lemuel; *The Handmaid's Tale; 1984; Robinson Crusoe;* Rossum, Old Dr.; Rossum, Young Dr.; Rossum's Island; speculative fiction; technology; utopia; women in utopia.

 SANCHO PANZA

This fictional Spanish peasant farmer serves as literary foil to Cervantes's Don Quixote, hero of *El Ingenioso Hidalgo Don Quixote de la Mancha* (1615), one of Western literature's most entrancing moralist adventures. An earthy realist, Sancho demonstrates goodness toward his family and his beloved mount, Dapple. He is crude and unlettered, easily fooled, and at times candidly deceptive and stupid. At the beginning of Don Quixote's second foray, Sancho leaves specific instructions about the betrothal of his daughter Mari-Sancha and bids farewell to his wife Teresa with a light heart:

> We're out to roam the world and play give and take with giants, dragons, and other monsters. We'll be hearing hissings and roarings and bellowings and howlings. But all that would be lavender if we didn't have to count upon meeting [human villainy].

Sancho agrees to serve as squire in exchange for riches, perhaps even an island to govern. Often Sancho suffers drubbings, insults, threats, and danger, but he remains loyal to Don Quixote even though he perceives the old man as befuddled and ludicrous.

In Part II, Chapters 42–53, through the generosity of a duke and duchess, Sancho attains his goal on July 20, 1614, by becoming governor of the landlocked island of Baratario. To the duke's chagrin, Sancho governs the area surprisingly well. By applying the experience and horse sense common to his class, he settles legal matters and parries a health-conscious doctor who tries to limit his diet. A trumped-up invasion and a letter full of home news from Teresa convince him that he is not meant to be governor or to roam too far from his family. He accompanies Don Quixote homeward and hugs his wife and daughter.

In Part III, Chapter 16, as his master lies on his deathbed in La Mancha dictating the disposition of his cash to Sancho, the former squire weeps:

> Don't die on me; but take my advice and live on for many a year; for the greatest madness that a man can be guilty of in this life is to die without good reason, without anyone's killing him, slain only by the hands of melancholy.

In vain, Sancho attempts to revive the idealistic spirit that guided and invigorated the old man throughout their bold adventures. Sancho tempts him with his ideal woman, noting "who knows but we may find Lady Dulcinea behind a hedge and disenchanted and as fresh as a daisy." Ennobling himself with the Christian spirit of self-sacrifice, Sancho takes the blame for Don Quixote's defeat. (Bloom 1986a; Byron 1988; Cervantes 1957; Duran 1974; Gilman 1989; Nabokov 1984; Predmore 1990; Riley 1986; Russell 1985)

See also Cervantes Saavedra, Miguel de; Don Quixote; Dulcinea del Toboso; escapism; fantasy; idealism; women in utopia.

SATAN

A monstrously grand, glib, manipulative, and devilishly appealing characterization of subversion, Satan is the chief adversary of God in John Milton's *Paradise Lost* (1667) and its sequel, *Paradise Regained* (1671). Formerly known as Lucifer, the "star of stars," Satan is the bright angel who once served as God's "light-bringer." Although he is a lordly hero in the Underworld, he chafes at his loss of supremacy in heaven and his humbling fall into hell, his unholy monarchy. Unbeaten, he capitulates only to pride, which leads him to create Pandemonium, a conference hall for his demonic staff. Along with Beelzebub and his array of evildoers, Satan plots further defiance, disputation, and chicanery against God. The fervid spirit and clever sophistry that fells Eve, then Adam, temporarily deters God's plan.

Reflecting Milton's classic models—Homer's *Iliad* and *Odyssey* (eighth century B.C.) and Virgil's *Aeneid* (19 B.C.)—Satan exhibits in *Paradise Lost* the glittering heroic traits of Achilles, Odysseus, and Aeneas: charm, intelligence, determination, and spunk. In Book 1, he commands attention as the perpetrator who "first seduced [Adam and Eve] to that foul revolt." Lying in coils upon the burning lake of the murky, sulfurous netherworld, Satan appears doomed to powerlessness. His indomitable spirit rejects impotence, throws off weakness, and declares, "to do aught good never will be our task." Already serpentine in form, he rises above the water level "with head uplift above the wave, and eyes that sparkling blazed." His cohorts' toil and magic call forth the archetypal home of evil, Pandemonium, Milton's made-up name for the residence of all demons.

A magisterial roll call of evil agents depicts a paradox: the pagan elements of Satan's infernal milieu, a dark kingdom filled with myriad demonic forces and forever aflame, but giving off no light. Satan's extremes of flexibility, energy, and mobility allow him a range of disguises and supernatural powers. A master deceiver, he suborns Eve and, through her, Adam. Milton provides the perfect punishment for Satan. At the end of *Paradise Lost*, Satan is confined to the body of the serpent, a lowly reptile that slithers through eternity in perpetual enmity with the human creatures he deceived.

The literary foil who counters Satan is Christ, the son of God and redeemer of humankind from its penchant for wrongdoing. The purpose of Satan's magnificence as a dramatic hero is his role in bringing about the Fortunate Fall, the loss of Eden in exchange for Christ's condemnation of Adam and Eve. Doomed to a trying existence of childbirth, toil, pain, and despair relieved in its dismalness only by the promise of salvation through God's grace, the first couple suffer for their vulnerability to the archdeceiver.

Satan conceals his envy of Eden's garden-keepers; flaunting his success, he sinks into his infernal home to plot mischief in the desert, where Christ confronts temptations of power, might, and erudition. As recorded in Book 4 of *Paradise Regained,* Satan prepares himself to understand his adversary by studying him and learning

> In what degree or meaning thou art call'd
> The Son of God, which bears no single sense;
> The Son of God I also am, or was.
> And if I was, I am; relation stands;
> All men are sons of God, yet thee I thought
> In some respect far higher so declar'd.

Satan attempts to humble Christ by flying him to Jerusalem and setting him on "the highest Pinnacle" as an object of ridicule. Satan is thwarted a second time because he is unable to call up enough wisdom from his lieutenant, enough oily charm, enough appeal to upset Christ's mission on Earth. At the end of the fourth book, the supreme tempter plummets to his doom as an angelic choir rejoices at his demise. Milton chortles that the master tempter resides in hell, and that Paradise blooms anew from the promise of a savior, the "queller of Satan." (Enroth 1970; Harrison et al. 1967; Martz 1967; Milton 1957a; Parker 1958)

See also Adam; Eden; Eve; Genesis; heaven; Milton, John; Pandemonium; *Paradise Lost; Paradise Regained;* religion; Revelation; theocracy; women in utopia.

SATIRE

Satire is a sharply pointed, and at times, embarrassingly or cruelly effective rhetorical device or genre in such utopian works as Aristophanes's *The Birds* (414 B.C.), Jonathan Swift's "A Modest Proposal" (1720) and *Gulliver's Travels* (1727), Voltaire's *Candide* (1759), and Samuel Butler's *Erewhon* (1872), as well as in isolated scenes of other literature, e.g., Margaret Atwood's *The Handmaid's Tale* (1985). As a rule, satire is intended to ridicule or belittle a human weakness, idiosyncrasy, folly, or crime. Satire enables the author to enlighten readers about the least admirable character qualities by applying incongruity, humor, and wit to laughable or deplorable situations such as governmental graft or aristocratic vanity. Dating to ancient Greece and Rome, particularly the witty comedies of Aristophanes and the barbed verse of Juvenal and Horace, the tradition of satire as a means of uplifting mortals from vice carries over from fable and fabliau to the utopian novel, which attempts to create the perfect world, and the dystopian novel, which pinpoints the flaws in philosophies and governments that strive in vain for perfection.

The style of the satire tends toward overt, sophisticated, mock-serious, or formalized ridicule stated by a first-person narrator. This method of isolating human foibles or taunting pretense, deception, conceit, or hypocrisy can vary from the gentle jest, pun, or mot juste of the needler to the stinging jabs and lacerations of the most indignant outrage in panegyric or diatribe, as is the case with the work of Jonathan Swift, England's most renowned satirist and shaper of irony. Concealed in the folds of humor—however genteel, good-humored, sarcastic, or blatant—satire enables the writer to afflict the pompous or infamous, then take refuge in the laughter of the audience, thus shielding the originator from backlash.

Satire is not limited to essay or editorial, but accommodates itself to sudden enlightening revelations of amusement, dismay, or disgust in chant, song, verse, epic, drama, comic strip, monologue, editorial, and short and long fiction. It may lurk within parody, understatement, mockery, burlesque, irony, caricature, or parody, as demonstrated by Bernard de Mandeville's *Fable of the Bees* (1705), or more directly in invective, the weapon of political cartoonists. A key rhetorical weapon for the utopian and dystopian novelist, the satire of Miguel de Cervantes, François Rabelais, Mark Twain, Aldous Huxley, George Orwell, and Margaret Atwood serves as a necessary vehicle for effective criticism of society's failings, as demonstrated in *Gargantua and Pantagruel* (1562), *Don Quixote* (1615), *A Connecticut Yankee in King Arthur's Court* (1886), *Brave New World* (1932), *Animal Farm* (1945), *1984* (1949), and *The Handmaid's Tale* (1985). (Aristophanes 1993; Atwood 1972; Butler 1968; Cervantes 1957; Drabble 1985; Holman 1981; Huxley 1932; Mandeville 1989; Orwell 1946; Orwell 1949; Pollard 1970; Rabelais 1955; Snodgrass 1987; Swift 1958; Twain 1963; Voltaire 1961)

See also *Animal Farm*; Aristophanes; Atwood, Margaret; *The Birds*; *Brave New World*; Butler, Samuel; *Candide*; *A Connecticut Yankee in King Arthur's Court*; dystopia; *Erewhon*; *The Fable of the Bees*; *Gargantua and Pantagruel*; *Gulliver's Travels*; *The Handmaid's Tale*; Huxley, Aldous; Mandeville, Bernard de; *1984*; Orwell, George; Rabelais, François; Swift, Jonathan; utopia; Voltaire, François.

 # SATURNALIA

During this idyllic Roman holiday, celebrated December 17–23 at the end of the Roman calendar, slaves and masters traded places and acted out their utopian ideal or a return to the golden age. As described in Sir James Frazer's *The Golden Bough* (1922), the arrival of Saturnalia, originally an agricultural festival, brought a momentary enfranchisement to Rome's slaves. In honor of Saturn, the fertility god who blessed Italy's fields with grain and established human communities, owners allowed drinking and arguing, and even shared cup and plate with their slaves, whom they served in a turnabout of the slave/master relationship.

Saturnalia graced Rome and the provinces with a benevolent, forgive-and-forget spirit. Harsh punishments such as lashings, mutilation, imprisonment, or death were suspended as slaves turned the social order topsy-turvy. Like the medieval Lord of Misrule, a slave might supplant a legislator or magistrate and make orders for his betters to carry out, such as the singing of a bawdy tune or the presentation of a comely kitchen slave. In later times, Saturnalia gave place to Christmas and Lenten Carnival, both instances of lavish merry-making and freedom from care. A similar custom, patterned after the Roman Saturnalia, arose in the American South at Christmas, allowing slaves an opportunity to drop their servile personae and act as equals to their masters. (Asimov 1969; Frazer 1947; Guerber 1921; Morford and Lenardon 1977; Pennick 1992)

See also golden age; slavery.

SCIENCE FICTION

This branch of fantasy literature applies scientific research, mathematical formulas, inventions, social tinkering, projections, and theory to plot development, character, and setting. By extrapolating logical advancements based on current technology, such as the programming of humanoid drones and the application of the fourth dimension to interplanetary travel, science-fiction writers explore the possibilities of time, space, and nature, both animal and human. A nineteenth-century example is the curious cycle invented by the Time Traveller in H. G. Wells's *The Time Machine* (1895), which carries the inventor so far into the future that he witnesses the sterile shores and strange-hued horizon of a forbiddingly lifeless sea. A significant genre for utopian and dystopian literature, the sci-fi canon includes notable works by major experts in the field: Margaret Atwood, Karel Capek, Frederik Pohl, Aldous Huxley, P. D. James, Kurt Vonnegut, Jr., Yevgeny Zamyatin, Jules Verne, Marge Piercy, Isaac Asimov, Ursula LeGuin, Arthur C. Clarke, Frank Herbert, Ayn Rand, Ray Bradbury, David Karp, and George Orwell.

The premise of most fantasy, prophecy, or speculative fiction involves the tampering with or correction of human foibles, limitations, and character flaws, especially the unequal distribution of wealth, out-of-control imagination, or the threat of doom through world war, depletion of Earth's resources, famine, or rampant moral corruption, pollution, or disease. By creating perfect worlds, often far in the future, sci-fi utopists evaluate the raw material of the here and now, usually ridiculing, satirizing, or condemning some aspect of reality. Through fantasy or philosophic projection, the writer escapes the confines of realism and probes possibilities, e.g., the idealized pantisocracy in Jean Jacques Rousseau's *Discours sur l'inegalité des conditions* (1754), where each citizen bears the same amount of prestige and power as any other citizen, or the use of a lodestone to power the floating island of Laputa in Jonathan Swift's *Gulliver's Travels* (1727). In the best of futuristic or speculative fiction, authors have successfully predicted breakthroughs in technology that have become accepted practice; for instance,

- deep-dive ocean craft in the undersea adventures of Jules Verne's Captain Nemo in *Twenty Thousand Leagues under the Sea* (1870)

- the robot factory in Karel Capek's *R. U. R.* (1920)

- rocketry in Yevgeny Zamyatin's *We* (1921)

- the use of mind-altering drugs in Anthony Burgess's *A Clockwork Orange* (1962) and Marge Piercy's *Woman at the Edge of Time* (1976)

- manipulative bioethics governing in vitro fertilizations and treatment of a developing fetus in Aldous Huxley's *Brave New World* (1932)

- mind control through sophisticated electronic spying, torture, and intimidation in George Orwell's *1984* (1949)

- virtual reality, which uses electronic sounds and visuals to rival real life in Ray Bradbury's *Fahrenheit 451* (1953)

- robotics as a replacement of labor in manufacturing and computerized communications, two strong features of Arthur C. Clarke's *Childhood's End* (1953)

- identification control based on scanners in Margaret Atwood's *The Handmaid's Tale* (1985)

Implicit in sci-fi utopia lies a promise of success and the opportunity for miscalculation, unforeseen intervention, or evolving tyranny. A single serious flaw, i.e., the misapplication of technology to labor-saving devices, dominates Karel Capek's *R. U. R.*; fascist enforcers of a fundamentalist theocracy control television news in Margaret Atwood's *The Handmaid's Tale*; and a house run by timed robotic devices overlooks the absence of a human resident in Ray Bradbury's "There Will Come Soft Rains" (1950). Illustrating why monumental change does not always benefit—as is the case with Michael Crichton's *Jurassic Park* (1990), Kurt Vonnegut's *Cat's Cradle* (1963), and Ayn Rand's *Anthem* (1937)—the heavy-handed engineering of utopian states sometimes results in chicanery, oppression, the devaluation of humanity, and the jeopardization of the human race and all of nature through powers that tempt the user to foolhardy application. Terrifying are the implications of Crichton's fictional laboratories, which are capable of stocking zoos with prehistoric beasts; Vonnegut's satiric study of a substance that solidifies liquids; or Rand's totalitarian world, so rigidly controlled that individuality suffers and human will atrophies. By mating the utopian genre with horror novels, this wing of utopianism is therefore more likely to end in dystopic nightmare than blissful paradise. (Amis 1960; Esbach 1964; Hollister 1982; LeGuin 1992; McKnight 1992; Warren 1992)

See also Anthem; Childhood's End; Fahrenheit 451; The Handmaid's Tale; 1984; R. U. R.; technology; "There Will Come Soft Rains"; The Time Machine; Woman at the Edge of Time; women in utopia.

 # SERENA JOY

An envious, cheerless character in Margaret Atwood's dystopian *The Handmaid's Tale* (1985), she is the sterile, arthritic Wife of Commander Frederick, who couples monthly with a surrogate breeder in an attempt to produce a child for his family and for the depleted society of Gilead. Serena Joy—who is neither serene nor joyful—limps dispiritedly about her tulip bed, her diamond-clad hands grasping a cane. On the arrival of Offred, Serena blocks the front door in an ineffectual show of power over her womanly domain, a late-Victorian home filled with refined adornments but devoid of contentment or children.

Clad in wifely blue uniform, Serena (who is modeled on traditionalist Mirabel Morgan, fund-raiser and televangelist Tammy Bakker, and Phyllis Schlafly, leader of antifeminist conservatives) vaguely resembles the blue-eyed blond soprano originally named Pam, her earlier incarnation, who once sang on a televised religious program and lectured to women on the value of the traditional wifely role. The Handmaid observes up close:

> A little of her hair was showing, from under her veil. It was still blond. . . . Her eyebrows were plucked into thin arched lines, which gave her a permanent look of surprise, or outrage, or inquisitiveness, such as you might see on a startled child, but below them her eyelids were tired-looking. Not so her eyes, which were the flat hostile blue of a midsummer sky in bright sunlight, a blue that shuts you out.

As the Commander's Wife, Serena Joy lives the role she once advocated—a circumscribed boredom of needlework, knitting scarves for the troops at the front, arranging daffodils from her garden, and supervising Handmaids. Like a hovering, malignant materfamilias, she presides over the monthly tableau that begins with a worship service in the sitting room. As hostess to the Handmaid, two maids, and chauffeur, she smokes nervously and flips television channels while awaiting the tardy arrival of the Commander, the true head of the household.

Once the trio of Wife, husband, and Handmaid gather on the canopied bed for the prescribed mating, Serena lies rigid and miserable, eager for a child but glad to unseat Offred at the end of the ritual and dispatch her to the oblivion of her chaste, unadorned room. Because Offred shows no sign of conception, Serena engineers a late-night mating with Nick, the chauffeur. In exchange for jeopardizing Offred and Nick's lives for conspiracy and adultery, Serena produces a Polaroid photo of Offred's daughter as an inducement.

The plot motivation in *The Handmaid's Tale* echoes a theme that is as old as the Abraham/Sarah/Haggar triangle of the Old Testament—jealousy between wife and concubine of the same man. Just as the Handmaids' indoctrinator warned, the fable concludes with a contretemps between Offred the Handmaid and Serena Joy the Wife. Serena locates the sequined and feathered costume that Offred wore for the Commander to an evening tryst at Jezebel's night spot. Angered and envious of Offred, Serena registers disappointment and disillusion. As Offred is spirited away in a police van, Serena calls her a bitch. A purge of liberal forces in Gilead leads to the Commander's death, leaving Serena husbandless. (Atwood 1972; *Contemporary Authors* 1989; *Contemporary Literary Criticism* 1987; Davidson 1986; Dreifus 1992; Hammer 1990; Ingersoll 1991; McCombs 1988; *Major Twentieth-Century Writers* 1990; Van Spanckeren and Castro 1988)

See also Atwood, Margaret; city planning; The Commander; Gilead; *The Handmaid's Tale;* Lydia, Aunt; Offred; religion; theocracy; women in utopia.

SERMON ON THE MOUNT

These are the prophetic words of Jesus of Nazareth during the first century A.D., as reported by St. Matthew in the New Testament. In Chapter 5, following the example of John the Baptist in teaching and warning people of a coming upheaval, Jesus climbs a hill and addresses his disciples and followers. Poetically, Jesus speaks the Beatitudes, a series of promises to the dispirited, mournful, meek, hungry, merciful, pure, peaceable, and persecuted. He warns that no good will come of stockpiling treasures on Earth. Rather, in Chapter 6, verse 20, he exhorts his listeners to "lay up for yourselves treasures in heaven, where neither moth nor rust doth corrupt, and where thieves do not break through nor steal: for where your treasure is, there will your heart be also."

This exhortation to otherworldliness extends to all facets of life, which Jesus urges his followers to devalue. In the face of coming death and rebirth, he urges in verse 34: "Take therefore no thought for the morrow: for the morrow shall take thought for the things of itself." Chapter 7 makes greater promises of riches and joy. In verses 7–8 Jesus says, "Ask and it shall be given you: seek, and ye shall find; knock, and it shall be opened to you. For every one that asketh receiveth; and he that seeketh findeth; and to him that knocketh it shall be opened."

To express the nature of the promise, Jesus instructs his listeners through parables. The parable of the sower, found in Chapter 13, verses 3–9, implies that not all are worthy of this promised kingdom of the blessed. His metaphors compare heaven to a great tree that sprouts from a tiny mustard seed and to leavening, which affects jars of meal and makes bread rise. In later verses, he notes that the kingdom of heaven is a hidden treasure, a pearl of great price. Like the fisherman keeping the best of the haul in the net and casting the unwanted catch back into the sea, Jesus declares that, at the end of the world, the chosen people shall be gathered up by angels, and the wicked cast into a fiery furnace. (Alexander and Alexander 1973; Chase 1955; Holy Bible 1958; Mays 1988; Metzger and Coogan 1993)

See also Augustine, St.; baptism; Bunyan, John; *De Civitate Dei; Divina Commedia;* heaven; *Pilgrim's Progress;* Promised Land; prophecy; religion.

SHAKESPEARE, WILLIAM

Actor and playwright, Shakespeare's canon constitutes the height of the English Renaissance. His life fits the pattern of the zeitgeist—a coming to age of drama that ideally suited the poet with opportunities to fulfill his genius. Born April 23, 1564, in Stratford-upon-Avon, Shakespeare was the son of glover and magistrate John Shakespeare. He studied at a Latin grammar school, but a low

William Shakespeare portrayed in an engraving by Martin Droeshout

point in his family's fortunes left him unable to attend a university. At age 18 he married Anne Hathaway of Shottery, who was eight years his senior. Following the birth of their daughter Susanna and twins Judith and Hamnet in 1584, Shakespeare left his wife and children at his father's house and sought his fortune in London.

Amid a thriving theatrical world, Shakespeare joined the Lord Chamberlain's Men around 1587. His career was briefly circumvented by an outbreak of plague, which closed theaters from 1593–1595. During this hiatus, the playwright wrote poetry and produced his longest verses, *Venus and Adonis* and *The Rape of Lucrece*, which were skillful and appealing enough to inspire a public sneer from the envious dramatist Robert Greene. Undaunted by writers who boasted better lineage, extensive travel, and more ponderous university degrees, Shakespeare continued to make news. Under the patronage of the Earl of Southampton, he wrote a lengthy sonnet sequence rich in the evocative verse style that colored the 37 plays comprising the rest of his canon.

Under the aegis of Elizabeth I and her Scottish successor, James I, Shakespeare enjoyed moderate success. His tragedies, comedies, histories, and romances pleased audiences at London's major theaters and at Shakespeare's capital venture, the Globe playhouse, which he constructed across the Thames River—in part to avoid censorship by the dour Puritans. Retired to Stratford in his fifties, Shakespeare built a sizable residence and continued writing, although his ties with London were never again as close as they were during the height of his career. A few years after inscribing his will, he died on April 23, 1616, and was buried in the chancel of Stratford's Holy Trinity Church.

Shakespeare's works won the greatest of posthumous honors—publication that elevated them to the status of classics and made them available to more readers and collectors and more acting companies. Knowledgeable contemporaries valued the First Folio, which was published in 1623. His wide-ranging plots and settings reflect the Renaissance interest in matters and lifestyles far and wide and address human concerns, including love, treachery, family, loyalty, success, and failure. Three of his plays—*As You Like It* (1599), *The Tempest* (ca. 1611), and *A Midsummer Night's Dream* (ca. 1595)—demonstrate a philosophical interest in utopianism. *As You Like It* and *A Midsummer Night's Dream* take place in idyllic sylvan settings and conclude with the marriages of well-mated characters. A more complex romance, *The Tempest* depicts forgiveness and reconciliation on the desert isle of Bermuda, a place of interest to Elizabethans during an era that saw the defeat of the Spanish Armada and the expansion of British fortunes in the New World. Imbued with the "noble savage" theory, Shakespeare blends Edenic settings and nature's bounty into satisfying stagecraft. (Bentley 1961; Boorstin 1992; Boyce 1990; Chute 1949; Chute 1951; Muir and Schoenbaum 1971; Sandler 1986; Shakespeare 1958; Shakespeare 1959; White 1955)

See also Arden; *As You Like It*; Eden; *A Midsummer Night's Dream*; naturalism; *The Tempest*.

 # SHAMBALAH, OR SHAMBHALA

See Eden.

 # SHANGRI-LA

A serene, sheltered lamasery, Shangri-La is a Himalayan Eden 28,000 feet above sea level opposite the magnificent Mount Karakal. The milieu of Shangri-La reveals a humanistic tolerance of all philosophies and religions, which syncretize into an appealing, noncontroversial blend. The temperate nature, agricultural productivity, and verdance of the valley of Blue Moon typifies James Hilton's *Lost Horizon* (1933), a utopian dream and respite from cold, treacherous travel up the Tibetan slopes and the mechanized madness that, with buzz bombs and blitz, ended World War I and preceded World War II. Shangri-La—like nirvana, Neverland, fields of the blessed, happy hunting grounds, the land of milk and honey, Happy Valley, Eden, Eldorado, Xanadu, or Beulah Land—entices the outsider with modern plumbing, libraries, sensual delights, rest, contemplation, and the longevity to enjoy it.

Chiefly oriental in design and concept, Shangri-La displays milky blue roofs over a pleasant cloister surrounded by a crime-free settlement populated by peasants and governed by the "loose and elastic autocracy" of the benign Father Perrault from the lamasery's inception in 1734 until his death and replacement by Hugh Conway in 1928. The grounds are tastefully dotted with lotus pools, bronze statuary, and paper lanterns, and echoes classical piano and harpsichord music. In Conway's eyes, Shangri-La is ideal:

> The vast encircling *massif* made perfect contrast with the tiny lawns and weedless gardens, the painted tea-houses by the stream, and the frivolously toy-like houses. The inhabitants seemed to him a very successful blend of Chinese and Tibetan; they were cleaner and handsomer than the average of either race, and seemed to have suffered little from the inevitable inbreeding of such a small society.

To enhance the good will and contentment of Shangri-La, priests attain a heightened sensibility through purification of carnality, greed, violence, and other negative passions. They use the breathing exercises of yoga and the mind-focusing discipline of clairvoyant meditation along with the regular consumption of *tangatse,* a rejuvenating medicinal tea, to achieve a utopian community free of the dangers and strife that beset the world outside their lamasery.

Hugh Conway's search for the Tibetan paradise that he once deserted symbolizes his abandonment of idealism in favor of pragmatism, the philosophy that kept him alive during the horrors of World War I. Rutherford, the Englishman who tries to help Conway overcome amnesia, is fascinated by the area's mythic allure. At a considerable cost of time and money, Rutherford treks over a thousand miles of eastern terrain to locate the fabled lamasery. Like Don Quixote seeking his Dulcinea, Rutherford falls prey to the romance of the utopia that supplants Conway's former life and lures him into a seemingly endless search. (Hilton 1933; Kunitz 1942; Manguel and Guadalupi 1987; Perkins et al. 1991)

See also Buddhism; clairvoyance; Conway, Hugh; escapism; Hilton, James; *Lost Horizon;* Perrault, Father; religion; syncretism; Tao.

 # SHAW, GEORGE BERNARD

A long-lived, vigorous, and much acclaimed native of Dublin, George Bernard Shaw dominated the critical and theatrical scene at the end of the nineteenth

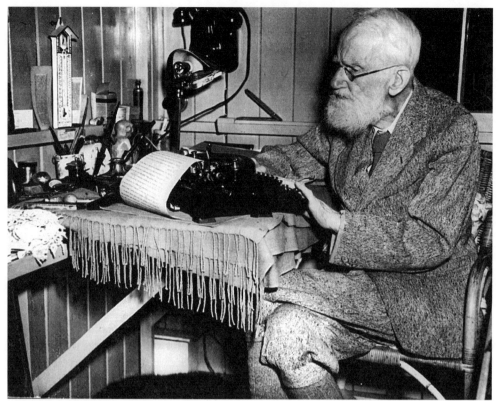

George Bernard Shaw, 1946

century and well into the twentieth. He has been called the greatest dramatist since Shakespeare. The author of *Back to Methuselah* (1921), a rigorous five-plays-in-one extension of the Garden of Eden myth, he appended one of his famous ponderous Shavian prefaces and used a ready arsenal of wit, logic, analysis, enlightenment, and repartee to entertain and enlighten audiences on the creative instinct. One line from Act I—"You see things; and say 'Why?' But I dream things that never were; and I say 'Why not?'"—is frequently cited by idealists who do not recognize the source as Satan, the glib-tongued traducer of Eve.

Born on July 26, 1856, the youngest of three children of grain merchant George Carr and Lucinda Elizabeth Gurly Shaw, a genteelly poor Protestant family, Shaw suffered the silences and disagreements common to unhappily mated parents. He did poorly in school, but learned music from his mother, a vocalist. At age 15, after his alcoholic father deserted the family, Shaw tried selling real estate, but gave up office work and Ireland. He resettled in London with his mother and sister Lucy, clerked for the telephone company, and began a journalistic career. As a commentator and essayist, he earned a reputation for strong opinions on war, women, education, propriety, persecution of minorities, abstinence from meat and alcohol, and the peculiarities of English spelling.

After establishing himself as an art, music, and drama critic, Shaw attempted to focus on novels, but—to the detriment of his work—involved himself in the socialist movement and the atheistic Fabian Society. As speaker, pamphleteer, and polemicist, he produced eminent essays on literature, economics, and politics. In 1898 he entered into a celibate marriage with Charlotte Payne-Townshend, an heiress whose money allowed him to settle in Hertfordshire and perfect drama as his most effective medium. Shaw's satiric *Arms and the Man* (1894) debunked the glories and pretensions of militarism. His best-received comedy, *Man and Superman* (1902), contains elements of one of Shaw's intriguing themes: élan vital, or the life force. Ten years later he composed *Androcles and the Lion*, a blend of comedy, dialectic, and fantasy mixed with beast fable, with major emphasis on the persecution of Christians during the Roman Empire.

Shaw wrote voluminously in the twentieth century, covering such varied issues as women's rights, Hitler, and fascism. In 1913 he produced his most famous play, *Pygmalion*, depicting male-female relations and the importance of speech to social acceptability. In 1925, two years after his successful *Saint Joan*, he won the Nobel Prize for literature. The first filming of *Pygmalion* earned him an Academy Award in 1938. On November 2, 1950, he died from hip injuries suffered in a fall. Four years later, *Pygmalion* was reworked as *My Fair Lady*, a musical stage romance that earned five Oscars and three Oscar nominations after its filming in 1964. (Brockett 1968; Gassner and Quinn 1969; Hill 1978; Hornstein et al. 1973; Johnson 1968; Magill 1958; Negley and Patrick 1952; Shaw 1988)

See also Adam; *Back to Methuselah;* Eden; Eve; fantasy; Genesis; karma; nirvana; prophecy; satire; *The Time Machine;* Wells, H. G.

SIDDHARTHA

Siddhartha is the focal character who evolves into the Buddha in Hermann Hesse's novel *Siddhartha* (1922). According to this fictional biography, which departs from the historical Gautama Buddha (563–493 B.C.), Siddhartha, the seeker, is separate from Gotama, a holy evangelist who impresses his hearers with his self-discipline and peace-loving nature. In middle age, Siddhartha abandons his sybaritic life. In place of gambling, lust for Kamala (the courtesan who is the mother of "little Siddhartha"), perfume, greed, and other self-indulgences, he seeks peace through asceticism, or avoidance of sensuality. Depressed to the point of suicide, he flees a strict Brahman father and anchors himself to a tree. Under its shade he hears the syllable *Om* resounding through his mind and sinks into a fulfilling, satisfying state of relaxation and love.

Directed by the ferryman Vasudeva, Siddhartha attunes himself to a nearby river. Its waters sweep by like human emotions—always in a state of flux, timeless and transcendent. Siddhartha concludes that the water continually flows, yet the river remains full; the stream is always the same, but perpetually new. As the stream is never used up, so does the human spirit continue to feel emotion, even after death. In midlife, Siddhartha tames youthful fervency and

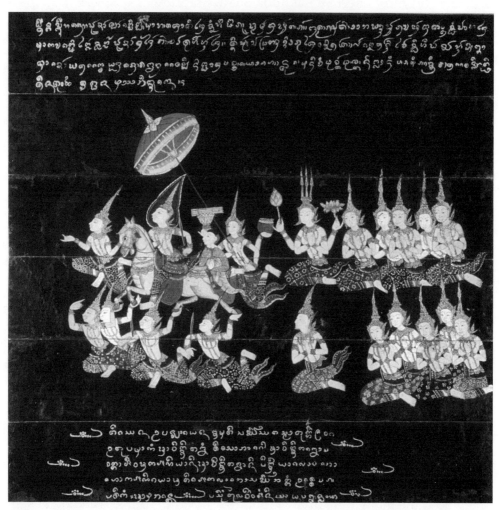

A Thai ritual text shows Buddhist gods carrying Siddhartha away in a late-nineteenth-century illustration. Hermann Hesse based his 1922 novel on the historical figure of Siddhartha.

listens to the river's song, a unified sound that echoes with the glad and anguished voices of thousands of people. As an old man, he sees a similar transformation possess the spirit of his friend Govinda, who achieves nirvana through his search for enlightenment. Siddhartha concludes that happiness and grief, which are all one in the continuous life cycle, must be experienced separately and without formal instruction. He recognizes in himself the contentment that comes with a merger of the sensate self in nature.

As a utopian vision, *Siddhartha* turns aside from the Western concept of religious hierarchies and locates the self, the true source of oneness with God. The author—whose cosmic philosophy contrasts the dehumanized, mechanistic dystopias designed by H. G. Wells, George Orwell, Ayn Rand, and Aldous Huxley—reveals in the closing lines of his novel an inner landscape, a melding of transitory human experience. The rapture of Siddhartha's vision is the repetitive life, death, and rebirth reflected in the Buddha's smile, a symbol of all that is sacred and worthy. (Baumer 1969; Field 1970; Fleissner 1972; Hesse 1951; Mileck 1958; Reichert 1972; Rose 1965)

See also asceticism; Buddhism; heaven; Hesse, Hermann; humanitarianism; religion; *Siddhartha;* women in utopia.

SIDDHARTHA

This philosophical novel was written by German philosopher and novelist Hermann Hesse in 1922 and published in English translation in 1951. By blurring the lines between the historical Gautama Buddha, the protagonist Siddhartha, and the author's own rebellion against a grimly religious, Calvinistic father, Hesse creates an unusual journey in search of truth. Siddhartha, born to the learned Brahmin class, receives the benefits of privilege, education, and family love, as well as the friendship of Govinda, a faithful companion who also seeks enlightenment. After perceiving Atman, the universal oversoul from which all humanity arises, Siddhartha takes an interest in meditation and in the truths of the *Rigveda* (ca. 1500 B.C.), the ancient collected wisdom of Hinduism. From so promising a background, Siddhartha plunges into a dismaying alienation from his past because he still lacks oneness with God.

Hesse emphasizes his protagonist's change of heart in his constant denials of self. Siddhartha informs his father that he must give up earthly indulgence and live the ascetic's sparse lifestyle. Joining the Samanas, a band of holy men, he and Govinda set out to discover God. Siddhartha approaches his task by meditating, fasting, and waiting. He purifies himself of the need for possessions, sexual pleasure, rest, sleep, food, and water. He and Govinda leave the Samanas and encounter Gotama, a respected evangelist called the "Illustrious One." Surrounded by seekers in the Jetavana grove outside the town of Savathi, the simple, unassuming speaker lectures on the Eightfold Path. Gotama's words influence Govinda to become a follower; Siddhartha, too, is touched by the master's teaching, yet he perceives a shallowness in Gotama's logic. In the chapter called "With the Samanas," Siddhartha says to Gotama:

You have [attained nirvana] by your own seeking, in your own way, through thought, through meditation, through knowledge, through enlightenment. You have learned nothing through teachings, and so I think, O Illustrious One, that nobody finds salvation through teachings.

On the basis of this profound coming to knowledge, Siddhartha abandons words and relies on introspection. With a half-smile and a gesture of dismissal, Gotama warns him not to be too clever.

To know himself, Siddhartha chooses to journey alone; he leaves Govinda to his newfound salvation and seeks to conquer self. He admits that the act of departure was a quid pro quo: In exchange for his friend Govinda, Siddhartha accepts the gift of self. In the second stage of his life, he fears that he is lost, homeless, and straying from the priestly calling. He falls into despair. As a means of purification and rebirth, he studies the inner self. He briefly encounters a ferryman, who urges him to learn from the river. Siddhartha rejects the man's kindness and continues on his way. He meets Kamala, an enticing courtesan seated in an ornamented sedan chair. At her request, he writes a poem dedicated to her and, like a greedy child, follows her into a life of luxury and self-indulgence.

At Kamala's suggestion, Siddhartha gives up traditional religious begging and locates a job. Living in the house of his employer, Kawaswami, in the city of Samsara (a symbolic name for the unending cycle of life, death, and reincarnation), Siddhartha learns the merchant's trade and enjoys its rewards. In Kamala he finds a kindred spirit who must also make a unique life that reflects the inner being. She compliments him by praising his lovemaking, although she realizes that he can truly love no one. By midlife he has abandoned spiritual pursuits, bathed his senses in earthly titillations, and grown arrogant.

Late in his life Siddhartha undergoes a third awakening, an awareness that lust, gambling, food, and acquisitiveness bring him no lasting happiness. Again he uproots himself and launches a pilgrimage, leaving Kamala and their unborn child behind in Samsara. On the shore of a river, he meets Vasudeva, the ferryman, sits in the shade of a tree, and longs to drown himself in the river. A single divine syllable pierces his miseries—the word *Om,* a mystical sound that suggests perfection. Repetition of the sound supplants the turmoil of thoughts and overrides his worldliness and suicidal urge. From the ferryman whose kindness he once brushed aside, Siddhartha accepts a nondirective approach to learning. Halting his frenzied search for answers, Siddhartha accepts peace and the attendant enlightenment he has been seeking.

Over a decade later, Kamala, the mother of his 11-year-old son, goes on pilgrimage to the Buddha, who is reportedly dying. Near the river, she is bitten by a poisonous black snake. The ferryman transports her and her son to his hut, where Siddhartha recognizes his own likeness in the boy's face. Siddhartha also knows that Kamala is sinking toward death. She ends her pilgrimage by finding peace in her former lover. Vasudeva recognizes in his faith the emotions of sorrow and loss.

Because of his neglect of fatherhood, Siddhartha attempts to make it up to young Siddhartha by teaching him asceticism. In the chapter called "The Son," the boy defies his father with harsh words: "You want me to become like you, so pious, so gentle, so wise, but just to spite you, I would rather become a thief and a murderer and go to hell, than be like you." The boy steals the ferryman's money and boat and flees in the night, leaving Siddhartha sad and empty, just as Siddhartha himself once left his own father. He helps ferry passengers across the river and feeds his self-pity by envying parents whose children are obedient. At this point in Siddhartha's development, he reaches a meaningful plateau—a realization that life, like the flowing river, is forever a blend of the good and bad. The river never ceases, just as life, which resembles a comedy, never alters its rich intermingling of emotion. In response, the river sings to Siddhartha.

In old age, Siddhartha concludes that life is a circle, a transcendent unity of joy and suffering. As Hesse describes his apotheosis in the chapter called "Om":

> All the waves and water hastened, suffering, towards goals, many goals, to the waterfall, to the sea, to the current, to the ocean and all goals were reached and each one was succeeded by another. The water changed to vapor and rose, became rain and came down again, became spring, brook and river, changed anew, flowed anew.

For Siddhartha, nirvana is a state of blessedness that stills the rebellion against destiny and replaces all vestiges of selfhood with godliness. Vasudeva departs to the woods, leaving Siddhartha at the riverside hut. His old friend Govinda, disillusioned by the Samaran cult, returns and greets Siddhartha as "Venerable One." Siddhartha realizes that Govinda does not recognize him. Siddhartha explains that enlightenment comes not from an obsession to possess knowledge, but from experience. Time, he adds, is unreal, an illusive divider between the world and the eternal. Instead of words, which fail to express the sublime, he kisses Govinda as a gesture of acceptance and love. Govinda reciprocates by bowing low. (Baumer 1969; Fleissner 1972; Hesse 1951; Mileck 1958; Reichert 1972; Rose 1965)

See also asceticism; Buddhism; heaven; Hesse, Hermann; humanitarianism; karma; nirvana; religion; Siddhartha; women in utopia.

 # SLAVERY

A given in the unburdened social systems of Plato's *The Republic* (fifth century B.C.) and Plutarch's *The Life of Lycurgus* (first century A.D.) as well as in James Harrington's *Commonwealth of Oceana* (1656), Daniel Defoe's *Robinson Crusoe* (1719), Jonathan Swift's *Gulliver's Travels* (1727), Edward Bulwer-Lytton's *The Coming Race* (1871), Mark Twain's *A Connecticut Yankee in King Arthur's Court* (1886), and Margaret Atwood's *The Handmaid's Tale* (1985), slavery seems endemic in a variety of utopian and dystopian schemes. In balance with the work necessary for the perfect life, utopian systems often call for a subclass of humanity to perform such menial work as cooking, lifting, slaughtering, and manufacture, or skilled or professional labor such as tutoring children or entertaining at table.

Some utopists, e.g., Plutarch, Plato, Virgil, Thomas Malory, François Rabelais, and William Shakespeare, brazen their elitism by obliquely mentioning a serving class as though servitude were an unworthy topic of consideration—something to be taken for granted:

- In Sir Thomas More's *Utopia* (1516), slaves merit their lowly caste through criminal acts, military capture, or voluntary submission, and carry out menial kitchen tasks and the slaughtering of animals, a chore Utopians disdain.

- As an outgrowth of political superiority over Atlantean colonies, Francis Bacon makes a point of subjugating white Greek captives to serve the swarthy populace of *The New Atlantis* (1627).

- In Herman Melville's *Typee* (1846), a man-centered society apportions the heavy, dull, and repetitive work to women, while men loll in their pavilion to eat, rest, and contemplate the gods.

- Morlocks, the subhuman underground laborers who tend machines and subsist on chunks of raw meat, live in darkness in H. G. Wells's *The Time Machine* (1895). Their only escape from a tormented, bestial subjugation occurs during a brief emergence in the dark of the moon, when they roam the surface of Earth and menace their masters, the weak, ineffectual Eloi.

- Likewise, a lesser form of slavery provides the work force in Oceania, setting of George Orwell's *1984* (1949), a severely segregated London scene where proles—the city's proletarian or working class—live in ghettos and enjoy a shadow state of complacence and autonomy by virtue of their dishevelment, thick patois, and ignorance.

- For Aldous Huxley's *Brave New World* (1932), a layered system of class distinction begins before birth. By means of Bokanovsky's Process (a form of eugenics), factory assembly lines clone enough deltas and epsilons—the lowest strata—and brainwash them sufficiently with hypnopaedia and conditioning to supply society with reasonably content drays to carry out mindless work in service to the privileged alphas and betas.

- An unprogrammed, less advanced system of servitude, Ayn Rand's *Anthem* (1937) allots to youngsters the menial public-works jobs that society needs, regardless of unfulfilled talents and ambition. Thus, a budding engineer may become a street sweeper, as is the case with Rand's central character, Equality 7-2521, while the dullards of the society control decision making in central committees.

- In Alex Haley's *The Aubiography of Malcolm X* (1965), the title character relegates female Muslims to the home chores of tending children, cooking, housework, and honoring husbands.

- In a twisted version of Rand's dystopia, the rabbits of Richard Adams's heroic animal fable *Watership Down* (1972) combat two forms of enslavement—the cages of Nuthanger Farm and the concentration camp ruled by the dreadful General Woundwort. Although these characters are small animals, their human parallels suggest an equally dismaying prospect of manipulation, intimidation, and, ultimately, execution.

- Margaret Atwood's *The Handmaid's Tale* (1985) delineates a world similar to Adams's hellish rabbit warrens. In Gilead, a totalitarian stronghold in New England, subservience is the role of fertile females who are surrogate breeders for sterile upper-class women. As sexual slaves, the breeders lose their identity when they take the designation of the men who mate with them, as with Offred, or "of Fred." For those who fail to produce after a three-year trial, or who are too old to conceive, the prospect is exile to the radioactive wastelands left over from nuclear war.

It is worthy of note that a subsection of utopists stress the equality of people in either partial or virtual pantisocracy. In Theodor Hertzka's *Freiland* (1890), people share work and pleasure, although Hertzka remains unclear on the nation's method of freeing wives from drudgery. W. H. Hudson also slights details on kitchen duties and general cleaning in *A Crystal Age* (1887), a matriarchy ruled by robust women and enervated men. With the intent of creating a collectivist nation, Jack London raises his fictional proletarian class into violent revolt against the pampered, spoiled oligarchy in *The Iron Heel* (1907). Voltaire not only abhors slavery, but makes a model of the balanced division of labor that harmonizes Candide's home in Turkey. In Chapter 30 of *Candide* (1759), Candide agrees with Pangloss, who says, "when man was put in the Garden of Eden, he was put there *ut operaretur eum,* to work; which proves that man was not born for rest." The story ends with Candide's beloved wife Cunégonde making pastry, the reformed prostitute Pacquette embroidering, the old woman caring for linen, Friar Giroflée acting as handyman, and Candide tilling the garden. (Adams 1972; Atwood 1972; Bacon 1905; Bulwer-Lytton 1979; Capek and Capek 1961; Defoe 1963; Haley 1965; Harrington 1992; Hertzka 1972; Hudson 1917; Huxley 1932; London 1982a; More 1963a; Orwell 1949; Plato 1937b; Plutarch 1971b; Rand 1946; Twain 1963; Voltaire 1961; Wells 1964)

See also Anthem; *The Autobiography of Malcolm X; Brave New World; Candide;* classism; *The Coming Race;* conditioning; *A Connecticut Yankee in King Arthur's Court; A Crystal Age;* dystopia; eugenics; Freiland; *The Handmaid's Tale;* Hazel; Hudson, W. H.; *The Iron Heel; The New Atlantis; 1984;* pantisocracy; Plato; Plutarch; *The Republic; Robinson Crusoe; R. U. R.; The Time Machine; Utopia; Watership Down;* women in utopia.

 # SMITH, JOSEPH, JR.

Transcriber of the gold plates that were compiled into *The Book of Mormon* (1830), a religious text revered by Mormons, Smith was the founder of the Church of Jesus Christ of the Latter-day Saints, a uniquely American religious sect. He was born December 23, 1805, in Sharon, Vermont; reared in Palmyra, New York,

Joseph Smith, Jr.

he received inadequate schooling. His awareness of religious turmoil and conflicting claims of righteousness and salvation began in 1819. Smith received a vision of God and Jesus, who urged him to ally with no sect. Four years later, a vision of the angel Moroni called him to a crucial task—the translation of gold plates on which were written details of the exodus of two Hebrew tribes from the Holy Lands to the New World. As the angel prophesied, Smith located the scriptural plates in a stone box near Manchester, New York. They remained entombed until 1827, when Smith received them directly from Moroni along with two stones, the Urim and Thummim, which enabled him to translate the text from Egyptian to English.

The birth of the Church of the Latter-day Saints hinged on Smith's use of history and prophecy. After the translated manuscript tiles were compiled into *The Book of Mormon*, Smith set out on a prophetic mission to found a new faith. He published his heavenly visions in *Doctrine and Covenants* (1835) and *The Pearl of Great Price* (1851), and gathered followers for his growing congregation. He settled the sect in Kirtland, Ohio, then moved about the Midwest until he found a climate of religious tolerance in Nauvoo, Illinois, which in 1839 became Mormon headquarters. Smith's leadership foundered on a single precept—the polygamous marriage of believers, which he intended as religious procreation to swell the ranks of Mormons with children of righteous parents learning church precepts and doctrine from infancy.

The conclusion to Smith's role in Mormon Church history reminds Americans of the inherent intolerance in the Midwest—the same surge of vigilantism and persecution that caused many settlers to abandon Europe and settle in the New World. After Smith hacked apart the press of the *Nauvoo Expositor* for libeling his ministry and mission, he was arrested and incarcerated in Carthage, Illinois. A vicious mob shot both Smith and his brother Hyrum. One wing of the remaining Mormons chose Brigham Young as their leader and followed him to Salt Lake City, Utah, to establish a new center of worship. Smith's wife, Emma Hale Smith, and nine children remained in the faith. Joseph Smith, Jr., followed his father's goals, pursued an ascetic lifestyle free of tobacco, alcohol, tea, and coffee, and established Graceland College in Lamoni, Iowa. (Cavendish 1970; Cavendish 1980; Cross 1957; Eliade 1986; Hastings 1951; Jurji 1946; McDannell 1994; Mullen 1966; Quinn 1987; Roberts 1985; Smith 1971; Smith 1982)

See also asceticism; *The Book of Mormon*; city planning; heaven; religion; vision; women in utopia.

SMITH, WINSTON

Antihero and enigmatic seeker of truth of George Orwell's *1984* (1949), Winston lives alone in a dreary urban flat. As a professional writer, he works closely enough with restructuring Oceania's history that he is unable to escape a nagging conscience that forces him to search for truth. A rewriter of history and current events for the Ministry of Truth, he holds in his hand a newspaper clipping—a photograph that proves that the government of Oceania deliberately misleads citizens by distributing misleading restructurings of history. He pours out his disillusion in silent scribblings in his journal, the sole testimony to the anarchy that grips his soul.

Loneliness exacerbates Winston's alienation. A sexually truncated man whose asexual wife left him 11 years earlier, he attempts intercourse with a prostitute, then abandons sex entirely in favor of an unsatisfactory celibacy. His tentative liaison with Julia bursts into a celebration of passion, which he conducts in the wild, in a bell tower, and later at a rented room over an antique shop. The relief he experiences from consorting with a reprobate state-hater like himself is markedly one-sided because Julia lacks his concern for truth. Nevertheless, romance restores his equilibrium and tempts him to take chances.

In a tightly controlled police state, Winston's arrest comes as no surprise. For the crimes of writing seditious statements in his journal and carrying on the affair with Julia, Winston Smith, an agonized victim of torture and betrayal, survives the worst—a helmet filled with rats. In his polemical arguments against Big Brother, Winston is ethically correct but powerless against state machinery, represented by the sadistic O'Brien and the Thought Police. Brutalized and soulless, of his own volition Winston loses his individuality and merges with the Party. In Book 3, Chapter 3, he glimpses the new Winston in O'Brien's mirror:

> A bowed, gray-colored, skeletonlike thing was coming toward him. Its actual appearance was frightening, and not merely the fact that he knew it to be himself. . . . A forlorn, jailbird's face with a nobby forehead running back into a bald scalp, a crooked nose and battered-looking cheekbones above which the eyes were fierce and watchful.

Bald, scarred, and dogged with the same symbolic varicose ulcer of the ankle that he had in the opening chapter, he leans forward in a permanent scoliosis and resembles the wreck of a "man of sixty, suffering from some malignant disease." At the end of his torment he conceals his feelings, returns to freedom, and sits opposite an empty chessboard in a defeatist posture. Bereft of will, he talks with Julia and weeps that their former anarchy has receded into an unemotional semblance of real life. With little choice, Winston yields to conditioning and loves Big Brother. (Alok 1989; Bloom 1987c; Brown 1976; Buitehuis and Nadel 1988; Calder 1987; Connelly 1986; Hynes 1974; Jenson 1984; Oldsey and Browne 1986; Orwell 1949; Stansky 1984)

See also Big Brother; conditioning; *1984;* Orwell, George; totalitarianism; women in utopia.

 # SNOWBALL

A character representing Leon Trotsky in George Orwell's fascist beast fable *Animal Farm* (1945), Snowball serves as scapegoat for the machinations of Napoleon, the tyrant pseudo-Stalinist. A youthful pig weighing 15 stone, Snowball contends with Napoleon for command over Animal Farm. Because

Snowball lacks guile and tries to direct farm production through logic and open communication with the other animals, he is easily duped by the more cunning Napoleon. After learning literacy from Farmer Jones's children's schoolbooks, Snowball paints "Animal Farm" over the old Manor Farm sign and posts seven commandments on the barn wall. He serves as bullyboy in driving the animals to outpace the human record for hay-cutting and organizes useless animal committees.

Before the Battle of the Cowshed, Snowball studies Julius Caesar's tactics and leads the defense in a confrontation with Mr. Jones, the ousted farmer. Snowball orders Boxer to cease his regret that violence downed the stable boy. For his role in the victory, Snowball earns the title of "Animal Hero, First Class." From his knowledge of farm journals, Snowball conceives a plan to build a labor-saving windmill and, grasping a stick of chalk with his hoof, draws a design for an incubator shed. After Napoleon unleashes savage dogs against him, Snowball flees through a gap in the hedge and remains a shadow figure maligned by escalating accusations from Napoleon and his henchmen. (Alok 1989; Buitehuis and Nadel 1988; Calder 1987; Connelly 1986; Hynes 1974; Oldsey and Browne 1986; Orwell 1946)

See also *Animal Farm;* bestiality; Napoleon; Orwell, George; satire; totalitarianism.

SOCRATES

Socrates is the main speaker in Plato's *The Republic,* a fifth-century B.C. dialogue in which the author applies the ideal or model state. Gently countering five other speakers at a holiday banquet in Piraeus, Socrates defines justice by explaining how the ideal government should be run by the philosopher-king, a mellow, altruistic ruler educated in pure mathematical logic, philosophy, and the classics. In Socrates's estimation, a city-state functions best when citizens— from king and warriors down to farmers, tradespeople, crafters, and the lowest servant—perform work suited to their talents.

The real Socrates (469–399 B.C.) was a poor philosopher, critic, and logician who lived his whole life in Athens, worked as a stonecutter and sculptor, and served briefly in the military. Because he believed that Apollo had chosen him for a divine mission, he devoted his considerable intellect to the study of justice and goodness, which he believed earned rewards in the afterlife. His research technique, the "Socratic method," involved questioning and challenging the opinions of other citizens. By rephrasing questions into an expanded dialectic, he isolated false conclusions in accepted thought, thus challenging Athenian morals and traditions.

Socrates's intense cross-examinations riled tempers. Consequently, annoyed citizens labeled him a bad influence on young people. Charged with impiety for subverting the city's belief in the gods, at the age of 70 he stood trial before a jury of 501, and was found guilty by a vote of 281 to 220. After confinement in a cell at the foot of the Acropolis, he was forced to drink hemlock, a poison that gradually paralyzed him from the extremities inward to major organs. Socrates had committed none of his thinking to writing, but Plato, his pupil, wrote down much of his thought, particularly the defense against the charge of impiety, which is recorded in the *Apology*. In Socrates's final moments, he called out to his judges, "be of good cheer about death, and know this of a truth—that no evil can happen to a good man, either in life or after death." (Jowett 1937; Rouse 1956; Snodgrass 1988a; Warner 1958)

See also idealism; philosopher-king; Plato; *The Republic;* utopia.

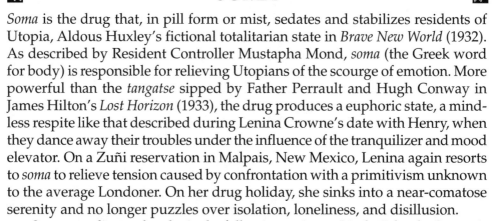

SOMA

Soma is the drug that, in pill form or mist, sedates and stabilizes residents of Utopia, Aldous Huxley's fictional totalitarian state in *Brave New World* (1932). As described by Resident Controller Mustapha Mond, *soma* (the Greek word for body) is responsible for relieving Utopians of the scourge of emotion. More powerful than the *tangatse* sipped by Father Perrault and Hugh Conway in James Hilton's *Lost Horizon* (1933), the drug produces a euphoric state, a mindless respite like that described during Lenina Crowne's date with Henry, when they dance away their troubles under the influence of the tranquilizer and mood elevator. On a Zuñi reservation in Malpais, New Mexico, Lenina again resorts to *soma* to relieve tension caused by confrontation with a primitivism unknown to the average Londoner. On her drug holiday, she sinks into a near-comatose serenity and no longer puzzles over isolation, loneliness, and disillusion.

Soma complicates the plot in the following action as Linda, John the Savage's mother, sedates herself so heavily that she undermines her health, which is already compromised by debauchery and heavy reliance on mescal. As her son speeds to her hospital room, he passes through a bevy of delta-level workers and exhorts them to abandon *soma* because it poisons and degrades them. After he throws the drug out the window, the workers become so agitated that riot police are called to sedate them with *soma* vapor. Like Connie Ramos in Marge Piercy's *Woman on the Edge of Time* (1976), Linda succumbs to the insidious control of drugs, aromatherapy, electronic entertainment, and sensual pleasures that are capable of reducing rebellious personalities into compliant tools of the state. The two women recede from the crises of their lives, Connie to a mental institution and Linda to an early death. (Bedford 1985; Holmes 1970; Huxley 1932; Nance 1988; Piercy 1976; Watts 1969)

See also *Brave New World;* classism; disillusion; escapism; Hilton, James; Huxley, Aldous; John; Linda; *Lost Horizon;* Mond, Mustapha; Piercy, Marge; totalitarianism; *Woman on the Edge of Time.*

SPECULATIVE FICTION

This grafted branch of utopian literature allies prophecy with a shrewd perception of technology and an anticipation of potential happenings based on the application of science to social needs, political power struggles, population control, economics, war, religion, and other human behaviors. The most pragmatic new-world predictors have been boldly dystopian; for example:

- Alfred Tennyson's "Locksley Hall" (1842) and "Locksley Hall Sixty Years After" (1886), two Victorian-era poems that foresee the destructiveness of flying devices capable of dropping bombs

- Thomas Malthus's *An Essay on the Principle of Population* (1798), a profoundly influential essay that warned Victorian England of the prospect of overpopulation and the resultant famine

- Jack London's Marxist vision of the collapse of the privileged, arrogant capitalistic oligarchy and the catastrophic rise and revolt of the working class in *The Iron Heel* (1907)

- Karel Capek's anticipation of robotic drones capable of fighting wars and replacing humans in the work force in the play *R. U. R.* (1920)

- Aldous Huxley's dystopia that relies on conveyor-belt eugenics, conditioning, and sleep-teaching; artificial contentment provided by the drug *soma;* and a melange of electronic entertainments in *Brave New World* (1932)

- James Hilton's prognostication of a greater world conflict to follow World War I in *Lost Horizon* (1933)

- George Orwell's nightmare state controlled by Thought Police, individualized forms of torture, and revisionist history in *1984* (1949)

- Arthur C. Clarke's ambiguous extension of human evolution from a golden age of contentment and harmony to inertia and annihilation of individuality, the themes of Book 3 of *Childhood's End* (1953)

- John G. Neihart's *Black Elk Speaks* (1932), a dictated memoir of a noted Sioux medicine man and visionary who had seen enough of the white man's arrogance and wastefulness to predict the collapse of nature, tribalism, and human decency

- Anthony Burgess's *A Clockwork Orange* (1962), a warning that the aimless drift of rootless teenagers could result in terror for society's most vulnerable members

- Richard Adams's urbanism through human-engineered extermination of nature in *Watership Down* (1972)

- Marge Piercy's reportage of repressive, sadistic doctors overdosing female patients on thorazine in *Woman on the Edge of Time* (1976)

- Doris Lessing's *Memoirs of a Survivor* (1974), a disturbingly generalized urban blight that returns humankind to atavistic roaming and pillaging

- Margaret Atwood's fundamentalist-guided, heavily policed breeding program in *The Handmaid's Tale* (1985)

Whether for palliative effects on a weakened society or outright alarm that trends are pushing humanity near the brink of despotism, despair, or extinction, writers of speculative fiction take seriously their duty to create scenarios that will awaken readers to danger. A simplified example of this genre is found in Ray Bradbury's short story "There Will Come Soft Rains" (1950), a futuristic view of the mechanized home where the absence of human residents is incidental to the smoothly run daily chores of awakening, serving breakfast, cleaning, and protecting the house from fire. Bradbury's grasp of mechanized menace grows darker and less promising in *Fahrenheit 451* (1953), the soulless world where housewives lose themselves in wall-to-wall soap operas, stuff their ears with electronic sounds to obliterate loneliness and despair, and lie helpless while coiled, snakelike hoses suck out their sedative overdoses to prevent suicide. Bradbury applies a generous amount of speculation about the effects of inhumane powers on cities where mechanized tracking dogs and helicopters chase down rebels and exterminate them with lethal injections. (Adams 1972; Atwood 1972; Bradbury 1953; Bradbury 1990a; Burgess 1962; Capek and Capek 1961; Clarke 1953; Hilton 1933; Huxley 1932; Lessing 1988; London 1982a; Malthus 1990; Neihardt 1961; Orwell 1949; Piercy 1976; Tennyson 1949b)

See also Black Elk; *Brave New World; Childhood's End; A Clockwork Orange; Fahrenheit 451; The Handmaid's Tale;* hypnopaedia; *The Iron Heel;* "Locksley Hall"; *Lost Horizon;* Malthus, Thomas; *Memoirs of a Survivor; 1984;* prophecy; *R. U. R.;* science fiction; "There Will Come Soft Rains"; *Woman on the Edge of Time.*

SUFISM

Sufism is a mystical branch of Islam that avoids the dogma and formalism established by the prophet Mohammed in favor of a personal oneness with Allah, Islam's God. The sect derived in the eighth century as a departure from luxury, sybaritism, and liberal interpretations of scripture. Influenced by Christian monks, Buddhist ascetics, and neo-Platonic philosophers, Sufist writers withdrew from society to contemplate *fana,* a revered state of union with God. Emulating Christian saints, monastics, and hermits, the Sufists denied self and searched for inner guidance, immersing themselves in the Koran and willing themselves into Allah's power. By the twelfth century, Sufists had organized into monastic colonies, the earliest being the Qadirite of Abd al-Qadir in Baghdad.

To shut out worldly distraction, Sufists dedicated themselves to poverty, the chanting of ritual hymns, and the performance of physical rhythms as a means of satisfying inner longings for peace, spirituality, purity, and truth. The path trod by the emerging saint covered seven allegorical valleys: quest, love, understanding, detachment, unity, bewilderment, and extinction, the oriental concept of merger of self in God. By *sama',* or dancing, playing pipes, or tapping drums, Sufists (derisively known as whirling dervishes) followed the teachings of poet Jalal al-Din al-Rumi, an Anatolian mystic and poet who died in 1273. In the sixteenth century, a Turkish offshoot, the Bektashi, followed a celibate order revering Ali, Mohammed's son-in-law, and based their worship on numerology. Later orders sprang up in other parts of the Islamic world—Shadhilite in Morocco and Tunisia, and Senusi in Libya.

The most orthodox of Sufist literature, *The Alchemy of Happiness* and *The Revival of the Religious Sciences* (twelfth century A.D.), was composed by al-Ghazali, a Persian theologian, poet, and scholar. Suffused with the heady ecstasy of godliness, these verses echo the soul's rejection of earthly enticements in the search for oneness with the divine, the supreme goal of Islam. In pursuit of the prophet Mohammed's dictum that the worshiper seek excellence, Sufists take literally the call to worship Allah as though he were visible or, being invisible, as though he views the suppliant. As with the American dancing Shakers or ecstatic charismatics and glossolalists (worshipers who speak in unknown languages), movement is central to Sufic oneness with the sublime. Dancing mystics recede from earthly reality by contemplating the emerging reality of the heart, a form of self-hypnosis that Umar al-Suhrawardi referred to as godly love that urges the dancer to perform the will of Allah. As Rumi characterizes the dance, the worshiper fragments self in a withdrawal from passions and imperfections. Thus, minstrels play their inner music, forming waves crested by the foam of passion. (Burckhardt 1969; Ghazali 1964; Idries Shah 1964; Nicholson 1950; Schimmel 1975; Schimmel 1982; Waley 1993)

See also asceticism; Ghazali; Koran; Malcolm X; religion; syncretism.

SUPPLEMENT AUX VOYAGES DE BOUGAINVILLE

A study of a primitive Polynesian haven, *Supplement to Bougainvilles "Voyages"* was written in 1772 by French philosopher and encyclopedist Denis Diderot (1713–1784). A thinly veiled attack on European mores, the dialogue between a French priest and a Tahitian expands on the observations of Louis Antoine de Bougainville (1729–1811), a French voyager and military attaché. In a reflective essay on Bougainville's observations, Diderot uses contrast as a means of recommending the natural lifestyle of the Pacific islands over Europe's much-flaunted "civilized" customs. In similar admiration of naturalism or oneness with the cycles of nature, as exalted in Michel de Montaigne's "Des Cannibales" (1580), Daniel Defoe's *Robinson Crusoe* (1719), Herman Melville's *Typee* (1846) and *Omoo* (1847), Henry Wadsworth Longfellow's *The Song of Hiawatha* (1855), and W. H. Hudson's *Green Mansions* (1904), but in conflict with William Golding's demonic *Lord of the Flies* (1954), Diderot's study of the "noble savage" suits the motif of the island paradise. He surmises that escape from European civilization is worth the voyage, as proven by such island visitors as painter Paul Gauguin and writer/raconteur Robert Louis Stevenson.

Like novelists Herman Melville in the nineteenth century and James Michener in the twentieth, Diderot seems fascinated by island spontaneity and the absence of formality. Governed by nature's whim, islanders enjoy a restful, healthful existence in the beauties of their isolated South Seas home and partake of seafood, fresh fruit, exercise, indolence, and sexual pleasures at will. Unlike Europeans, they suggest the peaceable figures in a Gauguin painting; sharing work and wealth commune-style, they avoid selfishness, self-aggrandizement, and the squabbles and litigation that spring from greed. (Bishop 1965; Defoe 1963; Diderot 1972; Fellows 1989; Golding 1954; Hudson n.d.; Longfellow 1992; Melville 1964; Melville 1968; Montaigne 1893b; Wilson 1972)

See also "Des Cannibales"; Diderot, Denis; escapism; Hudson, W. H.; Longfellow, Henry Wadsworth; *Lord of the Flies;* Montaigne, Michel Eyquem de; naturalism; *Omoo; Robinson Crusoe;* synergy; *Typee.*

SWIFT, JONATHAN

An English tract writer and satirist, Swift produced *Gulliver's Travels* (1727), a unique three-sided view of humanity. Influenced by the anti-utopianism of Thomas Hobbes's *Leviathan,* Swift's satire attempts to reshape society by revealing its shortcomings and to reform humanity by ridiculing its foibles. An Anglo native of Dublin, Jonathan Swift was born on November 30, 1667, of English parents, the grandson of a conservative English vicar. His father, a country lawyer for whom he was named, died before Swift was born; his mother, Abigail Erick Swift, abandoned him. Swift was raised by his uncle Godwin, who grudgingly paid his tuition to Kilkenny Grammar School and Trinity College, from which Swift obtained an M.A. in 1688.

Upon graduation, Swift accepted a post in Surrey as secretary to his mother's kinsman, Sir William Temple, who became his mentor. With raw edges refined, Swift was ready to put his gift for wit, satire, and contempt for human folly to work on his first compositions, *The Battle of the Books* and *A Tale of a Tub,* both of which were published anonymously in 1704. In 1694, fresh from a rebuff by the woman he loved, Swift entered the Anglican priesthood in Ireland, but departed ecclesiastical service in despair the following year after a dismal stint as parson of Kilroot, Antrim. His return to Temple's service in England put him in close company with the wits of the eighteenth century, notably Joseph Addison, Richard Steele, and Alexander Pope. As a literary sparring partner with the established church, Swift published biting essays in the *Tatler,* a forerunner of the modern magazine.

Before the death of Queen Anne, the political climate reshaped popular religious and contemporary philosophy. In 1710 a switch in political loyalties destroyed old friendships as Swift supported Tory trends. He formed loose associations with William Congreve, John Gay, and Thomas Parnell, and began editing the Tory *Examiner.* His reward for party loyalty was less than the English bishopric he had hoped for. In 1713 he began serving as dean of St. Patrick's Cathedral in Dublin, a rural post that brought him a small stipend. During this period, Swift's private life was graced by his lifelong admiration for Esther "Stella" Johnson; some biographers believe she may have been his wife or mistress.

Jonathan Swift

An advocate for Irish freedoms, Swift began publishing tracts protesting England's disgraceful treatment of the neighboring isle, where the church and absentee landlords held sway over a burdened populace. Among his most famous shorter satires are *Drapier Letters* (1724) and "A Modest Proposal" (1720), a tongue-in-cheek attack on the ruling class's insensitivity to the poor. In 1727, as an outgrowth of his writings for the Scriblerus Club, he published under his own name his classic fantasy, *Gulliver's Travels*, a lethal jab at orthodoxy and a vision of the petty, gross, and vapidly idealized visions of world order. The final two of four books implies that innate faults prevent the improvement of the human race, which falls short of the standards of a nation of horses.

Swift's final years brought pain, loneliness, and mental disintegration. He maintained correspondence with several women, including his long-standing love, Stella, and the mysterious and tumultuous Esther "Vanessa" Vanhomrigh, who relieved the intensity of his literary battles against the entrenched pillars of society with personal attacks of jealousy and spite. Both women predeceased Swift, leaving him lonely for conversation. Late in his seventies, deafness, dizzy spells, and melancholia (possibly from Ménière's disease or syphilis) destroyed his capacity to enjoy life and to craft the ironies that so enriched his prose, letters, journals, and verse. During five years of invalidism, his cousin Martha Whiteway watched over and cared for him. His death in Dublin on October 19, 1745, ended a distressing decline. Swift was buried alongside Stella in Dublin's St. Patrick's churchyard. (Drabble 1985; Harrison et al. 1967; Hornstein et al. 1973; Johnson 1968; Magill 1958; Manguel and Guadalupi 1987; Pollard 1970; Quintana 1958; Woods et al. 1947)

See also bestiality; Brobdingnags; dystopia; escapism; Gulliver, Lemuel; *Gulliver's Travels*; Houyhnhnms; Laputa; Lilliput; satire.

SYNCRETISM

Syncretism is a fusion of religious and/or philosophical beliefs, as demonstrated by numerous characters seeking a perfect religion by blending elements and tenets from two or more faiths. A process requiring open-mindedness, a generous nature, and a willingness to seek the good in any belief, syncretism affected the Orient's reverence for Confucius's *Analects* (second century A.D.) by evolving his scattered aphorisms into a blend of neo-Platonism, Taoism, and some Christian traits over the centuries. Likewise, the "whirling dervishes" who celebrated Sufism in ecstatic worship combined Islamic teachings with Ghazali's *Alchemy of Happiness* (twelfth century A.D.), the lore and ritual of hermits, saints' lives, and the monasticism of Christianity. A third example, the apocalyptic book of Revelation (A.D. 90–95) by St. John the Divine, exhibits qualities of the Christian faith overlaid by numerology, omens, astrology, demons and phantasms, dreams, visions, prophecy, and Eastern mysticism. These examples prove the suggestibility of worshipers to tenets of other faiths, particularly where a need goes unfulfilled under one strict doctrine.

A common occurrence among human institutions that receive input from differing philosophies, syncretism colors various utopian works:

- Genesis (ca. 950 B.C.), a primeval history of creation, is the first book of the Jewish Pentateuch. Genesis is credited with being the first book of Moses; however, traditions and archetypal characters bear the influence of such pervasive Semitic stories as the garden called Paradise, a flood that inundates the world, and events in the lives of the first human family.

- In the first century A.D., Lao Tzu's 200-year-old study of yin and yang and the pursuit of the Tao, or correct path, as represented in the *Tao Te Ching* (third century B.C.), evolved under Chang Tao-ling's emphasis into a religion complete with temples, statuary, saints, mysticism, healing, ritual, monasteries, and liturgy. Taoism reached a wide audience and influenced both Buddhism and Confucianism.

- On a convoluted journey from hell through purgatory to heaven, Dante's *Divina Commedia* (1320) honors such pagan writers as Homer and Virgil among the many souls that cluster in the Christian Underworld because they were not redeemed by Christ.

- Arthur's departure from his deathbed to Avalon in Sir Thomas Malory's *Le Morte d'Arthur* (1485) blends Celtic mysticism with a hint of Catholic lore when nunlike attendants tenderly bind his war wounds and ferry him away to a retreat on an invisible isle, where Arthur will heal, grow strong, and await a time when England will again need his idealism, piety, and heroic leadership.

- The worshipers of Bensalem in Francis Bacon's *New Atlantis* (1627) begin with tolerance to non-Christians and gradually influence Jewish Bensalemites, who accept the concepts of virgin birth and the divinity of Christ.

- Black Elk's career as a prophet took on new meaning after he came under the influence of the Ghost Dance, a physical liturgy begun by Wovoka in the mid-1900s as a revival of the spirit world. Black Elk and other followers expected the spirits to defeat white land-thieves and return the world of the plains Indian to its former Edenic state.

In each instance, the blending of philosophies enhances colonies, religions, and governments by creating less need for enforced dogma and by drawing together strands of belief and worship from multiple races and nations.

In the twentieth century, syncretism and ecumenism influence literary cosmologies in fiction and nonfiction. In James Hilton's *Lost Horizon* (1933), the acquiescence of Miss Brinklow, the didactic, narrow-minded fundamentalist missionary, helps her acclimate to the gentle serenity of Shangri-La, a utopian lamasery in the Himalayas of Tibet. The Chinese guide and majordomo, Chang, tactfully reminds the newcomers in Chapter 6 that "the jewel has facets . . . and it is possible that many religions are moderately true." This all-embracing aphorism, a metaphor for tolerance and ecumenism, counters extremism, orthodoxy, and overstated zeal with the virtues of all belief systems. Opposing Miss Brinklow's hidebound assurance that the world must accede to a single doctrine, Shangri-La's quiet beneficence erodes her dogmatism in the same way that it gently supplanted Father Perrault's Roman Catholicism two and a half centuries earlier.

Similarly, Arthur C. Clarke creates a world takeover in *Childhood's End* (1953), a speculative novel rich in the trappings of science fiction, but oddly mystical in its resolution. Clarke alleviates religious squabbling and world tensions based on prejudice by raising the education level globally. The resulting peace produces a tolerance that Clarke calls "purified Buddhism," a tendency to merge with the transcendent Overmind, which governs Earth from a distant solar system. The conclusion of Clarke's plot contains enough doubt, enough perturbing details (e.g., the enigmatic characterization of Karellen, a world supervisor with a forked tail and leathery wings resembling the stereotypical demon) to imply that the author himself is not convinced.

A nonfictional account of syncretism echoes in the life of Malcolm X, focus of Alex Haley's *The Autobiography of Malcolm X* (1965). Malcolm X searches for world brotherhood after withdrawing his support from Elijah Muhammad's racist, isolationist Nation of Islam, an urban phenomenon that began in Detroit and spread to ghetto blacks in major American cities. During his early ministry, Malcolm X preaches a similar hard line by blaming white devils for the troubles of African Americans. In 1965, having viewed the fellowship of numerous races and nations on a shared pilgrimage to Mecca, the sacred city of Islam, Malcolm X concludes that piety knows no color and that the merger of many views of the Mohammedan faith will initiate unity and world peace. Before Malcolm can begin the process of unifying believers or calling for assistance from the United Nations, he is assassinated.

Apart from these blended philosophies stands the work of St. Augustine of Hippo. In Book 2, Chapter 4 of his *De Civitate Dei* (A.D. 426), he struggles to rid himself of his early training in Platonic philosophy by debasing himself in sincere confession. A purist by nature, Augustine divides his intense, didactic commentary on godliness first by explaining the nature of pagan gods of classical Greece and Rome, and then painstakingly destroying their credibility:

> I myself, in my younger days, used to frequent the sacrilegious stage plays and comedies. I used to watch the demoniacal fanatics and listen to the choruses, and take delight in the obscene shows in honor of their gods and goddess, of the virgin Caelestis and the Berecynthian Cybele, mother of the gods.

At the end of the chapter, he lessens the charge of sacrilege against himself by implying how easily people can be charmed and enticed by fanciful pseudoreligious entertainments:

> If these enormities are religious service, what can sacrilege be? . . . If any one does not realize what kind of spirits find pleasure in such obscenities, then he is either unaware that there are unclean spirits wearing the deceptive masks

of gods, or else he is leading the sort of life that prefers the demons, rather than the true God.

By Book 5, Augustine's tedious refutation of classical literature assures the reader that the only way to eternal bliss is, like John Bunyan's Christian and Christiana on pilgrimage, a metaphoric journey to the City of God. (Augustine 1958; Bacon 1905; Bunyan 1896; Clarke 1953; Dante Alighieri 1968; Ghazali 1964; Haley 1965; Hilton 1933; Holy Bible 1958; Lao Tzu 1993; Malory 1982; Neihardt 1961)

See also The Analects of Confucius; Arthur; Augustine, St.; *The Autobiography of Malcolm X;* Avalon; Black Elk; *Childhood's End;* Christian; Christiana; *De Civitate Dei;* Confucius; didacticism; *Divina Commedia;* Genesis; Ghazali; Lao Tzu; *Lost Horizon; The New Atlantis;* Perrault, Father; Plato; religion; Revelation; Sufism; Tao; *Tao Te Ching.*

SYNERGY

Synergy is the combined efforts of workers, warriors, travelers, or believers to attain a common goal. Tending toward pantisocracy or total social equality, synergistic labors equalize the worth of citizens in utopian communes or cities, for example, cooperative species of birds in the building of Cloudcuckooland in Aristophanes's *The Birds* (414 B.C.), Bernard de Mandeville's hive workers in *The Fable of the Bees* (1705), monks in Thomas Carlyle's nostalgic reflection on the Middle Ages in *Past and Present* (1843), grain harvesters in William Morris's *News from Nowhere* (1890), and the Luddite commune of Altruria in William Dean Howells's pro-Christian works, *A Traveler from Altruria* (1894) and its sequel *Through the Eye of the Needle* (1907). In all instances, the common denominator of civic responsibility is a balanced interaction, communal belief systems, and reward for enthusiasm and diligence.

Synergy has a long history in utopian literature. Virgil's *Aeneid* (19 B.C.), the Roman literary epic composed in the style of Homer's Trojan War epics, lauds the flight of refugees on a godly mission to restore the sacred images and culture of a doomed kingdom to a new Troy. Without clear guidance to the exact Western site, the followers continue their random sailing pattern, swept far afield and thwarted by the envious Juno to peril, despair, and death for those who lack the vision of their leader, Aeneas. At one point, he opts to abandon the weak and dispirited in Sicily and continue with a select crew of faithful seekers. The winnowing out of uncommitted refugees works in his favor. In safe harbor at Alba Longa, Aeneas and his supportive crew begin the process of building a consensus of locals and securing land for a modest stronghold destined to become the mighty empire of Rome.

In similar epic style, Richard Adams's suspenseful beast fable *Watership Down* (1972) details a lengthy exodus that takes the leader, Hazel, his clairvoyant brother Fiver, and other rabbits away from an ill-defined doom that Fiver sees in a vision. In Chapter 5, Adams defines the obstacles they face:

Hazel and his companions had spent the night doing everything that came unnaturally to them, and this for the first time. They had been moving in a group, or trying to . . . if they lay brooding, unable to feed or go underground, all their troubles would come crowding into their hearts, their fears would mount and they might very likely scatter, or even try to return to the warren.

Pipkin, an undersized follower, takes his cue from Hazel and tells a story of El-ahrairah, the rabbit patriarch and equivalent of the Hebrew Abraham. Similar in philosophy to the Uncle Remus tales retold by Joel Chandler Harris from African originals, the familiar story concludes with appropriate advice to gentle, unwarlike, disorganized animals:

All the world will be your enemy . . . and whenever they catch you, they will kill you. But first they must catch you, digger, listener, runner, prince with the swift warning. Be cunning and full of tricks and your people shall never be destroyed.

At length, the group answers to a team goal of a safe warren and enough does to guarantee future generations of Watership offspring. The group's exploits include setting free domestic rabbits from a farm, crossing a river in a boat to elude a tyrant's sentries, and launching a massive counterattack, spearheaded by Bigwig, to halt insurgents intent on exterminating or enslaving them. In the end, their oral traditions preserve the courage and unanimity of the initial band, who trust their instincts and transport a glimmer of hope for a better life to the safety of Watership Down. (Adams 1972; Aristophanes 1993; Carlyle 1977; Howells 1907; Howells 1957; Morris 1968b; Virgil 1950)

See also Aeneas; *Aeneid; The Birds;* Hazel; humanitarianism; *News from No-where;* pantisocracy; *Past and Present;* prophecy; slavery; *Through the Eye of the Needle; A Traveler from Altruria;* Virgil; *Watership Down.*

 TAO

Tao is the indescribable, elusive inner pathway to oneness with the creative life force of the universe, a meaningful comfort to the poor, aged, handicapped, oppressed, or disenfranchised. Often represented as a paradoxical matrix, doctrine, or dogmatic structure, the Tao is an unassuming but intriguing construct. It exemplifies human experience, through which contemplative minds intuit the essence of everlasting reality. Taoism supposedly sprang from the writings of Lao Tzu, author of a book of aphorisms known as the *Tao Te Ching* (third century B.C.). The power that underlies Taoism is the art of unifying earthly behavior with godliness. Thus, the seeker of the way finds beauty in simplicity, honesty, selflessness, and freedom from greed.

As a means of explaining good and bad fortune, the Taoist locates the yin and yang, or negative and positive forces, that govern all actions in nature; for example, the forces of weather themselves can benefit or annihilate. Weather as strong and out of control as a cyclone or tsunami can wreak havoc on property and life. On the other hand, balmy, temperate weather can hasten the growth of vegetable beds and can comfort and delight the human observer. Yin, the cold, dark, female life force, urges the soul to withdraw and contemplate; yang, the hot, active, masculine life force, presses for expansion and aggression. To perceive nature in terms of these polarities, the Taoist ceases to struggle against or even perceive adversity, whether in the form of illness, loss, or political or economic threats. To the faithful, all is one, a part of the whole.

The creation of wholeness enlightens the Taoist to the ultimate in experience. The perception of *feng shui,* the Chinese term for balance or wholeness, ushers in an intellectual and spiritual epiphany or *ming*, the Chinese word for light. To prepare for an epiphany, the Taoist empties the soul, leaving the essential void in which a mystical wisdom forms. To be truly enlightened, the seeker must search for life's constant, the impartiality that breeds nobility, divinity, and the everlasting Way. After serving an earthly purpose, the seeker, submissive to all living aspects of nature, returns to nonbeing, or the state of precreation, a pure form of energy that is the ultimate harmony.

Near the end of the first century A.D., Lao Tzu's precepts took the form of a religion after Chang Tao-ling, a populist theologian, added the trappings of temples, icons, saints, alchemy, healing, ritual, holidays, monasteries, and liturgy arising from the *Tao-tsang,* an immense, amorphous body of collected Taoist scripture. Through the interjection of ethics and spirituality, the Taoist concepts influenced both Buddhism and Confucianism. In the fifth and sixth centuries, Taoism was China's state religion, but later declined when the intelligentsia perceived it to be the religion of the less educated. The sect spawned 350 Chinese commentaries and 250 by Japanese scholars; in Taiwan, Hong Kong, and the Western Hemisphere, it continues to find converts among seekers who attempt to comprehend world upheaval, especially China's political evolution from empire to republic to communist state. Today, Taoist views impact exercise or yoga, sexuality, diet, healing, natural cultivation of plants, contemplation, and an avoidance of artificiality. (Lao Tzu 1993; Blofeld 1973; Cleary 1991; Kaltenmark 1969; LaFargue 1992; Lau 1963; Mitchell 1988; Welch 1958)

See also asceticism; Buddhism; Confucius; Hilton, James; Lao Tzu; *Lost Horizon;* Perrault, Father; religion; syncretism; *Tao Te Ching.*

 # *TAO TE CHING*

Lao Tzu's *Way of Life,* or *The Way and the Power,* is a 5,000-word religious manual expressing ascetic views on contentment through *Te,* or virtue. Composed in China during the third century B.C., a violent period that produced China's first emperor, the *Tao Te Ching* has influenced numerous great thinkers and is currently one of the world's most translated books. As Lao Tzu expresses his notion of a perfect life, he calls for a stoic acceptance of worldly sufferings and acceptance of *wu wei,* which refers to a controlled state of inaction or passivity. Paralleling some of the precepts of Christ's Sermon on the Mount, Marcus Aurelius's *Meditations,* Gandhi's speeches to Indian strikers, and Dr. Martin Luther King's "creative extremism" during the Birmingham, Alabama, bus strike, the *Tao Te Ching* counsels "return love for hatred," a pragmatic way to offset the discontent brought on by stored animosity.

Lao Tzu's call for an end to self-defeat through force of law echoes other philosophies that encourage oneness with nature—for example, the animism of Native American worship, as described in Henry Wadsworth Longfellow's *The Song of Hiawatha* (1855), and the pacifism and achievement of peace in Hermann Hesse's *Siddhartha* (1922). In Lao Tzu's words,

> I contrive nothing, and the people are naturally civilized;
> I am fond of tranquillity, and the people are naturally upright.
> I have nothing to do, and the people are naturally enriched.
> I have no desire, and the people are naturally simple.

By supplanting dreams of greatness and power with nondoing, Taoism stresses joy in small things and obedience to natural law. By advising only ends, Lao Tzu leaves to each follower the steps by which contentment and *T'ai Ch'ai,* or harmony, are achieved.

In contrast to what neophytes assume to be nothingness, the *Tao Te Ching* prepares the disciple to receive an inner divinity, an individualized oneness with God that springs from the heart's depths rather than through prescribed liturgy or dogma. To reach for this unity or balance, the follower withdraws the outstretched hands, reposes in nature, and awaits what is already there. As Lao-Tzu describes this state of receptivity, it is the mysterious female, "the root of heaven and earth," a vital equanimity that cannot be analyzed, forced, or hurried. The receiver, by striving to immerse the imperfect self in the Way, acquires "the calling," an energizing, universal power. An unknowable quantity, the Tao has no measure or description; in Lao Tzu's words, "it is like pure space, limitless and serene." He advises a pacifist, noncombative, noninterventionist stance akin to the classical idea of stoicism: Any potential ruler can access the Tao by letting events "take shape by themselves" and allowing the world to find its own perfection. (Blofeld 1973; Cleary 1991; Hesse 1951; Holy Bible 1958; LaFargue 1992; Lao Tzu 1993; Lau 1963; Mitchell 1988; Welch 1958)

See also Buddhism; Confucius; heaven; Hesse, Hermann; Lao Tzu; religion; Sermon on the Mount; Siddhartha; *Siddhartha*; syncretism; Tao.

 # TASSO, TORQUATO

Author of *Jerusalem Delivered* (1581), Tasso was a native of Sorrento. Born 11 March 11, 1544, to Neopolitan poet Bernardo Tasso (1493–1569), Torquato Tasso lived with his refined, wealthy mother, who insisted on a sound education at a Jesuit academy in Naples. In 1554 the boy went to Pesaro to live with his father, who had been exiled for political intrigue. Two years later, Tasso's mother died. From home tutoring he advanced to the University of Padua and later to the University of Bologna, where he abandoned law and excelled in verse and philosophy. He assisted his father with editing and began publishing in his teens, achieving his first critical success with *Rinaldo* (1562), a romance epic.

In Renaissance Italy it was necessary for creative people to find financial supporters. Thus, in 1565 Tasso accepted the patronage of Cardinal Luigi d'Este, a scion of the Ferraras, one of Italy's most noble families. To distinguish the cardinal's genealogy, Tasso began composing *Jerusalem Delivered*, a literary epic. He lived comfortably in his new surroundings, traveled to Paris with his patron, and studied with Ronsard, France's notable lyric poet. An era of squabbling with his patron ended with Tasso seeking the support of the cardinal's brother, Duke Alfonso d'Este, also of Ferrara. In 1573 Tasso composed *Aminta*, a pastoral stage play, and finished *Jerusalem Delivered*, which he read aloud to the court.

From overwork, misgivings about Catholic interpretation of his work, and fear of the Inquisition, in 1576 Tasso fell ill with fever and fearful dreams, possibly symptoms of depression or paranoia. The duke forced him to remain in the court's custody and called on Franciscan healers to attend him. Legend suggests that the duke had an ulterior motive for the benign house arrest—it was the duke's way of halting an affair between the poet and the duke's sister

Leonora. Dressed in peasant garb, Tasso eluded his captors and fled to his sister Cornelia in Sorrento. A year later he returned to Ferrara to sue the duke for unlawful house arrest and attempted poisoning. Deluded and raving, Tasso remained in a mental institution until 1583; nevertheless, he completed the final version of *Jerusalem Delivered*, which the duke seized and published.

As the public poured out admiration for the work, Tasso, deprived of royalties, took refuge with the Prince of Mantua. In 1586 he produced *Re Torrismondo*, a romantic tragedy, then set out on a ramble across Europe. Still plagued with delusions and fever, he lived in poverty. In 1593 he finished *Gerusalemme Conquistata*, a poor sequel to *Jerusalem Delivered*. As Pope Clement VIII made plans for an official title and guaranteed stipend, Tasso was hospitalized at the monastery of St. Onofrio outside Rome, where he died on April 25, 1595. He was honored by Edmund Spenser, Johann Goethe, and George Byron, as well as later poets who emulated his stylish, graceful verse. (Boulting 1969; Johnson 1968; Magill 1958; Tasso 1987)

See also *Aeneid; Jerusalem Delivered;* Virgil.

 # TECHNOLOGY

An indispensible motif in speculative fiction, science fiction, and dystopian and utopian literature, the veneration of technology influences the plotting of perfect societies, which often come to expect freedom from inconvenience, toil, danger, disease, suffering, and death through the application of scientific theories and inventions. During the Renaissance, the exaltation of science resulted in near veneration of invention, which continued to spark utopian writers for centuries:

- In Fra Tomaso Campanella's *La Città del Sole* (1602), the exaltation of manual labor results in the creation of labor-saving devices, particularly the wonderfully mobile field wagon fitted with sails and "wheels within wheels," devices that anticipate the technology of the eighteenth century. Equally facile and useful are a winch that raises and lowers the town gates and self-propelled airplanes and ships.

- Likewise, Johann Andreae's *Christianopolis* (1619) employs crude lifts as well as astronomical devices, laboratory equipment, and catapults and siege weaponry, but refrains from engaging in warfare unless forced to fend off invaders.

- The strongest of utopist voices praising technology is that of Francis Bacon. In his *New Atlantis* (1627), the overlay of ceremony and pageantry thinly dresses a paean to Solomon's House, or the College of the Six Days' Works. Bacon's brief descriptions of hilltop observatories, underground laboratories, experimental agricultural and marine stations, and wellness clinics presage nineteenth- and twentieth-century innovations, particularly the Atlanteans' industrial laboratories, pharmaceutics, and experimentation on the application of sound, perfume, light, and taste to human behavior. However, *New Atlantis* only lists these possibilities, omitting the underlying breakthroughs that make them possible.

- A century after Bacon, Voltaire's *Candide* (1759) utilizes an extraordinary hoist capable of lifting travelers from the fabled city of Eldorado across treacherous South American mountains to the valley beyond. Built by 3,000 physicists, the device took only two weeks to construct and cost 20 million English pounds, a mere trifle to a nation where precious metals lie undisturbed in the streets. Packed along with 102 sheep, Candide and his valet embrace the king and are lifted out of a wanderer's paradise into the roiling world of intrigue where Candide's love, Cunégonde, awaits rescue.

- Edward Bulwer-Lytton's *The Coming Race* (1871) introduces a visitor to the concept of the home elevator. However, his greatest surprise is the use of wings and *vril*, a magic cure-all energy source available only to this subterranean society.

- More in the vein of city planning than power, Edward Bellamy's *Looking Backward, 2000–1887* (1887) features benevolent innovations from covered sidewalks to a home sound system capable of piping in sermons, lectures, and a varied entertainment program.

- Mark Twain's *A Connecticut Yankee in King Arthur's Court* (1886) details the use of clever devices including the match, gunpowder, bicycles, baseball and bat, and a generator in the protagonist's attempt to upgrade sixth-century England to the standards of Twain's day. Hank, the skilled laborer, ennobles himself by attempting to alleviate the cruelties and inequities of feudalism, yet the leap from King Arthur's time to Mark Twain's New England proves to be more than society can accommodate. Ultimately, Hank's own ingenuity encircles his stronghold with a charged fence, and he dies from the result—the rotting corpses of electrocuted knights. Hank's skill with telephone, telegraph, and blacksmithing cannot save him from numbing medievalism, symbolized by Merlin.

In the decades before 1900, signs of discontent with progress and a pervasive disbelief in human perfectability littered the philosophical landscape. Uncomfortable with the brimming idealism of Sir Francis Bacon and Fra Tomaso Campanella, polemicists fell back on the classic humanistic question of how humanity must deal with knowledge and power in order to survive. Perhaps one of the most damning of utopian commentaries on technology is found in an isolated passage in Chapter 57 of Herman Melville's *Moby Dick* (1851). He notes the discomforts and terrors of a sailor's life and admits that disaster has raised the toll of sea deaths into the hundreds of thousands. Still, Melville takes comfort in the sea's majesty and its ability to overwhelm "baby man" with "his science and skill." The author contends that science may augment human powers, but "the sea will insult and murder him, and pulverize the stateliest, stiffest frigate he can make."

Counter to utopians, dystopian writers of the Edwardian era tend to suspect and fear innovations that transfer too much power from operator to machine. Samuel Butler's *Erewhon* (1872) demonstrates the Luddite abhorrence of technology. Early in the nation's history, a seer predicted that machines would overrun humanity. To prevent such an eventuality, authorities destroyed machines, placed shards of gears and rods in the Museum of Old Machines in Sunchildston, and banned the creation of replacement models. Like the Amish, to maintain the land, Erewhonians resort to hoes, shovels, and horse-drawn vehicles. In a daring escape from Erewhon, the unnamed speaker shelters his girlfriend in the basket of a hot-air balloon and floats haphazardly over the mountains and into the sea before being rescued by a passing ship. Less fearful is Jules Verne's focus of *Twenty Thousand Leagues under the Sea* (1870)—the fictional Captain Nemo, whose symbolic name (Greek for "No Man") suggests that no human seeker of power is capable of controlling the technology of submarines or using it to produce happiness.

The twentieth century, presaged by Mark Twain, Herman Melville, William Dean Howells, and Samuel Butler, presents the jaundiced view of the human inability to profit from technology. The diminution of power reflects the Greek myth of Daedalus and Icarus, the doomed boy who drowned while attempting to fly too high on his father's homemade wings. A mild form of antitechnology during the Edwardian age precedes the virulent dystopianism of the twentieth century, as demonstrated by H. G. Wells's *The Time Machine* (1895), Karel Capek's *R. U. R.* (1920), Yevgeny Zamyatin's *We* (1921), Anthony Burgess's *A Clockwork Orange* (1962), Ernest Callenbach's *Ecotopia* (1975), Marge Piercy's *Woman on the Edge of Time* (1976), and Margaret Atwood's *The Handmaid's Tale* (1985). The technology that undergirds Capek's dark-spirited utopian stories, novels, and plays reaches its prophetic heights in *R. U. R.*, a mechanistic nightmare echoing the theme of "The Sorceror's Apprentice," a recurrent motif in legend, young-adult literature, opera, and film. The near domination of humanity by Rossum's Universal Robots exemplifies the fearful status of a world tampering with forbidden powers. Unintentionally, old Dr. Rossum's heirs exterminate the less efficient beings who venture too far and lose their knowledge of robotic science.

Likewise, mechanization dominates Old State, the dystopia of Zamyatin's *We*, where mathematical precision lays out streets in straight lines and houses are made of glass. Residents have access to an airplane, which can fly them beyond the city wall to the less civilized domain of the Ancients. For citizens who display a devil-may-care level of daring, the tyrant Benefactor maintains the Bell, a device that imprisons its victim under a dome while technicians draw out the oxygen. Near suffocation produces a brain free of imagination, which is the most dangerous ailment to threaten the rigorous order of Old State.

More diverse in theme and outlook than Capek's *R. U. R.*, Aldous Huxley's dystopian *Brave New World* (1932) produces consumers at specified levels and

brainwashes people to content themselves with a precise class system and programmed environment. The same assembly-line system that imprints their
genes to conform to caste specifications also engineers the technology to free
their lives from toil and stress and keep them occupied in mindless diversions.
Across London, mechanization portends an age of leisure and contentment;
still, life in Huxley's dystopia breeds a spiritual emptiness that requires constant drug consumption; regular, promiscuous sex; and sporadic vacations to
free citizens of fears and free-floating anxieties.

Huxley, more then any other dystopian writer, warns of manipulative mass
communication, godless belief systems, industrialization, Freudian psychology, hypnopaedia and oppressive forms of conditioning, eugenics, and birth
control. The personae in *Brave New World* attain the height of sensual pleasure
by negating their humanity. This renunciation of real passion and need enables inhabitants to view, touch, and smell the "feelies," multisense, futuristic
movies that pander to their depraved sensuality. Other contrivances—air
hearses, sanitized crematories, engineered embryos, obstacle golf, Riemann-
surface tennis, centrifugal bumble-puppy, and transport helicopters—separate
citizens from boredom, suffering, and death in a milieu where the present far
outvalues the past or future. In Huxley's preface, he warns:

> The people who govern the Brave New World may not be sane (in what may
> be called the absolute sense of the word); but they are not madmen, and their
> aim is not anarchy but social stability. It is in order to achieve stability that
> they carry out, by scientific means, the ultimate, personal, really revolution-
> ary revolution.

Unfortunately for them, the innovative genius that relieves their human weaknesses inadvertently robs them of humanity, which can be found only on distant reservations where the primitive lifestyle titillates tourists and scandalizes
those who examine too closely women breast-feeding their babies and men
dancing the snake dance, both behaviors belonging to the primitive, nontech-
nical past.

At the crux of the theme of technological menace lurk three key questions:

- Who controls world mechanization?

- What does that power afford the controller?

- What must the average citizen give up to profit from technology?

In Ayn Rand's *Anthem* (1937), a technologically regressive society subverts citizens' rights by generalizing education, forcing people into unsuitable jobs, and
suppressing creativity. In Rand's dystopia, ingenuity falls under the power
wielded by the World Council of Scholars, an effete, medieval group of pseudo-
scientists. The gift of an electric generator threatens the council's authority; the
inventor, Equality 7-2521, is forced to flee their vindictiveness and relocate on
the frontier, far from utopia's grasp.

The question of control supplies plenty of fodder for the dystopists who
followed Rand. In George Orwell's *1984* (1949) and Ray Bradbury's *Fahrenheit*

451 (1953) and "There Will Come Soft Rains" (1950), the perversion of electronics creates totalitarian control over futuristic societies. Orwell's Oceania, a post–World War II creation, exemplifies the curse of science as controller. The nation's gray joylessness reduces life to substitute goals, e.g., the promise of cash winnings from a state-run lottery, escapism through Victory Gin, protection from a shifting pool of adversaries by screaming rocket bombs, and low-level subsistence with no hope of future release. Equipped with mass communication and technological advancements, cynical politicians execute constant surveillance of homes through telescreens, which monitor citizens' private behavior and call them to daily calisthenics. In Chapter 3 of Goldstein's text, he clarifies the connection between the loss of individual freedom and perpetual war:

> [Laborers] add nothing to the wealth of the world, since whatever they produce is used for purposes of war, and the object of waging a war is always to be in a better position in which to wage another war.

The Oceanian economic treadmill saves none of its resources for human comforts. Goldstein surmises that the perpetuation of a war economy guarantees a world that is "bare, hungry, dilapidated."

Steeped in the same history as Orwell, Ray Bradbury focuses on the emptiness that overwhelms a people who are denied ideas. *Fahrenheit 451,* Bradbury's twenty-fourth-century dystopia, prophesies a nightmarish climate of ongoing warfare from which people escape through telescreens. The soap opera characters entertain and absorb viewers so completely that they think of the actors as more real than their own families. Viewers read from scripts as though they were taking part in real-life scenarios. The release gained from wall-to-wall television is a kind of fourth-dimensional evasion of the sterile, bookless world that has converted fire fighters to fire starters in an effort to stamp out literacy and empower tyranny. In his delightful short fable "There Will Come Soft Rains," (1950), Bradbury creates an agonizingly simplified version of *Fahrenheit 451*'s technology. Mrs. McClellan's house—superbly run by electric marvels that cook breakfast, vacuum the floors, and call the family to meals—remains technologically alive in Allendale, California, on August 4, 2026, after surrounding residences lie in glowing, radioactive ruin. The deceptively gentle title and the insistent calendar voice belie a horrendous cataclysm. Eerily alive and absorbed in officious duties, the house succumbs to fire. By dawn, only the calendar voice remains to announce August 5, 2026.

Less lyric and orchestrated than Bradbury's technological, apocalyptic hells and less regimented than Huxley's or Orwell's dismal dystopias is Anthony Burgess's *A Clockwork Orange.* The forced viewing of violent footage of war, torture, and savagery enables the reader to recognize the adverse possibilities of avoidance training. The mechanism is simple—an injection of a mind-altering drug, a chair, a screen, and a device to hold the eyes in place. Alex, the teenaged street waif who has landed himself in prison through repeated violations of peace and order, proves a worthy subject for brainwashing. In short order, he fights the film torture and graduates back to the streets, ostensibly a changed youth. The flaw in the system is the length of the rehabilitation process. The intervening change in English society traumatizes Alex; his pseudo-Christian virtues are easily toppled by renewed aggression from his "droog" pals and from a loss of ties with home. Evidently, Burgess does not presume that Ludovico's Technique is the answer to a well-ordered society bent on civilized behavior and respect for others.

Also spare in mechanical restraints leading to an enforced rehabilitation, Margaret Atwood's feminist fable *The Handmaid's Tale* presents little of the hardware found in the technically futuristic dystopias of Orwell, Huxley, and Bradbury. Instead, she draws on 1980s technology but illustrates how a dystopian climate could arise from misapplication or perversion of power. Atwood's Handmaids—in actuality, state-controlled breeders—are corralled in an old gymnasium within barbed-wire fences and subdued by whistle, cattle prod, and unspecified torments applied to the soles of the feet. Computer systems control medical care, banking, commerce, security, even prayers. Handmaids are tattooed with identification numbers and carry Identipasses on daily trips to the market, where they buy foodstuffs with plastic tokens. The technology is not futuristic: None of these devices is any more high tech than barcode scanners, credit cards, or televangelism.

The insidious horror of *The Handmaid's Tale* lies in technology's inability to supplant human reproduction with Huxley's birth factories in *Brave New World*. Still, Gilead's procreation system dehumanizes by forcing into service to a repressive fundamentalist theocracy its only natural resource—ovulating females. Without an in vitro system, Atwood's dystopia relies on subverted human mating similar to the eugenics of Rand's *Anthem*. Coerced by simplistic verbal jingoism punctuated with torture, public humiliation, and private interrogation, Gilead's robotic Handmaids shore up the flagging white population of Gilead by complacently serving as two-legged wombs. The women despair at the birth of deformed babies, the threat of radioactive colonies for Handmaids who don't conceive, and Unwomen, who are too old to enter the state's pool of breeders. Their only escape from either extreme is a slave-era run for freedom on the Underground Frailroad. (Aggler 1986; Atwood 1972; Bradbury 1990a; Burgess 1962; Butler 1968; Callenbach 1975; Capek and Capek 1961; *Contemporary Literary Criticism* 1987; Huxley 1932; McCombs 1988; Mathews 1978; Orwell 1949; Rand 1946; Stinson 1991; Van Spanckeren and Castro 1988)

See also Alex; *Anthem; Brave New World; Candide; Christianopolis; La Città del Sole; A Clockwork Orange;* collectivism; *A Connecticut Yankee in King Arthur's Court; Ecotopia; Erewhon;* escapism; *Fahrenheit 451;* futurism; *The Handmaid's Tale; Looking Backward, 2000–1887;* Ludovico's Technique; Lydia, Aunt; *The New Atlantis; 1984;* prophecy; *R. U. R.;* speculative fiction; "There Will Come Soft Rains"; *The Time Machine; We.*

THE TEMPEST

This conciliatory romance, written about 1611 near the end of William Shakespeare's career, suggests a time of his life when he felt the need to make peace and put his personal affairs in order. Set on the island of Bermuda, the play reunites the wronged Duke Prospero with his brother Antonio, a wicked usurper, and with Alonso, the king of Naples. By harnessing the magic of his supernatural servant Ariel, Prospero terrifies his tormentors, who have kept him and his innocent daughter Miranda exiled from court and immured on a desert isle. Prospero causes their ship to run off-course and founder on the island. Like the romantic comedy *As You Like It*, the plot of *The Tempest* concludes amicably, underscoring the themes of reconciliation and forgiveness.

Shakespeare, whose plays borrowed at length from contemporary sources, read Michel de Montaigne's *Essais* (1580), translated by Florio. The result of his study of "Des Cannibales" is a digression by Gonzalo, an idealistic royal adviser responsible for salvaging the hero and heroine, Prospero and Miranda. After Gonzalo and two scoundrels wash ashore, Gonzalo contrasts the corruption and superficiality of European society with the ingenuous "noble savages" of the New World, an idea that persisted into the eighteenth century in Denis Diderot's *Supplement to Bougainville's "Voyages"* (1772).

Parallel to Montaigne's summary of the qualities of Brazilian natives, Gonzalo notes that untutored natives possess a vigor and appreciation for life that jaded Europeans have lost over centuries of socialization. In Gonzalo's version of this argument, he dreams of a commonwealth devoid of traffic and magistrates, a place where no one studies or accumulates wealth and where poverty does not exist. He includes

> No use of metal, corn, or wine, or oil;
> No occupation; all men idle, all;
> And women too, but innocent and pure;
> No sovereignty . . .
> All things in common nature should produce
> Without sweat or endeavor. (II, i, 156–159, 162–163)

In this perfect microcosm, men and women coexist in harmony, innocence, and purity, and live off the land. Essential to Gonzalo's utopia is the absence of violence and war, for he promises, "Treason, felony, sword, pike, knife, gun, or need of any engine would I not have." Gonzalo summarizes that his dream world would "excel the golden age."

In an ornamented and uncharacteristically saccharine speech in Act IV, Iris, the rainbow messenger of the gods, enters with Ceres, goddess of the harvest, to set the stage for Prospero's masque. Ceres greets Iris and praises her

> Who, with thy saffron wings, upon my flowers
> Diffusest honey drops, refreshing showers,
> And with each end of thy blue bow dost crown
> My bosky acres and my unshrubbed down,
> Rich scarf to my proud earth . . . (IV, i, 78–82)

The scene, splendid with the arrival of Juno, goddess of matrimony, and her naiads, enraptures Ferdinand, who marvels,

Let me live here ever!
So rare a wondered father and a wise
Makes this place Paradise. (IV, i, 122–124)

Prospero, creator of a grand illusion, returns the vision to earthly proportions by reminding Ferdinand, his future son-in-law, of human mortality: "We are such stuff as dreams are made of, and our little life is rounded with a sleep." (IV, i, 156–158)

The antithesis of Gonzalo's idyll and Prospero's ephemeral playacting is exemplified in Caliban, a character whose name is an approximate anagram of cannibal, a term Shakespeare no doubt borrowed from Montaigne's essay. An elemental savage exploited as servant and dray, Caliban and his lurking evil suggests in creature in Mary Shelley's *Frankenstein*, an engineered monstrosity taught to speak the human language but burdened by lust, bestiality, and the absence of conscience or soul. As the obverse of the noble savage, Caliban nimbly mouths both wit and poesy, yet Prospero curses his efforts and labels him "a devil, a born devil." (IV, i, 188) (Boyce 1990; Diderot 1972; Lamb 1966; Papp and Kirkland 1988; Sandler 1986; Shakespeare 1961)

See also As You Like It; "Des Cannibales"; Diderot, Denis; golden age; Shakespeare, William; slavery; *Supplement aux Voyages de Bougainville*.

TENNYSON, ALFRED

England's poet laureate at the height of the Victorian era, Alfred, Lord Tennyson set the moral tone for a half-century of British literature. Born August 6, 1809, in Somersby, Lincolnshire, he was the third son and fourth child of 12 born to Elizabeth Fytche and George Clayton Tennyson, an abusive, alcoholic minister. Destined for landless penury, from childhood Tennyson read literary classics and displayed a prodigious talent with words. He was educated at home, then advanced to Trinity College, Cambridge, and distinguished himself at age 20 by winning the chancellor's award for "Timbuctoo," a poem in blank verse. In 1833 the death of Tennyson's college classmate, Arthur Henry Hallam, inspired one of the era's most beloved verse cycles, *In Memoriam* (1850).

Because of his meager earnings, the failure of an investment in the wood-carving industry, nervous collapse, and the melancholic tendencies of his forebears, Tennyson was age 41 when he married Emily Sellwood and fathered a son, named Hallam in honor of his deceased friend. Secure in his literary reputation for elegy, lyrical verse, ballads, epic, and verse drama on classic themes such as "Locksley Hall" and "Locksley Hall Sixty Years After," "Ulysses," "The Lady of Shalotte," and "Morte d'Arthur," in 1850 he accepted the appointment of poet laureate upon the death of William Wordsworth, one of his staunchest supporters. The post symbolized a changing of the guard from the Romantic era to the vigorous and ethically profound Victorians.

Resettled on the Isle of Wight, Tennyson profited from notoriety with strong sales of *Idylls of the King* (1888) and *Maud* (1853). He steadily produced quality verse and drama, concluding with *Tiresias* (1885) and *The Foresters* (1892). At his death on October 6, 1892, he was interred with state honors in Westminster Abbey's Poet's Corner. Late-Victorian and Edwardian critics questioned the extensive accolades heaped on Tennyson, whom they accused of obsequiousness to the royal family. However, the post-Edwardian age brought a renewed interest in his metrical perfection, sense imagery, and noble themes, particularly a growing doubt about the beneficence of the Industrial Revolution. (Albright 1986; Rosenberg 1973; Stephens et al. 1949)

See also Arthur; Camelot; escapism; *Idylls of the King;* "Locksley Hall"; Lotus-Eaters.

 # THEOCRACY

A theocracy is a government common to primitive, elemental, or isolated societies and founded on religious dogma, visions, prophecy, scripture, or a combination of these factors. Over time, theocracies have governed such god-centered people as the earliest Greeks and Romans, Native American tribes, Polynesian nations, Muslims, Jews, Buddhists, and Mormons. Such governments require a priest or religious council to interpret matters on which scripture, visions, prophecy, or church laws are unclear. In many cases, citizens in a theocracy respect the concept of the divine right of kings, which sets up a hierarchy from God to king to the people he rules; in some examples, classism stratifies residents further, as in a division of the king's subjects into aristocrats or lords, knights, clergy, artisans, commoners, and slaves. Theocratic nations accept civil governance administered by a godly person who is guided in some way by a deity; examples include the English Commonwealth set up by Oliver Cromwell and the Puritans; Geneva, Switzerland, under John Calvin; the miniature fiefdom in Rome's Vatican City; and the Massachusetts Bay Colony, which John Winthrop ruled. Cases of sacrilege or sinful behavior—for instance, the immodest dress, makeup, or misbehavior of a Muslim woman in an Islamic state—are tried in religious courts along with other crimes and misdemeanors.

Theocracy permeates utopian literature from earliest times to the present. There exists a body of utopias that depend on the religiosity, piety, and righteousness of its rulers and visionaries, e.g., Francis Bacon's *New Atlantis* (1627), John Bunyan's *Pilgrim's Progress* (1678), Thomas Carlyle's *Past and Present* (1843), Henry Wadsworth Longfellow's *The Song of Hiawatha* (1855), W. H. Hudson's *A Crystal Age* (1887), John G. Neihardt's *Black Elk Speaks* (1932), James Hilton's *Lost Horizon* (1933), Hermann Hesse's *Siddhartha* (1951), and Alex Haley's *The Autobiography of Malcolm X* (1965). However, these works fall short of true theocracy because their obedience to ethical and civil law parallels godliness in a clear separation of church and state. To locate god-centered governments, the reader must turn to Hesiod, John Milton, Dante Alighieri, Johann Andreae, and Margaret Atwood.

- Written about the time of Homer, Hesiod's *Theogony* and *Works and Days* (eighth century B.C.) describe a mythic time on Earth when the gods lived close to humankind in a relationship similar to that of the book of Genesis (950 B.C.). The communication between god or gods and followers is often described as face-to-face—for example, Prometheus's punishment for stealing Zeus's fire and giving it to humankind, and the creation of Adam and Eve and their punishment and expulsion from the garden of Eden for disobeying the rules laid down by God.

- The dramatic setting pitting God against Satan for tempting the first couple reappears in John Milton's epic *Paradise Lost* (1667) and peripherally in *Paradise Regained* (1671); it is also the focus of George Bernard Shaw's five-act play *Back to Methuselah* (1921). Although both works draw on the Old Testament story, the writers work the plot to their will and purpose. Milton, a godly man coping with a divisive era that resulted in the beheading of England's Charles I and the creation of Cromwell's Puritan commonwealth, chooses Eden over the legend of King Arthur for a focus. Milton clearly states his didactic purpose: "To justify the ways of God to man." Shaw, on the other hand, expands the biblical account with settings outside Eden and a blend of the original characters with Lilith, a mythic earth mother. Lacking the orthodoxy of *Paradise Lost*, Shaw's play depicts the difficulties inherent in immortality, which grows tiresome and counterproductive to the first couple after they have spent centuries on Earth.

Over time, theocracy, as an outgrowth of human expectations of religion and the afterlife, remained in vogue in European utopias.

- In the early days of the Italian Renaissance, Dante Alighieri wrote *The Divine Comedy* (1320), a guided verse tour of hell, purgatory, and heaven. At the top, Dante pictures the Almighty overseeing and ruling every descending stair and ring of the territories below his throne. Less noble and pious than Milton, Dante bore personal and political grudges against Florentine politicians, who had made his life more like hell than heaven. He derived sweet vengeance by incorporating punishments for great villains and the petty men who ejected him from his home state.

- *Christianopolis* (1619), a better example of theocracy than Dante's, is the fictional locale of Johann Andreae's utopian dream, which grew out of Fra Tomaso Campanella's priest-guided city, *La Città del Sole* (1602). Andreae published a practical layout covering more civic necessities than had earlier creators of theocracies. Against a tight overlay of Christian law, Andreae allows for art, beauty, and exercise. His 400 devout citizens study religious history and join for morning, noon, and evening prayers in an atmosphere made wholesome by total obedience to the teachings of Christ.

The twentieth century's contribution to theocratic utopianism exists primarily in the negative. Gilead, the dystopic setting of Margaret Atwood's *The Handmaid's Tale* (1985), was once a New England town under U.S. constitutional law. After fundamentalist fanatics overran the country and slaughtered its authority figures, Gilead came under religious tyranny in a pseudotheocratic takeover aimed specifically at females. Ostensibly, Gilead's philosophy of breeder wives obeys two stories from Genesis:

- the story of Abram; when his wife Sarai proved barren, he mated with his wife's maid, Haggar, and conceived Ishmael. In token of Sarai's pregnancy long after her childbearing years, the couple change their names to Abraham and Sarah, meaning "father of many" and "princess." (Genesis 17, 21)

- the saga of Jacob's sons; his two wives, Leah and Rachel; and their two handmaidens, Bilhah and Zilpah. In Jacob's later years, he changed his name to Israel. His sons were known as the founders of the Twelve Tribes of Israel. (Genesis 29–30)

Stretching beyond these historic beginnings, Atwood's modern theocracy resembles speculative fiction more than a resetting of biblical teachings or tenets. Her insidious theocracy is murderous, un-Christian, and power-motivated when the drive to enhance Gilead's population results in execution of homosexuals and dissident priests, suicidal Handmaids, jealous Wives, and husbands who frequent Jezebel's, a night spot reminiscent of the sinful pre-Gileadan days. (Andreae 1955; Atwood 1972; Campanella 1955; Dante Alighieri 1968; Hesiod 1957; Hesiod 1966; Hesiod 1973; Holy Bible 1958; Milton 1957b; Shaw 1988)

See also Adam; *Back to Methuselah; Christianopolis; La Città del Sole; Divina Commedia;* Eden; Eve; Genesis; Gilead; *The Handmaid's Tale;* Hesiod; Lydia, Aunt; *Paradise Lost; Pilgrim's Progress.*

 # "THERE WILL COME SOFT RAINS"

Ray Bradbury's short dystopic fantasy was published in 1950. Because of the author's typically spare, emotive use of language, this brief short story seizes the fancy of science-fiction readers and has commanded unique respect among longer, more detailed utopian literature. The story is a blend of fable and speculative fiction. On August 4, 2026, a modern house in Allendale, California, displays mechanical wizardry in the most mundane matters. Like a children's nursery rhyme, the magical house calls "Tick-tock, seven o'clock, time to get up, time to get up, seven o'clock!" A programmed stove makes toast, bacon, and eggs sunny-side up, then pours milk and coffee. It announces birthdays, bills to be paid, and social obligations. By 8:00 A.M., it disperses nonexistent children to school.

Bradbury's keen sense of the dehumanization caused by technology stresses the ineffectual "housework" of this futuristic residence. Empty, but unable to comprehend that its voice tapes reach no human ears, the house clears up the breakfast dishes and sends cleaning robots to vacuum and scurry after dust. At ten o'clock, the morning rain ceases on "a city of rubble and ashes . . . the one house left standing." At night, a radioactive glow warns no remaining human of the dangers of nuclear war. Mechanized hands continue to perform meaningless mowings, waterings, and garden sprucing. At noon, the dog, the only living being, whines for food. As the stove continues to make pancakes, the dog whirls in a frenzy and expires. Mechanical mice incinerate the decaying body in the cellar.

Like the tale of the Sorceror's Apprentice, the house in Bradbury's narrative churns efficiently toward chaos as the days of August approach the sixth, the date of the American bombing of Hiroshima, Japan. Amusements and habits keep the house occupied—cigars to light, hands of cards to deal, music to play, dinner to prepare. A disembodied electronic voice calls to Mrs. McClellan and reads the verse of Sara Teasdale, which ends: "Not one would mind, neither bird nor tree, if mankind perished utterly; and Spring herself, when she woke at dawn would scarcely know that we were gone." At ten that evening, the house sprouts a fire that outwits protective mechanisms, and the building succumbs to flames. By dawn, the calendar voice, which is all that remains of Mrs. McClellan's family and their splendid, technologically advanced home, proclaims: "Today is August 5, 2026, today is August 5, 2026, today is. . . ." (Bradbury 1975; Bradbury 1990a; Indick 1989; Johnson 1978; Mogen 1986; Slusser 1977a)

See also Bradbury, Ray; *Fahrenheit 451*; speculative fiction; technology.

THOREAU, HENRY DAVID

American philosopher, teacher, essayist, moralist, mystic, and one of the New World's most individualistic thinkers, Thoreau wrote *Walden* (1854), a rambling, introspective treatise on his withdrawal from society to subsist in the wild. Henry David Thoreau was born on July 12, 1817, in Boston, Massachusetts, and lived in what he considered to be just the right time. He attended Concord Academy and worked as a pencil maker in his father's factory. With his earnings, he enrolled at Harvard University in Cambridge and graduated at age 20 with a grounding in composition, the classics, and the professions, none of which appealed to him. He was dubbed a failure after he gave up classroom teaching and joined his father in making land surveys.

As the Emerson family's handyman, Thoreau came under the influence of his friend and neighbor, Ralph Waldo Emerson, Harvard professor, cogent lecturer, father of the American transcendentalists, and editor of their journal, *The Dial*. Thoreau, the youngest of the Transcendental Club, followed Emerson's precepts of "Know thyself" and "Study nature." He began writing in 1837 by keeping a journal, which he maintained until his death. During his quarter-century of note-taking, possibly influenced by his brother John's death from tetanus in 1842, Thoreau grew restless and pensive as he examined much of the philosophy of his age. In 1845 he rebelled against the Mexican War by opting for a jail term rather than support an immoral war.

By departing from Concord and building a cabin in March 1845, Thoreau prepared the way for a unique American work, *Walden,* for which he collected

Henry David Thoreau, in 1856 daguerreotype by Benjamin D. Maxham

material from July 4, 1845, to September 6, 1847. A series of introspective essays, the musings form a commentary on the self, which Thoreau sought by withdrawing from worldly distractions. The pond itself, like the cohesive force of Black Elk's plains and Shakespeare's Arden Forest, became the author's source and focus, embodying real contact with the heavens and unity with nature. *Walden* sold only 2,000 copies in its first five years in print and did not reach its zenith of popularity until the 1970s, when American youth mounted a counterculture and used Thoreau's pronouncements as an unofficial creed.

In 1847 Thoreau traveled in Europe and Canada and returned home to a nation obsessed by the questions of slavery and states' rights. His answer to abolitionists, "Civil Disobedience" (1849), preceded a speech defending John Brown, who was hanged for engineering an attempted revolt. Thoreau was devastated by Brown's execution, and as his health declined, he escaped harmful passions by withdrawing into his father's surveying trade. On tramps through the wild, he collected specimens of reptiles and plants for Harvard biologists. His data-filled notes supplied material for numerous articles in *The Union Magazine, The Dial,* and *Putnam's Monthly.* At his death from tuberculosis on May 6, 1862, his 43-volume collection of observations and works was parceled out to Harvard University's library; the J. Pierpont Morgan Library in New York; the Huntington Library in San Marino, California; and the New York and Concord, Massachusetts, public libraries.

A pacifist and unofficial Luddite, Thoreau used a nonviolent approach in fighting nineteenth-century social and economic perfectionism. He championed in its stead the inner peace he found while walking, gardening, fishing, contemplating the sky, and communing with the seasons on the banks of Walden Pond. His idealism permeates a score of oft-quoted aphorisms, e.g., "There is an infinitude in the private man!" and "We are born innocents. We are polluted by advice." He epitomized William Wordsworth's belief that "nature never did betray the heart that loved her." Neither too idealistic nor too cynical, Thoreau attuned himself to a level of contentment brought about by living up to his own sense of self. His values, as expressed in *Walden,* became the rallying cry of generations of disciples who departed city life, avoided military and economic competition, and studied ways of becoming one with nature. Both Mohandas Gandhi and Dr. Martin Luther King, Jr., emulated his regard for peaceful resistance to unjust laws. (Harding 1965; Lane 1961; Lawrence and Lee 1971; Ruland 1968; Thoreau 1965)

See also Arden; Black Elk; Carlyle, Thomas; escapism; golden age; heaven; naturalism; *Past and Present;* technology; transcendentalism; *Walden.*

THROUGH THE EYE OF THE NEEDLE

An epistolary novel, it is the second of William Dean Howells's shallow, altruistic utopias. The title was taken from the biblical warning that it is easier for a camel to pass through the needle's eye than for a rich man to enter heaven, which prepares the reader for the persistent vein of Christian didacticism that laces the text. Probably written shortly after the first volume, it was published in 1907, 13 years after *A Traveler from Altruria* (1894) as well as several influential English and American utopian novels by William Morris, Edward Bellamy, and H. G. Wells. Reintroducing the character of Altrurian emissary Aristides Homos, the story yields to a polemical discussion of American beliefs versus American practices. In Chapter 8, Homos, an astute observer, recognizes that although American slavery is at an end, the servant class receives only a few privileges and rights to set it apart from outright servitude. In contrast, the privileged class frequents showy clubs, where they loll in comfort, eat heartily, and indulge their whims.

Howells exploits the discomforts of urban life through Homos's discussion of the inefficiency and unlivability of New York tenement life with Mrs. Dorothea Makely, a voluble matron whom he meets on his first visit to the United States. In Chapter 7 she candidly describes the inconvenience and unaesthetic conditions:

> You've noticed the little front yard, about as big as a handkerchief, generally, and the steps leading down to the iron gate, which is kept locked, and the basement door inside the gate? Well, that's what you might call the back elevator of a house. . . . We have no alleys in New York, the blocks are so narrow, north and south; and, of course, we have no back doors; so we have to put the garbage out on the sidewalk. . . . Underneath the sidewalk there are bins where people keep their coal and kindling.

She invites Homos to a Thanksgiving feast, an ostentatious display of food, champagne, and table settings arranged and replenished by her hovering staff. A widow, Mrs. P. Bellington Strange, states the egalitarian conclusion that Voltaire reaches in *Candide* (1759) and on which Theodor Hertzka focuses in *Freiland* (1890): "I wish we had to work, all of us, and that we could be freed from our servile bondage to servants."

Howells concocts a union between an American and the Altrurian visitor after Homos grows fond of Mrs. Strange and, against the advice of her mother, marries her. Rejecting any suggestion that he settle in the United States, Homos returns to Altruria via a nine-day steamer voyage through the South Seas. Eveleth, his "capitalistic wife," dresses in corseted waist, leg-of-mutton sleeves, pointed-toed high heels, and a picture hat, to the consternation of Altrurians, who prefer sandals and a classic drapery similar to fifth-century Greece, a touch that brings to mind H. G. Wells's Eloi in *The Time Machine* (1895). Howells makes an issue of the tyranny of fashion to remind the reader that a needless changing of styles is both profligate and shallow-minded. Eveleth remarks that the simple life in Altruria has helped her lose 25 pounds because she stopped overeating.

An enlightening incident in Chapter 9 places the matter of classism in perspective. Homos and his wife are touring Altruria's capitals when they recognize an American plutocrat, Mr. Thrall, who has wrecked his yacht on Altruria's coast and pitched a tent to house his wife, daughter, and son-in-law until they can be rescued. He is unfamiliar with Altruria's socialist society and expects to be catered to by people who will work for money. To his embarrassment, Altrurians consider him a bloated social parasite and force him to earn his keep. Thrall reflects on money, charity, and the effect his wealth once had on society and on his relationship with others:

> I was long ago satisfied that I could really do no good with it. Perhaps if I had had more faith in it I might have done some good with it, but I believe that I never did anything but harm, even when I seemed to be helping the most, for I was aiding in the perpetuation of a state of things essentially wrong.

Homos and his wife visit Thrall's tent and make a serious faux pas by mistaking Mrs. Thrall for a servant, a social situation that the last name "Thrall" brings to mind. By Chapter 15, Thrall has been Altrurianized, but his wife clings to her former elitist life. In her final letter to Aristides, Mrs. Homos wonders if the captain of the *Little Sally* will cease shuttling between Altruria and the outside world and abandon the United States. (Bennett 1973; Cowie 1951; Escholtz 1975; Howells 1907; Howells 1957)

See also Altruria; classism; didacticism; *Through the Eye of the Needle; A Traveler from Altruria.*

 # *TIMAEUS*

One of Plato's dialogues dating to the fifth century B.C., Greece's golden age, *Timaeus* is taken from Socrates's interaction with two friends, Timaeus and Critias. Critias tells a story that his grandfather got from Solon, Greece's renowned and much-respected lawgiver. In a momentous act of self-determination, Greece overthrew Atlantis, an idyllic island larger than Asia and Libya combined, which lay in the Atlantic Ocean at the Pillar of Herakles (the ancient name for Gibraltar). Already overlords of Libya, the Atlanteans threatened Athens itself, subdued nations, and terrorized enemies as far east as the shores of the Tyrrhenian Sea until a catastrophic earthquake destroyed it. According to Critias, the legendary utopia of Atlantis sank into the sea.

Timaeus takes his turn and recites the Greek concept of creation, which contrasts the simpler Hebrew version of Adam and Eve in the Garden of Eden. Timaeus describes how God created the orderly world out of chaos and blessed it alone of heavenly bodies with intelligence and soul. A necessary tension among water, air, fire, and earth supplied the planet with balance in the form of a mathematical formula that mimics the proportions of the Pythagorean scale. From God's precise shaping of matter evolved the seven planets—Sun, Mercury, Venus, Moon, Saturn, Mars, and Jupiter. By regulating the heavenly bodies, God created a distinct pattern of time, including day and night, months and years, and the cycles of the stars.

From the same elements as made up the world, God created the human soul and blessed the best of human beings with a return to life among the stars. To the wicked, he designated a reforming process to rid their souls of self-inflicted evils. God dispensed rationality as a governing agent and gave each human a voice, hearing, and rhythm. The chemistry of the body God designed from a blend of astringency, harshness, bitterness, saltiness, acidity, and sweetness. He made the ears to hear all variations of sound; the eyes, equally discriminating, were capable of minute differentiation of light and color.

God set the soul in the head and mortality in the chest. These he inflamed with passion and desire. To govern these opposites, he placed the liver as guide and the spleen to regulate the liver. The apportionment of intestines, bone, flesh, marrow, joints, and muscles concluded with a covering of flesh. He finished the human frame with hair and nails, right and left sides, and the ability to draw air into the lungs. At his command, the young body, which was born in balance, grew old and died when balance collapsed and inner harmony ceased, thereby loosening the soul from its moorings. Critias notes that natural death gives no pain, but violence causes a wretched demise.

Disease, explains the storyteller, indicated an imbalance in the four elements and a disharmony of the bodily functions. The best way to regulate natural functions was through exercise. To undergird the soul with order and strength and to keep it safe from ambition and desire, the human being had to exercise the inner divinity, which dwelled in the head. The worst of these beings were females, who evolved from cowards and criminals. Simple-minded men evolved into birds; sybarites became wild animals; fools became reptiles; and the least rational men became fish. Critias concludes his creation fable with a nod to the intellectual, who bears God's image: "the greatest, best, fairest, most perfect." (Hare 1982; Jordan 1981; Lodge 1956; Nettleship 1968; Plato 1937a; Plato 1937b; Rouse 1956; Snodgrass 1988a; Warner 1958)

See also Adam; Atlantis; Eden; Plato; *The Republic;* utopia; women in utopia.

 # *THE TIME MACHINE*

H. G. Wells's 1895 dystopian novella and whimsical social allegory views future generations through the experiences of a fictional tinker, philosopher, and Time Traveller. The book pursues standard Wellsian themes, particularly the devaluation of working-class people in a technological era. Like Ray Bradbury, William Morris, W. H. Hudson, Karel Capek, and Jack London, Wells doubts that advancements or progress warrant the despair they inflict on workers who are displaced by machines.

The story opens on a Thursday soiree in late-Victorian Richmond, England, where the unnamed central character introduces a gathering of male dinner guests—an editor, medical man, provincial mayor, psychologist, and the story's narrator—to the fourth dimension: the breeching of the time barrier. He excuses himself and retrieves from his laboratory an unimpressive metal framework the size of a clock, which is a model of a two-levered time machine two years in the making. After demonstrating the prototype, he escorts his guests to the laboratory, seats himself in the saddle of the real contraption, activates its levers, and disappears.

In accordance with the Time Traveller's written instructions, the unnamed medical man chairs the next Thursday's meeting at the same locale until the arrival of the host. In scruffy, grass-stained coat, and blood-smeared socks, and with a pale, haggard complexion and grayer hair, the Time Traveller joins the assemblage in his dining room and squints at the light. He mutters inarticulately, "I'm—funny! Be all right in a minute," and wanders out to change clothes. After bolting two glasses of champagne and a plate of mutton, he explains that, since four o'clock that afternoon, he has passed eight days of time travel.

Wells presents the gist of his plot through the convention of polite table talk. The Traveller narrates the dizzy departure of his invention, which spins him through time before he can exert control. He arrives at a garden surrounded by massive marble statues and fallen architecture, attempts to remount for an escape, and upsets his machine, which lacerates his chin. The Eloi, a graceful, diminutive people clad in effeminate robes, welcome him to London in the year A.D. 802,701. To prevent tampering with his machine, he detaches its lever and joins his indolent companions for a meal of fruit. That evening, the Traveller discovers that his machine is missing. Terrified that he is forever lost in the distant future, he aims to copy the original to assure his return. The next day, he locates tracks that lead to a pedestal.

The rhythmic hum of engines draws the Time Traveller to a series of circular wells. Before he can investigate, he hears the pitiful cries of a drowning woman and rushes toward the Thames to rescue her. The victim, Weena, becomes his devoted companion and explains the idiosyncrasies of the Eloi, who fear the apelike Morlocks, foul-odored subterranean carnivores who creep out of the wells on moonless nights and attack them. The Traveller deduces that the future of humanity lies in the two disparate species, Eloi and Morlocks.

Undismayed by the alter ego of the Eloi, the Time Traveller attempts to climb down a well, but returns to Weena. She emphasizes that the Morlocks are dangerous only during the dark of the moon. The Traveller enters the remnants of the Green Porcelain Palace, a deserted shell of a museum. Inside he sees the shape of a brontosaurus, fossils, ore samples, books, and other preserved flora and fauna. Among the relics on the dusty shelves he locates useful weapons—an iron bar, matches, and a lump of camphor, which will terrify light-sensitive Morlocks with flame. On the way past an armor gallery and a display of idols, the Traveller carries Weena outside and through dense woods, where Morlocks leap out in unprovoked attack. To defend himself and Weena, the Time Traveller strikes a light and sets the woods on fire. Morlock hands seize his matches. The Traveller takes on his attackers in hand-to-hand combat. In the scuffle, Weena vanishes.

Through the haze, the Time Traveller returns to the museum to regain his bearings. He is sad and lonely without Weena, his faithful guide and interpreter. Inside the pedestal of the White Sphinx near the Eloi hall he discovers his time machine, which the thieves have oiled and polished. But before he can return to his own time, Morlocks slam shut the bronze panels and encircle him. Quickly, he eludes their grasp by mounting the saddle and traveling farther into the future.

Wells emphasizes his protagonist's curiosity and courage by taking him so far into the future that life has lost its original meaning. The Time Traveller halts the spinning years. On a desolate shore, he confronts grotesque, over-sized crabs. On he travels until he reaches a sterile landscape 30 million years in the future. Retracing his wayward jaunt to the past, he searches for clues to his native era as the dial flashes back to zero. Trembling violently, he alights in his lab for the Thursday gathering. The silent guests doubt his narrative but, undaunted by their skepticism, the Time Traveller prepares for a second departure. In a flash, he sets out on a three-year trip. The only proof that substantiates his first trip are specimens of an unusual flower, which he leaves behind. (Geduld 1987; Parrinder 1986; Snodgrass 1990; Wells 1964)

See also bestiality; Eloi; Morlocks; technology; Weena; Wells, H. G.; women in utopia.

 # TOTALITARIANISM

The coercive, tyrannous government of citizens by deities, fiat, intimidation, religious decree, military control, or police state, totalitarianism is a major theme in utopian literature. It exists in degrees of harshness, from the benign rule of Prince Hoh in Fra Tomaso Campanella's *La Città del Sole* (1602), religious councils in Johann Andreae's *Christianopolis* (1619), and Father Perrault in James Hilton's *Lost Horizons* (1933) to the harsher controls on Étienne Cabet's *Voyage en Icarie* (1840) and the young-adult classic, L. Frank Baum's *The Wonderful Wizard of Oz* (1900), whose facade of tyranny turns out to be a sham. The most gruesome and soul-grinding of totalitarian states override human instincts and yearnings in several notable examples:

- Voltaire's *Candide* (1759), a picaresque blend of adventures among communities that acquiesce to kings, tyrants, cruel monks, and the judges and torture experts of the Spanish Inquisition

- Yevgeny Zamyatin's *We* (1921), an overmastered state that crushes individuality with such devices as passes for lovemaking and medical care for normal emotions and creativity

- Ayn Rand's *Anthem* (1937), a committee-ruled commune where technology is suppressed, people are mated by selective pairing, and children have no choice of a career

- Ray Bradbury's *Fahrenheit 451* (1953), in which a bizarre twist of logic puts fire companies at the forefront of tyranny over books and bibliophiles

- Richard Adams's *Watership Down* (1972), a safe haven for rabbits who escape the tyrant General Woundwort and free domestic rabbits from farm pens

- a repressive state mental hospital where staff rely on thorazine and incarceration as a restraint to psychotic women like Connie Ramos, protagonist of Marge Piercy's *Woman on the Edge of Time* (1976)

- the stifling, crazy-making theocracy of Margaret Atwood's *The Handmaid's Tale* (1985), a fundamentalist stronghold that commandeers women and forces them to breed children for the state's elite families

- the omnipotent committee that chooses Jonas to be the next Receiver in Lois Lowry's *The Giver* (1993)

The epitome of crushing dominion occurs in the classics of twentieth-century dystopianism: Aldous Huxley's *Brave New World* (1932) and George Orwell's *Animal Farm* (1945) and *1984* (1949). The flawed systems that overwhelm the citizenry of these fictional states mirror actual regimes, e.g., the fascist and communist states that preceded and followed World War II. (Huxley 1932; Orwell 1946; Orwell 1949)

See also *Animal Farm*; *Brave New World*; classism; Huxley, Aldous; *1984*; Orwell, George; technology.

✺ TRANSCENDENTALISM ✺

Transcendentalism is a blend of romanticism and mysticism prominent in American literary thought during the mid-1900s—the turbulent era of soul-searching that preceded the Civil War. Led by Ralph Waldo Emerson, Ellery Channing, Nathaniel Hawthorne, Bronson Alcott, and Henry David Thoreau, author of *Walden* (1854), the New England transcendentalists included writers, theologians, orators, and artists who read and discussed Emanuel Kant, Thomas Carlyle, Samuel Taylor Coleridge, Johann Goethe, and William Wordsworth. Literature published by the American transcendentalists focused on nature, manual labor, introspection, and spiritual oneness with the universe. By avoiding the trap of money and property, Emerson and other members of the Transcendental Club cleansed themselves of greed, gluttony, and other self-destructive habits, including the ill-effects of tobacco and alcohol. Intuitively, each member of the group contributed toward the emancipation of slaves and women.

The Unitarian movement, an American brand of antiestablishment religion on the far end of the spectrum from Puritanism, began in 1825 as an offshoot of romanticism and transcendentalism. Led by William Ellery Channing, who supported an intuitive syncretism of all human visions of God, and the literary impact of the essays and lectures of Ralph Waldo Emerson during the 1830s and 1840s, Unitarians formed a creedless, laissez-faire congregation who respected the individual's perception of self, God, and society. Their name derives from a belief in a unified deity rather than the Trinity, which occupies a central place in Christianity. (Harding 1965; Holman 1981; Lane 1961; Ruland 1968; Thoreau 1965)

See also Carlyle, Thomas; golden age; naturalism; syncretism; Thoreau, Henry David; *Walden*; women in utopia.

A TRAVELER FROM ALTRURIA

The first of two idealistic Christian fables written in pseudonovel form in 1894 by Bostonian William Dean Howells, it is a plotless, reflective piece. The novel works backward by having the speaker travel from a haven to reality to assess the progress of the United States toward a perfect society. The book is grounded on the well-worn device used by Mark Twain's *A Connecticut Yankee in King Arthur's Court* (1886), H. G. Wells's *The Time Machine* (1895), and James Hilton's *Lost Horizons* (1933)—the foreign visitor who criticizes the speaker's milieu. Following the convention of inaccessibility, Altruria has remained undiscovered until recent times. An Altrurian—Aristides Homos, a polite, punctilious everyman—settles into a mountain summer retreat to study the United States. Homos encounters unusual companions because Howells deliberately populates his cast with colorful allegorical caricatures: writer Twelvemough, widow Peggy Makely, and Mr. Bullion, a banker.

While studying under Twelvemough, his guide, Homos applies to real situations the precepts of the Declaration of Independence by assisting shoe shiners, scullery maids, and baggage clerks with heavy loads, and by honoring all levels of work. Understanding Homos's notions of pure democracy, Bullion rationalizes American inequities:

> We have not a political aristocracy, that is all; but there is as absolute a division between the orders of men, and as little love, in this country as in any country of the globe. The severance of the man who works for his living with his hands from the man who does not work for his living with his hands is so complete, and apparently so final, that nobody even imagines else, not even in fiction.

This plain-spoken admission of classism summons no rebuttal. Americans may maintain a surface appreciation of democracy, but at the heart of the economy there exists an infernal dichotomy of moneyed owners and worn-down laborers.

In Chapter 7 Homos has a chance to interview Reuben Camp, who is Mrs. Makely's employee. Mrs. Makely insists that, despite differences in opinion, "we all have the same country." Camp vents his spleen in retort:

> America is one thing for you, and it's quite another thing for us. America means ease, and comfort, and amusement for you, year in and year out, and if it means work, it's work that you *wish* to do. For us, America means work that we *have* to do, and hard work, all the time, if we're going to make both ends meet.

With obvious vitriol, he adds that no hungry person knows liberty. Likewise, blacklisted workers become pariahs to employers after word gets around that they won't knuckle under to tyrannical business owners.

The Altrurian continues finding aspects of the nation that require attention. He tours the countryside, pitying a tramp and recoiling from the horror of clear-cutting, an entrepreneurial venture that decimates a forest and burns out the stumps at the edge of a lake. The speaker justifies the commercialism of the owner, who intends to sell the denuded tract for building lots. The speaker glorifies individuality and property rights as evidences of a "very perfect system," leading the Altrurian to demand pointedly, "Do I understand you that, in America, a man may do what is wrong with his own?"

The visitor shames the United States with a description of Altrurian philosophy, a collectivist stance by which the community's rights supersede those of the individual. Homos contrasts the American freedom of property disposal to Altrurian community laws regulating marriage and prohibiting "theft and murder and slander and incest and perjury and drunkenness . . . [and] cruelty to animals." In conclusion, the Altrurian notes that Americans detest immorality as much as do his own fellow citizens. Howells's lame conclusion that all will right itself in the end exemplifies the do-gooder's heartfelt intentions and total lack of perception that societies evolve by plan, not chance. (Bennett 1973; Cowie 1951; Escholtz 1975; Howells 1907; Howells 1957; Parrington 1964)

See also Altruria; classism; *Through the Eye of the Needle; A Traveler from Altruria.*

TWAIN, MARK

America's best-loved humorist, Twain is the author of *A Connecticut Yankee in King Arthur's Court* (1886), a dystopian fantasy that places a late-nineteenth-century tinker in sixth-century Camelot. Mark Twain, the pseudonym of Samuel Langhorne Clemens, was born in Florida, Missouri, on November 30, 1835, to attorney John Marshall Clemens and Jane Lampton Clemens, a sweet-tempered Virginia aristocrat. A talented mimic who absorbed the diversity and humor of many parts of the country, Twain grew up on the banks of the Mississippi River, which he hoped would carry him far from his rural beginnings. At age four Twain moved to Hannibal and enjoyed idyllic country life until his father's death forced him to leave school at age 18 and learn the printer's trade. In daily contact with manuscripts and type for the *Hannibal Journal,* he began writing under various pen names. He obtained his river pilot's license a few years before the Civil War, but worked only four years before river travel ceased.

The war, which destroyed Twain's childhood dream of piloting a stern-wheeler, might have ended his life as well. After enlisting in the Confederate army, Twain reconsidered his role in the military; two weeks later, he deserted. With his brother Orion, the newly appointed secretary to the governor of Nevada, he journeyed by stage to Carson City, prospected for silver, and wrote for the Virginia City *Territorial Enterprise.* Published under his well-known pseudonym, Twain's first serious short story, "The Celebrated Jumping Frog of Calavaras County," launched a career that covered humor, essays, young-adult literature, autobiography, satire, lectures, history, and travelogues.

In 1869 Twain wed Olivia Langdon and settled in Buffalo, New York, where he edited the *Buffalo Express.* From there he moved to his famous riverboat mansion in Hartford, Connecticut, where he wrote *Roughing It* (1872), *The Adventures of Tom Sawyer* (1876), *The Prince and the Pauper* (1882), and *Life on the Mississippi* (1883). He reached the height of his fame with *The Adventures of Huckleberry Finn* (1884), a classic work in the young-adult canon. He followed

Samuel Langhorne Clemens, known by his pen name Mark Twain

two years later with *A Connecticut Yankee in King Arthur's Court*. A chaotic masterwork, this satiric historical novel reflects the author's belief in freedom and human rights, both endangered abstracts during the medieval period.

Although he never struck it rich from his publications, Twain profited from his genial wit and charm. His later years brought world-famous visitors to hear his store of anecdotes and jokes. Dressed in a white linen suit, his face framed in silvery locks, he looked the picture of Old South contentment. In reality, poor financial planning, an ill-advised investment in a typesetting machine, and the deaths of Olivia and his daughters Susy and Jean saddened and depleted him. Some of his bitterest stories attest to his unhappiness—for example, "The Man Who Corrupted Hadleyburg." Twain launched an autobiography in 1906 and left it unfinished at his death in Redding, Connecticut, on April 21, 1910. He remains America's favorite local colorist and teller of tales. (Bloom 1986e; Emerson 1985; Kaplan 1966; Twain 1963)

See also Arthur; Camelot; *A Connecticut Yankee in King Arthur's Court;* Morgan, Hank; satire; technology.

TYPEE

Herman Melville's episodic, dystopian sea romance, set on Nukuheva, one of the Marquesas Islands in the southern Pacific Ocean, is subtitled "A Peep at Polynesian Life during a Four Months' Residence in a Valley of the Marquesas." A suspenseful literary outgrowth of a real adventure he shared with Toby Greene in 1842, the semiautobiographical story details how the two jumped ship from the whaler *Acushnet* to escape rough discipline, extra deck duty, and poor rations. Their sojourn covers the late spring and early summer among seemingly mild-mannered Polynesians, whom the young sailors later learn are human flesh–eaters. So vivid are the details of the novel that it created the sobriquet "the man who lived among the cannibals," a subject Melville exploited in lectures and public appearances.

The enchantment of tropical breezes, fresh food, abundant leisure, and friendship with seemingly harmless people occupied Greene and Melville until July, when Melville departed alone aboard the whaler *Lucy Ann* for Papeete, Tahiti. Upon his return to New England, he narrated his account in the form of a sea romance and published it in 1846. The novel brought him instant success with an adoring reading public, who discovered the idyllic beauties of a relatively unexplored part of the globe.

The first-person narrative describes the flight of Tommo and Toby, two dissatisfied sailors, from the whaler *Dolly* when it docks in the ample bay of Nukuheva. The men face a dilemma—the need to avoid the reputedly cannibalistic Typees in their search for the Happars, a tribe known for their welcome to visitors from the outside world. The trek up a 3,000-foot slope, across a mountain ridge, and into an unknown vale introduces the sailors to jungle dangers. Tommo contracts fever and swelling in the leg, yet pushes on over thick undergrowth and past heady drop-offs into an alluring paradise. Below, the sojourners see a village so green, so picturesque that they assume they have reached the encampment of the peaceable Happars.

Mehevi, a magistrate of the village, indicates that the men have reached the Typees, headed by Chief Mow-Mow, and that they are welcome to stay and recuperate. The sailors live with Tinor and Marheyo and their son Kory-Kory. Tommo, whose injured leg hampers movement, receives Kory-Kory as a personal attendant who carries him to a shaman for therapy. The pummeling and massage exacerbates Tommo's discomfort. Other than his leg pain, he settles into the contented rhythm of island life and studies the beauty and innocence of Polynesian girls. His choice, the ingenuous Fayaway, excels the other young women in loveliness and charm.

By imitating the social and religious expectations for Polynesian men, Tommo learns more about island society. The Typees, who follow a social pattern of sexual segregation, provide a men-only lodge in the Taboo Groves. Near the Polynesian worship center, the men loll in the Ti, a sizable pavilion suitable for feasting and fellowship. At first squeamish about the main course, Tommo and Toby learn that they are eating pork, which allays their fears that the Typees are serving human flesh. After a week of rest and recovery, Toby leaves the grove and sets out for Nukuheva to find medicine for his ailing comrade. In the middle of the day, locals transport Toby's inert form back to the village. He recovers from a serious head wound and tells Tommo of his misadventures among the Happar. Within a few days, there is a stir on the shore. Toby joins the natives, but never returns. Tommo questions the Typees, but learns nothing about his friend's fate.

The peace of an island utopia creates calm in Tommo. Surprisingly comfortable and lethargic as the guest of Tinor and Marheyo, he sinks into complacency. He relishes the care of hovering attendants; however, his mind toys with the apprehension that he is being watched and forced into a gentle bondage. His crippled leg hampers mobility, causing depression and a sense of timelessness. After he recovers enough to move about without Kory-Kory's help, Tommo discovers that he is restricted in a benign house arrest that cuts off access to the beach, where Toby disappeared.

In first-person narrative, Melville emphasizes how physical contentment diverts the suspicious mind from investigating crime or potential dangers:

> All the inhabitants of the valley treated me with great kindness; but as to the household of Marheyo, with whom I was now permanently domiciled, nothing could surpass their efforts to minister to my comfort. To the gratification of my palate they paid the most unwearied attention.

Because he lives in the ease and languor of a pampered lapdog, Tommo ceases to brood over the unexplained departure of Toby. Welcomed to the lake, Tommo enjoys a serene jaunt with Fayaway in a canoe. The tranquillity of village life lulls him into submission until the arrival of Marnoo, a native who returns from a visit to Nukuheva. A privileged, handsome, well-traveled man who has sailed on a trader to Sydney, Australia, Marnoo rivals Tommo for the villagers' attention. Tommo attempts to ally himself with Marnoo, who is a viable hope of escape. As the Feast of Calabashes approaches, Tommo learns more about Moa Artua, the Typees' chief god, and about social order, fishing, dance, drum telegraphy, tattooing, and the making of tapa cloth. The tenuous circumstances that have puzzled Tommo from the first reach a climax after he comes upon natives examining three human heads—two Polynesian and one white—that are slung over beams of the residence. Tribesmen try to dissuade Tommo from investigating.

The upshot of a war with the neighboring Happars results in victory, and returning Typees indulge in secret ceremonies. Tommo concludes that the Typees are devouring the remains of their kill. At the end of his fourth month as guest/prisoner, Tommo eludes surveillance and joins Karakoee, a crewman from the *Dolly*, who negotiates for Tommo's release with cotton cloth, a musket, and gunpowder.

Melville cuts short the falling action with a clean departure back to the sailor's calling. Tommo sadly parts from Fayaway and his host family; later, he re-creates the familial parting:

> I looked imploringly at Marheyo, and moved towards the now almost deserted beach. The tears were in the old man's eyes, but neither he nor Kory-Kory attempted to hold me. . . .

Leaping into the tender, he and his rescuers row against the tide as the Typees clench spears in their jaws and swim after their prey. Safely aboard the *Julia*, Karakoee discloses to Tommo the plot to barter for the American sailor, whom Marnoo declared was being held in Typee custody. Tommo survives the harrowing rescue, but Toby's fate remains in doubt. In Melville's sequel to the novel, Tommo discovers that Toby escaped with the help of Jimmy, an elderly interpreter for King Mowanna. Although Toby is displeased that Tommo remains in Typee custody, he takes passage from Nukuheva to New Zealand. He fears that Tommo will not survive among the pagan tribe.

A significant difference between Melville's idealized sea idyll and other utopian literature is the source of his contrasts. Rather than dwell on government, he angers New England's religious establishment by lambasting the questionable methods of missionaries, who ostensibly journey to Polynesia to share the best in Western culture. In Melville's view, these proselytizers tarnish the glories of an unrefined but generous race with prejudice, constant disapproval, and cynicism: "the heart burnings, the jealousies, the social rivalries, the family dissensions, and the thousand self-inflicted discomforts of refined life."

For Tommo, escape from the dictatorial command of a corrupt sea captain is worth the hazard of living among cannibals. Like Adam mated to a Polynesian Eve, he escapes America's commercialism and the frenzied push to colonize the New World by embracing the unsullied joys of a Marquesan paradise. In comparing Tahiti with Hawaii, Tommo—a thin mask for the author himself—questions how civilization assists the primitive folk of the South Seas:

> Let the once smiling and populous Hawaiian Islands, with their now diseased, starving, and dying natives, answer the question. The missionaries may seek

to disguise the matter as they will, but the facts are incontrovertible; and the devoutest Christian who visits that group with an unbiased mind, must go away mournfully asking—"Are these, alas! the fruits of twenty-five years of enlightening?"

Thus, Melville debunks the burgeoning American myth that a perfect world exists in technology, government, social order, religiosity, and progress. His didactic dystopian novel highlights a dark truth: that an energetic young man seeking relief from ship duty—one of his era's worst examples of power gone awry—is unable to find respite in one of the world's last unspoiled havens. Yet, for all its lush, carefree enticements, life among the Typees bears a unique form of atavism too horrifying for outsiders to contemplate. (Allen 1971; Bloom 1986d; Bryant 1986; Hillway 1979; Johnson 1968; Melville 1961; Melville 1962; Melville 1964; Melville 1968; Sealts 1982; Wolff 1987)

See also Eden; escapism; Melville, Herman; *Omoo; Supplement to Bougainville's "Voyages."*

UTOPIA

A utopia is an imaginary golden age, haven, come-hither island paradise, isolated valley, planet, retreat, or perfect world. These getaways from earthly discomfort and distress may be designed by a scientist, philosopher, pastoral poet, religious mystic, economic visionary or futurist, didactic essayist, traveler, or novelist. Although utopias may represent a glistening dream, as depicted in Herman Melville's *Typee* (1846), the general purpose of these dream worlds is didactic: human betterment or the amelioration of society's short-sightedness, mismanagement, idiosyncrasies, and faults. In Melville's work, fiction and reportage blend in a semiautobiographical study of the South Seas, which he recalls from his sailing days; or, like the nostalgic re-creation of history in Thomas Carlyle's *Past and Present* (1843), may typify a yearning for a simpler era in which work is uncomplicated by technology and the heart's desire lies as close as the vegetable garden.

The creation of perfect worlds is almost exclusively a Western proclivity, although writers like John Milton, John Bunyan, James Hilton, Hermann Hesse, and Malcolm X draw heavily on Eastern lore and philosophy and on Hebrew and Arabic scriptures, which are dotted with alluring distant playgrounds with romantic names like Shambhala and Nirvana. Utopias present a vast array of answers to the question of how to create a stressfree human life. Certain utopias avoid the lockstep expectations of the clockwork municipality and steer wide of the orthodox, mechanistic goals of socialism and flag-waving chauvinism to arrive at several alternate or blended motifs, as demonstrated by these titles:

- **nature's delights,** for instance, Virgil's *Bucolics* (42–37 B.C.), Denis Diderot's *Supplement aux Voyages de Bougainville* (1772), Herman Melville's *Typee* (1846) and *Omoo* (1847), Henry David Thoreau's *Walden* (1854), Henry Olerich's *A Cityless and Countryless World* (1893), and W. H. Hudson's *Green Mansions* (1904)

- **good will and altruism,** the outward display of neighborliness, decency, and calm of Sir Thomas More's *Utopia* (1516); Johann Andreae's *Christianopolis* (1619); William Dean Howells's paired novels, *A Traveler* *from Altruria* (1894) and *Through the Eye of the Needle* (1907); and Prestonia Mann Martin's *Prohibiting Poverty* (1932)

- **industrial refinements,** the core of a better world in Edward Bellamy's *Looking Backward* (1887), Ayn Rand's *Anthem* (1937), A. T. Churchill's *The New Industrial Dawn* (1939), Isaac Asimov's *I, Robot* (1950), and Arthur C. Clarke's *Childhood's End* (1953)

- **social engineering,** for instance, Plutarch's *The Life of Lycurgus* (first century A.D.) and Edward M. House's extension of Woodrow Wilson's policies to help the worker in *Philip Dru: Administrator* (1912)

- **fantasy,** e.g., Oliver Goldsmith's *Asem* (1759), George Tucker's *A Voyage to the Moon* (1827), James Fenimore Cooper's *The Crater* (1847), Edward Bulwer-Lytton's *The Coming Race* (1871), L. Frank Baum's *The Wonderful Wizard of Oz* (1900), Virginia Woolf's *Orlando* (1928), and Richard Adams's *Watership Down* (1972)

- **theocracy,** as delineated in St. Augustine's *City of God* (A.D. 426), Dante Alighieri's verse epic *The Divine Comedy* (1320), John Eliot's pamphlet *The Christian Commonwealth or The Civil Policy of the Rising Kingdom of Jesus Christ* (1659), and Charles Sheldon's *In His Steps: "What Would Jesus Do?"* (1897)

- **otherworldliness,** as described by Jonathan Swift's *Gulliver's Travels* (1727), William Simpson's *The Man from Mars* (1891), J. M. Barrie's children's play *Peter Pan* (1904), and Arthur C. Clarke's *Childhood's End* (1953)

- **peace by default,** the depleted world of Edward Shanks's *The People of the Ruins* (1920), a nation withered of strength and devoid of idealism after wars exhaust the populace; the ambiguous control of the Overmind that concludes Arthur C. Clarke's *Childhood's End* (1953); and a similar defeatist utopia in Franz Werfel's *Star of the Unborn* (1946) and Marge Piercy's *Woman on the Edge of Time* (1976)

- **prophecy,** the focus of Gerrard Winstanley's *Law of Freedom* (1632), Karl Marx and Friedrich Engels's *The Communist Manifesto* (1848), William Morris's idyllic commune in *News from Nowhere* (1890), Jack London's *The Iron Heel* (1907), and Franz Werfel's *Star of the Unborn* (1946)

No single description—religious, naturalistic, bureaucratic, individualistic, prophetic, or otherwise—fits all utopias, and no definition sufficiently covers all possible perfect worlds; rather, utopists or social reformers draw upon an inherent, predictable human discontent with reality and a desire for less external control and more intrinsic worth in everyday existence, the type of satisfaction the grain harvesters share in William Morris's *News from Nowhere*. Typically, the personae of utopias deserve the worryfree domain that becomes the canvas on which the author paints with broad strokes the generalized atmosphere and aim of heaven on Earth.

In some instances, particularly works that appeal to oriental tastes and beliefs, writers propose their utopias without giving memorable detail of topography or concrete objects. One such is Hermann Hesse's *Siddhartha* (1951), a beatific vision of transcendent happiness through acquiescence to all phases of life, whether anguished or joyful. The smile of the Buddha that adorns the prophet's face symbolizes the ultimate union that strips the ego of worldliness and blends the remaining psychic power with God. In another vein, Alex Haley's *The Autobiography of Malcolm X* (1965) draws on Eastern lore to calm, inspire, and uplift an oppressed American underclass—the blacks of urban ghettos. According to Haley's posthumous version, Malcolm was influenced by his father's support of the dreams of Marcus Garvey to restore blacks to their African home. Under the guidance of Detroit evangelist Elijah Muhammad, when Malcolm left prison, he escaped racist oppression by assisting his mentor's ministry to the Nation of Islam, also known as the Black Muslims. After Malcolm proved worthy of his own temple, he conducted a *hajj,* or pilgrimage, to the holy city of Mecca. Among worshipers of many nations and races, he attained world recognition by making a dramatic change in his earthly black paradise. While pressing for the United Nations to put a stop to racial discrimination in the United States, Malcolm enlarged his utopian initiative from all-black to all-inclusive. His untimely assassination in 1965 at Harlem's Audubon Ballroom ended his Muslim Mosque, Inc. and his disciples' hopes for world brotherhood, an earthly cooperative composed of all races and creeds.

In reply to the demand for more or better, visionaries like Marcus Garvey, Elijah Muhammad, and Malcolm X have wrestled with a recurring conflict of themes and motifs: idealism versus nihilism, public versus private ownership, free love versus state- or church-regulated mating, technology versus humanism, piety versus paganism, materialism versus spirituality, racism, classism, sexism, eugenics, authoritarianism, revolution, and the perpetual struggle between virtue and evil. Theorists deduce that these conflicting notions gain prominence during periods of social or economic upheaval, violence, or readjustment, particularly the Renaissance, Reformation, Industrial Revolution, and World Wars I and II. The desire for calm amid tumult, or tradition and structure amid chaos, leads idealists toward safer, more stable ground, whether civic, religious, or poetic in nature.

Utopianism results from a distinctly individual, impractical, and, in some instances, chimerical point of view. The literary prototype, Thomas More's *Utopia,* created a modern term from the Greek *ou* for "not" and *topos,* or place, by punning on *eutopia,* or "happy place." The idea of perfection is an established literary construct dating back to the conventions of *Gilgamesh* and the Eden of the Koran and Bible and to havens, pipe dreams, and idylls limned by Homer, Hesiod, Pindar, Plato, Aristophanes, Cicero, Virgil, Ovid, Lucian, Horace, Theocritus, Plutarch, Tasso, St. Augustine, Dante, and Omar Khayyam. Like other lyric longings for a desirable cosmos free of tyranny, suffering, coercion, and the clangor of competition, dissension, and trade, Khayyam's speaker yearns to destroy the sorry universe and, with God's help, "remold it nearer to

the heart's desire." So noble an aspiration echoes the sincerity of the roman-
ticist's speculation that love can move mountains and negate the raw spots
that chafe the nay-sayer's soul.

Numerous versifiers and dramatists have envisioned a leafy bower closed
off from intruders, dictators, violence, and noise, such as Sherwood Forest in
Robin Hood lore, the South American jungle in W. H. Hudson's *Green Mansions*
(1904), Samuel Taylor Coleridge's dreamy compound in "Kubla Khan" (1798), or
Shakespeare's Arden Forest in *As You Like It* (1599), where the duke, "exempt
from public haunt, finds tongues in trees, books in running brooks, sermons in
stones and good in everything." (II, i, 15–17) Parallels to Arden appear in the
Athenian wood that provides a respite from authoritarian law in *A Midsum-
mer-Night's Dream* (ca. 1595). In this forest wonderland, Oberon looks for

> . . . a bank where the wild thyme blows,
> Where oxlips and the nodding violet grows,
> Quite over-canopi'd with luscious woodbine,
> With sweet musk-roses and with eglantine . . .
> And there the snake throws her enamell'd skin,
> Weed wide enough to wrap a fairy in . . . (II, i, 249–256)

Perhaps Shakespeare's most idyllic setting is Bermuda, the setting for *The Tempest* (1611) and the home of Prospero and his daughter Miranda. The verdant
Caribbean isle is swept by sweet winds imbued with magical harmony and
blessing. Gonzalo grows so enamored of its charm, he vows that if he were its
caretaker,

> . . . no kind of traffic
> Would I admit; no name of magistrate;
> Letters should not be known; riches, poverty,
> And use of service, none; contract, succession,
> Bourn, bound of land, tilth, vineyard, none;
> No use of metal, corn, or wine, or oil;
> No occupation; all men idle, all;
> And women too, but innocent and pure;
> No sovereignty . . .
> All things in common nature should produce
> Without sweat or endeavour: treason, felony
> Sword, pike, knife, gun, or need of any engine,
> Would I not have; but nature should bring forth,
> Of its own kind, all foison, all abundance,
> To feed my innocent people. (II, i, 148–164)

Appropriately, he concludes that such benign governance would "excel
the golden age," the subject of utopian glimpses in Hesiod's *Works and Days*
(eighth century B.C.) and Ovid's *Metamorphoses* (A.D. 8).

A twentieth-century version of Shakespeare's forest idyll is found in W. H.
Hudson's *Green Mansions*, a light, romantic Edenic escape doomed to failure
by the intrusive nonutopian outside world, even though it appears too far from

human faults and despotic governments to fall prey. Set in the Orinoco region of Guayana, the novel pictures Abel, a young protagonist fleeing persecution. He locates a slender sylph—a bird-woman named Rima, whose jungle home gives Abel the refuge he craves. In Chapter 2, sensing the joys of a lush paradise, Abel reflects:

> . . . as far as I went it was nowhere dark under the trees, and the number of lovely parasites everywhere illustrated the kindly influence of light and air. Even where the trees were largest the sunshine penetrated, subdued by the foliage to exquisite greenish-golden tints, filling the wide lower spaces with tender half-lights, and faint blue-and-grey shadows.

The animistic beauties of the South American rain forest entice the reader, yet the triumph of reality over illusion predicts doom. In similar escapes from human foibles, as with Henry David Thoreau's *Walden* and the beneficent forest of Henry Wadsworth Longfellow's *The Song of Hiawatha* (1855), the departure from reality, like a brief camping trip or religious retreat, is short-lived and ultimately detrimental to the wearied soul. Such green retreats, like the will-o'-the-wisp, coax the vulnerable and the world-weary with promises of spiritual compensations, peace, or abundance, but they remain too elusive, too insubstantial, too nondirective to provide a lasting respite from travail. Like shadows of utopia, they portray true "no-places."

Not all prescriptions for utopia contain so hermetic an approach to community life. Many call for large populations, sacrifice, violent overthrow, and the necessary authoritarianism of police, king, magistrate, high priest, samurai, dictator, or wizard. In some works, the need for a controller produces an authority figure as gentle as Father Perrault, James Hilton's transcendent high lama; Plato's grandfatherly philosopher-king; L. Frank Baum's Wizard of Oz; Fra Tomaso Campanella's Prince Hoh in the City of the Sun; or Arthur C. Clarke's Karellen, the benevolent alien overseer of Earth during a radical period of human evolution in *Childhood's End*. More stringent characterization reveals the stronger, less tolerant potentates, e.g., the prince in More's *Utopia*; Plutarch's King Lycurgus, supreme ruler of the Spartans; William Golding's cocky Jack Merridew, a chorister turned savage on a Pacific isle; and the champion despot and tormentor, Big Brother, the faceless menace in George Orwell's *1984* (1949). In his assessment of authoritarian utopias, Herbert Read explains the need for a shepherd, captain, or tyrant as the expressed wish of the governed. Those who reject control become lawgivers; the most assertive, in turn, dominate lesser leaders. Such is the impetus that spawned the blatantly overbearing, hobnailed, or whip-cracking twentieth-century dystopias, the antitheses of Eden.

The New World, which held out hope to European emigrants that life could have a new beginning, grasped at the possibilities of an earthly paradise. According to a list of concerns in Chapter 6 of French philosopher and social critic Alexis de Tocqueville's *De la démocratie en Amérique* (Democracy in America) (1835), framers of a new civilization had serious questions to answer about their purpose and objectives:

- Do you want to uplift humanity above commercialism?

- Do you intend to inspire devotion and seriousness of purpose?

- Do you want to encourage refinement, courtesy, and appreciation of the arts?

- Do you wish your nation to influence or dominate other nations?

- Do you intend to establish a special place in history?

De Tocqueville summarizes that tranquillity is a better base than the power-mongering implicit in grandiose ideals. He writes that the United States should "provide for every individual therein the utmost well-being, protecting him as far as possible from all afflictions" and equalize the blessings of liberty to all.

Yet, from the beginning of New World colonization by Europeans, the normal process of social compromise halted any notion that the United States could be the perfect solution to the centuries-old problems of disease, war, prejudice, privilege, and greed that ground down European populations and unseated kings. In the exposition of *The Scarlet Letter* (1850), Nathaniel Hawthorne addresses the reality of a burgeoning New England Puritan community intent on perfection in body and spirit:

> The founders of a new colony, whatever Utopia of human virtue and happiness they might originally project, have invariably recognized it among their earliest practical necessities to allot a portion of the virgin soil as a cemetery, and another portion as the site of a prison. [Chapter 1]

Whatever immigrants from Europe hoped to accomplish by testing the New World's welcome, they brought along a predictable complement of human miseries—smallpox, tuberculosis, depression, jealousy, pride, racism, and religious fanaticism.

De Tocqueville recognized that racism and prejudice were the stumbling blocks to a true democratic haven. The slaughter of Native Americans, torment and execution of witches, and importation and breeding of black slaves obliterated the brightest picture of a New Dominion promising hope for all. In time, within the classic literary canon, notable characters ranging from F. Scott Fitzgerald's Nick Caraway and Jay Gatsby to James Fenimore Cooper's Natty Bumppo, J. D. Salinger's Holden Caulfield, Mark Twain's Huck Finn, Herman Melville's Ishmael, Nathaniel Hawthorne's Hester Prynne, and Joseph Heller's Yosarian batter against a dead end—a dream that, in time, collapsed on the prairies following the arrival of European settlers and the disappearance of the buffalo. A central motif to the novels and short stories of midwesterners O. E. Rolvaag, Hamlin Garland, and Sherwood Anderson, the demise of the American dream haunts the literature dating from the mid-1850s through current publications, which grow bleaker in such works as Marge Piercy's *Woman on the Edge of Time* and Margaret Atwood's *The Handmaid's Tale* (1985) as the human ability to torment, exploit, and destroy life discolors visions of the future. (Atwood 1972; Bellamy 1960; Berneri 1951; Bleich 1984; Clarke 1953; Cuddon 1979; Gerber 1958; Haley 1965; Hawthorne 1959; Holman 1981;

J.C. Holt 1989; Hudson n.d.; Negley and Patrick 1952; Neilson and Hill 1942; Piercy 1976; Tocqueville 1969; Walkover 1974; White 1955)

See also *The Autobiography of Malcolm X;* Black Muslims; *Childhood's End; De Civitate Dei;* dystopia; Eden; escapism; *The Handmaid's Tale;* heaven; Hoh; *The Life of Lycurgus;* Perrault, Father; Plutarch; Siddhartha; slavery; *Utopia; Woman on the Edge of Time.*

UTOPIA

Sir Thomas More's two-part moral document (1516) was composed in Latin in 1515 under the title *Libellus vere Aureus nec minus salutaris quam festivus de optimo reipublicae statu deque nova Insula Utopia* (A Pamphlet truly Golden no less beneficial than enjoyable concerning the republic's best state and concerning the new Island Utopia). A subsequent version, dated 1516, augmented the title with a formal nod toward "the Distinguished and Eloquent Author Thomas More, Citizen and Sheriff of the Famous City of London." In addition to the original introduction and discussion of Utopia, the expanded edition contained fuller dialogue and a short conclusion. Utopia appeared in various European languages and was translated into English in 1551 by Ralphe Robynson, reaching a greater market among general readers.

More's international success applies speculation and fantasy to the question of the best type of government for the perfect world. Spiked with linguistic puns and parodies, *Utopia* satirizes many of the ills of sixteenth-century England by contrasting them to an idealized nation that has so little use for worldly goods that Utopians ornament children in pearls and semiprecious stones and form out of gold ore a melange of useful items, e.g., slaves' manacles, badges of infamy, and chamber pots. More calls his imaginary world the Greek word "Utopia" (no place), a pun on "Eutopia" (the good place), thus suggesting the unattainable. He names the fictional guide Hythloday, a concocted Greek term meaning "spinner of idle tales."

At Flanders during the reign of King Henry VIII of England, the speaker, Master More, serves as royal emissary to debate and settle an international contretemps with King Charles V. After four months' separation from his family, the speaker journeys to Antwerp and, following a service at Our Lady's Church, meets Peter Giles, a courteous, intelligent, plain-spoken young Belgian. Giles introduces the speaker to Raphael Hythloday, a bronze, bearded Portuguese adventurer, classical scholar, and philosopher who claims to have visited Utopia, which critics identify with the warm climate of lower California or the Caribbean isles.

More crafts his story along the lines of the contemporary mania for travel, exploration, and riches, a theme that dominated English verse, drama, and nonfiction after Columbus made his first voyage to the West Indies. Hythloday, himself an adventurer, discloses that he has visited the far quarters of the world. Along with 23 voyagers, he parted from Captain Amerigo Vespucci, the Italian mapmaker, in Gulike after the third of Vespucci's four voyages. Hythloday and five others developed a rapport with the Gulikians, who treated them to a boat and wagon tour of the land. Beyond a wretched desert, they approached a temperate zone that conducted steady sea commerce with the outside world.

With didactic purpose, More directs attention to the areas of perfection that might benefit European readers by having Hythloday focus on Utopian laws, which he calls "good and wholesome." In his assessment, Utopians "define virtue to be living according to nature, so they imagine that nature prompts all people on to seek after pleasure as the end of all they do." This healthful reliance on naturalism, a hallmark of Renaissance humanism, demonstrates the author's belief that problem-solving via intelligence and the senses uplifts humankind more than faith, which was the prime goal of his predecessors in the fusty, cloistered monasticism of the Middle Ages.

For Thomas More, no place could achieve utopian happiness without reforming government and ejecting the oligarchy or aristocracy. Hythloday describes Utopia as a society that achieved its ideal by replacing the monarchy with a republic. Each Utopian works at farming during a six-hour workday. The remainder of the time, citizens devote themselves to the family, which is ruled by the father. Laws affecting individuals provide euthanasia, access to divorce, and humanitarian punishments for criminals. A low-key people, the Utopians make no show of wealth and, preferring diplomacy to war, avoid violent confrontations with other nations. Their abhorrence of bloodshed extends to hunting, fowling, and gaming. Since no citizen will kill animals, even for food, Utopia relies on slaves to operate abattoirs.

At this point in the narrative, More moves directly to the heart of his didacticism—the improvement of his own land. The fictional trio debate the social ills of England's economy, capital punishment for thieves, the plight of war veterans made destitute by military service, displacement of farmers by greedy landowners, the high prices of woolen goods, and England's social and moral structure. More puts greater emphasis on the subjects that he finds most disturbing and contrary to a healthy society: the Enclosure acts, venal churchmen, and the rise of an affluent minority. Hythloday concludes, "Thus the unreasonable covetousness of a few hath turned that thing to the utter undoing of your island, in the which thing the chief felicity of your realm did consist." More emphasizes that the state of "beggery and miserable poverty" that undercuts England's greatness is augmented by "wantonness, importunate superfluity, and excessive riot." As a result, working-class people are given to bawdy, profligate pastimes, including "stews, wine taverns, ale-houses and tippling-houses, with so many naughty, lewd, and unlawful games as dice, cards, tables [sic] tennis, bowls, coits. . . . " Such "enormities," More concludes, encourage felons. If More is correct, Renaissance England supplies itself with miscreants by allowing unseemly behaviors to breed crime.

To circumvent a social pattern that results in spiraling debauchery and villainy, Hythloday proposes a form of socialism: Property should be distributed equally among citizens and more equitable laws should lessen the powers of monarchy and impede a few rich men's excessive wealth and pride. Likewise, legislation should halt graft and bribery, especially the purchase of public office. The speaker opposes Hythloday's call for outright communism. Hythloday retorts:

> If you had been with me in Utopia and had presently seen their fashions and laws, as I did, which lived there five years and more . . . then doubtless you would grant that you never saw people well ordered but only there.

Giles adds his doubts that any land could contrive a better system than the ancient commonwealths of Europe, but Hythloday insists that "their commonwealths be wiselier governed and do florish [*sic*] in more wealth than ours." Growing interested in the possibilities of improving England, More requests additional data about Utopian customs and laws.

In Book II, after the trio dine and return to their bench, Hythloday describes the physical outlines of the crescent-shaped island of Utopia, which is 200 miles wide and 500 miles around, and fortified by natural defenses. Sheltering a large inland harbor paved with dangerous rocks, Utopia receives extensive sea traffic, which must be directed by skilled harbormasters. The island, governed by King Ademus (literally, "peopleless") and named for King Utopus, who engineered the 11-mile entrance to the bay, exemplifies the orderly, livable domain of a people perfect "in all good fashions, humanity, and civil gentleness," who inhabit 54 homogeneous walled cities no more than 24 miles apart, or no greater than a day's journey on foot. On the Anider (literally, "waterless") River 60 miles from the shore on a central plot 2 miles square reposes the capital city of Amaurote (the Greek term for "shadow town"), which is walled and encircled with a moat for maximum protection. In this centralized location, a yearly council of elders, three from each city, serves as the public forum.

Reverting to a belief that slaves are a natural caste in human society, More seems unperturbed that not all residents of Utopia live in freedom and equality. Hythloday boasts that Utopians—a remarkably healthy and robust people—live in well-appointed collaborative farms composed of 40 inhabitants and a pair of slaves, whom he scarcely mentions. These compounds, or "families," are founded on the dignity of manual labor for all and ruled by a goodman and goodwife. Each citizen is obliged to perform two years' worth of farm labor, which satisfies a type of state military requirement to the "land army." For every 30 farms there is a phylarch, or head bailiff. Annually, representatives from each farm move to the city to learn the latest in agricultural technology, which they teach the others of their commune. Under a balanced husbandry, the farms produce crops, cattle, chickens, horses, oxen, grain, timber, wine, and mead, and depend on a reciprocity of city laborers, who harvest farm produce in exchange for goods. In addition to farming, each goodman learns at least one trade, e.g., stonework, flax weaving, carpentry, or ironwork.

Although the serving caste lightens the work load of each compound, More's Utopia thrives ostensibly as a democracy. Every 30 farms elect a syphogrant (an overseer), who joins with nine other magistrates under the rule of a tranibore, or chief. By secret ballot, the magistrates select a prince, who retains rule for life under the advisement of the chiefs and lives simply, with a sheaf of grain borne before him to indicate the majesty of his office, but not of his person or family. Employing a rotation of advisory chiefs, the prince makes laws only after serious debate of council extending over no fewer than three sessions. Regulations concern the public good, such as requiring the storage of two years' worth of food in case of shortages; the remaining surplus serves as trade goods, which are sold to fortify the public treasury and hire mercenaries in case of war.

More makes a lethal thrust at English bureaucracy by stressing that Utopians have no need of attorneys or ambassadors because their laws are few and self-explanatory and the nation abstains from foreign alliances. Trials involve only a judge and the principal parties of the case. Gambling is forbidden. Travel is restricted by a passport system and limited to journeys by oxcart between cities. Parents curb children's excesses at home. The usual punishment for more serious offenses is enslavement; however, anyone who traduces the representational system or attempts to tyrannize the state is subject to the death penalty. Likewise, judges hand out rewards for good behavior, usually in the form of public statues to honor virtue.

On this fictional island, people dress in a uniform made of leather covered by a cloak of undyed wool. Women live with their husbands' families; sons remain allied with fathers and tend to follow the family trade or profession. Virginity is required before marriage. Women marry at 18, men at 22. As though examining a horse before purchase, unmarried people observe potential mates in the nude to determine the quality of the body. Unhappy mates are allowed to divorce and search for a better alliance. Violators of prenuptial mores are banned from entering into matrimony. Adulterers are sold into slavery; their mates are allowed to remarry.

More values population control and describes how Utopian families maintain an equal number of children. The excess children—those that exceed arbitrary standards—are parceled out from families with an abundance to childless couples. A rise in population results in the creation of a distant colony. In Utopia's cities, streets are wide and traffic is kept to a minimum of noise and obstruction. Flat-roofed homes are uniform in appearance—three stories high, stuccoed, similar in construction, and filled with windows that are either glazed or covered with oiled linen. A separate lodging is reserved for the infrequent visits of dignitaries and strangers. Municipalities are divided into quadrants, each containing a common store, food market, municipal hall, and spacious hospital outside the city walls. Special care with dirty animals and diseased people reduces contagion. Slaughtering takes place at a distance from residences to control odor.

In the city, Utopians dine in refectories, each of which serves 30 families. At mealtime a trumpet announces food service. Women cook for the compound; slaves carry out menial labor. Men sit on the benches against the wall; women occupy the inner seating so that they can depart to the nursery if they or their children become ill. Nurses tend children under the age of five in a separate dining area. Older children serve their elders, with the magistrate and his family occupying an honored place; old and young men are mingled together "to the intent that the sage gravity and reverence of the elders should keep the youngers from wanton license of words and behavior." Dinner hours are perfumed with incense and fragrant waters and include a serious reading, board games, and pleasurable conversation. Mealtime ends with music and rest.

In his Utopia, More removes the threat of plutocracy, a lethal presence in Jack London's *The Iron Heel* (1907). Money carries less importance in Utopia than in the outside world. No one is allowed to amass a fortune or, on pain of forfeiture, accrue honor through acquiring gold. More valuable than worldly goods is learning, which occupies Utopians throughout their lives, even in their games and amusements. Likewise, locals treasure purity of language, a knowledge of the earth, weather prediction, and the movements of the stars, but they give no thought to astrology or prognostication, which violates More's Christian philosophy. Rather, they put their trust in an afterlife, their reward for virtue and obedience to law. Social institutions demonstrate the Utopian concept of tolerance. A communistic system provides education to both sexes, largely in the applied sciences of logic, computation, geometry, astronomy, meteorology, and music. No course work encourages art, creativity, or deviation from the norm. Physical education prepares potential warriors for war. Both sexes study self-defense of person or nation, but Utopia as a whole finds warfare repellent and uncivilized, a situation they abjure unless absolutely unavoidable.

The application of reason encourages Utopians to believe in life after death and the punishment of evil. They tolerate all forms of worship, differences of opinion, and worldly pleasures. One segment follows monastic strictures and vegetarianism; their counterpart forms a sect who revere hard work, but make no rules against sexual intercourse nor dietary laws. The priestly caste, made up of men and some widows, earns respect by serving as censors of public morality. Bimonthly worship services feature songs, prayers, and brightly feathered vestments. On the whole, Utopians follow a virtuous, contented lifestyle and, like Plato's ideal in *The Republic* (fifth century B.C.), achieve the greatest good for the populace by applying religious principles and reason to common problems.

In the discussion of religious pursuits, More focuses on tolerance over fanaticism to orthodox faiths. Hythloday notes that some Utopians rejoiced to hear of Christianity: "Many of them consented togethers [*sic*] in our religion, and were washed in the holy water of baptism." Because one of Hythloday's companions expounded too hotly on orthodoxy, the annoyed islanders, who prize peace above all else, "laid hold on him, accused him, and condempned [*sic*] him into exile, not as a despiser of religion but as a seditious person and raiser-up of dissension among the people." The precedent for such rough handling stems from the foundation of Utopia, when King Utopus dissuaded his people from strife and argument by decreeing banishment or servitude as a punishment for those who employ other than "fair and gentle speech."

At the end of his discourse, Hythloday notes that deceased Utopians, both human and beast, receive dignified cremation. Those who have lived cheerful lives receive a joyful funeral followed by a lengthy discussion of their virtues and good deeds. On the whole, islanders prefer an unadorned life devoid of "nobility, magnificence, worship, honor, and majesty." Although More disagrees on unspecified particulars, he refrains from rebuttal because Hythloday has grown weary with talking. More concedes, "so must I needs confess and grant that many things be in the Utopian weal publique, which in our cities I may rather wish for, than hoope, to see followed in our governments."

More's *Utopia* has been labeled a utopian fantasy, social satire, pure communism, an impractical scheme of social regeneration, and a humanistic system for bettering the world. One theory proposes that he modeled his regulated society on the Incan civilization that sprang up in the vicinity of the fictional island of Utopia and was revealed to Europe in 1513 through the expeditionary observations of Vasco de Balboa. More's rational pagans, who resemble Plato's Republicans, are remarkably devoid of Christian principles. More's purpose in presenting a community outside the Judeo-Christian ethic is obvious: In order to lambaste the excesses and animosities of Christian Europeans, he extolled the virtues of a heathen people who lived amicably by reason. (Andrews n.d.; Johnson 1968; Logan 1983; Maguel and Guadalupi 1987; More 1963a; Negley and Patrick 1952; Rollins and Baker 1954)

See also didacticism; More, Sir Thomas; naturalism; Plato; *The Republic*; slavery; utopia.

 # VALHALLA

A male-centered bastion, Valhalla is the gold-embellished hall of Odin, or Wodin, oldest and supreme god in Norse mythology, as recorded in the *Edda*, the Norse epic compiled in the twelfth century. The 640-doored edifice is described as glittering with gold shields and spear shafts, which support the roof. In Valhalla the best, noblest, and most honored of war heroes reside after their earthly deaths in battle. The contrasting repository of dishonored or devalued souls is administered by Hel, goddess of the dead. Flanked by Starvation and Hunter, Hel receives the lesser dead, who expire from disease or old age and depart to the land of Niflheim for eternity.

In the *Elder Edda*, the poet rejoices, "I know one thing that never dies, the glory of the great deed." To single out the worthy casualties of war, the Valkyries (the battle maidens of Odin), like the Greek Fates, choose the mightiest and most valiant, whom they select for death. The Valkyries then accord a suitable victory, during which the heroes die. Retrieved and transported, these fallen exemplars of manhood and glory enter the Hall of the Slain in Paradise and spend eternity feasting on roast boar, quaffing great steins of pungent mead, practicing their battle skills, and fighting a perpetual clash against the invading giants in a cycle of war, death, and rebirth. (Cavendish 1970; Faraday 1902; Fraser 1947; McDannell 1994; Rosenberg 1992)

See also Elysian Fields; heaven; women in utopia.

 # VALKYRIES

See Valhalla.

 # VIRGIL

Classed alongside Plato, Homer, Dante, and Shakespeare as the greatest poets of the Western world, Publius Virgilius Maro, a Mantuan and son of a lumberman, was born October 15, 70 B.C., in Andes, a village lying near the Po River in

A third-century Roman mosaic represents Virgil reading the *Aeneid* in the company of two muses.

Cisalpine Gaul. A shy, soft-spoken, unassuming youth, he grew straight and dark-eyed, and at age 17 followed the gentrified path of law and rhetoric in Cremona and Milan and later at Epidius's school in Rome. Around 47 B.C., he joined the army, but resigned because of a delicate constitution, possibly consumption.

Newly mustered out, Virgil went south to Naples in Campania and studied philosophy under Siro, who left his villa to his favorite pupil. The residence proved to be a stabilizing influence in the life of the poet, who had studied nature and husbandry in childhood. With his mother and Flaccus, his only surviving brother, Virgil evaded the clash of civil war that followed Julius Caesar's assassination and Cicero's execution in the ten years between the republic's demise and the establishment of the Roman Empire.

Meanwhile, the government confiscated his home in Mantua and passed it to veterans returning from conflicts that rocked the Mediterranean world. The loss dismayed his family and inspired a poetic tribute to his rural childhood in his *Bucolics* (42–37 B.C.). He probably never saw his home again. Because he suffered chronic respiratory distress, he pleaded only one court case, then abandoned his law practice in favor of philosophy and literature and the contemplative life. Although his patron Maecenas gave him a comfortable residence on Rome's Esquiline Hill, he preferred the countryside to infrequent but necessary social gatherings of patricians, statesmen, and literati, including his schoolmate Augustus and poets Catullus and Horace.

As a writer, Virgil moved methodically through each line of verse by dictating every morning, then using the rest of his working hours to redraft and refine. By the age of 33, he had published only the *Bucolics*, a lyric, rhythmic poem extolling the rural pleasures of country festivals, rambles among cool glades, and restful solitude. The fourth chapter, the most mystical section, prophesies a golden age when the birth of a divine child will inaugurate peace and good will. Later centuries read into the work a prediction of the birth of Christ.

In his late thirties, Virgil composed the *Georgics,* a four-book agricultural manual modeled on classical forebears. Touching on animal husbandry, crops, vineyards, fruit trees, and beekeeping, the book presents a distilled image of the conservative Roman lifestyle. Essential to his themes are concepts of reverence to the gods and hard work. At the request or direction of Emperor August, the last decade of Virgil's career was spent writing his masterwork, the *Aeneid* (19 B.C.), Rome's literary epic, which paralleled the style and tone of Homer's *Iliad* and *Odyssey* (eighth century B.C.). Focusing on Aeneas, the Trojan son of King Priam and Queen Hecuba, Virgil interwove history with prophecy in a mesmerizing epic from which the poet often read aloud.

Under an imperial patronage that afforded him a luxurious home and servants, Virgil spent his last years refining his work, studying history, and visiting historical sites in Greece and Asia Minor. On September 21, 19 B.C., at Megara, he contracted a fatal infection and died at Brundisium, leaving the *Aeneid* unfinished. He was so concerned that faulty rhymes would spoil his masterpiece that he instructed his heirs to burn the manuscript. To the glory of the literature of Rome and the world, the emperor overruled the poet's wishes and paid Varius Rufus and Plotius Tucca to edit where necessary. The *Aeneid* elevated Virgil to the status of Rome's Homer and influenced Dante Alighieri, Geoffrey Chaucer, Edmund Spenser, John Milton, John Dryden, Alfred Tennyson, and T. S. Eliot. (Bernard and Alessi 1986; Dickinson 1964; Garrison 1984; Letters 1981; McDermott 1950; Snodgrass 1988b; Snodgrass 1994)

See also Aeneas; *Aeneid; Bucolics;* golden age.

 # VISION

Vision is a central motif in utopian literature and often the seminal act or impetus to the creation of a visionary religion, government, or regime. Visions can occur in dreams, in the twilight zone between sleeping and waking, in trances or apparitions, from visitations of divinities, or as hallucinations when the receiver is fully awake or has senses heightened by incense, magic spells or herbs, stimulants, or soporific drugs. Varied works depend on divine inspiration, which visits human intelligence under unusual circumstance. For example,

- the angelic visitations in Jacob's ladder, a portentous Old Testament event recounted in Genesis 28:10–22

- the final battle between good and evil that appears in the book of Revelation (A.D. 90–95) and in the Koran (610), Islam's holy text

- Samuel Taylor Coleridge's exotic "Kubla Khan" (1798), the start of a lush, drug-induced vision of an oriental palace; according to legend, a visitor interrupted the dream scenario before the poet could frame the rest of the verse

- Joseph Smith's *The Book of Mormon* (1830), an extensive scripture transmitted from biblical times to Smith on metal plates and translated through the application of a decoding device supplied by the angel Moroni

- a blow to the head that transports Hank Morgan to Arthur's Camelot in Mark Twain's fanciful *A Connecticut Yankee in King Arthur's Court* (1886)

- Edward Bellamy's *Looking Backward* (1887), a vision that whisks the catatonic Bostonian protagonist from 1888 forward 112 years, when an industrial phalanx controls society

- Dick, the protagonist of William Morris's *News from Nowhere* (1890), who awakens to the London of the future, a paradox in that citizens labor in agrarian communes, detest machinery and factories, and value cottage crafts as they did in the past

- Richard Adams's *Watership Down* (1972), an epic beast fable that begins with the whimpering of Fiver, an undersized rabbit whose vivid nightmares lead a handful of survivors from a doomed warren to safety

In each of these works, the compression of time and the view of a distant milieu provide the contrast between what is and what will be or can be.

One of epic literature's most egregiously propagandist visions occurs in Book 6 of Virgil's *Aeneid* (19 B.C.). To honor Emperor Augustus, founder of the Roman Empire following a decade of antirepublican bloodshed and civil war, Virgil, a noted historian and poet, carries the mythic Trojan hero Aeneas into the Elysian Fields. Posed on verdant hillsides are Rome's future heroes, awaiting birth. The literary convention of viewing the leaders who will follow Aeneas allows Virgil to lionize Trojan warriors—Ilus, Teucer, and Dardanus—and republican Rome's notables—Romulus, Cato, the Gracchi, Julius Caesar, and "Caesar Augustus, a god's son, who shall again establish the ages of gold in Latium over the fields that once were the realm of Saturn." With a deft bit of writer's magic, Virgil manages to prophesy what Augustus dictates, even the sad fate of his nephew Marcellus, who died before achieving anticipated greatness.

Visions continue in the twentieth century, an era less likely to picture green pastures than the grim images of dystopia. Portrayed in the opening chapter of George Orwell's *Animal Farm* (1945), a dream inspires Old Major, a venerable boar, to assemble the animals of Manor Farm and impart the wisdom he has gained. He lists three concerns:

- Humans exploit animals by using them to produce goods and by denying them a share of the bounty.

- Animals, endowed by nature with greater goodness than humans, lack the will to exploit.

- After seizing control of their labor, animals can circumvent human intervention and enjoy fuller, less toilsome lives.

By encouraging the animals to throw off the heavy yoke of human control, Old Major motivates the animals to examine their barnyard subjugation and to overthrow human rule and replace it with animal rule. Major overlooks the possibility that their utopia will leave them vulnerable to the chicanery of Napoleon, a despotic pig who disproves the second axiom of Major's vision. The imperfection of Old Major's dream forms the focus and action of the novel, which illustrates how good intentions, such as those that sparked the Russian Revolution, do not guarantee a perfect world. (Adams 1972; Bellamy 1960; Coleridge 1948; Holy Bible 1958; Morris 1968a; Orwell 1946; Smith 1982; Twain 1963; Virgil 1950)

See also Aeneid; *Animal Farm*; clairvoyance; *A Connecticut Yankee in King Arthur's Court*; heaven; Koran; "Kubla Khan"; *Looking Backward, 2000–1887*; Napoleon; *News from Nowhere*; prophecy; Revelation; Snowball; speculative fiction; Virgil; *Watership Down*.

 # VOLTAIRE, FRANÇOIS

An impish reformer, letter-writer, poet, conversationalist, and playwright, Voltaire is the author of *Candide* (1759), a witty, philosophical examination of human foibles and a retreat into a personalized utopia. Voltaire lived his egalitarian themes by battling ignorance and tyranny. He used the proceeds of his best-selling epic *L'Henriade* to underwrite altruistic projects, including a country school and hospital. For his outspoken opinions, he was often the target of privileged circles, particularly royalty.

Born Jean François-Marie Arouet in Poitou, France, on November 21, 1694, he was weak from infancy, but possessed a precocious, vigorous intellect. His father, a local magistrate and attorney, expected him to follow the legal profession. Law and literature studies with Jesuits at the Collège Louis-le-Grand from 1704 to 1711—along with the influence of a deist godfather—led Voltaire to reject the concepts of the soul and religion, which he labeled destructive. A volatile, self-directed genius, he rebelled against his father's choice of profession and began writing under the name Voltaire.

François Voltaire

Because he understood the importance of patronage, Voltaire cultivated the best of the aristocracy and composed paeans to individual freedom, history, novels, pamphlets, tales, polemics, encyclopedia articles, essays, and spiteful satiric verse, which earned him enemies and frequent exiles from Paris. During his rises in fortune, he lived well and loved boldly; when his patrons fell from favor, he dodged lawsuits and duels and retreated to the country estates of friends. In 1717 and 1726, he was imprisoned in the Bastille, where he composed his tragedy *Oedipe* and his epic *L'Henriade.* He spent much of his life in Holland, Switzerland, Germany, and England, where in 1733 he completed his *Lettres philosophiques sur les Anglais.* Critics often credit English thought with rounding out Voltaire's education.

A champion of tolerance and human rights, Voltaire settled in Lorraine at the home of Emilie, the marquise du Châtelat, his longtime love and intellectual equal. Far from controversy and the grasp of power, he produced some of his best works, including essays, drama, satire, and verse, and was elected to the Royal Academy and appointed royal historiographer. After Emilie died in childbirth in 1749, Voltaire retreated to the court of his friend, Frederick the Great of Prussia, at Potsdam and worked amicably and profitably until personal differences with his host provoked a permanent schism.

In 1760 Voltaire, fearing a bad reception in Paris, moved to Switzerland, where conservative Calvinists forced him over the French border to the château of his niece and mistress, Madame Denis, near Lake Geneva. A wealthy world celebrity, he welcomed numerous guests to his estate, championed justice and the rights of the underprivileged, submitted articles for Denis Diderot's *Encyclopédie,* and rained a flurry of barbed pamphlets on the French. In three days he wrote *Candide,* his imaginative masterpiece of absurdity, parody, didacticism, and satire. The city council of Geneva, still controlled by puritanic Calvinists, inadvertently promoted the work by condemning it.

When his self-imposed exile ended, Voltaire, already mortally ill, returned to Paris in 1778 to witness the staging of *Irene,* his final tragedy. The public championed him; the French academy presented him a medal. When he died within months of his triumph on May 30, 1778, Europe mourned his loss, but vindictive clerics conspired to shove his remains into a common grave reserved for apostates and scoffers of orthodoxy. Voltaire's supporters managed to spirit his body out of their grasp and provide a dignified interment. Eleven years later, during the French Revolution, mourners buried his ashes in the Pantheon alongside French heroes. (Andrews 1981; Ayer 1986; Gay 1988; Mason 1981; Richter and Ricardo 1980; Voltaire 1961)

See also Candide; *Candide;* idealism; Pangloss; slavery; technology; women in utopia.

 # VOYAGE EN ICARIE

This utopian novel was written by the French-American attorney, socialist, and visionary Étienne Cabet. *Voyage en Icarie* (1840) inspired the temporary establishment of a utopian commune along the Red River in Texas and a subsequent attempt in Nauvoo, Illinois. The strict patriarchy of its founder led to a fatal schism. As a result of the squabbling, Cabet was ousted in 1849; he moved his idyllic community to St. Louis, where he died.

The text of Cabet's work describes an English aristocrat's visit to Icaria, a Mediterranian republic separated from the nation of Marvols by a saltwater canal and lagoon. The nation encompasses 100 provinces balanced in size and population and divided into departments similar to France's system. Within each province are ten communes, each centered by a capital. Icaria's circular capital, Icara, reflects the riverbank society of Paris along the Seine. The communitarian government of Icara encourages symmetrical city planning, with residences clustered at the heart, away from noise and odor. From garden apartments and buildings no more than four stories high, like Thomas More's Utopia the city radiates outward to light industry and service facilities, including bakeries and slaughterhouses.

Icaria thrives under a welcome tyranny balanced with the nation's belief in scientific progress. The state owes its success to its dictator, Icar, who implemented the governmental machinery that oversees a rigid uniformity. Scientists regulate diet, both selection and serving size; the state regulates money and industry. This state-ruled socialism belongs to the inhabitants in theory, but in actuality functions as a benign dictatorship. Icarians dress in the state uniform, which symbolizes their role as managers. Family life—like business, agriculture, and public works—conforms to state dicta. Couples date for six months, and girls may marry at age 18, men at age 20. Both mates are expected to remain monogamous. Before the birth of children, the mother receives instruction in infant care. At age 5, Icarian offspring enter into a 12- to 13-year instruction program in morality and general knowledge.

Cabet stresses the importance of work to Icaria. In their late teens, Icarian students begin professional studies, which prepare them for a set number of job openings prescribed by state industrial committees. Icarian workers remain employed from the late teens until age 50 for women and 65 for men. Productivity parallels the availability of raw materials, with warehouse surplus being shipped to other communes. Much like the idealistic communes projected by the Soviets in the 1950s, the Icarian system links every variable to the survival and progress of the state. No decision is left to the individual; all matters of importance remain in the hands of the Icarian bureaucracy.

Selection of officeholders occurs biennially, when two deputies are elected from each commune to sit in the assembly. The public forum consists of assembly meetings. National, provincial, and communal newspapers publish state news; no other outlet for debate is allowed. Like a peacetime army, Icarians learn to do what committees decide is best for them. As Cabet stresses, to an orderly society the shoemaker is as valuable to the community's success and well-being as the doctor. Thus, all residents earn respect for what they are able to contribute. (Cabet 1973; Johnson 1974; Maguel and Guadalupi 1987; Mumford 1959; Negley and Patrick 1952; Piotrowski 1935)

See also Cabet, Étienne; city planning; Icara; Icaria; totalitarianism.

VRIL-YA

A subterranean fantasy land near Newcastle, England, Vril-Ya is the focus of Edward Bulwer-Lytton's utopian novel *The Coming Race* (1871). Beneath a mine shaft and along a lamp-lit road, an underground colony laced with streams thrives with unusually tall ferns, mushrooms, and flowers. The region receives no light from moon, stars, or sun, but supports elk, tigers, fish, songbirds, and crocodiles. Lush blossoms grace the city along its boulevards; Egyptian colonnades, walls, and columns appear coated with jewels. To the outsider, Vril-Ya surprises and delights with its unexpected Edenic qualities.

A whimsically inviting city, Vril-Ya, powered by a magnetic force called *vril*, is scented with sweet fragrance and decked with balconies furnished with luxurious furniture. The adventurer, who explores under the guidance of a child named Taë, comments on the building's trappings:

> . . . I was conducted into a chamber fitted up with an Oriental splendor; the walls were tesselated with spars, and metals, and uncut jewels; cushions and divans abounded; apertures as for windows, but unglazed, were made in the chamber, opening to the floor; and as I passed along I observed that these openings led into spacious balconies, and commanded views of the illumined landscape without.

A gracious hostess heaps golden plates with food for the visitor. For access to upper floors, inhabitants rely on elevators; they communicate by means of telegraphic screens. Automata, who serve as house staff, glide silently by.

The visitor describes the people of Vril-Ya as winged beings with rosy skin and black eyes; the women are stronger than the men. Both sexes dress in diaphanous tunics and leg coverings. The host's daughter, Zee, who belongs to the College of Sages, learns the visitor's language and strikes up a meaningful friendship. The host questions the guest's background politely, yet a bit of hostility clings to the spoken doubt that the outsider belongs to a civilized race. Zee demonstrates Vril-Ya's strong electric current and her own ability to subdue or heal the guest by pointing her finger at him and releasing the power.

The heart of Vril-Ya is a massive, solid construction on a public square where municipal duties are performed and the College of Sages meets. By manipulating *vril*, citizens have overcome the need for weapons. Freed from fear of invasion, they patronize the theater, partake in flying sports, and travel in airboats. Being without heavenly lights, they divide their day arbitrarily into 20 hours, 4 of which require silence. Left in peace, they read from home libraries and meditate. In Chapter 17, the visitor comments on the results of their asceticism:

> . . . they enjoy a general degree of health and vigour which makes life itself a blessing even to the last. Various causes contribute to this result: the absence of all alcoholic stimulants; temperance in food; more especially, perhaps, a serenity of mind undisturbed by anxious occupations and eager passions.

Devoid of greed, competitiveness, and violence, the subterranean beings devote themselves to affection and happiness. At the end of a blissful 130-year span, they weaken, die painlessly, and are cremated.

The government, which is matriarchal, depends on the Tur, or head magistrate. Little is required of the council because Vril-Yans need neither laws nor courts and are instinctively peace-loving and free of crime. Courtesy dominates the relationships of adults and children. Their religious creed centers on the Life-Giver, the god who dispenses the galvanic power that fuels the city. (Bulwer-Lytton 1979; Flower 1973; Manguel and Guadalupi 1987; Mumford 1959)

See also asceticism; Bulwer-Lytton, Edward; city planning; *The Coming Race;* fantasy; technology.

WALDEN

An autobiographical utopian philosophy, Henry David Thoreau's *Walden* (1854), subtitled "Life in the Woods," makes a deceivingly simple statement justifying his escape from urban surroundings to commune with nature. Basing his philosophies on a two-year hermitage on Walden Pond's north shore near Concord, Massachusetts, Thoreau taught generations of readers that withdrawing from society is a worthwhile venture in self-discovery. Having established an unadorned hut on the land of his friend and mentor Ralph Waldo Emerson, Thoreau awaits spiritual fulfillment and escape from the drudgery that society imposes on itself. While subsisting on the beans, corn, peas, potatoes, and turnips he grows in his small garden patch, Thoreau lives apart from the abhorrent acquisitiveness and luxury common to his neighborhood, returning occasionally to Concord for news.

Like Abbot Samson in Thomas Carlyle's *Past and Present* (1843) and the title character in Hermann Hesse's *Siddhartha* (1922), Thoreau looks forward to a purification and spiritual rebirth through introspection. His contentment derives from nature and the renunciation of urban needs and temptations. In search of great truths available only when the soul partakes of solitude, in Chapter 5 he sets forth the parameters of his study:

> I have my horizon bounded by woods all to myself. . . . It is as much Asia or Africa as New England. I have, as it were, my own sun and moon and stars, and a little world all to myself.

In his musings, Thoreau concludes that nature is a "sweet and beneficent society." He learns the preparation and uses of "simples" from an elderly local herbalist and determines that the spontaneity and cheer he derives from his rambles are healthful to him and to the aged gatherer.

In his contemplation of spring, Thoreau returns to the mythological concept of the golden age, a time when humanity was so closely allied with creation that people lived "spontaneously without law." Living neither by fear nor punishment, these perfect people "knew no shores but their own" and enjoyed eternal spring. In Chapter 11 Thoreau contemplates the precepts that govern nature and create a panoply of seasons, animal behaviors, and cosmic beauty. He avoids thinking of even the smallest event as trivial. To him, the

WALDEN;

OR,

LIFE IN THE WOODS.

BY HENRY D. THOREAU,

AUTHOR OF "A WEEK ON THE CONCORD AND MERRIMACK RIVERS."

I do not propose to write an ode to dejection, but to brag as lustily as chanticleer in the morning, standing on his roost, if only to wake my neighbors up. — Page 92.

BOSTON:

TICKNOR AND FIELDS.

M DCCC LIV.

The title page of the 1854 edition of Henry David Thoreau's *Walden*

behavior that produces sound mental and physical health forms a catechism to be learned and internalized. In carpentry terms, he extemporizes:

> Every man is the builder of a temple, called his body, to the god he worships, after a style purely his own, nor can he get off by hammering marble instead. We are all sculptors and painters and our material is our own flesh and blood and bones. Any nobleness begins at once to refine a man's features, any mean-ness or sensuality to imbrute them.

The universal appeal of his philosophy is his insistence on self-respect, which he derives from a close communion with self outside the furor and dissension of cities and well guarded by nature.

Thoreau's tone takes on a note of nostalgia in his final paragraphs. He regrets that most people endure a self-imposed exile into dullness. To the citizen suffer-ing wanderlust but unable to satisfy the urge, in Chapter 18 he encourages,

> Direct your eye right inward, and you'll find
> A thousand regions in your mind
> Yet undiscovered. Travel them, and be
> Expert in home-cosmography.

In explanation of his choice to return to society after exploring self and search-ing for truth, he reports pragmatically: "I left the woods for as good a reason as I went there. Perhaps it seemed to me that I had several more lives to live, and could not spare any more time for that one." A better explanation for his return to dutiful citizenship may have been the approaching war over slavery and the spiritual and polemic agitation over abolitionism, one of Thoreau's cher-ished creeds. (Harding 1965; Lane 1961; Ruland 1968; Thoreau 1965)

See also Carlyle, Thomas; escapism; golden age; Hesse, Hermann; natural-ism; *Past and Present*; *Siddhartha*; Thoreau, Henry David; transcendentalism.

 # *WALDEN TWO*

In B. F. Skinner's dry, didactic plan, human society is conditioned from birth to age six to seek pleasure and profit. Unlike the Edenic or naturalistic utopia—for example, the island escapes of Herman Melville's *Typee* (1846) and *Omoo* (1847) or W. H. Hudson's *Green Mansions* (1904)—Skinner's thinly plotted trea-tise builds on clinical observation and learned experience. His subjects move through lockstep training programs much as border collies, guide dogs for the handicapped, or air patrol dogs learn the doctrinaire behaviors of their jobs.

Published in 1948, *Walden Two* foresees behaviorally engineered nurseries where children thrive in hermetically controlled environments. Neither as cyni-cal nor as stringent as Aldous Huxley's electric shock therapy for crawling infants, Skinner manages to imply animalistic qualities to the children who receive his idealized indoctrination. With no need of clothing except diapers in the early stages of development, they play contentedly as adults reinforce the emotions of joy and love and seek to exterminate anger, envy, desire, and fear.

The code of conduct, which is explained in Chapters 13–14—an amalgamation of Plato, Aristotle, Confucius, the New Testament, the Puritans, Machiavelli, Lord Chesterfield, and Sigmund Freud—attempts to eradicate antisocial behavior by instilling self-control and love as a deterrent to force and violence.

As strident as the lectures and ravings of Thomas Carlyle in *Past and Present* (1843) and as adamant as Henry David Thoreau in his insistence on self-knowledge in the original *Walden* (1854), Skinner abhors a society that discounts the importance of nurture. According to *Walden Two,* the inner harmony that results from this humanistic, altruistic educational system strengthens tolerance for external annoyance. Freed of the world's usual levels of frustration, failure, and intellectual classification, children trained by Skinner's conditioning tend to be individuals with their own set of self-determined expectations. In Skinner's paradigm, all children have the option to become winners. (Carpenter 1985; Modgil 1987; Proctor and Weeks 1991; Rabkin et al. 1983; Skinner 1968; Skinner 1976; Skinner 1993)

See also Carlyle, Thomas; conditioning; didacticism; Hudson, W. H.; hypnopaedia; Melville, Herman; *Omoo; Past and Present*; Thoreau, Henry David; *Typee; Walden.*

WATERSHIP DOWN

This mythic beast fable was written by Richard Adams in 1972. Composed aloud during motoring trips to Stratford as entertainment for his daughters, Juliet and Rosamond, the plot parallels the child-centered tradition of the nineteenth century, which spawned Robert Louis Stevenson's *Treasure Island,* Lewis Carroll's *Alice in Wonderland,* and Rudyard Kipling's Indian episodes for *The Jungle Book.* Rich in themes of survival, synergy, martyrdom, and mythic pilgrimage, the story opens on Sandleford Warren, where Fiver, a runt, troubles his brother Hazel with free-floating, prophetic visions of doom. Hazel tries to warn the Chief Rabbit, who refuses to listen. An inexperienced but resilient leader, Hazel guides his brother, Pipkin, Blackberry, and Bigwig away from their home warren across the Enborne River. Newly arrived on Cowslip Warren, the five journeyers find what they believe to be an idyllic environment—sleek, fat, domesticated rabbits that humans protect and feed carrots, clover, and apples. Hazel and his band jettison their naive optimism after Bigwig is nearly decapitated by a twisted-copper-wire snare. In Chapter 18 the animals pause to reconnoiter. They realize that "they had come closer together, relying on and valuing each other's capacities. They knew now that it was on these and on nothing else that their lives depended." They profit by the experience and guard the successes they have won.

Like Virgil narrating the false starts of Aeneas in the *Aeneid* (19 B.C.) or John Bunyan in *Pilgrim's Progress* (1678), the author sees his column through several deceptive havens. The second stop on the rabbit migration is Watership Down, a lush, Edenic grassland and empty warren. In the tradition of the rabbit epic hero El-ahrairah, Hazel leads the warren without giving up his congenial, humble nature. Kehaar, a friendly kestrel, flies Hazel over Nuthanger Farm. Hazel catches sight of caged rabbits and returns to set them free of their hutches. During the raid, the momentary bliss of Watership Down crumbles after Hazel is shot in the leg and nears death before he is rescued.

Adams returns to pragmatism and the future by equalizing the balance of male to female rabbits. With the addition of Clover, Haystack, and Boxwood to the growing commune, Hazel foresees a need for does to produce more young. Holly and Bluebell shake his confidence by fleeing to Watership Down to report that Sutch and Martin, Ltd., of Newbury has exterminated Sandleford Warren by poisoning its chambers and shooting those animals that fled underground suffocation. A yellow bulldozer finished the job. Just as Fiver dreamed, doom was certain. In Chapter 21 Holly concludes prophetically: "Men never rest till they've spoiled the earth and destroyed the animals."

Hazel's most challenging adversary, General Woundwort, runs the Efrafa warren like a petty dictatorship by holding councils and posting patrols to enforce his rule. Bigwig falls into the general's hands, but by tricking the general's guards, escapes and completes the original Watership Down family. After Hazel's leg heals, he and Bigwig make a second foray against Efrafa. They cross the railroad tracks and the Test River bridge. Bigwig enlists a female, Hyzenthlay, in selecting worthy does for the warren.

Backed by his comrades, Bigwig boards a boat and slips by General Woundwort's pickets. With Kehaar's help as a spotter, the rabbits return with Hyzenthlay, three more does, and Blackavar, a maimed victim of Woundwort's

Hazel and Pipkin, characters in *Watership Down,* encounter a cat at Nuthanger Farm in the 1978 animated film version of Richard Adams's utopian novel.

torture. The final battle between the Watership Down warren and Woundwort's mercenaries requires Bigwig's ingenuity in burying the Efrafan insurgents in underground passageways. Hazel volunteers for a suicide mission and releases the watchdog from Nuthanger Farm. The dog chases away the warren's enemies. Lucy Canes, the farmer's daughter, realizes that Hazel is wounded. She rescues him from Tab, the barnyard tomcat, and returns him to his idyllic Watership Down, where the rabbits live peacefully.

The naturalism of Adams's novel balances the menaces to rabbit welfare. After numerous threats and near misses, Chapter 50 rounds out the novel with a description of a rabbit utopia, richly scented by wild clematis, patches of long grass, and the fall sky foretelling the first frosts of October. Wind rustles beech limbs as the rabbits, increased in number by renegades from Woundwort's compound, prepare their subterranean chambers for winter. Thinking over the price the rabbits' epic struggle has cost in pain, terror, and loss, Silver concludes, "Everything that's happened is unnatural—the fighting, the breeding—and all on account of Woundwort."

In a hollow near Ladle Hill, mother Vilthuril tells her young a story of Elahrairah, who guided the rabbits to their promised land carpeted with "green fields, very beautiful, with good sweet grass." At sunset, the sky glitters with "Perseus and the Pleiades, Cassiopeia, faint Pisces and the great square of Pegasus." The rabbits, who have departed from the chill, continue their storytelling underground. In the epilogue, the story of Hazel's bravery and brash courage elevates him to mythic proportions. The next spring, Hazel, old and weary, greets death by slipping out of his earthly body and frisking across Watership Down as though he were young.

The novel received mixed reviews—some sneering, cynical, and picky, others profoundly impressed by Adams's anthropomorphized cast of rabbits, their reverence to rabbit lore, and their instinctive flight to a better land. Adams was alternately lauded for the grandeur of his undertaking and reviled as a would-be J. R. R. Tolkien, T. H. White, L. Frank Baum, or Lewis Carroll. Overall, strong critical support credits him for the heroism of the humble Hazel, whose political savvy results in a viable life amid the flora and fauna of a rabbit haven. As with Robert O'Brien's *Mrs. Frisbee and the Rats of NIMH* (1971), the natural rhythms of animal life, which are thrown out of sync by greedy land developers and urbanization, remind readers of the fragility and evanescence of isolated corners of nature, where human encroachment threatens survival. (Adams 1972; *Contemporary Authors* 1981; *Contemporary Literary Criticism* 1976; Gilman 1974; Prescott 1974; Smith 1974)

See also Adams, Richard; Hazel; humanitarianism; naturalism; prophecy; synergy.

 # *WE*

An incisive, stark dystopian classic by Russian polemicist Yevgeny Zamyatin, *We* was written in 1921, but repressed by Stalin and the Soviet hierarchy until the late 1920s. Composed in journal form, the novel depicts a brash anti-Soviet view of grinding, dehumanized totalitarianism. So virulent is the author's attack on the entrenched bureaucracy and the application of pure reason to human existence that he was denied publication rights and was forced to read his work aloud to the Russian Writer's Union in 1923. The novel's demand for human rights brought down on the author and his cohorts the furor of communist party regulars, who insisted on orthodoxy and the gutless, compliant mediocrity that accompanied the party's covert cruelties, treachery, thought control, suspension of human rights, and capricious reprisals.

When the story opens, the hero, D-503, has yet to discover his humanity. Following the Great Two Hundred Years' War, only 20 percent of the world's population survives. Living in artificial, regimented harmony in One State under the "unfreedom" of the dictatorial Benefactor, the citizenry—like that of Margaret Atwood's *The Handmaid's Tale* (1985), Ayn Rand's *Anthem* (1937), George Orwell's *1984* (1949) and *Animal Farm* (1945), and Aldous Huxley's *Brave New World* (1932)—suppress their humanity and plod through a stultifying lifestyle resembling that of rats in a neat, tidy cage. Their daily affairs conform to the Table of Hours, the Personal Hour, and the Maternity Norm. The precision of the Table of Hours recalls a train schedule with its precise calculations of time spent and activities pursued. Only the Personal Hour allows individuality and a brief illusion of freedom of choice. By day's end, all motion ceases at the tolling of a bell.

The setting of this chilling dystopia is the twenty-sixth century and a glass-topped city, a veritable bell jar that permits the lurking Guardians to oversee all activities, except on days when shades are drawn for private sexual privileges (which must be prearranged and validated by a pink permission slip). Outside One State, a beastly, hirsute race occupies the land beyond the Green Wall, the antithesis of One State's straight lines and immaculate right angles. State people—known as "numbers"—subsist on petroleum-based foodstuffs and give little thought to the passions, accomplishments, and dreams of former times.

In an attempt to clarify his theories, D-503, a dedicated mathematician and chief of rocketry, dreams in formulas and equations. Allowing himself a moment of self-praise, he comments:

> ... it was not the generations before me, but I—yes, I—who had conquered the old God and the old life. It was I who had created all this. And I was like a tower, I dared not move an elbow lest walls, cupolas, machines tumble in fragments about me.

To the surprise of his colleagues, his introspection produces a dangerous anomaly—a thinking, feeling human being. He courts O-90, a simple-witted companion who understands nothing of his number-based genius. Partly out of boredom and stress, he exorcises haunting misgivings by keeping a journal. The focus of the novel—the protagonist's loss of identity—depicts D-503's disillusion with uniformity. As he walks the streets, the Music Plant broadcasts "The March of the One State." Other citizens, dressed in blue uniforms called "unifs" and identified by numbered badges, cluster in ranks of four, keeping time to the beat. D-503 senses the presence of I-330 in his row, yet remains loyal to O-90. I-330 implies that she will see him again soon. During a required meeting in the auditorium, D-503 stands with the others and sings the "Hymn of the One State," an affirmation of totalitarianism. He is startled to see I-330 appear onstage in the royal box and hear her playing romantic tunes from the ancient past. As he departs in an orderly rank of four, he acknowledges that the sane, predictable music of his era far outclasses the epileptic compositions of earlier civilizations.

Zamyatin draws on the sophisticated technological advancements that were already under way in the 1920s. D-503's musings dredge up visions of world hunger, which the One State conquered by warring against Love and reducing emotion to a mathematical equation. To control hormonal urges, the One State set up laboratories to study blood samples and pattern days for release of sexual urges. By indicating that O-90 suits his fancy, D-503 sets in motion a mechanized sexual outlet, controlled by pink ration coupons that O-90 presents on the days the Lex Sexualis has set aside for coupling. On the surface, the mathematical clarity of a meticulously controlled system delights the tidy, science- and formula-obsessed D-503. Yet, his writings indicate a dark recess that remains disturbingly unfulfilled and threatens to overwhelm his reason with feeling. He admits that the state's tinkering with human needs has produced a fault, which the local paper, the *One State Gazette,* announces. The Benefactor plans to realign social control the next day with a Justice celebration at the Plaza of the Cube.

An unanticipated call from I-330 sets up an impromptu May outing in the air car. Although this aggressive female unsettles D-503, he agrees to take an exploratory flight beyond the Wall to the Ancient House. Grandmother, the aged curator of the museum, wishes that state residents would frequent the repository of impedimenta of the past—the apartment with its jumble of colors, music, statuary, religious symbols, furniture, and books. D-503 compares this tangled melange of sense impressions to epilepsy. I-330 gets caught up in the romance of the fireplace and the opportunity to make love spontaneously and without state approval. Her whim takes her to the closet, which yields an antique yellow silk dress, black stockings, and black hat. D-503 reminds her that such behavior encourages originality, a major fault banned in One State. I-330 offers to get a pass from a physician so that D-503 can skip a required meeting on art and sciences. Sensing danger, he declines her obvious attempt at seduction and returns to the city. According to law, he has two days to report her unorthodox behavior to the Guardians.

At an unexpected turn in the plot, Zamyatin produces spontaneity in his rigid protagonist. The next morning, an unbidden flow of tears surprises D-503, who likens them to sap. After breakfast he calculates how much speed he would need to steer the *Integral,* a spaceship he and his staff are creating for ferrying colonists to less-controlled societies beyond One State. He loses himself in formulaic considerations of thrust, fuel, and mass. He discloses to O-90 that he must go to the authorities to inform on I-330. She frowns at the notion of spying and hands him a fragrant spray of lilies of the valley. Drifts of poetry dot D-503's memory. He visits the state god, which is reduced to a face on a cube with two riveting eyes. Above the deity sits the Benefactor, who lifts a stone hand to summon a petitioner. D-503 recalls the turbulent worship style of former ages and compares these purifying events to the current system of supplying each citizen with a Guardian to serve as archangel.

D-503 receives official notification that I-330 has selected him as a mate. Shoving the document into his pocket, he glimpses his hairy hand, a suggestion of his link with the shaggy folk beyond the Wall. He presents himself at I-330's residence and admits that he deliberately passed up the required report to the Guardians about her illegal behavior. She uses his breach of protocol as implied blackmail and offers him a green liqueur and cigarettes, both forbidden in One State. I-330's diabolical laugh precedes seduction. D-503 realizes that human behavior results from seething, inconstant but persistent emotional urges. He fears that he will self-destruct if he allows them free rein. He grabs I-330, bites and mauls her. She stops his paroxysm of passion by reminding him that the watch on his badge points nearly to curfew. D-503 rushes home, dropping his badge, then retrieving it as anonymous footsteps approach. Safe in his bed, he suffers insomnia, which is a state crime.

Zamyatin's denouement concentrates on a makeover of the robotic aeronautical genius. Over a period of restless days and nights, D-503 ponders emotions and poetry. He surmises that the gods, too, have become as mundane and predictable as verse and reflects:

> Their God gave them nothing except eternal, tormenting searching; their God had not been able to think of anything more sensible than offering himself as sacrifice for some incomprehensible reason. We, on the other hand, offer a sacrifice to our God, the One State—a calm, reasoned, sensible sacrifice.

I-330 interrupts his reveries and forces him to visit a Medical Officer. The jovial doctor declares D-503's disease dangerous. Zamyatin implies that D-503 is more threatening to One State than to himself.

D-503 and I-330 return to the Ancient House to celebrate their love. She calls him a "fallen angel." As he exits, he changes his mind and returns, but finds I-330 mysteriously vanished in a room with only one door. Her departure baffles him. Back in his own room, D-503 recognizes that his malady is obvious to O-90, who perceives that he lives in some ancient time. She weeps as she ends their relationship. After attempting to return to a normal work schedule, D-503 develops a frenzy for I-330, who evades him. He rushes to the doctor, who declares that D-503 has developed a soul. The situation is incurable. The doctor acknowledges that souls can be excised by surgery, yet advises that D-503 try a less life-threatening treatment for restlessness by taking long walks to the Ancient House.

D-503 arrives at the familiar trysting place and asks for I-330, who has already gone to the room. He finds the key in the door, but no I-330. In frustration, he shuts himself into the wardrobe and drops down into a deathlike state. Unable to halt the fall, he plummets to a lower level. Opening the door, D-503 finds himself staring at I-330 and the doctor. The couple walk in the Ancient House's garden and agree to meet two days hence. In Chapter 14, his sleep still disturbed, D-503 spends his nights contemplating "the ancient nightmare world, the world of square root of minus one." Shortly after O-90 writes a formal, tear-stained farewell, D-503 nears the date for the initial firing of the *Integral*. He attends a lecture and encounters O-90; she is writing a book entitled *We* and begs D-503 to help her conceive a child. He uses a pass meant for I-330 and couples one last time with his girlish, sweet-natured O.

Unanimity Day brings the action to a peak as the Benefactor forces a unanimous vote for his reelection. I-330 attempts to cast a dissenting ballot and is wounded. Reunited with her, D-503 journeys beyond the Wall and hears her explain to the Ancients the building of the *Integral* and One State's resolve to conquer and oppress other nations. She introduces to the gathering the builder of the *Integral*—D-503. The next morning, the *Gazette* announces that the Benefactor has noticed too many smiles, a symptom of the dreaded disease of imagination:

> It is a worm that gnaws out black lines on the forehead. It is a fever that drives you to escape ever farther, even if this "farther" begins where happiness ends. This is the last barricade on our way to happiness.

He possesses a one-size-fits-all solution for the problem. Using a bell jar, the Benefactor's minions empty the air to form a vacuum and lobotomize their victims' spirits, thereby sterilizing imagination and turning patients into mindless automata. In Chapter 40, after D-503 is subjected to the treatment, he looks back on his journal in amazement that he expended 200 pages describing emotions.

Zamyatin's novel, like Margaret Atwood's *The Handmaid's Tale*, concludes on a hopeful note: I-330 is killed, but his first lover, O-90, survives beyond the Wall and awaits the birth of a child, the seed of society's renaissance. The motifs of this vivid, energetic science-fiction novel presage the use of Big Brother and torture in *1984*, an attempt at stasis and brainwashing similar to that of Aldous Huxley's *Brave New World*, and the numbered beings and surrounding primitive forest of Ayn Rand's *Anthem*. Similarly, Wells's *The Time Machine* (1895) draws on bestial outlanders who serve as a constant threat to the Wall, the division between emotion and pure reason. (Grigson 1963; Kunitz 1942; Russell 1994; Shane 1968; Zamyatin 1972)

See also Anthem; Big Brother; *Brave New World*; D-503; *The Handmaid's Tale*; *1984*; science fiction; technology; *The Time Machine*; Zamyatin, Yevgeny.

 # WEENA

A light-limbed girl-woman, Weena is a member of the Eloi, an effeminate race of diminutive beings who populate England 8,000 years in the future in H. G. Wells's dystopic novel *The Time Machine* (1895). The Time Traveller forms a strong dependence on Weena, whom he saves from drowning in the Thames because her Eloi companions lack his strength. A sweet, frail human specimen, she depends on him to protect her from attack and to carry her through a burning forest. In exchange, she adorns him with flowers and provides him with information about Morlocks, the cannibalistic predators who lurk at the rim of subterranean holes and await darkness so that they can overrun Eloi turf and cannibalize their prey, which they devour in fetid lairs below ground.

The Time Traveller values Weena's assistance and plans to bring her along on the return flight to nineteenth-century England because, as he explains to his male dinner guests, "she cared for me." He attempts to rescue her from a prolonged attack in a forest, which Morlocks set on fire. Weena falls to the Time Traveller's feet, clutches them, and faints. In the hazy smoke, he carries her on his shoulder, then sets her on the ground and takes up his crowbar and light. In the confusion, she disappears; he surmises that Morlocks have kidnapped her. All that remains of his winsome, frail Weena are some unfamiliar white blooms that symbolize her beauty, sweetness, and fragility. (Costa 1985; Crossley 1986; Draper 1988; Smith 1988; Wells 1964)

See also classism; Eloi; Morlocks; slavery; technology; *The Time Machine;* women in utopia.

WELLS, H. G.

One of science fiction's self-made masters, Wells was a social theorist whose observation that World War I was "the war that will end war" brought him fame. A hater of social castes, he enlivened his fiction with hope and compassion for lower-class people and championed those most harmed by social tinkering, science, and technology. A disciple of Jules Verne, Wells advanced utopianism from mild whimsy to the level of serious anti-utopian criticism. As a late Victorian, he foresaw twentieth-century inventions and concepts and the ominous ramifications for humanity.

Born Herbert George Wells on September 21, 1866, in Bromley, Kent, to a poor working-class family of shopkeepers, Wells was self-educated through intense reading of world classics, which entertained and enlightened him while he recovered from a serious illness at age 8. At age 15 he worked the counter of a dry-goods store under the tutelage of a Portsmouth draper. The instruction of a chemist earned him a job as student aide at Midhurst Grammar School. To rid himself of poverty and drudgery, he ran away from home. On scholarship to the Normal School of Science in South Kensington, in 1884 Wells studied under biologist Thomas Henry Huxley, a noted Darwinian. A subsequent grant to London University underwrote his degree in biology, which he completed with honors in 1890. A single incident—a ruptured vein—dictated his future, which could no longer include the strenuous lifting, standing, and walking of merchandising. As compensation, he became a writer.

In his early twenties, Wells wrote fiction for the *Science Schools Journal.* One of his serialized stories, *The Cosmic Argonauts,* formed the nucleus of *The Time*

Machine, which he refined through two subsequent renderings and published in 1895. In 1891 Wells began teaching in a correspondence college and wed his cousin Isabel. After his writing career supplanted teaching, he divorced Isabel and married Amy Catherine Robbins, a former student. Wells's best work flowed from this period of domestic contentment: *The Time Machine, The Island of Dr. Moreau* (1896), *The Invisible Man* (1897), *The War of the Worlds* (1898), *When the Sleeper Wakes* (1899), *The First Men in the Moon* (1901), and *The War in the Air* (1908).

Surrounded in his Kent home by such noted British and American writers as George Bernard Shaw, Rudyard Kipling, Joseph Conrad, and Henry James, Wells developed a reputation for keen insights into social problems of the poor, joined the Marxist Fabian Society, and sparked social change through activism. He insisted that the world would never improve until all people spoke one language and one government controlled human affairs. His voluminous writings, stemming from his gravitation toward didactic nonfiction, include *Love and Mr. Lewisham* (1900), *Kipps* (1905), *Tono-Bungay* (1909), *Ann Veronica* (1909), *The History of Mr. Polly* (1910), *Boon* (1915), *Mr. Britling Sees It Through* (1916), and *The Croquet Player* (1938). Intermingled with these, Wells produced post-Victorian philosophy in *Anticipations* (1901), *Mankind in the Making* (1903), *The Food of the Gods* (1904), *A Modern Utopia* (1905), and *The New Machiavelli* (1911).

In his fifties and sixties, Wells continued producing antiwar nonfiction as well as autobiography with *Outline of History* (1920), *Men like Gods* (1923), *The Open Conspiracy: Blue Prints for a World Revolution* (1928), *The Science of Life* (1931), *The Work, Wealth, and Happiness* (1932), *The Shape of Things To Come* (1933), *Experiment in Autobiography* (1934), *Apropos of Dolores* (1938), and *Mind at the End of Its Tether* (1945). He spent his last 16 years in London, where he died on 13 August 13, 1946. (Costa 1985; Crossley 1986; Draper 1988; Smith 1988; Wells 1964; Wells 1967)

See also Eloi; Morlocks; slavery; technology; *The Time Machine;* Weena; women in utopia.

WEST, JULIAN

West is a high-strung 30-year-old Time Traveller in Edward Bellamy's *Looking Backward* (1887) who awakens in Boston 112 years in the future. The torment in West's mind is evident in his need for a subterranean bunker, brandy, and the services of a mesmerist to relieve chronic insomnia. In the opening chapter, being a sensitive and fair-minded man, West despairs of the elitism that places him and his fiancée, Edith Bartlett, "on the top of the coach," which is West's metaphor for elitism and the exploitation of an underclass. In the immediate future, he anticipates marriage after

> ... the completion of the house which I was building for our occupancy in one of the most desirable parts of the city, that is to say, a part chiefly inhabited by the rich. For it must be understood that the comparative desirability of differ-

ent parts of Boston for residence depended then, not on natural features, but on the character of the neighboring population.

The guilt that skewers West and dampens his enthusiasm for the future derives from the vast chasm separating his own class from Boston's impoverished, uneducated Irish poor "living in isolation among a jealous and alien race." Rejecting the nineteenth century's tendency to overrate progress as a "chimera of the imagination, with no analogue in nature," West predicts a cycle of rises and falls in civilization that can be neither controlled nor ameliorated.

When West realizes that he has slept through a catastrophic fire and remained in his bunker in an undisturbed catatonic state for more than a century, he sits contentedly on his hosts' housetop and marvels at the serenity of the Boston of A.D. 2000, a society devoid of class, poverty, and suffering. Melodramatically, he rejoices:

> What were my intellectual sensations . . . on finding myself so suddenly dropped as it were into a new world. In reply let me [say that I was] transported from earth, say, to Paradise or Hades.

His thrill at a new day replete with electrical conveniences, no money or competition, and a resurgence of family values is tinged with doubts that what he sees can be real. His trust in the kindly Dr. Leete assures him that Boston has made dramatic changes in the past century, particularly in the restructuring of labor and economics.

The comfort of positive change, however, is not enough to uplift West in his new, nonthreatening environment. Fortunately, his tendency toward melancholy abates in the love of Edith Leete, who is the great-granddaughter of the Edith he loved in the past. After a terrifying nightmare takes West back to the anguish and poverty of the nineteenth century, he awakens once more in utopian Boston and weeps the pent-up misgivings that have wracked and traumatized his three-day sojourn in the future. With the assurance of Edith's love, Dr. Leete's altruism, and the harmony of a socialistic society, the becalmed, energized Julian West symbolizes Bellamy's hopes for the future. The finer points of his characterization lighten the extreme didacticism of the novel, which tends toward lecturing, one-sided logic, and moralizing. Weak in normal dialogue, the book would be plodding diatribe if not for the humanity and need of Julian. (Bellamy 1960; Bowman 1979; Bowman 1986; Patai 1988)

See also Bellamy, Edward; humanitarianism; *Looking Backward, 2000–1887*; materialism; vision.

WIZARD OF OZ

The Wizard is the supreme ruler of the Emerald City in the land of Oz in L. Frank Baum's whimsical utopian fantasy *The Wonderful Wizard of Oz* (1900), an American young-adult classic in book and film. The Wizard, whom the Witch of the East drove to the City of Emeralds by calling on the Winged Monkeys, remains a mystery to his subjects, as Dorothy learns from questioning residents. They contend that he can take any shape he chooses—a bird, cat, elephant, fairy, or brownie—and that he is invincible.

Dorothy must wait for an audience with the Wizard, whom she imagines as mighty. After the Great Oz appears to her without theatrical trappings or fake voice, he reveals himself to be a short, wrinkled, bald-headed midwesterner from Omaha who happened to land in the Emerald City when his hot-air balloon veered off course. As titular head of the city, he maintains his distance and operates a complex sound-and-light show to perpetuate the myth that he is great, powerful, and not to be trifled with. He demonstrates his gift for illusion by making the Cowardly Lion feel courageous, the Scarecrow appear intelligent, and the Tin Woodman believe he has a heart. Before he can prepare a balloon escape for Dorothy, he accidentally triggers his own upward flight and disappears from his kingdom, leaving a saddened realm below. In sequels of Baum's first Oz book, the Wizard has additional adventures, but they were never so popular as the original story. (Baum 1983; Baum and MacFall 1961; Bewley 1970; Manguel and Guadalupi 1987; Mannix 1964; Snodgrass 1992; Snow 1954; Wagenknecht 1968)

See also Baum, L. Frank; Dorothy; Emerald City; fantasy; Oz; technology; *The Wonderful Wizard of Oz.*

WOMAN ON THE EDGE OF TIME

This ambiguous, feminist dystopian novel was published by Marge Piercy in 1976. The plot, at first set in a Hispanic neighborhood in Brooklyn, New York, juxtaposes scenes of madness, medical torture, flight into the countryside, and visits to a future society. The stark chronicle of draconian health providers sedating, restraining, and dehumanizing female patients in the violent ward of an insane asylum contrasts with scenes of encouragement, acceptance, creativity, love, and family, all of which the main character lacks in her picaresque existence in the barrio.

At age 35, Consuelo "Connie" Camacho Ramos, the novel's focus, is admitted to Bellevue, a public mental institution in New York. Her records indicate that she is a violent schizophrenic guilty of abusing her 4-year-old daughter and incapable of thinking clearly or acting responsibly. As revealed in the clinical reports in Chapter 20, hospital personnel conclude that Connie, unkempt and prematurely aged, has been in decline since the dissolution of her marriage to Martin Ramos and has sunk into a self-destructive rampage of petty crime, assault, child battering, alcoholism, and pill popping. On her release, Connie's record describes decreased psychosis and glimmers of normality. Three years later, she chafes at supervision by a caseworker. In frustration, Connie attacks her niece Dolly and Dolly's pimp with a glass shard. Connie is taken by ambulance to the New York University trauma center. Lodged with violent female patients, Connie consults Luciente, her contact with the future world, and escapes through the woods. Two days later, she is recaptured in a Fairview bus station and treated with brain implants, which are controlled by the staff at Rockover State Psychiatric Hospital.

The inner landscape of *Woman on the Edge of Time* releases Connie from the tentacles of welfare checks, prostitutes, barrios, self-destructive behaviors, and government-controlled supervision. Through plant geneticist Luciente, a resident of a mixed-race commune in Mattapoisett, Massachusetts, in A.D. 2137, Connie employs telepathy to learn his mission. Luciente explains:

> We study with any person who can teach us. We start out learning in our own village, of course. But after naming, we go wherever we must to learn, although only up to the number a teacher can handle. . . . Where you go depends on what you want to study.

The two hold long talks about the future and the past. Luciente abhors the twentieth-century dependence on pesticides and fears the virulence of water tainted with sewage.

Luciente is ambivalent toward his study and, because of his Wamponaug heritage, is burdened by slight variances in language, which weaken his understanding of Connie's generation. He describes his commune of 600 as small and diversified:

> Fasure we're a mixed dish. A breeder of turkeys, an embryo tester, a shelf diver, a flight dealer, a ritual maker, a minder, a telemetrist, a shield grower and a student of blue whales.

The span of ages is 18 to 62; the commune's territory ranges from James Bay to Poughkeepsie, which Luciente jokingly refers to as "the Manhattan Project."

Through a kenner, or "memory annex," Luciente taps into a language database that explains slang terms. He invites Connie to visit and assures her that she will not lose her way back to her own time. Connie describes her disillusionment with psychiatric care, which her brother, Luis Camacho, forces on her. Luciente replies that madhouses of the twenty-second century are

> . . . places where people retreat when they want to go down into themselves—to collapse, carry on, see visions, hear voices of prophecy, bang on the walls, relive infancy—getting in touch with the buried self and the inner mind.

He concludes with a blend of Jungian and gestalt philosophy, "We all lose parts of ourselves. We all make choices that go bad."

Connie's first physical contact with Luciente disorients her—Luciente has breasts, yet displays a forthright posture and masculine demeanor. Connie accepts the strangeness of woman-to-woman communication and leans her forehead against Luciente's. The resulting vision shows her

> . . . a river, little no-account buildings, strange structures like long-legged birds with sails that turned in the wind, a few large terra-cotta and yellow buildings and one blue dome, irregular buildings, none bigger than a supermarket of her day.

To Connie's surprise, Luciente's commune rejects metropolitan life because large cities fall short of human needs and churn up too many petrochemicals and pollutants. In place of skyscrapers, the chewing cows, goats, chickens, and clothes flapping on the line form a bucolic peasant culture that recalls "Tio Manuel's in Texas. A bunch of wetback refugees!"

In Piercy's futuristic setting, each citizen past infancy occupies a private space. Telescreens project facts and articles on plant genetics. Expecting the technologic world of science-fiction novels and second-rate movies, instead Connie recognizes remnants of rural Mexico. In Chapter 3 she concludes:

> I guess we blew ourselves up and now we're back to the dark ages to start it all over again. . . . A better world for the children—that had always been the fantasy: that however bad things were, they might get better.

Luciente explains that children of the future are produced by an alliance of comothers. To Connie, the adults *are* children, a unisex breed who laugh, romp, mate, fly on floaters, and express their artistic flair in mural drawing and music. Willingly admitted into their festive company, she partakes of platters of salad greens that are "good in the mouth and stomach. Pleasant food."

Piercy distances Connie from the future by jerking her back to the asylum. On a drizzly June day, Connie departs the violent ward by a subsequent telepathic meeting with Luciente, whose weather is sunny. She explains how weather has changed since Connie's time:

> It rained for forty days on the Gulf Coast till most of it floated out to sea. Let's see, the jet stream was forced south from Canada. They close to brought on an ice age. There was five years' drought in Australia. Plagues of insects . . .

A more startling revelation than weather control is the embryo tank, a surrogate womb where babies, each produced by three mothers, wait up to ten months to be born. Memories of her own motherhood shove Connie back into the guilt-ridden purgatory haunted by her own Angelina, a ward of the court who lives with foster parents in Larchmont. Connie grows depressed because of long-term care among raging psychotics destabilized on fluctuating doses of drugs and fearful of retaliation by ward keepers.

Luciente tries to relieve Connie's fogged brain of cheerlessness by escorting her to the commune, a farm setting where simple living based on ecological balance and preservation of nature delights her with its relaxing rhythms. A funeral undermines her contentment when she learns that communes require stasis: Every birth requires a death. Luciente's explanations of change confuse Connie. He labels her era "a crux-time." From the twentieth century and beyond, "alternate universes co-exist. Probabilities clash and possibilities wink out forever." The commune restricts its gardens to foods needed for nutrition; there are no luxuries like tea, sugar, or alcohol. Connie doubts that she could live without coffee, which is forbidden as a waste of arable land. Luciente explains that technology is still in a state of flux and that the commune struggles to survive.

Piercy parallels a tenuous society with a tenuous life in the asylum by indicating that Connie's own survival is threatened when she returns to the ward. She observes the metal brain implant that alters Alice's behavior. The scene is prophetic of her own deterioration; she dreads trying to think with a wired, remote-controlled cerebrum. Failing to convince her keepers that she is more coherent and less crazed by delusions, she escapes the ward and wanders two days before the inevitable capture and more dehumanizing incarceration. Meanwhile, the commune's enemy, Chase-World-TT, menaces an easy prey. Connie's otherworldly friends depend on contact with her to strengthen them for the coming battle, which breaks into full-scale attack in Chapter 17. In terror of the sonic sweeps, she flees in despair. Luciente, who is naturally optimistic, clings to faith that "Someday the gross repair will be done. The oceans will be balanced, the rivers flow clean, the wetlands and the forests flourish. There'll be no more enemies. No Them and Us." In the background, the medical team tries to free Connie of her inner demons, which they diagnose as vivid hallucinations.

Piercy offers a single sliver of hope for Connie's autonomy. She attempts to prove her sanity by spending Thanksgiving with her brother's family. Still at war, she arms herself with Parathion, a lethal pesticide, and returns to the hospital. In disjointed telepathic speech, Luciente denies that Connie witnessed war scenes or that her floater was aflame. She identifies the conflict as a hardness in Connie's mind that shuts out telepathy. The staff prepares coffee; Connie laces it with Parathion and dedicates her act of war to the commune.

Critics debate the reality of Connie's brush with the future. Is the commune a pastoral retreat? Is Luciente a light-bringer, as the name implies? Does Connie have an opportunity to redeem herself through selfless aid to Luciente's commune, or is she deluding herself with otherworldly adventures to dodge the misery of psychosis? Whichever interpretation rings true matters less than the warning that social evils, pollution, and brutality defeat Connie in both settings—the present and the future. (Buck 1992; *Contemporary Authors* 1984; *Contemporary Literary Criticism* 1981; Piercy 1976; Walker and Hamner 1984)

See also clairvoyance; escapism; futurism; Piercy, Marge; Ramos, Connie; technology; women in utopia.

 # WOMEN IN UTOPIA

Utopian literature, a loosely defined genre that extends from fanciful idyll, pastoral, science fiction, drama, prophecy, and speculative novels to short stories, poetry, epic, scripture, essay, fable, and oratory, has made no formal gesture toward real women's needs or the need for real women as planners and equal partners in a perfect world. In the heroic era, literature was profoundly male-oriented. Women, when they appear at all, take stereotypical, one-dimensional parts as goddesses (Persephone/Proserpina), expendable wives (Creusa and Sandy), daughters (unlisted in male-only genealogies), mistresses (lovers of Egyptian kings), consorts to the wise philosopher-kings (Plato's unnamed examples), dreamy-eyed seers (Virgil's Cumaean Sibyl), handmaids (Bilhah and Hagar), shepherdesses (Phyllis), camp followers and barkeeps (Siduri and the wife of Utnapishtim), or unnamed slaves (attendants on Bhima, the Balinese hero; the Islamic Houris). In the havens designed by Greeks, Romans, Norse, Balinese, Hebrew, Native American, and Mesopotamian epic writers, the glorification of spear throwers, archers, wrestlers, navigators, priests, and leaders of men (Cain, Aeneas, Hiawatha, Odysseus, Gilgamesh) covers most of the panorama. Frequently, women appear as war trophies or as the essential womb that bears the next great hero, as is the case with Virgil's Lavinia. Religious literature, which is no less guilty of devaluing women, anchors female characters in supportive functions under the guidance of patriarchs and a patriarchal deity. The Bible and Koran ennoble Adam as a garden-keeper who draws for a mate a vulnerable, cardboard Eve ripe for waywardness and destruction. Overall, manly deeds of strength and daring surmount womanly deeds of compassion, nurturing, and faith. Glimpses of women are limited to culprits like Eve and Pandora, supernatural Valkyries, Olympic goddesses, and Aeneas's brief encounter with his wife's shade and that of Queen Dido, his spurned lover; as the widow of the late king of North Africa, Dido supervised the building of the forerunner of Carthage at the time of her suicide. Plutarch, Rome's prominent biographer, proffers even less drama to Lacedaemonian women. In Lycurgus's lengthy plan for a law-abiding Greek deme, women who live, work, and raise families in his militaristic Sparta merit a brief commentary: Plutarch describes a boot-camp atmosphere and the naked bodies the women harden with athletic training.

A separate class of idolized women provides a romantic focus in utopian lore of the Renaissance, when stories of Queen Guinevere and Elaine tread the predetermined patriarchal path of the elevated "lady," a suffocatingly pious, abstract concept that reached its height with Dante Alighieri's Beatrice, the chaste, angelic guide who escorts him through hell and purgatory to heaven in *Divina Commedia* (1320). As defined by Thomas Malory's *Le Morte d'Arthur* (1485) and other traditional English lore, Arthur's role in Camelot equates with mundane policing to rid the English wilds of brigands and ravishers of weak maidens, who require manly protection. Women in Arthurian settings lack policy-making power and expend their talents in subservient roles, e.g., as nurses aboard King Arthur's barge, bargaining chips for marriage agreements, and producers of male heirs, an accomplishment denied to Arthur's ill-fated queen. Her immurement in a convent suggests that lifelong celibacy is the appropriate punishment for a barren consort suspected of adultery with Lancelot, the king's best friend.

The patriarchal vision of the demure, soft-spoken—or nonspeaking—noble lady of quality, grace, and charm perpetuates the "helpless female" myth via the wanderings of Christiana in search of her husband, through whose example she achieves salvation in John Bunyan's *Pilgrim's Progress* (1678), and the disenfranchised, mostly invisible women of Thomas More's *Utopia* (1516). More makes a brief nod toward women's aspirations by allowing women into the priesthood, but he limits applicants to the elderly. Relegated to small bits of utopian commentary are the extremes of frivolous mirror-lookers, ribbon-flaunters, and vain gadabouts. In François Rabelais's *Gargantua and Pantagruel* (1562) men share the Abbey of Thélème, a compound populated by self-indulgent beauties of aristocratic heritage whose pinnacle of achievement is a happy marriage. So too do ladies ornament but reserve their full intellectual attendance at the salons and audience halls of Baldessar Castiglione's *The Courtier* (1528). In the sparkling, potentially remunerative microcosm of the aristocrat, women are an object of pursuit only if they are beautiful, rich, and titled; the men who pursue these trophies attain to an unrealistic perfection through training and socialization tailored to create the ideal court gentleman. (No equivalent writer of Castiglione's volubility, wit, and talent explains how the best of women are readied for court.)

Ironically, the most beatific, enchanting lady from the Renaissance, Doña Dulcinea del Toboso from Cervantes's *Don Quixote* (1615), doesn't exist at all. For Don Quixote, the ethereal dream woman floats before his earthly path like a hologram, a manufactured version of womanhood devoid even of flesh and breath. At least in Cervantes's version, the less-perfect females who bind wounds, turn game birds over spits, serve tipplers and diners at inns, and ready guest chambers resemble the real thing—the suppressed female nonentity to whom education, power, or admission to the professions is unthinkable. In addition to the nameless servant girls and Don Quixote's housekeeper and niece, Sancho Panza's wife and daughter, Teresa and Mari-Sancha, offer a bit of contrast to the far ends of the continuum, from drudges to the saintly Dulcinea.

Manhood evolved significantly in the post-Renaissance era. In later utopias and dystopias, men no longer prove their worth by merely governing wisely, standing tough, or slaughtering invaders. However, the move toward realism continues to exclude or obscure the female perspective. The incarceration of women in traditional kitchens, salons, and bedrooms limits the depiction of utopia, as demonstrated by the self-sacrificing Zee, a priestess and lover of the visitor to Vril-Ya in Edward Bulwer-Lytton's *The Coming Race* (1871), and Mrs. Aristides Homos, the glowing convert to Altrurianism in William Dean Howells's *A Traveler from Altruria* (1872) and its sequel, *Through the Eye of the Needle* (1907). Likewise, in *A Connecticut Yankee in King Arthur's Court* (1886), Mark Twain denies the voluble, intrusive Sandy—Mrs. Hank Morgan—a useful aim beyond mothering her sickly daughter Hello-Central, named for Hank's fantasies of Puss Flanagan, his old flame back in nineteenth-century Hartford. Other nineteenth-century examples of women grow more distorted because male utopists picture them as decorative: the lithe and lovely Fayaway, an afternoon's diversion for Tommo in Herman Melville's *Typee* (1846); Minnehaha, gracious Indian princess in Henry Wadsworth Longfellow's *The Song of Hiawatha* (1855); and Edith Leete, who rhapsodizes over old love letters in Edward Bellamy's *Looking Backward* (1887). One near-heroine, Weena, a spindly shanked, pseudoadult Eloi who clings to the Time Traveller and festoons him with flowers in H. G. Wells's *The Time Machine* (1895), provides temporary leadership through the dystopic future, yet sinks into a swoon and dies ignobly in a forest fire, perhaps serving the cannibalistic Morlocks as a brief meal.

The first strong, decisive woman to thrive in utopian fiction is Chastel, an isolated, somewhat pompous Gaea, or earth mother figure, who resides in the

Mother's Room in W. H. Hudson's *A Crystal Age* (1887). In his stiffly structured matriarchy, Hudson focuses on botanist Smith, who is enamored of a gentle people and their appealing, soft-spoken women. In a strained effort to compliment the female sex, he tells Edra, the friend of his beloved Yoletta:

> It must be patent to every one that women have far quicker, finer intellects than men, although their brains are smaller; but then quality is more important than mere quantity . . . some people hold that women fight not to have the franchise, or suffrage, or whatever it is! Not that I care two straws about the question myself, and I only hope they'll never get it; but then I think it is so illogical—don't you?

Smith's ambivalence toward feminist issues suits Hudson's flimsy plot, which exalts a single controlling mother while dooming the remaining females to celibacy, a high price to pay for the liberation of one woman per household. In the same detached mode, Rima, a wispy dream girl in Hudson's *Green Mansions* (1904), hovers above the dazzled Abel in a suspended otherworldliness of dappled shade and indistinct persona. As unattainable as Don Quixote's Dulcinea, Rima bears a stronger resemblance to J. M. Barrie's sprightly Tinker Bell in *Peter Pan* (1904) than to an actual human female. In the final analysis, Hudson's lame attempt to champion women breaks down into a transcendence of sex that supplants normal human libido with romanticized sunsets, flowers, furtive conversations, and fits of melancholia.

Apart from a rare example—Virginia Woolf's *Orlando* (1928)—early-twentieth-century utopists and dystopists come no closer to liberating women from hopelessly inane situations. Children's stories carry the utopian dream closer to women by increasing their visibility, yet authors seem stuck on the motherly Dorothy in the Land of Oz and the cloyingly sweet Wendy Darling, the maternal figure who guards the Lost Boys but stays out of fights with pirates and Indians in Peter Pan's Neverland. Karel Capek's *R. U. R.* (1920) produces a similar earth angel—the overly idealistic Helena Glory Domin, a representative of the humanistic community whose meddling in robotics nearly destroys the world. Opposite Helena stand the dim-witted O, the potential baby-maker of Yevgeny Zamyatin's *We* (1921); servile female Sioux of *Black Elk Speaks* (1932); and the women of Aldous Huxley's *Brave New World* (1932)— Linda, a drugged-out sex slave on a Zuñi reservation, and the coquettish, amoral Lenina Crowne, a mindless chatterbox intent on making the perfect date for the evening. James Hilton's *Lost Horizon* (1933) nods briefly toward a fuller, more dignified cast of female personae with a disparate pair: the fanatic missionary, Miss Brinklow, who manages to balance the musical talent and haunting beauty of Lo-Tsen, the love interest who spoils Shangri-La for the cool, distant, brilliant Hugh "Glory" Conway.

Female protagonists make no memorable niche for themselves in utopian fare of the 1940s, 1950s, and 1960s. In George Orwell's *Animal Farm* (1945), the egregious role of Mollie, a vain wearer of ribbons, denies her an understanding and/or appreciation of Old Major's experimental farm ideal, an enterprise run by animals; the ignominious Mollie eventually deserts and works in a pub.

In Orwell's *1984* (1949), Julia seduces Winston, who was abandoned by his wife nine years previously; however, like the air-headed horse Mollie, Julia makes no cognitive connection between coercion and the need to rebel in clandestine afternoons in bed with Winston. Her role in the novel renders her the perfect sex toy who has nothing to add to the polemics of Oceania. Ayn Rand, an influential female dystopist and lecturer, further degrades feminine intellectual powers with Liberty 5-3000, the wild-maned sower of seeds who regresses toward an even more useless function as wife to the hero in *Anthem* (1937). The last straw is Liberty 5-3000's wish for a son to please her mate—ironically named Equality 7-2521.

Toward midcentury, women evolve into a more active but still incomplete characterization. Ray Bradbury's *Fahrenheit 451* (1953) depicts the hero, Guy Montag, as Mildred's disgruntled husband who flirts briefly with Clarisse, a will-o'-the-wisp teenage savant. Guy scarcely misses "poor, poor Millie," whose graphic attempt at suicide prefigures the destruction of Los Angeles after she betrays him to the authorities for hiding books. At a distance, she dies anonymously in a minutes-long war, completed in a single blitz. Baptized and invited to a spartan male fireside chat, Guy joins Granger and the other men, who make inroads against tyranny in a brotherhood of book-savers. The same year that Bradbury published his famous dystopia, Hermann Hesse's *Siddhartha* was completed, yet found no strong demand for its philosophical message until two decades later. Epitomizing woman-as-temptress, Kamala, Siddhartha's painted, richly perfumed temptress, lures him from his spiritual quest and bears him a son, the ungrateful young Siddhartha. Like the mythic Eurydice, bride of Orpheus, Kamala succumbs to the bite of a poisonous snake, leaving her former lover to his contemplation of the river. This bleak, degenerate vision of women in utopia holds to its unpromising sameness into the 1960s, when Alex Haley completed *The Autobiography of Malcolm X* (1965), a bombshell title that urged black males to seek pride in self and accomplishment in a white-dominated society. Yet, the pattern produces no surprise alterations, no breakthroughs in female liberation. Almost as stodgy and sexist as the hero-centered Elysian Fields and Valhalla in ancient lore, Malcolm X formulates a heaven on Earth for Muslim males, but delegates baby-making, home chores, home schooling, and other pink-collar jobs to the long-suffering wives, including his own, Betty X Shabazz.

The arrival of powerful, thoughtful women in the utopian matrix occurs simultaneously with the profemale movement, which encouraged women to educate themselves; choose goals without regard to society's preconceived notions of beauty, motherhood, and wifeliness; fulfill desires without regard to public prejudice or prohibition; and become equal participants in human affairs. The literary blossoming is slow and laborious, like the night-blooming cereus making its once-per-century show:

- Marge Piercy's Connie Ramos muddles through a chance at autonomy after fleeing to a future century, then falling into the medical Underworld's dehumanizing grasp in *Woman on the Edge of Time* (1976).

- Similarly powerless and oddly detached is Doris Lessing's unnamed apartment dweller and foster mother of the rabid Emily, a capricious, slightly psychotic street urchin, in *Memoirs of a Survivor* (1974).

- A typical West Coast counterculture amazon, Marissa Brightcloud in Ernest Callenbach's *Ecotopia* (1975) lights up the world of William Weston, whose antipathy toward the East Coast journalistic milieu pulls him irrevocably toward Ecotopianism and a woman with strength and self-assurance. Unlike ambivalent or duplicitous women from New York, Weston's lover knows what direction to take and what emotional and physical forces to apply to her goals. At first she repulses Weston by vigorously and unapologetically courting him, yet their consummation of love and trust becomes the basis for his acceptance of Ecotopian philosophy and of a woman who dares to express a healthy libido.

- A bit less heroic than Virgil's *Aeneid* (19 B.C.) or *Gilgamesh* (1200 B.C.), Richard Adams's beast fable *Watership Down* (1972) includes in his mostly male rabbit utopia a few does to breed a strong strain of replacements for Hazel's warren. To supervise the choice, Bigwig relies on Hyzenthlay, the clairvoyant insider doe. To himself, Bigwig marvels: "He had stumbled, quite unexpectedly, upon what he needed most of all, a strong, sensible friend who would think on her own account and help to bear his burden."

The break in centuries of stereotyping ends with the flourish caused by Margaret Atwood, Canadian dystopist who wrote *The Handmaid's Tale* (1985). Under her controlled satire, the image of woman as functioning womb grows into a monstrous dystopian perversion and produces the twentieth-century's most enduringly feminist survivalist heroine. More capable than Jack London's groveling Avis Everhard in *The Iron Heel* (1907), more purposeful than Lilith, the mythic earth mother who speaks the epilogue in George Bernard Shaw's *Back to Methuselah* (1921), the unnamed Handmaid clutches at sanity, release, and love in that order, putting herself first in a setting that threatens dissidents with hanging for adultery and permanent cleanup assignment to a dead land killed by radiation for Unwomen, i.e., those too old to conceive. Buoyed by love of her daughter and empowered by a feminist mother for a role model and a lesbian college roommate who manages to stay alive while fighting the system, the Handmaid figures her chances and plays the odds: If she stays as the Commander's brood-wife, she may lose all; if she commits adultery with the Commander's chauffeur without getting caught, she may free herself and reunite with her daughter. Loyal to a distant possibility, the Handmaid walks the thin line between compliant concubine and rebel.

Margaret Atwood's bold Handmaid sets a precedent, proving that if there is any hope for the female protagonist in utopia, it must lie far afield from the Pandoras and Eves, the ever-patient Penelopes, the Polynesian hut slaves of Melville's and Mandeville's travelogues, the servants and domestics of More's *Utopia* and Shakespeare's *The Tempest* (1611), and the manipulated females, e.g.,

Women play varied roles in utopian literature. William Morris, artist and author of the utopian novel *News from Nowhere*, portrayed Queen Guinevere of the English Arthurian legend as a romantic figure in this 1858 work.

the multiple wives of Mormon Joseph Smith; Serena Joy, the evangelist-turned-matron; and Aunt Lydia, mother superior and warden of an indoctrination center in Atwood's dystopic Gilead. As depicted by Maryann Crescent Moon, chair of a symposium studying Gilead's theocracy and by Orlando, title character in Virginia Woolf's surreal utopia, the strength of women as survivors, as planners and participants in significant action, deserves its place in the utopian literature of the coming centuries. More than added names to the cast of characters, women are essential to the other half of the human race and to the creation and enjoyment of a perfect world. (Adams 1972; Atwood 1972; Barrie 1981; Baum 1983; Bradbury 1953; Bulwer-Lytton 1979; Bunyan 1896; Callenbach 1975; Capek and Capek 1961; Castiglione 1976; Cervantes 1957; Dante Alighieri 1968; Haley 1965; Hesse 1951; Howells 1907; Howells 1957; Hudson 1917; Huxley 1932; Lessing 1988; London 1982a; Longfellow 1992; Malory 1982; Melville 1964; More 1963a; Neihardt 1961; Parrington 1964; Piercy 1976; Rabelais 1955; Rand 1946; Twain 1963; Virgil 1950; Voltaire 1961; Wells 1964; Woolf 1928; Zamyatin 1972)

See also The Abbey of Thélème; Adams, Richard; Aeneas; *Animal Farm; Anthem;* Arthur; *The Autobiography of Malcolm X; Brave New World;* The Commander; *A Connecticut Yankee in King Arthur's Court; The Courtier; A Crystal Age;* Don Quixote; Dorothy; *Ecotopia; Fahrenheit 451; The Handmaid's Tale; Lost Horizon; Memoirs of a Survivor; 1984; Pilgrim's Progress;* Serena Joy; *Siddhartha;* Smith, Joseph, Jr.; *Through the Eye of the Needle; The Time Machine; A Traveler from Altruria; Typee;* utopia; *Utopia;* Virgil; *Watership Down; Woman on the Edge of Time; The Wonderful Wizard of Oz.*

THE WONDERFUL WIZARD OF OZ

One of America's most successful, most enduring children's escapist fantasies, this novel, published by L. Frank Baum in 1900, featured 124 three-color illustrations by William Wallace Denslow, his noted collaborator. A momentous allegorical utopia created out of Baum's desire for nonviolent, thought-provoking young-adult literature, *The Wonderful Wizard of Oz* got its name from a filing cabinet drawer labeled O–Z. Baum began with a utopian plan—the episode entitled "The Emerald City"—and advanced to novel length. The vanguard of later young-adult fantasy, *The Wonderful Wizard of Oz* spawned a series of Oz titles, including *The Land of Oz, The Road to Oz, The Magic of Oz,* and ten others. However, no later title approached the original for its cohesion and themes, which continue to please audiences in film, stage, and book versions.

Baum, who lived on the American prairie, used his own past experience with loneliness and boredom as motivation for a natural opening scene for his wayward but good-natured heroine. The story features Aunt Em and Uncle Henry's orphaned niece, Dorothy, who comes to live on the bleak Kansas plains and grows increasingly dismayed with midwestern farm life. Dorothy's daily existence is so hard that she takes little pleasure in anything except her dog Toto. Her departure from home is cataclysmic: While trying to catch Toto and take him into the storm cellar, Dorothy and the house are swept up and away in a cyclone. The whirling motion rocks Dorothy to sleep. She awakens in Munchkin land, an idyllic country filled with green grass and flowers and populated by small people. The kindly Witch of the North thanks Dorothy for killing the Witch of the East (inadvertently, after the cyclone dropped the house on top of her). Unaware of her heroic deed, Dorothy weeps as she begs for help in returning to Kansas. The Witch of the North blesses her with a kiss on the forehead and sends her down the Yellow Brick Road to ask for help from Oz, the Great Wizard.

Along the way, Dorothy befriends others who need the Wizard's help. First she meets a Scarecrow who needs a brain, then a Tin Woodman who needs a heart, and a Cowardly Lion who needs courage. The four travelers lose their way while fording a river by raft; a helpful stork sets them on dry land, but the Yellow Brick Road is nowhere to be seen. Continuing without direction, they escape a sleep-inducing field of poppies and rescue a mouse. For this kindness, the mouse queen awards Dorothy a whistle and has the mice work together to pull the sleeping lion from the poppies.

A master at theatrical touches, Baum extends the suspense and heightens the tension as Dorothy and the trio close in on their destination. At length, they arrive at the Emerald City and await their audience with the Great Wizard, who sees only one visitor per day. Dorothy takes the first turn and addresses the giant head, which claims to be "Oz, the Great and Terrible." Oz takes an interest in the kiss that adorns her forehead and the silver shoes she wears. He agrees to help Dorothy if she will kill the remaining evil menace, the Witch of the East. His replies to the Tin Woodman, Scarecrow, and Lion are the same— they must destroy the witch before receiving their requests.

Dorothy and her followers journey through rough, pathless terrain. The Witch of the East, who spies them coming, sends 40 wolves to stop them. The Tin Woodman chops the head off each wolf. The Witch dispatches King Crow and his birds, whom the Scarecrow strangles. The Witch then orders black bees to sting the visitors, but the Scarecrow uses his stuffing as a covering for Dorothy, the Lion, and Toto. Seeing only one target, the bees attack the Tin Woodman and destroy themselves against his metal body. At last the Witch sends the Winkies, whom the Lion scares away. As a final effort, the Witch of the East dons her magic cap and orders the Winged Monkeys to defeat the four visitors. The monkeys subdue the trio accompanying Dorothy, but refuse to harm her or Toto because of the protective kiss on her forehead. The Witch puts Dorothy to work scouring pots in the kitchen, then trips her so that she can steal one of the silver shoes. Dorothy retaliates by throwing a pail of water on the witch. To Dorothy's surprise, the Witch melts into nothing.

Baum stresses his heroine's concern for others, one of her most endearing traits. Dorothy urges the Winkies to find tinsmiths to rescue the Tin Woodman and restuff the Scarecrow. Suitably restored, the foursome, with Dorothy wearing the witch's Golden Cap, sets out for the Emerald City, but loses the way again. By summoning the Winged Monkeys, Dorothy is flown to the Wizard, who responds as an awesome, disembodied voice. The travelers learn that the

The title page of the first edition of L. Frank Baum's *The Wonderful Wizard of Oz* with illustrations by W. W. Denslow shows the Tin Woodman and the Scarecrow, Dorothy's companions in search of the Wizard of Oz, who resides in the utopian Emerald City.

Wizard is only a pose—he is really an ordinary man. The Wizard tricks the Tin Woodman, Scarecrow, and Lion into believing that they have received their desires for heart, brain, and courage. While preparing a great silk balloon in which to fly Dorothy back to her home in Kansas, the Wizard unintentionally slips away without her. His subjects mourn his departure, but accept the wise Scarecrow in his stead. Through more adventures among a land of china people and a forest of beasts, the group marches to the home of Glinda, the good Witch of the South, who tells Dorothy to wish on her silver shoes. The wish works; Dorothy reappears on the farm in Kansas, leaving the Lion and Tin Woodman to their own kingdoms.

Baum's innovative, energetic brand of young-adult fiction resulted in the sale of 5 million copies. The story evolved into film, plays, puppet shows, recordings, toys, games, art prints, clothing, and musical comedies. *The Wonderful Wizard of Oz* inspired numerous writers, including Shirley Jackson, Ray Bradbury, William Styron, and Gore Vidal. The movie version, filmed in 1939, set the tone for the end of the Depression. Starring Judy Garland, Frank Morgan, Ray Bolger, Bert Lahr, Jack Haley, Billie Burke, and Margaret Hamilton, the film was nominated for best art and best picture, and won an Oscar for its utopian theme song "Somewhere over the Rainbow." (Baum 1983; Baum and MacFall 1961; Bewley 1970; Manguel and Guadalupi 1987; Mannix 1964; Snodgrass 1992; Snow 1954; Wagenknecht 1968)

See also Baum, L. Frank; Dorothy; Emerald City; escapism; fantasy; Oz; Wizard of Oz.

XANADU

This Asian coastal pleasure palace of Kublai Khan, a Mongol warlord, is featured in Samuel Taylor Coleridge's sensuous verse fragment "Kubla Khan" (1798), subtitled "A Vision in a Dream," in which the poet simplifies the spelling of a real warrior's name. Above ground, Xanadu sits surrounded by wolds and flourishes with fragrant gardens, streams, towers, ten miles of arable fields, meadows, and a bower where a musician strums a dulcimer. In the distance the woods resound with the cries of women disappointed by their demon lovers. Beneath the domed palace, ice caves contrast the sunny scene meant to relax the Mongol leader. A gushing fountain feeds Alf, a sacred river that flows five miles before pouring into the nearby "sunless sea." Tradition claims that the voices of the khan's ancestors reverberate in the splash of a waterfall. Although incomplete in its descriptions, the titillating, beguiling images hint at untold pleasures of an exotic retreat from the great khan's military and governmental responsibilities. (Coleridge 1948; Dille 1969; Hornstein et al. 1973; Magill 1958; Willey 1973)

See also city planning; escapism; "Kubla Khan"; vision.

ZAMYATIN, YEVGENY

Playwright, iconoclastic novelist, prophet, and essayist, Zamyatin wrote *We* (1921), an influential Russian dystopian novel that was first published in the West in 1924 and influenced numerous subsequent writers, including Ayn Rand, Aldous Huxley, George Orwell, and H. G. Wells. Weighted down by distrust of anarchy, enforced uniformity, oppression, and the political dreamers that preceded him—Karl Marx, Josef Stalin, and Leon Trotsky—Zamyatin concluded that revolutions do not end; by definition, revolution is ongoing. This credo expresses Zamyatin's study of the innate human urge for self-determination and fulfillment, which he epitomizes in Chapter 27 of *We* in the promise, "We shall break down all walls—to let the green wind blow free from end to end—across the earth."

Zamyatin was born on February 1, 1884, in Lebedyan in the province of Tambov, the Russian wheat belt 200 miles south of Moscow. The son of an Orthodox priest and a pianist, he knew firsthand the vitality of the soil and the Russian-speaking peasants who work it. From childhood, Zamyatin appreciated the moral example and literary mastery of Gogol and Dostoyevski, his idols. He studied at the Voronesh Gymnasium and excelled in composition before enrolling in naval engineering at the St. Petersurg Polytechnical Institute. After graduating in May 1908 he initially allied with the Bolsheviks, yet remained attuned to humanistic expression. In 1905 he was arrested by the Secret Service and thrown into solitary confinement for pursuing an anti-tsarist philosophy. On his release, he was exiled from his hometown and spent two years in the barrens of Lachta, where he gave up writing specifications for ships and began honing his literary talents. For four years he lurked on the rim of society so that he could finish his engineering degree.

In 1911 Zamyatin's blatant flouting of court orders brought him again into custody, and once more he was cast out of St. Petersburg. Granted amnesty at age 29, he returned home to teach science at his alma mater. He published "A Provincial Tale" and followed the next year with "At the World's End," a neorealist reflection of the spiritual isolation and alienation that preceded the Russian Revolution and World War I. Because of his intense verisimilitude, examination of the grotesque, and familiarity with contemporary street slang, both Zamyatin and his publisher were tried but found innocent of slandering Tsar Nicholas I.

During World War I, Zamyatin ceased writing and resided for two years in England, where he studied the design of icebreakers and helped the Russian government develop similar ships to free up ice-jammed ports. The St. Bartholomew's Day Massacre brought him back to Russia. The next October, frenzied with concern for his native land, he outfitted himself with a life preserver and swam through dark waters past German submarines to Russia. Remorseful that he did not view the first shots of the revolution, Zamyatin experienced a searing anti-Western impetus. This emotion impelled him to publish two anti-British satires, "The Islanders" and "The Fisher of Men," and a personal essay, "I Am Afraid." The upshot of this repatriation was a disgust with the English, whom he considered trivial and devoid of worthy goals. Meanwhile, in Russia, the end of the revolution produced a cheerless muddle, a suitable cultural and artistic climate in which he could probe his literary inclinations to help the backward, war-torn country evolve into an equal to modern Europe. In 1920 Zamyatin joined a seedy, unheated writer's commune called the House of the Arts, where he edited and wrote among an evolving literati who represented Russia's best, most energetic, and least affluent creative minds.

Amid the clash of differing philosophies, Zamyatin fit in with the Serapion Brotherhood, an experimental group who championed individuality over propaganda, bourgeois pomposity, and didacticism. He declared that writers owed their readers honesty, a quality that could not be compromised by political expediency. Like his fellow Serapionites, he embraced heresy as the only means by which the Russian intelligentsia could reassert human values. Rejecting the tsar and the past as well as the chaos of his own time, Zamyatin asserted that the future was the sole substance with which he could work. In 1921 and 1923 he broached utopianism with his essays "Paradise" and "The New Russian Prose," two bold alarums condemning past hopes. These short treatises served as a preface to a new era of creativity, fantasy, and altruistic philosophy.

Throughout Zamyatin's evolution into a visionary, he rejected entropy, the sterility of the status quo, and the mind-numbing synchronization of thought and feeling. To combat mental paralysis, he urged the search for vast horizons, which he outlined in "The Goal," composed in 1926. His disillusion with communism brought him into conflict with the party line and into the ranks of the most illustrious dissidents, including Boris Pasternak and Alexander Solzhenitsyn. No respectable house would publish Zamyatin's works, so he turned to the underground press, a phenomenon of the writers and idealogues who rejected outright the sovietization of literature and journalism.

Richly diverse in his lively, provocative, wide-ranging wit, comedy, and satire, Zamyatin harbored no illusions that his point of view would triumph over the iron fist of communism. Similar to the style of William Goldings's *Lord of the Flies* (1954) and Anthony Burgess's *A Clockwork Orange* (1962), Zamyatin composed two plays, *The Fires of St. Dominic* (1923) and *The Society of Honorary Bell-Ringers* (1926), before launching his dystopian novel *We*. The book stirred much rancor among party faithfuls, who took offense at the egalitarian implications and anti-Soviet tone. The Russian Association of Proletarian Writers began its clampdown on freethinkers, resulting in destruction of presses, widespread persecution, and rampant suicides among Russia's idealists. Zamyatin, too, considered himself doomed—an outsider and homebound exile.

After *We* was translated into English in 1924 and into Czechoslovakian three years later, it was pirated by a Czechoslovakian Journal, *Volya Rosii*, in 1927. Despite the author's innocence in the matter, the authorities pressed other writers to implicate Zamyatin in anti-Soviet propaganda. When he returned from his summer vacation, his outrage against cowards who once claimed to be colleagues resulted in his resignation from the writers' union. He persisted against the power structure—calling the censors "little men"—and published "On the Future of the Theater," a black-edged death notice for those who continued to believe in individual rights. He maintained a loyal following, who petitioned Stalin to reinstate those titles that had been squelched.

Zamyatin gained a significant boost from Maxim Gorky, an insider with Stalin, who gained a reprieve for the banned works. In 1931 Zamyatin willed himself to become a nonperson by emigrating to France and living out his remaining six years in poverty and isolation, far from his beloved Russia and deliberately cut off from other Russian émigrés. On March 2, 1937, in Paris, Zamyatin succumbed to heart disease, a conclusion to his long vigil for a return to free speech in his native land. His obituary was never published in Russia; his contributions to Russian literature were obliterated from anthologies and histories.

In the West, Zamyatin's writings have enjoyed a resurgence. His essays, plays, short stories, and novels are readily available. Translated into ten languages, *We*, Zamyatin's masterwork, is currently read in Russia in the original. The author receives scant mention in literary histories, but his strong grasp of irony as a weapon against totalitarianism gained credence in derivative works: *Brave New World* (1932), Aldous Huxley's notable escapist dystopia; Ayn Rand's earnestly philosophic *Anthem* (1937); and *1984* (1949) by George Orwell, Zamyatin's English disciple. (Grigson 1963; Kunitz 1942; Russell 1994; Shane 1968; Zamyatin 1972)

See also *Animal Farm; Anthem; Brave New World;* Burgess, Anthony; *A Clockwork Orange;* D-503; Golding, William; Huxley, Aldous; *Lord of the Flies; 1984;* O-90; Orwell, George; Rand, Ayn; *We;* women in utopia.

 # APPENDIX A

PRIMARY SOURCES

Adams, Richard. 1972. *Watership Down.* New York: Avon Books.

Andreae, Johann. 1955. "Christianopolis." In *Famous Utopias of the Renaissance.* New York: Hendricks House.

Aristophanes. *The Birds.* 1993. London: David Brown.

Atwood, Margaret. 1972. *Surfacing; Life before Men; The Handmaid's Tale.* New York: Quality Paperback Club.

Augustine. 1958. *The City of God.* Garden City, N.Y.: Image Books.

———. 1981. *The Confessions of St. Augustine.* Chicago: Moody.

Bacon, Francis. 1905. *The Philosophical Works of Francis Bacon.* Salem, N.H.: Ayer.

Barrie, J. M. 1981. *Peter Pan.* New York: Bantam Books.

Baum, L. Frank. 1983. *The Annotated Wizard of Oz.* New York: Schocken Books.

Bellamy, Edward. 1960. *Looking Backward, 2000–1887.* New York: New American Library.

Bhagavad Gita. 1992. Largo, Fla: Top of the Mountain Publishing.

The Book of the Dead. 1960. New Hyde Park, N.Y.: University Books.

Bradbury, Ray. 1953. *Fahrenheit 451.* New York: Ballantine Books.

———. 1990. *The Vintage Bradbury.* New York: Vintage Books.

Bulwer-Lytton, Edward. 1979. *The Coming Race.* Santa Barbara, Calif.: Woodbridge Press.

Bunyan, John. 1896. *Pilgrim's Progress and the Holy War.* Chicago: Puritan Publishing.

Burgess, Anthony. 1962. *A Clockwork Orange.* New York: Ballantine Books.

Butler, Samuel. 1968. *Erewhon.* New York: Lancer Books.

Cabet, Étienne. 1973. *Voyage en Icarie.* New York: Kelley.

Callenbach, Ernest. 1975. *Ecotopia.* New York: Bantam Books.

Campanella, Fra Tomaso. 1955. *La Città del Sole.* In *Famous Utopias of the Renaissance.* New York: Hendricks House.

Capek, Josef, and Karel Capek. 1961. *R. U. R.* New York: Oxford University Press.

Carlyle, Thomas. 1977. *Past and Present.* New York: New York University Press.

Carroll, Lewis. 1960. *The Annotated Alice.* New York: Bramhall House.

Castiglione, Baldessar. 1976. *The Book of the Courtier.* New York: Viking Penguin.

Cervantes, Miguel de. 1957. *Don Quixote.* New York: Mentor Books.

Cicero. 1966. *De Republica in Classics in Translation.* Madison: University of Wisconsin.

Clarke, Arthur C. 1953. *Childhood's End.* New York: Ballantine Books.

Coleridge, Samuel Taylor. 1948. "Kubla Khan." in *The Anthology of Romanticism.* New York: Ronald Press.

Confucius. 1992. *Confucianism: The Analects of Confucius.* New York: HarperCollins.

Dante Alighieri. 1968. *The Divine Comedy.* New York: Washington Square Press.

———. 1982. *Inferno.* New York: New American Library.

Defoe, Daniel. 1963. *Robinson Crusoe.* New York: Airmont Books.

Diderot, Denis. 1972. *Supplement aux Voyages de Bougainville.* New York: French and European Publications.

Dutt, Romesh C., trans. *The Ramayana and the Mahabharata.* 1910. London: J. M. Dent.

Faraday, Winifred. 1902. *The Edda,* Parts 1 & 2. New York: AMS Press.

Ferry, David. 1992. *Gilgamesh.* New York: Farrar, Straus and Giroux.

Forster, E. M. 1966. *The Collected Tales of E. M. Forster.* New York: Alfred A. Knopf.

Fourier, Charles. 1972. *Selections from the Works of Fourier.* New York: Gordon Press.

Ghazali. *Alchemy of Happiness.* 1964. New York: Orientalia.

Golding, William. *Lord of the Flies.* 1954. New York: Wideview/Perigee Books.

Goldsmith, Oliver. *Asem*. 1992. In *The Collected Poetical Works of Oliver Goldsmith*. Irvine, Calif.: Reprint Service.

Haley, Alex. 1965. *The Autobiography of Malcolm X*. New York: Ballantine Books.

Harrington, James. 1992. *The Commonwealth of Oceana and a System of Politics*. New York: Cambridge University Press.

Hawthorne, Nathaniel. 1959. *The Scarlet Letter*. New York: New American Library.

Hertzka, Theodor. 1972. *Freeland: A Social Anticipation*. New York: Gordon Press.

Hesiod. *Theogony*. 1966. New York: Oxford University Press.

———. *Works and Days*. 1973. Ann Arbor: University of Michigan Press.

Hesse, Hermann. *Siddhartha*. 1951. New York: New Directions Publishing.

Hilton, James. 1933. *Lost Horizon*. New York: Pocket Books.

Holy Bible. 1958. Cleveland, Ohio: World Publishing.

Homer. *The Odyssey*. 1946. New York: Penguin.

Howells, William Dean. 1907. *Through the Eye of the Needle*. New York: Harper & Brothers.

———. 1957. *A Traveler from Altruria*. New York: Sagamore Press.

Hudson, W. H. n.d. *Green Mansions*. New York: Amsco School Publications.

———. 1916. *A Crystal Age*. New York: E. P. Dutton.

Huxley, Aldous. 1932. *Brave New World*. New York: Bantam Books.

———. 1948. *Ape and Essence*. New York: Harper & Brothers.

———. 1989. *Brave New World Revisited*. HarperCollins,

James, P. D. 1993. *The Children of Men*. New York: Alfred A. Knopf.

Johnson, Samuel. 1982. *Johnson: Selected Writings*. New York: Viking Penguin.

Kalevala. 1950. Hancock, Mich.: Book Concern.

Karp, David. 1953. *One*. New York: Grosset & Dunlap.

Koestler, Arthur. 1962. *Darkness at Noon*. New York: Time.

Lao Tzu. 1993. *To Know and Not Be Knowing*. San Francisco: Chronicle Books.

Lawrence, Jerome, and Robert E. Lee. 1971. *The Night Thoreau Spent in Jail*. New York: Bantam Books.

Lessing, Doris. 1988. *Memoirs of a Survivor*. New York: Random House.

London, Jack. 1982. *The Iron Heel*. In *Novels and Social Writings*. New York: Library of America.

Longfellow, Henry Wadsworth. 1992. *The Song of Hiawatha*. London: J. M. Dent.

Malory, Sir Thomas. 1982. *Le Morte d'Arthur*. London: Collier Books.

Malthus, Thomas. 1990. *An Essay on the Principle of Population*. New York: Cambridge University Press.

Mandeville, Bernard de. 1989. *The Fable of the Bees*. New York: Penguin.

Marx, Karl. 1992. *Das Kapital*. Ventura, Calif.: Regal.

Marx, Karl, and Friedrich Engels. 1985. *The Communist Manifesto*. New York: Viking Press.

Melville, Herman. 1961. *Moby Dick or the White Whale*. New York: New American Library.

————. 1964. *Typee*. New York: New American Library.

————. 1968. *Omoo*. Evanston, Ill.: Northwestern University Press.

Milton, John. 1957. *Complete Poems and Major Prose*. New York: Odyssey Press.

Mitchell, Stephen. 1988. *Tao Te Ching*. New York: Harper & Row.

Montaigne, Michel de. Repr. of 1893 ed. *The Essays of Montaigne*. New York: AMS Press.

More, Sir Thomas. 1963. *The Complete Works*. New Haven, Conn.: Yale University Press.

Morris, William. 1968. *Three Works by William Morris*. New York: International Publishers.

Neihardt, John G. 1961. *Black Elk Speaks*. Lincoln: University of Nebraska Press.

Orwell, George. 1946. *Animal Farm*. New York: Harcourt Brace Jovanovich.

————. 1949. *1984*. New York: New American Library.

Ovid. 1977. *Metamorphoses*. Cambridge, Mass.: Harvard University Press.

Piercy, Marge. 1976. *Woman on the Edge of Time*. New York: Fawcett Crest.

Plato. 1937. "Timaeus." In *The Dialogues of Plato*. New York: Random House.

————. 1955. *The Republic*. New York: Viking Penguin.

Plutarch. 1971. *The Life of Lycurgus*. In *Moral Essays*. London: Harmondsworth.

Poe, Edgar Allan. 1962. *Selected Stories and Poems*. New York: Airmont Books.

Pucci, Idanna. 1992. *Bhima Swarga*. Boston: Little, Brown.

The Qu'ran. New York: Quality Paperback.

Rabelais, François. 1955. *Gargantua and Pantagruel*. New York: Viking Penguin.

Rand, Ayn. *Anthem*. 1946. New York: New American Library.

Rig Veda. 1900. New York: AMS Press.

Shakespeare, William. 1958. *A Midsummer Night's Dream*. New York: Washington Square Press.

———. 1959. *As You Like It*. New York: Washington Square Press.

———. 1961. *The Tempest*. New York: Washington Square Press.

Shaw, G. B. 1988. *Back to Methuselah*. New York: Penguin.

Skinner, B. F. 1988. *Walden Two*. New York: Macmillan.

Smith, Joseph, trans. 1982. *The Book of Mormon*. Salt Lake City: The Church of Jesus Christ of Latter-Day Saints.

Stevenson, Robert Louis. 1988. *A Child's Garden of Verses*. New York: Macmillan Child's Group.

Stewart, Mary. 1970. *The Crystal Cave*. Greenwich, Conn.: Fawcett.

———. 1973. *The Hollow Hills*. Greenwich, Conn.: Fawcett.

———. 1984. *The Last Enchantment*. Greenwich, Conn.: Fawcett.

Stowe, Harriet Beecher. 1991. *Uncle Tom's Cabin* New York: Random House.

Swift, Jonathan. 1958. *Gulliver's Travels and Other Writings*. New York: Modern Library.

Tao Te Ching. 1988. New York: Harper & Row.

Tasso, Torquato. 1987. *Jerusalem Delivered*. Detroit: Wayne State University Press.

Tennyson, Alfred. 1949. "Locksley Hall" and "Locksley Hall Sixty Years After." In *Victorian and Later English Poets*. New York: American Book Co.

———. 1989. *Idylls of the King*. New York: Viking.

———. 1949."The Lotus-Eaters." In *Victorian and Later English Poets*. New York: American Book Co.

Thoreau, Henry David. 1965. *Walden and "Civil Disobedience."* New York: Airmont.

Tocqueville, Alexis de. 1969. *Democracy in America*. New York: Harper Perennial.

Twain, Mark. 1963. *A Connecticut Yankee in King Arthur's Court*. New York: New American Library.

Upanishads. 1965. New York: Viking Penguin.

Verne, Jules. 1985. *Twenty Thousand Leagues under the Sea*. New York: Bantam Books.

Virgil. 1950. *Virgil's Works: The Aeneid, Eclogues and Georgics*. New York: Modern Library.

Voltaire. 1961. *Candide, Zadig, and Selected Stories.* New York: New American Library.

Vonnegut, Kurt. 1990. *Cat's Cradle.* New York: Henry Holt.

Wells, H. G. 1964. *The Time Machine.* New York: Airmont.

———. 1967. *A Modern Utopia.* Lincoln: University of Nebraska.

Woolf, Virginia. 1928. *Orlando.* New York: Harcourt Brace.

Zamyatin, Yevgeny. 1972. *We.* New York: Viking Press.

Zenda-Vesta of Zarathustra. 1993. New York: Orientalia.

 # APPENDIX B

TITLES FEATURED IN THE TEXT

Aeneid (19 B.C.)
Analects of Confucius (second century A.D.)
Animal Farm (1945)
Anthem (1937)
As You Like It (1599)
Asem, an Eastern Tale (1759)
The Autobiography of Malcolm X (1965)
Back to Methuselah (1921)
The Birds (414 B.C.)
Black Elk Speaks (1932)
The Book of Mormon (1830)
The Book of the Dead (fifteenth century B.C.)
Brave New World (1932)
Brave New World Revisited (1958)
Bucolics (also known as *Eclogues)*
  (42–37 B.C.)
Candide (1759)
Childhood's End (1953)
The Children of Men (1993)
Christianopolis (1619)
La Città del Sole (1602)
De Civitate Dei (A.D. 426)
A Clockwork Orange (1962)
The Coming Race (1871)
The Commonwealth of Oceana (1656)
The Communist Manifesto (1848)
*A Connecticut Yankee in King Arthur's
  Court* (1886)
The Courtier (1528)
A Crystal Age (1887)
Das Kapital (1867)
"Des Cannibales" (1580)

Divina Commedia (1320)
Don Quixote (1615)
Ecotopia (1975)
Erewhon (1872)
The Fable of the Bees (1714)
Fahrenheit 451 (1951)
Freiland (1890)
Gargantua and Pantagruel (1562)
Genesis (ca. 950 B.C.)
Gilgamesh (1200 B.C.)
The Giver (1993)
Green Mansions (1904)
Gulliver's Travels (1727)
The Handmaid's Tale (1985)
Idylls of the King (1888)
The Iron Heel (1907)
Jerusalem Delivered (1581)
Koran (610)
"Kubla Khan" (1798)
The Life of Lycurgus (first century A.D.)
"Locksley Hall" (1842)
"Locksley Hall Sixty Years After" (1886)
Looking Backward, 2000–1887 (1887)
Lord of the Flies (1954)
Lost Horizon (1933)
"The Lotus-Eaters" (1832)
Memoirs of a Survivor (1974)
A Midsummer Night's Dream (ca. 1595)
Le Morte d'Arthur (1485)
The New Atlantis (1627)
News from Nowhere (1890)
1984 (1949)

Omoo (1847)
Paradise Lost (1667)
Paradise Regained (1671)
Past and Present (1843)
Peter Pan (1904)
Pilgrim's Progress (1678)
"Rasselas, Prince of Abissinia" (1759)
The Republic (fifth century B.C.)
Revelation (A.D. 90–95)
Robinson Crusoe (1719)
R. U. R. (1920)
Sermon on the Mount (first century A.D.)
Siddhartha (1922)
Supplement aux Voyages de Bougainville (1772)
Tao Te Ching (third century B.C.)

The Tempest (1611)
"There Will Come Soft Rains" (1950)
Through the Eye of the Needle (1907)
Timaeus (fifth century B.C.)
The Time Machine (1895)
A Traveler from Altruria (1872)
Typee (1846)
Utopia (1516)
Voyage en Icarie (1840)
Walden (1854)
Walden Two (1948)
Watership Down (1972)
We (1921)
Woman on the Edge of Time (1976)
The Wonderful Wizard of Oz (1900)

APPENDIX C

TITLES FEATURED IN THE TEXT, LISTED BY DATE

Book of the Dead (fifteenth century B.C.)
Gilgamesh (1200 B.C.)
Genesis (ca. 950 B.C.)
The Republic (fifth century B.C.)
Timaeus (fifth century B.C.)
The Birds (414 B.C.)
Tao Te Ching (third century B.C.)
Bucolics (also known as *Eclogues*)
    (42–37 B.C.)
Aeneid (19 B.C.)
Metamorphoses (A.D. 8)
Revelation (A.D. 90–95)
The Life of Lycurgus (first century A.D.)
Sermon on the Mount (first century A.D.)
Analects of Confucius (second century A.D.)
De Civitate Dei (A.D. 426)
Koran (610)
Divina Commedia (1320)
Le Morte d'Arthur (1485)
Utopia (1516)
The Courtier (1528)
Gargantua and Pantagruel (1562)
"Des Cannibales" (1580)
Jerusalem Delivered (1581)
A Midsummer Night's Dream (ca. 1595)
As You Like It (1599)
La Città del Sole (1602)
The Tempest (1611)
Don Quixote (1615)
Christianopolis (1619)
The New Atlantis (1627)
The Commonwealth of Oceana (1656)

Paradise Lost (1667)
Paradise Regained (1671)
Pilgrim's Progress (1678)
The Fable of the Bees (1714)
Robinson Crusoe (1719)
Gulliver's Travels (1727)
Asem, an Eastern Tale (1759)
Candide (1759)
"Rasselas, Prince of Abissinia" (1759)
Supplement aux Voyages de Bougainville
    (1772)
"Kubla Khan" (1798)
The Book of Mormon (1830)
"The Lotus-Eaters" (1832)
Voyage en Icarie (1840)
"Locksley Hall" (1842)
Past and Present (1843)
Typee (1846)
Omoo (1847)
The Communist Manifesto (1848)
Walden (1854)
Das Kapital (1867)
The Coming Race (1871)
Erewhon (1872)
A Traveler from Altruria (1872)
"Locksley Hall Sixty Years After" (1886)
A Crystal Age (1887)
A Connecticut Yankee in King Arthur's
    Court (1886)
Looking Backward, 2000–1887 (1887)
Idylls of the King (1888)
Freiland (1890)

News from Nowhere (1890)

The Time Machine (1895)

The Wonderful Wizard of Oz (1900)

Green Mansions (1904)

Peter Pan (1904)

The Iron Heel (1907)

Through the Eye of the Needle (1907)

R. U. R. (1920)

Back to Methuselah (1921)

We (1921)

Black Elk Speaks (1932)

Brave New World (1932)

Lost Horizon (1933)

Anthem (1937)

Animal Farm (1945)

Walden Two (1948)

1984 (1949)

"There Will Come Soft Rains" (1950)

Fahrenheit 451 (1953)

Siddhartha (1922)

Childhood's End (1953)

Lord of the Flies (1954)

Brave New World Revisited (1958)

A Clockwork Orange (1962)

The Autobiography of Malcolm X (1965)

Watership Down (1972)

Memoirs of a Survivor (1974)

Ecotopia (1975)

Woman on the Edge of Time (1976)

The Handmaid's Tale (1985)

The Children of Men (1993)

The Giver (1993)

 BIBLIOGRAPHY

Abbott, Walter M., et al. 1969. *The Bible Reader.* New York: Bruce Publishing.

Abrams, M. H., gen. ed. 1968. *The Norton Anthology of English Literature.* New York: W. W. Norton.

Adams, Richard. 1972. *Watership Down.* New York: Avon Books.

Ady, Julia M. 1908. *Baldassare Castiglione: The Perfect Courtier, His Life and Letters.* New York: AMS Press.

Aggler, Geoffrey, ed. 1986. *Critical Essays on Anthony Burgess.* Boston: G. K. Hall.

Albinski, Nan Bowman. 1988. *Women's Utopias in British and American Fiction.* New York: Routledge.

Albright, Daniel. 1986. *Tennyson: The Muses' Tug-of-War.* Charlottesville: University Press of Virginia.

Alexander, David, and Pat Alexander, eds. 1973. *Eerdmans' Handbook to the Bible.* Herts, England: Lion Publishing.

Allen, Gay Wilson. 1971. *Melville and His World.* New York: Viking Press.

Alok, Roi. 1989. *Orwell and the Politics of Despair: A Critical Study of the Writings of George Orwell.* New York: Cambridge University Press.

Amis, Kingsley. 1960. *New Maps of Hell: A Survey of Science Fiction.* New York: Harcourt Brace.

Anderson, Bernhard W. 1966. *Understanding the Old Testament.* 2d ed. Englewood Cliffs, N.J.: Prentice-Hall.

Anderson, William. 1989. *Dante the Maker.* Winchester, Mass.: Unwin Hyman.

Andreae, Johann. 1955. "Christianopolis." In *Famous Utopias of the Renaissance,* edited by R. Frederic White. New York: Hendricks House.

Andrews, Charles M. n.d. Introduction to *Famous Utopias.* New York: Tudor Publishing.

———. 1901. Introduction to *Ideal Empires and Republics.* New York: William H. Wise.

Andrews, Ted. 1992. *How To Uncover Past Lives.* St. Paul, Minn.: Llewellyn Publications.

Andrews, Wayne. 1981. *Voltaire.* New York: New Directions.

Antosik, Stanley J. 1978. *The Question of Elites.* New York: Peter Lang.

Aristophanes. 1962. *The Birds.* In *Four Comedies.* New York: Harcourt Brace Jovanovich.

———. 1993. *The Birds.* London: David Brown.

Armstrong, Karen. 1994. *A History of God.* New York: Alfred A. Knopf.

Arnot, Robert P. 1976. *William Morris, the Man and the Myth.* Westport, Conn.: Greenwood.

Ashe, Geoffrey. 1987. *The Landscape of King Arthur.* New York: Henry Holt.

Ashton, Graham. 1974. *The Realm of King Arthur.* Isle of Wight, England: J. Arthur Dixon.

Asimov, Isaac. 1969. *Words from the Myths.* New York: Signet Key Books.

Atlas of Communism. 1991. New York: Macmillan.

Atwood, Margaret. 1972. *Surfacing; Life before Men; The Handmaid's Tale.* New York: Quality Paperback Club.

Augustine. 1958. *The City of God.* Garden City, N.Y.: Image Books.

———. 1981. *The Confessions of St. Augustine.* Chicago: Moody.

Ayer, A. J. 1986. *Voltaire.* New York: Random House.

Babbitt, Natalie. 1993. "Review of *The Giver.*" *Washington Post Book World,* May 9, 3.

Bacon, Francis. 1905. "The New Atlantis." In *The Philosophical Works of Francis Bacon.* Salem, N.H.: Ayer.

Baehr, Stephen Lessing. 1991. *The Paradise Myth in Eighteenth-Century Russian and Utopian Patterns in Early Secular Russian Literature and Culture.* Stanford, Calif.: Stanford University Press.

Baker, James R., ed. 1988. *Critical Essays on William Golding.* Boston: G. K. Hall.

Baker, James T. 1987. *Ayn Rand.* Boston: G. K. Hall.

Baker, Robert S. 1990. Brave New World: *History, Science, and Dystopia.* Boston: G. K. Hall.

Bammer, Angelika. 1991. *Partial Vision: Feminism and Utopianism in the 1970s.* New York: Routledge.

Barrie, J. M. 1981. *Peter Pan*. New York: Bantam Books.

Bartkowski, Frances. 1989. *Feminist Utopias*. Lincoln: University of Nebraska Press.

Baugh, Albert C., ed. 1948. *A Literary History of England*. New York: Appleton-Century-Crofts.

Baum, Frank Joslyn, and Russell P. MacFall. 1961. *To Please a Child: A Biography of L. Frank Baum*. Chicago: Reilly & Lee.

Baum, L. Frank. 1983. *The Annotated Wizard of Oz*. New York: Schocken Books.

Baumer, Franz. 1969. *Hermann Hesse*. New York: Frederick Ungar.

Beauchamp, Gorman. 1984. *Jack London*. San Bernardino, Calif.: Borgo Press.

Bechtel, Paul, ed. 1981. *The Confessions of St. Augustine*. Chicago: Moody.

Bedford, Sybille. 1985. *Aldous Huxley*. New York: Carroll & Graf.

Bell, Robert E. 1989. *Place-Names in Classical Mythology: Greece*. Santa Barbara, Calif.: ABC-CLIO.

Bellamy, Edward. 1960. *Looking Backward, 2000–1887*. New York: New American Library.

Benét, William Rose. 1991. *The Reader's Encyclopedia*. New York: Thomas Y. Crowell.

Bennett, George N. 1973. *The Realism of William Dean Howells*. Nashville, Tenn.: Vanderbilt University Press.

Bentley, Gerald E. 1961. *Shakespeare: A Biographical Handbook*. New Haven, Conn.: Yale University Press.

Bergmann, Harriet F. 1989. "Teaching Them To Read: A Fishing Expedition in *The Handmaid's Tale*." *College English* (December), 847–854.

Bernard, John D., and Paul T. Alessi, eds. 1986. *Virgil at 2000: Commemorative Essays on the Poet and His Influence*. Lawrence, Kans.: AMS Press.

Berneri, Marie Louise. 1951. *Journey through Utopia*. Boston: Beacon Press.

Bernstein, Charles, ed. 1983. *Baudelaire, Rimbaud and Verlaine: Selected Verse and Prose Poems*. New York: Carol Publishing Group.

Bernstein, Jeremy. 1969. "Out of the Ego Chamber." *New Yorker* (9 August).

Bewley, Marius. 1970. *Masks and Mirrors*. New York: Atheneum.

Bhagavad Gita. 1992. Largo, Fla.: Top of the Mountain Publishing.

Biederman, Hans. 1992. *Dictionary of Symbolism*. New York: Facts on File.

Binswanger, Harry. 1988. *The Ayn Rand Lexicon*. New York: New American Library.

Bishop, Morris. 1965. *A Survey of French Literature.* Vol. 1: *The Middle Ages to 1800.* New York: Harcourt Brace Jovanovich.

Blanchet, Leon. 1920. *Campanella 1568–1639.* New York: Burt Franklin.

Bleich, David. 1984. *Utopia: The Psychology of a Cultural Fantasy.* Ann Arbor, Mich.: UMI Research Press.

Blofeld, John. 1973. *The Secret and the Sublime: Taoist Mysteries and Magic.* London: George Allen & Unwin.

Bloom, Harold. 1986a. *Cervantes.* New York: Chelsea House.

———. 1986b. *Dante.* New York: Chelsea House.

———. 1986c. *Doris Lessing.* New York: Chelsea House.

———. 1986d. *Herman Melville.* New York: Chelsea House.

———. 1986e. *Mark Twain.* New York: Chelsea House.

———. 1987a. *Anthony Burgess.* New York: Chelsea House.

———. 1987b. *Daniel Defoe.* New York: Chelsea House.

———. 1987c. *George Orwell's* Nineteen Eighty-Four. New York: Chelsea House.

———. 1987d. *Michel de Montaigne's Essays.* New York: Chelsea House.

———. 1987e. *Oliver Goldsmith.* New York: Chelsea House.

Bogan, Mary Inez. 1984. *Vocabulary and Style of the Soliloquies and Dialogues of St. Augustine.* Cleveland, Ohio: Zubal.

Boorstin, Daniel J. 1983. *The Discoverers: A History of Man's Search To Know His World and Himself.* New York: Vintage Books.

———. 1992. *The Creators: A History of Heroes of the Imagination.* New York: Vintage Books.

Boswell, James. 1981. *Everybody's Boswell: Being the Life of Samuel Johnson.* Athens: Ohio University Press.

Boulting, William. 1969. *Tasso and His Times.* Brooklyn: Haskell.

Boulton, James T., ed. 1978. *Johnson: The Critical Heritage.* New York: Routledge.

Bowman, Sylvia. 1979. *Year 2000: A Critical Biography of Edward Bellamy.* New York: Hippocrene Books.

———. 1986. *Edward Bellamy.* New York: Macmillan.

Boyce, Charles. 1990. *Shakespeare A to Z.* New York: Facts on File.

Bradbury, Ray. 1953. *Fahrenheit 451.* New York: Ballantine Books.

———. 1975. *The Ray Bradbury Companion.* Detroit: Bruccoli Clark Books.

————. 1990a. *The Vintage Bradbury.* New York: Vintage Books.

————. 1990b. *Yestermorrow: Obvious Answers to Impossible Futures.* San Bernardino, Calif.: Borgo Press.

Breit, Harvey. 1956. *The Writer Observed.* New York: World Publishing.

Breitman, George. 1965. *Malcolm X: The Man and His Ideas.* Pittsburgh, Pa.: Merit Group.

————. 1967. *The Last Year of Malcolm X.* Pittsburgh, Pa.: Merit Group.

Brewer, E. Cobham, ed. 1899. *The Reader's Handbook.* Philadelphia: J. B. Lippincott.

Brockett, Oscar G. 1968. *History of the Theatre.* Boston: Allyn & Bacon.

Brooke, Barbara. 1989. *The Sioux.* Vero Beach, Fla.: Rourke.

Brown, Dee. 1970. *Bury My Heart at Wounded Knee.* New York: Henry Holt.

Brown, Edward James. 1976. Brave New World, 1984, *and* We. Ann Arbor, Mich.: Ardis.

Bryant, Arthur. 1966. *The Medieval Foundation of England.* Garden City, N.Y.: Doubleday.

Bryant, John, ed. 1986. *A Companion to Melville Studies.* Westport, Conn.: Greenwood.

Buck, Claire, ed. 1992. *The Bloomsbury Guide to Women's Literature.* New York: Prentice-Hall.

Buckler, William E. 1958. *Prose of the Victorian Period.* Boston: Houghton Mifflin.

Budd, Louis J. 1983. *Critical Essays on Mark Twain.* Boston: G. K. Hall.

Budge, E. A. Wallis. 1960. *The Book of the Dead.* New Hyde Park, N.Y.: University Books.

Buitehuis, Peter, and Ira B. Nadel, eds. 1988. *George Orwell: A Reassessment.* New York: St. Martin's Press.

Bulfinch's Mythology. 1964. London: Hamlyn Publishing.

Bulwer-Lytton, Edward. 1979. *The Coming Race.* Santa Barbara, Calif.: Woodbridge Press.

Bunyan, John. 1896. *Pilgrim's Progress and the Holy War.* Chicago: Puritan Publishing.

Burckhardt, Titus, trans. 1969. *Letters of a Sufi Master.* Middlesex, England: Perennial Books.

Burgess, Anthony. 1962. *A Clockwork Orange.* New York: Ballantine Books.

Burke, Vernon J. 1984. *Wisdom from St. Augustine.* South Bend, Ind.: University of Notre Dame.

Butler, Samuel. 1968. *Erewhon.* New York: Lancer Books.

Byron, William. 1988. *Cervantes: A Biography.* New York: Paragon House.

Cabet, Étienne. 1973. *Voyage en Icarie.* New York: Kelley.

Calder, Jenni. 1987. Animal Farm *and* Nineteen Eighty-Four. New York: Taylor & Francis.

Callenbach, Ernest. 1975. *Ecotopia.* New York: Bantam Books.

———. 1981a. *Ecotopia Emerging.* Berkeley, Calif.: Banyan Tree.

———. 1981b. *The Ecotopian Encyclopedia for the 80s.* Berkeley, Calif.: And/Or Press.

———. 1990. *Ecotopia: The Notebooks and Reports of William Weston.* New York: Bantam Books.

Campanella, Fra Tomaso. 1950. *La Città del Sole.* In *Journey through Utopia,* ed. Marie Louise Berneri. Boston: Beacon Press.

———. 1955. *La Città del Sole.* In *Famous Utopias of the Renaissance.* New York: Hendricks House.

Cannan, G. 1925. *Samuel Butler: A Critical Study.* Brooklyn: Haskell.

Capek, Josef, and Karel Capek. 1961. *R. U. R.* New York: Oxford University Press.

Carey, John, ed. 1987. *William Golding: The Man and His Books.* New York: Farrar, Straus & Giroux.

Carlyle, Thomas. 1977. *Past and Present.* New York: New York University Press.

Carpenter, Finlay. 1985. *The Skinner Primer: Behind Freedom and Dignity.* New York: Free Press.

Carpenter, Humphrey, and Mari Prichard. 1984. *The Oxford Companion to Children's Literature.* New York: Oxford University Press.

Carson, Clayborne. 1991. *Malcolm X: The FBI File.* New York: Carroll & Graf.

Carver, Terrell, ed. 1991. *The Cambridge Companion to Marx.* New York: Cambridge University Press.

Castiglione, Baldessar. 1976. *The Book of the Courtier.* New York: Viking Penguin.

Catullus. 1893. Cambridge, Mass.: Harvard University Press.

Cavendish, Marshall. 1970. *Man, Myth, and Magic.* New York: Marshall Cavendish.

Cavendish, Richard. 1980. *The Great Religions.* New York: Arco Publishing.

Ceram, C. W. 1968. *Gods, Graves, and Scholars: The Story of Archaeology.* New York: Alfred A. Knopf.

Cervantes, Miguel de. 1957. *Don Quixote*. New York: Mentor Books.

Chambers, R. W. 1935. *Thomas More*. London: Cape Publishing Ltd.

Chapman, Graham. 1968. *Black Voices: An Anthology of Afro-American Literature*. New York: New American Library.

Chase, Mary Ellen. 1955. *Life and Language in the Old Testament*. New York: W. W. Norton.

Chianese, Robert L., ed. 1971. *Peaceable Kingdoms: An Anthology of Utopian Writings*. New York: Harcourt Brace Jovanovich.

Children's Literature Review. 1984. Vol. 6. Detroit: Gale Research.

Chute, Marchette. 1949. *Shakespeare of London*. New York: E. P. Dutton.

———. 1951. *An Introduction to Shakespeare*. New York: E. P. Dutton.

Cirlot, J. E. 1971. *A Dictionary of Symbols*. New York: Dorset.

Clareson, Thomas D., ed. 1976. *Voices for the Future: Essays on Major Science Fiction Writers*. Vol. 1. New York: Bowling Green University.

Clark, R. T. Rundle. 1959. *Myth and Symbol in Ancient Egypt*. London: Thames and Hudson.

Clarke, Arthur C. 1953. *Childhood's End*. New York: Ballantine Books.

———. 1963. *2001: A Space Odyssey*. New York: New American Library.

———. 1990. *Astounding Days: A Science Fictional Autobiography*. New York: Bantam Books.

Cleary, Thomas. 1991. *The Essential Tao*. San Francisco: Harper.

Clifton, Chas S. 1992. *Encyclopedia of Heresies and Heretics*. Santa Barbara, Calif.: ABC-CLIO.

Clowes, Edith W. 1993. *Russian Experimental Fiction: Resisting Ideology after Utopia*. Princeton, N.J.: Princeton University Press.

Coale, Samuel. 1981. *Anthony Burgess*. New York: Continuum.

Coates, Joseph F., and Jennifer Jarratt. 1989. *What Futurists Believe*. Bethesda, Md.: World Future Society.

Coleridge, Samuel Taylor. 1948. "Kubla Khan." In *The Anthology of Romanticism*. New York: Ronald Press.

Collier, John. 1947. *Indians of the Americas*. New York: New American Library.

Collins, James. 1989. *Dante: Layman, Prophet, Mystic*. Staten Island, N.Y.: Alba House.

Commire, Anne. 1978. *Yesterday's Authors of Books for Children*. Vol. 1. Detroit: Gale Research.

Confucius. 1992. *The Analects of Confucius.* New York: HarperCollins.

Connelly, Mark. 1986. *The Diminished Self: Orwell and the Loss of Freedom.* Pittsburgh, Pa.: Duquesne.

Contemporary Authors, New Revision Series. 1981. Vol. 3. Detroit: Gale Research.

———. 1984. Vol. 13. Detroit: Gale Research.

———. 1986. Vols. 15–16. Detroit: Gale Research.

———. 1988. Vol. 21. Detroit: Gale Research.

———. 1989. Vol. 33. Detroit: Gale Research.

Contemporary Literary Criticism. 1976. Vol. 5. Detroit: Gale Research.

———. 1981a. Vol. 14. Detroit: Gale Research.

———. 1981b. Vol. 18. Detroit: Gale Research.

———. 1987. Vol. 44. Detroit: Gale Research.

Cooper, Ilene. 1993. "Giving and Receiving." *Booklist,* April 15.

Corsaro, Julie. 1994. "Lois Lowry's *The Giver.*" *Book Links,* May, 9–11.

Costa, Richard. 1985. *H. G. Wells.* Boston: G. K. Hall.

Cowie, Alexander. 1951. *The Rise of the American Novel.* New York: American Book Co.

Crane, Ronald S., ed. 1932. *A Collection of English Poems, 1660–1800.* New York: Harper & Row.

Crenshaw, Gwendolyn J. 1991. *Malcolm X: Developing Self-Esteem, Self-Love, and Self-Dignity.* Indianapolis, Ind.: Aesop Enterprises.

Crick, Bernard. 1980. *George Orwell: A Life.* Boston: Little, Brown.

Critical Interpretations Series. 1987. New York: Chelsea House.

Cross, F. L., ed. 1957. *The Oxford Dictionary of the Christian Church.* London: Oxford University Press.

Crossley, Robert. 1986. *Reader's Guide to H. G. Wells.* Mercer Island, Wash.: Starmont House.

Cuddon, J. A. 1979. *A Dictionary of Literary Terms.* New York: Penguin.

Dante Alighieri. 1968. *The Divine Comedy.* New York: Washington Square Press.

———. 1982. *The Inferno.* New York: New American Library.

Darlington, W. A. 1974. *J. M. Barrie.* Brooklyn, N.Y.: Haskell.

Davidson, Cathy N. 1986. "A Feminist *1984.*" *Ms.* (February), 24–26.

De Lange, P. J. 1925. *Samuel Butler: Critic and Philosopher.* Brooklyn, N.Y.: Haskell.

Dearden, C. W. 1976. *The Stage of Aristophanes.* London: Athlone Press.

Defoe, Daniel. 1963. *Robinson Crusoe.* New York: Airmont Books.

Dembo, L. S., and Annis Pratt, eds. 1993. *Doris Lessing: Critical Essays.* Ann Arbor, Mich.: Books on Demand.

Den Uyl, Douglas J., and Douglas B. Rasmussen, eds. 1984. *The Philosophic Thought of Ayn Rand.* Urbana: University of Illinois Press.

Deur, Lynne. 1972. *Indian Chiefs.* Minneapolis, Minn.: Lerner.

Dexter, D. Gilbert. 1972. *Life and Works of Henry Wadsworth Longfellow.* New York: Gordon Press.

Dickey, Norma, ed. 1993. *Funk & Wagnalls New Encyclopedia.* New York: Funk & Wagnalls.

Dickinson, Patric, intro. 1964. *Virgil's* Aeneid. New York: New American Library.

Dickinson, Thomas H. 1943. *Chief Contemporary Dramatists: Twenty Plays from the Recent Drama of England, Ireland, America, Germany, France, Belgium, Norway, Sweden, and Russia.* Boston: Houghton Mifflin.

Dictionary of Literary Biography. 1987. Vol. 52. Detroit: Gale Research.

Diderot, Denis. 1972. *Supplement aux Voyages de Beaugainville.* New York: French and European Publications.

Dille, Roland. 1969. *Four Romantic Poets: Wordsworth, Coleridge, Shelley, Keats.* New York: Holt, Rinehart & Winston.

Dix, Carol M. 1971. *Anthony Burgess.* White Plains, N.Y.: Longman.

Dixon, J. Arthur. 1974. *The Realm of King Arthur.* Isle of Wight, England: J. Arthur Dixon.

Donner, Henry W. 1969. *Introduction to Utopia.* Freeport, N.Y.: Books for Libraries.

Downs, Michael. 1977. *James Harrington.* New York: Irvington.

Downs, Robert B. 1956. *Books That Changed the World.* New York: New American Library.

Drabble, Margaret, ed. 1985. *The Oxford Companion to English Literature.* 5th ed. New York: Oxford University Press.

Draper, Michael. 1988. *H. G. Wells.* New York: St. Martin's Press.

Dreifus, Claudia. 1992. "Margaret Atwood." *The Progressive* (March) 30–33.

Dunbar, Janet. 1970. *J. M. Barrie: The Man behind the Image.* Boston: Houghton Mifflin.

Duran, Manuel. 1974. *Cervantes.* Boston: G. K. Hall.

Durant, Will. 1939. *The Life of Greece*. New York: Simon & Schuster.

Dutt, Romesh C., trans. 1910. *The Ramayana and the Mahabharata*. London: J. M. Dent.

Duval, Edwin M. 1991. *The Design of Rabelais's* Pantagruel. New Haven, Conn.: Yale University Press.

Eagle, Dorothy, and Hilary Carnell, eds. 1992. *The Oxford Illustrated Literary Guide to Great Britain and Ireland*. 2d ed. New York: Oxford University Press.

Ehrenberg, Victor. 1943. *The People of Aristophanes: A Sociology of Old Attic Comedy*. Oxford, England: Blackwell.

Ehrlich, Eugene, and Gorton Carruth. 1982. *The Oxford Illustrated Literary Guide to the United States*. New York: Oxford University Press.

Eliade, Mircea, ed. 1986. *The Encyclopedia of Religion*. New York: Macmillan.

Elliott, Robert C. 1970. *The Shape of Utopia: Studies in a Literary Genre*. Chicago: University of Chicago Press.

Ellis, Peter Berresford. 1991. *A Dictionary of Irish Mythology*. New York: Oxford University Press.

Emerson, Everett. 1985. *The Authentic Mark Twain: A Literary Biography of Samuel L. Clemens*. Philadelphia: University of Pennsylvania Press.

Engell, James, ed. 1985. *Johnson and His Age*. Cambridge, Mass.: Harvard University Press.

Enroth, C. A., ed. 1970. *Major British Authors: Spenser and Milton*. New York: Holt, Rinehart & Winston.

Esbach, Lloyd, ed. 1964. *Of Worlds Beyond: The Science of Science Fiction Writing*. Chicago: Advent.

Escholtz, Paul A., ed. 1975. *Critics on William Dean Howells*. Baltimore, Md.: University of Miami Press.

Evans, Ivor H., ed. 1817. *Brewer's Dictionary of Phrase and Fable*. New York: Harper & Row.

Faraday, Winifred. 1902. *The Edda*. Parts 1 & 2. New York: AMS Press.

Feder, Lillian. 1986. *The Meridian Handbook of Classical Literature*. New York: New American Library.

Fellows, Otis. 1989. *Diderot*. New York: Macmillan.

Ferguson, John. 1975. *Utopias in the Classical World*. Ithaca, N.Y.: Cornell University Press.

Ferrell, Keith. 1988. *George Orwell: The Political Pen*. New York: M. Evans.

Ferry, David. 1992. *Gilgamesh*. New York: Farrar, Straus & Giroux.

Field, George W. 1970. *Hermann Hesse.* New York: Macmillan.

Finkelstein, Norman. 1988. *The Utopian Moment in Contemporary American Poetry.* Cranberry, N.J.: Bucknell University Press.

Finn, Molly. 1993. "Review." *Commonweal* (24 April), 1300.

Fischer, Carl. 1968. *The Myth and Legend of Greece.* Dayton, Ohio: George A. Pflaum.

Fishburn, Katherine. 1985. *The Unexpected Universe of Doris Lessing: A Study of Narrative Technique.* Westport, Conn.: Greenwood.

Fleissner, Else M. 1972. *Hermann Hesse: Modern German Poet and Writer.* New York: Sam-Har Press.

Flower, S. J. 1973. *Bulwer-Lytton.* Merrimack, Mass.: Newbury Books.

Forman, H. Buxton. 1992. *The Books of William Morris.* Watchung, N.J.: Saifer.

Fourier, Charles. 1972. *Selections from the Works of Fourier.* New York: Gordon Press.

Fraser, James George. 1947. *The Golden Bough.* New York: Macmillan.

Fuller, Edmund, ed. 1959. *Plutarch: Lives of the Noble Greeks.* New York: Dell.

Gallen, David. 1992. *Malcolm X: As They Knew Him.* New York: Carroll & Graf.

Gardner, Averil. 1987. *George Orwell.* Boston: G. K. Hall.

Garrison, Daniel H. 1984. *The Language of Virgil.* New York: Peter Lang.

Gassner, John, and Edward Quinn, eds. 1969. *The Reader's Encyclopedia of World Drama.* New York: Thomas Y. Crowell.

Gay, Peter. 1988. *Voltaire's Politics: The Poet as Realist.* New Haven, Conn.: Yale University Press.

Geduld, Harry M. 1987. *The Definitive* Time Machine: *A Critical Edition of H. G. Wells's Scientific Romance.* Indianapolis: Indiana University Press.

Genesis in the Holy Bible. 1958. Cleveland, Ohio: World Publishing.

Gerber, Richard. 1958. *Utopian Fantasy.* New York: McGraw-Hill, 1973.

Ghazali. 1964. *The Alchemy of Happiness.* New York: Orientalia.

Gibb, John, and William Montgomery. 1980. *The Confessions of St. Augustine.* New York: Garland.

Gillispie, Charles Coulston, ed. 1970. *Dictionary of Scientific Biography.* New York: Charles Scribner's Sons.

Gilman, Richard. 1974. "Review." *New York Times Book Review* (24), 3–4.

Gilman, Stephen. 1989. *The Novel According to Cervantes.* Berkeley: University of California Press.

Gilson, Etiénne. 1983. *The Christian Philosophy of St. Augustine.* New York: Hippocrene Books.

Gindin, James. 1988. *William Golding.* New York: St. Martin's Press.

Gladstein, Mimi R. 1984. *The Ayn Rand Companion.* Brooklyn, N.Y.: Greenwood.

Golding, William. 1954. *Lord of the Flies.* New York: Wideview/Perigee Books.

Goldman, Peter L. 1979. *The Death and Life of Malcolm X.* Champaign: University of Illinois Press.

Goldsmith, Oliver. 1992. *Asem.* In *Complete Poetical Works.* Irvine, Calif.: Reprint Service.

Grant, Michael. 1962. *Myths of the Greeks and Romans.* New York: Mentor Books.

Graves, Robert, intro. 1968. *New Larousse Encyclopedia of Mythology.* London: Prometheus Press.

Greene, James J. 1971. *Victorian Prose: Carlyle, Arnold, Mill.* New York: Holt, Rinehart & Winston.

Grigson, Geoffrey, ed. 1963. *The Concise Encyclopedia of Modern World Literature.* New York: Hawthorn Books.

Grimal, Pierre. 1991. *Dictionary of Classical Mythology.* London: Penguin.

Guerber, H. A. 1921. *Myths of Greece and Rome.* New York: American Book Co.

Haley, Alex. 1965. *The Autobiography of Malcolm X.* New York: Ballantine Books.

Hall, Judy. 1991. *The Karmic Journey: The Birchart, Karma and Reincarnation.* New York: Viking Penguin.

Hall, Marie-Louise. 1972. *Montaigne and His Translators.* Chelsea, England: Gordon Press.

Halliwell's Film Guide. 1989. New York: Harper & Row.

Hamilton, Edith. 1942. *Mythology.* Boston: Little, Brown.

Hammer, Stephanie Barbé. 1990. "The World as It Will Be? Female Satire and the Technology of Power in *The Handmaid's Tale.*" *Modern Language Studies* (Spring), 39–49.

Hammond, N. G. L., and H. H. Scullard, eds. 1970. *The Oxford Classical Dictionary.* Oxford, England: Clarendon Press.

Hanning, Robert W., and David Rosand. 1983. *Castiglione: The Ideal and the Real in Renaissance Culture.* New Haven, Conn. Yale University Press.

Hardie, Philip. 1986. *Virgil's* Aeneid: *Cosmos and Imperium.* New York: Oxford University Press.

Harding, Walter. 1965. *The Days of Henry Thoreau*. New York: Alfred A. Knopf.

Hare, Richard Mervyn. 1982. *Plato*. New York: Oxford University Press.

Harkins, William E. 1962. *Karel Capek*. New York: Columbia University Press.

Harpur, James. 1994. *The Atlas of Sacred Places*. New York: Henry Holt.

Harrington, James. 1992. *The Commonwealth of Oceana and a System of Politics*. New York: Cambridge University Press.

Harrison, G. B., et al., eds. 1967. *Major British Writers*. New York: Harcourt Brace & World.

Hart, James D. 1983. *The Oxford Companion to American Literature*. 5th ed. New York: Oxford University Press.

Hastings, James, ed. 1951. *Encyclopedia of Religion and Ethics*. New York: Charles Scribner's Sons.

Hawthorne, Nathaniel. 1959. *The Scarlet Letter*. New York: New American Library.

Hedrick, Joan D. 1982. *Solitary Comrade: Jack London and His Work*. Chapel Hill: University of North Carolina Press.

Heilbroner, Robert L. 1989. *Behind the Veil of Economics: Essays in the Worldly Philosophy*. New York: W. W. Norton.

Henderson, Jeffrey. 1975. *The Maculate Muse*. New Haven, Conn.: Yale University Press.

Hertzka, Theodor. 1972. *Freiland: A Social Anticipation*. New York: Gordon Press.

Hesiod. 1957. *Paradise Regained*. New York: Odyssey Press.

———. 1966. *Theogony*. New York: Oxford University Press.

———. 1973. *Works and Days*. Ann Arbor: University of Michigan Press.

Hesse, Hermann. 1951. *Siddhartha*. New York: New Directions.

Hill, Eldon C. 1978. *George Bernard Shaw*. Boston: G. K. Hall.

Hillway, Tyrus. 1979. *Herman Melville*. Boston: G. K. Hall.

Hilton, James. 1933. *Lost Horizon*. New York: Simon & Schuster.

Hodgkins, Louise Manning. 1904. *A Guide to the Study of Nineteenth Century Authors*. Boston: D. C. Heath.

Hoffman, A. J. 1988. *Twain's Heroes, Twain's Worlds*. Philadelphia: University of Pennsylvania Press.

Hollister, Bernard. 1982. *You and Science Fiction*. Skokie, Ill.: National Textbook Co.

Holman, C. Hugh, ed. 1981. *A Handbook to Literature*. Indianapolis, Ind.: Bobbs-Merrill Educational Publishing.

Holmes, Charles M. 1970. *Aldous Huxley and the Way to Reality*. Westport, Conn.: Greenwood.

Holt, J. C. 1989. *Robin Hood*. London: Thames and Hudson.

Holt, Lee. 1989. *Samuel Butler*. New York: Macmillan.

Holy Bible. 1958. Cleveland, Ohio: World Publishing.

Homer. 1967. *The Odyssey*. New York: Harper & Row.

Hooke, S. H. 1963. *Middle Eastern Mythology*. Baltimore, Md.: Penguin.

Hopkins, Robert H. 1993. *The True Genius of Oliver Goldsmith*. Ann Arbor, Mich.: Books on Demand.

Hopper, Vincent F. 1952. *Essentials of European Literature*. Great Neck, N.Y.: Barron's Educational Series.

Hornstein, Lillian Herlands, et al., eds. 1973. *The Reader's Companion to World Literature*. 2d ed. New York: New American Library.

Howatson, M. C., ed. 1991. *The Oxford Companion to Classical Literature*. Oxford, England: Oxford University Press.

Howells, William Dean. 1907. *Through the Eye of the Needle*. New York: Harper & Brothers.

———. 1957. *A Traveler from Altruria*. New York: Sagamore Press.

Hudson, W. H. n.d. *Green Mansions*. New York: Amsco School Publication.

———. 1917. *A Crystal Age*. New York: E. P. Dutton.

Hughes, Kathryn. 1992. "Review." *New Statesman Society* (25 September), 55.

Hughes, Merritt Y. 1957. *John Milton: Complete Poems and Major Prose*. New York: Odyssey Press.

Huxley, Aldous. 1932. *Brave New World*. New York: Bantam Books.

———. 1989. *Brave New World Revisited*. New York: HarperCollins.

Hynes, Samuel, ed. 1974. *Twentieth-Century Interpretations of 1984: A Collection of Critical Essays*. Englewood Cliffs, N.J.: Prentice-Hall.

Idries Shah, Sayyid. 1964. *The Sufis*. New York: Doubleday.

Indick, Ben. 1989. *Ray Bradbury: Dramatist*. San Bernardino, Calif.: Borgo Press.

Ingersoll, Earl G., ed. 1991. *Margaret Atwood: Conversations*. Princeton, N.J.: Ontario Review Press.

James, P. D. 1958. *The Children of Men*. New York: Alfred A. Knopf, 1993.

Jeffers, Thomas L. 1981. *Samuel Butler Revalued.* University Park: Pennsylvania State University Press.

Jenson, Ejner J., ed. 1984. *The Future of* Nineteen Eighty-Four. Ann Arbor: University of Michigan Press.

Johnson, Christopher H. 1974. *Utopian Communism in France: Cabet and the Icarians.* Ithaca, N.Y.: Cornell University Press.

Johnson, J. W., ed. 1968. *Utopian Literature: A Selection.* New York: Modern Library.

Johnson, Samuel. 1982. *Johnson: Selected Writings.* New York: Viking Penguin.

Johnson, Wayne L. 1978. "The Invasion Stories of Ray Bradbury." In *Critical Encounters: Writers and Themes in Science Fiction.* New York: Frederick Ungar.

Johnston, Arnold. 1980. *Of Earth and Darkness: The Novels of William Golding.* Columbia: University of Missouri Press.

Jordan, Nehemiah. 1981. *The Wisdom of Plato.* Lanham, Md.: University Press of America.

Jowett, Benjamin, trans. 1981. *The Apology, Phaedo, and Crito of Plato.* New York: P. F. Collier.

Jurji, Edward J., ed. 1946. *The Great Religions of the Modern World.* Princeton, N.J.: Princeton University Press.

Kalevala. 1950. Hancock, Mich.: Book Concern.

Kaltenmark, Max. 1969. *Lao Tzu and Taoism.* Stanford, Calif.: Stanford University Press.

Kaplan, Justin. 1966. *Mister Clemens and Mark Twain: A Biography.* New York: Simon & Schuster.

Karp, David. 1953. *One.* New York: Grosset & Dunlap.

Kateb, George. 1923. *Utopia and Its Enemies.* London: Collier-Macmillan.

Kateb, George, ed. 1971. *Utopia.* New York: Atherton Press.

Kennedy, W. Sloane. 1972. *Henry W. Longfellow: Biography, Anecdote, Letters, Criticism.* Brooklyn, N.Y.: Haskell.

Kesterson, David B., ed. 1979. *Critics on Mark Twain.* Baltimore, Md.: University of Miami Press.

Kinkead-Weeks, Mark, and Ian Gregor. 1984. *William Golding: A Critical Study.* Winchester, Mass.: Faber & Faber.

Klaic, Dragan. 1991. *The Plot of the Future: Utopia and Dystopia in Modern Drama.* Ann Arbor: University of Michigan Press.

Kly, Y. N. 1986. *The Black Book: The True Political Philosophy of Malcolm X.* Atlanta, Ga.: Clarity Press.

Knapp, Jeffrey. 1992. *An Empire Nowhere: England, America, and Literature from Utopia to the Tempest.* Berkeley: University of California Press.

Knapp, Mona. 1984. *Doris Lessing.* New York: Continuum.

Knight, Damon. 1967. *In Search of Wonder: Critical Essays on Science Fiction.* New York: Advent.

Koran. 1992. New York: Alfred A. Knopf.

Kuhn, Anna Katharina. 1988. *Christa Wolf's Utopian Vision: From Marxism to Feminism.* New York: Cambridge University Press.

Kumar, Krishan. 1987. *Utopia and Anti-Utopia in Modern Times.* Cambridge, Mass.: Blackwell.

Kunitz, Stanley. 1942. *Twentieth Century Authors.* New York: H. W. Wilson.

Lacy, Norris J. 1986. *The Arthurian Encyclopedia.* New York: Peter Bedrick Books.

LaFargue, Roger. 1992. *The Tao of the Tao-te Ching.* New York: State University of New York.

Lamb, Sidney, ed. 1966. *The Tempest.* Lincoln, Nebr.: Cliffs Notes.

Lane, Lauriat. 1961. *Approaches to* Walden. San Francisco: Wadsworth.

Lao Tzu. 1993. *Tao: To Know and Not Be Knowing.* San Francisco: Chronicle Books.

Lasky, Melvin J. 1976. *Utopia and Revolution.* Chicago: University of Chicago Press.

Lattimore, Richmond, trans. 1973. *Hesiod.* Ann Arbor: University of Michigan Press.

Lau, D. C. 1963. *Lao Tzu: Tao Te Ching.* Baltimore, Md.: Penguin.

Lawless, George P. 1987. *Augustine of Hippo and His Monastic Rule.* New York: Oxford University Press.

Lawrence, Jerome, and Robert E. Lee. 1971. *The Night Thoreau Spent in Jail.* New York: Bantam Books.

Leader, Edward R. 1992. *Understanding Malcolm X: His Controversial Philosophical Changes.* New York: Vantage Press.

Leeming, David Adams. 1990. *The World of Myth.* New York: Oxford University Press.

Legat, Michael. 1987. *The Illustrated Dictionary of Western Literature.* New York: Continuum.

LeGuin, Ursula K. 1992. *The Language of the Night: Essays on Fantasy and Science Fiction.* New York: HarperCollins.

Lessing, Doris. 1988. *Memoirs of a Survivor.* New York: Random House.

Letters, F. J. 1981. *Virgil.* Norwood, Pa.: Telegraph Books.

Levin, Harry. 1969. *The Myth of the Golden Age in the Renaissance.* Bloomington: Indiana University Press.

Lewis, Arthur O., ed. 1971. *American Utopias.* New York: Arno Press and the *New York Times.*

Lewis, Dominic B. 1969. Doctor Rabelais. Brooklyn: Greenwood.

Lichtheim, George. 1969. *The Origins of Socialism.* Essex, Conn.: Praeger.

Liljegren, Sten Bodvar. 1969. *Studies on the Origin and Early Tradition of English Utopian Fiction.* Lundequistska Bokhandeln.

Lindsay, Jack. 1969. *John Bunyan: Maker of Myths.* New York: Kelley.

Lodge, Rupert Clendon. 1956. *The Philosophy of Plato.* London: Routledge & Kegan Paul.

Logan, George M. 1983. *The Meaning of More's* Utopia. Princeton, N.J.: Princeton University Press.

London, Jack. 1982a. *The Iron Heel.* In *Novels and Social Writings.* New York: Library of America.

———. 1982b. *Novels and Social Writings.* New York: Library of America.

Longfellow, Henry Wadsworth. 1992. *The Song of Hiawatha.* London: J. M. Dent.

Lord, Louis E. 1963. *Aristophanes: His Plays and His Influence.* New York: Cooper Square.

Lorraine, Walter H. "Lois Lowry." *Horn Book,* July / August.

Lovett, Robert Morss, and Helen Sard Hughes, eds. 1932. *The History of the Novel in England.* Boston: Houghton Mifflin.

Low, W. Augustus, and Virgil A. Clift. 1981. *Encyclopedia of Black America.* New York: Da Capo.

Lowry, Lois. 1993. *The Giver.* Boston: Houghton Mifflin.

Lundquist, James. 1987. *Jack London: Adventures, Ideas and Fiction.* New York: Frederick Ungar.

Lurker, Manfred. 1980. *The Gods and Symbols of Ancient Egypt.* London: Thames and Hudson.

McCombs, Judith, ed. 1988. *Critical Essays on Margaret Atwood.* Boston: G. K. Hall.

McDannell, Coleen. 1994. *Heaven: A History.* Salt Lake City: University of Utah.

McDermott, William C. 1950. *Virgil's Works.* New York: Modern Library.

Mack, Maynard, gen. ed. 1962. *The Continental Edition of Old Masterpieces.* New York: W. W. Norton.

MacKendrick, Paul, and Herbert M. Howe, eds. 1952. *Classics in Translation.* Vols. I & II. Madison: University of Wisconsin Press.

McKnight, Stephen A. 1992. *Science, Pseudo-Science, and Utopianism in Early Modern Thought.* Columbia: University of Missouri Press.

Magill, Frank N., ed. 1958. *Cyclopedia of World Authors.* New York: Harper & Brothers.

Magnusson, Magnus, gen. ed. 1990. *Cambridge Biographical Dictionary.* New York: Cambridge University Press.

Major Twentieth-Century Writers. 1990. Detroit: Gale Research.

Malory, Thomas. 1982. *Le Morte d'Arthur.* London: Collier Books.

Malthus, Thomas. 1990. *An Essay on the Principle of Population.* New York: Cambridge University Press.

Mandeville, Bernard de. 1989. *The Fable of the Bees.* New York: Penguin.

Manguel, Alberto, and Gianni Guadalupi. 1987. *The Dictionary of Imaginary Places.* New York: Harcourt Brace Jovanovich.

Mannix, Daniel P. 1964. "The Father of the Wizard of Oz." *American Heritage* (December), 36–47.

Manuel, Frank E., ed. 1966. *Utopias and Utopian Thought.* Boston: Houghton Mifflin.

"Margaret Atwood: Interview." 1983. Audiocassette. Englewood Cliffs, N.J.: Prentice-Hall.

Martz, Louis L., ed. 1967. *Milton: A Collection of Critical Essays.* Englewood Cliffs, N.J.: Penguin.

Marx, Karl. 1992. *Das Kapital.* Ventura, Calif.: Regal.

Marx, Karl, and Friedrich Engels. 1985. *The Communist Manifesto.* New York: Viking Press.

Mason, Haydn. 1981. *Voltaire: A Biography.* Baltimore, Md.: Johns Hopkins.

Massaryk, Thomas G. 1938. *On Thought and Life: Conversations with Karel Capek.* Salem, N.H.: Ayer.

Mathews, Richard. 1978. *The Clockwork Universe of Anthony Burgess.* San Bernardino, Calif.: Borgo Press.

Mays, James L., ed. 1988. *Harper's Bible Commentary.* New York: Harper & Row.

Melville, Herman. 1961. *Moby Dick or the White Whale.* New York: New American Library.

———. 1962. *Billy Budd: Sailor.* Chicago: University of Chicago Press.

———. 1964. *Typee.* New York: New American Library.

———. 1968. *Omoo.* Evanston, Ill.: Northwestern University Press.

Metzger, Bruce M., and Michael D. Coogan, eds. 1993. *The Oxford Companion to the Bible.* New York: Oxford University Press.

Mileck, Joseph. 1958. *Hermann Hesse and His Critics.* Chapel Hill: University of North Carolina Press.

Miller, David. 1990. *W. H. Hudson and the Elusive Paradise.* New York: St. Martin's Press.

Miller, Dieter. 1990. "Lois Lowry." *Authors and Artists for Young Adults,* Vol. 5. Detroit: Gale Research.

Miller, James E., et al., eds. 1970. *Literature of the Eastern World.* Glenview, Ill.: Scott, Foresman.

Milton, John. 1957a. *Complete Poems and Major Prose.* New York: Odyssey Press.

———. 1957b. *Paradise Lost.* New York: Odyssey Press.

Mitchell, Stephen. 1988. *Tao Te Ching.* New York: Harper & Row.

Modgil, Sohan, ed. 1987. *B. F. Skinner: Controversy and Consensus.* Bristol, Pa.: Taylor & Francis.

Mogen, David. 1986. *Ray Bradbury.* Boston: G. K. Hall.

Montaigne, Michel de. 1893a. "Des Cannibales." In *The Essays of Montaigne.* New York: AMS Press.

———. 1893b. *The Essays of Montaigne.* New York: AMS Press.

More, Thomas. n.d. *Utopia.* In *Famous Utopias.* New York: Tudor Publishing.

———. 1963a. *The Complete Works.* New Haven, Conn.: Yale University Press.

———. 1963b. *Utopia.* In *The Complete Works.* New Haven, Conn.: Yale University Press.

———. 1968. *Utopia.* In *Three Works by William Morris.* New York: International Publishers.

Morford, Mark P. O., and Robert J. Lenardon. 1977. *Classical Mythology.* New York: Longman.

Morgan, Arthur E. 1945. *The Philosophy of Edward Bellamy.* Westport, Conn.: Greenwood.

Morris, Robert K. 1971. *Consolations of Ambiguity: An Essay on the Novels of Anthony Burgess.* Minneapolis: University of Minnesota Press.

Morris, William. 1968a. *News from Nowhere.* In *Three Works by William Morris.* New York: International Publishers.

———. 1968b. *Three Works by William Morris.* New York: International Publishers.

Moylan, Tom. 1986. *Demand the Impossible: Science Fiction and the Utopian Imagination.* New York: Methuen.

Muir, Kenneth, and Samuel Schoenbaum. 1971. *A New Companion to Shakespearean Studies.* Cambridge, Mass.: Harvard University Press.

Mullen, Robert. 1966. *The Latter-Day Saints: The Mormons Yesterday and Today.* Garden City, N.Y.: Doubleday.

Mumford, Lewis. 1959. *The Story of Utopias.* Gloucester, Mass.: Peter Smith.

Myles, Anita. 1990. *Doris Lessing: A Novelist with Organic Sensibility.* Advent, N.Y.: Associated Publishing House.

Nabokov, Vladimir. 1984. *Lectures on Don Quixote.* San Diego: Harbrace.

Nance, Guinevera A. 1988. *Aldous Huxley.* New York: Continuum.

Nath, Prem, ed. 1987. *Fresh Reflections on Samuel Johnson: Essays in Criticism.* London: Whiston Publishing.

Negley, Glenn, and J. Max Patrick, eds. 1952. *The Quest for Utopia.* New York: Henry Schumann.

Neihardt, John G. 1961. *Black Elk Speaks.* Lincoln: University of Nebraska Press.

Neilson, William Allan, and Charles Jarvis Hill. 1942. *The Complete Plays and Poems of William Shakespeare.* Boston: Houghton Mifflin.

Nelson, William, ed. 1968. *Twentieth Century Interpretations of Utopia.* Englewood Cliffs, N.J.: Prentice-Hall.

Nettleship, Richard Lewis. 1968. *Lectures on* The Republic *of Plato.* New York: St. Martin's Press.

Nicholls, Peter, gen. ed. 1979. *The Science Fiction Encyclopedia.* Garden City, N.Y.: Doubleday.

Nicholson, R. A. 1950. *Rumi, Poet and Mystic.* London: George Allen & Unwin.

O'Daly, Gerard. 1987. *Augustine's Philosophy of the Mind.* Berkeley: University of California Press.

Oldsey, Bernard, and Joseph Browne, eds. 1986. *Critical Essays on George Orwell.* Boston: G. K. Hall.

O'Neill, William F. 1977. *With Charity toward None: An Analysis of Ayn Rand's Philosophy.* Lanham, Md.: Littlefield.

Orwell, George. 1946. *Animal Farm.* New York: New American Library.

———. 1949. *1984.* New York: New American Library.

Ovid. 1977. *Metamorphoses.* Cambridge, Mass.: Harvard University Press.

The Oxford Annotated Bible. 1962. New York: Oxford University Press.

Papp, Joseph, and Elizabeth Kirkland. 1988. *Shakespeare Alive!* New York: Bantam Books.

Pappu, S. S., and R. Rao, eds. 1987. *The Dimension of Karma.* Flushing, N.Y.: Asia Book Corporation.

Parker, William Riley. 1958. *Milton: A Biography.* New York: Oxford University Press.

Parrinder, Patrick, ed. 1986. *H. G. Wells: Reality and Beyond.* Champaign, Ill.: Champaign Public Library.

Parrington, Vernon Louis, Jr. 1964. *American Dreams: A Study of American Utopias.* New York: Russell & Russell.

Patai, Daphne, ed. 1988. *Looking Backward: 1988–1888: Essays on Edward Bellamy.* Amherst: University of Massachusetts Press.

Patterson, Lotsee, and Mary Ellen Snodgrass. 1994. *Indian Terms of the Americas.* Englewood, Colo.: Libraries Unlimited.

Pelikan, Jaroslav. 1992a. *On Searching the Scriptures—Your Own or Someone Else's.* New York: Book-of-the-Month Club.

Pelikan, Jaroslav, ed. 1992b. *Sacred Writings: Buddhism.* New York: Quality Paperback Club.

———. 1992c. *Sacred Writings: The Qur'an.* New York: Quality Paperback Club.

Pennick, Nigel. 1992. *The Pagan Book of Days.* Rochester, Vt.: Destiny Books.

Perkins, George, et al., eds. 1991. *Benét's Reader's Encyclopedia of American Literature.* New York: HarperCollins.

Perry, John. 1981. *Jack London: An American Myth.* Chicago: Nelson-Hall.

Peterson, William. 1979. *Malthus.* Cambridge, Mass.: Harvard University Press.

Pfaelzer, Jean. 1984. *The Utopian Novel in America, 1886–1896: The Politics of Form.* Pittsburgh, Pa.: University of Pittsburgh Press.

Picard, Barbara Leonie. 1964. *Celtic Tales: Legends of Tall Warriors and Old Enchantments.* New York: Criterion Books.

Piercy, Marge. 1976. *Woman on the Edge of Time.* New York: Fawcett Crest.

Piotrowski, Sylvester A. 1935. *Étienne Cabet and the Voyage en Icarie: A Study in the History of Social Thought.* Westport, Conn.: Hyperion Books.

Plato. 1937a. *The Apology, Phaedo, and Crito of Plato.* New York: P. F. Collier.

———. 1937b. *The Dialogues of Plato.* New York: Random House.

———. 1937c. *Timaeus.* In *The Dialogues of Plato.* New York: Random House.

———. 1955. *The Republic.* New York: Viking Penguin.

Ploski, Harry A., and James Williams, eds. 1989. *The Negro Almanac.* Detroit: Gale Research.

Plutarch. 1958. *Fall of the Roman Republic.* Baltimore, Md.: Penguin.

———. 1971a. *The of Lycurgus.* In *Moral Essays.* London: Harmondsworth.

———. 1971b. *Moral Essays.* London: Harmondsworth.

Poe, Edgar Allan. 1962. *Selected Stories and Poems.* New York: Airmont Books.

Pollard, Arthur. 1970. *Satire.* London: Methuen.

Predmore, Richard L. 1990. *The World of Don Quixote.* Ann Arbor, Mich.: Books on Demand.

Prescott, Peter S. 1974. "Rabbit, Read." *Newsweek* (18 March), 114.

Prideaux, Tom. 1953. *World Theatre in Pictures: From Ancient Times to Modern Broadway.* New York: Greenberg.

Proctor, R. W., and D. J. Weeks. 1991. *The Goal of B. F. Skinner and Behavior Analysis.* New York: Springer-Verlag.

Pucci, Idanna. 1992. *Bhima Swarga.* Boston: Little, Brown.

Putnam, Samuel. 1993. *François Rabelais, Man of the Renaissance: A Spiritual Biography.* Salem, N.H.: Ayer.

Quinn, D. Michael. 1987. *Early Mormonism and the Magic World View.* Salt Lake City: Signature Books.

Quintana, Ricardo, intro. 1958. *Gulliver's Travels and Other Writings.* New York: Modern Library.

The Qu'ran. 1992. New York: Quality Paperback Club.

Rabelais, François. 1955. *Gargantua and Pantagruel.* New York: Viking Penguin.

Rabkin, Eric S. 1979. *Arthur C. Clarke.* San Bernardino, Calif.: Borgo Press.

Rabkin, Eric, et al., eds. 1983. *No Place Else.* Carbondale: Southern Illinois University Press.

Radice, Betty. 1984. *Who Was Who in the Ancient World.* New York: Penguin.

Rand, Ayn. 1946. *Anthem.* New York: New American Library.

Rattray, Robert F. 1974. *Samuel Butler.* Brooklyn, N.Y.: Haskell.

Ray, Karen. 1993. "Children's Books." *New York Times,* October 31.

Reading, Peter. 1992. "Review." *Times Literary Supplement* (24 September), 26.

Reason, Joyce. 1961. *To Be a Pilgrim.* Canby, Ore.: Christian Literature.

Reginald, Robert, ed. 1992. *Science Fiction and Fantasy Literature: 1975–1986 Supplement.* Detroit: Gale Research.

Reichert, Herbert W. 1972. *The Impact of Nietzsche on Hermann Hesse.* Mt. Pleasant, Mich.: Enigma Press.

Reilly, Patrick. 1989. *George Orwell: The Age's Adversary.* New York: St. Martin's Press.

Richetti, John. 1987. *Daniel Defoe.* New York: Macmillan.

Richter, Peyton E. 1971. *Utopias.* Boston: Holbrook Press.

Richter, Peyton, and Ilona Ricardo. 1980. *Voltaire.* Boston: G. K. Hall.

Rigby, S. H. 1992. *Engels and the Formation of Marxism: History, Dialectics and Revolution.* New York: St. Martin's Press.

Riley, E. C. 1986. *Don Quixote.* Winchester, Mass.: Unwin Hyman.

Roberts, B. H. 1985. *Studies of the* Book of Mormon. Urbana: University of Illinois Press.

Roemer, Kenneth M. 1976. *The Obsolete Necessity: America in Utopian Writing, 1888–1900.* Kent, Ohio: Kent State University Press.

Rollins, Hyder E., and Herschel Baker. 1954. *The Renaissance in England: Non-dramatic Prose and Verse of the Sixteenth Century.* Boston: D. C. Heath.

Ronner, Amy D. 1986. *W. H. Hudson: The Man, the Novelist, the Naturalist.* New York: AMS Press.

Rooney, Charles J. 1985. *Dreams and Visions: A Study of American Utopias, 1865–1917.* Westport, Conn.: Greenwood.

Rose, Ernst. 1965. *Faith from the Abyss: Hermann Hesse's Way from Romanticism to Modernity.* New York: New York University Press.

Rosenberg, Donna. 1992. *World Mythology: An Anthology of the Great Myths and Epics.* Lincolnwood, Ill.: Passport Books.

Rosenberg, John D. 1973. *The Fall of Camelot: A Study of Tennyson's* Idylls of the King. Cambridge, Mass.: Harvard University Press.

Rosinsky, Natalie M. 1984. *Feminist Futures—Contemporary Women's Speculative Fiction.* Ann Arbor, Mich.: UMI Research Press.

Ross, Jean W. 1984. "Interview." *Contemporary Authors, New Revision Series,* Vol. 13. Detroit: Gale Research.

Rouse, W. H. D., trans. 1956. *Great Dialogues of Plato.* New York: New American Library.

Ruland, Richard, ed. 1968. *Twentieth Century Interpretations of* Walden. Englewood Cliffs, N.J.: Prentice-Hall.

Ruppert, Peter. 1986. *Reader in a Strange Land: The Activity of Reading Literary Utopias.* Athens: University of Georgia Press.

Russell, P. E. 1985. *Cervantes.* New York: Oxford University Press.

Russell, Robert. 1994. *Evgeny Zamyatin.* Portland, Ore.: International Specialized Book Services.

Sandler, Robert, ed. 1986. *Northrop Frye on Shakespeare.* New Haven, Conn.: Yale University Press.

Schimmel, Annemarie. 1975. *Mystical Dimensions of Islam.* Chapel Hill: University of North Carolina Press.

———. 1982. *As through a Veil: Mystical Poetry in Islam.* New York: Columbia University Press.

Schwartz, Benjamin I. 1985. *The World of Thought in Ancient China.* Cambridge, Mass.: Harvard University Press.

Screech, M. A. 1980. *Rabelais.* Ithaca, N.Y.: Cornell University Press.

Sealts, Merton M., Jr. 1982. *Pursuing Melville: 1940–1980.* Madison: University of Wisconsin Press.

Seltman, Charles. 1960. *The Twelve Olympians.* New York: Thomas Y. Crowell.

Severy, Merle, ed. 1977. *Greece and Rome.* Washington, D.C.: National Geographic Society.

Shakespeare, William. 1958. *A Midsummer Night's Dream.* New York: Washington Square Press.

———. 1959. *As You Like It.* New York: Washington Square Press.

———. 1961. *The Tempest.* New York: Washington Square Press.

Shane, Alex M. 1968. *The Life and Work of Evgenij Zamjatin.* Berkeley: University of California Press.

Shaw, George Bernard. 1988. *Back to Methuselah.* New York: Penguin.

Shepard, Leslie A., ed. 1990. *Encyclopedia of Occultism and Parapsychology.* Detroit: Gale Research.

Siebenheller, Norma. 1981. *P. D. James.* Del Mar, Calif.: Frederick Ungar.

Sinclair, Andrew. 1983. *Jack: Biography of Jack London.* New York: Washington Square Press.

Skinner, B. F. 1968. *The Technology of Teaching.* Englewood Cliffs, N.J.: Prentice-Hall.

———. 1976. *About Behaviorism.* New York: Random House.

———. 1993. *Walden Two.* New York: Macmillan.

Slusser, George E. 1977a. *The Ray Bradbury Chronicles.* San Bernardino, Calif.: Borgo Press.

———. 1977b. *The Space Odysseys of Arthur C. Clarke.* San Bernardino, Calif.: Borgo Press.

Smith, David. 1988. *H. G. Wells, Desperately Mortal.* New Haven, Conn.: Yale University Press.

Smith, Eric. 1984. *A Dictionary of Classical Reference in English Poetry.* Cambridge, England: Barnes & Noble.

Smith, Janet Adam. 1974. "Exodus." *New York Review of Books* (18 April), 8–9.

Smith, Joseph, trans. 1971. *Doctrine and Covenants of the Church of Jesus Christ of Latter-Day Saints: Containing the Revelations Given to Joseph Smith, Jun, the Prophet, for the Building Up of the Kingdom of God in the Last Days.* Westport, Conn.: Greenwood.

———. 1982. *The Book of Mormon.* Salt Lake City: The Church of Jesus Christ of Latter-Day Saints.

Snodgrass, Mary Ellen. 1987. *The Great American English Handbook.* Jacksonville, Ill.: Perma-Bound.

———. 1988a. *Greek Classics.* Lincoln, Nebr.: Cliffs Notes.

———. 1988b. *Roman Classics.* Lincoln, Nebr.: Cliffs Notes.

———. 1990. *Characters from Young Adult Literature.* Englewood, Colo.: Libraries Unlimited.

———. 1992. *Late Achievers: Famous People Who Succeeded Late in Life.* Englewood, Colo.: Libraries Unlimited.

———. 1993. *Crossing Barriers: People Who Overcame.* Englewood, Colo.: Libraries Unlimited.

———. 1994. *Voyages in Classical Mythology.* Santa Barbara, Calif.: ABC-CLIO.

Snow, Jack. 1954. *Who's Who in Oz.* Chicago: Reilly & Lee.

Something about the Author. 1984. Vol. 34. Detroit: Gale Research.

———. 1993. Vol. 70. Detroit: Gale Research.

Something about the Author Autobiography Series. 1986. Vol. 3. Detroit: Gale Research.

Spatz, Lois. 1978. *Aristophanes.* Boston: Twayne.

Sprague, Claire, ed. 1986. *In Pursuit of Doris Lessing: Nine Nations' Readings.* Boston: G. K. Hall.

Stansky, Peter, ed. 1984. *On* Nineteen Eighty-Four. New York: W. H. Freeman.

Steinbeck, John. 1976. *The Acts of King Arthur and His Noble Knights.* New York: Farrar, Straus & Giroux.

Stephens, James, et al., eds. 1949. *Victorian and Later English Poets.* New York: American Book Co.

Stevenson, Robert Louis. 1989. *A Child's Garden of Verses.* San Francisco: Chronicle Books.

Stewart, Mary. 1970. *The Crystal Cave.* Greenwich, Conn.: Fawcett.

———. 1973. *The Hollow Hills.* Greenwich, Conn.: Fawcett.

———. 1984. *The Last Enchantment.* Greenwich, Conn.: Fawcett.

Stinson, John J. 1991. *Anthony Burgess Revisited.* New York: Macmillan.

Stoekl, Allan. 1985. *Politics, Writing, Mutilation: The Cases of Bataille, Blanchot, Roussel, Leiris, and Ponge.* Minneapolis: University of Minnesota Press.

Stone, Irving. 1978. *Jack London: Sailor on Horseback.* New York: Doubleday.

Stowe, Harriet Beecher. 1958. *Uncle Tom's Cabin or Life among the Lowly.* New York: Harper & Row.

Sturluson, Snorri. 1987. *Edda.* London: J. M. Dent.

Subbarao, V. V. 1987. *William Golding.* New York: Envoy Press.

Sullivan, C. W., III. 1992. "Review." In *Masterplots II.* Englewood Cliffs, N.J.: Salem Press.

Swift, Jonathan. 1958. *Gulliver's Travels and Other Writings.* New York: Modern Library.

Symons, Julian. 1992. "Review." *London Review of Books.* Vol. 14 (10 September), 22.

Tao Te Ching. 1988. New York: Harper & Row.

Tasso, Torquato, 1987. *Jerusalem Delivered.* Detroit, Mich.: Wayne State University Press.

Tawney, R. H. 1993. *Harrington's Interpretation of His Age.* New York: Gordon Press.

Tennyson, Alfred. 1949a. "Locksley Hall." In *Victorian and Later English Poets,* ed. James Stephens et al. New York: American Book Co.

———. 1949b. "Locksley Hall" and "Locksley Hall Sixty Years After." In *Victorian and Later English Poets,* ed. James Stephens et al. New York: American Book Co.

———. 1949c. "The Lotus-Eaters." In *Victorian and Later English Poets,* ed. James Stephens et al. New York: American Book Co.

———. 1989. *Idylls of the King.* New York: Viking Press.

Thompson, E. P. 1992. *William Morris: Romantic to Revolutionary.* Oxford, England: Oxford University Press.

Thompson, Eileen, et al., eds. 1991. *World Masterpieces.* Englewood Cliffs, N.J.: Prentice-Hall.

Thoreau, Henry David. 1965. *Walden and "Civil Disobedience."* New York: Airmont Books.

Tocqueville, Alexis de. 1969. *Democracy in America.* New York: Harper Perennial.

Tripp, Edward. 1970. *The Meridian Handbook of Classical Mythology.* New York: New American Library.

Troyes, Chrétien de. 1975. *Arthurian Romances.* New York: Everyman's Library.

Turner, Alice K. 1993. *The History of Hell.* New York: Harcourt Brace.

Turner, Michael, ed. 1986. *Malthus and His Time.* New York: St. Martin's Press.

Twain, Mark. 1963. *A Connecticut Yankee in King Arthur's Court.* New York: New American Library.

Ussher, Robert Glenn. 1979. *Aristophanes.* Oxford, England: Clarendon Press.

Utopian Visions. Mysteries of the Unknown Series. Alexandria, Va.: Time-Life Books.

Van Pelt, Gertrude W. 1975. *The Doctrine of Karma.* San Diego, Calif.: Point Loma Publishing.

Van Spanckeren, Kathryn, and Jan G. Castro, eds. 1988. *Margaret Atwood: Vision and Forms.* Carbondale: Southern Illinois University Press.

Veronica, Sister May. 1993. "Review of *The Giver.*" *VOYA,* 167.

Virgil. 1950. *Virgil's Works: The Aeneid, Eclogues and Georgics,* trans. J. W. Mackail. New York: Modern Library.

Voltaire. 1961. *Candide, Zadig, and Selected Stories.* New York: New American Library.

Wagenknecht, Edward. 1968. *As Far as Yesterday.* Norman: University of Oklahoma Press.

———. 1986. *Henry Wadsworth Longfellow: His Poetry and Prose.* New York: Continuum.

Waley, Arthur, trans. 1992. *Confucianism: The Analects of Confucius.* New York: HarperCollins.

Waley, M. I. 1993. *Sufism: The Alchemy of the Heart.* San Francisco: Chronicle Books.

Walker, Sue, and Eugenie Hamner, eds. 1984. *Ways of Knowing: Critical Essays on Marge Piercy.* Mobile, Ala.: Negative Capability Press.

Walkover, Andrew. 1974. *The Dialectics of Eden.* Stanford, Calif.: Stanford University Press.

Walsh, Chad. 1962. *From Utopia to Nightmare*. New York: Harper & Row.

Wangerin, Walter. 1993. "Review." *New York Times Book Review* (28 March), 41.

Warner, Rex. 1958. *The Greek Philosophers*. New York: New American Library.

———. 1971. *Plutarch: Moral Essays*. London: Harmondsworth.

Warren, Jack. 1992. *Rage in Utopia*. Smyrna, Ga.: Grafco Products.

Watts, Harold H. 1969. *Aldous Huxley*. New York: Macmillan.

Welch, Holmes. 1958. *The Parting of the Way: Lao Tzu and the Taoist Movement*. London: Methuen.

Wells, H. G. 1964. *The Time Machine*. New York: Airmont Books.

———. 1967. *A Modern Utopia*. Lincoln: University of Nebraska.

White, Frederic R., ed. 1955. *Famous Utopias of the Renaissance*. New York: Hendricks House.

White, T. H. 1965. *Once and Future King*. New York: Berkley Books.

Whitten, Wilfred. 1974. *Daniel Defoe*. Brooklyn, N.Y.: Haskell.

Widmer, Kingsley. 1988. *Counterings: Utopian Dialectics in Contemporary Contexts*. Ann Arbor, Mich.: UMI Research Press.

Willey, Basil. 1973. *Samuel Taylor Coleridge*. New York: W. W. Norton.

Williams, Cecil B. 1964. *Henry Wadsworth Longfellow*. New York: Macmillan.

Williams, R. D., and T. S. Pattie. 1982. *Virgil: His Poetry through the Ages*. Wolfeboro, N.H.: Longwood.

Wilson, Arthur M. 1972. *Diderot*. Oxford, England: Oxford University Press.

Winch, Donald. 1987. *Malthus*. New York: Oxford University Press.

Wolfenstein, Eugene V. 1990. *The Victims of Democracy: Malcolm X and the Black Revolution with a New Preface*. Denver: Colorado University Press.

Wolff, Geoffrey. 1987. *Herman Melville*. New York: Viking Press.

Woods, George B., et al., eds. 1947. *The Literature of England*. Chicago: Scott, Foresman.

Woolf, Virginia. 1928. *Orlando*. New York: Harcourt Brace.

Worsley, Peter, ed. 1982. *Marx & Marxism*. London: Routledge.

Wright, G. Ernest, gen. ed. 1971. *Great People of the Bible and How They Lived*. Pleasantville, N.Y.: Reader's Digest Association.

"Writer, Illustrator Wins Children's Book Awards." 1990. *Chicago Sun Times*, January 9.

Wynn, Dilys, ed. 1977. *Murderess Ink*. New York: Workman Publishing.

Zamyatin, Yevgeny. 1972. *We.* New York: Viking Press.

———. 1992. *A Soviet Heretic: Essays by Yevgeny Zamyatin.* Evanston, Ill.: Northwestern University Press.

ILLUSTRATION CREDITS

161 Giovanni dal Ponte. Gift of Friends of the Fogg Art Museum. Harvard University Art Museums, Cambridge, Massachusetts.

174 Manuscript Department, Yates Thompson 36 f. 149, British Library.

177 Culver Pictures.

184 *Earthly Paradise,* from *The Garden of Earthly Delights* triptych by Hieronymus Bosch. Prado, Madrid, Spain. Alinari/Art Resource, New York.

205 *Eve* by Lucas Cranach the Elder. Gemaeldegalerie, Staatliche Museen, Berlin. Foto Marburg/Art Resource, New York.

211 Film Stills Archive, Museum of Modern Art, New York.

217 Culver Pictures.

228 PML 12 ChL ff1 Biblia Latina, vol I. Mainz: Gutenberg & Fust (ca. 1455 folio 5 M.500, f4v. The Pierpont Morgan Library, New York.

243 T. Morten in *Gulliver's Travels* by Jonathan Swift, 1865. Rare Book Collection, Library of Congress.

247 Adapted from *Cliffs Notes on Atwood's* The Handmaid's Tale, 1994.

261 Oriental and India Office Collections MS 14004.ff34-35, British Library.

270 UPI/Bettmann.

275 The Bettmann Archive.

280 UPI/Bettmann.

298 *Doctor Samuel Johnson* by Sir Joshua Reynolds. Tate Gallery, London/ Art Resource.

305 Oriental and India Office Collections 1009 folios 115v-116r, British Library.

306 Manuscript Department Add MS 50847, f. IV, British Library.

321 UPI/Bettmann.

322 Library of Congress.

331 Film Stills Archive, Museum of Modern Art, New York.

340 U.S. News and World Report Collection, Library of Congress.

349 Library of Congress LC-USZ62-39759.

357 *Blind Milton Dictating* Paradise Lost *to His Daughters,* by Mikhaly Munkacy. New York Public Library.

359 Film Stills Archive, Museum of Modern Art, New York.

361 *Buffalo Chase*, after George Catlin in *Letters and Notes on the Manners, Customs, and Conditions of North American Indians*. Western History Collection, Denver Public Library.

363 Painting by Hans Holbein the Younger. The Frick Collection 12.1.77, New York.

368 Culver Pictures.

385 Film Stills Archive, Museum of Modern Art, New York.

397 The Bettmann Archive.

415 Performing Arts Collection, New York Public Library.

419 Film Stills Archive, Museum of Modern Art, New York.

424 Beinecke Library, Yale University, New Haven.

434 Culver Pictures.

438 Photograph by G. B. Kress. UPI/Bettmann.

450 Pierpont Morgan Library 8210.2, New York.

455 Photofest, New York.

467 Library of Congress USZ62-80147.

470 UPI/Bettmann Newsphotos.

472 Oriental and India Office Collections MS 14025 (detail), British Library.

478 Painting by Adrian Lamb, 1971. National Portrait Gallery, Washington, D.C./Art Resource.

487 Engraving by Paul Fourdriner, after C. Jervas. Prints Division, New York Public Library.

508 Daguerreotype by Benjamin D. Maxham; Concord Free Public Library, Concord, Massachusetts.

518 Library of Congress LC-USZ67-5632.

536 Musee National du Bardo, Le Bardo, Tunisia. Giraudon/Art Resource.

540 Culver Pictures.

546 Beinecke Library, Yale University, New Haven.

549 Film Stills Archive, Museum of Modern Art, New York.

567 *La Belle Iseult* (Queen Guinevere) by William Morris (1858). Tate Gallery, London/Art Resource, New York.

570 The Bettmann Archive.

 # INDEX

Note: Page numbers in **boldface** denote major entry headings. Numbers in *italics* indicate illustrations.

INDEX

INDEX

INDEX